No Small Courage

No Small Courage

A History of Women in the United States

edited by

Nancy F. Cott

OXFORD
UNIVERSITY PRESS

OXFORD
UNIVERSITY PRESS

Oxford   New York
Auckland   Bangkok   Buenos Aires
Cape Town   Chennai   Dar es Salaam   Delhi   Hong Kong
Istanbul   Karachi   Kolkata   Kuala Lumpur   Madrid   Melbourne   Mexico City
Mumbai   Nairobi   São Paulo   Shangahi   Taipei   Tokyo   Toronto

First published by Oxford University Press, Inc., 2000
First issued as an Oxford University Press paperback, 2004
198 Madison Avenue, New York, New York 10016

www.oup.com

Oxford is a registered trademark of Oxford University Press

Library of Congress Cataloging-in-Publication Data

No small courage: a history of women in the United States /
edited by Nancy F. Cott.
p. cm.
Includes bibliographical references and index.
ISBN 0-19-513946-1 (cloth) ISBN 0-19-517323-6 (pbk.)
Women—United States—History.   I. Cott, Nancy F.

HQ1410.N6 2000
305.4'0973—dc21   00-021130

1 3 5 7 9 10 8 6 4 2

Printed in the United States of America on acid free paper

Frontispiece: The textile mills of New England offered relatively high wages and a sense of independence to young working women in the nineteenth century.

Contents

Preface

Nancy F. Cott

I n much of the Western world's written record of history, women's presence is minimal. Women hardly surface as historical actors. An eminent male historian in the 1940s excused this lack by saying that it was "through no conspiracy of historians" that the composition of courts, parliaments, colleges of cardinals, and the great explorations, where history took place, were "pretty much stag affairs." Yet just two decades after he made this pronouncement, historical interest moved its focus toward social history, putting a spotlight on ordinary people rather than ruling elites.

The trend toward social history converged with the feminist movement in the 1960s and 1970s to produce a harvest of knowledge. Developments in women's history prove the maxim that what one finds in the past depends on what one looks for. If the traditional view of history typically obscured women, that was because it assumed men were the human norm and took men's activities for human pursuits. No one denied that women were subject to history, but it required a different angle to see them as active agents in its making. New perspectives have now been found, which change the historical record altogether.

Investigating history is a matter of research, discovery of evidence, and interpretation, but it is also a field for imagination. We look to the past as one way of understanding ourselves. The experience of delving into history is something like traveling to a foreign land. We find other human beings and the societies they have constructed, and can compare them to ourselves. Their social creations may be somewhat similar to ours, or very different; they may arouse our sympathy—even our envy—and, equally, our antipathy. What makes the comparisons worthwhile is the double-headed fact that our forebears are both like us and not like us. History thus offers a field for mental expansion. It is a canvas that portrays a larger panorama of human possibilities, and enables us to envision alternatives to our present-day lives. In this respect, written history is like literature or drama: it provides us with characters, actions, and turning-points. It is up to historians and readers to plumb the depths of these elements, to put them in coherent order, to find the insights, and to point out relevant comparisons.

The range and variety of viewpoints offered in this capacious volume give plenty of opportunities for such opening of minds. This survey covers the history of women in the United States, and the colonies that preceded the nation, from the seventeenth to the twentieth century. It looks at women of different types and in many roles: as wives, mothers, and housekeepers, but also, for example, as wage-earners, immigrants and migrants, community builders, political rebels, policy makers, intellectual innovators, voluntary organization leaders—women of no small courage, as the title suggests. Characters of varying origins, regions, races, national and self-definitions play across these pages. The book addresses historical questions that require women's outlooks, actions, and aspirations to be part of the answer. How did families change, and what difference did that make in people's lives? How did expectations for the two sexes differ, and did these expectations change over time? What form did women's political participation take when they could not vote? And how did politics change when women did gain political rights? What was the economic importance of women's unpaid work, and of their paid employment? How did women collaborate with other women, and with men, for social or political goals?

By putting its focus on women's work and leisure, family patterns, political activities, forms of organization, and outstanding accomplishments, *No Small Courage* aims to attain a fuller picture of the diverse people of the United States. Well-recognized events, from the settling of the continent to the American Revolution, the Civil War, industrialization, the nation's entry onto the world stage, and world wars, are all here, seen through the lens of women's experiences. The volume begins with a thoughtful consideration of native American women's experience of European contact, as compared to the experience of native American men. Both the destructive impact of European colonization and the give-and-take between the two cultures can be understood and assessed more completely when the essential economic, social, and family roles of women come into the picture. In the colonial period, English women's religious values, educational strivings, and economic contributions come into clearer focus, illuminating the trans-Atlantic conveyance of cultural patterns and their transformation in the new physical and demographic environment. The multiracial character of the United States, and the inequalities among its women of different races and economic situations are forecast here in the portrait of contact and clash between white and native and the early importation of Africans as slave laborers.

Chapters on women's lives in the era surrounding the American Revolution and in the early United States show a diversifying palette of women's experiences. Opportunities for education and calls to political action and to new religious sects find women eager to respond. The reform movements of the era are peopled with women, and so are occupations on farms across the continent, in hydropowered factories, and in shops on city streets. Women take part in the sectional divide between the free-labor North and the slave-labor South, defenders and accusers on both sides. The portrayal of the Civil War deepens in complexity with female actors visible as home-front producers, spies, nurses, and partisans.

As the story moves into the late nineteenth century, the increasing heterogeneity of the people of the United States and their striving across a continent can be seen in the lives of women. Advocates for women's rights and temperance, club women, artists, educators, budding professionals, and new thousands of women wage-earners spring up in the landscape. By the next generation modernity is measured in women's new activities: politics, youth culture, social science, technological improvements—all address the female half of the population as much as the male. In World War I, women are both pacifists and military auxiliaries; women of all sorts suffer through the economic crisis of the depression and also attempt to fix it, as policy makers.

The final two chapters bring the story to the second half of the twentieth century. The extraordinary national effort of World War II can be seen in the unprecedented move of women into war production and into military services. Women's lives likewise represent the generational and epochal shifts evident in the political, social, and cultural rebellions of the 1960s and 1970s. The many variants of feminism enacted in those decades changed the nation's landscape for the remainder of the millennium and beyond. Thus, looking through women's eyes, *No Small Courage* composes a new writing of the history of the United States over four centuries.

No Small Courage

CHAPTER 1

The Tried and the True

Native American Women
Confronting Colonization

John Demos

T he first of the women we now call Native American were actually natives of Asia who lived and died some twenty thousand years ago. They belonged to small bands of prehistoric people who roamed the rugged wilderness of eastern Siberia and survived chiefly by hunting. Some twenty thousand years ago (and in still earlier eras as well) ocean levels were lower, and a land bridge linked Asia and North America where the forty-mile-wide Bering Strait flows today. Across the bridge, from time to time, moved animals of various ancient types—followed by the humans who hunted them.

From this remote beginning flowed the peopling of the Americas. The earth was locked in a bitter Ice Age, but between huge glaciers lay corridors of open land. The hunters and their descendants could walk these corridors from what is now Alaska to milder climes in the south. The process was long and difficult, but by about the year 7000 B.C. people were scattered throughout the Americas. Archaeologists have found their traces—their tools, their graves, the bones of the animals they killed—in campsites as far south as the Strait of Magellan at South America's lowest tip.

Like other prehistoric groups around the world, these people lived in the manner of the Stone Age. They were nomads who wandered from place to place, in continuous pursuit of their game, which included mastodons, woolly mammoths, antelopes, wild horses, tapirs, and pigs. Eventually, with the passage of many centuries, some of these species became extinct, and the hunters shifted their sights toward smaller game, such as deer and fox and other fur-bearers. They began also to develop new ways of sustaining themselves. Wild roots, berries, nuts, seeds, and fruit became a major part of their diet. This change brought changes in their social patterns. The human bands became somewhat larger and less nomadic. And the balance of duties between men and women gradually shifted. In the first period, men were the hunters and women their helpers. In the second, men still hunted

3

Mexican ceramic figures, dating from between 200 B.C. and A.D. 600, show women making tortillas from ground maize. Once Native American societies began farming, they settled into villages in which women often maintained the fields, harvested the crops, and prepared the food.

and women still helped, but women also took the lead in gathering the plant foods on which human survival increasingly depended.

More centuries passed, and their ways of life were further transformed. By around 5000 B.C. some Native Americans had begun the practice of farming; their crops included squashes, corn, peppers, and sunflowers. No longer reliant on the luck of the hunt or success in finding wild plants, these groups could build settled villages. From villages grew still larger units, the seeds of tribes and nations.

These developments proceeded furthest and fastest in present-day Central America. As early as 1000 B.C. a group called the Olmecs built an impressive empire in eastern Mexico; huge stone figures, which they carved into human shapes and apparently used in religious ceremonies, survive to the present. The Olmecs were followed, in the march of history, by the Mayas, whose rule peaked between A.D. 200 and 600. Theirs was a civilization to rival any in Europe at the time. They lived in prosperous city-states, ranged across what is now southern Mexico and Guatemala. Their leaders were hereditary kings—and, at least occasionally, queens—who were thought to communicate with the gods. Priests conducted elaborate rites, including human sacrifice, in gracefully built, pyramidal temples. Gifted scholars created a sophisticated mathematical system and achieved the most accurate knowledge of astronomy the world had yet seen. Merchants traded between cities and ventured also to regions outside Mayan control. Beneath these fortunate classes labored a large mass of peasant farmers. As with many Native American groups in later eras, corn was the key to their diet—and the focus of their everyday efforts. By A.D. 1000 the Mayan cities were mostly in decline, and new empires—the Toltecs and the Aztecs—had formed in the Valley of Mexico to the north. By this time, too, advanced cultures were appearing elsewhere in the Americas; among these were the Incas of modern-day Peru and the Mound Builders of the Ohio and Mississippi river valleys in the present-day United States. These, like the earlier kingdoms of Mexico, were agricultural peoples, but they also built cities and maintained extensive networks of trade.

Indian Foremothers and the Coming of the Europeans

Beginning in 1492, the lives of Native Americans were changed forever by the arrival of foreigners from Europe. Christopher Columbus was only the first in a long line of overseas explorers, and the explorers were followed by traders, settlers, conquerors, and colonizers. It was, all in all, an invasion of massive proportions.

Columbus failed to realize, as he dropped anchor among the islands of the Caribbean, that he had reached a "New World" (new, of course, only from a European viewpoint); instead, he believed himself to be in the Asian region known as the Indies. Thus he called the people who greeted him Indians, a mistake that has persisted to the present day. Had he known better—had he somehow gained the hindsight of our own time—he would have found these American groups to be almost as different from one another as they were from his own "tribe" of Europeans.

There were the peoples of the islands and of the Atlantic and the Pacific coasts, fisherfolk whose lives expressed the rhythms of the sea. There were numerous tribes of hunters, especially in the northern half of North America, where the environment allowed no other means of survival. There were the farmers of lower North America, Mexico, and the South American highlands. There were cultures linked to every conceivable environment: to mountains and prairies, and deserts and forests; to arctic cold and tropical heat. Their social and political systems ranged from highly centralized empires and sprawling confederacies to village-level chiefdoms and roving, family-style bands. Their ideas about men and women were no less varied. In some groups, women were leaders; in others, followers. Some households were matrilineal, organized around mothers; others, patrilineal. Women's work was central and primary in some groups, while in others it mainly involved assistance to men. The languages these Indians spoke were too numerous for historians to count accurately; estimates range upward from two thousand, not including local differences of dialect. Even the physical appearance of the Indians

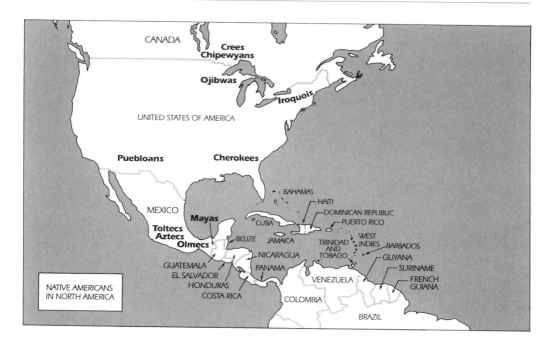

CANADA
Crees
Chipewyans
Ojibwas
Iroquois
UNITED STATES OF AMERICA
Puebloans   Cherokees
BAHAMAS
MEXICO   HAITI
Mayas   DOMINICAN REPUBLIC
CUBA   PUERTO RICO
Toltecs
Aztecs   WEST
Olmecs   BELIZE   JAMAICA   TRINIDAD   INDIES   BARBADOS
AND
NICARAGUA   TOBAGO   GUYANA
GUATEMALA   PANAMA   SURINAME
EL SALVADOR   VENEZUELA   FRENCH
NATIVE AMERICANS   HONDURAS   GUIANA
IN NORTH AMERICA   COSTA RICA
COLOMBIA
BRAZIL

was enormously varied. Some were very dark, others light-skinned; some were tall and rangy in stature, others short and heavyset; some clearly displayed the Asian features of their ancestors, others did not.

Yet to Columbus and to other Europeans who came in his wake, they were all of a piece—Indians. And they did share at least a few biological characteristics. To their great misfortune, for example, they were widely vulnerable to the unfamiliar diseases brought by the explorers and colonists from overseas. Europeans had for centuries been attacked by smallpox, typhus, measles, and plague; huge numbers of people had sickened and died in recurring epidemics. But Europeans had also, over many generations, developed immunities to these diseases; their bodies learned how to fight back. Native American bodies, by contrast, had no such capacity at the time when the explorers who carried the deadly germs first began to move among them.

The results were simply catastrophic. Whole villages were wiped out in a single epidemic, and entire tribes disappeared within a decade. In some cases, such as the Incas of Peru, the European germs arrived ahead of the European people, having passed from one native group to another with lightning speed. The process began among the peoples of the Atlantic coast, but it was repeated with every newly exposed group. Epidemics moved in this way, steadily and relentlessly, from east to west until they reached the very shores of the Pacific. Historians today can only guess at the numbers affected, but it seems that within a century of Columbus's arrival a native population of nearly 100 million in *all* the Americas had been reduced by at least half. In some particular regions the toll was higher still; in Mexico, for example, it approached 90 percent. And far to the north, among a tribe near the coast of New England, only a single man—the famed Squanto—survived to greet the first of the Pilgrim settlers.

These losses were not, moreover, entirely from disease. The Europeans did not shy from using violence—including enslavements, kidnappings, killings, and full-scale warfare, depending on the time and place. The Spanish conquistadors of the sixteenth century attacked and overwhelmed the Aztecs of Mexico, the Incas of Peru, and many lesser tribes as well. A hundred years later the English fought native warriors in the newly established colonies of Virginia, Connecticut, Massachusetts, and New York, while the French battled the Iroquois Confederacy along the borders of Canada.

But it would be wrong to describe warfare as the chief mode of contact between colonists and Indians. Virtually from the start, most natives reacted to most newcomers with something other than hostility: with open interest and curiosity, with mixed admiration and scorn, and with hope of gain for themselves. The newcomers seemed physically unappealing—they were too ruddy, with too much body and facial hair—while their social style was rough and undignified by native standards. On the other hand, their material possessions and technology—large oceangoing ships, finely woven textiles, loud and deadly firearms—were undeniably impressive.

The European newcomers, meanwhile, responded from the viewpoint of their own beliefs and values. To them Indians were "heathen," and thus prime candidates for conversion to Christianity. Indians were "savage," and thus in need of learning "civilized ways." Indians were "lascivious," and thus a source of sexual temptation. Indians were skilled at farming, hunting, and surviving in the "wilderness," and thus could serve as guides for inexperienced colonists. Indians occupied land important to colonists, and thus must be removed elsewhere.

Each side wished, in the early stages, to use the other for its own benefit. Trade was perhaps the clearest example of this impulse: Indian foods, furs, skins, and tribally owned lands were traded for European cloth, guns, cookware, jewelry, and liquor. Inevitably, these exchanges were open to misunderstanding—or to outright abuse. Land was a particularly sore point. Usually, the colonists expected to obtain full privileges of ownership, while the Indians were offering rights of *use* only. In this, each side was following its own principles with respect to land. In many other cases, however, their dealings seemed mutually satisfactory.

There also developed between the Europeans and the Indians a pattern of mutual learning, even of borrowing. Each side learned, to some extent, the languages of the other. Together they created a "pidgin" speech in which elements of various tongues were joined. And each learned something of the other's cultural ways. Colonists embraced the flowery rhetoric and ritual of native diplomacy, while Indians began to use European money. Colonists learned corn cultivation from native farmers, while Indians grew grains, melons, and vegetables using seeds brought from Europe. Colonists used Indian-style canoes and snowshoes for travel; Indians raised and rode horses of European breed. Indeed, the list of such borrowings grew remarkably long. To go through this list is to glimpse a process of two-way influence: natives and newcomers becoming progressively more alike. Yet the pattern would not last indefinitely. If the exchanges were roughly even at the start, they became increasingly *un*even with the passage of time.

Trade furnished many examples of the shifting balance. In the earliest years of settlement, the natives could frequently set the terms of trade: the times and places for meeting, the goods offered and received, even the rates of exchange. But after some decades it was the colonists who set the terms. Moreover, the eventual effect of such trade was to make Indians dependent on outside sources of supply; their clothing, their tools and weapons, even their foods were increasingly obtained from European sources. At the same time, and as part of the same process, native technologies that had previously supplied their needs were left to shrivel and die. Warfare and diplomacy followed a similar track. At first, Indians pulled colonists into their own conflicts, as enemies or allies. By the later colonial period, though, the colonists' wars with Indians were simply part of larger European struggles. Meanwhile, treaty negotiations became a pretext for removing native groups from the path of white settlement.

These changes reflected the increasingly uneven population numbers as warfare and epidemics took a continuing toll on the natives. Each year there were more colonists and fewer Indians. Each year the pressure of advancing settlement increased. By the middle of the eighteenth century Indians had become a rare sight in the coastal parts of eastern North America. And in the newly formed United States of the early 1800s, Indians began to be confined to what the government called reservations.

Nevertheless, Indian cultures and Indian people did not simply fade away. In fact, some of these cultures showed great strength in resisting and ultimately adjusting to the encroachments of the Europeans. The Iroquois Five Nations succeeded for more than a century in playing off the English and the French against each other while guarding their homeland in upstate New York. They succeeded, too, in controlling the fur trade between colonial merchants and native groups farther west: Furs moved through Iroquois hands and paid Iroquois tolls and tribute on the way to markets overseas.

Farther south—indeed, all along the Atlantic seaboard—Indians pulled back and regrouped in order to save at least some of their traditional ways. A tribe that was decimated by disease or wars would join with others that had been similarly reduced to create a new group with added strength of numbers. Languages, religious beliefs, dietary customs, and technologies were blended as a result—blended, but not lost. Moreover, the members of such groups would frequently find a means to enter the market system. Some continued their old pursuits of hunting and fishing, selling their catch to the highest bidder. Others worked as porters,

laborers, or traders in their own right. These developments were especially important near, or beyond, the frontier of white settlement. But the frontier was itself
highly elastic—more nearly a region than a single line. Within that region appeared what one historian has called a "middle ground," in which white and Indian
cultures were thoroughly mixed. Daniel Boone with his coonskin cap became a
famous symbol of the middle ground, but there were equally clear, if less well
known, symbols on the Indian side as well.

In many respects the Native Americans and the European colonists were more
alike than different. On both sides the vast majority of people lived in villages and
towns. On both sides, too, agriculture was the leading means of sustenance.
European markets were more fully developed, but Indians were also quite familiar
with trade. Europeans took great pride in their Judeo-Christian religious heritage,
but Indians, too, maintained elaborate spiritual traditions. European medicines
were more effective for certain kinds of illnesses, but Indian remedies seemed better for others. Europeans possessed important technological advantages—firearms
were the most obvious example—but European visitors found much to admire in
native basketry, leatherwork, and pottery.

On one point, however, Europeans found much that was different—and nothing whatsoever to admire. Indian cultures, they said almost in one voice, allowed—
or even required—shocking mistreatment of women. At the heart of this criticism
lay divergent patterns of work. In most of Europe, before modern times, farm work

Women of a Great Lakes tribe scare birds out of the cornfields in this 1852 illustration by Henry
Rowe Schoolcraft. Taking care of the crops, as well as the household, was often the women's job in
Native American cultures.

was primarily for men, while women labored in various home-based activities. In America, with the natives, the pattern seemed almost opposite. In many tribes women took care of the fields, hoeing, planting, tending, harvesting. Women also cut and hauled firewood, built and maintained housing, and did household chores besides. Men, meanwhile, were responsible for hunting and fishing—which Europeans wrote off as mere "sport"—and also for military defense. The gist was, as Europeans saw it, that Indian men exploited their women shamefully. The men seemed idle and lazy, while women were reduced to the level of slaves.

Such charges appear with striking regularity throughout the settlers' comments on Indians; no doubt they were widely believed. But a closer look at the settlers' actions suggests a more complicated picture. Consider the matter of Indian war captives. Many native groups, especially in North America, waged war in order to seize outsiders for adoption into their own families and communities. In time these captives came to include thousands of Europeans, chiefly French and English. Of the latter, most would eventually have the chance to return home, but some were so comfortable in their new surroundings that they chose to stay on. And among such "white Indians," as they were called, the largest number by far were women.

These facts raise a question: Why did so many female captives prefer to remain with their captors—especially if women's lot among the Indians was truly equivalent to slavery? Why were they ready to leave family, friends, and home surroundings for a life allegedly at the mercy of "savage" men? Unfortunately, we cannot hear from most of them directly, but one famous "white Indian"—Mary Jemison, captured by the Iroquois in the 1740s—wrote in a published memoir about native women: "Their task is probably not harder than that of white women . . . and their cares certainly are not half as numerous, nor as great." Moreover, in her own case, Jemison had become "warmly attached [to her captors] in consideration of the favors, affection, and friendship with which they had uniformly treated me, from the time of my adoption."

Perhaps, then, there was more to the life of Indian women than what the settlers typically claimed. This chapter looks at four groups: the Puebloans of the Southwest; the Iroquois of the northeast woodlands; the fur-trading tribes—principally Ojibwas, Chipewyans, and Crees—near and north of the Great Lakes; and the Cherokees of the interior Southeast. Close views of different cultural settings provide a sense of the possibilities open to Indian women—and of the gains and losses that colonization brought to these women.

Puebloan Women and the Children of the Sun

At some point in their long migration southward, the Native Americans reached the region of present-day New Mexico. Surviving traces of an Indian presence there go back at least to 9000 B.C. What followed was the usual sequence of cultural change. As animal herds shrank, the original bands of hunters gradually became hunter-gatherers. By 2000 B.C. they had learned corn cultivation, probably through contact with farming communities farther south, and sometime after that they were growing squash and beans as well. They ceased to be nomads and built settled villages. They began also to produce colorful pottery and textiles. By around A.D. 1000 their descendants had created a culture we now call the Anasazi. Its people lived in cliff houses high above the Rio Grande and adjacent river valleys, where modern visitors can still see impressive remains. Because the climate had been slowly drying out for centuries, the Anasazi irrigated their cornfields with water from the rivers. Their farming became more productive, their villages grew in size, and their crafts were increasingly specialized and sophisticated. In about the year 1500 a new factor entered the lives of these people. Groups of nomadic Indians from the north, ancestors of the present-day Apaches and Navajos, arrived in their vicinity. Contact with the newcomers was sometimes friendly, sometimes not; there was trade, but also sporadic violence. Accordingly, life within the villages became more cautious and defensive than before.

The people of this region did not think of themselves as a single group. In fact, they represented at least a dozen different tribes (Hopi, Zuni, Tewa, Tano, Piro, and so on) and nearly as many separate languages. Nonetheless, they shared many beliefs and customs, and outsiders later called them all by the Spanish name for their villages, "pueblos." Each of the hundred or so pueblos managed its own governance. Each was led by "inside" and "outside" chiefs; the former were responsible for matters within the community, the latter for military defense. Spiritual concerns were pervasive. Deities called "katsina" were thought to control the details of everyday life, especially the appearance or absence of life-giving rains. The katsina were worshiped in underground chapels called "kivas."

The village population was divided into large family groups called lineages. Older people ("seniors") and younger ones ("juniors") were linked together by complex bonds of social obligation. These bonds were expressed, as in many other native groups elsewhere, by elaborate ceremonies of gift exchange. Gifts were given and received for all important life events: birth, puberty, marriage, and death. The most successful citizens of the pueblos were those best able to confer such gifts. Some were thought to possess special powers as warriors, rain conjurors, and medicine men, further adding to their prestige.

The most important of all social differences was that between male and female—and the position of women was notably strong. Households were organized around senior women, who owned most family property and controlled its use; a newly married man would typically move into his wife's family's house. Women's responsibilities included, above all, the nurturance, the "feeding," of others. Each day they ground corn, cut and dried meat, and prepared additional foods for family consumption—activities for which they were widely honored. Women also built and maintained housing and generally supervised family affairs. Men, meanwhile, tended the corn plots, conducted trade with outsiders such as the Apaches and Navajos, invoked the katsina, and defended the community when it came under attack. This pattern of mutual service was thought to represent the balance and harmony of the universe. The earth itself seemed to embody female qualities such as the power of reproduction. The sky and the rain were male; from their union came the corn and other crops on which human life depended. These beliefs gave a sacred meaning to human sexuality; sex was seen to symbolize the cosmic balance. Religious ceremonies were sometimes concluded with ritual acts of sexual intercourse. And, just as women gave food to sustain the lives of others, so, too, they offered their bodies sexually—even to strangers—as a sign of welcome and alliance.

Weddings were events of great moment, featuring especially elaborate gifts. The families of both bride and groom were closely involved, and the ceremony expressed the different but balanced roles of each partner. According to Hernan Gallegos, a Spanish visitor in the late sixteenth century: "Colored and ornamented blankets are set before the couple. The groom covers his bride with her blankets, and she places his on him, in such a way that they clothe one another. . . . The people place before the bride a grindstone, an olla [a large earthenware vessel], a flat earthenware pan, and drinking vessels. They also put a grinding stone in her hand. . . . The gifts set before her signify that with them she is to grind and cook food for her husband. . . . Before the groom are placed a bow, spear, warclub, and shield, which signify that he is to defend his home and protect his wife and children. They give him his crate and leather band for carrying burdens. Then they place a hoe in his hand to signify that he is to till and cultivate the soil and gather corn to support his wife and children." Impressive as these rites were, it was not expected that marriage would last for life; most Pueblo people were wed several times. A man or woman whose affections changed was free to take a new spouse.

In sum, women's power was based on their place in the household, their control of property and of the earth's fertility, and their sexuality. Men, by contrast, predominated in local politics and in communication with the gods. Balanced though these roles apparently were, they also fostered a sense of competition. In ceremonies of childbirth, for example, women would mock the genitals of boy babies and praise those of girls. And men, for their part, would periodically segregate themselves to protect their energies from women's powerful demands.

In the spring of 1539 the people of the pueblos received a strange report: a "black katsina" was approaching from the west. Escorted by Indians of other tribes, and dressed in animal skins and gaudy jewelry, he called himself Estevanico and claimed extraordinary spiritual powers. At each stop on his way he erected large prayer sticks (crosses) and chanted unintelligible words.

Upon entering one of the Zuni pueblos, Estevanico was taken prisoner. Undaunted, he announced that other katsina—white ones, whom he called Children of the Sun—would soon arrive to rescue him. He demanded gifts of food and jewelry and access to local women, whereupon his captors executed him as a witch. But Estevanico's prophecy was fulfilled the next summer, when a large group of white katsina entered the pueblo country. Riding on huge, unfamiliar monsters (horses were unknown in North America before the Europeans arrived), clad in glittering steel armor, and laden with fire-breathing guns, these strangers did indeed appear to be Children of the Sun. Greatly alarmed, the villagers prepared to defend themselves. A short battle followed and the strange katsina triumphed completely. When people nearby heard the news, they rushed to declare their submission by decking the conquerors' prayer sticks with ceremonial flowers and feathers.

Estevanico was, in fact, the black slave of Spanish explorers who had reached Florida some years earlier. And the white katsina who followed him were Spaniards from central Mexico. Their ambitions fired by rumors of "golden cities" in the north, they were attempting a new expedition of discovery. Their leader was a young officer named Francisco Vásquez de Coronado. Their expedition resulted in bitter disappointment. No gold was found in the pueblos, and Coronado wrote later that his informants had "not told the truth in a single thing." He did not immediately give up hope, however, and he spent the following year exploring still farther north in present-day Kansas. But in 1542, still disappointed, he and his men returned to Mexico to quell an Indian rebellion there.

The white katsina did not reappear for another forty years. Life in the pueblos had resumed its traditional pattern when, toward the end of the century, a new phase began. Spanish Catholic friars took aim at New Mexico as a field for missionary work. Several preliminary expeditions in the 1580s gathered useful information on the natives. And in 1595 a newly appointed Spanish governor came to stay, accompanied by a modest contingent of soldiers, settlers, and priests. The governor's guns and horses overawed the Puebloans, and their chiefs swore allegiance to the Spanish king. The settlers built houses and chapels for Christian worship, and the priests began their work of "saving [Indian] souls."

From this point forward New Mexico was a colony of Spain; successive governors and other civil officials ruled in the name of a faraway king. The initial group of around two hundred soldier-settlers in 1600 grew to nearly three thousand a century later. Meanwhile, the native population shrank from perhaps eighty thousand to ten thousand in roughly the same time period. Notwithstanding their initially small numbers the colonizers prevailed because of their much superior weaponry. But the natives did not remain wholly compliant in the face of conquest. From time to time individual pueblos would resist and revolt; then soldiers, officials, and even the friars were liable to suffer capture or death. To be sure, retaliation for such acts was swift and sure. Spanish losses were avenged tenfold or more among the Indians.

Apart from these spasms of violence, the pueblos endured a regular round of demands by the colonizers. Under the *encomineda* systems imposed by Spain on its American colonies there was tribute to pay—property, or labor, or both. And there

A Hopi katsina doll stands in stark contrast to the image of Saint Michael found in a Zuni church established by missionaries. Although native religion was strikingly different from Catholicism, some priests worked to integrate the two—by comparing the katsina to Catholic saints, for example.

were demands also on the persons of the Indians, especially for sexual favors from the women. At first the natives responded willingly; in their minds the tribute could be seen as part of a gift exchange, and the sexual favors as a form of welcome. But receiving no suitable return, they soon took a darker view.

The deepest pressure on their lives, however, came not from the settlers and civil officials but rather from the priests. For these men, few as they were, planned a sweeping transformation of native culture. They began by attacking Pueblo religion. Indians were urged to renounce katsina "devils" and embrace the Christian God. In some villages priests would raid the sacred kiva, confiscate ceremonial objects, and erect crosses in their place. One bragged to his superiors of having seized and burned "more than a thousand idols of wood."

And this was only the beginning. In order to become model Christians, the natives would have to change all their customary ways and attitudes—their sexual attitudes, for example. What the Puebloans saw as a natural, life-affirming function tinged with social and sacred meanings the friars called the "sins of the flesh." Individual sinners must, according to Catholic belief, be shamed, whipped, or otherwise cowed into repentance. And chastity, faithfulness between spouses, lifelong marriage, and physical modesty—ideas previously unknown to the Puebloans— must henceforth be embraced as supreme virtues. The changes would extend to the core of social organization. The priests aimed, for instance, to undermine the authority of seniors over juniors. Indeed, they presented themselves as the best and truest of "fathers," while urging younger Indians to reject their natural fathers. At the same time, they claimed a "mothering" role, offering gifts, care, and comfort to children. These efforts achieved some undeniable success. Young Puebloans would occasionally expose and incriminate seniors who continued their katsina worship in secret.

In all this the priests tried—again, with some success—to blend traditional Puebloan culture with parts of their own system. The prayer-sticks used in the katsina cults could be likened to Christian crosses. The katsina themselves could be compared to Catholic saints. The ancestral Corn Mother, another key figure in Pueblo religion, could be seen as an imperfect representation of the Virgin Mary. The magic of native medicine men could be matched, or exceeded, by the healing rites of the friars. Even rain conjuring could be reshaped as Christian prayer. Moreover, in exercising their various powers, the priests would seem to be acting like "inside chiefs," while the Spanish governor took on the role of "outside chief" and the soldiers claimed the role of young warriors.

Key parts of the friars' assault on native culture concerned the position of women. The friars' efforts to suppress exuberant—and sometimes generous— female sexuality increased over time and were paralleled by their disapproval of women's fertility societies, groups devoted to venerating "mother earth." To be sure, the friars mixed woman-suppression with gestures of apparent sympathy. When Indian women were exploited sexually or otherwise by Spanish settlers, it was the priests who came to their defense. Moreover, native women could find reward and solace in the Catholic adoration of Mary. So, too, could they win approval for assisting the mission churches in tasks such as baking communion bread and cleaning vestments and altar linens. Yet considered as a whole, Catholic Christianity was distinctly patriarchal, with God the Father, Christ the Son, and an entirely male priesthood. Hence the weight it pressed on Pueblo culture went largely against women. Historians have noticed a striking link: In those pueblos least affected by Christianity, families continued to be organized according to matrilineal principles, and some degree of fertility worship survived. In pueblos where missionary influence was strong, matrilineal families gave way to patrilineal ones, and fertility rites of all kinds disappeared.

Of course, native women had dealings with many other Europeans besides the priests. And although these others also maintained patriarchal standards,

Unmarried Hopi girls in Arizona can be identified by their hair whorls. To the Puebloan culture, the strict Catholic codes that imposed chastity before marriage and prohibited divorce were new and strange concepts.

their effect on the women was quite complex. What were the circumstances that brought the two groups—Spanish settlers and Puebloan women—together? And how much did they influence one another?

Most settlers in the original group, at least ninety percent, were men. This meant that they had to look to the Indians for female companionship. Some took Puebloan women into their houses and beds as mistresses. Others formalized such relationships with rites of marriage. Of course, there were many looser connections as well: casual short-term sprees, prostitution, forcible rapes. A common result of all such varied relationships was half-breed children, whom the Spanish called *mestizos*. Eventually mestizos would form a large part of the total New Mexican population.

Native women also played important work roles in relation to the colonists. Many Spaniards hired household maids from the pueblos; the duties of these women included cooking, cleaning, childcare, and other domestic chores. A few served as interpreters. Indians were frequently in demand as seamstresses and weavers. Their blankets and other textiles proved important both for personal use and in trade. The same was true of the pine nuts and berries gathered by Indian women. Ironware, leatherwork, and some foodstuffs had to be imported from Mexico, and Indian-made articles were offered in exchange.

Puebloan women had for generations played a leading role in house building; many were expert plasterers. This custom seemed surprising and inappropriate to the early Spanish settlers, and some wished to change it. But the natives proved resistant. "If we compel any man to work on building a house," wrote one of the priests, "the women laugh at him . . . and he runs away." In fact, the shame of such incidents went so deep that some of the men involved would actually leave for good and take up with the nearby Apaches. In time the colonists accepted the native pattern and sought to benefit from it. Women continued to work as builders for the Spanish as well as for their own people. Indeed, in the nineteenth century, when visitors arrived from other parts of America, they too were amazed at the sight of women builders. But plastering has remained an important activity for Indian women of the Southwest right up to the present day.

Other traditional work activities of the women also won appreciation from the colonists. As far back as the 1540s, a member of Coronado's expedition had noted their production of "earthenware . . . jars of extraordinary labor and workmanship." Their textiles were no less impressive, especially the delicate embroidery and painted design. Puebloan women owned and tended large flocks of turkeys (another surprise for the Spanish). In every case, the products might easily enter settler households and then become part of the larger colonial trade.

Significantly, Indian women adopted materials and methods from the colonists in order to diversify or improve on their own craftsmanship. Their textiles had traditionally been made from cotton, but when the Spanish introduced sheep to the Southwest, wool became an equally popular fiber. Moreover, the use of sheepskin fragments to set plaster made building easier and the final result stronger. Peaches, melons, and apricots brought from Spain, as well as tomatoes and chilies from Mexico, could be incorporated into their cooking, with important consequences for native diet. All such developments modified, but did not obliterate, traditional native ways. And they may actually have worked to strengthen the position of Puebloan women. It is worth noting that women in the neighboring tribes—for example, the Apaches and Navajos—modeled their own work roles on the Puebloans. They too would become potters and textile makers of great skill, and they too would eventually learn plastering.

The middle decades of the seventeenth century were a time of simmering discontent in the pueblos. There was repeated drought, leading to crop failure, leading to famine. Apache and Navajo neighbors, themselves on the brink of starvation, carried out frequent, deadly raids. The Spanish governors bickered continually with the priests, and, as often as not, the Indians were caught in the middle. Finally, in the summer of 1680, after months of secret planning, the pueblos rose together in open revolt. Eight thousand warriors, including some of their erstwhile enemies, the Apaches, swept into battle under the leadership of a Tewa medicine man named Popé. Within a few days Spanish settlements through-out New Mexico lay in ruins and hundreds of settlers, including dozens of friars, were dead. The following months brought a determined campaign to replace for-eign with traditional Indian ways. Christianity, the Spanish language, European foods, clothing, and social customs—all must be destroyed without a trace. But that could not—and did not—happen. Droughts continued. The Puebloans and the Apaches quarreled. And even inside the pueblos there was dissension, which in some cases amounted to civil war. The Spanish, for their part, would not accept defeat; after a decade of withdrawal, they used their bases to the south as launch-ing-points for the reconquest of New Mexico. By 1692 they had succeeded.

Reconquest did not bring simply a return to earlier patterns. The priests, for one thing, would operate only in a much reduced role. The settlers and soldiers would, from now on, live in well-protected fortresslike communities. And the pueblos themselves, especially those at some distance from the Spanish, would try to main-tain their own protected world. Insofar as possible they continued their ancient rites and other cultural practices in private—or, in the case of the kivas, literally underground. But the pueblos were not entirely immune to outside pressure. The Spanish continued to demand tribute labor and most pueblos, however reluctant-ly, complied. At stated times and places work gangs reported to Spanish officials for assignment—the men to dig irrigation ditches and cultivate the governor's fields, the women to perform domestic chores. In theory, no one was exempt, including, in the words of the law, "even pregnant women."

In fact, this system of draft labor posed special dangers to women, pregnant or not. Sexual abuse of draftees by Spanish men seems to have been common. "When Indian women enter Santa Fe [the colonial capital] to mill wheat or spin wool," reported a local priest, "they return to their pueblos deflowered and crying over their dishonor." Worse still, some of these attacks led to pregnancy, and often when that happened the woman and her child were disowned by her family. The Spanish called such unfortunates *genizaros,* which means "mixed" or "hybrid." They had no place to turn except the Spanish towns, where they might subsist as household domestics under conditions not far from slavery. Continued abuse, sexual and oth-erwise, was almost a certainty.

These were perhaps the worst of the human casualties of Spanish colonization, but they were just a part of the larger story. Another part, no less important and affecting, involved the many Puebloan women who managed to accommodate the pressures of colonization—and even to shape the terms of that accommodation. Their importance as mothers, as workers, and as guardians of cherished traditions would long outlast the rule of the colonizers. Indeed, the Puebloans remain one of the most vibrant of all native societies in the present-day United States. They have responded very forcefully to modern economic conditions; they profit, for example, from tourism in and around their settlements. Yet they have kept their own identity, and their pride, as a people distinct from their Anglo neighbors. Women's role has always been central to this process of development and change. Baskets, pottery, and textiles made by Puebloan women now earn widespread admiration—and money. Traditional skills, applied under altered conditions: this has been the strategy of Puebloan women through many generations.

One specific case may stand for the rest. Near the end of the nineteenth century, fragments of ancient pottery began to appear in archaeological excavations near the Hopi pueblos of central Arizona. Their long-forgotten style and methods were taken up by a local craftswoman named Nampeyo. Her work in turn sparked a major resurgence of Puebloan ceramic traditions. Nampeyo's pots revived designs not seen in centuries; moreover, she extended the old forms to make new ones as well. Her work was sold in shops, hotels, and railroad stations throughout the Southwest. Nampeyo's achievement was a modern echo of a theme first sounded in the era of colonization when Puebloan women saved the old by accommodating the new, and through it all *survived.*

Iroquois Women and the Village World

According to the people we now know as Iroquois, history began with a godlike being called Sky Woman. Pushed from her home in the heavens by her jealous, uncaring husband, she fell toward an endless lake below. But birds and ducks flew to break her fall, and a turtle emerged from the waters to provide a resting place. Animals brought earth to put on the turtle's back—which, with Sky Woman's help, grew into the continent of North America. Presently, Sky Woman bore a daughter, and the daughter in turn bore twin sons. One of them, the Good Twin, improved the land and brought human beings to life. His brother, the Evil Twin, tried to destroy these works of creation. Eventually the two fought. Fortunately, the Good Twin triumphed and began teaching humans how to farm, how to govern themselves, and how to communicate with the spirit world. This origin myth illustrates the importance of women to the Iroquois. Other Iroquois myths have a similar emphasis; they tell, for example, of long migrations throughout North America—frequently under the leadership of a woman.

The actual origins of the Iroquois are difficult to discover. They seem, as their myths suggest, to have been migrants from elsewhere. Their most likely ancestors were a people called the Owasco, who by about A.D. 1000 were established to the south and east of the Great Lakes. The Owasco, like the Iroquois later on, lived in compact villages and supported themselves through hunting and farming. As the centuries passed, these communities fell into recurrent warfare, while trade and other forms of contact among them dwindled almost to nothing. Eventually, they

A typical Iroquois village contained a cluster of bark-covered longhouses. The best site for a village was on a hilltop, which made it easier to defend against enemy war parties.

came together to make a "Great Peace"—there are powerful legends about that as well—and entered a new phase of their history. The peace would thereafter be kept by a "League" of their "Five Nations": the Mohawk, the Oneida, the Onondaga, the Cayuga, and the Seneca. These five made up the famed Iroquois Confederacy. A sixth group, the Tuscarora, joined in the eighteenth century.

For protection Iroquois villages were set on hilltops and enclosed by high palisade fences. Each contained a cluster of several dozen residential buildings called longhouses. These were large, tunnel-like structures framed by tree limbs and covered with huge strips of bark. On the land beside the palisades stretched farm fields, and beyond the fields rose the dark shapes of the forest. The Iroquois themselves spoke of the "village world" and the "forest world" as separate places with entirely different modes of life.

The village world was first and foremost a world of women. The local population was organized into large clans. The clans themselves were composed of families, with women at the center in each case. When young Iroquois married, they usually took up residence in the wife's longhouse; there they would join other members of her clan and family—mother, aunts, sisters, female cousins, and related menfolk. Their children were considered to belong to her family's "line" and would, when grown, inherit property from the same source. The husband, meanwhile, remained closely allied with his own mother's household; according to one account, "his mother and his sisters are more dear to him than his wife."

Women also bore a primary responsibility to *provide*—for themselves, for their children and other relatives, and for the community at large. The land belonged to them, not to their husbands and brothers. So did the crops, especially the so-called three sisters—corn, squash, and beans—on which human life was thought to depend. Work parties of women labored in the fields all through the summer season. Corn cultivation was a particularly elaborate focus of activity. In addition to performing the basic tasks of planting, tending, and harvesting, women dried and braided the mature husks, shelled the kernels for storage, ground the stored kernels into flour, sifted the flour in preparation for cooking, and boiled the result into a variety of stews, all the while retaining a few bits for the *next* summer's planting. Every Iroquois girl learned the various steps at an early age. And every Iroquois woman was honored for her part in this work in a variety of seasonal festivals.

Women's responsibilities extended well beyond home care and farming. Berries, fruits, nuts, and other gathered products were also important to the Iroquois diet—and were also part of the female domain. Meat was obtained by men in far-ranging hunts, but women were much involved in skinning, packing, and otherwise preparing the animal carcasses for consumption. Women joined men in springtime fishing expeditions at strategic sites on nearby streams. Women were centrally involved in craft production: basketry, pottery, rope making, and leather work. Taken together, these activities secured their preeminence in the village world.

The men, for their part, were dominant in the forest world. Hunting was only a part of what they did there. Men led in dealings with outsiders—with fellow Iroquois from other villages and regions, and with strangers from beyond Iroquois lands altogether. Men, therefore, were traders, diplomats, and above all, warriors. Yet precisely because these duties took them away for long periods, their position within the village was weakened.

To be sure, men decided matters of policy. Iroquois clans were headed by chiefs, who would, as the occasion demanded, come together in council to govern their village and tribe. Tribal councils in turn chose representatives to the council of the Five Nations League itself. At every level such leaders were men, but women were not left out—on the contrary, their role was critical. For one thing, local chiefs were selected by clan matrons. Typically, when a chief died, these elder women would review the ranks of adult clansmen and then nominate a successor. The matrons met more or less regularly to discuss policy; their opinions, as conveyed subsequently to the chiefs, carried much weight.

Even in warfare, apparently the prime responsibility of men, women played an important part. Some Iroquois wars were fought to avenge wrongs done to an individual or a family. Others were "mourning wars" designed to secure captives who might replace and "requicken" (or, figuratively, bring back to life) deceased members of local clans. Either way, the wishes of women, especially the matrons, would likely prove decisive. One whose husband or son had died in battle could virtually require her kinsmen to start a mourning war. And when the battle was over, the same woman might decide the fate of any captives—whether to "send them to the flames," as the Europeans commonly described ritual torture and execution by burning, or to adopt them into her own or another village family. Women participated even in the torture process itself, by taking their place in the gauntlets of aroused villagers who taunted and beat newly arrived captives and in the crowds that carried out decrees of full-scale immolation.

The range of women's rights and duties has long impressed observers from outside the country of the Iroquois. Some early visitors, noting especially women's work obligations, reduced it all to "enslavement"—Iroquois women as slaves to their husbands. But others reached an opposite conclusion. According to a missionary at the beginning of the eighteenth century, "it is they [the women] who really maintain the tribe . . . In them resides all the real authority." Modern anthropologists and historians are inclined to side with the second viewpoint; many go so far as to use the term *matriarchy,* meaning a society in which women rule. The Iroquois matrons, writes one historian, had more prestige and power "than women have enjoyed anywhere [else] at any time."

Longer than most Indian groups—perhaps longer than any—the Iroquois managed to hold their space against the pressures of colonization. Their contact with Europeans began soon after the opening of the seventeenth century, and they were still a substantial presence at the time of the American Revolution 150 years later. Indeed, at least a portion of their ancient tribal ground has remained with their descendants to the present day.

The first Europeans they saw were undoubtedly traders. By 1620 Iroquois were visiting a Dutch outpost called Fort Orange on the site of present-day Albany to exchange furs for guns, cloth, liquor, and other European-made goods. This was the start of a pattern that would greatly change their lives. From self-sufficient producers and consumers of what they produced, the Iroquois were transformed into vigorous participants in the international market system. This in turn pulled them into increasingly complicated, often violent, relations with a variety of Indian and European neighbors.

In the 1620s the Mohawks fought and defeated the Mahicans to their east; this assured Iroquois dominance in trading with the Dutch. In the 1630s and 1640s Iroquois war parties began raiding Huron and Algonquin convoys to the north and thus intruded themselves into the trade of French Canada. In 1649 a large Five Nations attack force overwhelmed and dispersed the Hurons and also defeated a number of neighboring tribes in what is today Ontario. In the late 1650s they turned on the Eries to the west; in the 1670s, they conquered the Susquehannocks to the south; and in the 1680s, the Illinois farther toward the Great Lakes. The motive of the Iroquois in every case was economic: to control the Indian side of the ever-widening fur trade. Their success in these Beaver Wars would establish their superiority throughout the woodland regions of eastern North America.

Success also brought them more fully to grips with the European colonizers. The French opposed Iroquois moves against the tribes of Canada and mounted periodic invasions against the Mohawks, Oneidas, and Senecas. The Indians replied with sharp, bloody strikes of their own; by the 1690s French colonists at Montreal and other Canadian sites were living in daily fear for their lives. Fortunately for both sides, peace was finally achieved through elaborate treaty negotiations in 1701.

In spite of all their victories, the Iroquois suffered grievously from this century-long period of warfare. Young warriors died by the hundreds—and there had not been more than a few thousand to begin with. To these losses "on the warpath" must be added the huge toll taken by recurrent epidemic disease. Village populations could be suddenly halved (or worse), and the overall number of Iroquois was in a steep decline. Each of the Five Nations tried to replenish its ranks by incorporating war captives; in certain villages former captives became a majority. But this created new complications as differences of culture, language, and personal loyalty created social divisiveness. Local power structures changed as well. The traditional chiefs seem gradually to have lost authority, and war leaders took their place. Moreover, because men were so frequently away at war, the village world was even more fully controlled by women. There is evidence that the power of the matrons increased and that the women's councils attained greater and more direct influence in matters of policy. Some eighteenth-century visitors to the Iroquois reported the presence of women chiefs they called "she-sachems," a new and significant development.

But there was more to the Iroquois experience of confronting colonization than trade and warfare. As with other native groups, religion proved an especially powerful factor. Dutch and English preachers paid at least occasional visits to the Iroquois throughout the period, but it was French Catholics based in Canada who made by far the greatest impact. The most active of these were Jesuits, members of a monastic order with worldwide plans and ambitions. Jesuit missionaries were present in Iroquoia as early as the 1640s, and they stayed there even during periods of open French-Iroquois hostilities. Their eagerness to convert the "poor savages" was matched by their readiness to suffer and die for their faith; the combination was undeniably powerful. Jesuits penetrated even the most remote and unfriendly of Iroquois villages. Some remained for years or decades, learned the tribal languages and customs, and endured the taunts—or worse abuse—of their hosts. A few paid the ultimate price of death by torture when native opinion turned fully against them. Through their sacrifice, they became martyrs in the eyes of their fellow churchmen.

From the Indian standpoint these visitors were altogether strange. The Iroquois called them "blackrobes," after their severe monkish clothing. Their beards and body hair also seemed peculiar, as Indian men had little of either, and much of their behavior appeared unnatural, if not absurd. Their status as bachelors and their renunciation of any sexual interest were especially baffling. Moreover, their difficulty in meeting the challenges of survival in the wilderness sometimes verged on the laughable. For all that, Indians could not fail to notice the Jesuits' tenacity—or to listen, at least occasionally, to their message. The Jesuits controlled a remarkable technology, including clocks, medicines, iron tools, and housewares, all of which were openly displayed in their residences. They displayed as well extraordinary powers of communication and memory through scribbled marks on parchment paper. And their connections to "white chiefs," officials of the colonial governments, could yield valuable gains for the natives—trade preferences, for instance.

These factors weighed on the side of accommodating the missionaries. And many Iroquois went well beyond accommodation. With so much turmoil and violence around them, and with their own shamans apparently unable to reverse the trend, some decided to accept the Christian god. These converts might then become foes of others among their kin and neighbors who remained true to the old tribal beliefs. Iroquois villages became increasingly divided, with traditionalists on one side and newly declared Christians on the other. As this conflict worsened, a growing number of the Christian villagers decided to leave. The Jesuits were starting mission communities for Indian converts in various parts of Canada, and the Iroquois were among the first to respond. These places would, with the passage of time, develop a strikingly mixed cultural pattern: though Catholic in religion, they nonetheless preserved many aspects of native tradition. Their dwellings were likely to be longhouses. Their diet was still centered on the "three sisters," especially corn. The women kept their old roles as farmers and gatherers, while the men continued to hunt and, when the occasion required, go off to war. Indeed, the paired worlds of village and forest remained largely intact.

The Jesuits, however, were not content to leave Indian life as it was, and struggled for generations to effect change. Sex, marriage, and divorce were particular points of concern. Traditional Iroquois courtship practice was notably free, by Christian standards; sexual contact was generally allowed, or even expected. Out-of-wedlock births were, accordingly, quite numerous, and were accepted without stigma. Marriage making was another matter—there the matrons took charge. The interests of the families were carefully weighed before a particular match could win approval. Divorce was common and easily and informally managed, with no bar whatsoever to remarriage. The Jesuits opposed these customs at every point. Courtship should, in their view, be closely supervised; the church, not the matrons, should oversee marriage; and remarriage should be entirely forbidden. The Indians gave lip service (at most) to the Jesuit position and quietly continued with their own ways.

The Iroquois response to Christianity itself was deeper and more complicated. The Jesuits insisted on teaching the essentials of the faith and claimed extraordinary success in doing so. The Canadian missions gained wide publicity; visitors from outside were reportedly moved to tears by the "sober conduct" and "pious disposition" of the converts.

Strikingly, too, the women responded with particular fervor. The Jesuits' writings on native villages are full of vivid stories of women converts gathered in prayerful sisterhood or pleading with reluctant relatives, especially husbands, to accept the "true faith," or reproaching local shamans for their "devil worship," or destroying the liquor supplies that made their neighbors drunk. Some women endured "painful persecution" by other villagers who supported traditional ways. A few paid for their beliefs with life itself—"in the fires," as Jesuit accounts put it, of native torture ceremonies.

The traditional pattern of female leadership was present throughout the northern missions. The largest of these—called Kahnawake, near Montreal—witnessed a legendary outburst of female "devotion" around 1680, when a young Mohawk woman named Kateri Tekakwitha arrived. Earlier converted by Jesuits in her home village, Kateri brought to Kahnawake a remarkably intense focus on religious matters. Almost immediately, she became the center of a kind of cult, in which she and other mission women literally tortured themselves for their faith. They beat each other with whips, walked naked in the winter cold, fasted for days at a time, refused to sleep, and recited rosaries till their voices went hoarse—all this in the name of an ever-deepening piety. The men of the community watched with mixed fascination and envy; the Jesuits moved from wonder and excitement to growing alarm. Eventually, Kateri took sick and died, and the movement she led simmered down. However, she was remembered thereafter as a kind of martyr. Visitors came to her grave—indeed, they still come—to pray for her blessing. For some she worked apparent miracles. And the Catholic Church, in the twentieth century, began the process of making her a saint.

One can only speculate on the reasons why women led the way in converting from their native religion to Christianity. But Iroquois women had always been leaders of a sort, and certain elements of Catholic Christianity may have seemed especially appealing to female converts: the tradition of reverence for the Virgin Mary, the honor accorded to numerous female saints, and the various sisterhoods of nuns, some of which had spread to the European colonies in North America. Yet the piety of the Christian Iroquois was more than a simple matter of conversion. For even as they embraced their new faith, they infused it with elements distinctively their own. They decorated the churches with wampum beads, wore traditional ceremonial dress to Mass, and added native harmonies to familiar hymns

This Mohawk cradleboard, with elaborate carved and painted decorations, was probably made around 1875. In rearing their children, Iroquois women continued to pass along their heritage and traditions even after the tribe had learned to live among whites and had adopted many white ways.

and chants. They invented new rites of penance and thanksgiving, reflecting the pattern of Iroquois feasts. The practices of Kateri and her followers resembled native "vision quests," in which young Iroquois sought spiritual knowledge through self-denial and deprivation. The result of all these changes was a distinctly native brand of Catholicism. Its features can be seen even today in the churches of Indian communities in New York State and Canada.

The American Revolution was a critical and ultimately devastating event in the history of the Iroquois. For the first time the nations themselves were divided: four sided with the British, two with the revolutionary patriots. The fighting flowed back and forth through the tribal heartlands, leaving death and destruction in its wake. The climax was a brutal campaign, led by the patriot General John Sullivan, to burn the towns and croplands of the Indians, especially the Seneca, who remained loyal to Great Britain. Its successful conclusion left thousands of Indians without the means to support themselves; many died soon thereafter from starvation or disease.

The post-Revolution years were no kinder to the Iroquois. Through a series of treaties, the new United States government peeled away large chunks of their lands and forced them to accept the status of a conquered people. These legal actions were followed by renewed pressures from Christian missionaries, this time from Quakers and other Protestants. Once again the idea was to detach the natives from their traditional ways and move them toward modern "civilization." The process was furthered by changes in the environment, especially the disappearance of the woodlands. No longer could hunting, fishing, and gathering form any considerable part of the Iroquois' life-sustaining activities. These changes struck especially hard at the position of Iroquois men, who were obliged now to transform themselves from hunters and warriors into farmers and day laborers. Many succumbed to despair or escaped into alcoholism. The position of women, by contrast, was less directly undermined. Their farming and traditional craft production could be continued under the new conditions. And women's role in the household, in the clan, and in local governance seems to have remained as strong as it had been before. Moreover, their responsibilities in child rearing made them guardians of traditional Iroquois ways for the future.

In the long run, of course, all Iroquois—female as well as male—suffered from the changes around them. But, also in the long run, their culture, like many others in Native America, would continue in at least modified form. To this process Iroquois women made a persistent, vital contribution.

Fur-Trade Women and the Middle Ground

Among the many factors shaping relations between Indians and people of European descent, none was more important than the North American beaver. Worldwide demand for the furs of this water-dwelling mammal began growing by or before the year 1500. Furs could be made into robes worn against the cold of winter, and above all, into warm, waterproof hats. In the sixteenth century beaver furs came principally from Russia and surrounding regions; by the seventeenth century they were coming increasingly from America. Although European fur dealers especially prized the soft undercoat of the beaver, other fur-bearing animals—muskrats, martens, deer, moose, and even bears—were important in the fur trade that developed in North America.

At first animals were taken near the little settlements along the Atlantic coast. But the supply there, especially of beaver, was soon exhausted, so the trade moved steadily west. In the eighteenth century it penetrated the heart of the continent, eventually reaching the Rocky Mountains and the great bays of central Canada. Before that time, however, the fur trade had made its greatest impact in the vast wilderness surrounding the Great Lakes. Among the Native American tribes most powerfully affected were the Ojibwas, Chipewyans, and Crees.

Because the fur trade was so profitable, people from various nations wished to control its European end. For many decades the French led the way in this competition. The government of New France (their colony in what today is Canada) tried to organize and regulate all aspects of the trade. Indians from the west were encouraged to bring their goods to huge market fairs held annually in the city of Montreal. These were boisterous events, with much feasting, drinking, and speechmaking, the exchange of gifts, and the renewal of political alliances. After the 1670s such trade fairs declined in importance, and furs were increasingly exchanged in the "Indian country" itself. French traders journeyed alone or in small groups to native villages and hunting camps deep in the forest. Meanwhile, Englishmen tried to enlarge their own part of the trade. Then, in the 1750s and '60s, the English defeated the French in a bitter war for control of North America, and the shape of the trade changed yet again. In the years to follow, it was managed largely by huge corporations like the Hudson Bay and Northwest companies. Moreover, in the nineteenth century, English operations moved gradually from transporting and selling furs into trapping the animals in their native habitats.

Throughout this long sequence, the fur trade drew Indians and Euro-Americans closer and closer together. Wherever the trade was centered, there developed a kind of middle ground—a region where cultures met, customs clashed, lifestyles merged and blended one into another. Indians adopted certain "white" ways, such as European-style clothes, food, and weaponry, while whites, for their part, adjusted to the ways of the natives. "Nous sommes tous sauvages" ("We are all savages"), wrote one French trader about his experience of the middle ground in the late eighteenth century.

Often, in fact, relations between the two sides passed through the stage of familiarity to real intimacy. There were few white women in the region of the middle ground, so traders would frequently take up with native "squaws" (a term that was extremely common in previous centuries and now seems painfully racist). Some of these relationships were actual marriages, formalized in church and at law; others were informal but nonetheless deep and long lasting; still others were affairs of a single season. Whatever their depth and duration, they helped to anchor a widespread pattern of interracial exchange. But companionship and sexual favors for the traders were only the start of women's involvement in the fur trade. From these flowed a variety of related contributions, all of them important—not to say indispensable.

Sturdy footwear was key to success in the trade and survival in the wilderness: moccasins in summer, snowshoes in winter. And everywhere these were made by Indian women. The process was laborious. For moccasins it involved the tanning, cutting, and shaping of animal hides; for snowshoes, the preparation and webbing of leather strands to be stretched within a wooden frame. On one apparently typical expedition in the 1780s, according to the leader's account, the Indian wives of two French traders were kept "continually employed making shoes [moccasins] of moose skin, as a pair does not last … above one day." At about the same time a Scotsman trading on his own in winter lamented his lack of snowshoes: "I do not know what to do without these articles—see what it is to have no wives!"

A reliable food supply was no less essential. Here, too, Indian women made the key contributions. Some set snares to catch small game for the table; "my woman brings home eight hares and fourteen partridges," wrote an English trader with evident satisfaction in the summer of 1815. Others fished the wilderness rivers and dried their catch to preserve it for the future. Still others harvested wild rice from shoreline marshes. In springtime they took sap for sugaring from maple trees,

In this 1850 drawing, Ojibwa women harvest wild rice in Wisconsin. The labor of Indian women was crucial in providing a reliable food supply for trappers and traders.

and in summer they gathered berries from the forest floor. The most important food of all in the middle ground was Indian pemmican, of which Indian women were the sole producers. Starting with fresh buffalo carcasses, they cut out a supply of stripped meat, dried it in the sun or over a fire, pounded it with mortars, added melted fat, and stuffed the finished product into sacks of animal hide, also of their own making. Thus prepared and packaged, pemmican could be transported far and wide; the fact that it was highly nutritious and kept well only added to its value. From all these activities of the women, traders derived a varied and usually ample diet. From time to time, however, there were shortages or other situations of special need. One trader described a time when he was injured and without food "till the berries became ripe and the kind hearted Indian women brought me plenty." Another remembered how his Indian wife saved a large group from starvation because she alone possessed the skills of making and mending fishnets.

Besides performing such traditional domestic tasks—traditional in their own cultures as well as those of the Europeans—Indian women contributed directly to the operations of the trade. Of obvious importance was their knowledge and skill in dressing furs; officials of one English company described how they "clean and put into a state of preservation all beaver and otter skins brought ... undried and in bad condition." They participated, too, in making the canoes on which travel and transport so largely depended. In many native communities the women were carefully trained to prepare special tree roots called *wattape* for sewing the seams of these craft. They also gathered gum for use in caulking, and fashioned canoe sails. Moreover, when the canoes were ready for the water, Indian women sometimes took a turn at paddling. A trader, returning home from a long wilderness trek, reported encountering three heavily loaded canoes, each one paddled by an English man and an Indian woman—the latter in the steering position. It was clear to all how much the trade depended on the labor of these women. A wilderness guide summed it up in the early 1770s. Women, he noted, were essential as porters. Moreover, they "pitch our tents, make and mend our clothing, keep us warm at night; and, in fact, there is no such thing as travelling any considerable distance, or for any length of time, in this country without their assistance."

But even this does not exhaust the list of their contributions. Frequently, Indian women put their knowledge of the wilderness to direct use by serving the traders as guides. In addition, they could play the role of interpreters, or even of language teachers, for the men. In some cases, rival trading posts competed for the allegiance of women whose language skills were especially strong. Moreover, Indian women served, on several levels, as diplomatic agents for the traders. Even when entirely informal, this process was still important. Traders would need introductions to local chiefs and clan groups, which their native wives could readily supply. In fact, there were numerous occasions when female partners helped to smooth the way by furnishing contacts, delivering messages, or resolving differences and misunderstandings.

Occasionally their diplomacy rose to higher, more official levels. A Chipewyan woman named Thanadelthur provides a good example. In 1713 she was captured by Crees, traditional enemies of her tribe. A year later she escaped and, though almost starved, somehow made her way to an English trading post. There she offered her services as a guide along the route to her Chipewyan homeland. The English governor, anxious to extend the range of his trade, quickly took her on. In the long expedition that followed, Thanadelthur became very much a leader. Whenever disaster threatened, in the form of sickness, starvation, or enemy attack, she kept the group moving forward. When the route itself proved difficult, she set off alone and after many days of perilous travel reached her objective. When the Chipewyans and Crees seemed unwilling to trust each other, the Scottish trader William Stuart reported, "she made them all stand in fear of her; she scolded at some ... and forced them to the peace." And when, at length, the expedition had returned home, the English governor acknowledged Thanadelthur's part as "the chief promoter and acter" in it. Thanadelthur spent the next months advising on new possibilities for trade, and was about to lead another wilderness journey when she was struck down by illness. The governor tried frantically to nurse her back to health; when she died in spite of his best efforts, he "felt almost ready to break my heart." She had been, he wrote to his superiors, a person of "very high spirit and of the foremost resolution that I ever see." Her loss, therefore, was bound to be "very prejudicial to the company's interest."

Finally, some Indian women became direct participants in the trade, especially with small animals like rabbits and martens. After all, as one English visitor noted, in many tribes "the snaring and trapping [of small animals] . . . are the business of women," and their skills in such work were readily transferable to dealings with outsiders. A further step might lead them into direct partnership with European traders, where business, sex, and companionship were fully entwined.

It is important to understand all this from the viewpoint of the women involved. Why were they interested in forming such connections—with the trade, and with individual traders? And what were the consequences for their own lives?

Often the traders made a poor first impression. Most Indians found European men physically unappealing, especially their facial and body hair. One group contrasted their own "soft and delicate" skin with the "ugly" appearance of whites. Another ridiculed the possibility of intermarriage, saying that "our [women] would not live with them, for they have hair all over their faces and we have none there or elsewhere." Moreover, Indians found Europeans to be rude in manner and personal style: impulsive, complaining, lacking in dignity and self-control.

Increasing familiarity would soften these impressions, at least for some. And other factors also worked, over time, to draw native women toward the traders. Christianity was one such factor. Missionaries noted that most of their converts were female; Indian men, after all, were frequently away on the hunt or at war, while the women were accessible on a regular basis at home. Once conversion had been achieved, a woman might prefer to take a Christian husband. Demography was a second and parallel factor. In some Indian communities women outnumbered men by large margins. Polygamy could solve this problem, but not for women who had been Christianized. Indeed, the missionaries insisted with special vehemence on the principle of one wife per man.

Most native women, of course, were not Christians, and most did not marry white husbands. Those who did make one or the other choice, or both, were unusual—and may well have been unusual to begin with. In fact, Indian cultures had long recognized special roles for certain women, roles that went against accepted tribal principles. For example, a few women qualified as seers because of their ability to prophesy. Others were healers of physical and psychological illnesses. Still others were known as "hunting women"; they accompanied men on the hunt, gave their labor as needed, and sometimes provided sexual favors as well. An additional group would actually go into battle with men as "warrior women." All these women were exceptional; all violated the expectations that applied to others of their sex. But all were tolerated, and even to a degree admired, for their evident strength. And it appears that women who married white men were similarly regarded. Perhaps some individuals in this last category had previously belonged to one of the others as well—for example, a hunting woman who became a trader's wife.

The very process of personal growth sometimes forecast these outcomes. Indian girls, like Indian boys, typically undertook a vision quest upon reaching the age of puberty. This meant a period of withdrawal from regular life, of fasting and intense prayer, and—if all went well—of dreams and visions about the future. Most girls dreamed of spirits who revealed the secrets of successful marriage, childbearing, and other aspects of domestic life. But future hunting women might dream instead of buffaloes and wilderness treks, while budding female warriors "saw" battles and weaponry. And the visions of at least one Indian girl predicted her marriage to a trader. As a European visitor to her village later wrote, "she dreamed continually of a white man, who approached her with a cup in his hand. . . . She fasted for ten days . . . [and] when satisfied that she had obtained a guardian spirit in the white stranger who haunted her dreams she returned to her father's lodge." Her husband, some years later, would be a rich and influential Irish immigrant named John Johnston.

The father of this woman, himself an important chieftain, actually arranged her marriage, and other tribal leaders sought to encourage similar alliances. Or women might themselves take the initiative in such matters. Colonial officials reported cases in which native women independently decided to "desert [their husbands] to live with the whites." One such case involved an Ojibwa chief's daughter who simply moved into a trader's house, and, as he himself later wrote, "the devil could not have got her out." The trader, having tried but failed to persuade her to leave, made her his "country wife" and fathered several children by her.

Such cases suggest that Indian women hoped to change their life situation through connections to white men. Some no doubt succeeded. Those who married resident traders and became themselves resident in one or another trading post had a comfortably domestic routine. No longer were they obliged to follow their clan or tribal group in a seasonal round of migration; no more would they have to serve as carriers of heavy loads. Indeed, in some cases their experience reversed traditional patterns; the wives of company officials, for instance, would receive the service of others instead of offering it to family members.

Even women of humbler status were said to enjoy "a comparatively easy and free life" when attached to one of the trading posts. As producers of moccasins, snowshoes, and fishing nets, they achieved both recognition and respect. Meanwhile, their efforts in cooking or other aspects of housekeeping benefited from the white man's technology. Metal pots were more versatile than bark containers, and ready-

This pencil sketch from around 1825 illustrates the clothing typically worn by mixed-blood women: high-waisted gowns combined with Indian leggings. Although many articles of European clothing appealed to Indian women, shoes never became popular; they consistently preferred moccasins.

made cloth of cotton or wool saved the long hours previously spent in preparing animal skins. "Show them an awl or a strong needle," wrote one trader, "and they will gladly give the finest beaver or wolf skin they have to purchase it." Clearly, too, these women enjoyed the European garments and jewelry that were sometimes lavished on them. Traders took it as a matter of pride that their wives should make a fine appearance; their orders to company supply stores often included shawls, scarves, garters, stockings, and other items of stylish feminine apparel. Fur-trade women might also escape restrictions that would have applied to them in their native settings. Indians in the Great Lakes area, for example, had traditionally reserved choice foods, especially certain animal parts, for men; a woman who consumed these was considered likely to die. But, as one English observer wryly noted, "women living with the white men eat of . . . [the] forbidden morsels . . . without the least inconvenience."

Some visitors to the middle ground felt that native women exercised "un-natural" influence over their trader-husbands—indeed "that they give the law to their lords." A Chipewyan woman named Madame Lamallice seems a clear case in point. Married in the early 1800s to an officer of the Hudson's Bay Company, she nonetheless retained considerable standing with nearby Indians. Because she was a skilled interpreter and thus essential to company operations, her demands for spe-cial favors could not be refused. Eventually, she began a private trade in furs and other goods. And when her white competitors tried to stop her, she threatened to turn all the natives against them.

The maneuvers of Madame Lamallice reveal how Indian women, linked to white traders, might benefit from their position between cultures. In other cases their influence was directed against the natives on behalf of the traders. The Chipewyan Thanadelthur was especially active in protecting fair conditions of exchange. An English official described a time when Thanadelthur observed an Indian offering furs of inferior quality and "ketch'd him by the nose, push'd him backwards, and call'd him fool, and told him if they brought any [goods] but such as they were directed [to bring] they would not be traded." No Indian woman could have acted so forcefully toward a man in her own village or clan.

To be sure, Madame Lamallice and Thanadelthur may represent extreme cases of Indian womanpower. Other women, in different situations and with different men, fared much less well. Some were treated callously, even brutally, by their white partners; some were abandoned far from home; some were actually sold, like slaves, from one trader to another. In a few instances, Indian kinsmen of women thus victimized attacked and even murdered the perpetrators in revenge. Around the year 1800 an Ojibwa chief spoke bitterly of the entire situation: "The whites . . . take [Indian] women not for wives—but to use them as sluts—to satisfy their ani-mal lust, and when they are satiated, they cast them off, and another one takes her for the same purpose, and by & by casts her off again, and so she will go on . . . soiled by everyone who chooses to use her."

These, too, were extreme cases. For most native women connection to white traders brought a mix of losses and gains: material comfort along with isolation from blood kin; greater independence along with at least occasional insecurity and self-doubt. In some respects the health of trader-wives may actually have declined. They were more fully exposed to contagious diseases carried by whites—and also to the white man's "firewater" (alcoholic drinks). They seem to have been more frequently pregnant than women who remained in tribal settings, which meant an increased risk of illness and of death in childbirth. Moreover, there were unavoidable strains in mixed-race households. Most Indian groups in the middle ground regarded child rearing as a woman's responsibility. But whites took a different line; in their view, a father should act as his family's leader. From this difference flowed recurrent conflicts of authority. Some white fathers wished to send their children away to boarding school, an idea that native mothers could neither accept nor understand. On the other hand, certain Indian practices, such as flattening the backs of infants' heads, met with strong objections from the fathers.

There is a final irony about the outcome of these unions: The women involved would eventually be displaced by their own children and grandchildren. Members of these younger generations, commonly known as *métis* (French for "crossbreed"), were an ever-growing presence in the middle ground. And, in the nineteenth century, it was largely to métis women that traders turned for both personal and business partnership. Such women were especially well attuned to the demands of life between cultures. From their mothers they learned the skills needed for effective participation in the trade. Their needlework, for example, helped clothe the traders, and they continued the tradition of making wilderness footwear. At the same time, they contributed in more European ways: by washing and cleaning, and by tending small gardens of fruits, herbs, and vegetables in the vicinity of the major trading posts. An English official in one such place commented that "the women here work very hard; if it was not so, I do not know how we could get on with the company work."

Some métis women were fluent in several languages, both European and Indian, and were particularly useful as interpreters. Their knowledge of native customs enabled them also to act as intermediaries between cultures, again following the pattern of their mothers. Meanwhile, however, their fathers tried to acquaint them with at least the basics of European culture. Schools appeared in the middle ground during the early 1800s; there métis children learned reading, writing, and the principles of Christian "virtue." Churches were also a powerful influence, and most métis were intensely Catholic. Thus educated and "civilized"—from the white point of view—these "daughters of the country" became all the more attractive to European men arriving from overseas. Indeed, marriage between traders and métis women became increasingly "the vogue," as one visitor put it, and in some cases served to strengthen ties within fur-trade society itself. A young trader, for example, might wed the métis daughter of his company boss and thus improve not only his personal situation but also his prospects of professional advancement.

The middle ground, with its strikingly bicultural way of living, lasted well into the nineteenth century. But eventually it succumbed to new forces of social and economic change—above all, the coming of agriculture to replace fur trading, and then the coming of industry to replace agriculture. Farmers took wives from among their own people and brought them to settle. For the first time ever, the population of the Great Lakes country began to include significant numbers of white women. As this happened, native and métis partners seemed less and less desirable to white men; indeed, a white wife became a kind of status symbol.

By 1900 the forest was gone, the animals were gone, the fur trade was gone—and so too was the middle ground. The remnants of the original tribes were shunted onto small reservations, where they maintained their traditions as best they could. The métis, for their part, went in one of two directions. Some gravitated with their Indian kin to the reservations; others, especially those who had been "whitened" by two or more generations of intermarriage, became fully absorbed into mainstream society. But the extraordinary story of their predecessors—including those whom one historian has called the "women in between"—would be remembered to the present day and beyond.

Cherokee Women and the Trail of Tears

Throughout the region that is now the southeastern United States, and well up into the Middle West, the landscape is dotted with earth mounds of varying size and shape. Some are one hundred feet tall and six times that broad. Many are roughly pyramidal in form, though flattened on top. A few are quite irregular and elaborate and seem to represent the bodies of animals. All were made long ago, well before the first colonists arrived from overseas. Until quite recently most people believed that the Mound Builders had also come, many centuries earlier, from overseas and had subsequently vanished, perhaps when overwhelmed by "savage" Indians. Euro-Americans did not think that native peoples could by their own efforts have created such massively imposing structures. Yet we now know that the mounds were indeed built by ancient Indians, including the ancestors of the group known today as Cherokees.

In 1534 a Spanish explorer, Hernando de Soto, became the first European to visit the Cherokees in their highland towns near the southern end of the Appalachian mountain chain. He admired their physical appearance, their pottery and basket making, and their skills in hunting. He also noted their use of mounds as sites for ceremonial temples and sometimes for burials.

The Cherokees of this early date were a people apparently at one with their environment. Their way of life combined farming by women, hunting by men, fishing, and intermittent rounds of gathering wild foods. Their towns were small, compact, and largely self-sufficient. The people themselves seemed strikingly friendly, even gregarious; their activities, whether of work, play, politics, or religion, were typically done in a group. Harmony was their supreme social value, and therefore they always viewed the goals of the community as more important than the interests of individuals.

Women were strongly positioned within this social system. The basic family unit was the matrilineage, a line of kin based on mothers. Women owned important properties—housing, for example, and the fields they farmed—and at death passed these to their blood relatives. A married man usually lived with his wife's matrilineage. Some men were polygynous, but in most such cases the co-wives were sisters or cousins. Divorce was readily accepted and easily obtained. After divorce a woman regained the full support of her parents, brothers, and other maternal relatives.

Women frequently resorted to abortion and infanticide to limit family size. At the same time, their role as childbearers was honored everywhere; so were their contributions as providers of food. Priests could be either male or female, and women took the lead in important annual festivals, such as the Green Corn Dance held at the start of the harvest. Town government was managed by a council in which all adults participated. Only men held positions as chiefs and elders, but women freely declared their own opinions. Indeed, a few so-called Beloved Women—older and presumably wiser than the rest—made key decisions about warfare and the treatment of captives.

Because the Cherokees lived well back from the coast, they were not at first much affected by the arrival of white colonists. But around the year 1700 their situation began to change. Like Indians everywhere, they were highly vulnerable to the unfamiliar diseases brought from Europe. And, also like other native groups, they were drawn into international trade. Cherokee huntsmen had long sought deer and bear in limited quantities for local consumption. Now they killed the same animals on a very large scale and offered the hides in trade at colonial seaports.

As the eighteenth century went along, the shape of Cherokee life was transformed by these and other factors. Warfare with neighboring tribes such as the Tuscaroras, Shawnees, and Yuchi increased as hunters moved farther and farther out in search of game. White settlers, moving up into the mountains from the east, increasingly clashed with passing Indians. Colonial leaders in Virginia and the Carolinas pressed for land near or within the traditional borders of Cherokee territory; beginning in 1721, a series of official treaties transferred such land from native to white hands in chunks of hundreds and even thousands of square miles at a time. In the second half of the century the Cherokees were caught up in the colonists' wars, with ultimately devastating results. Twice they fought on the losing side—with the French in the French and Indian War of 1754–63 and then with the English and Loyalists in the American Revolution of 1776–83. Each time they paid a heavy price as invading armies swept into their towns, burning and pillaging at will. Defeat was followed by the loss of additional land, either through government-to-government negotiation or from the continuing encroachments of individual frontiersmen.

In the meantime, the fur trade steadily reshaped the Cherokees' economy and even their day-to-day existence. Because of European demand, many of their menfolk now did little but hunt. The women were also pulled into trade-related tasks: preparing and processing skins for the market. Women's work in farming was changed by the introduction of European tools such as iron hoes and shovels and of European fruits and vegetables such as potatoes, apples, watermelons, and peaches. Imported pots and hearth tools altered old ways of preparing food for the table, and machine-woven blankets replaced garments made from animal skins. As part of the same process, women's traditional craft skills—molding and firing clay pots, shaping bone into combs, needles, and other small tools, and weaving fiber mats—were gradually abandoned, then forgotten. Some Cherokees lamented these trends, especially when they increased dependence on outsiders. Said one chief in the 1740s, "every necessary of life we must now have from the white people."

Political and social organization changed as well. Leaders of the English colonies wished to deal with leaders of similar stature among the natives. But the Cherokees had no chiefs beyond the level of individual towns, so the colonists selected one for the role of "emperor." Thus began a process of centralizing power within the tribe that would last far into the nineteenth century. An important side effect of this process was a gradual lessening of women's role in governance. Town councils had been open to female participation, but the councils were steadily losing their former importance. And since contact with whites mainly involved trade and warfare, and since those matters had traditionally concerned Cherokee men, women were left more or less on the sidelines.

But they did not fall entirely silent. A certain Nancy Ward, Beloved Woman from the native town of Chota, appeared in 1785 at a treaty conference concluding Cherokee participation in the American Revolution. Describing herself as "a mother of warriors," she exhorted the delegates to create a firm basis for peace between her own people and the newly formed United States. Two years later another Cherokee woman wrote to Benjamin Franklin on the same subject. She had argued for peace at a recent assembly of tribal leaders, had filled peace pipes for the warriors, and had sent some of the same tobacco to the United States Congress. Her letter to Franklin urged him to "rightly consider that woman is the mother of All—and the Woman does not pull children out of Trees or Stumps nor out of old Logs, but out of their Bodies, so that [men] ought to mind what a woman says." These words reflected the ancient Cherokee belief that women's role as mothers gave them special authority in guarding the welfare of society as a whole.

Peace was not restored to the southern frontier until 1794, and for the Cherokees it came far too late. Their lands had been greatly reduced by repeated cessions to colonial, state, and federal governments. The territory that remained open to them had been nearly emptied of game animals. Their numbers had been reduced by the combined effects of warfare and disease. Dozens of their ancient towns lay devastated, with survivors scattered to new sites deeper in the mountains. Ordinary members of the group faced extreme difficulty in meeting their most basic needs for food and shelter, and the authority of their chiefs was increasingly in doubt. There were white populations on every side: Americans to the north and east, Spaniards to the south, French in the west. Many of these, especially the notorious American pioneers, were pressing relentlessly forward, with an eye to further transfers—or seizures—of tribal land.

Still, at this critical juncture, new opportunities were about to open for the Cherokees. The policy of the federal government would give them a choice—and a chance—not previously available. Federal policy was, in a word, to "civilize" them, to detach them from their "savage" ways and transform them into solid "republican" citizens in order to permit their eventual absorption into the larger American nation. In the context of the times, this seemed a strikingly generous and enlightened prospect.

"The Indian," wrote President Thomas Jefferson, "is the equal of the European in mind and body." His cultural "backwardness" was but an accident of history; given a proper mix of encouragement and incentives, he would rise quickly to the level of whites. Jefferson pressed this viewpoint directly on Indians themselves. "You will find that our laws are good," he told a gathering of native leaders in 1808. "You will wish to live under them, you will unite yourselves with us, join in our great councils and form one people with us, and we shall all be Americans; you will mix with us by marriage, your blood will run in our veins, and will spread with us over this great continent."

The leading parts of the new policy included, besides intermarriage, education for native children, the conversion of as many Indians as possible to Christianity, and, above all, a shift in their economy to intensive horse-and-plow agriculture. What the latter meant specifically was that Indian men should abandon hunting and fur trading in order to learn farming, while their women became "homemakers" in a typical white-American sense. To enact this program the federal government would offer plows, axes, seed, spinning wheels, looms, and other such implements to willing Indians. Missionaries would be encouraged to establish schools and churches in native communities. Resident government agents would supervise the entire program.

The plan was devised for all Indians of every tribe. As events developed, however, the Cherokees would be its main focus. Nowhere else was the commitment of funds as large; nowhere else did hopes, especially among whites, rise as high. At first, in the early 1800s, Cherokee response was uncertain and divided. Some of the tribe seemed ready, even eager, to embrace the proposed changes. Interestingly, this was especially true of Cherokee women. A government agent described their "great earnestness [in] . . . the manufacturing of Cotton." Indeed, their interest was so great that "I have not been able to supply half the number who apply . . . for [spinning] wheels, [combing] cards, and looms, etc." The process may even have unsettled relations between the sexes. Cherokee men, reluctant as they often were to give up their status as hunters for that of farmers, probably shared the view of a chieftain among the nearby Creeks: "If the women can clothe themselves," he said, "they will be proud and not obedient to their husbands."

But many Cherokees, women as well as men, resisted all pressures to change; for them tribal traditions remained strong. They believed, wrote one federal agent, "that they are not derived from the same stock as whites, and that the great spirit

. . . never intended they should live the laborious lives of whites." Some defended old ways within their home villages, while others chose the path of escape. Thus some Cherokees began leaving for new destinations far to the west.

Meanwhile, the tribe was under constant pressure to yield additional lands. White frontiersmen were forever pushing forward, contesting native ownership, and, not infrequently, initiating or provoking violence. These people did not share the attitude of national leaders like Jefferson. To them the Indian was a racial infe- rior, a "red nigger" who was "radically different from all other men," as newspaper accounts put it. Moreover, they believed, in the words of a frontier minister, that "his difference presents an insurmountable barrier to his civilization." They wished to see the natives "removed . . . as quickly and completely as possible."

The resident federal agents tried to steer a course midway between these extremes. Periodically, they would act to suppress violence and to chase the fron- tiersmen out. However, they also pressured the Indians to negotiate territorial transfers, especially of the old hunting grounds, for which, supposedly, the Indians would have no further need. In fact, the agents secured the signing of seven land treaties between the years 1800 and 1820. Each time Cherokee opinions were divid- ed, with some Indians in favor of the treaties and others bitterly opposed.

Among the opponents were many Cherokee women. In 1817 a special women's council addressed the chiefs and warriors of the tribe in the following terms: "We have raised all of you on the land which we now have. . . . We know that our coun- try has once been extensive, but by repeated sales has become circumscribed to a small tract. . . . Your mothers and sisters ask and beg of you not to part with any more of our lands." A year later, when the chiefs were considering a plan to allot tribal lands to individuals, the women responded again. "The land," they declared, "was given to us by the Great Spirit above as our common right, to raise our chil- dren upon and to make support for our rising generations. . . . We therefore unan- imously join in our meeting to hold our country in common as hitherto." Holding land in common had meant, in practice, ownership by the matrilineal family. Thus a new system of individual ownership might significantly reduce the status of Cherokee women, since government agents, like most white Americans, saw men as the heads of families and owners of property. Land granted to "individuals" usu- ally went to men.

Torn by internal divisions, and with their territorial base steadily eroding, the Cherokees seemed at this point to be set on a course of extinction. But after about 1820 they entered a new, remarkable, and much more promising period of their history—what one historian has termed a "renascence." They achieved, in the first place, a unified stance against further loss of their lands. And they also began, as never before, to accept the changes proposed by the United States government. For example, they took up farming on a broad scale. Some followed their white neigh- bors of the "Old South" in adopting a plantation model, including the use of black slaves and the intensive cultivation of market crops such as cotton. At the same time, increasing numbers of Cherokees embraced Christian religious beliefs and practices; a few became Protestant ministers. Schooling expanded, literacy broadened. And, in a particularly remarkable achievement, a Cherokee "mixed blood" named Sequoyah succeeded in reducing the tribal language to written form. This led, in turn, to a Cherokee translation of the Bible and to the first regularly published newspaper in any Indian language. Capping the entire sequence was a major restructuring of tribal government, which came to include an elected council in two parts, like the U.S. Congress; an executive authority headed by a single chief, somewhat like the presidency; and a carefully graded court system to administer the law. These changes were formalized in the Cherokee constitution of 1828, which was modeled on the U. S. Constitution.

Taken as a whole, the Cherokee renascence drew admiring notice from white citizens all across the country; "the most civilized tribe in America" was a comment frequently heard in descriptions of the Cherokees. But the effects of the renascence were not evenly distributed. Wealth and other forms of personal benefit went disproportionately to a small group of highly assimilated Cherokees: men who embraced Christianity and the culture of nearby whites and who, in some cases, took white wives. By contrast, those who resisted assimilation led marginal and increasingly impoverished lives.

The changes had an especially powerful impact on the position of women. As the old matrilineal clans lost importance, a woman could no longer rely on her brothers and other blood relatives as her ultimate source of security. Within the narrower confines of her immediate household she occupied a place subordinate to that of her "provider" husband. Her traditional control of family property was more and more in question; when Cherokee men emigrated to the west, for example, the wives and children they left behind would sometimes be evicted from family farmsteads. Tribal law struggled to blend old values with new circumstances. On the one hand, it said that "the improvements and labor of our people by the mother's side" should remain "inviolate" for as long as a woman lived. On the other hand, the death of her husband would bring a division of property among their children and *his* "nearest kin." These apparent confusions might easily lead to court cases, in which Cherokee women would have to retain attorneys to guard their vital interests. Other laws brought changes no less unsettling. Marriages had to be licensed by local authorities. The traditional practices of abortion and infanticide were made into crimes. Even where the laws were designed to protect Cherokee women—against rape, for example—enforcement was difficult. Individuals who could not read or write, and who had no experience with courts and lawyers, were understandably hesitant to press their claims.

Finally, the continuing decline in women's political participation was sealed in the Cherokee constitution of 1828. The right to vote was restricted to "free male

The role of women in tribal life continued to decline as the Cherokees became "civilized" under the U.S. government's supervision. These women in North Carolina were photographed wearing traditional dress in the early twentieth century; by that time, Cherokee women had been forced into the role of "housewives" and had lost much of their social and political influence.

citizens," as was the right to participate in government: "no person shall be eligible to a seat in the General Council but a free Cherokee male, who shall have attained the age of twenty-five." With this explicit bar to female officeholding the Cherokees went beyond even the United States Constitution—perhaps in backhanded recognition of their women's once powerful role. Nevertheless, some Cherokee women managed to retain at least a part of their traditional status. Local census rolls continued to include a good many female heads-of-household. An obituary from the tribal newspaper in 1828 presents an especially striking case: a woman named Oudah-less, described as a major property holder and "the support of her large family." Other women were noted, well into the 1830s, as owners of slaves and proprietors of substantial plantations.

Whatever its short-term effects, the process of renascence was ultimately—and tragically—doomed. The demands of white settlers did not abate following the establishment of the new Cherokee government and constitution. Indeed, a policy of "removing" Indians gained official favor during the decade of the 1820s and was written into law by the United States Congress in 1830. The idea was that various native groups should trade their homelands for "open" territory beyond the edge of white settlement in the West. Some, such as the Creeks and Choctaws, readily accepted these terms, but the Cherokees did not.

Meanwhile, the state of Georgia was trying to extend its own authority over the Cherokee nation. The result was a series of lawsuits that went all the way to the U.S. Supreme Court. In 1831, Samuel Worcester, a white missionary, was arrested for residing among the Cherokees without a permit from the Georgia governor. Worcester appealed to the Supreme Court, claiming that the law he had violated was unconstitutional because it interfered with the sovereign status of the Cherokees. In 1832, the Court ruled in *Worcester v. Georgia* that the Cherokees were an independent nation, not subject to the laws of Georgia. State officials, however, ignored the Court's decision, and the federal government refused to enforce it. Eventually a small faction agreed to negotiate removal and, in the 1835 Treaty of New Echota, exchanged the tribal homeland for other territory in what is today the state of Oklahoma.

Most Cherokees rejected this agreement and vehemently refused to leave. But in 1838 federal leaders decided to evict them, by force if necessary. American soldiers proceeded, as a first step, to herd reluctant tribespeople into hastily built stockades. After weeks or months of virtual imprisonment, bands of Cherokee emigrants began to leave for the West. Facing unusually severe winter weather and lacking adequate supplies, they were very much at risk. Of the fifteen thousand who set out, at least four thousand are believed to have died at one point or another along this "trail of tears."

The process of removal worked particular hardship on Cherokee women. According to the recollections of an army interpreter, many were simply "dragged from their homes by soldiers whose language they could not understand"; their children, meanwhile, "were often separated from them." In the stockades they were at the mercy of their white guards and "exposed to every species of moral desolation." A Methodist missionary reported the case of a "young married woman" who had been "caught" by soldiers, "dragged about," plied with liquor, and "seduced away, so that she is now an outcast even among her own relatives." According to the same source, "many [others] of the poor captive women are thus debauched through terror and seduction." The missionary did not use the word "rape," but that is clearly what he meant.

Once they were headed west, women continued to suffer. A few of them, especially among the elderly, rode in wagons, but most covered the entire one-thousand-mile distance on foot. An eyewitness reported that many "were travelling with heavy burdens attached to the back." Some were pregnant and had to give birth by the trail. Others watched helplessly as their children took sick and died. And still others were themselves beset with mortal illness.

Those Cherokees who survived the "trail of tears" would find little comfort or compensation in their new homes in the West. A radically different environment of grasslands instead of mountain forests, another group of unfriendly white neighbors, the inherent difficulties of a large-scale, forced uprooting—these factors would prolong the pains of removal for decades to come. For Cherokee women in particular the process continued a long, downward spiral of change. The laws of their transplanted nation confirmed their exclusion from public life. The cultural values propounded by white missionaries, federal agents, and even their own menfolk stressed a narrow view of female "housewifery." There is evidence that they bore the brunt of increased personal violence when Cherokee husbands vented their own frustrations on other family members. As a leading historian of the Cherokees has recently written, "In the removal crisis of the 1830s men learned an important lesson about power; it was a lesson women had learned well before."

Indian Women in a Changing World

Each of the numerous Indian cultures was different, in at least some ways, from all the others. And women's position within these cultures was also different. But there were similarities in the experience of such women, both before and after contact with foreigners. The Puebloans, the Iroquois, the Great Lakes tribes at the center of the developing fur trade, and the Cherokees: their separate stories of suffering and struggle, of accommodation and resistance and at least occasional triumph, reveal common threads that link the histories of Indian women everywhere.

The traditional patterns of Indian cultures almost invariably included a strong base in clan organization. Individual persons, both male and female, took their place in a group of relatives much larger than the nuclear family of parents and children. Typically, they married someone from outside the clan; but after marriage they remained close to their own blood kin. In many tribes—the Iroquois and the Cherokees, for example—the clans were matrilineal. Property passed through the female line, from mothers to daughters to granddaughters, and in some cases the same was true of family names. This was quite different from the European practice of transmitting both property and names through males. Moreover, in some tribes—again the Iroquois and Cherokees are powerful examples—a married couple usually lived with the wife's relatives. These patterns meant that women kept considerable power and influence through the link to their clan. Just as they remained loyal to the clan, the clan remained loyal to them. When subject to abuse or exploitation, they were defended by their own blood relatives; if divorced from their husbands, they were fully supported by the same relatives. Marriage itself was begun and continued on roughly even terms. Young Indian women moved into and out of courtships as they pleased. In many native cultures sex before marriage was fully permissible; European travelers noted that Indian women had "free disposition over their own bodies." Divorce was also easily obtained—at the instance of either spouse or both.

Most Indian cultures expected women to play an important role as producers. Women often had the primary responsibility for planting, tending, and harvesting essential food crops. Typically, too, they were much involved with craft production. Sometimes their skills extended to house construction and boat building. In all these activities women occupied a domain meant especially for their sex. Thus, for instance, the Iroquois defined an entire "village world" as belonging to women while reserving the "forest world" for men. These arrangements implied both separation and cooperation. Members of each sex were expected to contribute to the common good, and members of each would gain respect accordingly. These attitudes applied also to spiritual life. Women were prominently featured in tribal myths and folklore. In some cultures women took the lead in important religious ceremonies such as the Green Corn festival of the Cherokees; in others they served as priests.

Governance, however, was principally in the hands of men. In a few cases women served as chiefs, but in most the leaders were male. Still, women did not lack influence. Often special women's councils advised the chiefs on matters of policy. And on certain issues, such as starting wars, women might go beyond advising to actual decision making.

Behind the broad array of women's roles and duties lay a fundamental respect for women *as women*. Among most European peoples of the premodern era, to be female was to be considered inferior—a lesser version of the strong, wise, and more nearly "godlike" male. Indian cultures, in contrast, supported a balanced view of the sexes. Men were considered superior in some ways, women in others, and both were necessary to the survival of the group.

These were leading themes in the experience of native women before their cultures entered into contact with Europeans. But the process of contact vastly changed them and their cultures. Some groups accommodated change quite readily; others resisted for longer or shorter periods; none escaped its effects indefinitely. Some effects applied directly and equally to both sexes. Disease, for example, struck down women and men in equal numbers. War, on the other hand, killed more men, since they were with rare exceptions the warrior group.

Over the long term, the combination of disease and war would so drastically reduce Indian populations that community life itself was reshaped. Villages might see their numbers cut in half within the space of a decade or a generation, and among the surviving group the ratio of women to men might become badly skewed. In one case for which there is particularly good evidence—the Iroquois village of Kahnawake, near Montreal, in the eighteenth century—females outnumbered males by nearly three to one. It was in such extreme circumstances that the influence of women's councils might temporarily expand—and that some women would actually become chiefs. One imagines as well a powerful effect on family life: more and more widows, fewer and fewer potential husbands, numerous children growing up without fathers.

Like war, trade was a major area of change in the lives of Native Americans. Here too the process affected men and women in different ways. Typically, men were the leaders in trade, partly because men were the hunters of the fur-bearing animals that whites sought so eagerly and partly because whites preferred to deal with men in these matters. Women, by contrast, performed support roles: preparing goods for the market, carrying them to trading sites, and supplying the men with food and other necessities of everyday life. In contrast to the balance of their native cultures, women came to occupy a secondary place, distinctly behind that of men, in the economies of trade-focused tribes.

Trade also undermined traditional craft production, in which female participation had once been central. Fewer and fewer women would now earn status and influence by making fine baskets or pots or jewelry; instead, such articles, or their European equivalents, were imported from outside the community. The activities these goods supported also moved away from traditional patterns. Iron cookware transformed food preparation, and previously unknown foodstuffs altered the native diet. These changes were most evident in situations where Indians encountered whites on a group-to-group basis, but in other situations individual encounters took precedence. Wherever the newly arriving white population was predominantly male, Indian females became a focus of interest and sometimes of coercion. This was especially true in the case of fur traders, who actively sought native women as sexual partners, as helpers and collaborators in work, or simply as domestic companions.

Some of these women were themselves eager for such connections; evidently they preferred the role of trader's partner to that of tribal spouse. A few managed to use their opportunities as a way of entering the trade on their own account. Many others endured abuse, abandonment, and exploitation at the hands of their white partners. And often enough, for this latter group, there was no returning to their communities of origin; they remained thereafter set apart from both white and native cultures.

Besides fur traders, Indian women also encountered government agents, like those sent to the Cherokees to promote the federal policy of "civilization," and soldiers, like the ones assigned to enforce removal. Encounters with these outsiders left women with decidedly mixed results. From the agents they received the "gifts" of a supposedly more advanced technology, such as looms, spinning wheels, and other implements of domestic production. But the soldiers confronted them with the brute power of an alien government—and sometimes, too, with assaults on their very persons.

Along with the white man's government came the white man's churches; often, indeed, the churches arrived first. The friars in the Puebloan country of the Southwest and the Jesuits who sought out the Iroquois in the Northeast were just the vanguard of a centuries-long, continent-wide missionary project, a project that

Officials of the U.S. government believed in a white ideal for Cherokee women. Here, students at the Cherokee Female Seminary in Oklahoma in 1898 wear dresses and hats fashionable in white society. The school was modeled on Mount Holyoke Female Seminary (now called Mount Holyoke College) in Massachusetts.

achieved some of its earliest and strongest successes with Indian women. But the impact of alliances between white missionaries and native women was finally disruptive of traditional culture. Christian converts would have to reject many of the beliefs and values with which they had been raised. Female converts in particular would have to adjust to a religious system in which the Deity Himself and His principal earthly advocates, priests and ministers, were all male. Moreover, the same system identified a specific woman (Eve, in the Bible) as the "root of all evil" and attributed to every female born thereafter a share in the stain of her "original sin." The mission churches were, in short, little patriarchies.

There is no simple way to calculate the sum of these encounters, whether of groups or of individuals. Clearly, in many respects, Indians were obliged to give way. Every native culture brought closely to grips with encroaching whites would emerge—after decades or centuries—irrevocably transformed. Some would simply disappear. The power of such transformations can best be grasped through a process of before-and-after comparison: before the whites arrived, and after the effects of contact had been substantially worked out.

Family relationships, first of all, were pushed in the direction of European norms, as Indian households became more and more nuclear. Loyalties to the larger clan would not be abandoned entirely, but the primary bonds became the ones between husband and wife and between parents and children. From a woman's standpoint, this meant a significant narrowing of personal support. No longer could she count on her own parents, her uncles, her siblings and cousins to come automatically to her aid in times of need. Was her marriage proving difficult? She must try to make the best of it. Were her children failing to grow and learn as expected? She must find her own solutions. New living arrangements—separate, for the most part, from those of clan relatives—reinforced the trend. A wife's ties to her husband and his to her became the basis of all her experience.

Increasingly, too, these ties expressed a kind of inequality. Christian churches, schools run by whites, and U.S. government agencies all propounded an American model of marriage, with the husband serving as head and the wife as his "helpmeet." As part of the same model, men would take the role of providers while women would center their lives on home. This model corresponded to ongoing changes in native economies as farming replaced hunting and trade as the major source of subsistence for many Indian groups—and became to an ever greater degree the work of men. These changes served to reduce the economic worth of women's labor. At the same time, women were losing their connection to property. The old matrilineal principles slowly but steadily weakened. Under the new conditions men owned property and men controlled inheritance. In all this, Indians were pressured to follow the pattern—and the law—of whites, according to which married women had little or no standing of their own. Instead, their identities were merged into those of the men closest to them, principally their husbands. Women's part in governance shrank, also in conformity to white standards. As the clan system lost influence, so did the clans' leading women. Most of the new systems of government and social organization adopted by Indians excluded women from voting and holding office. Like their white counterparts, Indian women were pushed to the political sidelines.

During this long-term process of decline, Indian women were *losing* opportunities, influence, and status that had formerly belonged to them. The process was not uniform either in its timing or in its specific details, and individual tribes were affected in at least somewhat different ways. But its direction was everywhere the same. The decline for women was, of course, just a piece of the larger decline of Native Americans in general. Indian men lost out, too, in the unfolding encounter with peoples of European extraction.

In 1922, Ojibwa women use traditional skills to make birchbark containers for holding maple sap. Even in the face of twentieth-century technology, Indian women have preserved their culture, in part by continuing the craft traditions of their ancestors.

And yet there is more to the story than this. Indians did not simply surrender; rather, they responded to their losses with courage, flexibility, and a sometimes extraordinary resourcefulness. The survivors of shattered tribes would regroup and join together to make a new stand against continuing white encroachment. Ancient tribal traditions—the customs, beliefs, and values at the core of their his-torical experience—would be preserved carefully for the future. Native cultures might bend this way or that, but seldom did they break. Even now these cultures live on, albeit under tightly constricted conditions and outside the notice of the American mainstream.

Women's part in these efforts to preserve Indian culture has been consistently important. Some women, like those of the Cherokees in the early nineteenth century, struggled valiantly for the preservation of tribal lands. Iroquois women, also in the nineteenth century, anchored a process of strategic retreat. The women of the fur-trading tribes of the Upper Great Lakes helped to create a middle ground on which native people could try to hold their own, at least for a time. Among the twentieth-century Puebloans women initiated a kind of cultural revival by recovering the craft traditions of remote ancestors. It is certain, too, that in the privacy of countless Indian households old cultural ways were remembered and valued—and passed on, across the generations—by individual mothers and their children. The story of Native American women is not simply one of loss and decline. Adaptation, recovery, and survival—such words also apply. And the struggle continues still.

CHAPTER 2

The Colonial Mosaic

1600–1760

Jane Kamensky

A lthough the varieties of female experience among the native North American peoples who first encountered Europeans in the sixteenth, seventeenth, and eighteenth centuries were nearly endless, some unifying plot lines are visible. Chief among these is a sense of doubleness: of cooperation combined with resistance. Of living one's life according to two different sets of beliefs about what women were, should be, *must* be.

The European women who migrated to the North American colonies also knew two worlds. It was in England that women like Margaret Winthrop learned what it meant to be female—and pondered how their roles might change in a strange new world across the Atlantic. Winthrop was born Margaret Tyndal, daughter of a wealthy landowner in Essex, England. In 1618, at the age of twenty-seven, she pledged her love and obedience, along with a substantial dowry, to John Winthrop, an aspiring young lawyer from the village of Groton.

John Winthrop had become an ardent believer in the growing movement to purge the Church of England of its Catholic, or "popish," practices. He thought of himself as a Puritan: one who wished to reform the Anglican faith from within. He did not—at least not at first—wish to remove himself from the "old" world. In the end, though, Winthrop's passion for a godly life would take him far from what he saw as the increasing spiritual corruption of England. As a prolonged economic depression worsened and the noose of government repression tightened around Puritan believers, he looked across the Atlantic. The several North American outposts recently established by the New England Company (later the Massachusetts Bay Company) seemed to him to represent the best hope for building a godly community. In May 1629, John Winthrop wrote to Margaret of his dawning belief that Massachusetts would "provide a shelter and a hiding place for us and ours." By the end of August, they had decided to journey across the ocean. At the end of that journey, John Winthrop would emerge as a central figure in the exodus of Puritan families that came to be known as "the Great Migration." Between 1629 and 1640, some twenty-one thousand English men, women, and children migrated to New

THE
Woman Outwitted :

OR, THE

Weaver's Wife cunningly catch'd in a Trap, by her Husband, who sold her for ten Pounds, and sent her to *Virginny*.

To an excellent new Tune.

NOt far from hence, there dwelt,
 an honest Man a Weaver,
He had a Wife she was witty and fair,
 but her Wit did deceive her;
She was a Grain too light,
 she calls him Fool and Ninny;
Which made the Man then often say,
 I'll go unto Virginny.

Altho' he hard did work,
 he ne'er could live in quiet,
She said her Cloathing was too base,
 so was her homely Diet;
Tho' nothing she did want,
 as he could buy for Money,
Which made the Man then often say,
 I'll go unto Virginny.

She lov'd a lusty Lad,
 and vow'd she'd love him ever,
At last her Husband found a Trick
 these loving Mates to sever:
Your notes, quoth he, I'll quickly change,
 that now so sweetly sing ye;
Unto a Merchant straight he went
 that sailed to Virginny:

He coming then unto the Ship,
 Of Women you are lacking,
And I have one that I can spare,
 and her I will send packing:
The Times are very hard,
 I'll sell my Wife for Mony,
She is good Merchandize you know,
 when you come to Virginny.

If she be young, bring her on board,
 and I will entertain her;
But tell to me the lowest price,
 for I must be some Gainer.
Ten Pound he answered,
 I cannot bait one penny;
She is good Merchandize you know
 when you come to Virginny.

Then he came home unto his Wife,
 and said that he was packing;
This joyful news reviv'd her mind,
 and set her Heart a leaping;
And smiling to herself, she said,
 Then farewel Goodman Ninny,
My Love with me shall merry be
 when you are at Virginny.

One thing I do desire of thee,
 to see me, my Dear, take shipping.
Ay, that I will, my Love, said she,
 and seem'd to fall a weeping;

A bottle of Strong-waters good
 I will bestow upon thee,
For fear that you should be Sea-sick
 a sailing to Virginny.

Then come into the Ship,
 the Captain bid them welcome,
He led them into his Cabin,
 whereas such Guests came seldom:
He stepped forth unto her Husband,
 and paid him down the Money,
Who straight took Boat and row'd on shore
 and sent her unto Virginny.

But when she saw that he was gone,
 and that she there was Caid,
She bitterly did wail and weep,
 and said she was betray'd;
Take me, said she, with you,
 I'll never more offend thee,
He cry'd, farewel sweet Wife, adieu,
 God send you to Virginny.

Then presently they hoist up Sail,
 and had good Wind and Weather,
And seven long weeks they were at Sea,
 before that they came thither;
He for a Maiden sold her there,
 for fifty pounds in Money,
And she another Husband had
 when she came to Virginny.

They being parted thus,
 so many Leagues asunder,
He carries Mony in his purse,
 there's none to keep him under,
But governs all at home,
 and with his friends lives merry;
Now many one doth stile him,
 a Merchant of Virginny.

London : Printed by and for W. O. and are to be sold by C. Bates, in Py-corner.

England in search of a better life. For most of those years, John Winthrop would rank as a prominent leader. In October 1629, those in charge of the expedition elected him governor of the colony of Massachusetts Bay—an office he continued to hold, off and on, until his death in 1649.

Migration held a different meaning for Margaret. In some ways, her days in Boston would pass much as they had in Groton, each minute filled with the care of hearth, husband, and children. Her thoughts would most often revolve around the glory of God, much as they had in England. In these ways, her new life would be perhaps no more full of joy than her old one had—nor any less.

In other respects, though, Margaret Winthrop would find her life in America quite different. To her, the region's native peoples, along with its forbidding wood-ed landscape, looked nothing less than "savage." In time, the foreignness of the place and its people would bring about many changes in the ways Margaret Winthrop would work, and love, and pray: changes in the very way she thought. In the end, she would find the life of a woman in this New England to be profoundly unlike what she had left behind—different, and not always easier.

However difficult English women found their first years in New England, other colonial settlements held harder lessons by far. In early Virginia and Maryland, few English women of any rank settled until much later in the seventeenth century. No females are believed to have been among the "First Supply" of Jamestown settlers in 1607; only two—a gentlewoman and her servant—found their way to Virginia in the "Second Supply" that arrived in the winter of 1608. Well into the 1610s women remained one of Virginia's scarcest and most precious resources.

Starting in November 1619, that colony's leaders undertook a concerted effort to remedy the situation. Sir Edwin Sandys, who was the treasurer of the Virginia Company of London that funded Jamestown, began to recruit women to settle in Virginia. The "want of wives," he wrote, had proved to be among "the greatest of hindrances" to the new plantation. He hoped that the shipment of "an extraordi-narily choice lot of ... maides" would help "make the men more settled & lesse moveable." According to Sandys's plan, Virginia freemen, desperate for mates, would defray the costs of transporting these "maids." In exchange for 120 pounds of his best tobacco, the man of some means could effectively buy himself a wife. In 1619, 1621, and 1622, a total of nearly 150 English women—most of them young, poor, and alone—ventured across the Atlantic in response to Sandys's campaign. By the end of 1622, every one of them had married. But by 1625, an estimated three-quarters of them were dead of starvation and disease. Similar patterns would be found all over the southern Atlantic coast from Maryland south to the Caribbean.

Although there is very scanty evidence of the innermost feelings of women in the colonial South, we do know that their new world was a particularly difficult—indeed, deadly—place. Recruiters might claim that "women that go over into this Province as Servants, have the best luck as in any place of the world." The real story, however, was not nearly so rosy. The few letters that do survive, including one written by a young Huguenot named Judith Giton who fled the persecution of Protestants in France for the newly settled colony of South Carolina in 1685, speak of unremitting hardship. Since "our arrival in Carolina," she wrote, "we [have] suffered all sorts of evils ... sickness, pestilence, famine, poverty, and the roughest labor." In other corners of the early colonial South, Englishwomen's stories were much the same. Seventeenth-century ballads like "The Trappan'd Maiden" set their suffering to music, with verses featuring a "distressed damsel's" lament:

> A thousand woes beside, that I do here abide
> In the Land of Virginny, O;
> In misery I spend my time that hath no end
> When that I am weary, weary, weary, O.

"No rest ... I can have, whilst I am here a Slave" was the musical complaint of the weary young "Trappan'd Maiden." But, of course, she was not really a slave— not, at least, in the way slavery would soon come to be defined in the Chesapeake. Unlike even the poorest settlers who migrated from England, enslaved Africans did not make the journey by choice. By the 1660s it was clear that black women and their children would occupy very different places in the social order than their white counterparts did.

As early America took shape, the lives of all of these sorts of women—black and white, native and immigrant, rich and poor—would come to have much in common. As daughters, wives, and mothers they shared certain expectations and realities where work, love, sex, and even death were concerned. Yet their lives would also be marked by dramatic differences. This blend of sameness and difference in the lives of colonial women becomes visible when we consider the kinds of labor they performed.

To Toil the Livelong Day

Samuel de Champlain, a French adventurer-explorer seeking his fortune in New France in the 1610s, thought the native people he encountered there treated their women little better than mules. Huron women, he reported, "have almost the whole care of the house and the work." Women "till the soil, sow the Indian corn, fetch wood for the winter"; they "strip the hemp, and spin it." Huron women were also responsible for many other "necessary things"—heavy labor that only the very poorest French matron would ever have been forced to undertake.

French readers must have found Champlain's descriptions of native women's work astonishing. In European villages of the sixteenth and seventeenth centuries, women of even modest means typically worked in and around their houses. The good wife, as English minister William Secker was fond of quoting from Proverbs, "looketh well to the ways of her household." Her "trade," as he called housewifery, chiefly concerned "household affairs," especially chores "at the wash-house ... at the needle, at the wheel," and "at the spindle." She might be required, in a pinch, to lend a hand in the fields. But on a routine basis, such duties fell only to women who found themselves in exceptional circumstances: cursed with too few sons to work their land, too poor to hire extra hands, or both. But in the Huron villages Champlain visited, there *were* no houses to speak of—at least none that *he* considered worthy of that name. Instead, there were dirt-floored "lodges" or "cabins" that one Jesuit preacher described as "a miniature picture of Hell" in which family members "mingled pell-mell with the dogs." Here women as often as not worked out-of-doors, while Huron men seemed to do relatively little—little, that is, that Champlain recognized as proper, manly labor. As far as he could tell, native men spent their days in pursuits befitting European gentlemen—hunting and fishing were popular leisure activities for French aristocrats—while their wives toiled.

All across colonial North America, European observers from a variety of backgrounds reacted with shock to the ways in which native men and women divided up their daily labors. But exactly what do their reactions tell us? These "Old World" reactions tell us more about European standards than about the ways native peoples divided their daily labors. Everywhere Europeans looked, the indigenous people had their *own* ideas of how men and women should behave. Chief among these were notions about the kinds of work women and men should each perform. These differences were deeply unsettling to the colonists. Today we accept that one people can favor a particular kind of social order while another erects a different and equally valid one. But people in seventeenth-century England, France, Holland, and Spain believed that there was one right way for people to act. From their vantage point, there was an incontestable logic behind the duties men and women were each called upon to perform: the logic of nature, the logic of God. Their sexual division of labor—the ways in which European men and women divvied up their tasks—was understood as much more than a convenient social arrangement. It was a reflection of the divine plan that made men men, and women women.

Coming to a new world was not supposed to challenge that plan. English migrants in the seventeenth century were not trying to re-imagine what it meant to be male or female. Instead, they hoped their culture and their working lives could be easily transplanted. Immigrant women and men would each perform their customary duties; husbands and wives would find their roles and their relationships appreciably unaltered. Goodwives and yeomen, indentured workers and serving maids, elite "mistresses" and their gentleman partners: each would perform essentially the same duties they had in the Old World. Or would they? America had its own set of answers in store. Almost every woman who left England for Virginia or Maryland in the early seventeenth century would have expected to work—and work hard—from the moment she reached her destination. Between 80 and 90 percent of the English folk who emigrated to that region, and virtually all of the women, came as indentured servants. This meant that the great majority of the anonymous, young, single women who journeyed to the Chesapeake arrived not as free people but as bound laborers, having contracted to work off the cost of their passage by serving, typically for four to seven years, in the household of the person who had put up the money for their transport. At first these young women toiled for men who were their masters. After their debts had been satisfied, they might work alongside their husbands on small plantations. In either case, their labors would be shaped by the broader goal of the region's economy: extracting from the soil the maximum possible volume of tobacco, the intoxicating leaf Londoners were craving.

From the first, the speculators who invested in Virginia and Maryland saw their ventures as a potential source of great profit. In the early years in Jamestown they had tried their hands at cultivating silk and unearthing minerals. By the early 1620s, however, it was clear that another product would provide the quickest returns on their investments. Virginia tobacco commanded decent prices from British merchants—prices high enough to ensure that, for a time, every available acre in the Chesapeake would be devoted to its cultivation. What's more, every available hand—and many more—would be needed to till the soil. These econom-ic necessities defined the existence of English women in the Chesapeake. Unlike other parts of British America, theirs would not be a world of close-knit villages and family farms where people grew just enough to get by. Instead, they would find themselves scattered along large tracts of tobacco land, governed by the boom and bust cycles of cash-crop agriculture.

Especially while she remained a servant, the environment in which the female immigrant labored meant that prevailing English notions of "women's work" could hardly apply to her. Conditions in the early Chesapeake were mean, even by the standards of those who came from the lower rungs of English society. The average planter was likely to inhabit an unpainted wooden dwelling no larger than twenty-five by eighteen feet—about the size of a modern two-car garage. These so-called "Virginia houses" usually consisted of a single room on the ground floor with some storage space under the eaves above. The first floor "hall" or large room served as the family's kitchen, dining area, workroom, living quarters, and bedchamber; maidservants and children might climb a ladder to sleep on straw pallets in the windowless storage space upstairs. Many servants made do with less, bunking in barns and in outdoor sheds.

The indentured servant's clothing and meals were likely to be as rude as her dwelling place. Her skirts and aprons would have been fashioned of a blend of the coarsest linen and wool. And her diet, as one traveler to the region reported, con-sisted mainly of a "somewhat indigestible soup" of ground corn. Not surprisingly, serving girls often succumbed to the Chesapeake's many endemic diseases. Malaria, pellagra, dysentery, and deadly "agues and fevers" killed off many during the crucial first six months of "seasoning," as getting used to the climate was called. All told, a combination of poverty, deprivation, hunger, and disease insured that, until the last quarter of the seventeenth century, only a fraction of Englishwomen would outlive their indentures.

Those who did manage to survive these harsh beginnings inherited a world in which women's working lives were dramatically different from what they had been in England. For one thing, the seventeenth-century Chesapeake was a world in which white women were scarce. Nearly twenty years after the founding of Jamestown, there were still more than three times as many men as women. Because so few Englishmen were able to find wives, and because English migrants continued to die at shockingly early ages, the proportions of men to women—which historians call the "sex ratio"—did not begin to even out until the early eighteenth century. As late as 1691, there were three Englishmen for every two Englishwomen in Virginia. In Maryland, female immigrants were outnumbered six to one in the 1630s and by as much as three to one from 1650 to 1680.

On the positive side, this imbalanace meant that virtually every female migrant would eventually find a husband—should she live long enough to attain her freedom; indentured servants were forbidden to marry. But it also meant that English notions of the proper sexual division of labor simply *could* not apply. In a colony where land was abundant and labor was scarce, a certain degree of flexibility regarding one's day-to-day tasks was an absolute necessity. Vast fields were all but begging for hands to plant them. It was almost a foregone conclusion that some of those hands would be women's.

The Chesapeake planter's wife could not afford to center her labors around her house and its surrounding yards. Her work was needed elsewhere. Particularly if she were indentured under or married to the poorer sort of planter, her daily chores were likely to include work in the fields. Incomplete records make good estimates hard to come by, but roughly half of the white women in Maryland and at least that percentage in Virginia would routinely have engaged in heavy agricultural work.

Their specific duties varied with the season. But there was always plenty to do, for tobacco required nearly constant attention. For men and women alike, the workday stretched from sunrise to sunset, with time off during the heat of the day in the warmer months. In the winter—the beginning of the tobacco production cycle—an Englishwoman would have spent those hours helping her master or her husband plant crops and enrich the seedbeds. By late April, she might have been called upon to transplant the tiny seedlings to the main fields, a delicate task that demanded the intensive effort of the whole plantation labor force over a period of several months. In June, July, and August, her deft hands would hoe and weed the tiny hills surrounding each plant and keep the plants free from worms. September brought the arduous labor of cutting and curing the mature leaves; this was typically men's work. But the planter's wife might well lend a hand in the stripping, stemming, curing, and packing that followed later in the fall. By Christmas, the whole cycle was ready to begin again—calling for at least some of her attention at every point in the coming year.

The planter's wife who lived in a more elevated household might have avoided

Growing and harvesting tobacco was a time-consuming, labor-intensive task. This illustration portrays some of the steps involved. In the background, slaves hang tobacco leaves for drying. The woman in front strips the cured tobacco leaves from the plant and packs them into a barrel.

regular outdoor labor. But every white woman in Virginia and Maryland helped to sustain this "tobacco culture" with her daily chores. By preparing food and washing linens, she freed up the men and boys to work outdoors. By tending a vegetable garden on cleared land near her house lot, she supplemented the family's diet and perhaps even made a little cash to pay for imported items like cloth and iron ware—English goods nobody in the Chesapeake had time to produce.

As the century wore on, the planter's wife would have become increasingly enmeshed in informal networks of female trade, swapping her yarn for a neighbor's knitted goods, her butter for some peas. She might also, during especially pressured times, put in long days in the fields. Her working life, then, would represent a kind of hybrid: a blend of Old World expectations and New World realities.

Until the last decades of the seventeenth century, enough English people saw enough opportunity in the Chesapeake to keep this system limping along. Despite reports about the adversity that awaited them, they kept on coming. But beginning in the 1660s and 1670s, changes began to overtake the region—changes that made the immigration of indentured English servants both less desirable and less necessary.

A slump in tobacco prices during the 1680s and 1690s meant fewer opportunities for immigrant laborers. Many would-be migrants chose instead to stay in England, where wages were rising. At the same time, the staggering mortality rates of the colonies' early years were leveling off. White servants who arrived in the 1650s and 1660s more often survived their indentures and became planters in their own right. As more serving girls lived to become planters' wives, and as their children survived to marry and have children of their own, sex ratios drew more nearly equal. By the 1690s, the region's white population was growing by natural increase—a surplus of births over deaths—rather than by immigration. By the mid-eighteenth century, the labor of the average planter's wife more closely resembled that of her kinswomen back in England than that of her forebears in Virginia and Maryland. Freed from daily chores in the fields, she spent most of her time cooking, sewing, dairying, gardening, tending poultry and hogs, and caring for children. Without electricity, running water, or store-bought goods, this was backbreaking work, but it was probably easier than fieldwork.

What—or, more precisely, *who*—allowed all but the poorest white women in the southern colonies to make this retreat? The answer is black women and men. Planters' wives were increasingly able to restrict themselves to duties befitting proper English matrons because they enslaved Africans to do the rest of their work. Shifts in the nature of white women's labor were tied, directly and indirectly, to perhaps the greatest change in the economy and society of the colonial Chesapeake: the rapid growth of race-based, perpetual slavery.

Africans and their descendants had been working the land since a Dutch ship unloaded a group of twenty blacks at Jamestown in 1619. But at first they comprised only a tiny fraction of the region's labor force; as late as 1660 fewer than one-fifth of Maryland's bound laborers were black. For most of the seventeenth century the status of these forced African immigrants remained ambiguous. Some black workers were servants who survived their indentures to become free men and women. Some eventually owned land, managed their own plantations, hired their own servants, and headed their own families.

Before the turn of the eighteenth century, however, the status of the region's black laborers had changed and their numbers had dramatically increased. By 1700, roughly two-thirds of Maryland and Virginia's bound laborers were black slaves whose perpetual servitude was enforced by law. Farther south, in South Carolina, Africans and their descendants comprised a majority of the whole population by 1708.

The conditions under which these involuntary African immigrants lived and labored varied widely, depending on the particular crops they slaved on: tobacco and wheat in the Chesapeake, rice and indigo in the Carolinas, and sugar in the Caribbean. But, as the colonial period wore on, Africans throughout the colonies found their status defined chiefly by the color of their skin. Because they were black, their differences from one another became in many ways less significant than their enforced separation from all whites.

At first, few women could be found among the enslaved labor force; the planters thought that strong male hands made better investments. Until the 1660s, two African men were imported for every African woman. But as white settlers began to turn the servitude of blacks into chattel slavery—a lifelong, even hereditary state—the logic of enslaving more women became clear. Enslaved men could labor only so many hours in the course of a day. But, as the masters saw it, enslaved women were *always* working, even when they were feeding their families or delivering babies. In the loathsome cycle of slavery, African women were perpetual producers: giving birth to more slaves, who could harvest more crops, the profits from which would provide more capital, which could be used to buy more slaves.

White planters made little distinction between suitable work for male and for female slaves. Englishmen might lament that Indian women worked as hard as slaves. But none seemed troubled by making the African women work as hard as Indians. An overwhelming majority of African women worked in the fields during the colonial period. As planter Thomas Nairne wrote in his *Letter from South Carolina*, "Hoes, Hatchets Broad Axes, and other necessary Tools" were perfectly appropriate equipment for female slaves. Occasionally a planter might specify, as Virginia's William Fitzhugh did in his will, that a favored female slave "be exempted from working in the ground." But such provisions were clear exceptions; most female slaves between the ages of ten and fifty could expect to spend the majority of their time working in the fields. Some evidence suggests that as plantation economies became more complex in the late eighteenth century, male slaves were diverted to the skilled trades, leaving the heaviest manual labor to their womenfolk.

Slave women deemed incapable of field labor—the very young, the infirm, and the very old—might be put to household service. In the first half of the eighteenth century, these indoor workers accounted for a distinct minority of female slaves, well under 20 percent. Being assigned to the plantation household was not necessarily desirable. Unlike field work, which often took place in gangs of six or more slaves away from the master's watchful eye, housework meant nearly constant supervision and a heightened risk of sexual exploitation as well. And sundown did not mean the end of the house slave's day. Slave women who worked in their mistresses' homes were always on call. Their duties ranged from hard, physical labor like doing laundry and toting water, to such routine drudgery as emptying chamber pots and making beds.

Slave women demonstrated their hatred for the hardships and injustices of their working lives through courageous acts of resistance to their owners' demands. Sometimes, a woman's challenge to her enslavement might take a passive form.

Virginia planter Landon Carter, for example, wrote in his diary about Mary, who escaped field work by faking "fits"; Sarah, who managed to extract eleven months of reduced work assignments because of an overlong pregnancy; and Wilmot, who regularly "pretended to be too heavy [with child] to work." Such strategies enraged planters. But for slave women they bought precious extra time for tending the small gardens that nourished their families and caring for their children instead of waiting on their master's kin. Other African-American women rebelled in more violent ways. They ran away. They murdered masters who raped them. They refused the whip. They burned down the houses in which they were forced to toil. In 1755 a female slave whose name we do not know was burned at the stake in Charleston for poisoning her master—an act that must have raised fear among all the whites who enslaved black women to work in their kitchens.

In the southern colonies, then, "women's work" meant many things. English folks had distinct ideas about the labor women *should* do. But the work women actually *did*—whether they were Native Americans, planters' wives, indentured servants, or African slaves—was a different matter altogether. The urgency of farming crops for export often outweighed notions of proper feminine behavior.

Seventeenth-century New England was the destination of a very different sort of English migrant than the restless young adventurers who sailed to the Chesapeake. Seeking primarily to set up independent, pious communities rather than to turn a quick profit, many of those who settled in the colonies of Massachusetts Bay, Plymouth, New Haven, Connecticut, and Rhode Island were looking for a new way of life in which God-fearing folk could band together in communities organized for their collective good in this world and the next. In many ways, however, their new lives would resemble the ones they left behind. These were migrants who brought with them as much of Old England as they possibly could.

One of the most important ways in which New England mirrored Old was in the age structure and sex ratio of its population. More than 85 percent of those who came over during the 1630s brought along at least their immediate kin. The predominance of families, coupled with relatively healthy living conditions, created communities that were able to reproduce themselves by natural increase almost from the start.

Later in the seventeenth century, variations on this pattern of immigration would appear in the "middle colonies" between New England and the Chesapeake. As late as 1660, the region stretching from northern New York to the lower Delaware Bay held fewer than six thousand white settlers of diverse European origins. Dutch merchants, farmers, and fur traders predominated in New Netherland, where they lived in trading centers like New Amsterdam (later Manhattan) and remote rural outposts like the borough of Rensselaerswyck, which included Albany. Farther to the south, Dutch settlers competed with Swedish and Finnish migrants for title to the rich lands along the Delaware River. Beginning in the mid-seventeenth century, when the English crown seized control of the region, these small settlements embarked on a period of rapid growth. With soil more fertile than New England's and a climate less noxious than the Chesapeake's, the colonies of New York, New Jersey, and Pennsylvania proved ideal for the production of grains, especially wheat. Reports of the good living to be made there, along with the promise of greater religious tolerance than was the norm in most other places, soon attracted large numbers of migrants from England, Scotland, Wales, Ireland, Switzerland, and Germany as well as from the other colonies. By 1700, the region was one of the fastest growing and most ethnically diverse in all of British America, with a population of more than fifty thousand white inhabitants, a sizable number of slaves, and a growing community of free blacks. More than half of the white settlers who flocked to New Jersey and Pennsylvania in the late seventeenth and early eighteenth centuries came in family groups. But ships' passenger lists also reveal that a sizable number of young, unmarried male servants sought their fortunes in the middle colonies. As a consequence, men outnumbered women in the early years of white settlement, though never by as much as they did farther south.

New England and the middle colonies had a broader range of English people than could be found in the Chesapeake—children along with adults, women in numbers nearly equal to men, the middling ranks of yeomen and artisans side by side with poorer servants and higher-ranking leaders. The composition of the population made it easier for white settlers in those regions to import English ways. Young couples with some children already born and more on the way formed the core of a rapidly growing society that quickly replicated the customs of the world they had left behind. Ideas about the proper nature of women's work adapted almost effortlessly to conditions in these parts of the "new" world.

Thomas Baily and his wife, heads of the large family that inhabited a three-room house on a 150-acre farm in Chester County, Pennsylvania, in the 1760s, were average in many respects. Like most people in their corner of the middle colonies, they planted wheat, rye, and barley and raised some livestock on the side. Where the aim of the Chesapeake planter's household was to produce as much as possible—as much tobacco, as much cash, as many slaves—the goal of the family was, more often, to produce just enough. Instead of striving to get ahead, the Bailys and people like them thought in terms of subsisting, of maintaining, of holding on to their position in the world. The harvest from their fields, along with the wool produced by their twenty-four sheep and the cheese and butter Thomas's wife made from the milk of their five cows, would put food on the table and a bit of cash in their pockets. If Thomas, his wife, their several children, and their servants all worked hard throughout the summer and fall, they could set aside enough dried grains and cured meats in their second-floor storage space to see the family through the winter till the ground was fit for planting again.

Many of Goodwife Baily's duties remained the same throughout the year. Her first waking moments would be spent starting the cooking fires that would smolder throughout the day. Next she might see to the milking, setting aside pans of fresh milk for cream to form; later she would churn this cream into butter, salt it, and pack it into wooden molds for storage or sale. After heating up a breakfast of leftovers, she might spend the bulk of her morning preparing food for the day ahead: making a one-dish "pottage" and baking the coarse bread her family would eat at noonday dinner and evening supper, and brewing the beer that accompanied virtually every meal. The majority of the afternoon might be taken up with weeding the garden, washing and mending clothes, or taking grain to the miller's. And, on top of these regular chores, she would have to steal time for her various seasonal tasks: raising calves in the spring; processing milk into cheese, making sausage, and preserving bacon in the summer; putting up preserves in the fall; and completing the seemingly endless duties connected with cloth production, such as carding and spinning the wool she would send out to be woven into coarse fabric, while her garden lay fallow in the winter.

"This day is forty years since I left my father's house and come here, and I have seene little else but hard labor and much sorrow. . . . I am dirty and tired almost to death." Mary Cooper, the woman who found time to pen these plaintive lines in her diary before retiring late one night in 1769, lived on a family farm in Oyster Bay, New York. Though she lived several hundred miles from Goody Baily, their lives had much in common. Cooper, too, spent her days cooking and washing and preserving and sewing and marketing and trading.

Almost *any* woman in colonial America might have made these comments. Had the writer been a black slave in the Chesapeake, she could not have "left her father's house" of her own free will. If she were an indentured white servant in Maryland, she might well not have even *survived* forty years after marriage. If she were a very wealthy woman in New England, the Carolinas, Pennsylvania, or Virginia, she might have been just a little less dirty and felt just a bit less tired. But regardless of her race, region, or status, the central fact of nearly endless toil would have marked the lives of all of these women.

Of Marriage and Motherhood

During the fall of 1664 Martha Cross realized the extent of her dilemma. This young woman from the godly village of Ipswich, Massachusetts, found herself in a decidedly un-Puritan situation: As yet unmarried, she was going to have a baby. Even worse, the father of the child, one William Durkee, did not seem particularly interested in sharing his future with her. Indeed, as Martha's sister later told the Essex County magistrates, Durkee had gone so far as to say that "he had rather keep the child than keep her!" In time, Durkee retracted these cruel words, telling Martha that "if he kept one he would keep the other." But the promise seemed lukewarm at best. No wonder Martha felt, as her sister reported, "in sore distresse of mind."

In an era when marriage was an unquestioned norm, abortion was risky at best, and single parenthood was all but unheard of, Martha Cross did not know what to do. She talked the matter over first with the women among whom she spent her

[12]

An Indians having Strong Drink in his Cuſtody, (except Cyder made of Fruit of their own growth.)   ibid.

The Drink to be ſiezed, for the Poor of the Town. And the Indian to be Examined before a Juſtice.

An Indians being Drunk.   p. 63

A Fine of Five Shillings, for the Poor of the Town. Or, A Scourging, not exceeding Ten Laſhes.

(XV.)

Off. Any Man being found in Bed with another mans Wiſe.   p. 65

Pen. Both Man and Woman ſeverely Scourged, (not exceeding Thirty Stripes.)

Unleſs it appear that one party was meerly ſurprized, and conſented not ; and then the Puniſhment of that party Abated.

Adultery Committed.   p. 66.

Convicted before the Juſtices of Aſſize, - both Man and Woman to be ſet on the Gallowes an Hour, with a Rope about their Neck, and the other end caſt over the Gallowes. And in the way from thence to the common Gaol, to be Scourged, not exceeding Forty Stripes. And forever after to wear a Capital A of two Inches long, of a contrary Colour to their

[13]

their Cloathes, ſewed on their upper Garments, on the Back or Arm, in open view. And as often as they appear without it, openly to be Scourged, not exceeding Fifteen Stripes.

(XVI.)

Off. To Marry any other, the former Husband or Wife, being alive; (unleſs they have been abſent for Three Years, and in this Term have not heard of one another.) And except in Caſe of Divorce, or where the Marriage has been declared Void; or been made under the Age of Conſent. p. 66.

Explanation 134.

Pen. Death, as in Caſes of Felony; in whatever County the Offender is apprehended.

(XVII.)

Off. Retailers of Strong Drink, ſuffering People to ſit drinking in their Houſes, or their Dependences. Or Selling any other Drink, than what they have a Licenſe for. p 74

Pen. The like Forfeitures as by Law inflicted on them that Sell without Licenſe.

Any Officers, taking a Bribe, to Conceal ſuch Offences.   ibid.

To

The so-called "Scarlet Letter Law" in seventeenth-century Massachusetts required those convicted of adultery to wear the letter A sewn on their clothes. It was only one example of the laws the Puritans enacted in an effort to regulate private behavior to conform to God's laws.

working days: her sister and several female neighbors. Then, like the dutiful daughter she had always been, she sought counsel from the most important man in her life—one whose opinion mattered even more than Durkee's—her father. Robert Cross's reaction did not make matters any easier. News of his daughter's transgression plunged him, neighbors told the court, into "a sad and sorrowfull Condition" and he found himself unsure "which way to turn or what to say." Martha, her sister, and two neighborhood women impressed upon him their sense of the best possible resolution: that he should allow his frantic daughter to marry the wretched Durkee. By tradition, this was his decision to make. Martha was his to give in marriage—and his to withhold.

Cross chose the latter course. Perhaps, struck by reports of Durkee's less-than-enthusiastic proposal, Cross thought Martha deserved better. Perhaps, like many fathers of his era, he wished to retain some vestige of control over his adult children. Perhaps he worried about the fate of Martha's older sisters. If she married before them, would they seem less desirable to potential suitors? Whatever his reasons, however, Cross's wishes soon became moot. His verdict was overruled by the county magistrates, who, fearful of becoming responsible for the financial support of a fatherless infant, allowed Martha and William to marry before their child was born.

Martha Cross's situation was, to be sure, an unhappy one. But in many respects it was not an unusual one—not even in Massachusetts Bay, which was known as the "Bible Commonwealth" because of its strict adherence to Old Testament notions of morality. Courtship, marriage, love, sex, pregnancy, motherhood: these were central experiences shared by all young women in colonial North America. Facets of what we think of as private life, they were not nearly so private in the colonial period. Getting married, having sex, giving birth, and raising children were parts of a woman's life about which her wider community—from her parents, to her siblings, to her neighbors, to the magistrates and ministers who presided over her town—would have something to say.

The particular sequence of steps—from affection to intercourse to marriage to motherhood—might differ according to a woman's race, region, religion, social status, even personality. Yet just as the seasons of the year governed the working lives of women in various corners of the colonial mosaic, the seasons of the female life course—the biology of sexual maturation, reproduction, and aging—governed the lives of early American women.

Adolescence was the spring of a young woman's life. During their teenage years and into their early twenties, girls in colonial America grew to womanhood, learning what it meant to be wives and mothers in their communities. The progression was gradual, because most of the boundaries that separate youth from adulthood in our day would have been meaningless to the typical colonial daughter.

Education, for example, now provides an important measure of maturity, but in the colonial period few common people, and still fewer girls of any social class, received much formal education. In the Puritan colonies, civil authorities deemed knowledge of the Bible so important that they passed laws requiring that children attain basic literacy. Taught by their parents, by the head of the household in which they served as apprentices, or, increasingly after 1690, in a "dame school" in the home of a local woman during slack periods of the agricultural year, most boys and girls probably learned how to read. *Writing*, however, was considered a separate art reserved primarily for boys. Some local laws made the distinction official by proclaiming that boys should learn to read, write, and cipher (do math) while girls should master reading and needlework.

Not surprisingly, a wide gap separated male and female rates of literacy in colonial America. In mid-seventeenth-century New England, roughly 60 percent of white men could write well enough to sign their names on a will; only 30 percent of women could. As late as 1775, when nine out of ten white men in the region could write, less than half the women had the same degree of skill. The gap would not be closed until the second quarter of the nineteenth century. Throughout the

North American colonies, girls' education lagged behind their brothers'. Daughters of the colonial elite, for example, received more schooling than their poorer counterparts, but unlike their brothers they rarely learned Greek and Latin and never attended college.

Euro-American girls, however, had a much better chance of learning to read and write than their Native American and African-American counterparts did. In Puritan New England as well as in the Catholic settlements of New France and the Spanish borderlands, schools for native children—when they existed at all—were typically directed toward transforming "savage" Indians into "civilized" Christians. In this sense, Indian girls and boys paid a heavy price for their schooling. Formal education for African-American slaves was virtually nonexistent, especially in the South, where less than 1 percent of blacks of either sex could read and write. In New England, where the population of slaves and free blacks remained small, black children might receive some rudimentary schooling by attending classes along with their white neighbors. Later in the colonial period, Pennsylvania's Quaker leaders would do more to promote education for African Americans, including opening a school especially for black children in Philadelphia in 1758.

Most of a young woman's training would take place not in any classroom but within her own home, at her mother's side. Beginning by assisting with the care of her younger siblings, she would learn to relieve her mother of such time-consuming tasks as washing and spinning. Becoming a woman did not require her to forge her own path. Instead, adulthood meant following her mother's path.

An important part of the slow, almost imperceptible transition from girlhood to womanhood was the dawning of sexual maturity. Despite a prevailing belief among Anglo Americans that premarital intercourse was a grievous sin (in New England sex between two unmarried people was a crime), youth was a time of sexual exploration for many women. Experimentation often led to pregnancy, marriage, and motherhood in quick succession. As many as one in ten New England women were, like Martha Cross, pregnant when they reached the altar. Thanks to the watchfulness of New England neighbors, parents, and authorities, this was only half the proportion that would have been found in England at the time.

Farther south, the scarcity of women in the Chesapeake meant that every young girl had plenty of opportunities, and faced plenty of pressures, in matters of the heart. The existence of a Virginia law punishing "dissolute masters" who "have gotten their maides with child" tells us that female servants may have been particularly vulnerable to sexual exploration and exploitation. In Charles County, Maryland, roughly one-fifth of all the maidservants who arrived from England between 1658 and 1705 were eventually charged with bastardy, the crime of bearing a child out of wedlock. Many of them, the courts found, had been made pregnant by their masters. Thousands of miles from their families, isolated on small plantations, impoverished adolescent girls were easy prey for aggressive or unscrupulous men. In other ways, though, these young women were also unusually free to make their own choices. Out of necessity, they exercised a degree of control over their lives and their bodies that would have been quite alien to the likes of Ipswich's Martha Cross. Without fathers and mothers to decide their fates (even women born in Virginia and Maryland were often orphaned before they reached their teens), they would have received little guidance about how to direct their affections. But unlike Martha, they did not need anyone's permission. More than one-third of white women in the early Chesapeake were pregnant at the time of their weddings.

Virtually everyone in the colonial period would have known young women who became mothers almost as soon as they became wives—if not before. They would also, undoubtedly, have been acquainted with many more adolescent girls who experimented sexually before marriage but, miraculously escaping pregnancy, were able to keep their dalliances secret. Especially in the densely settled towns of New England, young couples seeking a bit of time alone faced a tough time of it. Houses were small and crowded. Windows were low to the ground, affording easy access to prying eyes. Indeed, privacy as a concept was all but nonexistent; family members, neighbors, and town "fathers" considered it a religious and social duty to monitor even the most intimate goings-on. Still, as Martha's case and many others show, young women and men who were persistent, clever, and bold enough found chances to steal away on their own. In a world where somebody else always seemed to be nearby, even a few moments alone could be precious. And most ordinary young women—those of Martha Cross's middling status or below—found it relatively easy to follow their hearts. A stubborn father might threaten to withhold his consent. But, in the end, such women had considerable say in choosing their mates. Blessed with little in the way of property or status, they had only themselves to offer in marriage. Poverty tended to reduce courtship to its essentials: affection, desire, proximity, convenience, necessity.

For women in the colonial elite, however, adolescence was different. Those of at least modest wealth knew that courtship was much more than a flirtation between young lovers. It was, more centrally, the beginning of a connection between families: an arrangement for transmitting property from one generation to the next. William Byrd II, an aristocratic planter who made his home in early-eighteenth-century Virginia, knew that love was part heartfelt affection and part iron-clad contract. In a letter he wrote to his intended, Lucy Parke, in 1705, he likened the couple to turtle doves who "abound with expressions of tenderness to one another." In a letter to Lucy's father written the same year, Byrd spoke of his "respect and tenderness" for her. But he also took pains to add that his "fortune may be sufficient to make her happy"—especially when coupled with the substantial portion of her father's goods and property which Lucy would undoubtedly bring to the marriage as her dowry.

Courtship among the colonial elite was a ritual dance with a fixed order to its steps. Parents, especially fathers, choreographed the minuet while their sons took a leading role in its performance. Women were followers in the complicated "business" of marriage. Their hopes and desires often took a back seat. Affection, too, was of secondary concern. In an ideal situation, love would follow marriage. It did not necessarily have to precede it.

Virtually every woman in seventeenth- and eighteenth-century America eventually married. Weddings took many different forms. In New England, couples were required to make formal contracts of "espousal" declaring their engagement and then to announce their intentions in the meetinghouse on three separate occasions. For wealthier English colonists, a written contract typically spelled out the property consequences of the match in minute detail; for humbler sorts spoken promises would suffice.

The ceremony was almost always a small one, typically celebrated in the bride's home. In New England, where marriage was a civil matter, a magistrate was the necessary official; in the Chesapeake, ministers of the Church of England were the celebrants of choice. And, where the authorities needed to solemnize the affair were lacking altogether, many couples must have adopted planter Giles Tomkinson's logic. Brought to court for the crime of bastardy in 1665, he explained to the magistrates of Charles County, Maryland, that he and his wife *were* married and their child, therefore, was legitimate. "To matrimony is only necessary the parties' Consent and . . . a lawfull Churchman," Tomkinson said. If no "churchman" could be found consent alone would have to do.

African-American couples had only their mutual consent to offer. Except in Massachusetts, where a law permitting marriage between slaves was passed in 1705, the unions of black men and women were legitimized neither by law nor by religious leaders in the British colonies. By the mid-eighteenth century, sex ratios among the black population had leveled off enough to allow more slaves to find mates. But despite the unwavering commitment many slave men and women demonstrated toward their families, the bonds between husband and wife, like those between parents and child, were fragile. Masters could and often did sell one partner in a marriage, dissolving what was meant to be a lifelong partnership.

Whatever its particular conventions, a wedding marked the start of what we might call the summer of a woman's life. During this season of her life she would assume the roles of an adult woman: most centrally, those of wife and mother. She would learn to fit her daily chores around the nearly constant childbearing and childrearing that would continue until she reached menopause in her mid- to late forties.

In New England, most women had reached their early twenties before they married for the first time. In the Chesapeake, a more complicated pattern held sway. For women like Elizabeth Montague, who came to Virginia from England in the early 1650s, marriage had to wait until the end of a lengthy indenture. Many women of her generation were thus over twenty-five years old by the time they were free to wed. Their daughters did much to reverse this pattern in a single generation. If they were lucky enough to survive childhood, they were sure to be surrounded by potential suitors. And, with no indentures to satisfy, they had no reason to delay their choice. Elizabeth Montague's youngest daughter and namesake married in 1671 in her mid-teens.

What did becoming a wife mean for a mere girl like Elizabeth Montague? For one thing, marriage meant a change of residence. All but the poorest young couples throughout British America followed the English custom of setting up their own, separate households rather than the Native American tradition of residing in a multi-generational dwelling with maternal or paternal kin. In Elizabeth's case, the move was delayed by poverty. Her husband, Doodes Minor, and his family were not planters in their own right but tenants who rented a plot of land from Elizabeth's father. At first, she and her husband lived with her in-laws. In time, the hardworking young Doodes scraped together enough profits from this land to allow him to purchase 650 acres for the couple to farm. There Elizabeth learned the business of being the mistress of her own humble home.

She had to master it quickly, for in rapid succession, she gave birth to six children. Families of this size and larger were common; the woman who survived her childbearing years (most in the Chesapeake did not) would have delivered, on average, eight or nine children over the course of her reproductive life. As many as twelve or thirteen live births were not unheard of. If Elizabeth followed the typical pattern, she would have given birth to her oldest child within fifteen months of her wedding. Thereafter, a new baby would likely follow every two years or so. Starting a scant year after her marriage, she would spend much of the remainder of her life performing the manifold duties of a housewife—cooking, spinning, dairying, hog-tending—while either pregnant, nursing, caring for an infant, or all three. Not only ceaseless labor but a measure of sadness marked Elizabeth Montague Minor's days. She lived to bury half of her offspring; only three of them survived long enough to bear children of their own. Almost inconceivably tragic in our day, such a family history would have been commonplace in hers. Throughout the 1600s, roughly one-quarter of the children born in the Chesapeake died before their first birthdays; fewer than half reached the age of twenty. New England proved much healthier: Nine out of ten infants born there survived at least until age five, and perhaps three-quarters lived to see adulthood. Still, in the early modern world the loss of a child was a regular part of a woman's life.

So was the death of a spouse. Elizabeth lost Doodes while she was still a young woman—a fate perhaps heartbreaking but hardly surprising. In the disease-ridden environment in which she lived, either husband or wife was likely to die within seven years of marriage. Of course, with so few women around, widows like Elizabeth did not stay widows long. She remarried quickly, not once but twice. In the end, Elizabeth Montague Minor Cocke Blaze outlasted three husbands. Living out her remaining days on her third husband's plantation, she was positively ancient by Virginia standards. When death came in 1708, she was about fifty-two years old.

We know a good deal about what women like Elizabeth Montague *did*, but very little about how they *felt*. Was she "in love" with her first husband (or, for that matter, with her second, or her third)? Did her husbands and her children consider her a figure of authority? Or did she remain constantly under the shadow of the man of the house? Undoubtedly, Elizabeth Montague would soon have discovered that the mistress of a colonial household occupied a rather precarious rung on the ladder of authority that structured her society. In a world in which the principle of hierarchy was unquestioned—where it was simply assumed that some would always rule from above while others would serve dutifully below them—the good-wife had to occupy both places at once. As mother and mistress, she would learn to be a ruler of sorts. As wife, however, she was more clearly a subordinate. Her marriage vows would have included pledges to "obey" and "serve" her husband—promises he was not asked to make to her. Doodes Minor, for his part, was supposed to support his wife, to live with her in harmony, to have sex with her alone, and to refrain from physically abusing her beyond the bounds of necessary "correction." He was not, however, expected to "obey" her: to set her word above his own.

The woman's vow of submission in marriage expressed a view of the world that imagined man to be superior and woman to be inferior in almost every respect. Many English writers of the day referred to women as "the weaker vessel," a phrase denoting a being with less intellectual ability, less physical capacity, and less moral fortitude than a man. This notion of female inferiority manifested itself in a variety of ways in colonial America.

In Elizabeth Minor's day, the shortage of women meant that husbands and wives shared authority more equally than they would later in the colonial period. According to the ancient traditions of the English common law, a wife was entitled only to her "dower thirds"—one-third of her husband's real property—if he died before she did. But many men in the seventeenth-century Chesapeake went further than the law required, bequeathing at least half their estates to their wives. With no brothers or fathers nearby who might be entrusted with the family's care, these early planters left their widows in control. In terms of married women's property rights as in many other aspects of life, the early Chesapeake was marked by flexibility in the face of necessity.

By the eighteenth century, however, increased reliance on the English common law imposed narrower strictures on women throughout British America. Published in London in 1765, English jurist William Blackstone's four-volume compendium entitled *Commentaries on the Laws of England* gave precise definition of a wife's legal rights. Blackstone defined the married woman as a woman literally "covered" by her husband's authority. Her "very being or legal existence," he wrote, was "consolidated into that of her husband; under whose wing, protection, and cover, she performs everything." Unless her husband signed a special document permitting her to do so, a married Anglo-American woman could not own or buy property in her own name, enter into a contract, or write a will.

In New York, one legacy of the early years of Dutch control was a very different set of traditions concerning the rights of married women. Long after the English conquest of New Netherland in 1664, Dutch custom, rooted primarily in Roman civil law rather than in the English common law, governed women's lives. Roman-Dutch law gave married women a number of privileges they did not normally enjoy anywhere else in Europe. Unlike the English goodwife, the Dutch *huysvrouw* could and often did run a business, sue on her own behalf, inherit equally with her brothers, and make a will leaving her property to whomever she chose. She might even sue her husband in court—something that would have been literally impossible for an English woman, considered to be legally one with her husband. Like English traditions, Roman-Dutch law assumed that wives were, in some measure, subordinate to their husbands, but the mutual duties of married couples received greater emphasis than their presumed inequality. To the Dutch and their American-born descendants, marriage was like a business venture in which husbands were the senior partners while wives were prized junior executives.

Of course, systems of law only tell us what a marriage was *supposed* to be—not necessarily what it *was*. Even among the English, female submission was upheld more often in sermons and statutes than in actual practice. In day-to-day reality if not in law and letters, wives in British America were meaningful partners in their marriages. They were not, in any sense, their husbands' equals. But then again, equality had little meaning in the world of Elizabeth Montague Minor Cocke Blaze. What could equality possibly mean when the wealthy planters whose "Great Houses" loomed over the Chesapeake's richer lands could amass thousands of acres while she and her family eked out a hardscrabble existence on a small plot of rocky soil? What could equality mean in a world where men and women whose skin was darker were bought and sold like cattle?

Instead of demanding full legal parity, most wives in the colonies would have rested content with the knowledge that they were, as Puritan minister Samuel Willard put it, the "nearest to equality" among "all the Orders which are unequals." That the wife should submit to her husband's authority was a given. That the obligations between them were mutual was equally apparent. To an English woman of that time, the belief that her husband was both her ruler and her yokefellow—roles we might see as mutually exclusive—seemed perfectly logical.

Although marriage was based on more than romance, couples who proved compatible often forged bonds of affection, honor, and not least, sexual passion. This was the way that Anne Bradstreet experienced her life as wife and mother. Born in Northampton, England, in 1612, Anne Dudley, a wealthy girl, was schooled by private tutors. When she was just sixteen years old, Anne wed Simon Bradstreet. Luckier than the thrice-widowed Elizabeth Montague, Anne Bradstreet found in

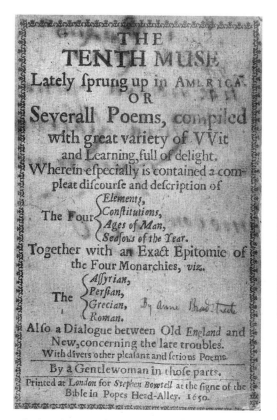

Left, the title page of Anne Bradstreet's *The Tenth Muse, Lately Sprung up in America,* a collection of poems published in London in 1650. Right, a handwritten page from Bradstreet's *Meditations Divine and Morall.* These meditations, addressed to her son Simon, are reflections on her constant struggle to purify her soul.

Simon a lifelong partner. They remained married for forty-four years until her death parted them in 1672. Less than two years after her marriage Anne Bradstreet abandoned her comfortable life in England forever. Devout Puritan believers, she and Simon sailed for Massachusetts in 1630. They were among the Bible commonwealth's most prominent inhabitants.

In some respects, Anne Bradstreet's wealth and education set her apart. Even in a setting as rustic as North Andover, the rude hamlet outside Boston she called home after 1644, her high position doubtless meant that her burdens were somewhat lighter than those carried by many humbler goodwives. Like very few women in her day, Anne Bradstreet was an accomplished woman of letters who became a published and widely admired poet. Yet she used her writings to affirm the prevailing belief that women were better suited to domestic roles than to public fame. In a series of poems addressed "To Her Husband, Absent on Public Employment," she praised Simon's leadership in the family. He was, she wrote, "my head, my heart, mine eyes, my life, nay more." At the same time, though, she portrayed a marriage that was not a dictatorship but a true partnership. "If ever two were one, then surely we," she wrote in a brief verse dedicated "To My Dear and Loving Husband." "If ever man was loved by wife, then thee." And, as she went on to make clear, the oneness she felt with Simon was physical as well as spiritual. When he was away from her, their lonely bed left her with "chilled limbs." She longed openly for the "sweet contentment" she experienced when they were together.

Of course, such expressions of tenderness do not mean that Anne Bradstreet and others like her were their husbands' equals in any formal sense. Nor was any wife in British America. Married women could not vote. They could not, without special arrangements, own property. They could not stand for office, or serve in the militia, or become ministers. They were not even encouraged to speak in public. They were, in every sense, subordinate to men both within and beyond their families. We should not imagine, however, that this enforced inferiority in law and customs meant colonial goodwives were, in the words of one common injunction to women, merely "chaste, silent, and obedient."

Then as now, some marriages flourished while others foundered. A match based on economic and familial concerns might develop into a harmonious partnership. Or love could sour, and a marriage might degenerate into a kind of hell on earth from which escape was difficult at best. In New England, where marriage was regarded as a civil contract that the courts could dissolve, divorce was granted when a spouse could prove adultery, unusual cruelty, or desertion. In New York and Pennsylvania, only adultery was considered grounds to terminate a marriage. In the southern colonies the Church of England followed the same rules as it did in the home country; divorce was granted only by a special act of the legislature. Even in Rhode Island and Connecticut, where divorce was available on a relatively liberal basis, few sought to end their marriages. Magistrates in those colonies ruled on an average of only one divorce petition per year throughout the seventeenth century. For women especially, staying in a troubled marriage often seemed preferable to trying to survive as a single person.

Wives sometimes took the lead in fomenting marital discord. Joan Miller of Plymouth colony, for example, was charged in 1655 with "beating and reviling her husband, and egging her children to help her." Others, like Goody Lawrence of Essex County, Massachusetts, made words their weapons. In 1681, the magistrates censured her for calling her husband "bald-pated old rogue." Were women like Lawrence and Miller rebelling against the position of women in their society? Though they rarely discussed their motives, some women in the seventeenth and eighteenth centuries appear to have found their roles as wives and mothers unbearable. For reasons that are now lost to historians, Salem's Dorothy Talbye was one of them. In 1635 she gave birth to a daughter to whom she gave the ominous name Difficulty, presumably a comment on the labor that produced the child. By 1637, there were signs of serious trouble in Talbye's household. That year the magistrates of the county court found her guilty of "frequent laying hands on her husband to the danger of his life" and sentenced her to the humiliating punishment of being chained to a post in a public square. But the court's rebuke apparently had no effect. Claiming that she had been inspired by the voice of God, Talbye broke her daughter's neck the following year. In December 1638 the authorities of the Bay Colony hanged her on Boston common as a warning to other wayward wives and murderous mothers.

For some women, marriage may have been the kind of earthly paradise Anne Bradstreet described. Others may have been too poor and too careworn even to think much about marital bliss. Still others—women, who, like Dorothy Talbye, were locked in frequent, violent confrontations with their mates and appear to have suffered bouts of deep depression—must have seen marriage as a prison where they were destined to serve time, as the wedding vow said, "till death them did part." It is important to remember, however, that none of these marriages existed in isolation; they were each part of the life of a broader community. Whatever the particular character of her relationship with her husband, every colonial woman knew that life did not stop at the threshold of her house.

Though she most likely lived a "nuclear" household—one that included herself, her husband, their offspring, and perhaps a servant or two—the typical goodwife would not have thought of her home as a retreat. The barrier separating family from community was easily breached; women throughout the colonies spent their lives enmeshed in a dense social fabric made up of neighbors, kinfolk, and friends. In happiness and in sadness, in seasons of want and seasons of plenty, colonial women wove the strands of their own lives into the intricate tapestry of their neighborhoods.

At no time would a goodwife have thought her local "community of women" more important than when she prepared to give birth. The onset of "travail," as the early Americans called labor and delivery, brought not only pain but genuine fear. Although respected midwives often succeeded in even the most complicated deliveries, death in childbirth was still an everyday occurrence. How comforting, then, that most women did not have to travail alone. Childbirth in the colonial era was not a private ordeal to be suffered through in a distant hospital. Instead, wherever neighbors lived near one another, the birth of a baby was an event shared by the whole female community. Particularly in the densely settled villages and towns of New England, the onset of labor pains was the signal for a goodwife to gather "her women" about her. In 1757, when Goody Patten, the wife of a farmer living in Bedford, New Hampshire, "was Delivered Safe of a Daughter . . . after [an] abundance of hard Labor and a great deal of Discouragement," eight neighborhood women were by her side. Men—even fathers-to-be—were kept firmly at bay while local female "experts" (most women would have seen numerous births before they experienced one of their own) served as healers, friends, therapists, and more. Offering refreshments such as the aptly named "groaning cakes" and dispensing traditional herbal remedies, they helped the expectant mother ease her pain and pass the time between contractions. Their counsel and experience allayed her fears. A devout woman would also have turned to God in her hour of need. Religion was a palpable presence in the lives of many women in the colonial era—one never so keenly felt as it was during the weary hours of travail.

Women and Religion

In the beginning was chaos. On that much, the Iroquois and their European neighbors in colonial North America would have agreed. Their respective creation myths both began with a vast, swirling emptiness. The version of the story favored by the Cayuga, one nation of the Iroquois confederacy, held that "in the beginning there was no world, no land, no creatures of the kind that are around us now." The Bible's book of Genesis, the story that guided the European Christians who sought to bring what they called civilization to Cayuga lands, also looked back to a primordial moment when "the earth was without form, and void, and darkness was upon the face of the waters."

In both versions it was from that formless oblivion that the world and all the living things in it, including humans, emerged. The Iroquois and the Europeans believed that humankind was created by a divine being and sometime thereafter divided into two sexes, male and female. But which sex came first? And what would their ensuing roles be? About such important details, pious Europeans and Iroquois held different views. These differences would be visible not just in their sacred stories, but in their daily lives as well. Religious traditions formed a central part of the cultures that instructed biological males and females in the ways of acting like men and women.

In the Christian version of the tale, the human race began with a man. Eve followed later, formed from a rib taken from the sleeping Adam. Recognizing their former oneness Adam called her "bone of my bones, flesh of my flesh." From the beginning, then, Christian tradition made woman the second sex—and the weaker sex. Eve soon proved herself worthy of this designation. Easily tempted, she succumbed to the charms of the wiliest creature in the garden of Eden, and then convinced Adam to sin along with her. The price for the transgression was steep: Adam and Eve and all humankind were driven from the garden forever. But though God punished them both for breaking His laws, Eve paid more dearly. "I will greatly multiply thy sorrow," God's voice told her. "In sorrow thou shalt bring forth children." The pain of childbirth, in the Christian view, was a sentence all women suffered for Eve's disobedience. So, too, was their subordination in marriage. Adam and Eve had shared equally in the government of the garden of Eden, but they would do so no more. In the uncharted world beyond the gates she would be his underling. "Thy desire shall be to thy husband," God rebuked her, "and he shall rule over thee."

At the beginning of time, the gods to whom the Iroquois prayed lived in the Sky-World, a kingdom far above the empty earth below. Those gods, male and female, were said to be "like people—like Iroquois." Among them was Sky-Woman, who fell headlong out of the Sky-World "toward the great ocean far below" and came to rest on the back of a great turtle. She created the earth, gathered its fruits, and bore a daughter who in turn bore the twin sons who came to rule the earth. Even in death, Sky-Woman's daughter did not stop nourishing her children. When they buried her in the earth she had helped to cultivate, "three sisters" grew from her grave. The sisters were corn, beans, and squash—staples that would feed the Iroquois and many other eastern woodlands peoples for centuries. One of her twin sons would call himself "Master of Life" or "Great Creator." But the first earthborn woman and her mother were the true providers for the Iroquois nations.

These very different creation myths belong to only two among many traditions that formed the spiritual base of people's lives in the colonial period. Every native group had its own account of the world's beginnings, and European beliefs were no more uniform. Though nearly all the whites who settled in colonial North America were Christians, they interpreted the Bible in many different ways. To the Protestants of New England, followers of the teachings of Swiss theologian John Calvin, the devotional practices of the Catholics in New France and the Spanish colonies seemed as alien as those of the Narragansets and Wampanoags who lived among them in Massachusetts and Rhode Island. In turn, the faithful in Virginia and Maryland, who followed the orthodox traditions of the Church of England, considered New England's Puritans to be overzealous reformers. Yet the Quaker radicals who came to the colonies from England in the 1650s and 1660s thought the Puritans too conservative—as did the Baptist rebels who sprang up in their midst. And the few European Jews who migrated to the colonies, concentrating in Dutch New Amsterdam, often met with intolerance from their Christian neighbors. While many sects believed that theirs was the true and only way to heaven, early Americans knew many different roads to salvation.

These varied religious traditions held two important things in common. The first was the almost unquestioned loyalty they commanded from their followers. In an era when religion has been separated from much of everyday life, it is hard to imagine the level of belief that permeated the premodern world. To be sure, some early Americans were more deeply spiritual than others. But virtually nobody in seventeenth- or eighteenth-century America would have considered herself an atheist. Whatever they understood "God" to mean, they would not have questioned the presence of the divine in their world.

Even in the most physical, tangible sense religion was a constant presence. From the stark clapboard spires that capped New England's Congregational meeting houses, to the sturdy brick of Virginia's Anglican churches, to the poles marking the underground kivas in which the Pueblo held sacred rituals, places of worship dotted the landscape. Each and every day, the English villages lining the eastern seaboard would have been alive with the sound of church bells. Religion was a constant backdrop to people's lives in less obvious ways, too. Particularly in the north-

ern colonies, reading from scripture and hearing ministers expound upon its messages were central parts of life. The Bible and other religious works were virtually
the only printed material available throughout much of the colonial period. For
those who could read and those who had God's word read to them, devotional
writings, tracts on theology, and tales of wondrous natural events offered needed
solace in a fallen world.

The second major thing the religious traditions held in common was their central importance for women's lives. Figures like the Christian Eve and the Iroquois
Sky-Woman offered explanations for the differences between men and women and
rules for the ways each gender should act. But religion was much more than a
source of prescriptions about the duties of ideal women. It was also a source of
emotional support for *real* women. In a world full of terrifying uncertainty—the
prospect of dying in childbirth, the likelihood of losing a beloved infant, the hardships of living thousands of miles from the land of one's birth, the terrors of invasion by warlike white strangers—religion was a place to turn for help and guidance.

Every part of colonial America had its own rhythms of religious devotion—
rhythms that helped women and men make sense of their lives. But nowhere did
religion play a greater role than it did in early New England. Almost without exception, the leaders of Massachusetts, Plymouth, Connecticut, New Haven, New
Hampshire, and Rhode Island were dissenters from the Church of England. For
many of the ordinary people among the first generations of white New Englanders,
immigration meant more than an opportunity for a better life in economic terms.
It was also a chance to live according to what they understood as God's laws—a
way of life they found impossible under the Church of England. Both law and custom enforced the preeminence of Puritan worship, called Congregationalism or
the "New England Way." Only churches embracing the Puritans' interpretation of
Calvin's teachings were permitted. And from the early 1630s until 1662, only the
spiritually "elect"—men and women who had personally experienced God's saving
grace and felt assured that their salvation had been predestined—could join the
Puritan churches. Church membership translated into a voice in civil life; only
male church members could become "freemen" and vote in local affairs. Not surprisingly, the communities these freemen-saints designed favored the Congregational way. Biblical mandates became civil laws. Mortal sins like adultery and blas-
phemy were punishable by death. Sunday, the Christian sabbath, was reserved solely for thoughts of God; no work could be performed. Attending church was
mandatory for the elect and the unredeemed alike, and the courts regularly punished those who stayed away.

No matter whether they enthusiastically supported or dared to question the
Puritan mission, all law-abiding New Englanders gathered in their local meeting-
houses every Sunday, and often once during the week as well, to hear their
preacher expound upon scripture. One popular sermon topic was the nature of
women. Between 1668 and 1735, women's lives were the subject of no fewer than

4   *Milk for Babes.*

s Ifa. 58.
12, 13.
Exo. 32. 6.

and much more from play on [*s*] the Lords day; that we may draw nigh to God in holy duties.

Q. *What is the fifth Commandement ?*

A. Honour thy Father and thy Mother, [*t*] that thy dayes may be long in the Land, which the Lord thy God giveth thee.

t Exo. 20.
12.
u Pro. 23.
22

Queft. *Who are here meant by father and mother ?*

x Kings 5.
13. and 2.
12.
1 Cor. 4.
15.
2 Chron.
29. 18.
x Tim. 5. 1.

Anfw. All our Superiours, whether in [*u*] Family, School, Church, and Common-wealth.

Queft. *What is the honour due to them ?*

x Sam. 25. 8.
Gen. 4. 20,
21.
w Mal. 1. 6.
Heb. 12. 9.
Eph. 6. 1.
1 Tim. 5. 4.
x Exo. 20.
13.
y Mat. 5.
22.
2 Cor. 7. 10.
1 Sam. 26.
24.
Mark 3. 4.

Anf. Reverence [*w*] Obedience, and (when I am able) Recompence.

Queft. *What is the fixth Commandement ?*

Anfw. Thou fhalt do no (*x*) murther.

Q. *What is the meaning of this Commandement ?*

Anfw. That we fhould not fhorten the (*y*) life, or health of our felves or others, but preferve both.

Q. *What*

John Cotton first published his catechism, *Spiritual Milk for Babes,* in 1646. The slim volume was used by generations of Puritans to teach their children religious doctrine. Cotton was the founder of a long line of New England ministers. Cotton Mather was his grandson, and his great-nephew John Cotton was a minister in New Hampshire.

seventy-five *printed* treatises. Some of these tracts were funeral sermons that eulogized an especially pious female parishioner; others were more general "how-to" homilies dealing with marriage or mothering. And clerics delivered many more lectures on female piety that were never reproduced in print. Attending carefully to their preachers' instructions, pious goodwives and their mates had many chances to learn about how to divide the work within their families or, as preachers often put it, about the "relative duties" of men and women.

John Cotton, a minister in New Hampshire, offered one such homily on June 19, 1694. On that warm Sunday, John Clark and Elizabeth Woodridge, two of the most prominent inhabitants of the town of Newcastle, were celebrating their wedding. With his entire congregation gathered for this joyous occasion, Cotton took the opportunity to offer some thoughts about the role of women. The sermon must have hit home with its audience, for it was later printed in Boston and distributed throughout the colonies. We can assume, therefore, that Cotton was saying things that common people—women included—wanted to hear.

Cotton drew for his message on Genesis 2:18. The passage described the creation of Eve, foremother of all women in Protestant tradition: "And the Lord God said, It is not good that the man should be alone; I will make him an help meet for him." Precisely what, Cotton pondered in his sermon, constituted a "meet" or fitting companion for a man? What was woman's true nature? Had Eve's daughters living in New England inherited her legacy of temptation and corruption? On balance, Cotton insisted, they had not. "Women," he told Newcastle's faithful, "are creatures without which there is no comfortable Living for man." In a godly society women were an asset and not, as celibate Catholic priests maintained, a necessary evil. What God had proclaimed at the world's beginning was still true: women "are a necessary Good; such as was not good that man should be without." Woman was not the *same* as man, Cotton was quick to note. Elizabeth Woodridge was not to venture forth into the world but to "keep at home, educating of her children, keeping and improving what is got by the industry of the man." Yet she would not be a mere servant in her husband's house but rather his "most sweet and intimate companion." In God's sight the two were equals of a sort: "joynt Heirs of salvation" in the world to come.

Many New England women took comfort in the spiritual equality of the sexes Cotton and other preachers propounded. Celebrated as "Daughters of Zion," pious matrons took religion very seriously indeed. They attended church without fail and sat rapt while the minister discoursed on the week's text. They read and meditated on the Bible, making their way through the Old and New Testaments at least once each year. They prayed and fasted and experienced God's grace and repented their sins with zeal only the most devout men could have matched.

Pious women were praised by ministers and neighbors alike. If they resembled any Old Testament figure, it was the industrious Bathsheba (the "virtuous woman" described in Proverbs 31:10–31) rather than the perfidious Eve. Where Eve tempted, persuaded, and seduced, Bathsheba planted, prayed, and spun. Her every word testified to a womanly brand of piety: faith tempered with respectful submission. Still, most New Englanders assumed, as minister Samuel Willard noted in a sermon, that woman was "the weaker Vessel." She was ill suited, Willard and others made clear, for the types of intellectual activity that came naturally to men. One Mistress Hopkins, wife of the governor of Connecticut, was said to have driven herself mad by reading and writing—activities which, John Winthrop noted in his journal, "are proper for men, whose minds are stronger." The sister of Thomas Parker, pastor of Newbury, Massachusetts, received an even harsher judgment of her mental prowess. "Your printing of a book beyond the custom of your sex," her brother told her in a letter in 1650, "doth rankly smell." But even if her mind was thought to be inferior, New England's preachers knew that woman's soul—that part of her which God alone saw—was the equal of any man's.

In fact, New England's "virtuous women" may have been even more devoted to religious practice than their husbands and fathers. At the very least they were more dedicated churchgoers. At first, men and women joined the churches in equal numbers. Within a generation, however, women outnumbered men in many if not most of the churches in Massachusetts and Connecticut. By the mid-eighteenth century women comprised nearly three-quarters of many congregations. Cotton Mather may not have been exaggerating when he said in 1692 that there were "far more godly women" than men in the world.

Reasons for the preponderance of women in Puritan churches are hard to pin down. Some preachers, Mather included, thought that facing death in childbirth brought women closer to God. Many historians now agree. Others suggest that the growing percentage of women in the churches really represents a decline in *male* piety. Whatever the combination of factors bringing them there, women continued to flock toward God's word long after men focused their attentions elsewhere.

"Let your women keep silence in the Churches: for it is not permitted unto them

Anne Hutchinson preaches in her house in Boston, in a romanticized nineteenth-century depiction. Hutchinson's preaching so outraged the leaders of Massachusetts that they excommunicated her.

to speak." Thus spoke Saint Paul on women's place in spiritual life in 1 Corinthians 14:34–35. New England's clergymen regarded these as words to live by. It was one thing for women to profess virtue, piety, and reverence for God and His ministers. But it was quite another for them to profess their faith loudly, publicly, and persuasively in New England's churches—to *act* like ministers. When women became *too* zealous in their religious practice, they sounded more like daughters of Eve than like daughters of Zion.

Anne Hutchinson was one of the first Puritan women to test the boundaries of female piety in New England. An exceptionally learned and devout supporter of Puritan minister John Cotton, Hutchinson and her husband, William, followed this charismatic preacher from England to Boston in 1634. At first, Hutchinson seemed content within the role the clergy prescribed for laywomen in Massachusetts. As John Cotton later remembered, she had been the ideal "meete helpe" in those early years. Leading small, informal women's prayer groups or "conventicles," and serving as a sometime midwife, Cotton recalled, "shee did much good in our Town." Hutchinson, however, found this auxiliary role in religious affairs confining. She had serious qualms about the way the colony's churches were being run and sought a larger, more official pulpit from which to air her views. By 1635, she had come to believe Massachusetts was falling short of its religious goals. Few among the clergy adhered to John Cotton's lofty principles. Where he emphasized the inner workings of divine grace in the souls of true believers, most preachers seemed content with inspiring outwardly pious behavior in their congregations. Like the clergy of the Anglican church, they were more concerned, Hutchinson said, with appearances, or "works," than with redemption, or "faith." It was up to every devout man and woman, Hutchinson believed, to reject the false authority of these inferior clergy: to go over their heads, so to speak, and seek direct communication with God.

Determined to help her neighbors achieve the kind of "immediate revelation" she herself had experienced, Hutchinson began to enlarge her role in the community's religious life. Many in Boston and surrounding towns apparently found her persuasive. By 1636, the prayer sessions in her home had grown to include sixty to eighty men and women—a sizable percentage of the church members in these tiny hamlets. Meeting twice a week to hear Hutchinson preach, these men and women had become a sort of shadow congregation worshiping in their own unconventional style right under the noses of the orthodox ministers. This state of affairs quickly became intolerable to the colony's leading clergy and magistrates. True, as Hutchinson was fond of reminding them, Saint Paul had declared that "there is neither male nor female: for you are all one in Jesus Christ." But hadn't Paul also proclaimed that "Christ is the head of every man and the man is the woman's head"? That was one lesson Hutchinson had ignored at her peril. It was one thing to hold small meetings in which godly women could reflect upon, and agree with, what their preachers had said the Sunday before. But it was quite another, as John

Winthrop later wrote, for Hutchinson to keep "open house for all comers": to become a preacher with disciples who hung on her every word, to reject the teachings of God's rightful ministers. That was what the clergy called "antinomianism"—a derisive term meaning "against or opposed to the law" that had been used to describe some of the most hated English heretics.

Salem minister Hugh Peter summed up the male elite's feelings on the matter when he rebuked Hutchinson before the First Church. "You have stept out of your place," Peter said, "you have rather been a Husband than a Wife and a preacher than a Hearer; and a Magistrate than a Subject." She was, others said, a new Eve: a seducer, a trickster, a cunning temptress. Her continued presence in their new world Eden, the elders of Boston's First Church declared, was intolerable. They excommunicated her from the church, and the court banished her from Massachusetts. That March, Hutchinson, her family, and several of her unrepentant followers were driven out of Boston by order of the Puritan government—sent not to Hell, but to Rhode Island, a colony founded by dissenters from the Puritan establishment and known for permitting a greater range of religious practices than Massachusetts allowed. After William Hutchinson died in 1642, Anne moved with her six youngest children and a small band of believers to a lonely spot in present-day Westchester County, New York. The following year the group was caught in a skirmish with the natives on whose land they were trespassing. Anne Hutchinson and twelve others, including most of her family, were killed; only her youngest daughter survived the attack.

In the most literal sense, Hutchinson was silenced forever that day in 1643. But her challenge to the Puritan elite lived on. Hutchinson was only the first (and possibly the loudest) of a long line of female religious dissenters in New England. Chief among the dissenting women who followed in Hutchinson's footsteps were those who joined the sect known as the Society of Friends, or the Quakers. One of the more radical groups in the spectrum of dissenting English Protestantism, the Quakers granted female believers an extraordinary degree of autonomy and equality. Spiritual rebirth, which Quakers understood as the direct inspiration of Divine Light, came to men and women alike. All those who felt Divine Light working within them could become lay ministers, sharing their transformation with others. Converts of both sexes were encouraged to preach about their religious experiences, and one of the movement's early and most prominent leaders was an English wife and mother, Margaret Fell.

Where the Puritans looked to biblical foremothers like Eve and the submissive Bathsheba, Fell and the Quakers considered such role models irrelevant. Eve's curse and St. Paul's injunctions regarding women's silence applied only to those who had not yet experienced the workings of grace. Reborn in "the Light," Quaker women could pursue more active spiritual roles modeled on the lives of such biblical prophets as Miriam and Hannah. And so they did; the first wave of fifty-nine itinerant Quaker preachers who ventured across the Atlantic between 1656 and 1663 included twenty-six women.

Mary Dyer was one of them. A follower of Anne Hutchinson in the 1630s, Dyer journeyed to England in 1652 and became a member of the Society of Friends. Convinced that God's Divine Light spoke through her, she returned to New England in 1657 to preach Quaker doctrine. But colonial authorities were unwilling to hear the Quakers' message—especially when preached by a woman—and Quaker lay ministers were hounded out of every corner of New England. Dyer was no exception. Banished first from Massachusetts and then from New Haven, she returned to Boston in the summer of 1659. She was again expelled, but defied the court and returned several times more during that summer and fall—even though doing so, Massachusetts law made clear, was inviting the death penalty. On October 19, Dyer and two of her compatriots were sentenced to be hanged. "The will of the Lord be done," she responded to the magistrates who handed down the punishment, "joyfully I go."

At the last minute, Dyer's sentence was commuted to banishment—the one verdict she refused to obey. In May 1660 she returned yet again to Boston, determined to protest statutes outlawing Quaker practice. This final challenge proved to be more than the colony's authorities could bear. Governor John Endicott again ordered her execution to be carried out the very next day. Dyer went willingly to the gallows. "In obedience to the will of the Lord I came," she told the crowd gathered to watch her hanging, "and in His will I abide faithful to the death."

Anne Hutchinson and Mary Dyer were what New England's leaders called "unquiet" women. Pious reflection, rapt attention, and wifely instruction were not enough for them, and they demanded more. Compelled by their faith to take leading roles in religious affairs, they would not rest contented with the models of feminine virtue that the clergy offered. It was a choice for which many women paid dearly.

New England did not possess a monopoly either on religious life or female piety. The North American colonies were home to a wide array of religious traditions, each with unique understandings of women's proper roles. Perhaps nowhere was this plurality of beliefs more dramatic than in the middle colonies, where the sheer diversity of the European settlers meant that no single religious order could easily gain an upper hand. Instead, groups that held widely varying notions of godliness—Presbyterians, members of the Dutch Reformed church, Anglicans, German "Dunkers" (a form of Baptist faith), Jews, and Roman Catholics—lived side by side, if not always in perfect harmony. In this atmosphere of pluralism and relative tolerance the Quakers sought refuge from the persecution they had encountered in England and in New England. Under the leadership of William Penn, to whom English King Charles II deeded huge tracts of land on the Delaware River in 1681, the Society of Friends began what they called a "Holy Experiment" in the colony they named

Pennsylvania. By 1715, more than twenty-three thousand migrants professing many different faiths had followed the Quakers' lead to the Delaware Valley.

The culture that grew up around the Society of Friends in Pennsylvania, Delaware, and parts of western New Jersey was noted for its acceptance of a variety of religious practices, and for its tolerance in another area as well: its endorsement of women's participation in religious life. In the Quaker meetings of the Delaware Valley, a popular Friends' saying—"in souls there is no sex"—took on real force. Although women and men came together for weekly worship, female Quakers also ran their own separate meetings. These so-called "women's meetings" had authority over many issues of church governance. Accused of giving too much authority to women Friends, William Penn explained the role of these separate women's meetings in a pamphlet entitled *Just Measures*, published in 1692: "Why should women meet apart? We think for a very good reason . . . women whose bashfulness will not permit them to say or do much, as to church affairs before men, when by themselves, may exercise their gift of wisdom and understanding, in a direct care of their own sex."

Convening each month as a group, the women of a congregation did indeed look after their own, meting out discipline to female Friends, dispensing charity to the local poor, making decisions about members' marriages, and keeping in touch with other women's meetings in the colonies and in England.

This does not mean that Quakers in the Delaware Valley were feminists in the modern-day sense. A women's meeting sometimes had to seek approval for controversial decisions from the local men's meeting. Quaker men, like their Puritan counterparts, were still recognized as the heads of their households. In social terms, the Quakers may not have considered men and women to be perfect equals. But Quaker women were encouraged to speak out in religious affairs as Puritan women almost never could.

If Quaker women in the middle colonies had more of a voice in spiritual matters than their New England counterparts, white women in the southern colonies were probably even less audible in public worship than were their Puritan sisters to the north. Anglicanism—the state church of England—was the denomination favored in the Chesapeake and lower south. In the seventeenth century, high death rates and the resulting social chaos made it difficult for churches to take root. But between 1700 and 1750, Anglican parishes, which were supported by taxes and remained largely unchallenged by other sects, grew quickly. Elite laymen, who could hire and fire their ministers at will, had real power in Anglican churches, but laywomen were expected to keep silent. Richard Allestree, an English minister who was the leading authority for Virginia's Anglicans, explained in a book entitled *The Ladies Calling* that Paul's decree was based on two factors: "the inferiority of the Woman in regard of the creation" and "the presumption that [women] needed instruction." In other words, Allestree said, women should be students and not teachers in religious matters.

Allestree and others recognized, however, that women played important religious roles within their households. What he called women's "native propensions" toward virtue made them important models within their families, and many women in the southern colonies were praised for their quiet piety. Occasionally, Anglican women took more public stances on spiritual matters. Mary Taney, wife of the sheriff of Calvert County, Maryland, was so distressed at the state of religion in that colony in the 1680s that she wrote to the Archbishop of Canterbury, the spiritual leader of the Church of England, to ask for help. The church, she wrote, was in a "sad condition." But she assured the archbishop that her "stray flock" might "prove a nursery of religion and loyalty through the whole Province"—if only they could raise sufficient money to build a church and retain a minister. Taney's plea eventually wound up before the King himself, and he quickly granted her request.

Black women and men brought a very different set of religious beliefs to the southern colonies. Their traditions concerning the supernatural were as diverse as the African cultures from which they came. There were, however, important common threads; most West Africans believed in more than one God and made the veneration of ancestors an important part of their worship ceremonies. Family and kin were at the very center of African religious life. Enslaved Africans and their American-born descendants cherished their religious rites and kept many traditional practices alive under slavery. Slave funerals, for example, were often followed with lively music and dancing—a joyous, exuberant custom common in Africa.

Until the 1730s, southern whites made little effort to convert their slaves to Christianity. But in the late eighteenth century, evangelical sects such as the Methodists and the Baptists appealed to blacks and poor whites alike. Slaves brought many of their own traditions to the Christian services they attended, in large numbers, at the end of the colonial period. Call-and-response hymn singing and joyful shouting are examples of African forms that influenced the style of worship practiced by both whites and blacks in many southern denominations.

The Catholic settlements of North America offer another model for women's participation in religion. In the missions of New France, for example, Catholic women who heard God's call could make religion their vocation. Some who did so were laywomen like Jeanne Mance, who left France for Montréal in 1642 and presided over that city's first hospital. Others were nuns who left the cloistered security of their orders in Europe in hopes of "civilizing" natives in America. Marie Guyart—later known as Marie of the Incarnation—allowed her calling to take her from her secluded, comfortable life in the Ursuline convent in Tours to the distant shores of Lake Québec. Arriving in 1639, she was the first female missionary in New France. During more than forty years there, she served her God as mystic, teacher, and scholar. Her endeavors included founding a school for native children, compiling and publishing a French-Algonquian dictionary, and composing more than thirteen thousand letters describing life in the French colonies.

From the Ursuline convent to the Puritan "conventicle," from the Algonquian dream quest to the African-influenced styles of worship in the Chesapeake, many different paths connected humans to the divine in early America. Whatever form religious life took in a given locale, women played essential roles. They took solace from the wisdom of preachers and holy texts. And their exemplary lives, in turn, inspired others, male and female alike. Yet in almost every religious context, with the notable exceptions of the Quakers and some native groups, the female faithful worshipped within explicit—and often narrow—limits. Nuns were not priests. Daughters of Zion were not ministers of the Word. Female piety did not always add up to female power. As the settlements of the future United States matured, however, many of the conditions that prevailed in seventeenth-century communities would be called into question. The future of religion and of women's places within it would be chief among them.

Captives, Rebels, and Witches

By the last quarter of the seventeenth century, white women and men had lived in British America for more than fifty years. Settlement was no longer new, and the desperate urgency of the era of "plantation" had given way to other kinds of problems. At least in older settlements, colonists no longer had to worry about subduing a wilderness. Instead, they had to live there, far from London, center of their "civilized" universe, permanently. There were few founding heroes left to help them; the colonies were no longer filled with men and women who had braved an average of ten weeks at sea to make the journey from Britain. Even in the disease-ridden Chesapeake, a dip in mortality rates meant that more and more of that region's white colonists had been born not in England but in Virginia or Maryland. In many areas immigration continued steadily and even accelerated. But so, too, did a very different kind of growth: the coming of age of a white population made up not of European migrants but of locally born Anglo Americans.

Would men and women born in these remote provincial outposts remain, in some sense, English? Or would they hold different values and create a different culture from that of their British forebears? Would the towns and villages and plantations in which they lived mature into new Englands? Or were they already becoming something else entirely? These questions went to the heart of the identity crisis that gripped British North America in the late seventeenth century.

They were also much on the minds of European authorities after 1660, the year that marked the restoration of the Stuart monarchy in England under Charles II. Upon his resumption of power, one of the first issues Charles resolved to tackle was the administration of the colonies overseas. The issue was no longer *whether* English settlements would flourish in the New World, but how: the political forms they would be permitted to take, the amounts of profit they could be made to generate, and especially, the degree of control London would exercise over them. Beginning with a series of Navigation Acts that Charles II's ministers pushed through Parliament in 1660, the crown would spend the next hundred years trying to shape the loosely knit settlements that dotted North America's Atlantic coast into something more coherent and efficient, a system that might deserve to be labeled an empire. This effort brought conflicts both within the colonies and without. In North America, the matter surfaced as an issue in scattered rebellions throughout the backcountry in the 1670s and 1680s and came to a head a century later when resistance to the crown's efforts to impose tighter controls on exports and revenues mushroomed into a War of Independence.

What did women living in the colonies make of these grand imperial contests? In one sense the great questions of empire were considered beyond their province. Prevailing views of women's capacities made it unlikely that the average New England goodwife or Chesapeake planter's wife would have much chance to debate the fine points of the economic theory of mercantilism—the belief that the crown should regulate colonial imports and exports. But in other ways, women were very much at the center of the great international conflicts of the day. All of the immense questions of colonial identity also had immediate local consequences. The collective identity crisis of the late seventeenth century was felt along the banks of Virginia's James River as well as in the state rooms of Whitehall in London. Women's roles were intimately bound up with this crisis. How would changes in the American landscape—political, economic, ecological, social, and religious changes—reshape their lives? And how would they, in turn, reconfigure the map of colonial America?

In New England, 1675 felt like the beginning of the end. Most of the leaders of the founding generation had since gone on to their rewards in heaven. How could the second, American-born generation live up to the lofty standards of these founding fathers? Every sign suggested that they could not. Anne Hutchinson's early, debilitating challenge had been followed by many others, including the Quaker heretics who had threatened the Puritan establishment in the late 1650s. Under attack from without, the Puritan experiment also seemed to be eroding from within. By 1662, so few of the elect were seeking admission to the Congregational churches that New England's leaders agreed to soften the rules for membership. A new Half-Way Covenant enacted that year allowed the children of the faithful to become church members without having experienced saving grace, thought to be the key ingredient in humanity's full "covenant" or contract with God.

But even these looser standards seemed too high for such a fallen people to attain. Eleazar Mather, son of founding Boston minister Richard Mather and pastor to the frontier parish of Northampton, Massachusetts, doubted that even the most pious of his generation were equal to the task before them. In a 1671 sermon he told his congregation that "the dayes wherein you live are backsliding times, evil dayes, times of great degeneracy," he said. "How hard it is to keep up an House when it's falling down." As the wife of a Puritan minister, Mary White Rowlandson must have been electrified—and terrified—by such concerns. Born in England in

1635, she had come to Massachusetts when just a toddler. Thus for all intents and purposes, she belonged to the colony's second generation—the generation of sons and daughters that, as the preachers kept reminding her, was fast sliding into disgrace. In the part of New England where Rowlandson dwelled, signs of this decline were all too visible. From the bustling seaport of Salem her family had moved north to Wenham, a small farming village founded in 1643. Then, in 1653, the Whites left behind even the minimal comforts of that hamlet when they relocated to a new settlement called Lancaster, an unincorporated village about ten miles west of Concord comprised of only nine families. Harvard-educated Joseph Rowlandson, the man Mary White married in 1656, was Lancaster's first minister. From the Anglo-American perspective, his tiny parish represented the far western edge of civilization, an exposed frontier at the edge of a howling wilderness.

Just how vulnerable the village was to the forces threatening New England became dramatically apparent to Mary Rowlandson during the winter of 1676. Since the previous June, a bloody war between the English and a confederation of Wampanoags, Nipmucs, and Narragansets (a struggle the Puritans called King Philip's War and the natives knew as Metacom's Rebellion) had raged in villages throughout Massachusetts and Plymouth. Increase Mather, minister of Boston's Second Church, called the war one more sign of God's profound displeasure with the Puritans: another indication that "our sins [were] ripe for so dreadfull a Judgment." And a dreadful judgment it was. Before the conflict ground to a halt in the summer of 1676, both sides suffered devastating losses. On the morning of February 10, God's "dreadfull judgment" of New England's failings arrived quite literally on the Rowlandsons' doorstep. It was "the dolefullest day that ever mine eyes saw," Mary Rowlandson later remembered, "now is that dreadful Hour come." A war party of Narragansets, whom she called "a company of hell-hounds," laid siege to the village at dawn. Setting fire to barns, overcoming sentries and guard dogs, and killing settlers who got in their way, the party at last arrived at the Rowlandson home, where thirty-seven villagers had taken refuge. In the ensuing melee only one escaped unharmed. Twelve of the English, including several of Rowlandson's relatives, were killed on the spot. Rowlandson and her six-year-old daughter Sarah were shot, and others lay mortally wounded. With her house in flames and her community decimated, Rowlandson, her three children, and twenty of their fellow townsfolk were taken captive by the native warriors and driven westward through the winter snow.

During the ensuing 150-mile trek into what Mary Rowlandson called "the vast and desolate Wilderness" of present-day Vermont, she would see everything she knew as civilization recede behind her. Within ten days of her capture she endured the slow and agonizing death of her wounded daughter. Consigning the child's wasted body to an unmarked grave on an unnamed hill, Rowlandson also left her familiar world behind. "All was gone," she wrote, "my Husband gone . . . my

Children gone, my Relations and Friends gone, our house and home, and all our comforts within door and without, all was gone, (except my life,) and I knew not but the next moment that might go too." From a world of neat fields, well-maintained fences, and fortified English garrisons, she found herself transported into an exotic land full of people and images and traditions she did not understand.

What did this journey across the gulf separating two such different cultures feel like to this Daughter of Zion? Although Rowlandson remained steadfast in her Puritan faith, the experience of captivity was a deeply unsettling one. Her people had been destined, she thought, to civilize the Indians. But now, she could not help thinking, the Narragansets were making a savage out of her. She was living the Indians' way: hunting for acorns, greedily gobbling half-cooked horse liver "with the blood about my mouth," dwelling with a Narraganset "master" and "mistress," speaking their language. Eleven weeks and five days passed before Joseph Rowlandson, who had been out of town during the attack, could ransom back his wife. After protracted negotiations with her captors, he succeeded in "redeeming"

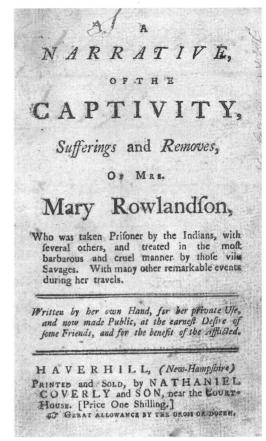

A NARRATIVE, OF THE CAPTIVITY, Sufferings and Removes, OF MRS. Mary Rowlandson, Who was taken Prisoner by the Indians, with several others, and treated in the most barbarous and cruel manner by those vile Savages. With many other remarkable events during her travels.

Written by her own Hand, for her private Use, and now made Public, at the earnest Desire of some Friends, and for the benefit of the Afflicted.

HAVERHILL, (New-Hampshire) PRINTED and SOLD, by NATHANIEL COVERLY and SON, near the Court-House. [Price One Shilling.] Great Allowance by the Gross or Dozen.

Mary Rowlandson's account of her captivity by the Narragansetts, first published in 1682, was a huge success, going through twenty-two printings by 1828.

her for the considerable sum of twenty pounds. With great fanfare, she was returned to Boston, where she rejoined her husband and their two surviving children. She lived the remainder of her days firmly ensconced within the "civilized" English world, first in Massachusetts and later in Connecticut. But memories of her time among the Indians must have haunted her till the day she died in 1711.

Rowlandson's experience as a captive was not unique. Between the onset of King Philip's War in 1675 and the end of the Seven Years' War, called the French and Indian War in British America, in 1763, more than sixteen hundred whites became Indian prisoners in New England alone. (Of course, the Indians were not the only ones taking prisoners; between the early sixteenth and late eighteenth centuries Spanish, French, and English raiding parties murdered, captured, ransomed, and sold countless thousands of Indian captives.) At least a third of the

Anglo-American captives were women; many more were children, of both sexes. The experience of captivity among the natives would hardly have been a welcome one for white men and women who still, appearances to the contrary, considered themselves English. But as the colonial period wore on it was, increasingly, a familiar one.

What is remarkable about Mary Rowlandson's case is the fact that she wrote and published an account of her story. Written in 1677 and first published in 1682, *The True History of the Captivity and Restoration of Mrs. Mary Rowlandson* (also known as *The Sovereignty and Goodness of God*) transformed its author from a private sufferer to a public martyr. The book was an instant success, going through four editions during its first year in print. Like Anne Bradstreet before her, Mary Rowlandson became something of a paradox in Puritan society: a woman who publicly and loudly proclaimed her feminine deference and modesty. In the coming years, there would be many others like her in New England, women whose not-so-silent suffering made them public figures, even heroines, in their communities. Hannah Dustin was one of them. By 1698, Dustin had replaced Rowlandson as the most famous woman in New England. In some ways, she was a more likely heroine. Where Rowlandson had trusted in God, Dustin relied on herself. Captured during a skirmish in King William's War in 1697, Dustin was dragged from the bed in which she had given birth to her eighth child just five days before and forced to march more than one hundred miles from her home. Unlike Rowlandson, she did not wait for redemption. Aided by another female captive, Dustin picked up a hatchet, murdered ten of the twelve Indians holding her, and returned to Boston carrying their scalps as proof of her deed. Proclaimed a heroine by the colony's leaders, she broke bread with magistrate Samuel Sewall and heard the eminent divine Cotton Mather memorialize her from his pulpit. She also received a bounty of twenty-five pounds—more than the Narragansets had charged to "redeem" Rowlandson—for the scalps.

Faced with a changing world at the turn of the eighteenth century, New Englanders were beginning to experiment with different possibilities for women's lives. Amidst the chaos caused by social transformations and Indian wars, some Anglo-American women were deemed worthy of public acclaim, not just for pious silence but also for acts of indisputable, even heroic strength. Women like Rowlandson and Dustin were creating a world in which extraordinary women could become role models for male and female alike. Would such a thing have seemed possible in Anne Hutchinson's day?

Yet for some women, even this expanded sphere of activity still seemed insufficient. There were plenty of female captives who, having been forced to cross the cultural divide separating Puritan from Indian, chose to stay on the other side of it. Nearly one-third of those taken captive remained among the natives who abducted them. Interestingly, it was not a choice Indian captives would make. As

French traveler Hector St. John de Crèvecoeur wrote in 1782 in his *Letters from an American Farmer*, "thousands of Europeans are Indians," but "we have no examples of even one of those Aborigines having from choice become Europeans."

Eunice Williams, daughter of minister John Williams of Deerfield, Massachusetts, was one who did not return. Taken prisoner in a raid on her town during the winter of 1704, Eunice was only seven years old when she made the long march north to a Kahnawake Mohawk village near Montreal. Her father, her mother, and four of her siblings also numbered among the captives. For the Mohawks knew that the Williamses—an esteemed Puritan family sure to fetch a high ransom—were worth more as diplomatic pawns than as adopted sons and daughters. Negotiations for their release took time, but in late 1707, some two and a half years after their capture, most of the surviving members of the Williams family (Mrs. Williams had been killed during the trek out of Deerfield) achieved their long-desired aim: a return to "civilization" in Massachusetts. Following in the footsteps of Mary Rowlandson, John Williams quickly published an account of his time among the Kahnawake, a popular treatise that made his sufferings a model all believers could follow. There was only one problem, one obstacle to Williams's happy ending. His daughter Eunice remained "captivated" in French territory. Now aged nine, she had not been "redeemed" with the rest of his children.

Nor would she ever be. Like many captive women and girls, Eunice came to prefer life among the Kahnawake. Her family reacted with disbelief, unable for many years to accept the reality that she was no longer being held against her will. But when her brother saw her again decades later, he had to face the truth: Eunice did not *want* to be redeemed. She was no longer Eunice Williams but Marguerite A'ongote Gannenstenhawi, Mohawk wife of a native named François Xavier Arosen, mother of three Kahnawake children. Born Puritan, she had become Catholic; the Mohawks who captured her had been converted to Catholicism by Jesuit missionaries. She had forgotten English and adopted the Mohawk tongue. Born a daughter of Zion, she had become something perhaps more powerful, more fulfilling, more meaningful: a Kahnawake mother, a farmer and hunter, a convert to a religion that made saints—even a Virgin queen of heaven—of ordinary women. No, she did not want to go back. No longer Deerfield's Eunice Williams in any meaningful sense, she lived on among her adopted people until the colonies of New England had become the United States. When she died in 1785, she was ninety-five years old. How distant a memory those first seven Puritan years must have seemed by then!

South of New England, the 1660s and 1670s brought different perils and possibilities for colonial women. The Puritans may have understood the growing pains their settlements faced in religious terms, as a falling away from the lofty goals of the first generation as their settlements aged and expanded. But their countrymen and women in the Chesapeake had no such pretensions about God's favor to begin with. Most English folk in Virginia and Maryland would have agreed that life in their part of the colonial world had started off badly and—with the exception of brief periods during which tobacco prices soared—had only gotten worse. By the 1670s, the crop that fetched three shillings per pound in 1625 was commanding only a tiny fraction of that. Charles II's tightening web of customs law ensured that an ever-increasing percentage of whatever planters could earn at these prices went directly into the pockets of the crown. Leading men who had amassed huge tracts of land were able to enhance their fortunes even at slim profit margins. But ordinary planters in Virginia and Maryland cultivated more and more tobacco (exports doubled between 1670 and 1690) and realized less and less gain from its sale.

In some respects, there was nothing new about this situation. In an era before the modern economic strategy of regulating supply to meet demand was fully understood, raising crops to sell for cash was always a boom-and-bust business. The problem was one of demographics. By the second half of the century, immigrants to the Chesapeake were beginning to live longer. Better provisioned and prepared for the hardships of the region's climate, servants were outliving their indentures and demanding their share of a shrinking economic pie. Enough servants were enduring enough years to become free, marry, and raise families of their own. They were also living long enough to give birth to *ambitions* of their own—ambitions they could not satisfy so long as they remained poor, landless tenants consigned to farm the immense plantations of an emerging local elite. With land prices high and tobacco profits low, common people found themselves unable to get ahead and seething with resentment. How, they wondered, was the region's new gentry class managing to make a killing in London's markets when common men and women were suffering so? How were planters like royal governor William Berkeley and his wealthy supporters able to grow fat and rich while they—humble men and women, but *English* men and women—worked like beasts of burden just to keep themselves fed? Many couldn't help feeling that Berkeley and his ilk were becoming rich by stealing the products of *their* labor.

By the 1670s the Chesapeake was ceasing to be a death trap only to become a powder keg. To a significant extent it was women—ordinary planters' wives—who were behind the shift. Their increasing fertility fueled the growth of the colonies' underclasses. Marrying earlier and giving birth to more children who survived infancy, Anglo-American women in the 1650s and 1660s were becoming the mothers of a restless generation. Surrounded by seemingly endless natural abundance (with so much open land around, why could they not afford to own any?), these young men and women were less willing than their parents had been to do all the work while their supposed "betters" reaped all the rewards. They were angry. They were poor. They were hungry. And they were armed. Most of all, they were waiting for a chance to get theirs and willing to take it, if need be.

In Virginia, that chance came during the scorching summer of 1675. Several white settlers came upon a small group of Indians trading. When one of the native traders seized as payment some hogs belonging to Thomas Mathew, he and a group of armed white men pursued the trading party, recaptured the hogs, and killed several Indians. An Indian war party then killed one of Mathew's servants in retaliation, and the discontent that had long been smoldering among poor white Virginians ignited in earnest. Throughout the summer and fall the pattern of Anglo raids and Indian counter-raids escalated. Casualties were heavy on both sides, and the white settlers in vulnerable frontier areas looked to their leaders in Jamestown for protection. But Governor Berkeley and other wealthy planters in the Tidewater region wanted to move slowly, preferring to defend their own property rather than to stick their necks out on behalf of the so-called rabble in the back-country. To those living in less settled parts of the colony, the guarded response of Berkeley and his fellow elites amounted to further proof that common people didn't count in Virginia. Reaction to the news of Berkeley's hesitation to act was nothing short of mutiny. By the spring of 1676, ragtag vigilante bands sometimes numbering in the hundreds had united under two men who supported their cause and opposed the governor: Nathaniel Bacon and Giles Bland. Under their direction, local uprisings became a full-fledged insurrection that would come to be known as Bacon's Rebellion.

From first to last, women were at the center of this escalating crisis. By tradition, they could not serve in the militia or vote on matters of local policy. In the Chesapeake as in other areas of the Anglo-American world, they had no official status in the public sphere. Nonetheless, in all kinds of unofficial ways, they made significant contributions to the struggle on both sides of the controversy. Indeed, some of the revolt's male leaders held their wives responsible for the initial decision to mount a full-scale insurrection. How could they sit back and wait for help, petitioners on Bacon's side asked the government, while "the cryes of their wives and children" grew ever more "grievous and intolerable"?

Women in frontier communities had plenty to cry out against. Not only did they suffer disproportionately in the Indian raids; they also suffered humiliating attacks by Berkeley's supporters. A number of women complained against a single loyalist officer, Colonel Edward Hill. One Mrs. Hunt accused him of stealing a precious hogshead of tobacco—the loss of which was certain to make a tough year even more difficult. Servant Sara Weekes did not get off so easily. Hill held her under guard, accusing her of being an "idle, infamous slutt" known for "robbing, thieving, and whoring." From Hill's perspective, the attacks on these rebel women were justified by what the armed rebels did to his own wife. While Hill was away fighting the governor's battles to the north and west, Bacon's men had taken over his plantation, gotten drunk on his fine Madeira, and vented their fury on his pregnant wife.

Other women were not merely victims caught in the crossfire, but combatants in their own right. Though they rarely took up arms, the support they offered was an effective weapon of war. Those who sympathized with the rebel faction were instrumental to the cause, providing food and shelter to the troops as Bacon's forces made their way to Jamestown. Mrs. Anthony Haviland, wife of one of Bacon's intimates, took even greater risks, smuggling papers from one end of the colony to the other. Even Colonel Hill admitted grudgingly that Haviland was "an excellent divulger of news."

In the end, forces loyal to the governor triumphed, but not until Bacon's men had seized Jamestown and burned the village to the ground in September 1676. Thus despite their efforts on behalf of the rebellion—efforts which transcended the normal duties of planter's wives—women like Haviland ultimately found themselves on the losing side. Or did they? As is the case in so many historical questions, the answer is both yes and no. In the wake of Bacon's Rebellion, the social order in Virginia changed subtly, and the roles of women changed along with it. The rebellion had showed the colony's leaders just how volatile the growing ranks of landless, poor freemen and women could be. A shortage of labor to work their abundant lands continued to be a pressing problem for Virginia's elite. But the rebellion drove home the need to find a less costly way of solving that problem than consigning ex-servants to perpetual tenancy in a region where land was plentiful.

Increasingly after 1676, wealthy Virginians came to see the permanent enslavement of black men and women as the best solution to their labor woes. With life expectancies rising, the higher initial price typically commanded by a lifetime slave began to seem worthwhile. With social tensions increasing, wealthy planters were looking for ways to give poor whites a stake in the colony's future. The forced importation of ever greater numbers of Africans answered both of these needs. Denied the possibility of freedom, slaves were not supposed to harbor ambitions for their futures, and a permanent black underclass would elevate the status of even the poorest whites. Perhaps, elites were willing to gamble, rich and poor Anglo Americans might find a kind of solidarity in the simple fact of their whiteness. In all of these respects, Virginia's governor noted in 1683, "Blacks can make [tobacco] cheaper than Whites."

The sudden, dramatic growth of the enslaved population indicates that many elite Anglo Americans agreed with the governor. From a population of roughly 500 at mid-century, the enslaved labor force in Virginia and elsewhere in the colonial south mushroomed. The eleven years between 1698 and 1709 alone saw the importation of twenty times that many slaves to Virginia. By 1775 there were more than 250 thousand blacks in the Chesapeake—nearly half the region's total population. Farther south, the proportion of black inhabitants was even higher. From Maryland to South Carolina, African-born slaves and their American-born descendants had all but replaced white servants by the second quarter of the eighteenth century.

How did this shift affect women's lives? For the planter wife, the turn toward slavery likely meant a life of increased ease. For the thousands of black women who were brought to the Chesapeake in chains in the years after Bacon's Rebellion, the answers would be altogether different. Captured from such diverse West African regions as modern-day Nigeria, Angola, and Sierra Leone, they lacked even a common language in which to share their sorrows. In time, however, their descendants would form a distinct African-American culture enduring enough to sustain its members through the hardships of slavery and strong enough to encourage many to claim their freedom whenever a chance presented itself. And in their world, no less than in the world of the white plantation owners, women often led the way.

As workers in the fields and as breeders of human property, black women were forced to serve their owners' needs. Within the plantation household and in the fields of the southern colonies, black women contributed to the comfort and wealth of the white ruling class. But within their own quarters, they worked to sustain their kin under the harshest possible conditions. In doing so, black women kept alive diverse African traditions while forging new, uniquely African-American ones.

In many African cultures, the bond between mother and children was considered especially strong. This tradition took on new importance under slavery. Male slaves were often sold away from their families, but many masters proved reluctant to separate young children from their mothers. Slave women typically lived with their sons and daughters until the children were at least ten years old. Mothers, more often than fathers, taught their children how to survive the slave system. Black women were also central to the dense networks of kin that grew up among slave family members who had been sold to neighboring plantations. The sense of connection provided by these wider circles of aunts, uncles, ex-spouses, cousins, and step-siblings helped slaves to compensate for the vulnerability of their individual households.

In Salem, Massachusetts, women confronted a range of perils and possibilities during the social upheaval of the late seventeenth century. There, in 1692, the most extensive witch-hunts ever seen in the colonies took place. Witchcraft had a long history in British North America. Prosecutions of women suspected of practicing witchcraft began in the 1630s and continued sporadically throughout the seventeenth century. In Salem, as in other locations, women comprised the vast majority of those accused—as well as a significant proportion of the accusers and some of the most vocal "victims." The crisis at Salem belonged, in part, to a very old Puritan pattern in which the Devil almost always seemed to appear in the shape of a woman.

But there were different things about Salem. For one thing, there appeared in Salem new sorts of "devils" to fight against: the rapid growth of the population, the spread of commerce, the feuding of neighbor against neighbor. And there was also, at Salem, an entirely new scale to the prosecutions. Between the day the first charges were leveled in January 1692 and the end of the trials early the following October, approximately 156 people in 24 towns had been accused. Nineteen of them—fourteen women and five men—had been hanged; one man had been pressed to death with heavy stones. Just what had plunged Salem and many nearby villages into such a panic?

VVitches Apprehended, Examined and Executed, for notable villanies by them committed both by Land and Water.

With a ftrange and moft true triall how to know whether a woman be a Witch or not.

This book, printed in London in 1613, offered English readers accounts of some of the "notable villanies" committed by witches, along with various "trialls" designed to determine whether a woman was a witch.

If we could interview someone from late-seventeenth-century Salem Village, the part of town that was home to most of the accusers, she would probably say that the story began one icy January morning in the kitchen of the Reverend Samuel Parris, minister of Salem Village. There, several girls and young women, including Parris's nine-year-old daughter Betty and his eleven-year-old niece, Abigail Williams, began an innocent game of divining: looking to the occult for signs as to the identity of their future husbands. Excitement soon gave way to fear as the girls experienced what they described to local ministers as a feeling of being "bitten and pinched by invisible agents ... taken dumb, their mouths stopped, their throats choked, their limbs wracked and tormented." News of their "cruel Sufferings" spread through the village, and many who heard descriptions of their "fits" knew immediately what the cause must be: witchcraft.

As the winter wore on, Betty Parris, Abigail Williams, and several of their friends displayed their "afflictions," real or pretended, for ever larger audiences. By June, young women living as far away as Boston, where some of the accused were jailed, had experienced similar symptoms. And plenty gathered to see them perform. Perhaps, like Mary Rowlandson, these young girls were eager to claim a larger space for women's voices in a changing world. Perhaps they truly *were* suffering—not from what we today would understand as witchcraft, but from some other mental or physical illnesses. To their audiences, however, the explanation was readily at hand in the shape of three local women whom the girls accused of tormenting them.

Only the first of the three, Sarah Good, fits traditional stereotypes of the witch. Pregnant, poor, and homeless, she was known in Salem Village as an outspoken malcontent—a personality type that often turned women into witches in their neighbors' eyes. The second accused was Sarah Osborne. Like many suspected witches, Osborne had defied local norms where inheritance was concerned. With the help of her second husband, she contrived to retain control of lands and moneys that she should have passed on to her children. Accused on February 29, 1692, she died in jail early that May. The third among the initial suspects proved to be in many ways the most important. Where the others denied they were witches, she confessed to the crimes of which she was accused and thus helped fuel the mounting spiral of accusations, counter-accusations, confessions, and hangings. Where Good and Osborne had been locals, she was in every sense an outsider. Her name was Tituba, and much about her remains shrouded in myth. Sometimes she is described as a black slave, while other accounts call her an Indian servant. Her husband, John Indian, was almost certainly a local Native American. But she was a stranger who had come to Salem from the sugar island of Barbados—a symbol of the thickening web of trade between Britain, Africa, the islands, and the mainland that supplied the southern colonies with slaves, New England with cash, and England with sugar, rum, and finished goods.

Whatever the tangled path that brought Tituba to Salem, her presence there had far-reaching consequences. Her stories of witches' sabbaths, spectral yellow birds, and flights through the sky on a broom entranced her judges and provided motifs others would later echo. After Good, Osborne, and Tituba told their stories in March, accusations and trials came thick and fast. By the end of April, Essex County's jails were packed with suspects, one of whom, young Dorcas Good, was no more than four years old. On June 10, the first hanging was carried out as Bridget Oliver Bishop—a woman long known for her belligerence toward her husband— was led to the gallows. By the end of the summer, so many more would follow in her footsteps that the place of her execution would earn the name "Witch Hill."

Each of the women who met her end on that hill maintained her innocence. Among the most eloquent was Sarah Good. As she stood on the gallows, the Reverend Nicholas Noyes urged her to confess her sins before the large crowd assembled to hear her last words. But Good, known all her life as a "turbulent spirit," did not go quietly. "You are a liar," she spat in Noyes's face. "I am no more a Witch than you are a Wizard, and if you take away my Life, God will give you blood to drink."

The trials at Salem were testimony both to the enlarged possibilities of Anglo-American women's lives in the late seventeenth century and to the limits within which women continued to live and think, write and speak. As afflicted girls, as Indian captives, as supporters of a male-led rebellion, some women experienced new power in the last quarter of the first century of the British colonial experience. But Salem reminds us that in the late seventeenth century women could only be accusers, or victims, or "witches"; they could not be preachers or judges. The new century would bring significant changes to their everyday lives. Yet as the colonial world expanded, the formal channels of education and public power remained beyond women's reach. This central fact, made so dramatically manifest in 1692, would remain unaltered for many years to come.

Awakening and Diverging

The year was 1734, a time of relative tranquility in the British settlements of North America. The non-Indian population was growing steadily, rising from 210,000 in 1690 past 400,000 in 1720; by 1776 it would top 2.5 million. Part of the increase was natural, as large families had become the rule everywhere in the colonies. In addition, each year saw waves of new immigrants arrive as the ongoing exodus from England was supplemented by a flood of refugees from other European lands—thousands of Scots-Irish, Swiss, Germans, and French along with a scattering of Welsh, Swedes, and Dutch—and by increasing numbers of Africans forced to migrate against their will. This influx failed to quell the soaring colonial economy. Exports fetched high prices. Land was cheap and plentiful. Most Anglo Americans were able to do what their counterparts in Europe could only dream of:

to live on their own family farms. Descended from a world of tenants, they had created a world of independent yeomen beholden to none.

But though the British colonies in 1734 may have looked like peaceable, prosperous kingdoms, the elders in the western Massachusetts village of Northampton were worried. For in their sleepy town, groups of young people had begun to display strange, inexplicable symptoms. The town's Yale-educated pastor, Jonathan Edwards, noted their "great terrors" and "sudden distresses," signs of what he called a "struggle and tumult" that bordered on "despair." His parishioner Abigail Hutchinson had manifested many of these "distempers." Only nineteen years old, she was gripped by what Edwards described as "exceeding terror ... her very flesh trembled" before his eyes. Other young women spoke of frightening visions, including an apparition of a gaping "dreadful furnace" only they could see.

Just what had driven the youth of Northampton into such a state? Some among the faithful could not help wondering whether they were witnessing a resurgence of the tensions that had plagued Salem. Once again, they pointed out, young women were wailing and weeping in public while powerful men doted on their every word. Once again there were rumors that the Devil was afoot. But, in the end, folks in Northampton and towns along the eastern seaboard where similar disturbances had arisen advanced another explanation for the turmoil. People came to believe that ecstatic young women were embracing the Lord; their "fits" were signs not of demonic possession but of religious conversion. Girls like Abigail Hutchinson were the vanguard of a movement of religious renewal that eventually overtook so many parts of British America that it earned the name "Great Awakening."

The revivals in Northampton were among the first sparks in what quickly became a firestorm of religious enthusiasm. The ensuing Great Awakening was not a single event but rather a series of "mini-awakenings" that took place from the 1730s through the 1760s and stretched from Britain to Maine to Georgia. Rejecting what they saw as the tendency of so-called "Old Light" preachers to over-intellectualize doctrine, "converted" or "New Light" ministers spoke to their congregations in the language of the heart. Appealing to passion as well as to reason, their oratory was a powerful draw to masses of common men and women who found themselves eager, as Edwards later wrote, "to drink in the words of the minister."

This sudden desire to "drink in" God's word was not confined to New England. Signs of a new religious foment surfaced somewhat earlier in the middle colonies, where the growing ethnic diversity of the population had produced an expansive array of Christian traditions. By the early eighteenth century, Pennsylvania, New Jersey, New York, and Delaware were home to an almost dizzying variety of denominations, including Presbyterians, Lutherans, Mennonites, Huguenots, Quakers, Baptists, Anglicans, and several smaller utopian sects. The mix of peoples and beliefs was volatile. In Presbyterian congregations throughout New Jersey and Pennsylvania, Scots-Irish immigrants and their descendants embraced the fiery rhetoric of evangelical or "New Sides" ministers. By the 1730s, many laymen and women were flocking to hear the sermons of revivalist preachers such as the young, intinerant English minister George Whitefield; Dutch Reformed leader Theodorus Frelinghuysen; and the Scottish-born William Tennent and his sons. The frenzy that greeted Whitefield's arrival in 1739 showed how eager common men and women were to hear God's word as interpreted by the revivalists. For Hannah Harkum Hodge, the daughter of a Calvinist minister in Philadelphia, hearing Whitefield preach was the central moment in her long life. When she died in 1805 at the age of 84, her obituary described a devotion that led her to follow the preacher "on foot" from Philadelphia "to Chester, to Abingdon, to Neshaminy, and . . . even to New-Brunswick, in New-Jersey, the distance of sixty miles." Hannah later became a leader in her community's religious life, and her home was known as "a place for prayer and religious improvement."

The revivalists showed a unique ability to entice men back into the fold, but although record numbers of male converts returned to the churches during the 1730s and 1740s, female voices accounted for a majority of those professing an "awakened" or reborn faith. And, for the first time during the revivals of the Great Awakening, women delivered their testimony not in private conferences with their ministers, but openly, loudly, and publicly. Sarah Pierpont Edwards was another of the tens of thousands of young women swept up in the religious fervor of the mid-eighteenth century. Born in New Haven in 1710 to a family of prominent Puritan ministers, young Sarah was widely known for her devotion to God. When she was just thirteen, she attracted the attention of Jonathan Edwards, who was then studying for the ministry at Yale. Writing in his private journal, Edwards praised Sarah's "strange sweetness" and "singular purity." Perhaps he knew that day that he had found his "meete helpe"; four years later the two were married.

If any woman could have felt certain that divine grace dwelled within her, surely it was Sarah Pierpont Edwards. But, perhaps prompted by her husband's hellfire-and-brimstone preaching, she began in the late 1730s to fret about the state of her soul. Over the next several years, she unflinchingly contemplated her own sinfulness, striving, as she put it, to be "swallowed up, in the light and joy of the love of God." So moved was her husband by Sarah's relentless probing of her innermost failings that he asked her to write a detailed account of the experience—a narrative which even today brings to life the momentousness of what some women experienced during the Great Awakening. In January 1743, Sarah Edwards reached the depths of despair. "I felt very uneasy and unhappy," she wrote, "at my being so low in grace." Shaken from her earlier sense of security in God's love, she began to feel "a deep abasement of soul . . . a sense of my own unworthiness." Her spirits alternated between elation and terror as she tried to bring herself closer to God. The break in this cycle of repentance, assurance, and renewed doubts came during a sermon preached by a local itinerant, Samuel Buell, whose lecture convinced Sarah Edwards that "God was present in the congregation." She swooned during the homily. When she returned home that evening the talk was again of God. Reverend Buell and several other area ministers had gathered at the Edwards' house to chat about "Divine goodness." As the pious group talked and sang psalms, Sarah felt so moved that she had to fight off the urge to dance for joy.

Her euphoria reached an ecstatic peak the next night, which she remembered as "the sweetest night I ever had in my life." Staying awake almost till dawn, Sarah experienced perfect union with God—"a constant flowing and reflowing of heavenly and divine love." So intense was this feeling that it seemed she had escaped her body. A single minute of this "heavenly elysium," she wrote, "was worth more than all the outward comfort and pleasure, which I had enjoyed in my whole life."

The next morning she could not contain her joy. When one of her husband's friends called at the house she greeted him saying, "I have dwelt on high in the heavenly mansions . . . my soul has been lost in God." Yearning to tell all who would listen about the experience, Sarah described the previous night's raptures for "about a quarter of an hour." Secure at last in her salvation, Sarah Edwards continued to be an inspiration to her husband and their nine surviving children until her death in 1758. Although Edwards's description of being "swallowed up in God" is particularly eloquent and detailed, many more humble female believers described similar feelings. Anxiety and doubt. Assurance and rapture. And, above all, an intense desire to *testify* to their experience. The initial probing was always unsettling. But after what one young convert called this "dreadful distress of soul" came sweet relief. Conversion was a deeply felt mental and *physical* experience for the women who renewed their covenant with God during the mid-century awakenings. Forgotten, for a time, was the belief that women had to keep silent in church. Suddenly their expressions of heavenly delight were heard everywhere. In a movement that elevated emotion over intellect there was no "weaker" sex; female converts became, in many respects, the equals of men.

The Great Awakening illustrated other forces at work in society. The revivals testified to the fragmentation of provincial society. Old allegiances (one church, one established minister, one unquestioned loyalty) were yielding to new choices. Long-held beliefs in deference before authority and devotion to a single, common good were crumbling as the colonies grew and became more diverse. With the expansion of society came a new ability to decide one's fate, particularly in matters of religion. The struggle between old and new styles of preaching was just one among a number of emerging fissures within the population: There were also growing gaps between rich and poor, black and white, town and country. Along with a new equality in the religious experiences of men and women, the second quarter of the eighteenth century saw an increase in the disparity between male and female lives—and between the lives of some women and the lives of others.

The women of comfortably prosperous landowning and merchant families in New England hardly formed a new leisure class, but they lived more graciously than the vast majority of poor and middling farm wives in New England and the middle colonies. For them, life got easier as the colonial period wore on. For many more humble families, the aging of the colonies meant a declining standard of living. As New England's population exploded, jumping from 100 thousand in 1700 to roughly 400 thousand by 1750, more people had to make do with less, particularly where land was concerned. In older towns like Dedham and Ipswich and Watertown, five generations of children were cramming themselves onto ever-smaller plots. In 1650, the average farming family subsisted on what they could grow on a 150-acre lot. By 1750, the average had shrunk to one-third that size—barely enough to sustain a family, let alone turn a profit. In the middle colonies, large numbers of new immigrants found themselves with no land at all, working as paid laborers and living as tenants on the growing farms of local agricultural entrepreneurs.

For parents and children alike this was a crisis. With diminishing stores of land, most parents had little to promise their children. And without a prize of land and cash to extend to dutiful sons or a hefty dowry to bestow upon obedient daughters, fathers also had less control over their children's decisions. After 1730, an increasing percentage of young women in New England appear to have married without their parents' consent. Rates of premarital pregnancy approached 40 percent by the 1750s. Ever larger numbers of young women married out of birth order, not waiting for their older sisters to find mates. In this sense, poorer women may have exerted a greater degree of control over their own lives in the eighteenth century than their mothers and grandmothers dreamed of in the seventeenth, but in other respects their lives were becoming harder rather than easier. Most ordinary farm wives continued to eke out a hardscrabble existence on the eve of the American Revolution—and well beyond it. This, at least, was the way Ruth Belknap seemed to feel about her life in Dover, New Hampshire. Married to a local parson, Belknap was a literate goodwife, hardly among the poorest colonial women. Yet she took umbrage at the way some of her wealthier, more urban counterparts lived. There was nothing genteel, she knew, about the life she lived in Dover. In her 1782 poem "The Pleasures of a Country Life," Belknap tried to tell the more genteel urban colonists how the other half lived:

> Ye starch'd up folks that live in town,
> That lounge upon your beds till noon,
> That never tire yourselves with work,
> Unless with handling knife & fork,
> Come, see the sweets of country life,
> Display'd in Parson B[elknap's] wife.

"Sweets," indeed! Belknap's poem dwells on the many chores that filled her hours from dawn to midnight. In 1750 as in 1650, the average farm wife's day was much as Belknap portrayed it: A house "with all confusion fill'd." Hands blistered by days filled with "toil and sweat." Perhaps the greatest difference between Belknap's life and that of her great-grandmother was not so much the content of her days as their *context*. In her grandmother's day, almost every woman had this sort of schedule. Now, it seemed, the wealthy few were setting standards that the poorer many simply could not afford to uphold. For women like Ruth Belknap, the conspicuous presence of local elites could make days on the farm seem long indeed.

The social and economic rifts that divided the population of eighteenth-century New England would have appeared almost invisible to Eliza Lucas. The cleavages separating the haves from the have-nots in her world were so profound as to make most women in New England and the mid-Atlantic colonies seem roughly equal in comparison. Lucas's perspective was forged in the plantation south, where social distinctions were literally measured in black and white. Born on the sugar island of Antigua in 1722, Eliza was the eldest daughter of a planter aristocrat. Schooled in London, Eliza returned to Antigua at the age of fifteen, every inch the English lady. In 1738, the Lucas family moved from the West Indies to South Carolina to take over some inherited properties. Eliza quickly became the toast of Charleston, then a lively city with nearly 7,000 inhabitants. Taking her place among the town's gentry, she noted in a letter to an English friend that Carolinians "live very Genteel and very much in the English taste."

Soon after Eliza's arrival in South Carolina, however, her life took a dramatic turn. When the sudden outbreak of hostilities between England and Spain forced George Lucas to return to Antigua, he left Eliza to manage his three plantations. This was a considerable task, for these were properties of six hundred, fifteen hundred, and three thousand acres, immense capitalist enterprises staffed with gangs of enslaved black workers. And Eliza, not yet seventeen years old, became their mistress. The enterprise, Eliza wrote in 1740, "requires much writing and more business and fatigue of other sorts than you can imagine." But Eliza Lucas proved equal to the task. She introduced a variety of new crops to the plantation, experimenting with ginger, cotton, and figs before striking gold—or rather, blue—with indigo. With the help of agricultural innovators like Lucas, this dark blue dye favored in British textiles soon joined rice as one of the region's most profitable export crops.

In 1744, Eliza Lucas married a close family friend, Charles Pinckney, a prominent lawyer. With Charles frequently away on business in Charleston, she continued her agricultural experiments, overseeing the cultivation of flax and hemp on his properties. She also threw herself into the many duties of mothering the couple's four children. This job was a complex one. No longer was it sufficient for a planter's wife—at least for one of her stature—merely to ensure her children's survival. Among the wealthy, every aspect of children's lives was considered a matter for maternal concern. Eliza penned an evocative passage on childcare. She resolved, she wrote, "to be a good Mother to my children, to pray for them, to set them good examples, to give them good advice, to be careful both of their souls and bodies ... and to instill piety, Virtue and true religion into them; to spare no paines or trouble to do them good." Before her death in 1793, Eliza Lucas Pinckney had lived to see her daughter marry and prosper and her two surviving sons become important public officials in the young United States.

What allowed Eliza Lucas to "spare no paines or trouble" with her children? The answer, in large measure, was the work of female slaves. The growth of plantation slavery was the ever-present backdrop to each of Lucas's many accomplishments. In the West Indies and later in South Carolina, Lucas lived in a world where African Americans comprised a majority of the population. Fully half of Charleston's seven thousand inhabitants were enslaved blacks. Colonywide, the population in the second quarter of the eighteenth century was roughly 65 percent black. African Americans were a constant presence in her life, but Eliza Lucas rarely commented on the institution of slavery. Her letters made no mention, for example, of the Stono Rebellion, a 1739 insurrection of some eighty slaves that erupted less than five miles from the Lucas homestead. Yet in all kinds of everyday ways, the institution of slavery made her life what it was. Slave women working in the fields put into practice the agricultural experiments she devised; indeed, the familiarity of many West African blacks with the delicate cultivation of rice and indigo provided expertise Anglo Americans lacked. Slave women cooked Eliza Lucas's dinner and saw to the needs of her visitors. Slave women nursed her children, setting aside the needs of their own offspring in the process.

Eliza Lucas Pinckney was both an extraordinary woman and typical of her times. Unusually learned and independent, she enjoyed rare opportunities, but like many wealthy southern women she gained her independence by enslaving other women and men. Like New England and the middle colonies, the Chesapeake and the Carolinas were fast becoming a world of the few and the many. But in the mid-eighteenth-century South, the few were always white and free, and the many, increasingly, were black slaves.

Perhaps nowhere in the British colonies was the widening gulf between the few and the many as visible as in the port cities of New York, Boston, and Philadelphia. From the European perspective, these urban villages hardly deserved to be called "cities" at all. London in the mid-eighteenth century was home to over half a million people, while Philadelphia, the largest of the colonial American cities, had just thirty-five thousand inhabitants on the eve of the Revolution. But although less than 5 percent of the population of the future United States lived in these urban environments, the port cities represented the cutting edge of social change. There thousands of new immigrants lived side by side with Anglo Americans, enslaved African Americans, and a growing free black community. There merchants of the middling sort became men of great wealth. And there wage labor, landlessness, and abject poverty first became realities for many.

In the cities as in the plantation south, great fortunes were built upon the labor of those less fortunate. Dock workers, roustabouts, and domestic servants in New York and Philadelphia were typically not enslaved. But freedom meant little when wages were too low to put food on the table.

Women dwelling in the urban ports found themselves on both sides of this widening gap between wealth and poverty. On the losing end were women whose situations were so desperate that they were forced to accept public charity. By the early decades of the eighteenth century, cities like Boston, New York, and Philadelphia had outgrown traditional mechanisms of caring for those in need. Poor women, particularly widows, could not always count on their extended families to help them make ends meet. Many of them found creative ways to bring in a modest income. By working as domestic servants in wealthy households or by taking boarders into their own homes, some were able to keep themselves afloat. But others were forced to turn to almshouses like the ones founded in Philadelphia in 1730 and in New York in 1736.

Other women found in the port cities of the mid-eighteenth century a world of expanding opportunities. For those who possessed needed skills and whose deceased husbands or fathers had left them considerable resources, urban life was full of possibilities. As so-called "she merchants" (widowed or unmarried traders) and workers in growing professions such as newspaper printing, women forged new paths for themselves and helped fuel booming urban economies. The single or widowed "woman of affairs" was not an eighteenth-century invention. In the early years of the colonies, women sometimes exercised considerable power in extraordinary circumstances. A century later, America's urban port towns were home to many women who ran shops, traded, and otherwise made names for themselves as women of affairs. Most of them had no husbands. Many were so-called "spinsters," part of the increasing percentage of Anglo-American women choosing never to marry. Others were widows of wealthy merchants or established artisans who expanded their economic roles after their husbands' deaths. Advertisements appearing in colonial newspapers from the 1720s to 1800 show that these women pursued professions as teachers, cooks, seamstresses, embroiderers, and vendors of commodities ranging from fine wines to farm equipment.

Sarah Kemble Knight was one widow of means for whom the booming economy of the colonial ports meant opportunity. Born in 1666 to a Boston merchant and his wife, she was twenty-two years old when she wed Thomas Knight, a shipmaster who sailed out of Boston harbor. Unlike most women of her era, she gave birth to only one child, which may have allowed her to devote time to matters beyond her daily round of housekeeping and childrearing duties. Like many women in the eighteenth-century port towns, Knight played a variety of roles in the local economy. Proficient in reading and writing and familiar with the popular literature of her day, she turned these skills into a job as one of the growing

AGNES LIND, MILLINER,

Hath just imported in the Prince of Wales, Capt. Curling, from London, a new assortment of millinery and other goods, viz.

BROWN tuffety,
Pink and blue mantuas,
Lutestrings,
Alamodes,
Poplins,
Flowered dresdens,
Plain and figured mecklenburgs,
Gauze caps and fillets,
Silver stomachers & pompoons,
Gauze stomachers with ditto,
Plain and flowered sattin cardinals,
Plain and figured silk polonoise,
Womens and girls scarlet cardinals,
Scarlet cloaks and quilted coats,
Womens and girls coloured and black sattin hats,
Sattin shoes,
Plain and figured ribbons,
Dresden and pinked handkerchiefs,
Head lace and footing,
Fine India chintzes,
White & coloured callicoes,
Clear and long lawns,
Britannias and Pomeranias,
Pistol lawns and silesias,
Men & boys castor & felt hats,
White and black glazed mitts,
Coloured, wash leather, and sattin ditto,
Clouting diaper,
Irish shirting and sheeting linen,
Blue and green plains,
Swanskin,
Blue and white linsey,
Men and womens worsted stockings,
Womens & girls plain, pink do.

Thread and cotton ditto,
Boys caps with black and white feathers
Cruels and canvas,
Fine hyson tea,
Green and bohea tea,
Durham mustard,
Pigtail and cut tobacco,
High and low teast snuff,
Short and long pipes,
Womens and girls everlasting shoes,
Red, black, plain and tooel clogs,
Men and womens leather shoes,
Dresden and stock tape,
Holland and diaper ditto,
Broad tape and bobbins,
Silk and cotton laces,
Silk, cotton and thread mitts,
White and coloured laps,
Pins, patches, and masks.
Sets of necklaces and ear-rings,
Pearl and blue stone ditto,
Cinnamon, nutmegs, cloves, mace, and black pepper.
Scented and plain hair powder,
Poland starch, & powder blue,
Wash balls and teeth powder,
Powder boxes and puffs,
Fine enamell'd & japanned snuff boxes,
Fine India china in setts,
Enamelled and blue and white bowls,
Enamelled and blue and white coffee cups,
Enamelled and blue and white cups and saucers, tea-pots, milk-pots, &c. &c.

Agnes Lind, a shopkeeper in Charleston, was one of the most persistent advertisers in the *South Carolina Gazette*. This advertisement, which appeared on August 21, 1762, lists an assortment of goods that had just arrived in her store from London.

number of young women who picked up a few extra pennies each week by teaching penmanship and reading to local children. Knight's vocation would take on heightened importance for women in the years after the American Revolution. But Knight was not only teacher, mother, and mistress of her household. She was also a boardinghouse operator, taking in modest rents from up to half a dozen relatives and others who shared her large Boston home. She was a shopkeeper, running a small retail establishment from her home. She was a traveler, striking out on her own in 1704 on an arduous five-month journey to New Haven and keeping a journal of the expedition for posterity. Though the ostensible purpose of the trip was to settle a kinswoman's estate, Knight found plenty of time to do some business along the way. She reported her success at a "vendue" or auction in New York, where she purchased one hundred reams of fine Dutch paper at a price that would allow her a substantial profit. She was indeed, as she wrote in her travel journal, "fitt for business." At her death in 1727, she had parlayed the proceeds from her various enterprises into the considerable estate of eighteen hundred pounds.

Like the wives of many urban artisans, Deborah Read Franklin, wife of printer and future statesman Benjamin Franklin, contributed valuable skills to her husband's career. With Benjamin away for months or even years at a time on state business, Deborah Franklin looked after his book and stationary business at home in Philadelphia. In his *Autobiography*, Benjamin Franklin remembered his wife as "a good and faithful Helpmate" who "assisted me much by attending the shop." Such a helpmate, he knew, was indispensable in his rapidly changing world. As he noted in a letter to a male friend in 1745, marriage had become a necessity for the enterprising man. "It is the Man and Woman united that make the compleat human Being," he wrote. "Together they are more likely to succeed in the World." In the commercial environment of eighteenth-century Philadelphia, success in one's profession had become the measure of a man. This kind of success, Franklin knew, was hard to attain without the help of a wife with a good head for business.

Did the male leaders of these colonial port cities recognize the value of the work performed by women like Sarah Kemble Knight and Deborah Read Franklin? What, for that matter, did these urban women of affairs think of their own contributions? Few eighteenth-century men and women pondered such questions in their diaries and letters. But the petition a group of New York's female traders addressed to newspaper editor John Peter Zenger in 1733 reveals that at least *some* urban women were aware of their importance to the local economy—and that they were beginning to chafe against the second-class status accorded to female workers. "Mr. Zenger," they wrote, "We, the widdows of this city, have had a Meeting, and as our case is something Deplorable, we beg you will give [our petition a] Place in your *Weekly Journal.* . . . it is as follows: We are House keepers, Pay our Taxes, carry on Trade, and most of us are she Merchants, and as we in some measure contribute to the Support of Government, we ought to be Intitled to some of the Sweets of it; but we find ourselves entirely neglected, while the Husbands that live in our Neighborhood are daily invited to Dine at Court; we have the Vanity to think we can be full[y] as Entertaining, and make as brave a Defence in Case of an Invasion and perhaps not turn Tail so soon as some of them."

We do not know what the *Journal's* readers made of this striking request. They may have found these protestations of bravery in the face of an invasion outlandish. No foreign invasion or domestic insurrection was then visible on the horizon. Within a generation, however, the ability of women like New York's "she Merchants" to conduct themselves as loyal and prosperous Americans would become essential to the colonies' claims to stand as a nation. For it was amid the political turmoil of the 1760s and 1770s that American women's lives would first become a topic of heated public debate.

CHAPTER 3

The Limits of Independence

1760–1800

Marylynn Salmon

T he two women walked slowly through the cornfields, heading toward the forest that surrounded the village compound. Following Seneca custom, the younger woman had prepared a place in the woods to give birth. Now that her time had come, she was going there with her mother, a village healer and midwife.

The older woman followed the younger, who moved steadily ahead despite the pains that came every few minutes. She was well prepared to give birth, for she was strong and healthy and, although this child would be her first, unafraid. Her mother had taught her the ways of women, and she knew that the pain of this birth, though strong, would last only a short while. She was confident she would bear her labor as a dignified Seneca woman should, without crying out. If she did give in to the pain, her people believed the child would suffer. Girls born of such mothers were known to be ill-natured, and boys proved cowardly in warfare. If her husband heard of her weakness, he would be ashamed.

They turned toward the sound of the brook that ran past their village on the eastern side and stopped a few hundred yards into the woods. The spot was close to their fields yet private, shielded on two sides by young hemlocks and bounded on a third by the brook, where the child would be dipped soon after birth. The washing was meant not only to clean and stimulate the child, but also to harden it against the coming rigors of Indian life. The mother approved of her daughter's choice and the way she had swept the earth and covered the ground with pine needles and hemlock boughs. On the ground, they laid the blankets they had brought. As night was approaching and the season was cold, the mother built a fire to warm them.

The midwife admired the endurance of her daughter, who laid down only between her pains, gathering herself for the effort to kneel through each contraction. The labor was long because it was her first. Despite the fact that she had remained in the village throughout the entire first day of her birth pains, working on her pelts, preparing food for her husband, and helping care for her sister's children, the wait in the woods *seemed long, too long to the mother. Toward morning, the mother decided to intervene and prepared a medicine to speed her daughter's contractions. She danced around the young woman, singing a special song to plead for help in bringing forth the baby. Soon her efforts were rewarded. With great determination the daughter rose to grasp the leather thong tied to the tree above her, trembling as she pushed her legs against the earth, groaning as the infant's head broke through. After one final push, the midwife held the newborn in her hands. Her daughter lay back on the blankets, exhausted, while she cut the umbilical cord and wiped the baby's face clean. "It is a girl," she announced. "You have done well." The new mother held her baby and an overwhelming sense of joy and relief passed through her. The baby was whole and unharmed. She would grow up to be a great help and comfort, and the line of women in their family would continue, strong and uninterrupted.*

Only a few hours after her delivery, the Seneca woman returned to her log house in the village. She held her baby wrapped in the beautifully decorated blanket she had made for it and displayed the girl proudly to the other women, children, and her husband. Her thoughts were on the family's happy future signified by the successful birth, but her mother's thoughts were much less joyful. She knew more than her daughter about the problems of their people, and to her the new generation seemed faced with more difficulties than they could overcome. Her pleasure at the birth of a granddaughter was tinged with sadness.

The Seneca nation of Indians, which controlled the region of western New York State between Seneca Lake and Lake Erie, would have included women such as those in this story. The Seneca was the largest and the most powerful of the six tribes that made up the Iroquois Confederacy. Seneca men ranged over a territory that extended from the Mississippi River east to the Atlantic Ocean and from Hudson Bay south to the Carolinas. They traveled to hunt and to conduct warfare and diplomacy, and often were gone from their villages for weeks or months at a time. In fact, Iroquois men were away from home for such extended periods that women came to control much of the day-to-day affairs of village life.

Among the Iroquois, women were the farmers. They produced the corn that was the mainstay of their people's diet and supplemental crops of squash and beans. Women also raised tobacco to smoke and herbs for teas and medicines. To add variety to their diet, they gathered fresh fruits, nuts, and insects such as grasshoppers.

Women usually farmed communally, although individuals could work their own plots of land if they preferred. They had little incentive to farm alone, however. Even if a farmer could produce extra food for later use, such hoarding would be frowned upon if other families in the village were in need.

The Iroquois had no concept of private land ownership. A woman might work a particular piece of land, and as long as she used the plot, it was considered hers. But when the village moved to another location, as it did from time to time, she no longer held a claim to her old fields. Near the new village she simply etched out another plot for her family. Economic security came primarily from contributing to the good of the village as a whole, rather than from individually owning and working a farm plot.

In addition to being the primary food producers for their villages, Iroquois women also maintained social stability through tightly knit female relationships. The mother-daughter bond was particularly strong. The Iroquois considered it more important than any other relationship, including that between a wife and husband. In times of trouble, women turned to each other for food, medical care, and advice on love and childrearing. The reason was simple: women were always there, whereas husbands, fathers, brothers, and sons were often away.

The close mother-daughter bond helped dictate where family members lived. Traditionally, large Iroquois dwellings, known as longhouses, sheltered as many as fifty or sixty people, all descendants of one elderly woman. By the mid-eighteenth century, however, smaller houses had become common. They often lodged only a single family or a mother and one daughter with her family. Unmarried sons as well as daughters lived with their mothers. The houses, then, and the fields that surrounded them, were controlled by the women of Iroquois villages.

Children also came under the control of women more than men. Infants and toddlers spent all of their time with their mothers because weaning did not occur until children were three or four years old. During later childhood, Iroquois boys and girls stayed in or around their villages, where they played and performed easy chores. Fathers came and went, providing essentials such as meat and trade goods for their families and offering instruction or advice as necessary. Although their contributions were important, they represented only distant figures compared to mothers.

After reaching eight or nine, boys came less directly under female control. At this time they began to imitate adult male behavior by forming hunting gangs that roamed the woods in search of small game. Until they reached manhood, these gangs maintained independence from both parents to a great extent. Older girls, meanwhile, remained with their mothers in the village compound, where they performed traditional women's work: farming, preparing animal pelts, caring for younger children, making baskets and pottery, and gathering, preserving, and cooking food.

Iroquois children of both sexes were reared indulgently. Mothers sought to harden their children by bathing them in cold water, but they rarely punished them for misbehavior. Parents assumed that by observing and imitating adult standards of conduct their children would outgrow unpleasant habits without much interference. White observers commented on the passionate love Iroquois women felt for their children and noted the mothers' refusal to strike or restrain them. Scholars believe the Iroquois avoided physical restraint and blows out of respect for their children. The Iroquois believed that children could be insulted as easily as adults, and parents wanted their offspring to remember them with love and respect, not fear and resentment. Perhaps as a result of the respect they were given as children, Iroquois adults often displayed a fierce desire to remain free and independent of all restraints.

The close and enduring ties of women complemented the loose and often short-term relationships between women and men. Men's frequent and lengthy absences placed a great strain on some marriages, and divorces and subsequent remarriages were common. A divorce could be initiated by either spouse, but often women entered into new marriages while their husbands were away from home. Because women were primarily responsible for the day-to-day care and feeding of young children and because land was held in common, questions of paternity and inheritance did not disrupt this system of remarriage.

Love, sexual attraction, and rejection were of great importance to the Iroquois. They readily consulted medicine women and men or even witches about problems in their relationships. Rejected spouses were usually encouraged to find new mates and accept the new unions of their former wives or husbands. Retaliation against a former spouse was discouraged largely because men's absences made easy divorce and remarriage a social necessity.

The clearly defined social roles of Iroquois women and men helped them deal with the tension of continual warfare between European powers in America. During the first half of the eighteenth century, France and England fought three separate wars for control of the northeastern interior and the vast wealth of the Indian fur trade. Throughout the conflict Iroquois warriors and diplomats never established a permanent allegiance to one side or the other. This allowed them to negotiate gifts from both nations in exchange for military favors. They also wanted to keep their people's freedom to trade wherever it was most profitable. As a result of careful negotiating, only the native inhabitants had maintained complete freedom to travel and trade at will. This delicate balance, in which the Iroquois kept two great European powers dependent on them for decades, finally was destroyed by Great Britain's increasing strength in the region. The English became determined to dominate the continent. In the French and Indian War (1754–63), England finally destroyed the French threat. After the war, France could no longer hinder the construction of English forts along the frontier or interfere with England's dominance of the fur trade.

As a result of their victory, the English changed the way in which they negotiated with the Native American inhabitants of frontier areas. Because the whites no longer needed the help of tribes such as the Seneca, they refused to pay them rent for the forts they constructed in Indian territory. They also raised the prices of trade goods and refused to give their former Indian allies traditional presents of hardware, dry goods, powder, lead, and rum. The Iroquois had become dependent on these goods. Without ready access to them, the Iroquois way of life was threatened. Even more disturbing was England's decision to allow white settlers to move onto Iroquois and Delaware lands in the Monongahela and Susquehanna valleys. (The Delaware controlled western Pennsylvania.) The Indians could not tolerate such disrespect for their ancient rights to this land.

Traditional Iroquois ways gave both women and men the right to decide when to go to war. In Iroquois politics men did the public speaking and announced the decisions of the tribes in great meetings, but women freely exhorted the men to action or delay. The influence of individual women varied according to the persuasiveness of their arguments and their personal status within the tribe. English behavior after the war with France had so angered the Iroquois that both women and men demanded action.

An Indian uprising—named Pontiac's Rebellion after the Ottawa leader who instigated it—began in the spring of 1763. In addition to the six nations of the Iroquois Confederacy, it involved the Huron, Chippewa, Potawatomi, Delaware, and Shawnee nations and some Mingo (Pennsylvania Iroquois exiled to the Ohio Valley). The Seneca played a particularly important role in igniting the war, which they planned over a period of two years and to which they contributed many warriors. Initially, the Native American fighters had a series of striking successes. They destroyed all the British outposts in the Great Lakes region west of Fort Niagara and north of Fort Pitt (at Pittsburgh) and killed at least two thousand white settlers along the Virginia and Pennsylvania frontiers.

The English never were in serious danger of losing control of the region, however. Forts Detroit, Pitt, and Niagara withstood attack, and eventually Indian supplies ran low. When English reinforcements arrived at the forts in the fall, the Indians gave up the fight. Pontiac was the last chief to lay down arms. His siege of the English fort at Detroit ended in late October, after most of the other Indian warriors already had given up and returned to their villages.

At about the same time that Pontiac was abandoning his efforts, the English government issued the Proclamation of 1763. This order recognized the exclusive right of the indigenous peoples to inhabit frontier lands previously controlled by the French. The English government recognized that without great effort it could not control the vast new territories it had acquired from France. Rather than risk continual warfare with the native inhabitants, it forbade English settlement in these areas. In theory the English proclamation line was an effort to prevent conflict until better arrangements could be made for the native inhabitants. In practice the idea was unworkable from the beginning, as many whites had already moved into the forbidden areas. Indian elders knew that traditional ways of life could not long withstand the rising English presence on their lands. For them, the peace after Pontiac's Rebellion spelled defeat. Fearing the changes their children and grandchildren would face in the coming years, they had difficulty feeling joy at the birth of a new generation.

By the 1760s white settlements in the British colonies stretched deep into the

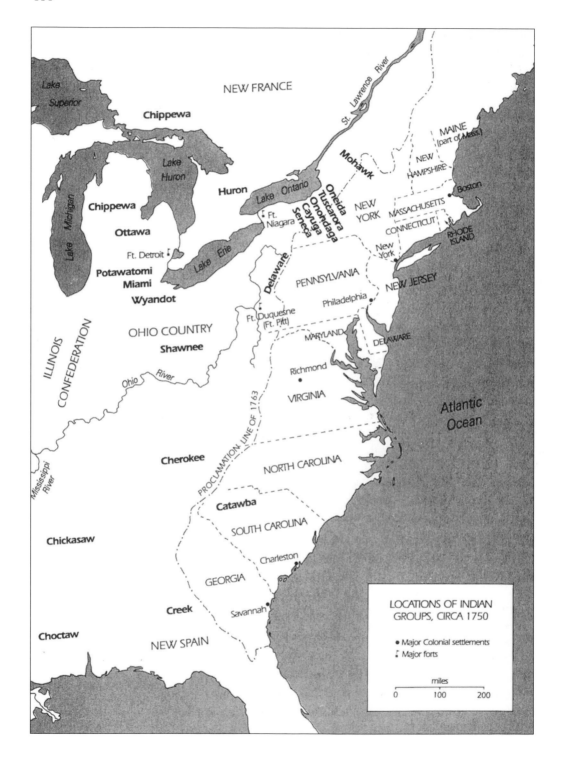

LOCATIONS OF INDIAN
GROUPS, CIRCA 1750

• Major Colonial settlements
⌐ Major forts

miles
0   100   200

continent. A million and a half people populated the Atlantic seaboard, and thousands more migrated to the colonies every year. Between 1760 and 1775 more than 125,000 people fled poor economic prospects in the British Isles and Germany to settle in British America. Adding to this surge in white immigration was the forced migration of at least 85,000 Africans, who were brought to the colonies primarily as agricultural laborers. The transportation of Africans and voluntary immigration of Europeans together resulted in a 10 percent increase in the colonial population in just fifteen years. The white population also grew dramatically by natural increase. In the eighteenth century European women living in America reproduced at a rate previously unknown in human history. Because of the early age at which most women married, the general health of the population, and in many areas the ease of remarriage after the death of a husband, the average white woman gave birth every two to three years. In British America, especially in the colonies north of Virginia, more children lived to adulthood than in Europe at that time. As a result, during the late colonial period, the population doubled approximately every twenty-five years.

These people needed land, for the majority made their living as farmers. Colonial settlers therefore welcomed the British victory over the French. It meant the opening of vast new areas for settlement. The lands already were inhabited by indigenous peoples, but this fact meant little to the colonists. They regarded Indian culture as barbaric, Indian religious beliefs as contemptible, and Indian use of the land as wasteful. White settlers believed that the Christian God wanted them to occupy the lands of the interior, just as they already had settled the coastal areas.

Such attitudes led European settlers and their families to move steadily onto the lands of the Iroquois in New York, the Delaware in Pennsylvania, and the Cherokee and Catawba in the Carolinas. They ignored the Proclamation Line of 1763, not only because they had no respect for the rights of the Indians, but also because they disputed the right of the English government to exercise such a vigorous form of control over their lives. When it came to a question of land ownership, English attempts to govern the interior were doomed to failure.

By the time white settlers began to move west of the Appalachian Mountains in large numbers, Native Americans understood their ways well. They knew that the whites would demand exclusive ownership of the lands they farmed, generally fencing in their land to make the point absolutely clear. They also knew that the whites would pay only nominal sums for the areas they claimed and that they would destroy traditional hunting grounds without regard for the Indian way of life. But by the mid-eighteenth century Indians such as the Iroquois of western New York also realized that the white presence would not go away. These people had to be dealt with in one way or another. When open warfare against them did not succeed, the Indians tried diplomacy. On at least two occasions, for example, the Iroquois negotiated peace with the whites by selling off large tracts of land belonging to less powerful Indian dependents. In this way the Shawnee lost their traditional hunting grounds in Kentucky, and the Ohio Valley lands of the Delaware and Mingo were turned over to the whites. Other powerful Native Americans also sometimes sacrificed the interests of weaker tribes in order to maintain some degree of control over white expansion into the interior. By the beginning of the American Revolution in 1775, some interior tribes were completely dispossessed, and others, such as the Seneca, felt severely threatened.

For women as well as men the issues of white expansion and land use were of vital importance. Although Native American men conducted warfare and negotiated treaties and trade agreements, women played important roles in making decisions for peace or war, especially among the powerful Iroquois. They wanted to preserve their traditional way of life as long as possible, and so they supported the efforts of men to control the movements of white settlers.

But for Iroquois women, adjustment to white culture, or acculturation, was less threatening than it was for men. White control over Indian lands meant that Iroquois men could no longer hunt or conduct warfare at will. These were the two aspects of male work that were the most important to the male Native American identity. Women, in contrast, led fairly settled lives, just as the whites did. They farmed, lived in one place most of the year, and concerned themselves with community and family above all else. The major impact of acculturation for Native American women was the sudden necessity to share their traditional work roles of farming and childrearing with men. This transformation required a total redefinition of female and male relationships. The main question loomed: How would women and men change their customary sex roles to make their way of life more like that of the whites who swarmed over Iroquois hunting lands in ever increasing numbers?

The Community of Women:
Childrearing and the Sexual Division of Labor

As the French and Indian War drew to a close, Hannah Breck Parkman of Westborough, Massachusetts, gave birth to her last child, a son named Elias. She and her husband Ebenezer already had nine children, and in addition Ebenezer was the father of four children by his first wife, Mary. The devout wife of a Congregational minister, Hannah undoubtedly viewed her large family with pride. But her health was poor, and the difficulties of providing for so many children were numerous. Families such as hers stretched the resources of farming communities to their limits.

Many years earlier Hannah Parkman's deliveries had begun in tragedy. Only a few months after her marriage in 1737, she suffered a miscarriage. Her first daughter died shortly after birth, and another miscarriage followed a year later. The birth of William in early 1741 signaled the beginning of happier times. In rapid succession Hannah delivered nine healthy children, all born between two and two-and-a-half years of each other. Only Elias's birth was delayed. He arrived almost three years after his older sister Hannah. At the time couples often acted to limit births late in a woman's childbearing years, when her health was more at risk and the family's need for additional children was much reduced.

Households such as the Parkmans' were common in the colonies in the mid-18th century. If a woman lived through the rigors of childbirth, she generally conceived again quickly. Aside from abstinence and abortion, effective forms of birth control were unknown. Religious beliefs also made people fatalistic about the problems associated with many pregnancies and births. They thought that God had meant them to have large families. Fertility was viewed as a mark of God's favor, especially when it was accompanied by good health for both a mother and her children. To become a mother and grandmother many times over was to obey God's commandment: "Be fruitful and multiply, and fill the earth and subdue it" (Gen. 1.28).

Women also saw childbirth as a way of atoning for the sin of Eve. According to biblical interpretation of the time, Eve committed the first sin by tempting Adam to eat of the fruit of the Tree of Knowledge. In this way original sin, and the expulsion of Adam and Eve from the Garden of Eden, was regarded as primarily the fault of women. By giving birth, women gained redemption not only for themselves, but for all of humanity. In this way they were thought to be blessed by God. In the eighteenth-century world, then, American women of European descent earned respect and authority through motherhood.

Large families, however, were difficult to support. Conscientious parents worried about two problems: how to feed and shelter their children properly, and how to prepare them for making their own living when they were grown. By the 1750s a concern of farming families was the scarcity of good farmland. The fact that an entire continent lay before them gave little comfort to people then living on the eastern seaboard. Parents hoped that their children could settle near them rather than move to a frontier area. But land became more and more expensive, and most families could not afford to buy farms in settled areas for all their children. Some sons and daughters had to migrate. Initially, they moved to distant towns and then, as the century progressed, to frontier areas such as Maine, western Massachusetts, New York, Pennsylvania, and even Ohio.

In the South the story was the same. The population there grew more slowly, primarily because the hot climate promoted a variety of lethal diseases, but families still watched with dismay as their children moved away from the home farm or plantation. The Virginian Landon Carter, for example, regretted his daughter Judith's settlement in a distant area after her marriage in 1774. He confided his concerns to his journal while noting the new bride's youthful enthusiasm for her upcoming move:

A mid-eighteenth-century painting by John Greenwood portrays the bond between grandmother and grandchild, both named Abigail Gerrish. Such multigenerational ties were greatly prized in an era when successful reproduction marked the fulfillment of women's highest destiny.

Poor Judy and her new sister Sally came here. I could not help observing how easily that poor girl is made to believe her distant happiness when I am certain she sees nothing but misery. She knows not whether she goes up this fall or next spring; I said it might keep her the longer from being miserable for she would be so as soon as she got there; She answered no she should not. I am certain the last time she was here she told me there was no neighbors about the place within 20 miles of it. But possibly it was with her All for Love or the world well Lost.

The rapid rise in the slave population after the mid-eighteenth century made the opening of southern frontier lands essential. Plantations with slave labor forces grew up steadily throughout western Virginia, the Carolinas, and Georgia.

In the era of the American Revolution (1775–83), most families lived on farms. They raised most of their own food and produced the flax and wool needed to make cloth, and in addition produced some crop or crops to trade. The ideal of the subsistence farm, on which a family raised everything it needed for a comfortable living, rarely was realized. Most people traded crops, goods, and services. Generally, this was accomplished locally, and many individuals never visited the thriving commercial centers of Boston, New York, and Philadelphia. But they came to depend more and more on people who did, traveling peddlers or local merchants who went to large towns and cities to get goods to trade in rural areas. By the mid-1760s urban areas in America had become thriving places to trade, hold court proceedings, and conduct government business. Although most people still lived on farms, they depended more and more on commercial areas for necessary services. And the closer a family lived to a trading center, even a small one, the more comfortable it could be. Parents therefore were saddened to see their children settle far from towns and villages.

For women, life on an isolated farm was particularly difficult because of the nature of their work roles and health care needs. Men living in rural areas still traveled to town to conduct necessary business such as selling crops and trading goods produced on the farm. Their work in town gave them opportunities for social interaction, the chance to gossip or discuss the political questions of the day. But women generally stayed close to home, restricted by pregnancy, the needs of nursing infants and small children, and their daily work routines. Even more important was women's need for help during pregnancy and childbirth. Once a woman moved into an area far from her nearest neighbor, she placed herself in a dangerous situation. She could expect little assistance when giving birth, and if she became ill during pregnancy or after childbirth there would be no medical care or household help available. Few women gladly moved away from their relatives, friends, and physicians.

The movement to the frontier, therefore, was regarded by most women as a necessary evil. Many men also saw their isolation as unpleasant and difficult, but on the whole more men than women were challenged and invigorated by the prospect of building a new life on the frontier. The story of the Cumming family was probably typical. After their marriage, the couple moved from Boston to the frontier, where they soon faced danger during the French and Indian War. As a friend reported, "Mrs Cumming is greatly affraid of the French and trys to get Mr

Cumming to be willing to move to Boston, but he will not hear nor think any thing about the French, and dont care *two pence* for all the french. They are as safe at York as anywhere, there is no dainger, etc."

Frontier settlers also faced attack and capture by Indian warriors. White women feared living on Indian lands just as much as Native Americans dreaded the settlers' appearance in their territory. If these women could have avoided moving to the dangerous frontier, they would have done so. But with land scarce and the population growing, they saw no other way to make a living and raise a family.

Many white people drew comfort from their conviction that the Christian God meant for them to live on Indian lands. To the whites, the Indians were wasting huge tracts of valuable farmland. White settlers could not believe that God condoned the Indian way of life. Instead, they were convinced that native inhabitants must be taught the benefits of living as Europeans did. Only when Indians were converted to Christianity and taught to farm did whites feel that the two peoples could live side by side in peace. Colonial leaders, and later, leaders of the new United States, therefore adopted a policy of seizing the vast majority of Indian lands with little or no compensation. They assumed that eventually the indigenous peoples could be acculturated to the ways of white farmers. Then, the leaders believed, Indians would be content with the small parcels of land the whites were willing to leave them.

Until menopause, which generally occurred sometime between ages forty and fifty, women's adult lives were dominated more by the rhythms of pregnancy, birth, and breast-feeding than by where they lived. Given women's medical needs, midwives and female healers held positions of status and authority. In fact, the only thing approaching a public role available to prerevolutionary women was that of healer or midwife. Women skillful in the use of medicines and knowledgeable about the human body provided valuable services to their neighbors and communities as well as to their own families. They often were as successful as professional physicians in treating their patients. Like many crafts and trades, healing was learned through an apprenticeship. As a result, the daughters of healers and midwives frequently followed in their mothers' footsteps, becoming local experts consulted for their special knowledge and skill. This pattern was just as common for African Americans and Indians as it was for whites.

Although families called on local healers and physicians, they also relied on home remedies to treat the sick. A mother was expected to have at least some medical knowledge. Sarah Pierpont Edwards, wife of the minister Jonathan Edwards, for example, sent medical advice to her daughter in a postscript to one of her husband's letters:

> Your mother would have you use a conserve of Raisons; a Pound of good
> sugar to a Pound of Raisons, after they are ston'd. Mix with it, nutmeg,
> mace, Cinnamon, Cloves, ground in a spicemill, with some orange-Pill; one

In this illustration from a 1793 midwifery manual, *Man-midwifery dissected, or The obstetric family-instructor,* the left side of the figure is a male midwife, the right side a female. Each half holds the tools of the trade. There were many more women midwives than men until after 1780.

Nutmeg to half a Pound of conserve, and the other spices in the same Quantity. Take a little as suits your stomach, in the morning, and an Hour before Dinner, and in the after-noon.

... Your mother has also an inclination that you should sometimes try a Tea made of the Leaves of Robins Plantain, If it be known at Newark by that name; she says she has found it very strengthening and comfortable to her in her weakness.

Jonathan Edwards added his own advice: "I should think it best pretty much to throw by [avoid] doctors, and be your own Physician, ... hearkening to them that are used to your Constitution."

Medical knowledge was especially important for rural women such as Sarah Edwards, who had no physicians or apothecaries living nearby, as urban women did. Literate women often kept medicinal recipes, called "receipts," in the same books in which they wrote down their cooking recipes. A receipt for cough syrup might be found between recipes for ginger cake and stuffed fowl. In addition, women grew standard ingredients for medicines in their gardens. Herbs such as vervain and Jerusalem oak were known to expel worms in children; caraway relieved colic; and marigold quickened the healing of cuts, bruises, and sprains.

Most women also had experience in attending births. Unlike Native American women, who generally gave birth alone or with one attendant in an isolated location, white women gathered relatives and friends together for births in their own homes. Labor and delivery generally were attended by several female relatives in addition to the midwife. Hannah Parkman, for example, always was attended by six or seven women. Gathering the women together was her husband's job, but he often had the assistance of male friends. When Elias was born, Ebenezer Parkman reported the event in this way:

At Eve[nin]g had such Indications of approaching Travail [that] N[eighbo]r Batherick being here I desir'd him to call at N[eighbo]r Pratts, who is ready to hasten to Granny Mayn[ar]d. wc. [which] was done: & Alex[an]d[e]r went to ye Widow Newton, whose son bro[ugh]t her Capt[ain] *Wood* went for Mrs Baker who (I perceive too unwillingly) came—both Mrs. W[illia]mss, Mrs. Pratt & Mrs. Morse came—all of ym [them] this E[venin]g.

Once the rush of bringing the midwife and neighbors was over, a husband's work ended. Husbands stayed at hand, but they were not crucial figures in the birth of their children unless it was not possible for women attendants to be there. (The modern turnabout is interesting: Today husbands generally are present at their children's births, and female relatives and friends are excluded.) Ebenezer, for example, was not present at any of his children's births. Although loving, concerned, and even frightened (for he loved his wife dearly), he remained in the background, visiting Hannah between moments of crisis but retreating when her pains increased. When Hannah was in labor with Elias, Ebenezer turned the birth over to more capable hands and went to bed until, "Ab[ou]t 2 in ye morning Widow Newton rouses me with the News of a Safe Deliv[eran]ce & ye Birth of a Son, of extr[aordinar]y Size and Fatness—To God be all Hon[o]r Praise & Thanksgiving!"

Births were almost public affairs to the community of women. During a normal labor, women visited, sewed, exchanged bawdy stories, and gave details of their own past deliveries. Their presence demonstrated women's concern for each other, the importance of female bonding at this crucial time, and the significance accorded a woman's labor—her travail. Friends (Mrs. Baker notwithstanding) wanted to be at the scene, a part of the ritual of birth. They regarded attendance at a birth as both a duty and a privilege. On a more practical level, for the new mother the psychological benefits of having friends nearby was great.

Having at least one nursing mother present at a birth also was helpful. Midwives sometimes gave laboring women a drink of breast milk as a way of speeding up contractions. At the time of delivery the midwife and perhaps one or two other women remained actively involved, while the others receded to the corners of the room or went into another room. A friend usually held up the mother as she gave birth, although in large towns midwives' stools were available to give her support.

In New England and the middle colonies, where most families lived in towns, white women rarely delivered alone or with only their husbands to help them. At worst, married women who lived nearby could attend, and at best numerous relatives, friends, and a skilled midwife saw a woman through her delivery. This was not so much the case in Virginia and Maryland, where men established their farms up and down the banks of the Chesapeake Bay and all navigable rivers in order to ship their cash crop—usually tobacco—as cheaply as possible. This settlement pattern of isolated farms with few population centers extended into other areas of the South as settlement in the Carolinas and Georgia expanded during the eighteenth century. The distance between farms meant that there were often few friends or neighbors close enough to attend a birth.

Isolated farm women did everything they could to avoid giving birth alone or with only their husband in attendance. Some women traveled to their parents' homes or asked female relatives who lived far away to visit them to help with their deliveries.

Sometimes even the wealthy delivered without a midwife. Landon Carter was one of the richest men in Virginia, but his daughter-in-law, who lived with him, failed to call for a midwife in time for several of her deliveries. The third time this happened, Carter was furious. The infant was born dead, and after the birth the mother seemed in critical condition. In his diary Carter wrote, "I was just riding out to see the destruction [around his farm after a severe rainstorm] but was called back by my son to his wife then taken in labor the third time without a midwife, so punctual are women or rather obstinate to their false accounts. I found every-body about her in a great fright and she almost in despair. The child was dead and the womb was fallen down and what not." The mother made a complete recovery, but the experience of having no skilled medical care available during a crisis was traumatic for the entire Carter family.

Like their white mistresses, African-American women preferred to have the company of relatives and friends during childbirth. The work routines of slaves often made this impossible, but women other than midwives sometimes were allowed to leave the fields to assist at births. Black and white women regularly attended each other in childbirth, especially when few women lived within easy traveling distance. White women valued the help of a skilled black midwife, and black women similarly relied on the aid of their white mistresses when their labor began. Childbirth was one occasion that called for the breakdown of racial barriers.

Rural women of all ranks assisted each other whenever they could, but at times there was no help nearby. Then a woman and her husband had to do the best they could on their own. For the literate, books were available by the mid-eighteenth cen-tury. In fact, one of the best-selling books of the period was a manual on sexual mat-ters, pregnancy, and childbirth called *Aristotle's Complete Masterpiece: Displaying the Secrets of Nature in the Generation of Man.* Undoubtedly, many women relied on *Aristotle's Masterpiece* to help them through a lonely, frontier delivery.

Hannah Parkman was fortunate to live in a settled farming area, with neighbors, midwives, and physicians close by, places to trade in town, and Boston only a day's ride to the east. Her residence in central Massachusetts was the colonial ideal: the Parkmans' house was close enough to a major trading area to gain many of its advantages, but far enough away to avoid the threat of disease. Eighteenth-century towns and cities could become life-threatening during epidemics of smallpox, diphtheria, measles, and yellow fever. At such times everyone with the means left town to live with friends or relatives in the country. During the second half of the century, wealthy residents of northern cities often owned country houses or boarded in the country every summer, when diseases swept through large towns, killing hundreds. Rural areas suffered epidemics as well, but disease spread less rapidly and killed fewer people in the country.

The situation south of Pennsylvania was somewhat different. Both country and town were unhealthy in the southern regions, where disease and early death were significantly more common than in the North. Whereas a northern mother might lose only one child out of four before he or she reached the age of twenty-one, a southern mother would lose two. Most southern children saw at least one of their parents die before they reached adulthood, and many children were orphaned. Parental and child death led to relatively unstable family lives in the South. Because of this high death rate and the isolation of the farming population, women in the South had to live more independent lives than those in New England.

Living in a town or city certainly made running a household somewhat easier.

Town women who lived above the subsistence level knew conveniences and luxuries that rural women could only dream of—inexpensive cloth imported from England, bakeries, and readily available professional medical care. But even for women in urban areas household management was difficult and time-consuming. Many still had to garden, raise poultry, and tend milk cows. And they also raised numerous children while managing their complicated households.

In order to care for their families, neighbors, and relatives, women needed a broad education in both mundane tasks (such as whitewashing the house and raising vegetables) and activities requiring considerable skill (such as caring for the sick and spinning). Many women knew at least a little about healing, producing cloth, dairying, and brewing, and they all performed the day-to-day, backbreaking labor of gardening; preparing and preserving food; raising and killing poultry; hauling water; and in between, of course, bearing, breast-feeding, and caring for their young children. An English folk song, addressed to a newly married groom, mentions one more chore many rural women could not avoid:

> Oats, peas, beans, and barley grow
> Oats, peas, beans, and barley grow
> Nor you nor I nor anyone knows
> How oats, peas, beans, and barley grow
>
> Now you're married, we wish you joy
> First a girl and then a boy
> You must be kind, you must be good
> And help your wife to chop the wood.

How did women manage to keep up with all their work (including chopping the firewood) and take care of their children, too? They usually had help. In all but the most isolated areas, women labored for each other on a daily basis. The assistance of other women was essential because of a rigidly observed sexual division of labor. Except in rare instances, usually during an illness, men did not do women's work. They faced their own round of daily chores, which were more than enough to keep them busy from morning to dark much of the year. Therefore, the community of women enforced a code of behavior based on the exchange of work and the sharing of their teenage daughters' labor.

Women were most in need of household assistance when their children were young. One infant usually did not prevent a woman from fulfilling her housekeeping obligations, but when a second baby arrived, she needed help. The older child, now usually two to two-and-a-half years old, required constant supervision, and the infant needed much of its mother's time for breast-feeding. (Bottle feeding was not practiced unless a mother was ill or had died. Lack of sterilization made it unhealthy, and bottle-fed babies rarely lived.) As Esther Edwards Burr, mother of Aaron Burr, observed after the birth of her second child, "[W]hen I had but one

Slave women were responsible for agricultural chores as well as for minding their own children and the master's, as depicted in this 1854 print.

Child my hands were tied, but now I am tied hand and foot (how I shall get along when I have got 1/2 dzn or 10 children I cant devise [understand])." During these years women turned to relatives or servants for assistance. If a woman had an unmarried sister or niece, this relative might come to live with her. In the country, neighbors' daughters might act as servants, either on a short-term or long-term basis. In urban areas professional servants could be hired. People of means paid their female servants wages, whereas poorer families relied on exchanges of goods and services.

Enslaved women were not restricted to women's work. White slaveholders did not hesitate to use women as agricultural laborers, although they preferred to purchase male slaves whenever possible. In addition to their agricultural work, however, some slaves helped their white mistresses in the house. Even wealthy women had to labor very hard, and the help of slaves was essential when there were few relatives and neighbors nearby to share work. Enslaved women therefore assisted with both child care and housekeeping, just as white servants did. Acculturated African-American women generally received these jobs because they could speak the language of their owners and had grown accustomed to white customs and manners. As slaves, they were not paid wages, worked long hours, and often were forced to live apart from their own families. Their primary compensation was the opportunity to develop skills valued by whites. On southern farms, baby nurses, healers, midwives, and spinners had a more elevated status than field hands. These skilled workers sometimes received better food, clothing, and medical care.

Despite the expense, most young mothers regarded the help of at least an adolescent girl as a necessity and its absence as an extreme hardship. One young mother complained to her sister about her difficulties in finding help. "I have nobody with me nor have had since Commencement, tho' throu mercy I have my helth as well as ever I had in my life or I could not possibly get a long in any shape. But you know there is nobody to have. *Girls* are very scarce for all are *Ladys* now a days." Because of the demand for their labor, adolescent girls were considered vital members of their communities. Their status is suggested by one rural minister's diary entry for March 17, 1756: "Betty Bellows dyed about 10 am., age 18 years. Extremely sorrowful in that House and Neighbourhood, there being no other daughter in that Family, and but one or two more young Women in that Corner of ye Town." The help of young women, both in their own families and the families of neighbors, was so important that this man could sense the sorrow of an entire neighborhood at the death of so useful a member.

Inadequate household help was not only inconvenient or burdensome for a mother. It could actually prove to be dangerous for young children, who consequently went without adequate supervision. While a housewife tended the fire or milked her cows, a youngster might pull over a kettle of boiling water, pick up a knife carelessly left within reach, or wander away into the fields or the woods. Esther Burr described one such accident involving a toddler who was visiting her in 1755: "About six weeks ago she fell into the fire and burnt her hands and face most tirrably, but is like to recover with the loss of one of her fingers."

In the spring of 1756 Ebenezer Parkman attended the funeral of a neighbor's child who "dyed by means of being burnt by a Warming pan." As he noted, the death could easily have happened in his own family. Only the previous fall one of his sons had narrowly escaped drowning. Parkman wrote, "Little John Sav'd from Drowning. Bill had dug a Hole in Neighbor Barnabas Newtons meadow in Time of

Drought, which was now fill'd with Water; into this John fell and Samuel pull'd him out." John was barely two years old; Samuel recently had turned four.

In the absence of adequate child care, mothers sometimes relied on physical restraints to control the movements of their very young children. A high chair or go-cart, the colonial equivalent of a modern baby's walker, could keep a child from crawling underfoot or into an open fireplace. But such devices could not replace a mother's watchful eye, and accidents still occurred. One journalist thanked God for the "memorable deliverance of my little Hannah. The Cellar Door was left open, & she in her Go Cart pitch'd down, & went to ye bottom—yet without any gr[ea]t Hurt."

Throughout the nineteenth century women's household chores became less difficult and time-consuming as a result of industrialization and the transportation revolution, which allowed the inexpensive movement of goods to rural areas. Formerly overworked and therefore somewhat neglectful mothers could then focus more energy on caring for their infants and young children. As a consequence, families became more child-oriented and the importance of the mother-child bond increased.

One example of this shift in attitudes can be seen in the use of go-carts. In the early nineteenth century, Mary Hunt Tayler, an influential writer on child care, criticized the devices. Referring to go-carts as "pernicious inventions," she wrote that they "are rapidly growing obsolete . . . and I sincerely hope they will ere long be consigned to complete oblivion, together with scull caps, forehead cloths, swaddling bands and stays, in which our great grandmamas used to imprison their hapless offspring." Cruel or not, "imprisonment," of course, was the purpose of these restraints. Without it, more children would have been injured, and more mothers made frantic by the antics of their offspring.

When a family's oldest child reached the age of seven or eight, household help became less critical. Even young children helped their mothers in numerous ways, but especially with child care. Given the sexual division of labor, girls were particularly useful as mothers' helpers, which explains why the English folk song "Oats, Peas, Beans, and Barley" expresses the hope that a newly married couple's firstborn would be a daughter. Apparently, most people thought that women needed help in the house even more than men needed it in the fields or the shop.

Despite the many claims on their time, most white women were able to work in or near their own houses, where they could keep an eye on their children while laboring at other chores. Black field-workers and the poorest white farm wives, however, had to take their infants and toddlers into the fields with them. Just like Iroquois women, many women of African descent came from a tradition in which women were the agricultural workers. They would have observed traditional customs of child care when more than one woman shared the work. If a farm had enough laborers—and in the South this was more and more often the case as the eighteenth century progressed—an elderly woman might be placed in charge of caring for several very young children while their parents worked. On larger farms and plantations slave women might be allowed to return home to breast-feed their infants at certain times during the day, or a baby might be brought to its mother for nursing. In either case, from a very early age black children had to learn to be independent of their mothers for most of the day. Only on Sundays were women allowed to spend all of their time with their children. If they attempted to subvert the slave system by demanding more time for their children, they might be punished. One planter described a long-standing dispute with his female slaves over their breast-feeding schedules:

> I discovered this day what I never knew before, nay what I had positively forbid years ago, but negroes have the impudence of the devil. Last year the suckling wenches told the overseer that I allowed them to go in five times about that business; for which I had some of them whipt and reduced it to half an hour before they went to work, half an hour before their breakfast; and half an hour before they go in at night. And Now they have made the simpletons believe I allow them to eat their morning's bit. So that a wench goes out to bake for that, then they must have their time to eat it, then another bakes for their breakfast. But these things I have forbid upon their Peril.

Whites interfered with slave mothers' care for their children in many ways, but by far the greatest threat facing these women was the possibility that their offspring might be sold. Under the law any child born of a slave mother also was a slave, and therefore could be sold at any time. Slave marriages had no legal validity, which gave slaveowners the right to separate slave spouses at will. As a result, enslaved women lived with the constant fear that they might be separated from their children and husbands. When an owner migrated to a new area, suffered financial setbacks, or died, black workers went up for sale. Most owners made no attempt to keep families together. As a rule, only breast-feeding infants were sure to stay with their mothers, for otherwise the babies were likely to die. Their death would rob their white owners of valuable property.

Slave women also lived with the knowledge that they could not control their children's play, work, explorations about the farm or plantation, or interaction with whites. When stingy owners did not give slaves adequate allowances, they even had difficulty feeding and clothing their children. Slave women and men supplemented their allowances by raising vegetables and poultry, but their only time to work for themselves was at the end of the day and on Sundays. The difficulties and heartache of raising children to be slaves led some women to resist childbearing by practicing abortion. But most women just did the best they could to care for their children under slavery. The alternatives—running away, engaging in violent resistance, or committing suicide—would have left their children even more vulnerable to the slave system.

The second half of the eighteenth century witnessed a subtle improvement in the conditions of slavery for some American blacks. More and more farms developed large slave work forces, thereby giving slaves a greater chance to interact and create close, and therefore protective, family ties. Previously, most farms were so small that their owners could afford to buy only one or at most a few slaves. Developing tight bonds with family members was then far more difficult for transported Africans and even African Americans.

Large plantations were made possible by a rapid increase in slave importations during the decades just preceding the Revolution. The shock of capture, sale, and the trans-Atlantic voyage for individuals must have made any meager improvements in the slave system as a whole seem unimportant. In addition, newly transported Africans were handicapped by language barriers and cultural differences, for they had followed many different ways of life in their own homelands. Therefore, the slaves born in the colonies profited most from living on the expanding plantations. Throughout this period they developed a distinctive African-American culture, which gave them both comfort and strength in dealing with the trauma of life under white domination.

The changes that came with the growth of plantations and economic diversification benefited enslaved men more than enslaved women. Historians have shown that improved farming methods in the Chesapeake produced a new sexual division of labor. In the seventeenth and early eighteenth centuries tobacco and corn, virtually the only crops planted, were produced using primitive farming techniques. Workers of both sexes labored side by side at most agricultural chores. For example, both women and men hoed, weeded, spread manure, and cleaned out swamps. As the eighteenth century progressed, more planters shifted to growing wheat or other grains and to raising livestock. Men then received new and valued work assignments. Plowing, which became necessary when wheat replaced tobacco as a cash crop, was defined exclusively as a man's job because it required greater strength than hoeing. Cutting lumber, fishing, milling, shearing sheep, and sowing and mowing grains used as fodder for livestock also demanded at least some degree of skill. They all became defined as men's work. Artisan work, such as coopering (making wooden casks), shoemaking, and smithing, also was performed by men, and as the economy grew, more labor of this kind was needed. Meanwhile, women continued to work at their traditional unskilled jobs. The new women's jobs that came with greater economic diversification included cleaning winnowed grain, shelling corn, breaking up newly opened fields by hand, and cleaning stables. These tasks were the most monotonous and distasteful.

Another important distinction between men's and women's labor under slavery concerned the way in which it was performed. As unskilled laborers, women more often than men worked in gangs, under the close eye of an overseer or gang leader. Thus they had little freedom to determine the pace of their work and the order in which assignments were completed. Men also tended to perform a greater variety of tasks than women, thereby reducing the monotony of their work.

According to the plantation records of George Washington, work suitable for men was distinguished carefully from work suitable for women. Washington grouped his male slaves together into one labor force and placed women in a separate group that also included adolescent workers of both sexes. The men's jobs included plowing, harrowing, sowing, cutting timber, carting goods, and making ditches and roads. Men often worked alone and could vary their tasks from day to day. Women were responsible for weeding fields, erecting fences, cleaning stables, spreading manure, harvesting and husking corn, and many other laborious and unpleasant chores. Unlike men, women worked at the same chores day after day until they were completed, rarely or never labored alone, and usually came under the supervision of an overseer. Men therefore came to be seen as the more skillful workers, a distinction that must have affected women's and men's attitudes toward their work and perhaps their private relations as well.

The white men who dominated eighteenth-century southern society assigned few slave women to either artisan or domestic work. Some women became artisans, particularly spinners or weavers, but they were exceptions. And most southern households, even relatively prosperous ones, got by with little domestic help. Wives and daughters of plantation owners were expected to do most of the gardening, cooking, cleaning, and sewing.

Plantation owners neglected these traditional areas of women's work because they did not value them. Whereas white women might have welcomed the help of enslaved women in the dairy or garden, white men preferred to keep their female slaves busy in the fields. They did not care if their tables lacked butter or fresh vegetables. Content with whatever their wives and daughters might produce, plantation owners in essence were denying the importance of traditional women's domestic labor. Thus both black and white women lived in a culture that devalued their work, while demanding that they labor intensively from sunup to sundown. For enslaved women this harsh work life was devoid of creative labor, with little chance of completing one task from beginning to end. Burdened by both race and sex, the lot of these workers was the worst of all.

An Era of Challenges: War and the Prospect of Independence

Women's lives in early America frequently were disrupted by warfare. The colonial period witnessed many wars, some between European powers and others between Europeans and Native Americans. Women participated in all of these wars, although only in rare instances did they actually engage in hand-to-hand combat. Instead, they provided food, shelter, nursing, and other assistance when fighting occurred near their homes or while traveling with an army as camp followers. With their husbands they paid taxes to support the troops. They were captured and held as prisoners for exchange or sale. When men were drafted for military service, they left their wives in exclusive charge of both children and family businesses, which required an unusual level of energy, fortitude, and independent initiative. Most colonial women were more accustomed to playing the part of helpmate than head of the family.

During the American Revolution, women once again met the challenges presented to them. But this war differed from previous conflicts. It demanded that women and men make new kinds of political decisions. In the years leading up to the war, women were forced to confront ideas about the nature of government and their roles in it. Whereas previous wars were almost exclusively territorial disputes, this one focused on the proper relationship between a government and the governed. For the first time people in America had to think about the advantages and disadvantages of living under a representative democracy and take a position either supporting or rejecting the idea of independence. Not surprisingly, different women came to different conclusions. Some were avid patriots; others were equally adamant about their loyalty to the British Crown. Still others, particularly members of the Society of Friends (also known as Quakers), were pacifists, people philosophically opposed to all wars.

Serious conflict between the American colonists and England began shortly after the end of the French and Indian War (1754–63). England had gone deeply into debt to pay for the war, and government leaders approved a series of tax measures meant to raise money in America to help reduce that debt. The new laws were opposed by many colonists, who were accustomed to paying taxes only at the local and colony level. Americans did not oppose paying England customs duties, and giving the mother country control over trade, for that was part of a mutually beneficial trading relationship between England and her colonies. But they did not want to become subject to the English Parliament in other ways. In particular, they did not welcome taxation by a governing body that cared more for the interests of the mother country than their own. Being part of the great British Empire gave the colonists many economic advantages, but those might all be lost if Parliament began to oppress them through burdensome taxes.

Fear of financial oppression at the hands of a distant government was one of the major causes of the American Revolution. But there were also other causes. Americans feared losing their liberties as well as their money. The issue of taxation demonstrated that they were not in complete control of their own lives. They had no elected representatives in Parliament and therefore possessed no way of controlling English legislation. English leaders enacted many regulations the colonists hated, such as the Proclamation Line of 1763. In addition, they removed the colonists' right to trial by jury in certain kinds of legal cases and denied them the right to print paper money. The English also disallowed laws enacted in America that conflicted with English laws, including the right to divorce, which many colonists supported but the English Parliament opposed. All of these actions threatened colonial autonomy, and people feared what might come next. But even more than the specific laws enacted by Parliament, many of the colonists resisted what those laws stood for in general: control by a distant, increasingly alien government.

The colonists had not always perceived England as an alien nation with interests different from their own. Throughout the colonial period relations between the mother country and her colonies had been cooperative and mutually beneficial. This was in large part because England had left the colonists alone. Self-government was customary, and it served both groups of people well. But after the French and Indian War, England increased her demands on the colonies. English leaders wanted a tighter relationship in which the colonists would increase the wealth of England not only through trade but through direct taxation as well. And they opposed Americans' attempts to legislate in ways different from their own.

Issues such as these were not considered women's concerns in the mid-eighteenth century. Social customs dictated that women defer to men in many areas of life, and one of these was politics. Undoubtedly, many women formed and voiced opinions about local political questions—where to locate a bridge or whether a school should be built, for example. But women felt less comfortable expressing their opinions on broad questions about the nature of government and the rights of the governed. The primary reason was the difference in the intellectual training of women and men. Only men were expected to read and study the great political thinkers of the day, to understand their arguments and consider their shortcomings. Because women rarely received an advanced education, they were made to feel inferior intellectually. As a rule, women's opinions were not respected, even when they possessed the training necessary to develop them.

Many men of ordinary social rank felt just as uncomfortable expressing political ideas as women did. More men than women were literate at all social ranks in colonial America, but most still had only a basic education. They could read and write and keep accounts, but they did not spend their evenings reading political philosophy. They might read the local newspaper occasionally but little else. Unless they believed their lives were threatened in some direct way, ordinary workingmen did not trouble themselves with politics. They left political decision making to their social betters, just as women did. The fact that only men of property were allowed to vote in local and colony-wide elections prevented many men in the lower ranks of society from feeling they had a right to express political opinions. The same attitudes prevailed among women of all social ranks, for even the wealthiest women could not vote in early America.

When England began to tax the colonists after the French and Indian War, poor men and women as well as the elite felt the effects of the new policies. Although they might not have understood the implications of English legislation in all areas, they did recognize when they were being asked to shoulder a new financial burden. And they did not like it. While elite men debated the place of the colonies in the

In this 1775 British engraving, entitled "A Society of Patriotic Ladies," women in North Carolina draft a pledge not to drink tea. Behind them, other women empty their tea containers. The unflattering appearance and behavior of the women indicated the English disapproval of such unfeminine political activity.

British Empire, ordinary men and women focused on the simple question of whether or not they would pay the new taxes. And as it turned out, virtually all Americans agreed that the taxes were oppressive and should not be submitted to without a fight.

Between 1764 and 1776 the colonists strongly opposed English taxation policies. In these years women came to feel that they had not only a right but also a responsibility to form and express political opinions. Men, who at first felt uncomfortable discussing politics with the women in their families, came to see that if women were asked to support a war, they had to understand and believe in the cause for which they were fighting. Many years passed before the colonists achieved the consensus necessary to declare independence from Great Britain, years filled with debates about the nature of government and the rights of the governed. Women participated in those debates alongside men.

To protest English taxes, American commercial and political leaders signed agreements of nonimportation and nonconsumption. Merchants made pacts not to import English goods, and citizens agreed not to consume them. In order to make these agreements effective, most people had to participate in them, and women's contribution was important. Women not only had to refrain from purchasing imported items they usually bought, such as tea, but also had to increase their production of homemade goods. By refusing to drink tea, a staple of their diet before the Revolution, colonial women showed their commitment to the Patriot cause. Similarly, Loyalist woman drank tea to show their support for a continued close relationship between England and the colonies.

An important way in which women and teenage girls expressed their opposition to English policies was through participation in spinning bees. Gathering on the town common or at a minister's home, teenagers and young women would set up their spinning wheels and work together all day. Their goal was the production of homespun—cloth that was made in America rather than imported from England. By participating in a spinning bee, and by working long hours at home spinning, weaving, knitting, and sewing, American women were helping to make the colonies independent of English goods. Public rituals such as spinning bees helped them understand the significance of their work. Most of the spinners at these occasions were unmarried. Married women were too busy with their babies and household chores to spin or weave. They left this work to adolescent girls and unmarried women—the spinsters of the age.

The significance of women's home production also was demonstrated by the appearance in public of prominent men and women dressed in homespun clothes. Wearing homespun would have been considered a sacrifice, for it was rough and unattractive compared to cloth imported from England. One year the entire graduating class of Harvard College attended commencement dressed in homespun. Political leaders of the revolutionary cause wore homespun for many public appearances. And many individuals, women and men, wore homespun as a way of demonstrating their support for the colonial government. As thirteen-year-old Anna Green Winslow put it in her journal in the winter of 1771, "As I am (as we say) a daughter of liberty, I chuse to wear as much of our own manufactory as possible." The efforts of girls like Anna were necessary to make the nonimportation agreements of colonial governments workable.

Direct and personal accounts of spinning bees are rare, but a variety of sources such as newspaper reports can create a picture of a typical bee. The following is a story of what one girl's experience might have been:

The young woman sat quietly beside her father on the seat of the wagon, glancing back to check on her spinning wheel whenever they jounced over potholes in the well worn road leading to town. She was excited and a little nervous, but her natural temperament was mild and so she just sat silently, thinking of the day ahead, not chatting with her father as other girls might have done. In fact, she was like her father in this regard. They both preferred action to words, and showed their thoughts by what they did rather than what they said. Today the daughter would show her opposition to the English Parliament by spinning in a public spinning bee held at the minister's home. The thread she produced could be woven into homespun cloth, a useful commodity now that the colonists were intent on reducing their dependence on imported English goods.

The wagon lurched as it came to a stop. Father and daughter jumped down to lift the heavy spinning wheel to the ground. They set it off to the side of the house, in a less conspicuous location than some others were choosing. While the young woman wanted to do her share to fight the hated taxes, she did not like being the center of attention. Proper women knew their place, and it was not in front of crowds. She would have preferred the quiet of her family's sitting room to the glare of the sun at the minister's house. But father said these public displays were important for teaching people their duty, and she had agreed to come for his sake. He was giving so much of his own time and money to oppose the new taxes. As a member of the local Sons of Liberty, it was his duty to make sure local shopkeepers and tavern keepers were observing the nonimportation agreements. His own store had suffered in trade since the agreements were signed, for now all his English goods were stacked in the back of the shop. He could not sell them, although he had paid for them with his own credit before the confrontation with England began. She had to help him. Fortunately, there were more and more wagons coming down the road. Many wheels would turn today, for the cause of liberty.

Fifty spinning wheels whirled and clicked through the morning. The girls and women worked hard, for at the end of the day they would see who had spun the most. Here was an opportunity to show industry and skill at the wheel, which were both valued traits in wives. At midday the wheels stopped and for a moment, an unnatural quiet settled on the crowd. The spinners were tired and hungry. Then a fiddle picked up and the laughing and talking began. They gathered around tables filled with local produce and piled their plates with the simple, homegrown fare. There were no teas imported from the Far East for this crowd. They drank herbal tea and coffee. This was one of their greatest sacrifices, for the colonists loved their imported teas. More than one person felt the effects of an upset stomach after drinking strong coffee that day.

By late afternoon the wheels turned slowly. The women's arms and backs ached with the efforts of the day. The town's minister rang the signal bell to stop the spinners, and as they joined their families he began his sermon in honor of the occasion. He praised the spinners for their work, calling them "Daughters of Liberty," and applauded the seriousness with which they, their families, and neighbors had treated the occasion. By showing their support for nonimportation, they had struck a blow for freedom and advanced the patriot cause. He concluded his words of praise and thanksgiving with a rousing call for further acts of female patriotism: "Yes, Ladies, you have it in your power more than all your committees and Congresses, to strike the Stroke, and make the Hills and Plains of America clap their hands." By making homespun and giving up tea and other imported goods, they could show the British "that American patriotism extends even to the Fair Sex, and discourage any future Attempts to enslave us." His words pleased the listeners, who seldom received much praise for the domestic chores they worked at day after day. Before and during the Revolution, the need for home production made women's work seem more important than it usually did.

After participating in a public ritual such as a spinning bee, girls and women could not help but have political thoughts and feelings. They said that after working all day they "felt Nationly," a new sentiment for many. Other women developed political opinions in response to different influences. In towns and cities, for example, women shopkeepers who might otherwise have wished to remain outside the fray were forced to decide whether they supported colonial resistance efforts. They were visited by local committees that made sure no one was selling imported English goods. With their activities scrutinized and their business reduced, the shopkeepers had to decide for themselves whether American resistance was necessary or foolish. In short, the colonists' efforts to persuade Parliament not to tax them aroused the female as well as the male population. It was virtually impossible not to form an opinion, and social customs dictating female silence on political questions went by the wayside. As Sarah Franklin wrote to her father, Benjamin Franklin, in the fall of 1765 (during the period of opposition to the taxes on legal documents, newspapers, and other goods imposed by the Stamp Act), "Nothing else is talked of. The Dutch talk of the stomp ack, the Negroes of the tamp. In short, everybody has something to say."

In the end most Americans resisted English taxes. Acceptance of a declaration of independence was another thing, however. Many Americans could not make the leap from tax resistance to military support for independence. Only after a full decade of agitation did leaders of the resistance effort convince the colonists that independence from England was the one way to guarantee their liberties. Even after the outbreak of war, the Loyalist minority was powerful. The group was composed of many leading citizens, men and women whose business, religious, and political ties to England made the prospect of independence unattractive. An estimated one-fifth of the colonists remained actively opposed to the Revolution throughout the war; another two-fifths were neutral. This neutral group showed a tendency to support whichever forces were winning, siding in particular with the troops that controlled their local communities. Basically, they just wanted to be left alone. Some neutrals, among them many Quakers, were pacifists. They opposed all warfare, particularly over issues such as taxation. Only about two-fifths of the population gave active support to the Patriot cause. With the neutrality or opposition of so many citizens, George Washington had a hard time forming and maintaining an army. That was one reason that the war lasted so long, more than six years.

For black Americans the choices were just as confusing and difficult as they were for whites. They were unsure which side, if any, they should support. The Patriots talked in glowing terms of freedom from slavery, but they meant freedom from their own enslavement to British tax officers rather than an end to the labor system that forced tens of thousands of Africans and African Americans into bondage. The British seemed to offer the best opportunity for enslaved people to improve their lives. In an attempt to undermine the Patriot cause, British commanders promised freedom to all slaves who joined the Royal Army. The offer applied to women and children as well as men, for the British were just as interested in preventing colonial farmers from maintaining a work force as they were in increasing the army's size. As a result, thousands of Africans and African Americans refused to join the revolutionary cause and sided with the Crown. Whenever the British army came near them, they abandoned their farms and plantations. These people fled from lives without hope, turning to the only available option for freedom.

The Sawyer family of Norfolk, Virginia, was one slave family that was determined to take the risks involved in escaping to the British lines. Living separately under three different owners, the mother, the father, and three children must have thought the British offer was their one chance to be together. In 1776 they made it to British-held territory. What they found there could only have terrified them. With inadequate food, shelter, and medical care, hundreds of escaped slaves were sick and dying from smallpox. Most of them would die that winter before they had the chance to begin a new life of any kind. The Sawyers were lucky. They were all still alive in 1782, when the British included them on a list of people deserving the continued protection of the Crown after the English surrender to the Americans.

Epidemic disease was a continual threat in all army camps, and one of the gravest problems for blacks who joined the British. Another serious difficulty was managing to escape with children. Women more often than men fled from slavery with children in tow, largely because fathers were so often separated from their families under the slave system. During mothers' escapes, babies and toddlers had to be carried, fed, and kept quiet. Young children had to be encouraged to be brave and uncomplaining as they traveled long distances with little food. When they finally reached British lines, women with children were faced with still more challenges. Children were more susceptible to disease than adults, so mothers had to struggle just to keep their offspring alive. And in addition to caring for their children, the women had to perform the work assigned to them by the British army.

The difficulties slave women faced in traveling with children explain why relatively few of them had attempted to escape from slavery before the Revolution. Until the English offered protection, there was no safe haven nearby. For women accompanied by small children, even a distance of a few miles could be an impossible obstacle to freedom. In their escapes, men and the few women who joined them traveled hundreds of miles to unknown areas. Some joined Indian communities; others traveled to distant colonies or Canada, usually on foot. All endured tremendous privations. Recapture was common, and stiff physical punishment the norm. Because it was virtually impossible to escape with children along, most women chose to remain where they were, enslaved but allowed to live with their daughters and sons.

After the English made their offer of protection, however, mothers suddenly saw that escape was possible. Thousands risked suffering, sickness, even death to win freedom for themselves and their children. Their bravery as they hid from their pursuers and comforted their frightened children cannot be overestimated. Ironically, the same force that drove them into the arms of the British—freedom—also compelled their masters and mistresses to join the revolutionary cause.

The onset of war forced white women to face other types of hardships and challenges. Twenty-year-old Jemima Condict of Pleasantdale, New Jersey, recorded in her journal her thoughts and fears as the conflict began. In the fall of 1774 she wrote, "It seams we have troublesome times a Coming for there is great Disturbance a Broad in the earth & they say it is tea that caused it. So then if they will Quarel about such a trifling thing as that What must we expect But war & I think or at least fear it will be so." Six months later her fears were realized. She then wrote:

> Monday Wich was Called Training Day I Rode with my Dear father Down to see them train, there being Several Companys met together. . . . How soon they will be Calld forth to the feild of war we Cannot tell, for by What we Can hear the Quarels are not like to be made up Without bloodshed. I have jest Now heard Say that All hopes of Conciliation Betwen Briten & her Colonies are at an end for Both the king & his Parliment have announced our Destruction. fleet and armies are Prepareing with utmost diligence for that Purpose.

The war began in Massachusetts on April 19, 1775, with the battles of Lexington and Concord. Word spread quickly throughout the colonies. Jemima Condict wrote of the first bloodshed of the war shortly after it occurred: "As every Day

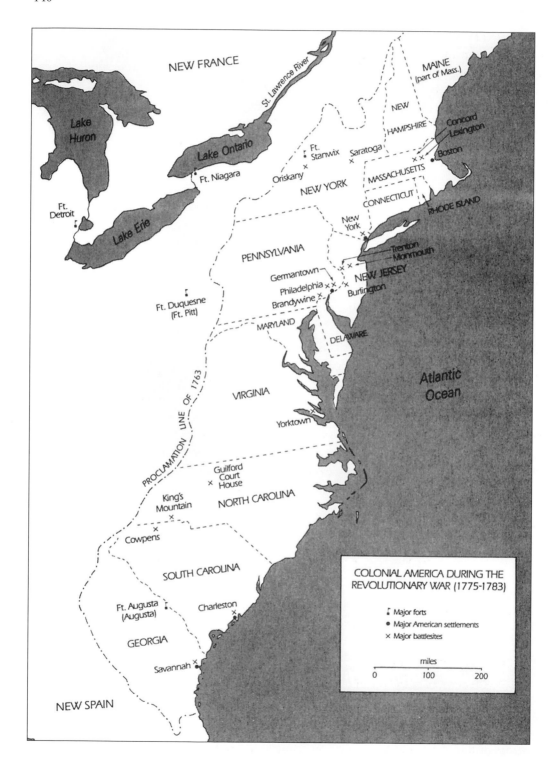

COLONIAL AMERICA DURING THE
REVOLUTIONARY WAR (1775-1783)

⌐ Major forts
● Major American settlements
× Major battlesites

miles

0   100   200

Brings New Troubels So this Day Brings News that yesterday very early in the morning They Began to fight at Boston, the regulers [British soldiers] We hear Shot first there." Jemima probably heard as well of the Battle of Bunker Hill, which took place near Boston on June 17. The British suffered their largest casualties of the war in that battle—more than 800 wounded and 228 killed.

After that, the two armies had no more major engagements for a year. Both sides dug in and waited. Then the British decided to leave New England, which they saw as the region of the colonies most hostile to their cause. In June 1776 they moved their army to New York, not far from Jemima Condict's home. Soon she was writing of the deaths of her neighbors' sons: "We hear News from our army ... & Several of them we hear is Dead. Sense there Departure Benjamin Canfcild & Stevan Morris, David Luis Died with the Camp Disorder & william acorn we hear was killed by the injins; Jabez freman, the Son of the Late Deceast John freman is Dead, Also Sias Heady Died up there with Sickness."

New Jersey women and men suffered tremendous hardships in the fall and winter of 1776–77. Failing in its attempt to defend New York City, the American army abandoned the city in late summer. Washington and his troops then retreated across New Jersey, with the British in pursuit. Unable to make a firm stand against the invaders, Washington's forces surrendered town after town. The English, and their hired German troops, known as Hessians, plundered and looted throughout the colony. Rape was common, as was the murder of unarmed civilians, including women and children. In this dark season, the Patriot cause seemed close to defeat. One woman, a Quaker named Margaret Morris, decided to remain in her home in Burlington, New Jersey, even though the British troops were approaching and many of her neighbors and friends were choosing to flee. Her journal, which she kept throughout the winter and spring of 1776–77, is a rich account of a woman's life in occupied territory during the war.

On December 7, 1776, Morris wrote, "A letter from my next neighbors Husband at the Camp, warnd her to be gone in haste, and many persons coming into Town today, brought intelligence that the British Army were advancing toward us." Morris, a widow, decided to remain in her house and trust in God to protect her. Her sister, who lived with her, agreed. As devout Quakers, the women had faith that God would not let the innocent suffer with the guilty. Although they never met with any personal injury that winter, they frequently feared for their lives. On the night of December 11, when "a large body of Hessians" arrived in Burlington, they hid in their cellar until the firing of cannons and muskets stopped. They learned the next day that Patriot troops had almost fired at their house. The troops thought that the light burning there meant Hessian soldiers were inside.

Women living close to the lines of battle had many opportunities to act bravely in the face of danger. Accounts of women serving as spies, carrying messages across enemy lines, and hiding men from their enemies were common throughout the war. Margaret Morris was one such courageous figure. A few days after the near attack on her house, American soldiers searched it for a Loyalist sympathizer, who was, in fact, hiding in a secret room. Morris's quick actions saved her friend from discovery. She reported the encounter later:

> A loud knocking at my door brought me to it. I was a little fluttered & kept locking and unlocking that I might get my ruffled face a little composed, at last I opend it, & half a dozen Men, all Armd, demanded the keys of the empty House [next door]. I asked what they wanted there they said to search for a D—d tory who had been spy[in]g at them from the Mill.

Morris was relieved that the soldiers believed the Tory was hiding at her neighbor's house and not in her own. She warned her friend of his danger by pulling a string attached to a bell in his hiding place: "I rung the bell violently, the Signal agreed on, if they came to Search." Then Morris played the fool to further mislead the search party:

> "I put on a very simple look & cryd out, bless me, I hope you are not Hessians—say, good Men, are you the Hessians?"
> "Do we look like Hessians?" asked one of them rudely.
> "Indeed I dont know."
> "Did you never see a Hessian?"
> "No never in my life But they *are Men,* & you are Men, and may be Hessians for any thing I know—but Ill go with you into Col[onel] Co[xe's] house."

She proudly concluded her story: "So I marchd at the head of them, opend the door, & searchd every place but we could not find the tory—strange where he could be." That night she went into Burlington with her "refugee," as she called him, and found him safer quarters. On the way home she seized an opportunity to do another good deed: "I was told to day of a design to seize on the person of a Young Man in town, as he was deemed a tory. I thought a hint w[oul]d be kindly rec[eive]d and as I came back calld on a fr[ien]d of his, & told him—next day he was out of . . . reach."

Quakers such as Margaret Morris often sympathized with the Loyalists. They thought the Patriot call to arms was sinful and unnecessary. Yet many Quakers, Morris among them, clearly supported the efforts of their revolutionary neighbors as well. Morris referred to Washington's army as "hers," and provided food and shelter to hungry Patriots whenever she could. After Washington defeated the British at the Battle of Trenton on December 26, 1776, American soldiers landed at Morris's wharf and spent the night in her neighbor's empty house, which she took care of. One man later wrote in his journal, "The good woman next Door Sent us 2 Mince pies Last Night, which I took very kind."

A few days later, when other soldiers had stopped to sleep in the house, she visited them to tend the fires and mourned for their suffering: "About bed time I went in the next house to see if the fires were safe, & my heart was melted with Compassion to see such a number of my fellow Creatures lying like Swine on the floor fast aSleep, & many of them without even a Blanket to cover them." As a mother, Morris's heart went out not only to the young men, but also to their mothers, who did not know the suffering of their children. When the soldiers left, she wrote pensively in her journal, "Several of *my* Soldiers left the next house, & returnd to the place from whence they came. . . . There were several pritty innocent looking lads among them, & I simpathized with thier Mothers when I saw them preparing to return to the Army."

Later that spring Morris was called on to perform another service for the military. Like many other women during the war, she used her knowledge of medicine and healing to help the sick. Several Patriot boatmen and their wives were ill and needed medical attention, but no doctor was available. As a skilled healer, Morris kept medicines at hand to give to the poor. Her reputation in town caused them to turn to her for help, but she hesitated to leave her house. "They Ventured to come to me—& in a very humble manner begd me to come and do something for them—At first I thought they might have a design to put a trick upon me & get me aboard of thier Gondolas—& then pillage my house, as they had done some others." But after discovering that the sick people were lodging in the governor's house, which she considered safe, Morris went to see them. She correctly diagnosed their illness as "the itch fever," and treated them so that they all recovered. "They Thankfully acknowledged my kindness," she wrote.

Morris's experiences were common for women who lived near the scenes of battle. When asked, local women performed many services for the soldiers on both sides. But the armies did not depend only, or even predominantly, on local residents for provisions and medical care. Many women traveled with the troops and worked for wages as cooks, laundresses, and nurses. They were known as camp followers, and are remembered, unfortunately, more for the sexual services they provided than for any others. But the soldiers relied on the food they prepared, the wounds they dressed, and the shirts they washed. Camp followers provided an important and necessary labor force for the armies. Continually short of manpower, Washington's army depended heavily on its womanpower to take care of the day-to-day needs of the soldiers.

Some women, especially those with no children and no independent means of support, became camp followers by accompanying their husbands into service. Traveling with the army, they could share their husbands' lives and offer them extra care and encouragement. They also were fed by the army, a significant consideration for many of these poor women. Others were escaped slaves or free blacks looking for a way to support themselves during the war. Still others *were* prostitutes or became prostitutes to earn money after they began working for the army.

This woodcut of a woman holding a musket was printed in "A New Touch on the Times . . . By a Daughter of Liberty," published in Massachusetts in 1779. The identity of the woman is not known, but her firm posture reveals her determination to aid the Patriot cause.

A few women rejected traditional female roles during the war and took on men's jobs. Women such as Mary Hays McCauley were not content to remain behind the lines during a battle. She earned the nickname Molly Pitcher because she carried water to thirsty soldiers on the front lines. On June 28, 1778, at the Battle of Monmouth, New Jersey, Molly's husband fell, either because he was wounded or merely overcome by the fatigue of the battle. Molly then assumed his place and loaded a cannon until the end of the engagement. Her bravery later earned her an annuity, an annual payment, from the federal government.

The winter of 1776–77 marked one of the lowest points of the war for the Patriot cause. General Washington had not yet proved himself an able commander, and the British were sending more and more troops to the colonies. On the assumption that a strong show of force would frighten the colonists into submission, England was dispatching a larger number of men to America than it had ever before sent overseas. The English had never fought a war like this one and had underestimated the difficulties of subduing a population spread over a vast territory. Even though many colonists openly or tacitly supported England in the war, not all chose to fight on the side of the British armies. The Loyalists gave England little actual help, and the Patriots were a fiercely driven minority.

The Patriots' determination became clear after the English easily entered and gained control over Philadelphia, Pennsylvania, in the late summer of 1777. Philadelphia was the capital of the fledgling United States and a port of strategic importance. The city was also filled with Loyalist sympathizers and neutrals because of its large Quaker population. But despite the English victory there, the people in the countryside refused to surrender. Washington's army had lost the city, but had defended it well in two engagements. And a major American victory at Saratoga, New York, in mid-October gave the Patriot cause new strength. In that battle more than six thousand Loyalist soldiers had been forced to lay down their arms.

When France entered the war on the side of the Americans in February 1778, Washington and his advisers became even more confident of their ability to win. The English might have captured major ports, such as New York and Philadelphia, but they could not control the countryside. The Americans suspected that these outlying areas were where the Revolution would be won.

The loss at Saratoga and stiff resistance in Philadelphia caused English commanders to reassess their overall strategy. They decided to shift the main focus of the fighting to the South. The English believed there were many more Loyalists or neutrals in the southern colonies than in the North, which meant the southern population would be easier to subdue. In fact, more southerners *did* have mixed feelings about the war. Many slaveholders feared losing their workers to the British. Even worse, they feared slave revolts. In Georgia the number of blacks equaled the number of whites. In South Carolina the majority (more than 60 percent) of the population was black. Support for the Revolution was noticeably cooler in these colonies than it was in New England or the middle colonies.

The first southern engagements of the war in 1779 convinced the English that they were right. Savannah and Augusta, two of Georgia's major cities, fell easily. The British then committed a large force to the defeat of Charleston, South Carolina, which fell in May 1780. General Benjamin Lincoln, the leader of the Americans in Charleston, was forced to surrender his entire army of 5,500 men along with the city. As English troops fanned out over the countryside, hopes faded. Many previously neutral people joined the invaders, convinced that they would be the ultimate winners.

Faced with these disasters, the Patriots held firm. Instead of giving up, they dedicated themselves to the war effort with renewed energy. One sign that the Patriot cause was alive and well was an intercolonial effort by women to raise money for the troops. Not since the Revolution's early days, when the Daughters of Liberty held their spinning bees, had women organized in support of independence. Although many women made sacrifices throughout the war, they did so individually.

After the fall of Charleston, a group of elite women in Philadelphia led by Esther DeBerdt Reed, wife of Joseph Reed, the governor of Pennsylvania, decided that a major, unified effort was necessary to encourage the troops. They formed a committee to go door-to-door in the city to ask the women and girls of each household to contribute money for the soldiers. The committee suggested that women with large or medium-sized incomes go without luxuries, such as fancy hairstyles and jewelry, and give equivalent money to the cause. Poorer women were asked to contribute whatever they could. No one was overlooked.

To prepare the city's inhabitants for the collection, Reed wrote an article titled "Sentiments of an American Woman." It said that American women should express their gratitude to the troops for their tremendous personal sacrifice in defending the colonies. Fending off potential criticism of her committee's efforts as unfeminine, she noted that many women in the past had acted heroically for their people and their countries and received praise for doing so. Joan of Arc was her favorite example, but she also cited Old Testament figures, female monarchs, and Roman matrons. She then argued that opposition to the women's relief effort would be unpatriotic. Her defensiveness and the care with which she justified the women's work before they had even begun shows that this effort was an unprecedented activity for women.

Philadelphia women collected a large sum for the troops in the early summer of 1780. They then expanded their efforts, writing to friends and relatives in other areas encouraging their participation in the fund-raising campaign. Esther Reed's "Sentiments" was published in newspapers throughout the colonies in July. In response, women in other colonies set about organizing their own committees. When all the money was collected, Reed wrote to General Washington informing him of the women's gift. His grateful reply included a request that the money be used to make shirts, because the troops were poorly clothed and winter was approaching. If the women made the shirts themselves, Washington noted, the army could save additional money by avoiding the cost of hiring seamstresses.

Reed was disappointed by this suggestion. She wanted to give the men something special, a monetary supplement to the pay they were receiving from the government. She did not want the women's gift to become a substitute for clothing the troops already should have been given for their services. Reed wrote to Washington, "Soldiers woud not be so much gratified by bestowing an article to which they look upon themselves entitled from the public as in some other method which woud convey more fully the Idea of a reward for past Services & an incitement to future Duty." She proposed that instead of shirts, money be delivered directly into the hands of the men. She wanted each soldier to receive two dollars in hard currency, rather than the depreciated continental paper money they usually received as pay.

Washington rejected Reed's proposal. He insisted that the women make shirts. To give the soldiers hard currency would only encourage their dissatisfaction with what the government could provide. "A taste of hard money," he wrote, "may be productive of much discontent as we have none but depreciated paper for their pay." In addition, he feared that some men would spend the money foolishly on drink.

Although disappointed that she could not do something more directly beneficial for the soldiers, Esther Reed accepted Washington's suggestion and organized the production of the shirts. Tragically, she died of dysentery before her work was completed, but others took it up. In late December 1780 thousands of shirts, each embroidered with the name of the woman who had made it, were sent to the quartermaster general in Philadelphia. Praising the women for their patriotism, Washington offered his thanks on behalf of the troops. He assured the women that his men would appreciate the shirts and bless them for their efforts.

The women's original goal—raising funds—was untraditional. Yet ultimately they were forced back into a traditional female role, that of seamstress. Washington probably believed that the money would be best used for shirts, but he ignored the sentiments of the women involved when he asked them to make the clothing. The women wanted to do much more. In the end, however, they did achieve something greater than just sewing for the army. They created the Ladies Association, the first intercolonial women's organization in North America. Before the Revolution there was no such thing as a women's club. Even church or maternal associations were unheard of. By organizing to provide active support for a cause they believed in, these women learned the value of working together. They also demonstrated to themselves and to men that they could perform tasks traditionally defined as men's work. The Ladies Association, therefore, taught the new nation something important about women's interests, values, and goals. Just like men, Patriot women could express their political beliefs through their actions. After the war some women remembered the lessons they had learned and founded women's organizations to serve other ends. And they did not forget the political lesson that activism was required to meet the challenges of the age.

Despite the Patriots' best efforts, the campaigns of 1780 went badly for the American cause. The British did well in the early southern campaigns, as thousands of white Loyalists and escaping black slaves came to their assistance. But although the British could capture territory, they could not defend it. Bands of marauding Patriots kept the British from establishing firm control over rural areas.

In the winter and spring of 1780–81 American armies were successful in a number of engagements. They defeated the British first at Kings Mountain and then at Cowpens, both near the border between North and South Carolina. At Guilford Court House, North Carolina, General Nathanael Greene decimated the main English army under Charles Cornwallis in March 1781. Then, as Cornwallis moved his troops north into Virginia, he made a disastrous mistake. Stationing his large force of 7,200 men on a peninsula between the York and James rivers, he left the army vulnerable to attack from both land and sea. Washington recognized his foe's error and quickly moved the largest body of his troops from New York to Virginia. As a French fleet attacked the English vessels sent to rescue Cornwallis, Washington trapped the English general. Cornwallis surrendered his army on October 19, 1781. This battle was the last major engagement between the British and the Americans. In response to Cornwallis's humiliating defeat, the English Parliament voted to cease military operations. Independence had been won.

Independence Realized: New Directions for American Women

The Treaty of Paris, which ended the American Revolution, gave Americans an unusual opportunity in modern history: the chance to create a republican form of government. At the time only two nations—Switzerland and Holland—were republics. Hereditary positions in governing bodies (such as the House of Lords in the English Parliament) were common in Europe. They gave certain families the automatic right to govern. Many people believed that large and populous nations needed the kind of discipline that monarchs could impose. The United States, therefore, was embarking on untried ground as it readied itself for republican rule.

Political theorists at the end of the eighteenth century taught that republics were fragile. Their survival depended on a homogeneous population that believed in honesty, frugality, and sacrifice for the common good. Citizens of a republic had to be both personally virtuous and dedicated to preserving high moral values in their leaders. Honorable and intelligent men needed to elect leaders who could rule dispassionately, with an eye to promoting the welfare of the country as a whole. Narrow self-interest had no place in a republic. Leaders had to be willing to make political compromises, because continual disagreements on basic issues could rip a republic apart. These requirements were particularly important to a republic as geographically large and as ethnically and culturally diverse as the new United States.

The first issue of the *Lady's Magazine and Repository of Entertaining Knowledge* (1792), published in Philadelphia, combines American patriotic stars with classical imagery to represent republican women. In an allusion to *A Vindication of the Rights of Woman,* a radical but widely read book by the British writer Mary Wollstonecraft, a woman presents a petition called "The Rights of Woman" to the figure of Liberty.

People all over the world asked themselves: Are the citizens of the United States virtuous enough to be citizens of a republic? Is there enough honor in the souls of the voters to prevent them from accepting bribes? Are they intelligent enough, and respectful enough, to choose the right representatives? Although many leaders of the Revolution believed Americans were extremely virtuous, they could not be sure their new system of government would work. Danger signs were all around them.

Following the war, Americans quickly returned to prerevolutionary standards of dress and consumption. After years of sacrifice for the revolutionary cause, people in the middle and upper ranks of society once again wanted to display their wealth and good taste. Gone was homespun; on display were imported silks and satins. Even more disturbing was the fact that common working men and farmers, who lacked the advantages of higher education, were being elected to high government offices. Some people worried that they did not have the proper intellectual background for leadership roles at this critical time.

One response to concern over the capabilities of voters was widespread improvement in public education. Rather than concluding that representative democracy was too risky an experiment (the position of Loyalists and many neutrals as well), supporters of the United States worked to improve the intellectual capacity of the average citizen. Soon after the Revolution, voters in northern states first called for the use of tax money to finance public schools. In 1789 Massachusetts became the first state to require towns to provide free elementary education to all children. The South could not immediately imitate this and other progressive developments. Devastated by years of British occupation during the war, southerners concentrated on reestablishing their economy. But elsewhere, in the middle and northern areas of the country, more and more free schools opened their doors. "The Spirit for Academy making is vigorous," wrote Congregational minister Ezra Stiles in 1786. He had witnessed the opening of twelve new academies in Connecticut in just five years.

Republican leaders also acted to improve the educational environment of the nation in other ways. Before the American Revolution, education was viewed by most people as a means of promoting the personal well-being of their children, not the well-being of society as a whole. As a result, more sons than daughters were educated, and to a higher level. Most people considered higher education unsuitable for girls, believing it would make them unfit for their duties as wives and mothers. As one man, a Harvard graduate, put it, "Girls knew quite enough if they could make a shirt and a pudding." The Connecticut poet John Trumbull expressed his feelings in verse:

> And why should girls be learned or wise,
> Books only serve to spoil their eyes.
> The studious eye but faintly twinkles
> And reading paves the way to wrinkles.

Colonial parents were also concerned about the expense of educating daughters, because most teachers then were hired privately.

Many people thought girls needed to read so that they could study the Bible and later instruct their own children at a basic level. Writing, however, was considered a frill, and arithmetic was taught only to a privileged few girls. "I regret the trifling narrow contracted Education of the Females of my own country," wrote Abigail Adams to her husband John in 1778. "You need not be told how much female Education is neglected, nor how fashionable it has been to ridicule Female learning."

Similar attitudes affected the education provided for boys at the lower ranks of society. Their future work as farmers, clerks, or laborers did not require higher learning. Most people thought that common working men needed only basic literacy and some facility with numbers so they could keep accounts. These assumptions changed with the establishment of a republic. Now, in addition to rudimentary reading, writing, and arithmetic, schools sought to teach children to think independently, reason, and express their opinions clearly and forcefully. According to Thomas Jefferson, even primary schools should be designed to "instruct the mass of our citizens in these their rights, interests and duties, as men and citizens." Now history, rhetoric, and oratory—subjects that previously had been taught only to boys headed for college—were included in the basic curriculum for all students in public schools.

For the first time independent thinking also became a desirable characteristic in women. The instruction of girls was not meant to prepare them to take part in political life. Women were not citizens on a par with men in the new United States. Except in New Jersey, they could not vote or hold public office. In most ways the establishment of a republic had left women's political status unchanged. But in a few important if subtle areas, progress was made. Women's work as mothers assumed greater political importance. Mothers were largely responsible for the early education of their children. They could rear either strong, virtuous children who would become valuable citizens or lazy, ignorant youngsters who would be corrupted easily and thus become undesirable members of society. Because of this influence, much of the future of the nation was seen as resting with its mothers. As one young woman explained:

> A woman who is skilled in every useful art, who practices every domestic virtue ... may, by her precept and example, inspire her brothers, her husband, or her sons, with such a love of virtue, such just ideas of the true value of civil liberty ... that future heroes and statesmen, when arrived at the summit of military or political fame, shall exaltingly declare, it is to my mother I owe this elevation.

Women's work as mothers was considered most important in the rearing of sons, who would participate directly in the political life of the republic. But even women without sons received recognition. Virtuous women were thought to influence all the men around them. Acting the part of good citizens would be easier for husbands, brothers, and fathers if they received the support of their female relatives.

For women to do their job properly, they needed to possess high moral standards. They could learn these standards best if they were educated and religious. Ideally, all women should be able to read, write, keep accounts, and think logically about current issues. They were also expected to attend church and heed the moral directions of their ministers.

The middle and upper ranks of American society had even higher standards for women's education by the end of the eighteenth century. Among wealthy women, poor reading, writing, and speaking skills became socially unacceptable. Elite men wanted their daughters to receive an education similar to that of their college-bound sons. At the same time, young men came to value educated young women as marriage partners. They wanted their wives to be capable not only of raising their children properly, but also of conversing intelligently about the topics of the day. As Benjamin Rush, a Philadelphia physician noted for his efforts to improve female education, explained, "One cause of the misery of many families, as well as communities, may be sought for in the *mediocrity* of knowledge of the women. They should know more . . . in order to be happy themselves, and to communicate happiness to others."

In response to this demand, educators in the major urban areas of the Northeast opened female academies, which were roughly the equivalent of high schools today. Their founding was a major breakthrough for women's education. The curriculum of female academies focused a great deal of attention on subjects previously considered frills: rhetoric, grammar, geography, history, arithmetic, and oratory. Now the areas of study that once had been thought essential for elite women—music, dancing, and needlework—were regarded as recreational activities or not taught at all. Although many girls continued to study these subjects and to receive praise for doing so, intellectual development was regarded as equally or more important.

One of the earliest and most successful female academies was the Philadelphia Young Ladies' Academy. Most of its students were from local families, but some came from as far away as Maine, South Carolina, and the West Indies. They lived with relatives or friends in the city and attended the school by day. For the first time, girls from elite families regularly left home to attend school. Before the Revolution wealthy men occasionally had sent their daughters abroad to study and learn the highest social graces, but the behavior of these fathers was considered almost eccentric. Now, sending a daughter to a female academy became an important way for a family to demonstrate its social standing and good taste.

Soon boarding schools for girls also opened. They appeared in rural areas as well as towns and answered a need for families who did not have relatives living in a northeastern city. One of the most successful was the Moravian Seminary in

Bethlehem, Pennsylvania, which had a reputation for strictly supervising the morals of its students while providing an advanced curriculum. As one mother, Elizabeth Chester, reported to an acquaintance, "The people of the society appear very amiable in their manners; and honest simplicity, void of affectation characterizes them. . . . As to the morals of a child, the Parent may repose entire confidence in the directors, who pay the strictest attention to check every deviation from delicacy & decorum."

Parents were particularly concerned that their daughters receive moral instruction at boarding schools, where girls lived for extended periods of time. At the Moravian Seminary, for example, students stayed for a maximum of about three years, beginning when they were as young as ten to twelve years old. Chester was also careful to note, "The [school] government is a government of persuasion, calculated more to attach the affections than pain the body." Her comment indicates that the teachers did not punish the students by striking them, a common method of managing unruly schoolboys during this period.

Letters between young scholars and their parents reveal that the girls understood the importance of their new educational opportunities but also missed the comforts and emotional support of home. Fourteen-year-old Eliza Southgate, away from home for the first time, wrote of her new experiences:

> Medford, May 12, 1797
>
> Honored Parents:
>
> With pleasure I sit down to the best of parents to inform them of my situation, as doubtless they are anxious to hear,—permit me to tell them something of my foolish heart. When I first came here I gave myself up to reflection, but not pleasing reflections. When Mr. Boyd [her brother-in-law] left me I burst into tears and instead of trying to calm my feelings I tried to feel worse. I begin to feel happier and will soon gather up all my Philosophy and think of the duty that now attends me, to think that here I may drink freely of the fountain of knowledge, but I will not dwell any longer on this subject. I am not doing anything but writing, reading, and cyphering. There is a French Master coming next Monday, and he will teach French and Dancing. William Boyd and Mr. Wyman advise me to learn French, yet if I do at all I wish you to write me very soon what you think best. . . . Mr. Wyman says I must learn Geometry before Geography, and that I better not begin till I have got through my Cyphering.
>
> We get up early in the morning and make our beds and sweep the chamber, it is a chamber about as large as our kitchen chamber, and a little better finished. There's 4 beds in the chamber, and two persons in each bed, we have chocolate for breakfast and supper.
>
> Your affectionate Daughter
> ELIZA SOUTHGATE

When mothers wrote to their daughters at school, they frequently stressed the importance of diligence and urged their daughters not to waste their time. In turn, many girls recognized that they had been given a privilege their mothers had not enjoyed, and that their absence from home represented considerable maternal sacrifice. After all, during these years they could be of greatest help to their mothers in running their households. For some families, doing without a teenage daughter's labor must have been as difficult as paying the cost of her higher education. With this in mind, Eliza wrote apologetically to her mother when she learned that her younger siblings were ill:

> Medford, Aug. 14, 1797
>
> Dear Mother:
>
> I am very sorry for your trouble, and sympathize with you in it. I now regret being from home, more than ever, for I think I might be of service to you now the children are sick. I hope they will be as much favored in their sickness now, as they were when they had the measles. I am very sorry that Jane has broken her arm, for it generally causes a long confinement, and I fear she has not got patience enough to bear it without a great deal of trouble. I suppose that Isabella will be very much worried about her babe. I would thank you to write me very often now—for I shall be very anxious about the children.
>
> I am your affectionate and dutiful daughter
>
> ELIZA SOUTHGATE

Although Eliza regretted her yearlong absence from home, she also enjoyed the intellectual atmosphere of school. At times her work gained precedence over her family obligations, and she forgot to write to her parents. When she wrote the following letter, the homesickness she had felt only a few months earlier was apparently gone:

> Medford, Sept. 30, 1797
>
> Dear Mother:
>
> You mentioned in yours, of the 16th inst. that it was a long time since you had received a letter from me; but it was owing to my studies which took up the greater part of my time; for I have been busy in my Arithmetic, but I finished it yesterday, and expect now to begin my large manuscript Arithmetic. You say that you shall regret so long an absence; not more certainly than I shall, but a strong desire to possess more useful knowledge than I at present do, I can dispense with the pleasure a little longer of beholding my friends and I hope I shall be better prepared to meet my good parents towards whom my heart overflows with gratitude.
>
> Your ever affectionate daughter
>
> ELIZA SOUTHGATE

Eliza's devotion to her work led her to ask her parents if she could continue her education at a better school. After studying for nine months at Mr. Wyman's school in Medford, Massachusetts, Eliza spent "a quarter" at Susanna Rowson's Young Ladies Academy in Boston. This school was one of the best academies of the day. It was headed by an accomplished woman of letters who was then famous as an actress, musician, playwright, and novelist. The variety and high quality of Rowson's publications marked her as one of the foremost female writers of the new United States. The appearance and popularity of their works also signaled that for the first time women had become prominent in the American literary scene.

Rowson is best known as the author of *Charlotte Temple* (London, 1791; Philadelphia, 1794), which is now known as the first American best-seller. The plot, a common one for the day, involved the seduction and betrayal of an innocent young woman by a scoundrel. Rowson, however, used this familiar material to criticize, implicitly, the sexual roles of women and men in the late eighteenth century. In addition to *Charlotte Temple* and a number of other novels, plays, and morality tales, Rowson wrote textbooks out of her dissatisfaction with available offerings and her devotion to teaching her students well. They included *An Abridgement of Universal Geography, together with Sketches of History* (circa 1805); *A Spelling Dictionary* (1807); and *Biblical Dialogues between a Father and His Family* (1822).

Rowson's students generally adored her, and Eliza Southgate was no exception. She wrote to her father, "I am again placed at school under the tuition of an amiable lady, so mild, so good, no one can help loving her; she treats all her scholars with such a tenderness as would win the affection of the most savage brute. . . . I never was happier in my life I think, and my heart overflows toward my heavenly Father for it." No doubt Eliza would have preferred to spend more time at the Boston academy, but her year of study was up in May 1798. She then returned to her family without a coveted diploma.

To receive a diploma from one of the female academies, girls had to pass examinations in the subjects covered by the curriculum. These tests were given over a number of days, and aroused a great deal of anxiety in the students, judging by the letters they wrote to their relatives. As one student, Margaret Akerly, complained to her sister, "I have so much to learn I dont know what to do with myself I hardly know what I write I think of nothing only what I have to learn; this morning I was up at 4 oClock sitting by the Lamp studying & every night I have 3 or 4 books under my head." (One wonders if Margaret passed her examination in grammar, given the poor use of punctuation in her letter.)

Graduation ceremonies often included speeches by the valedictorian and salutatorian. Such occasions marked one of the rare opportunities eighteenth-century girls or women had to deliver public speeches. Copies of some of the speeches have survived and show that the orators saw themselves as leaders, but leaders without a future. Although girls strove for academic excellence, they had nowhere to employ their educations after graduation. Colleges were closed to women during this era, and so were the professions. Women might become skilled healers, but they could not attend medical school and become licensed physicians. They might offer religious instruction in their homes, but they could not serve as ministers for any congregations, except those of the Quakers. They might run successful businesses as single women, but when they married, the law demanded that they have their husbands' permission to continue working outside the home.

The one option open to women in the early years of the United States was marriage and motherhood. Most women accepted their role without complaint. Family life offered them many comforts. But it could not satisfy their intellectual longings, and even in the first generation of academy-educated girls and women, some pressed for change. For example, in her salutatory address to the Philadelphia Young Ladies' Academy in 1793, Priscilla Mason argued against social customs that gave men (to whom she refers as "lords") the right to control women's lives:

> Our high and mighty Lords (thanks to their arbitrary constitutions) have denied us the means of knowledge, and then reproached us for the want of it. Being the stronger party, they early seized the sceptre and the sword; with these they gave laws to society; they denied women the advantage of a liberal education; forbid them to exercise their talents on those great occasions, which would serve to improve them. . . . Happily, a more liberal way of thinking begins to prevail. The sources of knowledge are gradually opening to our sex. . . . But supposing now that we posses'd all the talents of the orator, in the highest perfection; where shall we find a theatre for the display of them? The Church, the Bar, and the Senate are shut against us. Who shut them? Man; despotic man, first made us incapable of the duty, and then forbid us the exercise. Let us by suitable education, qualify ourselves for those high departments—they will open before us.

As a Quaker, Mason went on to explain that for members of that sect, a forum for female religious oratory was already available. Unlike other churches of the era, the Society of Friends encouraged women as well as men to offer religious instruction during meeting, as they called their religious services. Women, like men, could become ministers and travel as missionaries to preach the faith. Through separate women's meetings, they were also responsible for overseeing certain areas of family life, including marriage, inheritance, and the management of children. Indeed, women with Quaker backgrounds often served as leaders in the early women's rights movement in the United States. Their work experience in the Society of Friends had prepared them to be leaders in a culture that expected women to be silent, especially in public.

But even among Quakers, women were not considered the equals of men and generally played secondary roles. Although the education of girls such as Priscilla Mason led them to expect further significant gains for women in the near future,

Westtown Boarding School, a coeducational institution founded in 1799, was one of the most important Quaker schools in Pennsylvania. Especially designed to educate rural women, it taught "domestic employments" as well as academic subjects.

these did not materialize. Each step forward for women took time and a great deal of effort on the part of individuals. Sometimes an apparent gain in women's rights was followed by backsliding, and retrenchment made it even harder to push forward again.

One such temporary advance occurred in New Jersey in 1776. At the height of revolutionary fervor, the state wrote its first constitution. Although other states granted the right to vote only to men, the delegates to New Jersey's constitutional convention extended the franchise to "all free inhabitants." As one state representative explained, "Our Constitution gives this right to maids or widows *black or white.*" Wives were excluded because they were seen as less capable of independent action than single women. Most people assumed that a married woman would vote as her husband told her to, not as her own conscience dictated. Unmarried women, whether spinsters or widows, would not feel so compelled to follow the instructions of male relatives and friends. They would act for themselves at the polls, just as they did in managing their private affairs.

These attitudes reflected theories about women's property rights. The eminent English legal authority Sir William Blackstone had explained the legal position of married women this way in his *Commentaries on the Laws of England*, which was published shortly before the Revolution: "By marriage, the husband and wife are one person in law; that is, the very being or legal existence of the woman is suspended during the marriage, or at least is incorporated and consolidated into that of the husband; under whose wing, protection, and *cover* she performs every thing."

Under the laws of England as enforced in the United States, married women could not own property in their own name without special (and rare) contracts called marriage settlements. Everything a woman brought to marriage became her husband's. Movable goods became her husband's absolutely, and a man could sell or give away his wife's movables at will. Men's control over women's real estate was restricted, however. A husband could not mortgage or sell his wife's land unless the woman consented and signed deeds stating she did so of her own free will. But during marriage, a man could manage his wife's real estate and take all the rents and profits for his own use. These laws stemmed from a belief that families could be provided for best if the head of the family—the man—controlled all of the family's assets. In exchange for his wife's property, a husband became legally responsible for providing his wife with the necessities of life. If he neglected her, a woman could sue for support and be protected by the courts.

Restrictions on the political rights of married women flowed naturally from restrictions on their property rights. Just as men were obliged under the law to support their wives financially, the political system of the age assumed that husbands represented their wives as well as themselves when they cast their votes. The couple acted as a unit, represented by the husband. A second argument against allowing married women to vote was that they were not viewed as independent persons. Political theorists regarded women as incapable of exercising the franchise because they were subject to their husbands' influence. As one commentator asked, "How can a fair one refuse her lover?"

For the same reason, men without property also could not vote. Just like women, they were not independent persons. To earn a living, they were forced to work for others, and therefore their votes might be coerced or purchased.

Given these commonly held assumptions about women's rights, the New Jersey Constitution of 1776 was a surprise. In this state alone, revolutionary leaders extended the democratic ideal to include women. The restriction of their reform to single women "worth fifty pounds clear estate" and over the age of twenty-one is consistent with the theories of the day. The fact that they gave the vote to any women at all is not. What happened?

According to some historians, the New Jersey delegates were influenced by revolutionary ideals of justice more than anything else. They firmly believed that property holders of either sex should have a vote. By giving some women, but not all men, the vote, they were upholding the sanctity of property. They also were acknowledging the growth of women's political awareness during the war and the tremendous sacrifices made by New Jersey women in the early campaigns. Finally, Quakers, who believed in the equality of the sexes, had a strong influence in state politics during this period. The franchise clause probably was drafted by John Cooper, a prominent Quaker.

This explanation has not proved convincing to all historians of revolutionary era women. Some believe the initial wording of the New Jersey Constitution was an oversight rather than a deliberate step to enfranchise women. They argue that belief in the political subservience of women was too firmly entrenched to allow such a radical step to occur, particularly without public commentary in the press. Instead, they argue, women took advantage of the loose wording of the constitution. Voting regularly in local and statewide elections over the years, they gradually established a legal precedent that male politicians could not ignore. By 1790, when the state wrote a new election law, the men were ready to define voters explicitly as "he or she." As the statesman Elias Boudinot proclaimed in a Fourth of July oration delivered in Elizabeth Town, New Jersey, in 1793, "The rights of women are no longer strange sounds to an American ear, and I devoutly hope the day is not far distant when we shall find them dignifying in a distinguishing code, the jurisprudence of several states of the Union."

During the years when women were enfranchised in New Jersey, they seized the opportunity to act independently. Women's names appeared on town voting lists, newspaper reports noted the appearance of women at the polls, and political detractors and supporters of female suffrage alike commented on women's political activities. Women in other states expressed their envy of New Jersey women. One, Susan Boudinot Bradford, wrote, "I congratulate the ladies of New Jersey that they are in some thing put on a footing with the gentlemen and the most extraordinary part [of] it is, that it has been done by the gentlemen themselves but these are a few who have been more enlightened than the rest."

In fact, the very success of female suffrage in New Jersey contributed to its demise. After the establishment of America's first political parties (the Federalists and the Republicans) in 1789, women became an interest group courted by politicians, especially in close elections. Each party feared that the other would gain the support of women. And each side derided women's participation in elections when they thought they had been hurt by it but at the next election attempted once again to gain the support of women.

In the election of 1800, for example, Federalists Alexander Hamilton and Senator Matthias Ogden "so ingratiated themselves in the esteem of the Federalist ladies of Elizabeth-town, and in the lower part of the state," a Newark newspaper reported, "as to induce them (as it is said) to resolve on turning out to support the Federal ticket in the ensuing elections." Meanwhile, Republican politicians tried to win women voters with fiery speeches. As one orator proclaimed, "Our daughters are the same relation to us as our sons; we owe them the same duties; they have the same science, and are equally competent to their attainments. The contrary idea originated in the same abuse of power, as monarchy and slavery, and owes its little remaining support to stale sophistry." He then recited a long list of heroic women who had proved the equality of the sexes by their actions and writings. The speaker concluded, "The history of women is forever obtruding on our unwilling eyes bold and ardent spirits, who no tyrant could tame—no prejudice enslave. . . . Female-Citizens, follow examples so glorious; accept the station nature intended for you, and double the knowledge and happiness of mankind." They could do that best, he claimed, by voting for the Republican ticket.

Women continued to participate in New Jersey politics until 1807, when the election law was rewritten. Women, blacks, and aliens lost the vote at that time. The wording of the election law was part of a compromise between liberal and conservative Republicans, who had gained political control of the state but were in danger of losing power over their party. The move also was part of a widespread cultural shift away from radicalism. New Jerseyans, like Americans generally, did not want to face the full social implications of their revolutionary heritage. No other state had imitated New Jersey's example by giving women the vote. Elsewhere, even as slavery was abolished in the North, blacks were losing the franchise and other basic rights. Americans had their republic. But they were not yet ready to make it a full democracy.

During this era, all other legal reforms affecting white women focused exclusively on their private lives. (For black women, the end of slavery in the North was the most significant postrevolutionary reform.) One of the most important of these legal changes concerned divorce. Under English law as enforced in the colonies, absolute divorces that gave couples the right to remarry were virtually impossible to obtain. They were available only to men and required two procedures. First, a man had to sue his wife for adultery and obtain a conviction in an ecclesiastical, or church, court. Then, he had to obtain a private act of Parliament giving him the right to remarry. These suits and petitions were so expensive that only wealthy Englishmen could seek them. The poor, who cared less about their reputations and had little property to worry about, practiced informal divorce. One spouse, usually the husband, simply deserted, and both spouses entered into new, technically illegal unions. Friends and relatives condoned such behavior, and informal marriages were common in both England and America. But women and men between the highest and the lowest ranks of society had no solution to the problem of an unhappy marriage.

After the Revolution, all the new states made divorces easier to obtain. Some legislatures voted to allow both formal separations with property divisions, and absolute divorces that permitted remarriage. Others provided only for separations. But everywhere it was acknowledged that women and men needed legal recourse for disastrous marriages. As Pennsylvania lawmakers wrote in the preamble to that state's 1785 divorce statute, "It is the design of marriage, and the wish of parties entering into that state that it should continue during their joint lives, yet where one party is . . . guilty of acts and deeds inconsistent with the nature thereof, the laws of every well regulated society ought to give relief to the innocent and injured person." Freedom from English law allowed Americans to institute reforms in marriage that England adopted only in the twentieth century.

Both women and men benefited from the new laws, which acknowledged male as well as female adultery and prohibited physical cruelty. American lawmakers congratulated themselves on their liberality to the female sex, but the courts still favored men. They routinely demanded more evidence of men's wrongdoing than women's and automatically gave men custody of their children.

Revolutionary ideals led to few other improvements in the status of women immediately following the war. For the most part, Americans seemed intent on recreating the kind of stable sexual relationships they had known before the war, relationships in which women were subservient to men. Female independence and initiative, valued during a time of war, were less desirable when the crisis had passed. Perhaps Americans feared changing too much in their lives all at once. By being conservative on sexual issues, they may have felt freer to pursue radical political reforms.

Sexual equality has proved to be a very difficult goal to achieve in the United States. Not until the nineteenth century were property laws gradually changed to give women independent rights to real and personal property. Women were granted voting privileges even later, in 1920. And even today the laws on marriage, divorce, and the family have not resolved all issues of inequality.

Nevertheless, probably the most important first step on the road to sexual equality was taken after the Revolution. Higher education for women gave them the means to work for their own independence. As soon as women could demonstrate that their intellectual abilities were equal to men's, denying them legal and political rights became increasingly difficult. The founding of female academies at the end of the eighteenth century, then, marked the beginning of a new era for women. As Judith Sargent Murray, an early advocate of women's higher education, wrote in 1798: "I expect to see our young women forming a new era in female history.... The partial distribution of advantages which has too long obtained, is, in this enlightened age, rapidly giving place to a more uniform system of information ... and *the revolution of events is advancing in that half of the human species, which hath hitherto been involved in the night of darkness, toward the irradiating sun of science.*"

The Limits of Republicanism:
Racial Conflicts in the North, South, and West

Republican ideas of freedom and equality led to the gradual abolition of slavery in the North, but not in the South and the opening West. African Americans across the nation were quick to argue that slavery had no place in a republic. But only in areas where whites owned few slaves and where the economy was not dependent on slave labor did courts and legislatures act to outlaw human bondage. The Constitution supported slavery, in acknowledgment of the financial dependence of many areas on a slave work force. As practiced in the new United States, then, democracy was limited by the economic interests of slaveholding whites.

In the years following the Revolution, slavery as an institution grew and strengthened in the South. The rationale for slavery changed and hardened, becoming explicitly racist in tone. The potential for revolutionary change present in the republican ideals of the era was not, therefore, realized.

Northern states acted separately to end slavery. Vermont was the first state to forbid it, by incorporating an antislavery provision into its 1777 constitution. In Massachusetts the courts abolished slavery in a series of "freedom cases" brought by slaves and their sympathizers in the 1780s. As Chief Justice William Cushing of the Supreme Judicial Court ruled, "The idea of slavery is inconsistent with our own conduct and constitution. . . . there can be no such thing as perpetual servitude of a rational creature." New Hampshire adopted a constitution in 1783 that declared "all men are born equal and independent." Although no court cases tested the meaning of these words, slavery in New Hampshire disappeared over the next two decades. Only eight slaves were listed in the New Hampshire census of 1800; in the 1810 census there were none.

Elsewhere the process of freeing the enslaved was painfully slow. State legislatures enacted gradual abolition statutes in Pennsylvania (1780), Rhode Island (1784), Connecticut (1784), New York (1799), and New Jersey (1804). These laws provided for the freedom of the children of slaves when they reached ages ranging from eighteen to twenty-eight. In this way, parents who were enslaved for life saw their children become free. Their victory must have been bittersweet, filled with both joy and agonizing frustration. As late as 1840, New Jersey still listed legally owned slaves on its census.

In response to political pressure and their own personal dislike of slavery, some southern slaveholders and northern owners of adult slaves freed their slaves. Antislavery legislation, combined with these private actions, produced a large free black population in the United States by the beginning of the nineteenth century. Many more free blacks lived in the Chesapeake area than in the Carolinas or Georgia, but everywhere their numbers grew. As a consequence, black slaves could escape to freedom more easily than ever before. They could now pose as free during their flights and also use the homes of free friends and relatives as hiding places. Before the war, escape had been virtually impossible. Now the North Star became a guide to a free land.

For women, the shift from slave to free status had momentous importance, even more so than for men. Beyond giving women the right to choose where and for whom they would work, freedom gave them control over their persons and their children for the first time. Black women could now defend themselves more effectively from sexual assault. They could live with their own family separately from whites, thereby denying white men easy access. And if they were raped by a white or black assailant, they could bring a suit in a court of law, an option that was not available to them under slavery. Abolition did not end the sexual abuse of black women, but it did limit it in important ways. Just as significant, free women could face childbirth with a different set of expectations. No longer did they have to fear forced separation from their children.

Freedom did not, however, change the daunting work responsibilities of black women. They remained largely an unskilled work force. Under the southern slave system, women worked almost exclusively as agricultural laborers. A few found employment as domestics, and on rare occasions (especially during the war years) women worked at skilled tasks, such as spinning and weaving. But many more black men than women worked at skilled trades under slavery. In the North the story had been much the same. Most women who lived in urban areas worked as unskilled domestics, but if they lived in rural areas they worked in the fields.

After the Revolution, many rural black women migrated to northern towns and cities. Like white women faced with the necessity of supporting themselves, they learned they could find work there more easily. As a result, African-American women outnumbered men in northern urban areas at the end of the eighteenth century.

For a few of these women the move brought opportunity. For the first time some African-American women began to support themselves as retailers, boardinghouse keepers, bakers, peddlers, and teachers. But only one in twenty found these types of jobs. Most former slaves found that freedom gave them little opportunity to raise their standard of living. Most black women in towns and cities worked as laundresses. As the Pennsylvania Abolition Society reported in 1795, "The Women generally, both married and single, wash clothes for a living." This physically demanding job was no easier than fieldwork. Whatever their occupation, under both slavery and freedom women worked from dawn to dusk to support themselves and their families. Among blacks, as among poor whites, the contribution of all family members was needed to survive.

Life in northern towns and cities did have one significant advantage: the existence of close-knit black communities, which provided emotional and financial support to people in need. In all urban centers blacks moved gradually into their own neighborhoods. At first they sought simple companionship, the opportunity to live with people who did not judge them as inferiors. Soon, however, they were establishing churches, schools, and charitable societies to help each other in their daily struggles for survival. Life in the urban North was difficult for black families, but for those who could live where they wanted and with whom they wanted for the first time, freedom made the daily struggle to survive worthwhile.

Unfortunately, many newly freed blacks did not have the resources to move into their own homes. Most enslaved black women had worked as domestic servants and lived in the homes of their owners. With no savings and low wages, some were obliged to remain where they were after emancipation. Many whites made residence in their homes a condition of employment. Some controlled the behavior of their servants outside the house as well. In the first generation after slavery, therefore, some women still experienced little personal freedom.

For others, however, living separately from whites was their greatest priority. As soon as they learned they were free, they walked away without looking back. They had been waiting so long for freedom and had suffered so much as slaves that they had to strike out on their own, surviving off the land or charity until they found employment and places to live.

Reports of freedom cases such as that of the Massachusetts slave Elizabeth Freeman, also known as Mumbet, had electrifying effects on some blacks. The following story tells of how one typical woman might have been inspired to start a new life:

Once I heard about Mumbet I just walked off the place. Master couldn't keep me there because us slaves were free. Mumbet won herself the right in the courts. That judge said she was a free woman who could work where she wanted. And she made me a free woman too. I knew that. Didn't take much figuring. Massachusetts allowed no white people to own us after that Revolution. We were all free. So we started to move, and we mostly, us women, moved to the towns if we could. Took our youngins and went. Except some had to stay where they were, because they had no friends or family in Boston or Salem or places like that. Some people been staying with white folks for a long time, and it's frustrating. But they have masters that cause them no trouble, and it's better to stay where they are. Particularly women who have husbands and youngins with them.

But me, I went because I had enough of master. He was so bad there wasn't no living with him. Got myself a job right off. Washing, that's all. Lived with my sister and her friends and there were about ten or twelve of us in that little house. But we were free, that's all. We were glad. Then I met my husband. His name is Benjamin Smith. Before the Revolution they called him Ben. All the time Ben, and boy. He didn't like that. So now he's Benjamin, a full and proper name. And me, I changed my name too. Was Queenie. Now I'm Elizabeth. Elizabeth Smith. I say it real careful 'cause it's important, your name. Mumbet, she changed her name to Elizabeth, so I did too, 'cause I love that woman so much. Benjamin works on the ships that go from Boston to Philadelphia. He's a good sailor, and works hard and I've got no complaints. Except he's gone from home most of the time. I still work all the time, sometimes washing, sometimes cleaning, sometimes picking rags. My babies go with me and my older girl she helps. We're getting by, and we've got a better place to live, just with my sister and her family. Except we're always taking in new folks, from the country, who have no place else to go. Especially women. Set them up. Get them started. I watch out for the women.

Another thing I want to say. We have a church now. The African Zion Church, we call it. We all put our cents in and after awhile we got enough to buy a little land. Had to. Whites don't want us in their churches, and especially don't want us burying our dead in their churchyards. And we need a place for our dead. It's not right, putting them in the poor folks burying ground as though they don't belong to no one. It's not right, 'cause your ancestors are important. They have to be buried right. And you have to take care of their graves, and watch over their bones. Or you'll be in trouble when your time comes. So, myself and my sister and Benjamin and the other people in this part of town, we started to build a church. And it is just small. Just a shack really. But we've got a preacher even the whites like. They ask him to preach at their meetings sometimes, and he does. And I know why. He says it's good for the whites to know black folks have the ways of the Lord in their hearts. And he is a great preacher. And we all appreciate his work. And he travels sometimes and we miss him, but then he comes back here. There are not enough black preachers for all the folks who want to know the ways of the Lord. Yes, we're doing better, really. Except the white folks still have lots of hate in them. Us free people have to be careful all the time. It's no good, still, between us blacks and the whites.

The rise of a large free black population in the North aggravated racial tensions in both the North and South. White northerners no longer wanted to uphold a slave system, but for the most part their attitudes toward the newly freed slaves did not change. Racist feelings of superiority determined the treatment of blacks under both slavery and freedom. And as slavery became even more firmly entrenched in the South, explicitly racist arguments in favor of the institution were heard more and more. White southerners argued that blacks were intellectually incapable of caring for themselves and their families. They claimed that blacks were inherently lazy, dishonest, and foolish. If blacks were on their own, these whites maintained, they would stop working and turn to lives of petty crime. According to these arguments, whites were fulfilling a vital social obligation by keeping blacks enslaved.

Although northern whites saw daily evidence that free blacks were capable and hardworking, they readily accepted southern judgments on the inferiority of African Americans. Such beliefs allowed them to deny blacks basic rights, including the rights to vote, own real estate, and go to school. Racism solved a moral dilemma for some whites. If they believed in the inferiority of African Americans, they were relieved of the obligation to help them build better lives for themselves as free people.

After the Revolution the black population grew rapidly in the American South. Devastated by years of warfare, small farmers and large planters alike began rebuilding their work forces. Those with the means immediately purchased slaves to replace the ones they had lost during the war. Poorer farmers had to wait. As the economy improved, the demand for workers increased suddenly while the supply remained the same. As they had in the colonial period, southerners turned to the slave trade to solve their labor shortage. Tragically, as slavery ended in the North, it expanded in the South through the forced enslavement of thousands of newly imported Africans.

The U.S. Constitution allowed this importation. Although some political leaders had advocated the closing of the slave trade, a compromise was reached. Slaves could be brought into the United States during the twenty years following the Constitution's ratification. As stated in Article I, Section 9, "The migration or importation of such persons as any of the States now existing shall think proper to admit shall not be prohibited by the Congress prior to the year 1808." Tens of thousands of new slaves came to the United States in those two decades.

With the end of legal slave importation in sight, the role of enslaved women as childbearers took on new importance. By the end of the eighteenth century slave owners understood that their slaves' fertility increased their wealth and guaranteed the continued prosperity of their children. As Thomas Jefferson remarked, "I consider a woman who brings a child every two years as more profitable than the best man of the farm." This attitude became particularly prevalent in Maryland, Delaware, and Virginia, where planters began to encourage slaves to have large families as a way of making money.

Slave owners such as Jefferson offered women rewards for marrying and for frequently bearing children. On one occasion he directed his overseer to give a newly married slave woman a cooking pot and a bed—presents meant to indicate his approval of her choice of one of his other enslaved workers as a husband. Jefferson also encouraged stable slave marriages. He once wrote, "There is nothing I desire so much as that all the young people in the estate should intermarry with one another and stay at home." People who married "at home" were "worth a great deal more . . . than when they have husbands and wives abroad." Jefferson realized that marriages between his own workers allowed them to live more contentedly under the yoke of slavery.

Other men went even further to encourage slave women to marry and to bear children. One Virginia planter promised his slave Jenny that he would give her freedom if she bore six children—the number of offspring he had. He kept his word. After Jenny delivered her sixth child in eleven years, she and her youngest child gained their freedom in 1803. Imagine this woman's position. She was free, but her other five children remained enslaved for life.

In other cases, white men coerced their female slaves into reproducing. Some women found themselves coupled with a man unwillingly, simply because the master said it was time for them to produce children. Many owners even raped their own slaves or forced them to become their mistresses. Tragically, most of these men later turned the offspring from these unions into slaves. The social system of the southern colonies and states frowned on men who acknowledged their sexual liaisons by granting freedom to their children.

Even the slave owners who promoted stable family life took little trouble to ensure that families stayed together. Although planters might try to keep slave families intact while their children were young, older children generally were the first to be sold off the home plantation. One Charleston man explained his decision to sell a female slave this way: "She has a practice of goeing frequently to her Father and Mother, who Live at a Plantation I am concern'd in, about Twenty Miles from Town." Rather than respecting this young woman's clear desire to be with her family, the owner put her on a ship for Lisbon, Portugal, where she was sold.

On large plantations, where slaves lived and worked on different land holdings, adolescents often lived apart from their parents and grandparents. Frequently lonely, these children missed their older relatives' help in dealing with the cruelties of slavery. Nevertheless, slave parents and grandparents did whatever they could to protect the younger generation. For instance, when one elderly woman learned that her granddaughter had been beaten by an overseer, she asked her master to move the girl to another section of the plantation managed by a different overseer. After the master refused, the woman punished him in her own way. As the master reported the incident, "Sukey, the old Granny ... to be revenged because I would not take her granddaughter away turned out all my Cattle last night on my Cowpen ground which have done me a prodigeous mischief. She has had the impudence to say the child is poor and starved when I declare I never saw a finer, well, fat, nor healthyer child. I will repay this treatment." Undoubtedly, this slave woman received a whipping for attempting to help her granddaughter. Had she lived near-by, she could have assisted the child in more useful ways than by pleading with an unsympathetic owner.

One of the most tragic aspects of the slave system was the helplessness of women such as Sukey to prevent the breakup of their families. Encouraged to pro-duce children, most slave women experienced the agony of forced separation from their daughters and sons. Sojourner Truth, an abolitionist who was born at the end of the eighteenth century, explained her own despair to audiences at antislavery meetings in the years leading up to the outbreak of the Civil War in 1861. In her most famous speech, which was recorded by a white listener, she cried,

> Dat man ober dar say dat womin needs to be helped into carriages, and lift-ed ober ditches, and to hab de best place everywhar. Nobody eber helps me into carriages, or ober mud-puddles, or gibs me any best place! And a'n't I a woman? Look at me! Look at my arm! I have ploughed, and planted, and gathered into barns, and no man could head me! And a'n't I a woman? I could work as much and eat as much as a man—when I could get it—and bear de lash as well! And a'n't I a woman? I have borne thirteen chilern, and seen 'em mos' all sold off to slavery, and when I cried out with my mother's grief, none but Jesus heard me! And a'n't' I a woman?

Although enslaved women usually could not prevent owners from making de-cisions about their workers based on economic considerations, they never gave up trying. As mothers, daughters, sisters, and wives, women protested, complained, and pushed the boundaries of acceptable behavior whenever they could. For exam-ple, even though Virginia planter Robert Carter believed in "moderate correction in every case," he was forced to reconsider his ideas after an overzealous driver mis-treated a slave child. After the child's mother complained to Carter, he admitted that "in the present case ... allowances for the feelings of a Mother" should have been made. By forcing owners to acknowledge maternal love, women sustained

In a scene illustrating an antislavery publication, the artist depicts one of the worst abominations of slavery: a slaveholder taking slave children away from their mother, presumably for sale.

themselves and their families emotionally. They could not prevent the suffering of their children and grandchildren, but they could protest it. In the process they maintained the affection and the will of family members.

In giving birth to children under slavery, women affirmed their life-giving force. No white person could destroy their power and determination to produce life, to survive despite the hardships of slavery in the American South. Although some women practiced abortion and infanticide to deny owners additional human property, many more bore children as a means of self-affirmation. In African-American culture, as in the traditional societies of West Africa from which these people came, motherhood gave women personal fulfillment and high social status. As wives and mothers, they satisfied their own needs and the needs of black slave communities even more than the needs of owners. Enslaved families, however tortured, produced the means for individual slave survival.

Just as African-American women struggled to defend their families under slavery, Native American women attempted to protect their families from total destruction during the revolutionary era. The war was very hard on the eastern tribes, which suffered attacks from both English and Patriot troops. Some Indians tried to stay neutral, but the stance proved impossible to maintain. And no matter which side a tribe joined in the war, the enemy loomed near.

The Iroquois's experiences reflect those of all the eastern tribes at the end of the eighteenth century. During the Revolution, the Iroquois Confederacy could not agree on whom to support in the war. Initially, the Iroquois were neutral because it was unclear whether participating in the war on either side could work to their benefit. But by the summer of 1777 many of the Indians had rethought their position. The Oneida and Tuscarora chose to remain neutral, which at that point meant they were effectively siding with the Americans. But warriors from the Seneca, Cayuga, Onondaga, and Mohawk tribes decided to join the British, and "the mothers also consented to it," as the Seneca warrior Blacksnake reported. The final decision to go to war was made not by the chiefs, but by the warriors and the respected older women whose sacrifice of sons, brothers, and husbands was acknowledged in Iroquois political culture.

Immediately after joining the British, Iroquois warriors participated in a major battle at Oriskany, New York, in which casualties were high on all sides. Neither the English nor the Americans could claim complete victory. The British had not been able to take Fort Stanwix as planned, but they did succeed in inflicting high casualties on the Patriot troops. The Indians, however, were distraught over the bloodshed and destruction without victory. They returned to their villages disillusioned with organized British warfare. Their despair was reported by Mary Jemison, a white woman who became a member of the Seneca and lived with the tribe for her entire adult life. She wrote, "Our town exhibited a scene of real sorrow and distress, when our warriors returned and recounted their misfortunes, and stated the real loss they had received in the engagement. The mourning was excessive, and was expressed by the most doleful yells, shrieks, and howlings."

For the rest of the war the Iroquois preferred to engage in traditional Indian tactics of guerrilla warfare. They attacked individual farms and small frontier settlements in swift-moving raiding parties, destroying homes and fields but killing only those male settlers who resisted them. The warriors were highly successful. By the end of the Revolution, Indian and Loyalist raiders had destroyed white settlements in an area covering nearly fifty thousand square miles and stretching from the Mohawk Valley in New York to the Monongahela River in Ohio. When the English surrendered, the Iroquois were surprised and severely disappointed. From their perspective the war was going well.

Although the Iroquois warriors waged war successfully between 1778 and 1782, ultimately their campaign of destruction could not protect their people. Infuriated by their own inability to protect frontier whites, Patriot troops assumed the same tactics as the Native Americans. Soldiers could not attack warrior bands easily, but they could destroy Iroquois towns and villages. Beginning in the summer of 1779, they systematically burned houses, outbuildings, and planted fields; cut down orchards; and dispersed the inhabitants. George Washington became known among the Iroquois as Town Destroyer for his role in directing these campaigns. By the next spring only two out of thirty Iroquois villages remained unharmed.

Using stereotyped images, a broadside printed about 1800 demonstrates white settlers' fear of Indian attack.

The winter of 1779–80 was one of great hardship for the Iroquois. Most of them had no homes and suffered from exposure during the bitterly cold winter. Food was scarce, and epidemics of smallpox, dysentery, and measles ravaged the camps. Iroquois warriors continued to raid white settlements throughout the following three summers. But in the meantime, those left behind—the women, the children, the sick, and the elderly—faced the steady destruction of their way of life.

The war threatened the Iroquois with extinction. Between the revolutionary era and the end of the century, the population of the Six Nations was cut approximately in half, from between eight to ten thousand to about four thousand people. Most of the dead were not warriors killed in battle, but people of all ages and both sexes who suffered from disease, starvation, and exposure.

Although the Iroquois survived, their culture, in many ways, did not. Peace found the Iroquois crowded onto relatively small reservations, unable to follow the customs of the hunt, migration of town sites, warfare, and family relationships. As a people, they now questioned the validity of their traditions because they had fared so badly in their contests with Europeans. Many Iroquois came to despise their own culture as an inferior one without a place in a new world order.

Reservation life changed many aspects of Indian behavior. One important shift occurred in the division of labor between women and men. On reservations, men's traditional labor—hunting and warfare—lost significance. Men continued to hunt, but game was scarce and became more so as the years passed. The men usually were able to provide their families with meat, but they no longer traded in furs. In addition, accepting peace on white men's terms meant that warriors were acknowledging their inability to defend their families. As a result, political and religious leaders, as well as the warriors themselves, suffered greatly from shame. During the postrevolutionary period, alcoholism was common, stemming from depression and an absence of hope. As a missionary at the Buffalo Creek reservation in upstate New York explained, "Indians, as has been observed, bear suffering with great fortitude, but at the end of this fortitude is desperation. Suicides are frequent among the Senecas. I apprehend this despondency is the principal cause of their intemperance." Among Indian men, unrestricted drinking led to thefts, fights, and wife and child abuse. Such behavior could occur at important council meetings as well as in everyday situations. During negotiations for a major treaty with the federal government in 1797, for example, a white participant reported, "Red Jacket and many of the Indians ... from intoxication fell to fighting in groups, pulling Hair biting like dogs w[h]ere ever they could get hold."

At about this same time a federal agent reported that "the Indians of the Six Nations ... have become given to indolence, drunkenness and thefts, and have taken to killing each other, there have been five murders among themselves within Six months—they have recd their payments and immediately expended it for liquor and in the course of a frollick have killed one or two."

Meanwhile, women also suffered from depression, and alcoholism among them was common. They had seen their homes destroyed, their fields burned, and their children die after great suffering. The drunk, "aged women, in particular . . . were often seen lying beside the paths, overcome." Like the men, they questioned themselves and the value of their traditions. But unlike the men, women still had some traditional patterns to fall back on. Their work roles were unchanged. They still tended their children, farmed, cooked, produced craft goods, and participated in the political decisions of their tribes. For women life on reservations meant fewer changes than it did for men. Throughout the difficult period of adjustment, they worked in their fields and found a purpose in the labor that kept their families from starvation. Thus when Quaker missionaries arrived at one reservation in the spring of 1798, they saw the women busy at their planting "while the men were standing in companies sporting themselves with their bows and arrows and other trifling amusements."

Programs initiated by the federal government and individual religious groups such as the Society of Friends encouraged Iroquois men to become farmers. The adjustment was very difficult. Most of the older men never embraced the new occupation, but young men slowly began to learn the farming techniques of the whites. A Quaker assistance program persuaded some Seneca to abandon their old ways. Missionaries from the Society of Friends built a model farm where the whites pursued their agricultural work in full view of the Indians. The Quakers were careful to point out that long ago their own ancestors had been forced to adjust to new ways but that eventually farming had made life easier for both men and women. According to the Quaker missionaries, Seneca women encouraged their men to learn to farm as whites did. At one meeting the Quakers noticed that although many of the Seneca men regarded their suggestions as comical, some others and "particularly the women" appeared "solid" in their support of the Quakers' ideas.

At the end of the eighteenth century a Seneca religious prophet named Handsome Lake became very influential in helping his people accept a new way of life. Respected as a messenger from the spirit world, Handsome Lake called for the reformation of Iroquois behavior. He condemned alcoholism and the practice of witchcraft. He also argued that unless the Iroquois changed, they would cease to exist as a people. His apocalyptic view was accompanied by specific instructions on what the Iroquois should do to survive. He said that men must learn to farm, and women must become good housewives who could spin and weave. Handsome Lake was able to convince many Seneca that only by following new ways could their people survive.

Many aspects of traditional male and female behavior troubled Handsome Lake. He objected to men's physical abuse of their wives and children (especially when the men were drunk), the adultery of both spouses, and the prevalence of divorce. He urged his people to change their attitudes toward the nuclear family— a household consisting only of a mother, a father, and their children. Under traditional Iroquois teachings the kin relationship between mother and daughter took precedence over all others. Handsome Lake now maintained that the husband-wife bond must take first place in people's loyalties. He believed that most problems between wives and husbands stemmed from the interference of mothers, and he taught that "The Creator is sad because of the tendency of old women to breed mischief." According to the prophet, mothers encouraged daughters to argue with their husbands; they meddled with relationships through love medicines, sterilization, and abortion; and they condoned divorce.

In effect, Handsome Lake and his followers sought to destroy the old kinship system by teaching people to value their spouse above everyone else. Just as the nuclear family was now to become the economic center of Indian life through its management of a family farm, it was also to become the moral and emotional center of both women's and men's lives. Male solidarity through warfare and the hunt was no longer possible. Therefore, the close ties of mothers and daughters also had to end.

By the end of the eighteenth century, acculturation seemed the only route to survival for the Iroquois and other eastern tribes. By abandoning many ancient patterns of behavior, Indians such as the Seneca were able to persevere into the nineteenth century. What Indian women thought of their new lives is unknown. Illiterate and struggling on a day-to-day basis to provide for their families, they did not keep a record of their feelings. Missionaries and federal agents, who were almost all men, wrote primarily about men's words and actions. Their papers reveal little about the trials of women as they faced a new world. Women's acceptance of the teachings of both the Quakers and Handsome Lake, however, did demonstrate their commitment to helping their people. In their desire to create a decent life for themselves and their children, they recognized the necessity for a new direction. Their recognition of this need signaled their strength, intelligence, and will to survive.

Prayer and Charity: Creating Public Roles for Mothers

During the years of revolutionary turmoil, Americans paid less attention to the condition of their souls than to the state of their civil liberties. Clergymen worried about a "deadness" in the religious life of the nation and castigated their congregations for failing in their religious duties. By the 1790s many people felt a new urgency to turn their thoughts and energies back to the churches.

In this atmosphere the Second Great Awakening began, first in frontier areas long-starved for religious direction and then in the more densely settled regions of the East. (The first Great Awakening, a similar burst of religious fervor, had spread through the colonies over several decades beginning in the 1730s.) During the Second Great Awakening, religious revivals brought thousands of new converts into many different kinds of religious associations. Groups considered radical at the time, such as the Baptists and Shakers, grew dramatically in strength from the late eighteenth century to the mid-nineteenth century, and established churches also expanded.

For women, the Second Great Awakening was a means of increasing their already significant religious influence. Women had long constituted the majority of worshipers in most churches. During the revivals, their numbers swelled to an even greater proportion of the faithful. This growth ensured their dominance over the religious life of the nation.

Since the end of the seventeenth century, more women than men had sought solace in the churches for a variety of reasons. First, they had been socialized to sacrifice themselves for the good of others. Women therefore felt more comfortable with Christian teachings that promoted self-sacrifice. Second, because of the risks of childbearing, women faced death and permanent physical injury more often than men. Their frequent encounters with death led them to consider more seriously the state of their souls. (Not coincidentally, women often joined churches shortly after they married.) Perhaps equally important, women needed the comforts of religion to face the frequent deaths of their children and female friends. The infant mortality rate remained high throughout the eighteenth century, and every woman had friends or relatives who had died in childbirth or suffered injuries. These forces remained powerful incentives behind women's loyalty to their religious associations.

Female friendships and communal support of one another were a vital part of women's lives. In each town, and even in frontier areas whenever possible, women turned to each other for help in times of trouble. During childbirth and recovery, illness, and death, women needed the support of other women. Sometimes relatives helped, but often women needed to depend on their neighbors. As a result, female aloofness was rare in the eighteenth century. Women sought out the companionship of other women whenever possible, and the church was an important place to make connections. Membership in the same church gave women a claim to assistance they might not otherwise be able to make. Women's bonding, then, extended into and out of the churches. There, women could be confident of finding female friendship and respect as well as the fellowship of the faithful generally. The spiritual guidance of ministers was important, but so was membership in a female world of religious belief.

Ministers probably also won the support of female parishioners by teaching them that only through Christian principles had women been elevated to something resembling an equal standing with men. A theme that ran through many of the sermons delivered during the Second Great Awakening was the role of the churches in improving the social position of women. Only as a result of Christian instruction, the ministers argued, had men become willing to treat women with the respect they deserved. Other cultures and religions had not succeeded in raising the status of women, but Christianity, as one minister put it, had "exalt[ed] woman to an equal rank with man in all the felicities of the soul, in all the advantages of religious attainment, in all the prospects and hopes of immortality." It was therefore in the best interests of women to support the churches and the male ministers who led them.

A Connecticut teenager, Prudence Punderson, depicted in this piece of needlework the journey from cradle to grave. Even young people were acutely conscious of the fragility of life; indeed, the artist died at twenty-six.

Although women were excluded from positions of leadership in most churches, ministers felt obliged to consider their needs and opinions when composing sermons, developing church policies, or administering church funds. Because women dominated the churches and made most of the donations to their collection plates, ministers increasingly were obliged to them for their own positions, status, and even salaries. Perhaps as a result, ministers' depictions of women softened in the eighteenth century. Gone was the old, Puritan emphasis on the decadent role of Eve in tempting Adam to sin. In its place appeared a gentler view of women as prudent, generous, and uniquely suited to religious duties. Good women, many ministers believed, were the main supporters of religion in their families and communities. Without them, Christians were in danger, as one minister explained in eulogizing his own mother: "At the Gap, which the Death of a wise and good Mother makes, does many times enter a Torrent of Impieties and Vices." Ministers often turned to Proverbs 31 for inspiration in teaching women about their domestic and social obligations:

> A good wife who can find? She is far more precious than jewels... She puts
> her hand to the distaff, and her hands hold the spindle. She opens her hand

to the poor, and reaches out her hands to the needy. . . . She opens her mouth with wisdom and the teaching of kindness is on her tongue. She looks well to the ways of her household, and does not eat of the bread of idleness. Her children rise up and call her blessed; her husband also, and he praises her.

Sermons now portrayed the typical Protestant woman as a wise, hardworking matron with a keen desire to bring her children to Christ and perform charitable deeds.

The ministers' emphasis on female virtue complemented the republican belief that mothers were in a uniquely important position to promote the welfare of the nation. Like the politicians who argued that a republic's citizens needed to be moral, ministers believed that Christianity required personal virtue. Mothers were in the best position to teach their children the right moral lessons because early influences were regarded as the most important. Women's control over the nursery and the education of their children gave them the unique opportunity to instill youth with both proper Christian and proper republican qualities before other, less uplifting forces could interfere. In her defense of higher education for girls, Abigail Adams argued that intelligence in men could arise only from intelligence in women: "Much depends . . . upon the early education of youth, and the first principles which are instilled take the deepest root." She concluded, "If we mean to have heroes, statesmen, and philosophers, we should have learned women."

The comments of minister William Lyman are further evidence of the faith Americans had come to place in maternal influence. In 1802 he wrote, "Mothers do, in a sense, hold the reigns of government and sway the ensigns of national prosperity and glory. Yea, they give direction to the moral sentiments of our rising hopes and contribute to form their moral state. To them therefore our eyes are turned." Just as politicians promoted the maternal role, ministers elevated mothers' lessons to a plane equal or even superior to their own. In mothers' hands rested not only the future of the nation, but that of the churches as well.

Women received high praise for their work as mothers, but unfortunately motherhood was virtually the only vehicle through which eighteenth-century women could earn social recognition. Other avenues of public service remained closed to them. They could not participate directly in the political life of the new United States, for they could neither vote nor hold public office. Their property rights were severely restricted by law, so they had difficulty participating in commerce. The occupations open to women were generally menial ones. The few that were respectable—healer, midwife, and teacher—were all extensions of a mother's role in caring for her family. Some women with intellectual gifts were beginning to exercise influence through their writings, but most could not hope to imitate their example. No college had opened its doors to women, and therefore only those whose fathers arranged for their private instruction could hope to rival educated men in intellectual pursuits. If they did receive the equivalent of a college-level education, they risked social ridicule; highly learned women in general earned reputations for eccentricity.

Faced with these daunting limitations on their lives, women made a social virtue out of necessity. Using their influence in the churches, they succeeded in creating a public role from their private work in the home. Beginning in the 1790s, churchwomen founded a variety of self-help and charitable societies that, over the years, exerted a wide social influence. Through maternal associations, charitable organizations, and reform societies, individual women came to wield significant power.

No such opportunities had existed for colonial women. Female associations did not exist before the Revolution. Women came together to pray, but their groups were informal and single-minded in purpose. Charitable work was conducted only by individuals, local ministers, and the all-male Overseers of the Poor. Generally, men told women what to do for the poor, or matrons decided privately to assist specific people. Group efforts would have been perceived as usurpations of men's authority. Women were not regarded as capable administrators. Ironically, public recognition of the importance of motherhood—that most private of domestic obligations—gave women their first opportunity to find fulfillment outside the home. As mothers, women were permitted to form associations to further their important work. Maternal societies (the first mothers' clubs) attracted many women. Initially intended to help women became better mothers, many eventually became charitable or reform societies as well.

Women also turned to churches to find new avenues for effecting social change. Under the sponsorship of ministers, churchwomen created some of the first significant public roles for their sex. Although female religious associations were largely a nineteenth-century phenomenon, their foundation was laid by religious women of the colonial period.

The work of Rebecca Gratz (1781–1869) is illustrative of the kind of influence women could exert through charitable and religious work. It also demonstrates that Jewish as well as Christian women promoted reform and worked to create good public institutions for the sick and the poor. Gratz lived in Philadelphia and commanded both personal wealth and family prestige. At twenty she was already committed to charity work and helped establish one of the city's first female relief societies, the Female Association for the Relief of Women and Children in Reduced Circumstances. She served as its first secretary. As a mature woman, Gratz, who never married, was instrumental in founding numerous other charities, including the Philadelphia Orphan Asylum, the Female Hebrew Benevolent Society, the Jewish Foster Home and Orphan Asylum, the Fuel Society, the Sewing Society, and the Hebrew Sunday School Society. This last was probably her most significant accomplishment. The first such organization of its kind in the nation, it served as a model for all subsequent Jewish Sunday schools. Her work earned her the praise, admiration, and gratitude of Philadelphians.

Gratz's life reveals the new roads to significant social activism that were becoming available to women at the beginning of the nineteenth century. Although few women could match Gratz's energy and influence, many imitated her spirit in their own benevolent activities. Significantly, women found their greatest strength in working together. Colonial women gave their nineteenth-century descendants a legacy of strong female friendships, a tradition that proved essential for women's new social roles.

In fact, the earliest formal women's associations probably grew out of informal religious meetings women sponsored in their homes. Women long had gathered together for prayer and religious discussions. Throughout the eighteenth century these meetings served as intellectual and social outlets as well as spiritual ones. At the turn of the century women began to convert their prayer meetings into more ambitious associations. The example of the Female Religious and Cent Society of Jericho Center in Vermont was probably typical. Initially, this group of women met to pray out of a desire to "do good" and express their collective support for religion. Soon they were raising money for the missionary movement, a popular cause in the early nineteenth century.

In order to conduct their business properly, the Vermont women decided in 1806 to write up articles to govern their society. They proclaimed that the members would meet every other week "for social prayer and praise and religious instruction and edification ... [and that] all persons attending the meeting shall conduct themselves with seriousness and solemnity dureing the Exercises nor shall an Illiberal remark be made respecting the performance of any of the members, neither shall they report abroad any of the transactions of the society to the prejudice of any of its members." They insisted that members adhere to a strict code of mutual support in their efforts to improve the religious life of the country. In a culture that still questioned every attempt by women to gain a public voice, a united front was necessary to gain acceptance. Female solidarity was essential if they were to expand their horizons beyond the fireside.

Women who joined together to promote religious and charitable causes sought primarily to improve the human condition, not their own status. That the two went hand in hand may have gone unnoticed at first. Their efforts seemed in concert with traditional belief in women's potential to do good and help others. Only later, when women already had carved out a major sphere of influence in charity work, did ministers and politicians begin to fear what they had helped to create. In idealizing motherhood, men had opened the way for the higher education of girls and the group activities of mature women. Both experiences provided women with the tools and the confidence they needed to seek control over their own lives. Within a few decades some American women were arguing that as moral beings, they had the right to a political voice. At that point there was no returning to their colonial forebears' standard of female conduct. Women activists had found a voice and the will to express it.

CHAPTER 4

Breaking New Ground
1800–1848

Michael Goldberg

S canning the first fifty years of the nineteenth century and finding the familiar markers of women's history—including the growth of women's charitable and volunteer organizations, the blossoming of educational opportunities, and the organizing of the first women's rights convention at Seneca Falls in
1848—one might be tempted to characterize the period as one of steady progress
for women's rights. But on closer inspection of the variety of women's lives across
race, class, ethnic, religious, and regional lines, one is struck by the losses as well as
the gains—and in some cases the losses caused by the gains—experienced by
American women during this period.

The vortex of industrialization drew everything toward it and left nothing
unchanged. In the Northeast, it created fresh opportunities within newly circumscribed boundaries for middle- and upper-class women. For Northern white working-class women, the new economy forced them toward ever more difficult strategies of survival while offering some means to oppose factory owners. In the South,
slaveholders girded themselves against the perceived threat of the newly expanding
industrial North by hardening the strict divisions of race, gender, and class, ren-
dering resistance by black slaves ever more difficult. And in the West, the expanding American empire reshaped white settlers' lives while devastating the cultures of
the former inhabitants of those lands.

Women during this period experienced and to a greater or lesser degree affected shifting ideas and practices concerning education, religion, work, citizenship,
community, and family relations. For most of these women, this last category—
especially between wives and husbands, and mothers and children—was particularly unsettled. As new rules were created, and old ones renegotiated or reinforced,
the varying degrees of a woman's power and powerlessness in relation to those
closest to her were revealed, reflecting her status in society at large.

Reasons of the Heart

The changes to middle-class women's role in the family occurred most forcefully
and most positively where industrialization first took hold. Before the Industrial

Revolution, which began in the 1790s in New England and transformed an over-whelmingly agricultural society into an industrial one, most people made their living off the land as farmers or livestock producers. However, as the Industrial Revolution got under way and American entrepreneurs harnessed the energy of New England's many rivers to provide water power for textile mills, more and more people worked in factories and offices in the growing towns and cities of the Northeast. Industrialization helped create an urban middle class with money to spend. Middle-class families used their greater earnings to purchase ready-made goods—everything from soap to shoes—that were once produced at home, by women. And middle-class people no longer needed large families to help them work the farm. Indeed, a large family could now be seen as an economic burden.

Once New Englanders had viewed the family as a strict hierarchy: The father was ruler of all, the mother was underneath him, and the (theoretically) obedient children were at the bottom. After 1800, however, that ideal changed. Book and magazine writers began picturing families in which men controlled the public realm of politics and business but women took responsibility for the private sphere of the home. A marriage was viewed more as a partnership; true, the woman was still the junior partner, but the older model of the man as absolute ruler was no longer fashionable among middle-class Northeasterners. Yet despite women's newly glorified power within the home, they still could not vote, own property in their own names once married, file a lawsuit, or execute a will.

The changing view of marriage helps us understand why some young women were reluctant to marry. As marriage was seen as more of a partnership, courtship became a time to prove the existence of extraordinary compatibility and radiant love. As a woman in Catherine Sedgewick's popular novel *Clarence* (1830) put it, "Ever since I first thought of it at all, I have always said I would never marry any man that I was not willing to die for." Since perfect men did not pass through one's life every day, those women who aimed high were in for a certain amount of intellectual and emotional anguish before they made their final choice.

A courtship unfolded like an elaborate chess game. It was up to the women to establish the bounds of decency and mutual self-respect while encouraging the love professed by the man. Society had quite clearly drawn the line at sexual intercourse; anything up to that point, however, was for the couple to decide. Opportunities for establishing and testing the limits were many. Indeed, one favorite activity of courting couples—known as "bundling"—allowed them to sleep in the same bed unchaperoned. One suitor, Elias Nason, wrote of "all the walks and kisses and larks and sings and thoughts and meetings and partings and clingings" that he and his sweetheart had shared. His fiancée, responding to one of his love letters, replied, "O! I really do want to kiss you. . . . How I should like to be in that old parlor with you. . . . I hope there will be a carpet on the floor for it seems you intend to act worse than you ever did before your letter . . . but I shall humbly submit to my fate and willingly too, to speak candidly."

At some point during this struggle over sex, a man was expected to propose. One woman noted that it was "true we have the liberty of refusing those we don't like, but not of selecting those we do." If a woman were forthright in her interest for a man, she would be instantly labeled an immoral adventuress; this would bring her respectability rating down several notches, lessening her marriage prospects. Because the man felt he was putting so much on the line by proposing, a "proper" woman was expected to return a well-reasoned reply within a short period of time. A woman knew, however, that her response was perhaps her last chance to have control over her life. Once she said "yes," the legal cards would be stacked against her, regardless of her suitor's declarations of love. The expectations of middle-class marriage had been raised so high that women found reports of marital disasters very disconcerting. One married woman wrote to a single friend that marriage was "a sad, sour, sober beverage" that brought "some joys, but many crosses."

Numerous women suffered "marriage trauma," spending days or weeks depressed and emotionally paralyzed at the thought of their impending commitment. They well understood their relative powerlessness once they said "yes." Hannah Hunnington, a young New England woman, wrote to her fiancé, "Every joy in anticipation depends on you, and from you must I derive every pleasure." Mary Windsor, a New Hampshire woman, bemoaned, "O, it is solemn, it is awful, thus to bind one's self for life." Once a couple decided to marry, however, the wedding was planned quickly. Weddings were often performed during the week so they would not interfere with the minister's Sabbath duties. The date was announced a week or two before the ceremony, and the gathering was limited to friends and family from the area.

After marriage, suitors often cooled the fiery protestations of love made in their letters. Although many couples developed strong, deep bonds of affection, the idea of separate spheres—that women should stay at home, and men go out in the world—kept them apart for many hours. Advice books and religious sermons emphasized that wives were to make the home a haven of restfulness for their husbands. This separation of duties provided women with other companionship, however. Friendships between women grew as they came to understand what they shared with each other and how their lives differed from men's. Unlike a wife's relationship with her husband, a friendship with another woman was based on equality.

A successful marriage for a woman like Hannah Hunnington was one in which the husband was prudent with his money and gracious toward his wife. A disastrous marriage was one in which the man drank, managed his money poorly, and physically and verbally abused his wife and children. Only in the most extreme cases—when a man was guilty of desertion, violence against his wife or children, flagrant adultery, or well-documented alcoholism—could a woman hope to divorce her husband. Although divorces were growing faster among the urban northern middle class than any other group, they were still rare. Only one in a thousand marriages ended in divorce before the Civil War.

If a woman successfully sued for divorce, she would soon wonder what price she had paid for her freedom. Alimony was rarely awarded, although judges occasionally ordered one-time cash settlements to women who had been abused by their husbands. If a woman had brought property into the marriage, she was not likely to take it back out; once she and her husband said their "I do's," her husband legally controlled all she owned. Her chances for finding work were few, especially if she was approaching or beyond middle age.

Before 1800, a divorced woman could not even have gained custody of her children, since most judges believed that fathers were the "natural custodians" of their offspring. The new ideal of domesticity, of women's "natural" place as guardian of the home, reversed this trend, so that now judges began to cite women's "unique capacity" for nurturing their children. Unfortunately, the law did not back this concept up with provisions for child support. Still, even though divorce had huge disadvantages for a woman, many a battered or scorned middle-class wife was glad that the option existed and was becoming more accepted.

Even the best northeastern marriages demanded that a woman deny many of her own ambitions in order to serve her husband and children. Yet for women the promise of idealized love remained, as did the notion of women as morally superior to men. These ideas gave middle-class women a greater sense of possibilities for their role in the community and nation. Women came to understand that as a group distinct from men they had something to offer society. They could be the nurturers, the moral educators, of their country. As America expanded, so too did these women's vision of their place in the home, and the home's place in the world.

Conditions on frontier of Ohio, Indiana, Illinois, Missouri, and Iowa were quite unlike those in the small-town and urban Northeast. The prairie frontier was overwhelmingly agricultural, but because farming was such hard work, only a few women—most of them widows—worked the land without a husband. Although frontier women, unlike their northeastern sisters, rarely suffered from marriage trauma, they were quite careful in choosing spouses. The ideal man was hardworking, thrifty, and even-tempered. Lucinda Casteen, a frontierswoman writing to her sister in Kentucky, advised her, "it will be in your interest to come or go where you can have a home of your own, but never give your hand or heart to a lazy man."

Not many frontiersmen attempted to run their farms without a wife. A man might clear the land and plant the crops alone for a few years, but few acknowledged the charms of "baching." Bachelors found that life on the prairie could get terribly lonely, with no companionship and neighbors many miles away—and it was extremely difficult to make a farm pay without the help of women. The nature of farming meant that women and men worked the same land, that women helped produce food and earn cash. Women thus saw the farm as a mutual effort.

A farm wedding involved the expectation that both husband and wife would contribute crucial labor to the running of the farm. For women this meant hard physical work as well as bearing and raising children.

Frontier women were less concerned than their eastern contemporaries with raising perfect families. On the frontier, children were valued as workers and companions, making for a more pragmatic approach to child rearing. While the size of northeastern middle-class families was shrinking dramatically during this period, frontier families were holding steady, averaging around seven children each. Compared to northeastern women, frontier women married earlier, had children earlier, and continued to give birth for more years—often past the age of forty-five. But whereas northeastern women might have seen family size as a choice to be negotiated with their husbands, frontier women considered a large family just another part of life on the prairie. Giving birth to numerous children increased a woman's chance of dying in childbirth; it also made for some very busy years when the children were still young. As Frances Trollope, an Englishwoman who lived for several years in the frontier town of Cincinnati, noted, "You continually see women with infants on their knee, that you feel sure are their grand-children, till some convincing proof of the contrary is displayed. Even the young girls, though often with lovely features, look pale, thin and haggard."

Though the lives of northern and frontier women differed from each other in some ways, both stood in stark contrast to the lives of southern slave women. For a slave in the South, physical violence was an everyday and often random occurrence. Slaves could be whipped or even tortured by their masters for misdeeds real or imagined. Slave women were also vulnerable to sexual advances and attacks by their masters, overseers, or masters' sons. Although slaveholders professing Christian values officially condemned such "race mixing," they also knew that sexual contact between black women and white men was common; one needed only to look at the large number of mulatto children on any plantation to prove it. To shift the blame away from slaveholders, some whites insisted that black women, being "naturally" sexually aggressive, were often as not the seducers. Slaveholders must be wary of such temptations, urged one white preacher, and not fall prey to such enticements. Slaveholder fantasies aside, most sexual relations between white men and black women were the result of some form of white coercion. Many masters believed that ownership gave them the right to sexual relations with their slaves.

Marriage relations between enslaved African Americans in the South changed little during the early nineteenth century. Legally, a master owned a slave and could compel that person to do whatever he wished, but most slaveholders wanted their slaves to pair off. Although masters often sanctioned slave unions with their blessing, such marriages were not recognized legally. Nonetheless, most slave owners had at least one eye on their finances in supporting a slave's choice in marriage. A typical plantation manual advised slaveholders that a slave marriage based on love would add "to the comfort, happiness and health of those entering upon it, besides ensuring greater increase." Such marriages produced both stability and more slaves, two requirements of a successful plantation operation.

How, in this brutal system, could African-American women and men nurture love and commitment? Love may not triumph over everything, but the romantic love that many black women and men felt for each other did indeed endure slavery. What brought most slave couples together was physical and emotional attraction. Lucy Ann Dunn, a slave from North Carolina, remembered the thrill of her courtship: "It was in the little Baptist church where I first seen big black Jim Dunn and I fell in love with him then I reckon. He said that he loved me then too, but it was three Saturdays before he asked to see me home." Both Jim and Lucy were careful to adhere to the mores of their culture. Lucy recalled: "We walked that mile home in front of my Mammy, and I was so happy that I ain't thought it half a mile home. We ate corn bread and turnips for dinner, and it was night before he went home. Mammy wouldn't let me walk with him to the gate, I knowed, so I just sat there on the porch and says goodnight. He come every Sunday for a year and finally he proposed. I told Mammy that I thought that I ought to be allowed to walk to the gate with Jim and she said all right, if she was settin' there on the porch lookin'."

Although many black couples exhibited as much restraint as middle-class couples up North, it was not uncommon for children to be born out of wedlock because slave culture did not make outcasts of unwed mothers. Instead, the slave community expected the new father and mother to wed, whereupon the newborn was immediately accepted into the community. Black couples made an extra effort to respect personal boundaries in an effort to replace some measure of the self-respect their owners tried to strip from them. Indeed, a number of white observers noted that while slave couples often adhered to Christian notions of sexual restraint, their aggressive masters frequently did not.

Slaves viewed marriage as a means to build community stability. Despite the inherent tragedy of their situation, weddings were both solemn and joyous occasions. At a minimum, a conscientious master would contribute some whiskey, and perhaps a hog or two. If the slave were a favorite of the master or mistress—particularly if the bride were a personal servant of the mistress—the slaveholder would sponsor a more elaborate wedding with goodly quantities of food and drink, dancing and singing.

Although slaves were not legally bound together, they usually stayed together. A marriage arranged by the master was usually doomed, but those based on mutual love prospered. The slave community saw adultery by either the woman or the man as a serious transgression. Because slave men owned so little and generally received their food, clothing, and shelter from their masters, slave women were less economically bound to their husbands than white women were. Slave marriages thus proceeded on a more equal basis than most white marriages.

All too often, masters separated slave families by selling different members off to faraway plantations. Many slaveholders professed a belief in the sanctity of the marriage covenant, but others cared little for the niceties of family ties and would sell whichever slave might bring a profit. Even those adhering to moral beliefs about marriage might break up a family to pay off debts. And when a master died, there were no guarantees that a slave family's rights would be acknowledged. Despite these threats to the slave family—in fact because of them—slave women and men fought to create and maintain a stable family. If a family member was sold away to a distant plantation, she or he would instantly be adopted by a network of "aunts," "uncles," and "cousins." Later, after the Civil War, newly freed slaves traveled across the South in search of the husbands and wives who had been torn from them.

For many plantation mistresses, staging an elaborate slave wedding was a chance to relive their own moment of glory. Southern plantation women married earlier than northern women, usually around the age of twenty. By their mid-twenties, when middle-class Northerners were marrying, single plantation women were being labeled "old maids."

Before marriage, the single young "belle" was spared nothing by her doting parents—she could purchase the latest fashions, then quickly discard them for a new ensemble. She lived in a sheltered world, punctuated by frequent balls and daily rounds of social calls to other fashionable women. Plantation parents kept a much more watchful eye on their charges than their counterparts to the North.

One observer noted that in contrast to Northerners, "in the South it is deemed indecorous for them to be left alone, and the mother or some member of the family is always in the room; and if none of these, a female slave is seated on the rug at the door."

If sex was out, flirting was expected, and many belles raised it to an art form. One belle, Cary Bryon, declared "she meant to have as many lovers as she could bring to her feet to be a reputed belle." For Cary, "lovers" were of the verbal variety only, supplemented by an occasional well-chaperoned peck on the cheek. One Southerner wrote to another about a friend whose "wife never took his arm till she took it to be led to the church on her wedding day, and that he never had an opportunity of kissing her but twice" before the ceremony.

Unlike their northern cousins, belles rejected marriage proposals not because of feelings of inadequacy but simply as a matter of course. If, in her rejection, the belle held out any hope at all of relenting, the young man took this first refusal as merely the opening salvo in a long campaign.

Within the plantation class, then, a belle could flirt at will without damaging her reputation. It was for the male suitor to maintain the honor of southern white women, or else. (If a woman's "honor" was violated, an overly aggressive suitor could expect to get a call from an enraged brother or father. If the young man was fortunate, the avenger would not shoot at once, but would merely insist upon a duel at ten paces.) This state of affairs offered southern plantation women some protection against marauding men, but it also placed them, much more than their northern counterparts, in the role of helpless victim.

For both the belle and the suitor, financial considerations played an important role in the final selection of a marriage partner. It was not uncommon for a man to give a monetary value to the object of his affection. One fellow, newly married and brimming with pride for his bride, noted that, besides her many "excellent qualities, she is worth twenty-five hundred dollars. She has a good piece of land about ten or twelve miles from Nashville." Another man, calculating his attraction to a prospective bride, wrote, "If she were not guilty of the unpardonable crime in Mississippi, to wit, poverty—would be a great belle. She is pretty and smart." Belles had as keen an eye for the financial bottom line as their male counterparts; many a poorly matched couple was the result of a young woman choosing financial prospects over character and temperament.

Eventually, the belle settled on a favorite and the wedding date was announced. Weddings were important in a society where social events played a central role in reaffirming a way of life. They were usually lavish, with extensive guest lists and menus. Relatives from afar were expected to attend. The big house was abuzz with preparations for a week before the celebration, and weddings between members of particularly important families were the source of neighborhood gossip for quite a while afterward.

Marriage relations among the southern planter class were in many ways an exaggerated version of those among the northeastern middle class. While virginity before marriage was expected for northeastern women, southern planter society placed an absolute premium on the bride's "purity." Northeastern women were placed on a platform and praised for their selflessness and moral rectitude. Plantation women were put upon a gilded pedestal, and southern writers extolled the refinement, piety, and grace by which these women surpassed all others. The result was a tightly constrained life that offered southern women few opportunities to move beyond the boundaries their society had established for them. This vision of the plantation woman on a pedestal was created by the southern planter aristocracy to offset the violence and inhumanity of slavery. Plantation women thus experienced striking contradictions: They often had to overlook their husbands' extramarital affairs, including sexual relations—forced or otherwise—with slave women, and they had to be the keepers of Christian piety while wielding the lash against unwilling servants. Their marriages prospered or faltered according to the degree to which they were able to rationalize these contradictions throughout their lives.

Women at Work

With all the changes in women's lives from 1800 to the present, at least one thing has remained constant—housework is equated with women's work. Women still do most of the cooking, cleaning, and child raising in private homes across the country. Now, however, many women also have the opportunity to work as doctors, social workers, secretaries, or even construction workers. In the early nineteenth century, women who worked outside the home had far fewer choices than women today, and they earned far less money. And in almost every case, the wage-paying work they did—teaching, textile manufacturing, domestic service—was connected to women's traditional work in the home.

Women's work in the early nineteenth century was exhausting. Consider the wash day of a typical New England woman with three children. Her husband was able to buy her the latest box stove and a goodly supply of coal every month in order to heat the stove, and thus the water for washing. The water itself came from the pump in the front yard, which was drawn from their well. If the woman was lucky enough to have a "hired girl" to help her, the girl would have the task of drawing and carrying the water, lighting and maintaining the stove fire, and heating water in a large, heavy iron pot. Once the hot water had been poured into the manual washing machine, the housewife took control of the process. After washing the week's laundry, she and the girl, along with the oldest daughter, attached it to the clothesline outside with wooden clothespins, a recent invention. Once the sun had done its work, the housewife gathered the clothing and neatly folded each article.

If such labor seems time-consuming, imagine the enormity of wash day on the Illinois frontier. There a woman would probably be doing laundry not only for a larger family—upwards of eight children—but perhaps for a few seasonal workers as well. Her older children might help, but most likely she would not have a paid servant. Both cash and available labor were in short supply; few women were willing to work as domestics on the frontier when marriage appeared to be a better option. On wash day, the frontier woman's husband split the wood for fuel from logs he had felled earlier in the year. She dragged water in buckets from a nearby stream, boiled it over a fireplace, then scrubbed each article of clothing against a washboard, using soap she and her daughters had made, before rinsing it in a separate tub.

Frontier women also spent much of their time producing clothing. Few were without a spinning wheel and loom, the essential tools of the trade. Many an evening was spent bent over these machines, working steadily while teaching daughters the techniques that had been passed down from their grandmothers. Homespun cloth was an important commodity for sale or barter. Because most of the money from raising crops and livestock went toward mortgages, taxes, and farm equipment, income from homespun was used either to purchase manufactured goods from the East or to expand the farm operations. Charlotte Jacobs remembered that to acquire pigs for the farm, she "bought twelve shoats and paid for them with linsey and jeans of my own make." Other frontier women traded their excess homespun for clocks, pianos, and better butter churns, as well as additional land and implements. In this way a farm community worked itself out of the frontier stage of its development.

A farm woman tended a garden and managed the family poultry flock that provided meat and eggs, as well as down for quilts and pillows. She also fed and milked the cows, and then churned the cream into butter. When a steer was butchered, she used the fat to make soap and candles. She butchered hogs, then smoked and salted the meat. After harvest, she pickled, dried, and canned much of her garden produce for winter consumption.

Farm women on the frontier rarely had time for leisure—the occasional church meeting or Fourth of July celebration were their only days off. Wives and husbands alike toiled from sunup to sundown to make their farm a paying proposition. But as her husband rested in the evening from his labor in the fields, a woman would clean up after supper, spin yarn, mend clothing, or entertain the children. One observer, the French writer Alexis de Tocqueville, looked at the frontier woman and saw that "want, suffering, and boredom have changed her fragile frame but not broken down her courage." He noted that her children, "bursting with health, press around the woman. To see their strength and her weakness, one would say that she had drained herself to give them life and does not regret what they have cost her."

The market for farm products increased dramatically in urban areas. Before 1800, town and city dwellers often kept poultry and livestock in their backyards or on the town commons, and they kept a well-stocked garden going as well. As time went on, leading citizens of growing cities worked to ban animals that had become health problems and nuisances, and as land became more scarce and more expensive, the working class was forced into crowded tenement apartments. Women in cities like Boston and New York no longer made the farm products that their grandmothers had, but the new manufacturing technology did little to improve their lives. For working-class women, the new cash economy made life harder and meaner. Then as now, women earned far less than men and were grouped into industries, such as textile, millinery (hat-making), and shoe-making, recognized as "women's work." A New York charity reported in 1817, "The great disproportion which exists between the prices of labor of men and women is a matter of serious regret."

Most women wage workers in New York City labored in the clothing industry. Usually they took "outwork"—sewing together pieces of cloth into whole garments in their own homes. Because of cutthroat competition, the prices paid for such work were very low. A woman could barely keep herself, let alone her dependent children, clothed, sheltered, and fed. Factory owners made these conditions worse by abruptly cutting prices, withholding pay, and inventing numerous other frauds to keep from paying women their due. Reformer Matthew Carey noted in 1830 that seamstresses had little recourse against such unscrupulous practices: "If the price of shirts were brought down to six cents they would accept it, and thankfully too. Their numbers and their wants are so great, and the competition so urgent, that they are wholly at the mercy of their employers."

For women whose husbands were working, such practices made life difficult but not impossible. As long as their husbands brought in a steady income, reductions in women's pay meant hardship, not necessarily starvation. But conditions for working men were not much better than for women. Although paid more than women, most earned just enough money to provide the basics. Any unforeseen emergency, such as a medical problem, could send a family to the poorhouse. If the man became too sick to work or was injured on the job, the family could starve. Death was an ever-present possibility, given the abysmal working conditions and scant access to medical care of most working people. Such protections as unemployment insurance, Social Security, and Medicare were a century away. Given these pressures on the head breadwinner, many a man abandoned his wife and children for a fresh start in another town, leaving his family with few ways to survive.

Single women might enter domestic work, but here they paid a price as well. Hours were long, longer even than factory work or outwork. Many domestics worked from five in the morning until ten at night, six and sometimes seven days a week. One man who had grown up being served by domestics remembered how difficult the work was: "Oil lamps required trimming and filling; candlesticks … were to be cleaned; wood and coal to be brought from the cellar to all the

This illustration from an 1853 domestic guide shows a woman making pies while drying laundry by the fire and watching two children. Although advice from books and magazines helped women manage their housework and supervise their servants, it also created higher standards for housewives.

fires ... in all sitting rooms. All water required for the kitchen, or bedrooms, or for baths, was drawn from the nearest street pump, and all refuse water and slops were carried out to the street and emptied into the gutter. The street, for half its width in front of each building, was to be swept twice a week." Domestics also prepared three meals a day, as well as afternoon tea.

After 1800, elite society came to expect that "ladies" would refrain from menial chores around the house. One writer observed, "Women might work, but not ladies; or when the latter undertook it, they ceased to be such." There was thus an ever-widening gulf between mistress and servant, and the domestic was made to understand this difference in rank, which led to numerous tensions. Advice about the home in the newly popular magazines written for women increasingly described the role of the lady of the house as being a manager. She was to ensure that those beneath her performed their duties properly. One Irish domestic, Rose Butler, complained that her mistress "was always finding fault with my work, and scolding me." Butler's response was to scatter hot coals outside the fire grate, in the hopes that her mistress's enraged response would be to send her back to Ireland. Instead the domestic managed to burn the house down and was convicted of arson. Though not all domestic-mistress relationships ended in flames, numerous emotional fires burst out on both sides.

However, the job was not without its advantages to domestics. Because employers provided room and board as well as a small salary, a domestic had money for things other than the bare necessities. This surplus she often used to purchase the latest in "ready-made" fashions. Sporty dresses gave domestics an entree into the giddy whirl of urban nightlife, in part making up for the drudgery of their jobs. Employers often were scandalized by such shows of fancy dress. Many mistresses believed a domestic servant should save her money to help her achieve eventual middle-class status. Mistresses decried the "outlandish hot looking dresses" of their employees, seeing these "crimson and scarlet shawls, ribbons, and faded bonnet flowers," backed by "sultry yellow calico," as an invitation to sin and sexual misconduct.

Many working women chafed against such tight supervision. Some even chose prostitution rather than submit to the orders of a mistress, although that choice, too, brought its own dangers. Opportunities for prostitution ranged from high-class hotel establishments to the lowest waterfront saloon side-rooms, but all prostitutes were vulnerable to a wide range of sexual diseases. Those plying their trade independently, or in the less genteel establishments, were especially vulnerable to violence from customers, proprietors, or criminals. But when working women chose prostitution over domestic service, they were rejecting in no uncertain terms the moral assumptions of middle-class America. Most mistresses explained the choice by pointing to the "natural" moral laxness of the poor. Upper-class women were not ready to admit that servants were so scarce because working conditions were so trying.

Domestics became even more scarce in the 1820s, after the development of power mills in New England. These mills provided American women with their first opportunity at respectable, relatively safe work at reasonable wages. The entrepreneurs who began the massive New England mills in Lowell, Waltham, and other mill towns sought to attract young, unmarried women as their primary workers. Owners believed they would accept lower wages than men, particularly married men. And the owners could offer advantages that most other employers could not. Mill work offered women high wages in comparison to other jobs available to women, relative independence from their families, and a convivial group of like-minded young women. Most of the workers came from small farm towns in northern New England. Mill owners provided supervised boarding facilities that protected women workers from what the mill owners saw as temptation and sin, and the rural locations of the mills kept women sheltered from the lures of the city's bright lights. These conditions persuaded parents that mill work was an acceptable occupation for their daughters.

Farm women went to the mills for a number of reasons, which rarely had much to do with supporting their families. Mary Paul, a farm woman from Vermont, went to work at the mills when she was fifteen. Before quitting her job as a domestic servant, she wrote her father for permission to work at Lowell, explaining, "I think it would be much better for me in Lowell than to stay about here. I am in need of clothes which I cannot get about here." Sally Rice, another Vermont farm woman, explained to her family, "I am nineteen years old. I must of course have something of my own before many years have passed over my head. And where is

Women operate power looms to weave cloth in a factory. Before the introduction of the power loom, weaving by hand was an arduous task that had required the hard physical labor of men. Now, women could do the work—and for lower wages.

that something coming from if I go home and earn nothing. You may think me unkind but how can you blame me for wanting to stay here. I have but one life to live and I want to enjoy myself as well as I can while I live."

Although these women were separated from their families, they were not without connections to home. Many followed sisters and cousins into the mills. Older relatives helped newcomers secure jobs and taught them the rules of both work and social life in the mill community. Families also expected older relatives to keep an eye on the newcomers.

Mill workers came to expect a certain level of respect from both the outside world and the mill owners. They believed that they were in partnership with the owner—subordinate partners, to be sure, but nonetheless members of the company who were crucial to the success of the business. When the owners responded to increased competition and poor business conditions with sharp reductions in wages and increases in the rents they charged in their boardinghouses, many women workers were outraged. As conditions continued to decline during the 1840s, mill owners began hiring recent immigrant women, such as the Irish, who would accept lower pay and more work. The prior workers did not surrender without a fight, however. As owners shifted from stern but benevolent father figures to cutthroat businessmen, many workers began to reject the rhetoric of the mill as family. Instead, they used the sense of solidarity and worthiness gained from their work experience to create a movement that would fight for their rights. Their actions were part of a broader trend of women making their voices heard in the public arena.

Slave women, of course, had even less choice of jobs and working satisfaction. Women were sent to the fields like men and expected to do their share of the work; slaveholders cared little about preserving a "women's sphere" for slave women. Cotton was king in the plantation South, and although some regions produced rice, tobacco, and sugar as well, most slaves' memory of work revolved around picking cotton. Slave women recalled the intense physical labor that such work required. As one former slave recalled in an interview, "It don't make no difference if you big or little, you better keep up or the drivers burn you up with the whip, sure 'nough. 'Bout nine o'clock they hollers, 'cotton up' and that's the quittin' signal. We go to the quarters and just drop on the bunk and go to sleep with nothin' to eat."

Slaves were usually segregated into men's and women's gangs. Men tended to do jobs that required greater strength, such as plowing, while women were assigned to hoeing. However, a number of slave women took to plowing, a job that demanded great skill as well as strength. Indeed, there were few jobs that slave women did not do, including planting seeds, digging ditches, making fences, and clearing new ground for planting. While women were often not expected to accomplish as much as men, many women slaves exceeded the output of their male counterparts. Their work was a source of pride.

A few lucky women were trained as midwives, a skill that also provided status and a great deal of satisfaction. One ex-slave told of how when she was thirteen "my ol' mistress put me with a doctor who learned me how to be a midwife. I stayed with that doctor for five years. I got to be good. Got to be so he's sit down and I'd do all the work. When I come home, I made lots of money for old miss. Lots of times, didn't sleep regular or get my meals on time for three, four days. 'Cause when they call, I always went. Brought as many white as colored children."

White southern plantation women, while certainly benefiting from slave labor, also were responsible for much of the plantation's labor. The master hired an overseer to do much of his dirty work, but the mistress was in effect the overseer of the Big House, including the tending of livestock and poultry and the production of food and clothing. Additionally, the mistress performed tasks for which she did not trust her slaves. Even the most privileged mistress had to take on fairly strenuous tasks from time to time, such as processing the various by-products of slaughtered animals. The mistress and the slaves she supervised shared their work space in constant tension. In some cases, mistresses used brute force, resorting to repeated whippings, and occasionally slaves responded in kind. But more often, slave and slaveholder were involved in an elaborate chess match with each other to determine how power would be divided in the Big House.

Not all southern whites and blacks lived on large plantations. Even though the industrial development of southern cities and towns lagged far behind the North, a significant minority of southerners lived in urban areas. Work for white women in towns was similar to that of their northern counterparts, but without some of the advantages of northern industrial buying power. Ready-made goods were more expensive and less available in the South, where most women continued to produce their own food and clothing from scratch. Another significant section of the southern population lived on small family farms and worked their land without slaves. Life for women on these places was similar to that of women on the northern frontier—many children, backbreaking work from morning until bedtime, and not much chance to get ahead, unless one were willing to move to the frontiers of Arkansas or Texas.

In the North, most middle-class women during this period either could not afford or could not find hired help. Even those women lucky enough to hire a servant had plenty of work to do. Women had access to new technology but often found that "labor-saving devices" saved the labor of men, not of women. Take the four-burner stove, introduced in the mid-nineteenth century. Before it, cooking was very straightforward; a woman hung an iron pot over a fireplace and cooked one-pot meals for her family. But by mid-century, women's magazines and books insisted on new, more complicated, and time-consuming cooking techniques using the four-burner stove. Baking, for instance, had become a symbol of prestige for northeastern women. Harriet Beecher Stowe and Catharine Beecher, who produced the foremost domestic manual of the period, asked rhetorically: "Bread: What ought it to be? It should be light, sweet, and tender. This matter of lightness is the distinctive line between savage and civilized bread. The savage mixes simple flour and water into balls of paste, which he throws into boiling water. The air cells in bread thus prepared are coarse and uneven: the bread is as inferior in delicacy and nicety to that which is well kneaded as a raw servant to a perfectly educated lady." All that stood between civilization and savagery, between the elite and the mob, was the respectable housewife's tireless effort to produce refined bread for her family.

Stowe and Beecher, like other domestic writers, hoped to establish housewifery as a respected occupation based on scientific techniques and a firm moral foundation. Beecher led the way in these efforts with her pathbreaking *Treatise on Domestic Economy,* first published in 1841. She believed that once housewives were properly trained, they could claim and exercise the power in the domestic realm that they were denied in the public one. Beecher had no patience with talk of women's suffrage or women's rights. She believed that women's inequality in relation to men helped contribute to "the general good of all." By gaining power over the home, however, Beecher declared that American women were "committed to the exalted privilege of extending over the world those blessed influences which are to renovate degraded man." The efficiently run, morally uplifted home would save the American republic from degradation.

Beecher built on the views of domestic writers who had been advising middle-class women since the late eighteenth century. Sarah Josepha Hale, who edited *Godey's Lady's Book* from 1837 until her retirement in 1877 at the age of ninety, was perhaps the most influential domestic writer of her time. By 1860, *Godey's* had broken all readership records, with a subscription list of 150,000. Hale achieved these numbers with a philosophy that celebrated woman in her sphere while disapproving of "this notion of female voting." The home, explained Hale, "was the sacred residence designed by divine goodness for her happiness."

By elevating women's work to the level of national purpose, domestic writers created emotional and physical burdens for women. Yet by the late nineteenth century, women would use the ideal of the well-run, morally enlightened home as a model for the way the world should be run. By making the home morally superior to "the world"—men's sphere of politics and business—domestic writers were unwittingly giving future women the means to press their case for the necessity of women's perspective in running the government. Why try to raise morally upright sons if only to see them abandoned to the vicious, amoral world outside the home?

The new emphasis on women's domestic skills had a more immediate impact on middle-class women's status. Catharine Beecher, Sarah Josepha Hale, and others supported the idea put forth by women reformers that girls needed to be broadly educated in order to take command of the home. The new woman of the nineteenth century, women educators argued, needed to be literate and thoughtful as well as skilled at traditional domestic tasks. Yet while early educational reformers stressed that women's education would complement women's work, some women would discover that education let them rethink the kind of work women should be doing.

Stepping Stones of Education

The idea of women's education entered the arena of popular debate during the revolutionary era. Many social thinkers argued that a basic—though not overly demanding—education was a prerequisite for any respectable republican mother. One popular textbook, *The American Preceptor,* insisted that Americans were "indebted to their mothers for the seeds of virtue and knowledge." The book was quick to note, however, that women's education would ensure "our daughters will shine as bright constellations in the sphere where nature has placed them." The ideal of the educated mother obviously took hold—in New England, literacy among women rose from 50 to nearly 100 percent between the revolution and 1840.

In the South, the situation was much less advanced. While reformers in New England were pushing for the establishment of mandatory public education, southern leadership depended largely on private schools, which meant that only women from upper-class families received educations. Few women slaves learned to read, because slaveholders viewed literacy as an invitation to revolt. Still, a small percentage of the slave population did learn to read, many of them taught by white playmates when they were young. Overall, few southern women were able to take advantage of the expanded vision that literacy and education offered.

At first, women's education in the North was meant simply to reinforce upper-class women's domestic talents. Subjects like French, English, and embroidery were especially featured at female academies around the turn of the century. By the 1810s, however, a new ideal of women's education was taking shape. Educational reformers still talked of strengthening women's sphere but now saw this sphere as necessarily including a knowledge of moral philosophy, literature, psychology, physiology, and a range of other subjects. The new women's seminaries that opened during this time sought to provide an education nearly equal to that of men.

In 1819, Emma Willard, one of the earliest proponents of expanded female education, argued for a state-supported system of female seminaries. In *An Address to the Public; Particularly to the Members of the Legislature of New York, Proposing a Plan for Improving Female Education,* Willard claimed that an intellectually challenging education for women would bring about "a new and happy era in the history of her sex, and of her country, and of mankind." Although many legislators—and New York governor DeWitt Clinton—were favorably impressed with Willard's ideas, they were not willing to pay for them.

Willard did not win the legislature's support, but her pamphlet received warm reviews from the likes of John Adams and Thomas Jefferson. Having laid the groundwork for her plan, Willard turned to the town leaders of Troy, New York, to finance her dream. Troy's leading citizens, seeing Willard's school as an ideal opportunity for their daughters, agreed to fund her. Willard's Troy Female Seminary was the result of her fifteen years of teaching experience and experiments. It gave privileged young women the most demanding course of study available. One student reported that she had learned, "reading, writing, spelling, arithmetic, grammar, geography, history, maps, the globe, algebra, geometry, trigonometry, astronomy, natural philosophy, chemistry, botany, physiology, mineralogy, geology, and zoology"—and that was just the morning classes!

Troy Seminary became a model for others, while Willard herself took to traveling the country as an advocate of women's education. She stressed the role seminaries could play in filling the growing demand for women teachers. Although women had started teaching as part-time replacements for men, New England school boards were quick to realize that they could be hired at half the cost of men—a fact Willard liked to emphasize. By 1850, Troy Seminary had produced more than two hundred teachers.

Seminary students in the early 1800s often engaged in a strenuous course of education, including geography, as in this scene done with watercolor and ink on silk. Many seminary students would become teachers themselves.

Teaching proved to be an excellent opportunity for many young women. Women teachers received only half of what men received, but teaching still enabled single women to support themselves. The job also gave women more breathing space before getting married. Although marriage would most likely improve a woman's economic status, staying single—at least for a time—did not mean poverty.

An entrepreneurial woman could transform teaching into a better-paying occupation. A number of women who had experience teaching chose to open female seminaries, or to take on administrative positions. Opening a school was sometimes the only way that a widowed woman could support herself and her children. Numerous middle- and upper-class women avoided almost certain poverty by following this course. Others, like Emma Willard, opened a school when their husband's business collapsed.

Although Willard's Troy Seminary was a great success, only well-to-do women could afford it. Mary Lyon was responsible for bringing Willard's old idea for a publicly supported female seminary to fruition. Lyon envisioned "a residential seminary to be founded and sustained by the Christian public," with tuition and board to cost "as low as it may be." In order to keep costs low, train women in necessary skills, and improve discipline, the students themselves would perform the necessary domestic tasks. Lyon had experienced the problems associated with seminary boards of directors (who were usually all men). She therefore wanted her seminary to own its own property and to be self-supporting. By combining private contributions with local government support, she was able to raise enough money to build and sustain her project. In 1837 Mount Holyoke Female Seminary—later Mount Holyoke College—became the first endowed institution of female higher education in America.

Besides having a more diverse student body, Mount Holyoke differed from Troy in other ways. While Troy's curriculum had been broad, it had not been particularly deep. Lyon soon developed a four-year program of study, a first for women's seminaries. She instituted discussion classes about current political and social questions so that women could develop their own ideas. Mount Holyoke kept up with the latest scientific theories and provided its students with a small laboratory in which to conduct experiments. The school fulfilled Lyon's vision of a place for women to explore their own intellectual strivings.

Lyon died in 1849, at age fifty-two, exhausted by her lifetime of work for the cause of women's education. Her legacy, however, was substantial. The success of Mount Holyoke ensured that the notion of a thinking woman would not be treated as an impossibility. Holyoke went on to produce even more teachers than Troy. Because of Mount Holyoke's advanced curriculum, many of its former students became seminary teachers themselves. And Mount Holyoke students, having spent four years of intellectual excitement together, created strong networks that they would draw on throughout their lives.

Despite Mount Holyoke's radical implications, it was still based on fairly conservative principles. Though Lyon hoped to expand women's sphere, she still believed that the ideal of separate spheres was fundamentally sound. And while she insisted on a woman's right to an equal education, her ideas about equality had limits. Thus when one of her students, Lucy Stone, persisted in distributing William Lloyd Garrison's fiery antislavery newspaper, the *Liberator*, Lyon made clear that such activities were not acceptable. Lyon found fighting for equality for white women was enough of a battle—she was not about to alienate her supporters by allowing the advocacy of racial equality.

Stone, who was to become a leading abolitionist and women's rights advocate, found a more congenial home at Oberlin College, in Ohio. Oberlin was founded in 1833 by abolitionists and Protestant evangelists. It accepted all qualified students, regardless of race or sex—the first such college in the United States.

At Oberlin, Stone met Antoinette Brown, and the two became allied in the cause to make the college live up to its radical intentions. Both thrived at Oberlin, but each found that their professors and fellow students were more comfortable with equality in the abstract than in the particular. Stone was kept from taking public speaking courses throughout her time there. Although the faculty recognized her abilities by granting her the responsibility for writing the graduation speech, she was not allowed to deliver it. When she discovered this conditional honor, she turned the opportunity down altogether. Despite these bumps in the road, she and Brown graduated together in 1847.

Brown, however, was not through. She hoped to continue her religious education and earn a doctorate in divinity from Oberlin. At first, the faculty was dumbfounded. No woman had ever made such a request, and the Oberlin professors found themselves once again having to explain away what appeared to be obvious hypocrisy. She later recalled, "I was reasoned with, pleaded with, and besought even with tears not to combat a beneficent order tending to promote harmony in the family and the commonwealth. Masculine headship everywhere was held to be indispensable to morality, and grounded in the inmost fitness of things."

Although Brown finally was allowed to proceed, the school ultimately backed out on its promise, and prevented her and another woman from receiving their degrees. Only in 1908 did the school grant Brown an honorary degree. Stone noted with irony that Brown "felt that she was commanded to preach, and to arrest the progress of thousands that were on the road to hell." Given these sentiments—so in keeping with the mainstream of Protestantism—Stone wanted to know "why, when she applied for ordination, they acted as though they had rather the whole world should go to hell, than that Antoinette Brown should be allowed to tell them how to keep out of it?"

Although Brown and Stone had to struggle to receive their due at Oberlin, at least the school made it possible for such a struggle to take place. Despite its inconsistencies, Oberlin still offered unparalleled opportunity for women. Stone, in fact, was the first Massachusetts woman to earn a college degree. She and Brown continued to support each other in the abolition and women's rights movements. They solidified their alliance by marrying into the same family—Brown married Samuel Blackwell, and Stone married his brother Henry. But although Brown became Antoinette Brown Blackwell, Stone insisted on keeping the name Lucy Stone, a unique claim at the time. No doubt many an old-fashioned critic looked at Lucy Stone and Antoinette Brown Blackwell as perfect examples of the harm higher education could do to two otherwise sensible women.

Thanks to the pioneering work of Troy Seminary, Mount Holyoke, Oberlin College, and other schools, when the first crop of American women writers and activists began to emerge in the 1840s, they were not universally looked upon as freaks. Instead, there was now a large core of women committed to intellectual pursuits in New England and throughout the North. Indeed, some of the most prominent members of the transcendentalist movement, which sought to discover universal truths that would help one live a worthwhile life, were women, although Ralph Waldo Emerson and Henry David Thoreau are the most famous. In their day the Peabody sisters were celebrated transcendentalists. Elizabeth Peabody was a leader of Christian transcendentalism and a publisher of tracts, including Thoreau's famous essay "On Civil Disobedience." Mary Peabody Mann collaborated with her husband, Horace Mann, on his research into educational reform. After his death, she coauthored numerous works on early childhood education with Elizabeth. Sophia Peabody Hawthorne, a writer and artist in her own right, contributed significantly to the work of her husband, Nathaniel Hawthorne.

Margaret Fuller was the most influential woman identified with transcendentalism. She brought together the intellectuals who swirled around Emerson by initiating a series of "Conversations," symposia that touched on a vast array of topics. At first she offered the Conversations only to women, but she later opened them up to men as well. During 1839 and 1840 they were a center of intellectual activity in New England. In 1840 Fuller helped initiate and edit the influential transcendentalist journal *The Dial.* She also participated in the transcendentalists' utopian community at Brook Farm, but chose not to live there. She wisely saw it for what it was—a wonderful place for a conversation, but a thoroughly impractical experiment in communal living.

In 1844, Fuller began writing for Horace Greeley's influential *New York Tribune.* Greeley believed her to be "the most remarkable woman in America and in some respects the greatest woman whom America has yet known." Fuller was one of the first women columnists to move outside the domestic sphere, writing on everything from literary figures to prison reform to women's rights. In 1845, she published her groundbreaking work, *Woman in the Nineteenth Century,* which would influence numerous women's rights advocates in years to come. In it she argued, "We would have every arbitrary barrier thrown down. We would have every path laid open to Woman as freely as Man. As the friend of the Negro assumes that one man cannot by right hold another in bondage, so would the friend of Woman assume that Man cannot by right lay even well-meant restrictions on women." It was a heady call to arms.

Fuller reported for the *Tribune* in Europe between 1847 and 1850, another first for a woman. As she returned home on the ship *Elizabeth,* it seemed to many reformers in America that she was, as Greeley believed, without peer. But in a storm just a few hundred feet off New York harbor, the *Elizabeth* broke apart and sank. Margaret Fuller's body was never found. She was forty years old.

Although her words would outlive her, perhaps the example of her life was her greatest legacy. Fuller proved that intellectual pursuits could be a woman's vocation and demonstrated that a thorough education could equip a woman to achieve greatness. These lessons were a far cry from what early educational reformers had envisioned for women. Instead of planting women firmly in their sphere, education gave some women the tools to break through the restrictions society had placed on their potential. Critics of women's education had been right—too many ideas in a woman's head could be a dangerous thing.

Religious Activity and Utopian Communities

When Lucy Stone was a young girl, she came upon the biblical command in Genesis, "Unto the woman [God] said, I will greatly multiply thy sorrow and thy conception; in sorrow thou shalt bring forth children; and thy desire shall be to thy husband, and he shall rule over thee." Stone closed the Bible and solemnly asked her mother the best way to take her life. Young Lucy explained that she wished to obey God's will, but could not live in a world where she had to submit to such an oppressive commandment. Her mother tried to console her, explaining that the Bible was quite clear in this regard—it was a woman's duty to obey her husband. Lucy took another lesson from this. "My mother always tried to submit. I never could," she later remembered. In time, she would learn Greek, Latin, and Hebrew in order to master the Bible in its original form and discover if "men had falsified the text" in translation.

In 1800, the United States was an overwhelmingly Protestant nation. After the 1820s, greater numbers of Catholics and Jews would immigrate to America and join scattered communities of their brethren in the New World, but even then Protestantism would dominate American life. Protestantism was hardly one unified religion, however. Great battles were fought in the early nineteenth century over whose version of Christianity would triumph. Women provided most of the foot soldiers, and many of the officers, in these grand crusades to save the soul of the republic. Issues of women's proper place in these religious wars became battles in themselves, splitting numerous sects and forcing Americans to confront the contradiction between women's submission and women's moral duty.

The most electrifying religious crusade began in upper New York State in 1824 when evangelist Charles Finney set off a spark of religious fervor that would soon transform American religion. Religious revivals were not new in America; they had most recently intensified around the turn of the century as Methodists, Baptists, Presbyterians, and Congregationalists, among others, vied to bring new members into their congregations. But Finney's crusade was different. His revivals swept through the small towns of upstate New York with such speed and intensity that the region was nicknamed the "Burned-over District." Finney soon moved on to the bustling towns of Utica and Rochester, where he found young women and men especially open to his preaching. But he also noticed that women were taking a predominant role in organizing and participating in the revivals. In some towns, more than three-quarters of the converts were women. When Finney left the Burned-over District and took his crusade to New York City—where he was an instant success—he brought with him a commitment to increase the role of women in practicing and preaching religion.

Finney was a firm believer in the doctrine of perfectionism. He held that people were not predestined to sin or salvation, as the Calvinists had earlier claimed. Rather, they could free themselves of sin, and in turn free the world, through prayer

J. Cheney del. from R. Cosway R.A   Pendleton's Lith.

Prayer and religious faith were an important aspect of most women's lives in the nineteenth century, as this 1828 lithograph, "Devotion," indicates.

and good works. Further, he believed holiness resided most prominently in the individual, and that a person's connection with God was more important than the words or actions of ministers. This approach to religion had much to offer women who hoped to move beyond the confines of their appointed sphere while maintaining, like young Lucy Stone, their religious convictions. Finneyite Protestantism gave women a moral compass that was, in theory, not controlled by a minister or a husband, but by God. It was the woman's duty to read that compass correctly.

By the 1820s, women had established missionary societies throughout the North. The first of these was the Whitestone Female Charitable Organization, which soon branched out to encompass all of Oneida County, New York, renaming itself the Oneida Female Missionary Society in 1814. By this point, the group was supporting evangelical efforts in the newly expanding towns along the Erie Canal. By the time it changed its name to the Missionary Society of the Western District in 1817, it had more than seventy auxiliary organizations and was contributing over one thousand dollars a year to support ministries across the northern frontier. Suddenly, the female missionaries were a force to be reckoned with in the religious community. Thousands of lapsed Christians and nonbelievers had been "reborn," thanks to the efforts of the Female Missionary Society.

Protestant ministers did not always look favorably on women taking active roles in their congregations. Most prominently, Calvinists—the descendants of the first Puritan "pilgrims" who had settled New England—had once asserted that women were especially predisposed to sin. "Woman, Eve's progeny, by their naturally sensuous nature, have ever been Man's temptress," insisted one typical Calvinist tract. But as Eve's progeny filled ever more pews in the churches, even Calvinist ministers were recognizing "the selfless mothers and daughters" not as sinners but as saints.

Though most Protestant ministers encouraged women's role in religious life, the question remained just what that role would be. The Calvinist sects—Congregationalists and Presbyterians—were horrified at women speaking in public. Congregationalist minister Asahel Nettleton, who was a believer in emotionally restrained revivals led by ordained preachers, condemned those like Finney "who introduces the practice of females praying in promiscuous [that is, mixed male and female] assemblies." A Presbyterian association in New York objected to any participation by women in church services, arguing, "God has not made it [women's] duty to lead, but to be in silence."

Nonetheless, women did begin to preach. Perhaps the most influential was Phoebe Worrall Palmer, a Methodist lay minister who shared Finney's belief in immediate sanctification, the state of grace that overcomes one upon acceptance of Christ as one's savior, and in Christian perfectionism. Unlike Lucy Stone or Antoinette Brown Blackwell, who turned their evangelism toward equal-rights activism, Palmer believed women should go no further than religious preaching.

Perhaps because of her social conservatism, she was able to reach many people who were hostile to women's rights.

Born to an upper-middle-class family of ten in New York City, Phoebe Worrall married a fellow Methodist, Walter Clark Palmer, in 1827. Each of the two times Palmer gave birth, the infant died within weeks. She and her husband took this as a sign from God that they should focus all their efforts on saving souls. Soon thereafter, both attained spiritual sanctification during a Charles Finney revival in New York City. Palmer began her evangelical career with a weekly all-women prayer meeting she ran with her sister in their New York City home. In time, Palmer took on sole leadership of the meeting, which by the late 1830s had become known as the Tuesday Meeting for the Promotion of Holiness. In 1839, men were allowed to participate, and by 1840 the membership was so large that the meeting was forced to move to more spacious quarters. In later years, the meeting moved beyond its Methodist circle to include women and men from many evangelical Christian denominations.

Palmer gained even greater influence through her writings. While unwilling to support the cause of women's rights, she was adamant about women's rightful place in religious and charitable work. In *The Way of the Father* (1859), Palmer drew from biblical sources to refute conservatives' condemnation of women preachers, employing quotations such as Joel's prophecy from Acts 2:17, "And it shall come to pass in the last days, saith God, I will pour out of my Spirit upon all flesh; and your sons and your daughters shall prophesy." In the popular book *The Way of Holiness* (1845), Palmer used her own life as an example of the quest for spiritual perfection and the opportunities women could find in spreading the gospel.

Many evangelicals were deeply involved in the antislavery movement, and none more so than the Finneyites and the Quakers. The basic tenets of the Quaker faith stressed egalitarianism, and Quakers had long encouraged women to speak their religious faith. Though some Quaker women were appointed lay ministers, most focused their attention on the monthly women's meeting. Quakers provided some of the earliest opportunities for girls to be educated along with boys. At the core of Quaker theology was the ideal of individual communication with God, deemphasizing the ministry. Quaker ministers were unpaid and were expected to facilitate prayer meetings rather than to direct a service. The women's meetings were led by women ministers.

By the 1820s, however, conservative Quakers were stressing the importance of the word of the Bible as interpreted by each church's Elders, who provided leadership and counsel. As all the Elders were men, this policy tended to limit Quaker women's influence. In 1827, a group of Quakers called the Hicksites formed a separate group, rejecting the conservatives' growing drift away from egalitarianism and the individual's relationship with God. Named for their leader, Elias Hicks, they extended their egalitarianism to include the abolition of slavery. Whereas the conservative Quakers favored a gradual approach, the Hicksites joined with the more radical Finneyites to call for the immediate abolition of slavery.

Not surprisingly, the Hicksites tended to attract the most outspoken Quakers, including Lucretia Mott, one of the earliest American women's rights advocates. Mott learned her speaking skills at monthly meetings for married Quaker women. When she was only twenty-one, Quaker elders appointed her a lay minister. Mott credited the Quaker community with developing her views about women's role in society. "I grew up," she wrote, "so thoroughly imbued with women's rights that it was the most important question of my life from a very early day." Other Hicksites would join with Mott in the vanguard of the women's rights movement after 1848.

Christian perfectionism did not get very far in the plantation South. When the Finneyites and other evangelicals turned their social reform rhetoric on the evils of slavery, southern leaders demanded that their own churches toe the proslavery line or risk reprisals, and the southern churches soon rejected the perfectionist and reformist agenda of their northern brethren. Perfectionism implied that society had to be vastly improved, and southern slavery apologists agreed up to a point: Northern cities were swamps of iniquity badly in need of salvation, but their own southern plantation society was beyond reproach. When southern religious figures did use Christianity as a means of reform, it was to chastise those few recalcitrant slave owners who went beyond the bounds of Christian decency in handling their slaves—those who tortured their slaves, for instance.

At the same time, the church provided solace, stability, and a woman-dominated membership for plantation women. Virginia Cary, writing in *Letters on the Female Character* (1831) on "the peculiar difficulties of our southern housewives," noted that "religion is at least most necessary to enable women to perform their allotted duties in life. The very nature of those duties demands the strength of Christian principle to ensure their correct and dignified performance; while the nature of female trials, requires all [the] power of faith, to induce a requisite measure of patience and fortitude." In other words, religion enabled plantation mistresses to endure the atrocities of slave society with a modicum of inner peace.

Planters had mixed feelings about exposing their slaves to Christianity. Southern men believed that religion, carefully administered by white preachers, encouraged slaves to accept life as it was. The slave's reward could come in heaven, not on earth, white preachers claimed; the slaves would be assured of eternal salvation by their unceasing loyalty to their master. But Christianity offered the same subversive messages about moral standards, freedom, and individual empowerment to slaves as it did to northern white women. Not surprisingly, slaves were especially fond of the tale of Moses leading the Jews out of bondage from Egypt.

Some slave women used Christianity as a weapon of passive resistance against their owners. One old slave, having endured numerous beatings, told her mistress one day, "I'm saved. Now I know the Lord will show me the way. I ain't going to grieve no more. No matter how much you all beat me and my children the Lord will show me the way. And some day we'll never be slaves." Since God was certainly morally superior to the master, and the individual slave was answerable in the end only to God, a slave's Christianity could undermine the master's authority.

Black religion kept the emotional quality and various myths and beliefs of West African folk religions, and was shared by the whole family, indeed by the entire community. Slaves would have thought little of the idea of religion as a woman's "natural" province. Slave women were not expected to be moral paragons or natural educators—qualities that society typically assigned to middle-class white women that made them "especially suited" to Christianity. Nor did slave women need Christianity as a means to fill up a feeling of uselessness—they were plenty busy as it was. Finally, black men were not off in a separate world of business—their work was rooted in their immediate and extended family and their community.

Religion was a family affair for frontier families as well. Like black slaves, white men and women on the frontier did not make a sharp divide between work and home. There were rarely enough women in a frontier community to build the type of female religious network found in more settled areas. The camp meeting, an outdoor religious gathering, provided the type of community celebration that broke the monotony and isolation of frontier life. As an eastern newspaper reported, "A camp meeting [on the frontier] is the most mammoth picnic possible, as at a barbecue, the very heart and soul of hospitality and kindness is wide open and poured forth."

If evangelism ignited a spirit of community and kindliness toward one another, it could also unleash bigotry and intolerance. Evangelism was based on the belief that only those "born again" would make it into the kingdom of heaven. Nonbelievers could be saved, but only when they accepted Christ into their lives. As one young convert wrote in her diary, "He that is not with us said the Saviour is against us." Since the other side belonged to Satan, religious groups that did not conform to the broad expectations of mainstream Protestantism were often demonized. Both the Mormons and the Catholics found themselves cast as Satan's helpers just as the evangelist tide crested in the 1830s.

Some of the most threatening attacks against Catholics were directed at nuns. Most nuns in the early nineteenth century were immigrants from Europe who came to America as missionaries. With their distinctive uniform, European manners and speech, and belief in a strict class hierarchy, they suffered severe culture shock upon arrival in America. Perhaps the worst shock occurred in 1834, when a mob sacked and burned the Ursuline convent in Charlestown, Massachusetts. Trouble began after a rumor spread that a nun, Elizabeth Harrison, was being held in the convent by force. Anonymous letters were sent to the convent warning the inhabitants that "the convent would be pulled down" if the "mysterious lady could not be seen." Even though five town council members searched the entire building and interviewed Harrison—who assured them she was under no compulsion to remain—a mob rushed the building with cries of "down with the convent." The mother superior, Mary Edmund St. George, was able to hide away the nuns and students. Unfortunately, she could not save any of the convent's sacred or valuable artifacts from the plundering of the mob. What the thieves left, the fire later consumed. During this period, anti-Catholic mobs burned down at least ten convents.

Maryland was the most hospitable state for Catholics. The state contained a substantial Catholic minority, including many of Maryland's leading citizens. It was in Maryland that Elizabeth Ann Bayley Seton founded America's first Catholic order, the Sisters of Charity of St. Joseph. Mother Seton, born an Episcopalian, converted to Catholicism after her husband and her father died within several years of each other. Before converting, she had been active as a Protestant reformer in New York City. After coming to Baltimore to run a Catholic school for girls sponsored by St. Mary's College, she set out to raise funds for a religious community. In 1809, after securing the necessary funds from Samuel Sutherland Cooper, a recent convert, she established her convent near Emmitsburg, Maryland. The order soon built communities in New York, Baltimore, and Philadelphia.

The Mormons had an even harder time, in part because they were intentionally attempting to create a society apart from the mainstream. Mormonism was established when Joseph Smith, an itinerant worker from upstate New York, published the Book of Mormon in 1830, claiming that he had translated golden plates that contained prophesies from God. According to Smith, the plates instructed Americans to reestablish Christ's kingdom, which had once thrived in the New World. Mormons were to convert the Indians, who constituted the remnants of the lost tribe of Israel, and to follow the teachings of a new American prophet— Smith—to build a new Jerusalem.

Smith quickly attracted numerous followers, many of them rural and small-town people displaced by advancing industrialism who longed for a return to a more ordered world. Mormons believed in community cooperation and the sacrifice of individual success for the good of the community. Wherever they established their communities, however, they were harassed by distrustful neighbors and local governments. At one point, Smith even commanded a separate army in their colony of Nauvoo, Illinois. In 1843, Smith had told his followers of a revelation he had received from God commanding the practice of polygamy—multiple marriages—for men. Although he attempted to keep polygamy secret, word of the practice soon leaked out to the non-Mormon world and fueled much of the antagonism towards the Mormons. As tensions rose between Illinois officials and the Mormons, Smith began to search out possible havens for the Mormons in the West. Before the Mormons were able to emigrate, however, he and his brother were arrested for treason. On June 27, 1844, both men were killed by a mob led by many of the area's leading citizens. Soon after, the new Mormon leader, Brigham Young, led twelve thousand Mormons westward to establish the state of Deseret in Utah.

Other religious sects began with the assumptions of women's heightened status. These sects—especially the Shakers—were searching for a purer spiritual and communal life. They were part of a widespread movement during the nineteenth century that rejected mainstream Protestantism and the new American industrial growth to create utopian communities in the countryside. All shared the notion that humans could create a more perfect world by separating from mainstream society.

Communitarians believed that two of the most basic problems with society were the imbalance between women and men and the inadequacy of isolated home life. Nothing was more harmful to a woman's soul, they thought, than to spend all hours of the day washing, ironing, cleaning, and raising her children. And men had no business going off to work away from the home, making money in some "unproductive" capacity such as a banker or a clerk. Instead, they believed, women and men should produce their foods and goods together and raise their children together. For some of these groups, these ideas led to nothing less than the reinvention of the family.

The Shakers, an offshoot of the Quakers, were founded in England by Ann Lee, a woman of humble background. Lee prophesied that the millennium, the new human order mentioned in the Bible that would arise shortly before the end of the world, had arrived, and that a new Christian church would be established in America. The first Shaker settlement, Mount Lebanon, was founded in upstate New York in 1792. By the 1840s, Shakers had established eighteen societies in seven states, including four in Massachusetts, three in New York, and two apiece in New Hampshire, Maine, and Kentucky. Lee's followers believed that she was Christ's spirit returned to earth, and that her female soul would balance out Christ's male soul. They also believed that God was both male and female. True believers could only maintain the state of perfect grace made possible by Christ's second coming through "spiritualism, oral confession, community, peace, the gift of healing, physical health, the separation from the world," and celibacy.

The Shakers did away with the nuclear family. Instead, a Shaker family consisted of from forty to eighty people, related only by their commitment to their religion. Work was shared communally, as were the profits and property gained from the work. Although women and men in Shaker communities still worked in jobs traditionally associated with their sex, for women there was a great advantage to the communal work arrangement. The work was simply more fun when done in the company of others. Shakers usually sang, told stories, or had someone read newspapers and books aloud as they worked. In addition, the communal arrangement made for less work—it took five people much less time to prepare a meal for twenty than it did for five women to work alone preparing five separate meals for their families. The Shakers' system also saved money. Staple goods were cheaper when bought in bulk quantities, and communal kitchens required much less equipment than did groups of individual families.

The Shakers used their time well. They believed that frugality, industry, and cleanliness were basic to maintaining perfect spirituality. They used much of their free time to invent numerous items that made housework even easier. These inventions included an improved washing machine, a double rolling pin, the flat broom, a round oven for better cooking, a cheese press, an apple peeler—even the common clothespin. All served to save even more labor time for women. These activities also established women in a field for which they had rarely been given credit: as inventors.

The Shakers were able to convert their communal work system into profitable businesses. Communal kitchens had only to increase their work load a little bit to be able to maintain a restaurant. Since the Shakers had the means to process wool from shearing to spinning to weaving to dying to sewing, their clothes-making operation was extremely successful. Thus Shaker women were able to earn cash for their community and ensure its stability.

By the 1840s, American religious and utopian associations presented many American women with opportunities undreamed of at the start of the century. Although some religious and utopian ideas and practices called for women to remain in their traditional limited sphere, most provided women with a chance to redefine that sphere. Not all women living within America's boundaries were beneficiaries of these new opportunities, however. Indeed for many American Indian women, Protestant evangelism could become part of a threat to their way of life.

Conquerors and Conquered

In the early nineteenth century, Americans inhabited all the land between the Appalachian Mountains and the Atlantic Ocean. The Indian tribes struggled to hold on to the lands between the Appalachians and the Mississippi River, but as Americans pushed into Illinois, Ohio, Arkansas, the western Carolinas, and other border areas, the original inhabitants were often forced either to adopt white ways, or to be removed or annihilated by the U.S. Army, as were the Cherokees who walked the Trail of Tears.

Christian missionaries labored to convert American Indians to Christianity, with mixed results. The case of Narcissa Prentiss Whitman and her husband, Dr. Marcus Whitman, demonstrates that without the support of the U.S. Army, Indian resistance to white missionaries could turn violent. The Whitmans were in the vanguard of the thousands of white settlers who would descend on the Oregon Country, now the states of Oregon and Washington, in the 1840s and 1850s. Following what became known as the Oregon Trail, these settlers from the East leapfrogged the less hospitable Great Plains for the well-watered and forested coast of the Pacific Northwest.

While the overland emigrants came looking for new economic opportunities, the Whitmans and their party were more interested in saving souls. "I now offer myself to the American Board," wrote young Narcissa Prentiss, applying to the American Board of Foreign Missions in 1835, "to be employed in their service among the heathen." The American Board, which supported Protestant missions across the U.S. West and throughout the world, eventually underwrote the costs of

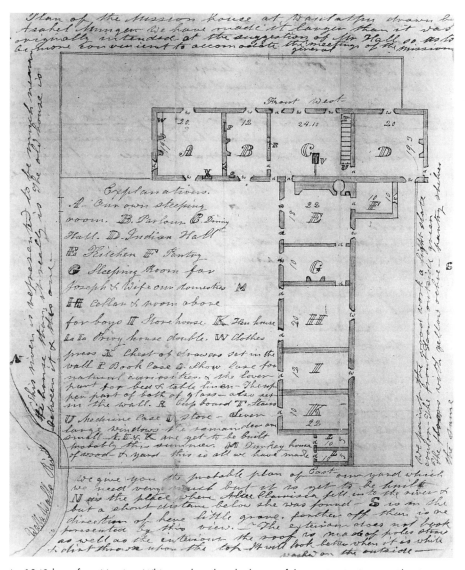

An 1840 letter from Narcissa Whitman describes the layout of the mission in Oregon. The Cayuse were initially eager to learn farming techniques and domestic tasks, but they were not interested in adopting Christianity.

the Whitmans' mission among the Cayuse Indians near Fort Walla Walla on the Columbia River. While Dr. Whitman practiced medicine and taught farming techniques to Cayuse men, Narcissa Whitman ran the mission school and organized the output of the mission kitchen. The Whitmans were initially energized by the flurry of activities at the frontier mission. At first, they were able to witness daily progress. In a letter to relatives back East, Narcissa Whitman wrote, "We never had greater encouragement about the Indians than at the present time."

Once the missionaries began to settle into the routine of mission life, however, things began to unravel. After the Cayuse learned the basics of American agriculture and domestic economy from the Whitmans, they demonstrated markedly less interest in hearing about the saving grace of God. Narcissa Whitman's life became a series of bitter disappointments. Her two-year-old child, Alice Clarissa, drowned. Whitman soon found herself the foster parent of eleven children whose own parents had perished along the Oregon Trail. Along with her many other duties, these new responsibilities exhausted her already depleted endurance. "My health has been so poor," she wrote her sister in 1846, "and my family increased so rapidly, that it has been impossible. You will be astonished to know that we have eleven children in our family, and not one of them our own. Seven orphans were brought to our door in Oct., 1844, whose parents both died on the way to this country. Destitute and friendless, there was no other alternative—we must take them or they must perish."

Longing for the community of women she had left back East, Narcissa Whitman grew increasingly lonely at the frontier mission. After the missionaries' problems led the American Board to cancel support for the mission, Marcus Whitman went east for nearly a year to plead his case. Although he won continued support, his absence made Narcissa all the more miserable. By the early 1840s, the number of settlers passing through the mission increased markedly as "Oregon Fever" set in. Though the settlers provided Narcissa with company, they also meant more work as the mission became an important way station for weary travelers.

The Whitmans had originally been quite taken by what they saw as the potential of the Cayuse to become "good Christians," but they soon changed their view. Narcissa Whitman increasingly saw the Indians as obstacles to white civilization and wondered if they would ever "progress" beyond "the thick darkness of heathenism." In a letter back East in 1840, she complained, "[The Cayuse] are so filthy they make a great deal of cleaning wherever they go, and this wears a woman out very fast. We must clean after them, for we have come to elevate them and not to suffer ourselves to sink down to their standards."

As more white settlers poured into the territory, the Cayuse and other tribes began to view the Whitmans not as deliverers of useful knowledge, but as harbingers of disaster. Narcissa noted the Indians' concern about the newcomers but seemed unaware of any imminent danger. "The poor Indians are amazed at the overwhelming numbers of Americans coming into the territory," she wrote in July 1847. "They seem not to know what to make of it." Once again, however, Whitman seems to have underestimated the Cayuse—they did indeed know what to make of the influx. When a measles outbreak brought by white settlers ravaged the Indian children while sparing the whites, the Cayuse blamed the Whitmans, thinking that the missionaries were turning to witchcraft to destroy their tribe; the Indians did not know that the measles had spared many whites because their bodies contained antibodies, whereas Indian children had no such protection against the unfamiliar disease. Having already made the connection between the Whitmans' presence and the whites' invasion, the Cayuse were convinced of the missionaries' ill intent. On November 29, 1847, a Cayuse war party attacked the mission settlement, killing fourteen—including the Whitmans—and taking forty-seven prisoners.

Eastern missionaries mourned the loss of their martyrs, while eastern newspapers used the Cayuse as a clear example to argue that the rifle, and not the cross, would best "convert" the Indians. Another assessment was reached by a fellow western missionary, H. K. W. Perkins, who wrote: "That [Narcissa Whitman] felt a deep interest in the welfare of the natives, no one who was at all acquainted with her could doubt. But the affection was manifested under a false view of Indian character. Her carriage toward them was always haughty. It was the common remark among them that Mrs. Whitman was 'very proud.' It was her misfortune, not her fault. She was adapted to a different destiny. She wanted something exalted—communion with mind. She loved company, society, and excitement. The self-denial that took her away from it was suicidal. She was not a missionary but a woman, a highly gifted, polished American lady. And so she died."

The Indians of California were first conquered not by Americans, but by Hispanics from the Spanish colony of Mexico. These *Californos,* as the Spanish came to be called, were eager to convert the local Indian tribes to the Catholic faith. Unlike the American missionaries, however, the Californos established elaborate missions for the purpose of utilizing Indian labor while at the same time teaching Catholic beliefs. The mission system called for Indians to pledge their souls to Catholicism and to hand over control of their lives to the Catholic padres who led the missions. After years of training and vigorous tests to prove that these converted Catholics had been civilized, the transformed Indians would be freed from the mission's control and given their own land. They could then become independent small farmers and loyal subjects of Spain.

Like most missionaries' visions, the Californos' system was fatally flawed. Few Indians seemed to have become sufficiently civilized in the eyes of the padres to be released from the missions. Further, mission Indians were sometimes cruelly abused by the padres and the Californo soldiers. Once the Indians committed themselves to the care of the missions, they could not leave voluntarily; those who ran away were brought back in irons by the soldiers. Often the soldiers captured Indians who had never pledged themselves to Catholicism, but these hapless captives were forced to convert and remain at the mission. Although the converts had to work long hours in the fields and at various income-producing tasks, they received only food, shelter, and clothing in return for their work.

When the Spanish first appeared in California in the 1770s, many Indians thought them to be godlike creatures—they wore shiny armor, rode horses, and fired muskets—things that the Indians had never seen before. Many Indians thus accepted Christianity because they believed the Spanish to be more powerful gods than those worshiped by the Indians. In time, however, Indians came to know the Californos as men, although extremely powerful men, and were less inclined to join the missions, especially after they heard of the harsh conditions there. To attract new converts, the padres specifically recruited Indian women, to whom the missions offered a number of advantages. Unlike many other Indian cultures, California Indian tribes were extremely patriarchal—power belonged to the men; women had little control either over the community's affairs or within their families. In material terms, mission life was a step up for women. As the head of the Santa Barbara mission during the late eighteenth century noted, Indian women in the mission had access to "grinding-stones, pans, pots, stew-pots, and even small ovens for baking bread." Indian men, whose job within the tribe was to fight and hunt, saw no such advantage in mission life.

The California missions had an even harder time attracting recruits after 1790, when even Indian women had become disenchanted with mission life. After 1800, the missions abandoned recruitment for outright coercion. Californo soldiers swept through the outlying areas and rounded up any Indians that could be found. Although the soldiers were ultimately responsible for the destruction of the California Indians, their chief weapons were not the sword and the gun. Rather, the soldiers decimated the Indian population by spreading syphilis, which was unknown to California Indians before the arrival of the Spaniards. The disease wreaked havoc among the native population. The Spaniards most often infected Indians by raping Indian women caught in raids. Although the padres attempted to enforce laws against such violence within the missions, there was little they could do outside the mission walls.

The lives of mission Indians became even more difficult after the Mexican Revolution in 1821. After Mexico freed itself from Spain, its leaders were determined to free the new republic from the influence of the church as well. The new government ordered the missions to be privatized and their land divided among mission Indians and Californos. Unfortunately, the Indians saw little of their promised lands; as a result many took to raiding Californo towns, while others took work as laborers where "all in reality are slaves."

The republic of Mexico did not have much time to profit from California. By the 1830s, "Yankees"—American entrepreneurs from the Northeast—were taking control of the territory's economic system. At first, the American presence seemed to offer much hope to the Californos. Most of the leading Yankees who established themselves in California sought to marry upper-class Californo brides, and fathers readily consented to these matches, relinquishing daughters and dowries to gain the status for their families associated with these wealthy newcomers. By the 1840s, however, a new wave of Americans rolled in from the East. Unconcerned with integrating themselves into Californo society, they viewed Californos as lazy barbarians—much as the original Californos had viewed the Indians. They saw Californo women not as prospective marriage partners but simply as another feature of the conquered landscape. For Californos, that landscape had changed markedly—the conquerors were now the conquered.

Not all Americans who headed west acted as conquerors. Numerous alliances between fur traders and Indians were often struck up to help both sides succeed in the fur trade, and many of the liaisons between white trappers and Indian women ended in marriage and demonstrated the potential for cross-cultural cooperation. White fur traders who took both an Indian bride and an Indian way of life were known at the time as "squawmen." Among whites, the term was derogatory, a sure indication that a man had buckled under to his wife's wishes. Among Indians, however, the label was simply a way of recognizing the man's choice to align himself with the tribe by accepting his wife's culture. By the 1840s, as hunters depleted the numbers of fur-bearing animals and settlers destroyed their habitat, the fur trade receded to the far north. The mixed-blood culture of Indians and whites— the métis, as the French called them—survived within some Indian tribes, but remained largely invisible to mainstream American culture. Yet métis culture reminds us that cultural interaction need not always be a tale of conquerors and conquered, but rather a story of negotiation and understanding.

Women in Public

Isabella Marshall Graham awoke one day in 1773 to find herself a widow. The day before she had been married to a Scottish physician, Dr. John Graham; the next day she was alone with five young children, nearly penniless, and with few means of producing an income. Despite these obstacles, she managed not only to survive, but to prosper. For the next twenty years, she did quite well as an educational entrepreneur, running successful schools for upper-class young women in Scotland and New York.

In 1797, Graham joined with Elizabeth Seton—who had not yet been converted to Catholicism—to found the Society for the Relief of Poor Widows with Small Children. Charitable organizations for poor widows had existed before; the well-to-do considered these women to be "deserving poor" and therefore the proper objects of pity. What was unusual was that Graham and Seton's organization was among the first to be founded and run by women. Graham and Seton were running meetings, raising money, and lobbying politicians, tasks that might have been considered inappropriate by the more conservative elements of society. But these utterly respectable ladies were careful to justify their efforts by saying that this type of work fell within the proper sphere for women.

A few observant folks realized that something was amiss with these benevolent societies, despite the respectable women and their careful language stressing "women's work." Conservative clergymen in particular remained uneasy with women's involvement in public matters. In 1815, Reverend Moses Stuart lectured the Salem Female Charitable Society that women's fundraising efforts had to be supervised by "men who are skilled in such matters." One year later, another minister told a New York City charitable organization that women should not "set themselves up as public teachers . . . and so usurp the authority over man." The reverend did allow that it was permissible for "a few females assembled in private . . . to meet together for prayer."

Philanthropic women—those involved in giving to help the poor or needy— were not about to retreat, however. In many ways, benevolent women were among the most conservative members of society, whatever certain ministers might have thought. Benevolent women believed they were obligated, as Christians and as members of the elite, to protect those who could not protect themselves. How were these women to know that their first careful steps into the public arena would help other women justify activities such as debating political issues, gathering petitions to send to Congress, and organizing strikes? But just as changes in work, education, and religion could lead to unexpected opportunities for women, so too could the most innocent involvement in public affairs present women with new possibilities.

Isabella Graham and other philanthropists were moved to act by very real problems. Poverty was on the rise in most American cities. Well-to-do women in New York, Boston, and other cities, watching poverty's steady advance, felt compelled to minister to the growing number of poor people around them. Seeing a need was one thing, but only the determined actions of a few strong leaders could convert opportunity into reality. Leaders like Graham and Seton encouraged women to take their first steps out of the domestic realm and engage in various administrative tasks within the safety of the benevolent societies.

Benevolent women believed that they could no more hope to eradicate the causes of poverty than to banish death. By the late 1820s, evangelical women, led by the Finneyites, were challenging this pessimism. Evangelical women believed the poor could be uplifted. In the view of evangelical reformers, immorality—not low wages, not misfortune—caused poverty. Rather than protect the worthy poor, evangelical reformers meant to make the poor worthy. The Second Great Awakening, culminating in Finney's revivals, had electrified many middle-class women into action. A number of them were recent graduates of the new female seminaries who had a sense both of mission and of solidarity with other women. The attention of evangelical women was soon riveted on the plight of their less fortunate sisters, prostitutes and other "fallen women." In 1831, John MacDowell, a recent convert of Charles Finney, issued a report on the sordid business of prostitution in New York City. The report was thoroughly denounced by business leaders and politicians who feared it would give New York a bad name. Many women, however, were drawn to MacDowell's call to "virtuous women of the city . . . to employ all the peculiar influences of your sex in promoting an Institution which is founded for the relief of the miserable of your sex exclusively." In response to this plea, evangelical women founded the New York Female Moral Reform Society in 1834. Six years later, the American Female Moral Reform Society (AFMRS) had 555 local chapters.

At first, the AFMRS sought to save prostitutes by getting them to renounce sin and embrace Christ. Reformers soon realized, however, that the prostitutes had customers, and that many of the customers had wives. Moral reformers asserted that a double standard existed: "Why should a female be trodden underfoot, and spurned from society . . . if she but fall into sin, while common consent allows the male to habituate himself to this vice, and treats him as not guilty?" asked the all-woman editorial board of the AFMRS paper, *Advocate of Moral Reform.* "Whence has this perversion in truth arisen?" For the women of the AFMRS, the onus lay with "the harder sex."

The Boston chapter of the AFMRS explained in 1838 that it was the society's duty "to guard our sisters, daughters, and female acquaintances from the delusive arts of corrupt and unprincipled men." In order to fulfill this duty, the New York FMRS took another step into the public realm—it spearheaded a petition drive to pass a state law making a man's seduction of a woman illegal. After presenting thousands of signatures to the legislature over several years, women reformers and their male allies won passage of an antiseduction bill in 1848. Although the law was rarely enforced, the campaign proved that organized women could make the legislature pay attention. Custom had long granted women the freedom to petition the legislature. In the past, however, individual women presented petitions concerning personal matters such as divorces or contested wills. Once again, women were taking accepted behavior and stretching it to fit new needs.

Even the male allies of evangelical women felt that men were better suited to address indelicate issues such as prostitution. The men of the newly founded Seventh Commandment Society ("Thou shalt not commit adultery") gently suggested that the AFMRS could now retire to more "appropriate" endeavors. The New York FMRS quickly let their evangelical brethren know that only women could truly understand the problem. "This is the appropriate work for *women,*" a rural reformer insisted, "Go on, ladies, go on, in the strength of the Lord."

The AFMRS's activities brought women together as never before. Their efforts gave women reformers an understanding of their potential power as a group. Although most women in the AFMRS came from the middle classes, the society connected women from farms, villages, and cities. Local chapters learned the importance of "assembling *women* in general convention meeting," as the *Advocate* put it, at least once a year. These conventions, said the *Advocate,* brought to women "a clearer discernment of the capabilities of [women's] mental powers . . . which have been for ages . . . *lost to the world.* . . . It indicates an increasing recognition of . . . the *glorious,* the *heroic* bursting of *iron limits.* . . . When I regard the influence which they will exert in raising woman from the lowly path in which she has hitherto walked . . . I experience sensations of peculiar joy; *for I am a woman.*"

The newfound solidarity of women reformers enabled them to perceive a common enemy—immoral men. Not only were men the seducers, the philanderers, but they were also responsible for sustaining an economic system that perpetuated women's poverty. Many women reformers came to realize that the same system that consigned working-class women to low-paying, unskilled jobs also restricted middle-class women's opportunities. The *Advocate* protested in 1846, "Men have monopolized almost every field of labor. They have taken ... almost every place where skill and talent is required, and they have excluded women." Prostitutes were simply poor women with no other recourse to survive. Only the continued health, sobriety, and business acumen of reformers' husbands kept most middle-class women from facing such a fate.

Evangelicals—women and men—were also involved in a tenacious struggle to shape the social mores and spiritual needs of the expanding middle class. The Burned-over District proved fertile ground for the same perfectionist fervors that had fueled the revivals. Rather than saving souls, moral reformers now intended to battle sin head-on; to eradicate temptation forever. Reformers sought to become chaperones to the growing population of footloose, upwardly mobile men who came to the boom towns in search of new opportunities. Women reformers began monitoring drinking habits and soon decided that total abstinence was in order; they observed courting behavior and began ostracizing those who sought to "take advantage" of a young woman. Reformers pushed for stronger Sabbatarian laws, insisting that church and not the dance hall or the saloon should be the proper gathering place on Sunday. And they looked askance at the young men's fraternal clubs.

Needless to say, many of the objects of the reformers' relentless campaign were less than overjoyed to be singled out for redemption. The reformers' vision of "proper" middle-class life had become so dominant, however, that many men— young and old—who sought respectability did not fight women's right to enforce moral codes. Instead, these men joined in their own efforts to "live the goodly life." The most successful of these efforts in terms of membership were the temperance societies.

During the 1820s and 1830s, organizations such as the New York City Temperance Society (NYCTS) were concerned largely with maintaining the boundaries between the "laboring classes" and the "respectable classes." Membership in the NYCTS was both a mark of class distinction and an opportunity to make valuable connections. Following the Panic of 1837, fortunes both newly made and well established were shattered. The temperance movement that grew out of the wreckage embraced a new understanding of economic mobility, both upward and downward. The new movement, particularly the Washingtonian Society, founded in 1840, eagerly embraced redemption. Washingtonians welcomed the admitted sinner and supported his conversion to abstinence. This approach fit perfectly the perspective of evangelical women reformers.

The Tree of Temperance bears fruit in the form of "Honesty," "Riches," and "Good Children," among other things. Reformers attacked alcoholism not as a disease but as an immoral activity that was incompatible with a respectable life.

Women began their involvement with the Washingtonians by establishing ladies' auxiliaries. At first, women were content to cook dinners for benefits and gatherings, organize social functions, and boycott grocers who sold alcohol. However, a group of more ambitious women soon established separate Martha Washington Societies, which began to focus more on the problem of men who had no interest in being redeemed. Women's temperance societies had their own particular strategies to gain young men's compliance with abstinence. As the *Massachusetts Cataract* explained, "When any of the tee-total ladies of these associations gives a social evening party at her house, it *happens* that those young nice men who refuse to sign the pledge, . . . and whose affection for the *bottle* is greater than their regard for the *belles* of those places, . . . don't get an invitation!" Martha Washingtonians used their position as organizers of social events to coerce men into accepting women reformers' notions of proper behavior. Like other women reformers, they accepted the ideal of domesticity, while pushing out the edges to make room for their expanded role in the public realm.

Not all women reformers saw themselves at a distance from the poor. In 1818, thirty women met in Salem, Massachusetts, to organize a moral reform society. Rather than attempting to improve the lives of another class, they sought to improve themselves. "We resolve to be charitably watchful over each other," they promised in their charter, "to advise caution and admonish where we judge there is an occasion, and that it may be useful; and we promise not to resent but kindly receive such friendly advise from our members." The society recognized the importance of building trust among its members: "We promise not to divulge or ridicule the supposed infirmities of any fellow member." The society pledged to provide mutual aid to each other during hard times and personal crises. After approving a constitution, the Colored Female Religious and Moral Society of Salem was officially initiated.

This society was different not simply because it consisted of African-American women, but because it practiced mutual aid and mutual improvement. The Salem society was one of many such black women's societies created during the first half of the nineteenth century. Because the black upper classes were not far removed from the black poor—a steady job at decent wages constituted an elite—black societies were less likely to make class distinctions. Nor did blacks make distinctions between the "worthy" and "unworthy" poor. African-American women realized that racism helped make poverty a way of life for blacks.

By the 1830s, African-American women's societies had added temperance, moral reform, and missionary activities to their agenda. Black women were also the first to initiate literary societies whose members met to discuss "improving literature." For most black women, such societies were the only means of intellectual development. Although the new seminary movement provided wonderful opportunities for middle-class white women, none of these institutions accepted blacks. Few black women would have had the necessary means to attend even if racism had not barred them. Early on, African-American women realized that only they could uplift themselves.

By the mid-1830s, white working-class women were learning this lesson as well. When New England mill owners lowered their wages in 1834, women workers did not meekly accept their fate or ask for charity. They did agree that if there were "any in want, the Ladies will be compassionate and assist them." As for the mill hands themselves, they preferred "to have the disposing of our charities in our own hands; and as we are free, we would remain in possession of what kind Providence has bestowed upon us, and remain daughters of freemen still." Mill workers were well aware that charity was not free.

Rather than receive handouts, mill workers decided to walk out, leaving the mills short-staffed, to pressure owners into maintaining the wage rates. The probusiness *Boston Evening Transcript* reported that in Lowell, eight hundred strikers had formed a procession "and marched about town. We are told that one of the leaders mounted a pump and made a flaming ... speech on the rights of women and the iniquities of the 'moneyed aristocracy,' which produced a powerful effect on her auditors, and they determined to 'have their own way if they died for it.'" Mill workers had struck sporadically since 1824. Only after the 1834 turnouts, however, did women begin to develop local organizations to sustain their protests. Textile workers in Lowell formed the Factory Girls' Association in 1836 and immediately signed up over twenty-five hundred members. Workers in other factory towns across New England followed Lowell's lead, developing local organizations to bring about strikes.

The hopes of the workers were dashed with the onset of the 1837 depression. With business down and labor plentiful, workers had little choice but to accept cuts in pay. But when the 1840s brought an upturn in both the national economy and the textile industry, a new generation of mill workers was ready to press their case again. Their activities would once again expand the things that women could do— the idea of "woman's sphere." Women textile workers at first had difficulty coordinating their actions with their male counterparts. Often, male workers did not see women's struggles as their own. During the 1840s, however, women workers joined forces with men through the movement to limit the workday to ten hours, six days a week. Together, these women and men fought to raise wage rates and improve working conditions. Numerous mill workers came to hold important posts in both women's and mixed organizations. Perhaps the most famous of these was Sarah Bagley, who seemed to be involved in every New England labor struggle during the mid-1840s.

Bagley was born in the early 1800s in Meredith, New Hampshire. She came to the Lowell mills just before the 1837 depression, and for seven years apparently worked without complaint. In 1844, when mill workers began organizing against longer working hours and increases in the pace of work, Bagley bloomed into a labor leader. She began by building up the newly formed Lowell Female Reform Association, an auxiliary of the New England Workingman's Association (NEWA). After increasing local membership from five to more than eight hundred, she organized chapters in Manchester, Waltham, Nashua, Fall River, and other New England mill towns. During this time, she wrote for numerous reform papers, and for a time she edited the NEWA's paper, *Voice of Industry*.

In 1845, Bagley helped organize a petition drive to the Massachusetts legislature requesting a ten-hour-day law. The legislature, which was overwhelmingly probusiness, was finally compelled to form an investigative committee—the first ever to consider a labor dispute—after being besieged with thousands of signatures. The legislators figured they had found a way out, however. Of the eight mill workers they summoned as witnesses, six were women. Believing that no woman would dare to face an austere body like the Massachusetts legislature, the committee warned, "as the greater part of the petitioners are females, it will be necessary for them to make the defence, or we shall be under the necessity of laying the petition aside." Sarah Bagley and her coworkers neither shirked their duty nor buckled under to the legislators' tough questioning. Among Bagley's colleagues that day were women such as Huldah Stone and Eliza Hemingway who would become the stars of the women's labor movement. Despite their powerful testimony, the legislature, led by probusiness editor William Schouler, offered no criticism of the industry in its final report. The women workers had the last word, however. After promising to "consign William Schouler to the obscurity he so justly deserves," they organized to defeat him in his bid for reelection as Lowell's state senator.

The labor struggles of the 1840s broadened women's perspective about who they were and what was possible. Just as evangelical reformers had developed an understanding of women as a group, so too did the textile workers. The workers, however, began to see themselves as members of both a *gender* and a *class*. One woman, writing in the labor paper *Zion's Herald,* proudly proclaimed, "I am heartily glad when anything is done to elevate that class to which it is my lot to belong. We are a band of sisters and must have sympathy for each other's woes."

Middle-class critics complained bitterly about the public activities of textile workers. Claiming that moral reform was an extension of motherhood was one thing, critics argued. But what possible justification could "these Amazons" have for so brazenly violating the niceties of domesticity? The strikers, however, seemed to have cared little for these middle-class notions. Instead, they looked to the ideals of the American Revolution. To the strikers, their actions were the natural course for "daughters of freemen" to take. Some workers used their strike experience to challenge the ideal of domesticity itself. One woman, writing in a prolabor paper in 1845, declared, "Woman is never thought to be out of her *sphere* at home; in the nursery, in the kitchen, over a hot stove cooking from morning till evening—over a washtub, or toiling in a cotton factory fourteen hours per day. But let her once

FACTORY SONG

Come all ye ladies of Lowell,
I'd have you to understand,
We are going to leave the factory,
And away to our native land.

While in the sable shades of night,
With curtains round our head;
The watchmen calls, the lamp is brought,
To light us from our bed.

Then we arise and all prepare
To receive corporeal food;
And some complain, while others say
That theirs is rich and good.

The factory bell begins to ring,
And we must all obey;
And each their own employment mind,
Or else be turned away.

We then into the carding room,
With cheerful hearts engage;
To labor in the dust and dirt,
The youth of every age.

And when the gate is hoisted high,
The water swiftly flows;
And each to their own station move,
And doth the machinery goes.

The rumbling wheels and rattling bands,
All in succession roll;
The regulator swiftly moves,
And regulates the whole.

It is a wonder how that man
Could such machinery make;
A thousand wheels in union move,
Without the least mistake.

The bales of cotton soon brought,
And from the picker flows;
Swift through the cards and brakers come,
And to the speeder goes.

With rapid flight the speeder flies,
'Tis pleasing to behold;
The ropeing round the bobbins wind,
One half can never be told.

The next we know the spinners call
For ropeing to be brought;

Its carried from the carding room,
And on their spindles caught.

Come listen friends and you I'll tell,
What spinners they can do;
The ropeing they will quick convert
To warp and filling too.

Another sight I now behold,
It is a pleasing scene;
The warp is taken soon as spun,
And wound around the beam.

These soon is carried out of sight
Into dressing room;
It's warped and dressed all complete,
And fitted for the loom.

The sleigh and harness is prepared,
Each thread for to commence;
The looms are placed in rows through,
The weavers stand between.

The shuttle now is swiftly thrown,
It flies from end to end;
And they stand ready all the while
Each broken thread to mend.

The best of weavers do not think,
Because they hither go;
That they are better than their friends,
That work in rooms below.

Six thousand yards from day to day,
If I am rightly told,
Is carded well, and spun and wove,
And carried to be sold.

When you my friends these lines behold,
Think not I've done my best;
But know that all I've left behind,
I'm leaving for the rest.

I hope all those who have the skill,
To view the least mistake;
Will start anew, the work review,
And much improvement make.

This corporation now is good,
It's rising with some others;
May friendship reign throughout the whole,
And all unite as brothers.

This factory song was probably written by a mill worker for a company newspaper.

step out, plead the cause of right and humanity, plead the wrongs of her slave sister of the South or of the [worker] of the North, . . . and a cry is raised against her,
'*out of her sphere*.'"

Women workers were beginning to make connections: between their oppression
as women and as workers, between their own oppression and that of African-
American slaves. Huldah Stone saw the vast possibilities of this new way of seeing
when she declared that the textile workers "do not regard [the ten-hour move-
ment] as an end, but only as one step toward the end to be attained. They deeply
feel that their work will never be accomplished until slavery and oppression, mental, physical, and religious, shall have been done away with and Christianity in its
original simplicity and pristine beauty shall be re-established and practiced."

Who would have foreseen that Isabella Marshall Graham's first careful steps
would have been overtaken by Huldah Stone's bold strides into the public arena?
Who might have suspected that the orderly mills and boardinghouses would have
produced "Amazons" who challenged the basis of the American social and economic system? Such upheavals, however, were harbingers of things to come. The
textile industry would soon undergo sweeping changes that would transform the
workers' movement. And the era's greatest struggle against oppression—the antislavery movement—had just begun.

The Politics of Resistance

It was 1835 and they knew there would be trouble. Boston's Mayor Theodore
Lyman had begged Maria Weston Chapman, the leader of the Boston Female Antislavery Society, to cancel the interracial antislavery meeting that night. He knew
that the mere presence of the radical abolitionist William Lloyd Garrison would be
sure to stir up an angry mob. And the presence of white and black women together—well, that was just tossing kerosene on the fire. And fire there very well might
be. Abolitionists had been burned in effigy before, and there was a good chance
that someone would next take a torch to the meeting hall.

Chapman held her ground, however, insisting that principle had to stand fast in
the face of cowardly intimidation. Once in the hall that night, as a howling mob
outside shouted obscenities and threatened worse, Chapman was even more resolute. Responding to Lyman's last-ditch appeal to cancel the meeting, Chapman
replied, "If this is the last bulwark of freedom, we might as well die here." After
Garrison spoke briefly, he was hustled out the back door. The mob caught on to the
ruse, however, and proceeded to drag Garrison through town at the end of a rope.
Back at the meeting hall, Chapman calmly ordered the women to group themselves
in pairs, one black and one white. The women then passed through the mob, "their
hands folded in their cotton gloves, their eyes busily identifying the genteel leaders
of the mob."

While abolitionist women were daring the wrath of northern mobs to vanquish
"the awful sin of slavery," southern slave women were resisting slavery on a more

personal level. Many years after regaining her freedom, Eliza Washington recalled how she had first stood up to her mistress. After her mistress scolded Washington for scrubbing the floor improperly, Washington "sassed her, and she struck me with her hand." That slap set off a chain of events that Washington savored many years later in the retelling: "Thinks I, it's a good time now to dress you out, and damned if I won't do it. I set down my tools and squared for a fight. The first whack, I struck her a hell of a blow with my fist. I didn't knock her entirely through the panels of the door, but her landing against the door made a terrible smash, and I hurt her so badly that all were frightened out of their wits and I didn't know myself but what I'd killed the old devil." Although Eliza received a whipping, her mistress refrained from slapping her after that.

Both northern abolitionist women and southern slave women put themselves at risk in opposing slavery. Though abolitionists did not always have to face angry mobs, they did continually experience both the subtle and not-so-subtle forms of harassment that befall those who champion unpopular causes. In return, they hoped to destroy the institution of slavery and return some measure of dignity to the lives of African Americans. The focus of slave women's energies was more immediate, and the threat of violent reprisal more likely. Slave women knew quite clearly that slavery was unjust, but they were more concerned with the day-to-day struggle to survive. They constantly had to measure their attempts at resistance against the probability of physical and emotional damage their masters and mistresses might inflict on them. Both abolitionists and slaves were working to oppose the system of slavery, but they had very different concerns—and they chose very different means.

Although slave women had taken an active part in slave rebellions in the past, by the mid-eighteenth century these uprisings were largely all-male activities. Slave men came to view uprisings as a chance to reassert the warrior role that their forefathers had taken in Africa. After 1750, because slaveholders passed numerous laws to hinder slave organization, rebellions also became less frequent. Instead, slaves chose to resist on a more individual level. One possibility was fleeing the plantation for freedom in the North. Once northern states began abolishing slavery after the American Revolution, slave men increasingly chose this as an option. Fewer slave women took this course, largely because they were unwilling to abandon their children. Also, those slave men trained as carpenters, blacksmiths, and at other skilled jobs were often sent out to earn money for the master. They had more opportunity to escape and were a more common sight on southern roads. A woman alone was more likely to attract unwelcome attention.

Some slave women did escape, and a few became celebrities. Ellen Craft, one of the most famous runaways of the time, convinced her husband, William, to join her in an elaborate ruse to gain their freedom. While Craft's owners were as kindly as slave owners could be, she feared that if she had any children they would be sold away from her. Craft, who was light-skinned, arranged to be dressed as a man, complete with a top hat. She obscured her face with a handkerchief, meant to simulate treatment for a toothache, and bound her arm in a sling, so that it would not be discovered that she could not write. Her husband came along posing as "Mr. Johnson's" servant. When William balked at this scheme, she implored, "Come, William, don't be a coward! Get me the clothes and I promise you we shall be free in a few days." And after securing passage on a northbound steamer, they were. Both became active in the abolitionist crusade.

Other women concocted imaginative deceptions to gain their freedom. Lear Green, a house servant in Baltimore, escaped by packing herself in a large sailor's chest and then having it shipped to Philadelphia. Such tales were quickly publicized in northern papers eager to demonstrate cracks in the southern slave system. Perhaps the most famous runaway, Harriet Tubman, escaped from her Maryland plantation in 1849 after the rest of her family chose to remain in the South. Over the next ten years she led expeditions to free hundreds of slaves, including many members of the family she had left behind. Her exploits would gain her much renown among northern abolitionists and much hatred among slaveholders.

Without running away, it was still possible to resist the daily indignities and physical hardships of slavery. Sometimes slave women attempted dire retribution against their tormentors. Although whites were forbidden to sell chemicals to slaves, slave women knew about the deadly effects of numerous plants. A particularly evil master or mistress might find out too late that a sampling of a poisonous plant had been added to the soup. Other slave owners might find ground-up glass in their drinks. In most cases, however, a perpetrator was either discovered or invented, and a slave paid the price with his or her life.

When slave women were unable to take such actions against their owners, they sometimes directed drastic measures against themselves. One woman, upon learning that she was to be sold and separated from her children, chopped off her fingers with a cleaver and ruined the sale. Other women refused to see any more of their babies sold off to distant plantations. After one mother was forced to give up three young children within several years, she took her fourth-born, and according to one observer, "gave it something out of the bottle and pretty soon it was dead." Since both infanticide and induced abortions were viewed by slaveholding society as a crime against the master's property, mothers found guilty of these crimes were usually sentenced to death.

Not all resistance took on such tragic proportions. Often women would simply make work in the field and the Big House go less smoothly than it might have. The trick was to make their actions appear as accidental as possible, so that the milk would seem to sour mysteriously. However, since slaves were usually whipped for even the appearance of wrongdoing, a punishment was often forthcoming. Given the enormous risks a slave took in resisting, it is not surprising that many chose simply to get along with the system as best they could. As one slave woman put it, "If your head is in the lion's mouth, it's best to pet him a little."

African-American women who lived in the North realized that their freedom enabled them to fight slavery in ways not open to their southern sisters. While northern blacks suffered enormous prejudice and occasionally violence, they also enjoyed certain basic rights and protections not accorded to slaves. The first Female Antislavery Society was organized in Salem, Massachusetts, in 1832. An outgrowth of the Colored Female Religious and Moral Society of Salem, the Female Antislavery Society pledged in its constitution to work both against slavery and for the improvement of blacks. Its combination of self-help with abolitionist activities would be replicated in other black women's antislavery organizations.

Some black abolitionists, such as Maria Stewart of Boston, attempted to fight slavery not by appealing to whites, but by imploring blacks to work towards self-improvement. Stewart began her campaign in 1832 after reading an editorial in Garrison's newspaper, the *Liberator,* extolling the special power of women's moral influence. Deeply religious, Stewart submitted several essays to the *Liberator* on morality, Christian duty, and African-American conditions. Garrison published these essays in his paper and then issued them as pamphlets. After he encouraged Stewart to present her ideas to black audiences, she began her speaking career.

Stewart believed that because whites ignored the conditions of blacks—both free and slave—blacks should "turn [their] attention to knowledge and improvement." Once blacks elevated themselves, "even those who now point at us with fingers of scorn will aid and befriend us. It is no use to sit with hands folded, lamenting our wretched condition; if no one will promote or respect us, let us promote and respect ourselves." Stewart was particularly concerned about earning respect for black women, urging them "to strive by their examples, both in public and private, to assist those who are endeavoring to stop the strong current of prejudice."

Despite Stewart's call for black women's prominence in the abolitionist movement—because of it, in fact—she was often harassed or criticized for her speeches. Most African-American men were no more ready to accept women as public speakers than white men were. In 1833, Stewart gave her farewell address, in which she acknowledged that the black community was not yet ready for a forceful woman speaker. She asked her audience, "What if I am a woman? Did not God raise up Deborah to be a mother and a judge in Israel? Did not Queen Esther save the lives of the Jews? If such women once existed, be no longer astonished, then, that God at this eventful period should raise up your females to strive." Other abolitionists, both black and white, would presenting the same argument to their male counterparts.

While some black women abolitionists preferred to work in groups separate from whites, others chose to join integrated organizations. Interracial groups such as the Boston Female Antislavery Association directly challenged northern assumptions about the need to separate the races. The Philadelphia Antislavery Association, which had almost as many black as white charter members in 1833, attracted fierce criticism and occasional reprisals for its effrontery. In 1838, in a repetition of the Boston mob scene, an abolitionist group was surrounded at the newly built Pennsylvania Hall. After tossing stones in the window, blocking the doors, and threatening the attendees as they departed, the mob—unhindered by any police presence—burned the building to the ground. A spokesman for the mob explained that the hall had been destroyed because the "audience [was] promiscuously mixed up of blacks and whites."

Such attacks caused some conservative abolitionists to suggest that black and white women remain apart while fighting slavery. Lucretia Mott, the leading white woman abolitionist in Philadelphia, criticized these "psuedo-abolitionists," who "left no means untried to expunge from our minutes a resolution to social intercourse with our colored brethren." When the Philadelphia mayor asked Mott that white women "avoid unnecessary walking with colored people," she replied, "We have never made a parade of walking with colored people and should do as we've done before—walk with them as occasion offered."

The Philadelphia society was able to maintain its vigorous integrationist stance, thanks in part to whites like Mott and her sister, Martha Coffin Wright. They favored an egalitarian stand, the belief that men and women, blacks and whites should participate equally in the fight against slavery. But these efforts would have been for naught if not for the presence of strong black women abolitionists like Charlotte Forten and her remarkable daughters, Margaretta, Harriet, and Sarah Louise. (Charlotte Forten's namesake and granddaughter, Charlotte Forten Grimké, became well known as an educator.) Charlotte Forten was a founding member of the Philadelphia Female Antislavery Society; Margaretta served in numerous official capacities; Harriet was active in the Underground Railroad during the 1850s with her husband, Robert Purvis; and Sarah Louise frequently contributed to the *Liberator* and the *Abolitionist*. With these activities, the family worked to strengthen ties between black and white abolitionists in Philadelphia and across the country.

Not all local antislavery societies were as open to black members as the Philadelphia group. The Boston, Rochester, Salem, and Lynn (Massachusetts) societies were integrated, but the New York City society split over whether to accept black women as members. Several midwestern cities, which established antislavery societies, also wrangled over the relations of black and white members. But integrationists were prominent enough in the national society to support the candidacies of such leading black abolitionists as Susan Paul, Martha Ball, and Grace Douglass to important positions in the national organization.

A number of white abolitionists suffered persecution for their integrationist or antislavery beliefs. Lydia Maria Child's successful literary career came to a crashing halt when she began to espouse both antislavery and integrationist sentiments. Although her husband had been an abolitionist for several years, Child did not embrace the cause until she met Garrison in 1831. Child later recalled that Garrison "got hold of the strings of my conscience and pulled me into reforms."

Two years later, she published *An Appeal in Favor of that Class of Americans Called Africans.* One of the first antislavery books published in America, the *Appeal* galvanized numerous important reformers to the abolitionists' cause, including Wendell Phillips, a Boston aristocrat, and Charles Sumner, a U.S. senator from Massachusetts. The effect on Child's place in Boston's literary and genteel society was far less pleasant. Her past associates were particularly upset at her denunciation of laws against mixed marriages and her support for integrating churches, theaters, and stagecoaches. She was barred from many lecture halls, and her reading public rejected her next works on domestic subjects.

The uproar caught Child by surprise. She later recalled that after the *Appeal* was published, "old dreams vanished, old associates departed, and all things became new." For Child, making a living at writing was a necessity as well as a vocation, since her husband rarely earned enough to support them. She plunged headlong into a number of abolitionist writing and editing projects, for a time editing the *National Anti-Slavery Standard.* Although she had some commercial successes (including her *Letters from New York,* in 1843 and 1845), she was never again the darling of middle- and upper-class literary society. Sarah Josepha Hale, surveying Child's abolitionist writings, lamented, "Her fine genius, her soul's wealth has been wasted." Child herself had no such regrets.

Unlike Child, Prudence Crandall did not embrace the abolitionist cause through a spiritual conversion. Rather, fate helped transform a rather staid, respectable New England life into a quest for reform. Crandall had been hired by the leading citizens of Canterbury, Connecticut, to run the Canterbury Female Boarding School. All went well for several years until Sarah Harris, a young black girl, asked to be admitted to the school. Harris told Crandall, "I want to get a little more learning, enough if possible to teach colored children, and if you will admit me to your school, I shall forever be under the greatest obligation to you. If you think that it will be the means of injuring you, I will not insist on the favor." Up to that point, Crandall had not taken an active part in the abolitionist cause. Having attended a Quaker boarding school, however, she was predisposed against slavery. She was given further encouragement by her maid, an African-American woman who was about to marry the local distributor of the *Liberator.* Realizing that she might face some complaints from Canterbury students and their parents, Crandall nevertheless decided to accept Harris as a pupil. In time, she hoped, those who protested the girl's presence would come to accept her. Instead, parents removed their children from the school one by one, and the school's more traditional supporters demanded that Harris be expelled. Crandall chose to close the school instead.

But she had just begun to fight. After gathering advice and support from abolitionists throughout the Northeast, Crandall returned to Canterbury to establish a school for "Young Ladies and Little Misses of Color." Twenty young women from surrounding areas and as far away as Boston and New York City attended the school. In response, the town of Canterbury virtually declared war on Crandall and her students. Town leaders first threatened to arrest her students as vagrants. Connecticut legislators then passed a law making it illegal to educate a black pupil from another state. Eventually, an appeals court threw the case out, perhaps realizing that it raised some knotty constitutional issues. Before Crandall's victory, however, she went to jail three times for defying the law. Canterburians tried more direct methods as well. They smashed the school's windows, tossed stones and rotten eggs at students and teachers, and spoiled the school's well with manure. No merchant in town would sell supplies to the school, and doctors refused to visit.

Crandall, aided by abolitionists from neighboring communities and her resolute students, refused to yield. As if in a fort under siege, they had to cart in food and water through a gauntlet of taunting townsfolk. The problems of the school became a rallying cry for abolitionists, and contributions were sent from across the North. Eventually, however, the siege became a frontal assault. One night, a mob set fire to the basement. After smashing some battering rams against the doors and walls, they trashed the classrooms while Crandall and her terrified students huddled upstairs. The next day, Crandall surrendered, unwilling to put her students' lives at risk. After closing the school, she moved with her husband to Illinois, where she continued to be active in abolitionist and women's rights causes.

Prudence Crandall's and Maria Lydia Child's experiences demonstrate the depth of racism that existed in the North. Even many Northerners who were opposed to southern slavery still had little use for the idea of black equality, and even less use for any attempt at racial integration. Soon after Garrison launched the *Liberator* in 1829, a split appeared in the antislavery ranks between those promoting black equality and those merely wishing to phase out slavery. At the same time, the issue of women's place within the movement also became a central point of contention between the two camps.

In 1833, speaking at a convention in Philadelphia, Garrison called for the founding of a national antislavery association. Despite the presence of numerous influential abolitionist women in the city, women were barred from joining the newly formed American Antislavery Society. Apparently, while Garrison had embraced the ideal of immediate emancipation and black equality, he had not yet equated these goals with women's rights. The women who had witnessed the proceedings had other ideas. Led by Lucretia Mott and Charlotte Forten, they immediately formed the Philadelphia Female Anti-Slavery Society.

The first speakers to bring the intertwined issues of abolition and women's rights to a national audience were raised in the heart of slaveholding society. Angelina and Sarah Grimké were born to a prominent South Carolina plantation family. Both had some misgivings about the treatment of slaves when they were growing up, and they recorded in their diaries their conflicts between their sense of Christian morality and the reality of southern slave society. During a visit to Philadelphia in 1819, Sarah became attracted to the Quakers' professions of simplicity and piety. Two years later, she moved to Philadelphia. Ten years after that,

Lucretia and James Mott are seated at far right in the front row of this portrait of the executive committee of the Philadelphia Anti-Slavery Society in 1851. Mott used her experience as an abolitionist leader to help organize the women's rights convention at Seneca Falls in 1848.

Angelina followed her sister north, unable to reconcile her personal beliefs with the horrors of the slave system that surrounded her.

Despite their abandonment of the South, the sisters did not become active abolitionists until Angelina joined the Philadelphia Female Antislavery Society in 1835. A year later, she published *An Appeal to the Christian Women of the South,* which instantly drew the public's attention. The Grimké family was well established in South Carolina, and a firsthand account of slavery's sinfulness from such a privileged person sent shock waves through both North and South. The pamphlet was particularly radical in that it urged southern women to lead the way in the fight against slavery. Postal workers often confiscated and then burned copies once they entered the South. Meanwhile, South Carolina politicians tried to outdo each other in denouncing the woman they saw as a traitor to her people.

In 1836 the sisters attended a lecture by Theodore Weld, a leading abolitionist orator. Weld's talk inspired Sarah to publish *Epistle to the Clergy of the Southern States,* which argued that the Bible did not condone slavery, as many southern ministers had insisted. The Grimkés did not neglect the North, however. Two years later, Angelina wrote *Appeal to the Women of the Nominally Free States,* an attack on northern racism and the complicity of northern racists in prolonging slavery. At this time both sisters were speaking to groups of women who flocked to hear their firsthand accounts of life in slave society. Angelina was particularly active, often speaking six nights in a row. Her unique perspective began to attract men to the audience, despite early efforts to restrict attendance to women. In 1838, she became the first woman to address the Massachusetts legislature on behalf of the hundreds of women's antislavery petitions that were pouring in.

All this notoriety was bound to gain the attention of the more conservative members of society. In 1837, the Congregational ministers of Massachusetts issued a strong condemnation of the Grimkés' behavior. "We invite your attention to the dangers which at present seem to threaten the female character with widespread and permanent injury," it warned. "We appreciate the [humbleness] of women in advancing the cause of religion at home and abroad in Sabbath schools and in all such associations associated with the modesty of her sex. But when she yields the power that was given her for her protection, then her character becomes unnatural." The ministers were particularly upset that the Grimkés had pursued these unnatural activities in "promiscuous audiences" of women and men.

Angelina Grimké wrote Weld, "We are placed very unexpectedly in a very trying situation, in the forefront of an entirely new contest—a contest for the *rights of woman* as a moral, intelligent and responsible being." Many male abolitionists believed, however, that this was a contest not worth fighting. Weld responded that women's rights was "an extraneous issue ... We cannot push Abolition forward," he urged Angelina, "until we take up the stumbling block out of the road." Encouraged by Garrison's conversion to their position, the Grimkés argued that women's rights were not an obstacle, but part of the foundation of abolitionism and social justice in general. Sarah Grimké produced *Letters on the Equality of the Sexes and the Condition of Women* in 1838, and Angelina contributed a series on the subject to the *Liberator*. Proving their continued popularity, they sold out a series of six lectures at Boston's Odeon Hall in the spring of 1838.

The Grimkés' remarkable speaking career came to an end several months later. It was Angelina who delivered the impassioned lecture the fateful night that the mob burned Pennsylvania Hall. Exhausted by the demands and dangers of her speaking engagements, she suffered a mental collapse shortly thereafter. Having married Theodore Weld days before the burning of Philadelphia Hall, Angelina retired with her husband and her sister to recuperate. Although the sisters produced some abolitionist tracts in the next few years, they effectively withdrew from the public movement.

Other women abolitionists followed the Grimkés into the breach they had created for the "woman question." Among the most prominent was Abigail Kelley Foster, who helped found the Lynn Antislavery Society in 1835. She became one of the early pioneers who insisted on women's right to speak publicly about politics. Refuting those who would consign her to "woman's sphere," she proclaimed in the *Connecticut Observer*, in 1840, "Whatever ways and means are right for men to adopt in reforming the world, are right also for women to adopt in pursuing the same subject." She was such a powerful speaker that she inevitably raised significant sums for the abolitionist cause whenever she lectured. Along with Lucretia Mott, she served as an inspiration and example to a whole generation of abolitionists and women's rights advocates, including Paulina Wright Davis, Lucy Stone, and Susan B. Anthony.

Although the "woman question" was not the only issue splitting radicals and conservatives in the antislavery movement, it became the wedge that forced a split. The supporters of women abolitionists came out on top, but the minority issued a bitter denunciation of the outcome that suggested the fight was not yet over. In 1840, those opposing women's influence in the society—a group that included many powerful men—formed a separate society. This all-male society would lead the way in pressing the cause of antislavery in the political arena. Meanwhile, the American Antislavery Society quickly placed Lydia Maria Child, Maria Weston Chapman, and Lucretia Mott on its executive committee, and it continued its efforts to convince the American people of the morality of women's participation in public debate and the immorality of slavery.

Before the final breakup, the two sides fought one more battle. In the summer of 1840, the American Antislavery Society attempted to have Lucretia Mott serve as one of its delegates at the World Antislavery Convention in London. The conservatives in the international delegations prevailed, and Mott was forced to watch the proceedings from the gallery. This affront to Mott proved to have a more formidable impact on the history of women's rights than on the fight against slavery. For Elizabeth Cady Stanton, who attended the convention during her honeymoon with her husband, the abolitionist Henry Stanton, the convention provided a wholly unexpected enlightenment. Stanton, destined to be among the key leaders of the women's rights movement throughout the nineteenth century, was asked on her return what most impressed her about England. She replied immediately, "Lucretia Mott." She later reminisced, "I shall never forget the look of recognition she gave me when she saw by my remarks that I fully comprehended the problems of women's rights. Mrs. Mott was to me an entire new revelation of womanhood."

Following the convention, an unexpected—even unthinkable—notion came into their heads. Elizabeth Stanton later recalled, "As Lucretia Mott and Elizabeth Cady Stanton wended their way arm in arm down Great Queen Street that night, reviewing the exciting scenes of the day, they agreed to hold a woman's rights convention on their return to America, as the men to whom they had just listened had manifested their great need of some education on that question." Eight years later, they achieved their goal.

The Year of Revolution

Eighteen forty-eight was a momentous year for American women, as it was for men and women across the world. During the spring, revolutions against tyrannical governments were initiated in Germany, Italy, France, and the Austro-Hungarian empire. At first the revolutions appeared to succeed, and the besieged governments made numerous concessions in order to stave off complete collapse. Liberal constitutions promising more democratic participation and personal liberty were adopted, and various emperors and kings temporarily fled their capitals. By autumn, however, the revolutions had collapsed, and the repressive governments reasserted themselves. Most of the liberal and radical revolutionaries were forced to flee Europe, and they were joined by those simply hoping to escape the chaos.

American shipping companies also began regular transatlantic service between the United States and Europe in 1848. The United States, long considered by Europeans to be a place of boundless opportunities, became the destination of the majority of European refugees. War was not the only reason for European immigration. A deadly cholera epidemic caused many to flee during 1847 and 1848. Crops in many of the European countries failed between 1845 and 1848. In Ireland, the potato crop was attacked by a blight that destroyed most of the island's staple food. More than a million people died of starvation and disease, and a million and a half fled the country. Two out of every three of these immigrants landed in the United States.

Irish and Germans had been immigrating to the United States in small but significant numbers since the colonial era. This sudden surge, however, was something different. Between 1847 and 1857, more than 3 million immigrants entered the United States, with a third coming from Ireland and a third from Germany. As the Civil War began in 1860, European immigrants made up 15 percent of the white population. The new immigration helped bring significant changes to American women. Immigrant women became a new source of cheap labor, largely replacing rural New England women as workers in the mills. Irish women were much more likely than Anglo-Protestant women to accept jobs as domestics, and thus answered the demand for house servants among the middle and upper classes. The new immigrants solidified the various ethnic neighborhoods that earlier Irish and German immigrants had established in urban areas, challenging the influence of the mainstream Anglo and Protestant culture. All of these changes would have a significant impact as the United States transformed itself from an agricultural to an industrial nation in the second half of the nineteenth century.

The year 1848 also brought the Mexican-American War to a close, thus making "immigrants" of thousands of Hispanics who lived in the Southwest. With the signing of the Treaty of Guadalupe Hidalgo, Mexico was forced to cede to the United States all of the territory north of the Rio Grande and the Gila River and south of Oregon for a cash settlement. Hispanics would now have to live under the laws of the United States and would have to face the land hunger of the incoming Americans. They would soon find themselves losing political, cultural, and economic power in the land they had once controlled. American Indian tribes within the new territory would find themselves similarly beset by American settlers and the U.S. Army. The U.S. Army would soon wage a war of annihilation against those tribes not willing to submit to life on newly established reservations.

In California, these transformations were accelerated by the discovery of gold at Sutter's Mill in 1848. Although those in the know tried to keep the information hidden, word soon leaked out. The next year, thousands of men—and a few women—from all over the world rushed in to the California gold country to strike it rich. The sudden population explosion and resultant social changes created new opportunities for some women, new tragedies for others.

With Americans rushing to grab a piece of the newly expanded territorial pie, old sectional disputes between North and South again came to the fore. Congress's Missouri Compromise of 1820 had precariously balanced the number of slave and free states. Northerners, whether abolitionist or merely opposed to the presence of blacks, were agreed that they did not want to see the spread of slavery into the West. Southerners saw expansion of slavery as the only way to maintain their political and economic influence. These controversies would help speed the two sides toward civil war in 1861.

Amidst all these events of national and international significance, few Americans took notice of a small group of women meeting in Seneca Falls, New York.

Elizabeth Cady Stanton and her daughter, Harriot. from a daguerreotipe 1856.

Elizabeth Cady Stanton holds her daughter, Harriot. Although Stanton did not denounce her role as wife and mother, she felt that women should be allowed to participate more fully in society and should not be confined to the home.

But there, in the heart of the Burned-over District, Lucretia Mott and Elizabeth Cady Stanton organized the first convention for women's rights in the United States. Fortunately, while others were looking elsewhere, the women delegates retained a sense of the history that they were making and carefully recorded the proceedings. Thus we are able today to add the Seneca Falls Convention to the list of revolutionary occurrences in 1848.

Although Mott and Stanton had been earnest in their desire to organize a women's rights meeting, they both found themselves burdened with numerous other duties. Mott continued to be a leader in the abolitionist movement and to raise her children and care for her husband. Stanton, recently married to journalist and reformer Henry Stanton, soon found herself overwhelmed with duties as a new wife and mother. She had been a child of privilege; as a teenager she had attended Emma Willard's seminary in Troy. The Stantons had originally settled in Boston, a center for abolitionist and literary activities. Here

Elizabeth Stanton was in her element, establishing friendships with Lydia Maria Child, Abby Kelley Foster, Maria Weston Chapman, Frederick Douglass, and other leading abolitionists. Henry Stanton found the wet Boston climate debilitating, however, and he moved his family to the small town of Seneca Falls.

In Boston, Elizabeth Stanton had been able to take advantage of city conveniences to make her life easier. In Seneca Falls, she had to work at numerous difficult tasks that her money had once paid for. Even when she could hire domestic help, she found herself a prisoner of the household. She later recalled, "I now fully understood the practical difficulties most women had to contend with in the isolated household, and the impossibility of woman's best development if in contact the chief part of her life with servants and children." Fortunately, she made good use of this lesson, turning her discontent with "women's portion" to the search for "active measures . . . to remedy the wrongs of society in general and of women in particular."

Luckily, Lucretia Mott was visiting the area soon after Stanton came to this understanding of her life and her life's purpose. Reunited with Mott, Stanton was further comforted by Mott's sister, Martha Wright, and Mott's friends Jane Hunt and Mary Ann McClintock—Quakers all. In the company of these women, Stanton "poured out," as she wrote in her autobiography, "the torrent of my long accumulating discontent, with such vehemence and indignation that I stirred myself, as well as the rest of the party, to do and dare something." The result of this fateful meeting was an advertisement, placed in the *Seneca County Courier,* announcing a "Woman's Rights Convention—A convention to discuss the social, civil and religious rights of women will be held in the Wesleyan Chapel, Seneca Falls, New York, the nineteenth and twentieth of July current." The advertisement noted, "During the first day the meeting will be held exclusively for women, who are earnestly invited to attend." The advertisement also offered a figure of national prominence, noting that "Lucretia Mott of Philadelphia and other ladies and gentlemen will address the convention."

Because nobody had organized a women's rights convention before, the five women had to make things up as they went along. Nonetheless, they were able to draw on the organizing tactics, administrative skills, and ideology of equal rights that they had developed in the abolitionist movement. For the Declaration of Sentiments of the convention, Stanton drew heavily on the Declaration of Independence. If it worked for the forefathers of America, Stanton figured, it would serve the foremothers of women's rights quite nicely.

Perhaps it was the Declaration of Independence's call for the rights and responsibilities of citizenship that inspired Stanton to make the radical demand for a woman's right to vote. Henry Stanton, considered a radical abolitionist and freethinker, was appalled. He threatened to leave town if his wife persisted in making this demand, and he kept to his word. The idea of woman suffrage at first proved too much for even the forward-thinking Lucretia Mott, who responded to

Stanton's proposal by writing, "Thou will make us ridiculous. We must go slowly." Stanton was encouraged to persist, however, by the support of the eminent abolitionist and ex-slave Frederick Douglass. Knowing Douglass's support would carry a lot of moral weight, Stanton decided to include the call for woman suffrage in the resolutions.

Stanton and Mott were concerned that they might end up addressing their own circle of friends. But the vast changes that had begun early in the nineteenth century had taken root in the fertile ground of the Burned-over District. From fifty miles around, people came by cart, by horse, and on foot—more than three hundred in all—to take part in this first official step toward liberation. The convention even attracted dozens of men, who, after some discussion, were allowed to participate on the first day. Perhaps we can take Charlotte Woodward's story as typical of those who chose to brave public ridicule and join in this groundbreaking event. Woodward, nineteen at the time, lived on a nearby farm but dreamed of one day working as a typesetter. It was an impossible dream, she knew—but then, who would have dreamed of a women's rights convention being held in Seneca Falls? When Woodward first read the fateful notice in the *Seneca Courier,* however, she began to believe in the power of dreams. While some of her neighbors laughed at the notion of women assembling to discuss their supposed rights, Woodward found six other brave souls to attend the meeting with her. As they set out in their wagon, they wondered if any other women would dare to attend. But their spirits soared as they spied other vehicles making their way toward the convention hall. Suddenly, they realized they were no longer alone.

Liberation does not come quickly, however, nor easily. Among the stalwart women gathered in Seneca Falls, none was willing to take up the gavel and lead the meeting; that honor was given to James Mott, Lucretia's husband. And when it came time to vote on the resolutions, all passed unanimously except No. 9—the resolution calling for women's enfranchisement, or the right to vote. After much debate, however, that passed as well, and the modern woman suffrage movement was born. Some seventy-two years later, Congress passed and the states ratified the 19th Amendment to the U.S. Constitution, ensuring that "the right of the citizens of the United States shall not be denied or abridged . . . on account of sex." Only one woman who signed the Declaration of Principles, Charlotte Woodward, was still alive to vote in the presidential election of 1920.

If Seneca Falls was a revolutionary event, it was also one that would take a good bit of time to make its impact known. Indeed, the reverberations set off by those five women sitting around their kitchen table—the same table that now stands honored in the Smithsonian Institution—are still being felt today. For a revolution is not won or lost in a few days time, or a few years. Its legacy lasts for generations, a continued source of inspiration for some, antagonism for others, and reflection for all.

CHAPTER 5

An Unfinished Battle
1848–1865

Harriet Sigerman

N ewspapers across the country carried reports of the Seneca Falls convention. Much of the coverage was critical, even nasty. One editorial called the convention "the most shocking and unnatural incident ever recorded in the history of womanity." Editors accused female participants of "unwomanly behavior" and of neglecting "their more appropriate duties." They feared that equal rights would "demoralize and degrade" women and "prove a monstrous injury to all mankind."

The newspapers' disparaging coverage frightened some people away. A few signers of the Declaration of Sentiments and Resolutions withdrew their support because of all the publicity, and others even spurned the organizers of the Seneca Falls convention. Still other women who did indeed support the cause of women's rights could not resist their husbands' opposition. But some women were not so easily cowed, and the convention galvanized them to work for women's rights.

A Movement for Women's Rights Begins

Seneca Falls was the opening salvo in the organized women's rights movement in the United States. Women had finally set forth the problem of sexual inequality in all of its forms—political, social, economic, and personal—and organized a movement to combat this inequality. The Declaration of Sentiments and Resolutions became a road map for the path they hoped to travel toward equality and self-determination. It would set the tone and goals of the American women's rights movement for decades to come. More important, the convention brought women together as a group to solve their problems. After Seneca Falls, women would hold other conventions and eventually establish local and national organizations to press their claims. From now on, American women would crusade for their rights behind the banner of an organized movement.

Perhaps it was not coincidental that the Seneca Falls convention was held in 1848, the year in which revolutions and insurrections swept Europe. In the United States the spirit of progress and reform abounded. The antislavery movement, the

The campaign against alcohol was one of the earliest and largest women's reform movements. Temperance advocates viewed alcohol abuse as a threat not only to the drinking men themselves but to their wives and families.

temperance movement to rid the country of the scourge of alcohol, and various experiments in communal living—all of these movements attempted to create a more enlightened and democratic society.

Although the Seneca Falls convention launched an organized women's rights movement in America, the ideas expressed at Seneca Falls—and the anger at women's inferior political and social status so eloquently voiced in the Declaration of Sentiments and Resolutions—had been simmering for a long time. These ideas and sentiments had found earlier expression in the writings of courageous women who had rejected the social and legal restrictions imposed upon their sex, and in the blossoming awareness of women who had joined the antislavery movement and charitable societies.

As the growing nation relied more on factories to produce its goods, many women had more time for such activities. Married women were expected to be nurturing, maternal wives and mothers. The harsh realm of business and manufacture drove men and women to view the home as a sanctuary, a place in which the values of love, harmony, and virtue reigned—a gentle, loving refuge from the harsh world outside. Women were expected to rule over this domain of love and peace.

This role invested women with special power and influence. "To render home happy is woman's peculiar province, home is her world," gushed the *Ladies' Magazine* in 1830. But home was expected to be her only province—the world out there was too rough and tumble for her tender mercies. Although popular books and magazines and religious and intellectual leaders increasingly assigned two separate roles, or spheres, to men and women, some women bristled at these rigid restrictions on their lives. They wanted to be part of the world beyond their front doors, and they risked the disapproval of family and friends to seek an education, acquire a skill or pursue a profession, and forgo marriage.

Throughout the middle of the nineteenth century, many women, both married and single, found the path toward participating in that world in moral reform and charitable organizations. In these groups, women developed important organizational and leadership skills. They learned how to draft their own constitutions and bylaws, elected officers, organized meetings and assigned duties, managed funds, and wrote and published progress reports. They also learned how to distribute petitions and testify before courts and state legislative committees. These and other newly acquired organizational skills instilled pride and self-confidence. In 1837 a volunteer for one organization exulted, "I rejoice my friends that I am woman; and I never gloried more in my sex than I do now."

Perhaps more importantly, women volunteers learned about the many difficulties that other women faced. They distributed firewood to widows, dispensed medicine to the sick, raised funds for orphanages, and tried to convert nonbelievers to Christianity. They also established training schools, nurseries, employment facilities, hospitals, and shelters for women and children. From these many volunteer

CIRCULAR.

THE FIRST REPORT OF THE ROCHESTER LADIES' ANTI-SLAVERY SEWING SOCIETY.

TREASURER'S REPORT.

Amount of Receipts at the Anti-Slavery Fair, March 18th and 19th, 1852.

For Foreign goods sold..........................$114,02	**Charges.**
" Domestic " 38,76	Paid Mr. Reynolds for Hall...........$50,00
" Books.....................................19,00	Sundry Bills.........................49,36
" Refreshments.............................103,47	———— 99,36
" Entrance at door..........................66,26	$309,21
" Donations from Philadelphia...............10,00	
" " McGrawville................10,00	Donation to Mr. Douglass................... 233,00
" " Peterboro.................... 5,00	
" " Canandaigua.................11,00	Balance in Treasury.................... 76,21
" " Rochester.....................31,12	
	MARIA G. PORTER, *Treasurer.*

$408,57

We present the above as the pecuniary result of the first effort of the Rochester Ladies' Anti-Slavery Sewing Society. The sum realized, though quite small when, viewed in connection with our large wishes, and the pressing wants of the anti-slavery cause, is, nevertheless, highly encouraging, and will serve to stimulate us to further endeavors of a like character. For the success which attended the recent Festival, we are greatly indebted to the kind co-operation of friends on both sides of the Atlantic. Our tables were supplied with articles of our own, and of foreign manufacture. Valuable contributions reached us from Cork, Belfast, Manchester and Birmingham, sent expressly to be disposed of for the benefit of *Frederick Douglass' Paper*. Many of our friends in Great Britain and Ireland inquire as to what articles prove most saleable in Rochester, that they may make their future arrangements accordingly. We would say to those friends that the beautiful *papier mache* from Manchester, together with the articles manufactured in lava, were greatly admired and commanded good prices. The finely wrought baby-linen, the exquisite sea-weed baskets, the drawings, the collection of Irish shells, and the beautiful embroidery, together with the knitted and netted work, in the Belfast box, were very acceptable. The handsome purses, reticules and crochet work from Cork, obtained a ready sale. Owing to some delay, a box of valuable contributions from Bridgewater, England, and another box from Penkeith, failed to reach Rochester in time for the Festival. To the kind friends who forwarded the boxes in question, we would say that, while we regret the non-arrival of their contributions for the late occasion, we are happy to state that measures will be forthwith adopted to dispose of them in a very short time, and the proceeds will be appropriated in the manner the donors desire. While referring to the valuable donations of our trans-Atlantic friends, we would not forget to mention that the three books of rare and choice botanical specimen, so beautifully classified by a friend in Dundee, Scotland, found purchasers. The lady who devoted so much valuable time to their arrangement will be interested to learn that one of the books is now in the possession of GERRIT SMITH, Esq., of Peterboro, the prince of American philanthropists. The presence of Mr. Smith at the Festival, contributed, in no small degree, towards its interest, usefulness and success. On the first evening, he delivered an able an eloquent address, which was listened to with deep attention by the audience assembled.

On the second evening, addresses were made by the Rev. R. R. Raymond of Syracuse, and by Frederick Douglass. Both addresses were heart-stirring, and left upon the audience a profound impression. It was thought, by some of our members, that, had the society accomplished nothing more than the calling forth of these speeches, in the presence of such an auditory, their labors would have been amply repaid; for a class of the Rochester citizens were reached, on that evening, by anti-slavery, who had, in all probability, never heard it before. In the address of Mr. Douglass, the devoted labors of our trans-Atlantic friends and co-adjutors were gratefully remembered, and eloquently commended. Our sisters in Great Britain may feel assured that their sympathy, for the enslaved of our land, is a welcome cordial to our hearts, in our labors to free our beloved country from the heinous crime, and deep disgrace of enslaving one-sixth of our population. The time has gone by, we trust, when it can be deemed improper or indelicate for the people of one country to sympathize with, and to labor for the improvement and elevation of the people of another. In the cause of *human freedom*, we may command the co-operation of the universe. That cause is bound by no geographical nor national lines. The slave has a right to appeal, from his cruel task-master, to assembled mankind. We, therefore, welcome with gratitude the contributions of our British friends; and we beg to assure them that, *small* as their donations may *seem* to *them* to be, they are here highly prized, and rendered greatly serviceable. For the Slave's sake, we solicit a continuance of the co-operation already existing. It is meet that our British friends should labor in this, to them, missionary work.

To our home friends who have assisted us, we tender our grateful acknowledgments. Among these, we would especially remember our young friends at McGrawville who sent us ten dollars. The existence of such an institution as Central College, so thoroughly anti-slavery and *anti-caste*, is a sign of progress exceedingly gratifying. It will be also seen that donations were sent from Canandaigua, Peterboro, Philadelphia and elsewhere. The contributions to the refreshment tables, from various sources, were very acceptable. Our Farmington, Henrietta, and Rochester friends did nobly in that department, making the expense of furnishing tables very slight. Being quite young in the cause, we very naturally glance around to see by whom our efforts are favorably regarded. Straws may sometimes show the course of the wind. Among the journals who willingly and kindly gave publicity to our intended Festival and Convention, we gratefully remember the *National Era*, *Pennsylvania Freeman*, the *American Baptist*, *The Independent*, *The Commonwealth*, the *Carson League*, the *Banner of the Times*, the *New-York Tribune*, and our own city papers.

This report stated, "The sum realized, though quite small, when, viewed in connection with our large wishes, and the pressing wants of the anti-slavery cause, is, nevertheless, highly encouraging." It acknowledged the contribution of "friends on both sides of the Atlantic."

tasks and others, they learned firsthand about the problems of women's lives—from meager earnings that hardly supported female wage earners to husbands and employers who were cruel or irresponsible. In this way, they began to challenge men's authority and to suggest ways that women could improve their lives.

African-American women as well as white women formed associations in the antebellum years. Most African-American clubs were formed in northern states, where slavery had died out or been abolished. But a few clubs for freed blacks existed in the slaveholding South as well. Most African-American clubs were educational in purpose. By 1849 more than half of Philadelphia's African-American population, men as well as women, belonged to one of 106 black literary organizations in the city. Other black clubs helped the African-American community by raising funds to build schools and libraries for their people. The Ohio Ladies Education Society, a club formed by black women in 1837, had a sterling record of accomplishment. By the 1840s it had opened more schools for African Americans than any other black, or white, organization in the nation. African-American women and men defied poverty and racism to organize clubs that served their communities. Their impressive club activities were even more remarkable because of the obstacles they overcame.

African-American women discovered their strength and power as women through helping themselves and their communities. In the 1830s their chief advocate was Maria Stewart, a black woman. She was also the first American-born woman to lecture in public—an activity simply not pursued by any other woman of her day. In her lectures Stewart urged black women to help strengthen the African-American community. "Daughters of Africa, awake!" Stewart exhorted her audience in Boston's Franklin Hall on September 21, 1832. "Arise! Distinguish yourselves. O do not say, you cannot make anything of your children; but say, with the help and assistance of God, we will try."

By 1833 Stewart's public-speaking activities had aroused such intense oppostion among Boston's black leaders that she decided to leave the city. To them, more troubling than her message was the fact that she was a woman who had dared to speak in public. Before she left, she defended her right as a woman to speak out: "What if I am a woman; is not the God of ancient times the God of these modern days? Did he not raise up Deborah to be a mother and a judge in Israel? Did not Queen Esther save the lives of the Jews? And Mary Magdalene first declare the resurraction of Christ from the dead?" Stewart was a towering example of courage and drive to other African-American women who wanted to improve their own lives and help their people.

From the abolitionist movement, which sought to abolish slavery in the South, women acquired a philosophy and a vocabulary of equality. Like moral reform and charity work, abolition reflected the temper of the times—a fervent desire to improve society, to end injustice and inequality.

Lucy Stone, who had graduated from Oberlin College with Antoinette Brown, decided to become a professional public speaker. When her family objected to this "unladylike" vocation, she wrote, "I expect to plead not for the slave only, but for suffering humanity everywhere. Especially do I mean to labor for the elevation of my sex." In the spring of 1848, Stone embarked on a career as a speaker for the Massachusetts Antislavery Society. She mesmerized audiences with her soft musical voice; one listener remarked that it sounded "like a silver bell."

Like other abolitionists, Stone was harassed wherever she spoke. Opponents tore down the posters advertising her talks, threw pepper into the auditoriums where she lectured, and even doused her with cold water one winter day. But, like the Grimké sisters, she insisted on her right to speak out—in support of abolition and women's rights. When the Massachusetts Antislavery Society protested that she had been hired to speak only on abolition, she retorted, "I was a woman before I was an abolitionist. I must speak for the women."

Margaret Fuller codified her thoughts on women's potential in her 1845 book *Woman in the Nineteenth Century.* In it, she offered a remarkably advanced vision of women's lives. She rejected the idea of a designated and limited sphere of activity and urged women to seek an education and work at whatever they desired: "Let them be sea-captains, if they will." She exhorted women to educate themselves for their own benefit, not merely to be better wives and mothers.

The path to Seneca Falls, therefore, was paved by many courageous women who, like Fuller and Stone, chose to speak for their sex—who had refused in thought or deed to accept the social, legal, and political inequalities that hindered women's lives. Two weeks after the convention, in early August 1848, another group of women organized a convention in Rochester, New York. At this meeting, a woman, the Quaker Abigail Bush, chaired the proceedings. Even Elizabeth Cady Stanton was doubtful about this unusual practice and called it a "hazardous experiment." But Bush's superb leadership skills quickly won her over. From then on, women chaired their own conventions. At the Rochester convention, participants debated a resolution on woman suffrage, and this time it passed with a wider margin than at Seneca Falls. Activists held another convention in April 1850 in Salem, Ohio; six months later, in October 1850, the first National Woman's Rights Convention was held in Worcester, Massachusetts.

As the new decade unfolded, the ripple effect of women's demands for equality spread, and new leaders and fresh visions of women's lives emerged. American women would not be stopped in their crusade to achieve their political rights and their full potential as human beings. They had crossed a barrier, and they would not be held back from entering that active arena of life.

New Voices and Ideas

Like a fire on the horizon, gathering speed and fury as it roared across the earth, the women's rights movement spread in every direction beyond Seneca Falls to distant regions and states. By their words and their courageous examples, women converted one another to the cause of women's rights. Olympia Brown, for example, was still a student at Antioch College in Yellow Springs, Ohio, when she heard Frances Dana Gage, an author and antislavery worker, speak. "It was the first time I had heard a woman preach," she later recalled, "and the sense of victory lifted me up." Other women reacted with similar hope and energy, and organized their own activities.

As the women's rights movement gained new converts and leaders, it also developed new ideas. During these early years, women's rights activists decided not to establish a formal organization with officers and bylaws, for fear that, as Angelina Grimké said, an organization would "fetter and distort the expanding mind." They drew most of their support from abolitionists, especially women. They also drew inspiration from the temperance movement, crusades for better schools and healthier ways to live, and spiritualism, a religious movement that aimed to prove the immortality of the soul by making contact with the spirits of the dead. All of these reform movements shared the same goal—to improve the way that people lived and help the nation fulfill its democratic ideals.

Despite this shared sense of purpose, however, the women's rights movement had its own goals to pursue, its own tasks to complete. As Elizabeth Cady Stanton had declared shortly after Seneca Falls, "Woman herself must do this work; for woman alone can understand the height, the depth, the length and the breadth of her degradation." The goals that defined the movement before and after the Seneca Falls convention remained the same. Women's rights activists continued to demand all citizenship rights for women. For married women, they demanded control over their own wages, the right to sign legal agreements or transact property in their own name, stronger inheritance rights after their husbands died, and equal educational and employment opportunities.

But the two central demands were suffrage and a woman's right to determine her own sphere—that is, her goals and aspirations for her life. These demands provoked the most fear and opposition because they challenged traditional notions of women's roles as wife and mother. In reacting to the demand for women's suffrage, one New York State legislator railed, "It is well known that the object of these unsexed women is to overthrow the most sacred of institutions. . . . Are we to put the stamp of truth upon the libel here set forth, that men and women, in the matrimonial relation, are to be equal?"

But women's rights activists did not intend to overthrow the institution of marriage. They accepted marriage and family as important social institutions. They wanted to reform marriage—to elevate the wife's role and therefore equalize her relation to her husband—not abolish it. Indeed, they felt, equality in marriage would lead to happier marriages and a more harmonious family life. Paulina Wright Davis, an activist and editor, argued that a healthy society depended upon a healthy family: "Its evils are the source of all evils, its good the fountain of all good." Reforming marriage was "the starting-point of all the reforms which the world needs."

Women's rights leaders also wanted women's sphere to encompass more than marriage and a family. "Woman is too large for the sphere in which society compels her to move," declared Elizabeth Oakes Smith. "Marriage no more fills up the sum of her whole being than it does that of a man." To demonstrate that marriage did not occupy the sum total of their lives, many activists, including Stanton, retained their birth names, adding on their husbands' last names, and preferred not to be called by their husbands' first names. Stanton, for instance, balked at being called "Mrs. *Henry* Stanton" and identified herself as Elizabeth Cady Stanton or simply Mrs. Stanton. Other activists also refused to be called only by their husbands' full names and, once again, drew a parallel to slavery: Only slaves, not free and equal persons, were compelled to take their masters' names and to forfeit their own identity.

Nevertheless, most women's rights activists accepted traditional ideas about women's special maternal qualities and their moral and spiritual superiority, even though they also hoped to enlarge women's opportunities beyond the home. Even Stanton, who decried any limits on women's freedom to live their lives as they wished, extolled women's "high moral sentiments and religious enthusiasms." It was left to Sojourner Truth to define womanhood without relying on traditional images of women. At a women's rights convention in Akron, Ohio, in 1851, a group of white ministers had tried to monopolize the proceedings by claiming that the Bible prohibited women from participating in any activities beyond the home. Impatient with their views, Truth rose from her seat, amidst gasps and exclamations from the audience, and solemnly walked to the front of the hall. "May I say a few words?" she asked, and after receiving permission to speak, she addressed the audience. "I have as much muscle as any man, and can do as much work as any man. I have plowed and reaped and husked and chopped and mowed, and can any man do more than that? I have heard much about the sexes being equal; I can carry as much as any man, and can eat as much too, if I can get it. I am as strong as any man that is now." She then demolished the idea that only educated people deserved equal rights: "If a woman have a pint, and man a quart—why can't she have her little pint full?" She gazed out at the audience. "I have heard the bible and have learned that Eve caused man to sin. Well if woman upset the world, do give her a chance to set it right side up again.... And how came Jesus into the world? Through God who created him and woman who bore him. Man, where is your part? ..." As Truth returned to her seat, the audience erupted into applause. Several spectators sat hushed and still, while others rushed up to shake her hand.

Although few free African-American women participated in the antebellum women's rights movement, they began to challenge inequality within their own communities. In 1848, the same year as the Seneca Falls convention, black women made their first official bid for equality in meetings with black men. At the annual meeting of the National Convention of Colored Freedmen in Cleveland, Ohio, a black woman proposed that women delegates be allowed to speak and vote as equals. Frederick Douglass supported her proposal. After much debate, convention delegates reclassified eligible voters as "persons" instead of men and allowed women to participate equally.

But despite official decrees to admit women as equal participants, black organizations did not carry out the policy consistently. At state and national conventions, delegates usually scorned women's equal participation and assigned them to such traditional tasks as arranging flowers at delegates' tables while the men determined policy. Even Frederick Douglass, a dedicated advocate of women's rights, put greater priority on ending slavery than achieving female equality within the African-American community and American society.

Other new names and faces joined the cause of women's rights during the 1850s. One of the most dedicated and courageous activists was Susan B. Anthony. Starting in 1851, she and Elizabeth Cady Stanton forged a powerful partnership for women's rights. Born in 1820 in western Massachusetts, Anthony was raised as a Quaker. Her grandmother and two aunts were influential leaders in the Quaker church, and young Susan B. Anthony was accustomed to hearing women speak their minds. Her parents also encouraged their daughters to think for themselves and to acquire an education. Daniel Anthony, Susan's father, was an ardent abolitionist, and he urged Susan to devote herself to a social cause. She followed his advice by joining the temperance movement in Rochester, New York, where she quickly rose to become president of the Rochester Daughters of Temperance.

In the spring of 1851, Anthony met Stanton, and the two women hit it off instantly. Stanton immediately recognized Anthony's commitment and skills as a reformer, and Anthony soon became her partner and confidante, someone to whom Stanton could pour out her frustrations at the many domestic obligations that filled her days. "Oh, Susan! Susan! Susan! ... How much I do long to be free from housekeeping and children, so as to have some time to read and think and write," she wrote Anthony. "But it may be well for me to understand all the trials of woman's lot, that I may more eloquently proclaim them when the time comes."

For the next fifty years the two women worked diligently for women's rights. Later Stanton wrote that she "forged the thunderbolts and [Anthony] fired them." For the first few years, Stanton formulated ideas and wrote speeches, and Anthony supplied the facts, delivered Stanton's speeches, and became a tireless recruiter for new converts to the cause. Anthony's impressive research and organizational skills ably matched Stanton's keen, analytical mind and eloquent pen. Together, they made a powerful team.

Meanwhile, other thinkers and proponents of women's rights also offered a wide array of ideas and initiatives to give women greater autonomy. For a brief period during the early 1850s, the causes of temperance and women's rights became closely linked. Men's addiction to alcohol had a profound impact on women. Wives became impoverished and were physically abused by drunken husbands who had squandered their families' money on alcohol. Temperance societies not only preached abstinence, they supported legislation to ban alcohol altogether or to prohibit the consumption of alcohol in certain neighborhoods or on certain days of the week. They also lobbied for laws to protect a wife's property and wages from a husband who would spend her earnings on alcohol. In her 1852 address to the Woman's New York State Temperance Society convention in Rochester, New York, Stanton boldly urged that drunkenness be made grounds for divorce. "Let no woman remain in the relation of wife with the confirmed drunkard," she declared. "Let no drunkard be the father of her children."

Other women took more direct action: Wielding axes and hatchets, they marched to the saloons in their communities and attacked the buildings. In Marion, Illinois, nine women went on trial for destroying a saloon—and were defended by a lawyer named Abraham Lincoln.

Besides their close alliance with abolitionists and temperance reformers, women's rights activists received support from an unusual source—mediums and other women who claimed to communicate with the spirit world. In their multi-volume work, *The History of Woman Suffrage,* Stanton and Anthony declared, "The only religious sect in the world . . . that has recognized the equality of women is the Spiritualists." The Spiritualist movement began in the same year, 1848, and in the same region, upstate New York, in which the Seneca Falls convention for women's rights was held. Spiritualism became a popular movement when two young girls, Kate and Margaret Fox, claimed to have made contact with the other side. Within months, other young women had also discovered a talent for contacting the spirit world, and séances were held in parlors throughout the North. Initially, adolescent girls were the most successful mediums. In Ohio in 1852, a student at a girls' school claimed that she and fifteen classmates had become mediums. Later on, older women also became mediums. The Spiritualist movement received something of a setback, however, when the Fox sisters were later revealed as frauds who had manufactured their famous "spirit knockings" by cracking the joints of their toes.

Like believers in organized religions, such as Christianity and Judaism, Spiritualists claimed that women were pious by nature. But unlike organized religion, Spiritualism thrust women into visible leadership roles and supported the most progressive reform movements of the day. Spiritualists envisioned marriages in which women were equal partners, controlled how many children they had, and were free to earn their own wages. Some advocated equal wages for equal work performed by men and women and called for more liberal divorce laws. Others urged women to reject corsets and other confining apparel and wear more comfortable clothes. And most Spiritualists advocated female suffrage. Spiritualists voiced these enlightened views because they believed that women as well as men had the ability to grasp truths without the guidance of a religious authority such as a minister or rabbi. But, they claimed, unjust laws and social customs had denied women the opportunity to develop their full potential as citizens and human beings capable of comprehending moral and religious truths.

Besides working for legal and political rights, activists also devised bold and original proposals to improve the health and personal well-being of women. Paulina Wright Davis, for example, urged women to be more knowledgeable about their anatomy and reproduction. Even physicians were loath to discuss such "indelicate" matters with their female patients, or they simply assumed that women had far less sexual desire than men. To combat the ignorance surrounding women's physiology and sexuality, Davis gave public lectures, using a plaster figure of a female nude. Some of her more delicate listeners, however, were shocked by such a display, and either covered their eyes, fled from the room, or fainted.

In 1853 Davis also founded one of the first journals devoted to women's rights, the *Una*. The title is the feminine form of the Latin word meaning *one*. In her columns, she urged women to demand the right to limit the number of children they bore and to take control over men's sexual access to them. She wanted women to enjoy the full rights and privileges of adulthood. "We ask to be regarded, respected, and treated as human beings, of full age and natural abilities," she wrote in the *Una*, "as equal fellow sinners, and not as infants or beautiful angels, to whom the rules of civil and social justice do not apply."

Elizabeth Cady Stanton also fought for women's personal freedom, especially in the sexual relations between husbands and wives. She endorsed, in her words, "the right of a wife to her own person"—that is, a wife's right to refuse sexual intercourse with her husband, especially if she did not want to have more children. In 1852 Stanton lamented that many women did not yet have this right. "Man in his lust has regulated this whole question of sexual intercourse long enough," she wrote to Anthony, ". . . let the mother of mankind . . . set bounds to his indulgence."

By the early 1850s, a few forms of birth control were available to women, notably the douche and different types of intrauterine devices. Women were also familiar with the rhythm method, in which they had intercourse only during the time of the month when they believed that they were not fertile, but ignorance about the female fertility cycle diminished the effectiveness of this form of birth control. Women sometimes resorted to abortion to end pregnancies, although abortions were beyond the means of many women. In 1858 the price of an abortion ranged from twenty-five to sixty dollars, an exorbitant price for a working woman barely able to make ends meet on a salary of three or four dollars a week. In addition, abortions could be dangerous when performed by a quack and were increasingly frowned upon by traditionally minded physicians for moral as well as medical reasons. As states began to make the practice of abortion a crime, women were less able to secure a safe, medically sound abortion, and resorted to using painful and dangerous homemade devices.

Even women who disagreed with many of the tenets of the women's rights movement sought ways to improve the quality of women's lives. Catharine Beecher opposed female suffrage and believed that women's greatest contribution lay in being mothers, wives, homemakers, and teachers. To her way of thinking, these social roles tapped women's special maternal qualities. Unlike Stanton and others, she did not crusade to break down all social and legal barriers to women's advancement. Instead, throughout the 1830s and 1840s she focused her energies on investing women's homemaking duties with greater power and dignity. She believed that healthy, happy homes—created by women—led to a healthy, happy society.

But if Beecher was not ready for women to become doctors or lawyers or politicians, she wanted them to be physically healthy and strong. She was a leading proponent of water cures. From the 1840s to the 1880s, water-cure centers sprang up around the North and Midwest and catered primarily to women, who stayed at these cure centers for several days or weeks, following a regimen of bathing, using wet compresses, taking steam baths and massages, and exercising. They also drank cold water and followed rigorous diets, and they learned about new forms of birth control.

Water cures brought women together to share the pleasures of indulging in healthful physical activities. While mainstream physicians preached to women about the incurable pain associated with menstruation and childbirth—a pain that women were predestined to suffer because of the biblical Eve's disobedience of divine commandments, they claimed—water cures helped women ease ailments and diseases that were connected with the female reproductive system.

Beecher also exhorted women to get adequate exercise and fresh air, eat nourishing meals, and stop wearing tight-fitting corsets, which endangered women's internal organs. Like Paulina Wright Davis, she urged women to learn about their bodies—in large part to protect their sexual virtue. Beecher believed that knowledge was the most potent weapon against sexual promiscuity. In 1855 she published her views in *Letters to the People on Health and Happiness.* Beecher was not prepared to challenge existing social and political distinctions between men and women, but she was a forceful, energetic advocate for giving women greater control over their physical health and well-being.

Efforts to reform women's clothing also aimed to give women greater physical comfort and freedom of movement. Tightly corseted dresses with their many layers of petticoats, which most women wore, could weigh up to twelve pounds, and the rigid steel and whalebone corsets prevented easy movement and breathing. These fashions were definitely not made for comfort. Nor were they safe. Not only did the corsets constrict women's ability to breathe comfortably, but wearers could easily trip over the long, full skirts, especially when they walked up stairs. Before the days of electricity, a woman often had to climb the steps holding a candle or oil lamp in one hand and perhaps a baby in the other. Without a free hand to hold up the layers of petticoat and skirt, she could easily catch a foot in the skirt, injuring herself and the baby, and set the place on fire.

Among the new ideas for women's apparel were bloomers, a costume composed

"BLOOMERISM,"
OR THE
NEW FEMALE COSTUME OF 1851,

As it has appeared in the various Cities and Towns.

BOSTON: S. W. WHEELER, 66 Cornhill—1851.

For every ounce of comfort it gave, the bloomer outfit also provoked sneers and derision. Clergymen condemned the costume because it violated the biblical commandment that men and women must not wear the same garments. Some men and boys even threw rocks and eggs at women who wore bloomers in public.

of a loose-fitting skirt that came below the knees and was worn over pantaloons that ballooned out and gathered at each ankle with a short ruffle. When Elizabeth Smith Miller, Stanton's cousin, introduced pantaloons to America after discovering them in Europe, they caused a minor sensation, especially among Stanton and other women who recognized their comfort. The new garment became known as bloomers after editor and temperance advocate Amelia Bloomer described them in the *Lily,* a magazine for women. Within days, hundreds of women deluged the paper with requests for more information about the costume, and Bloomer published sewing instructions. But many people ridiculed women who wore this unorthodox garment.

Beyond the controversy over bloomers, women's rights activists faced intense opposition for daring to want greater social and political equality for women. In 1854 Susan Anthony selected sixty women to circulate petitions throughout New York State demanding suffrage and equal economic and legal rights for wives. For ten weeks during the middle of winter, Anthony and her recruits canvassed the state, holding meetings and going door to door to collect signatures. They all had trouble finding adequate lodgings and being seated in restaurants because innkeepers frowned upon women traveling without a male escort. But the hardest part was having doors slammed in their faces by men—and women—who disapproved of their work. To these opponents and others, any form of female assertion conjured up images of women stepping out of their rightful domestic sphere and invading the male domain of commerce and politics.

Stanton's father even threatened to erase her name from his will if she insisted on addressing the New York State legislature. Stanton was outraged. "I passed through a terrible scourging when last at my father's," she wrote to Anthony. "I cannot tell you how deeply the iron entered my soul. I never felt more keenly the degradation of my sex. To think that all in me of which my father would have felt a proper pride had I been a man, is deeply mortifying to him because I am a woman. That thought has stung me to a fierce decision—to speak as soon as I can do myself credit. . . . Sometimes, Susan, I struggle in deep waters." Stanton continued to speak in public, though infrequently, and remained in her father's will when he died in 1859.

By 1857 women's rights activists faced one other obstacle to achieving their goals—the growing crisis over slavery. Mounting tension between the North and South brought the nation ominously close to Civil War. In 1857 the infamous *Dred Scott* decision alarmed abolitionists and delighted slaveholders when the U.S. Supreme Court ruled that slaves remained in bondage even when they were taken by their masters, or had escaped, to free states. The decision opened up the possibility that slavery could not be restricted to the southern slaveholding states, because slave owners could take their property—their slaves—to nonslaveholding territories and states, where they could continue to practice slavery. Abolitionists feared that the Supreme Court might declare that all states—including nonslaveholding states—could no longer exclude slavery, because that would violate the 5th Amendment's protection of the slave owner's rights to property, including human property. As a result, Lucy Stone Blackwell, Antoinette Brown Blackwell, and other women's rights activists shifted their attention from women's rights to abolition. Women's rights leaders canceled their 1857 annual convention because of a lack of money and followers. Stanton and Anthony despaired that all they had worked for was coming apart.

By the eve of the Civil War, however, the movement had achieved one significant victory: passage of an amendment to the New York State 1848 Married Woman's Property Act. This amendment gave women the right to keep their own earnings and invest any money or transact any business in their own name without their husbands' permission or involvement. They could also keep any property inherited or received as a gift. In addition, women could sign contracts and instigate lawsuits. The law was a major victory for married women. It took them out of the legal and economic category of "children, idiots, and lunatics," as previous statutes had classified them, and helped to abolish the notion of women's "legal death" in marriage. Next to suffrage, which women would not achieve for another sixty years, this law was a major milestone in American women's quest for autonomy. By 1860 other states, including Indiana, Maine, Missouri, and Ohio, had also passed laws to allow married women to keep their own earnings.

That same year, at the Tenth National Women's Rights Convention, Stanton introduced ten resolutions favoring more liberal divorce laws. Only Anthony and a handful of others supported her. The delegates voted, and the issue was tabled and recorded—that is, acknowledged in the record but not acted upon. At that time, women in New York State were entitled to sue for divorce only on grounds of adultery. A few other states also allowed women to sue for divorce on the grounds of the husband's desertion or failure to provide for his wife and children. Stanton urged that marriages be treated as a simple contract that could be quickly and quietly dissolved on the grounds of drunkenness, insanity, desertion, brutality, adultery, or incompatibility. Despite hostile public reaction, Stanton continued to believe that more liberal divorce laws were essential for giving women greater freedom and protection in marriage.

With the nation hurtling toward Civil War, women's rights activists now shifted their energies to wartime concerns. The battle for suffrage, for divorce reform and women's control over reproduction, for greater educational and employment opportunities, and for more comfortable and healthful clothing would have to wait while the nation fought a terrible civil war. But in these prewar years, the women's rights movement had set the stage for further battles—and some victories—in the crusade to make women equal citizens and human beings in their own right, separate from their husbands and fathers, sons and brothers. A chorus of new ideas about women's lives had been raised, and the strong, supple voices of reform would not be silenced.

Journeys to New Places

Like the Pilgrims who journeyed to the New World more than two centuries earlier, people flocked to America throughout the first half of the nineteenth century to seek a better life. At the same time, thousands of Americans journeyed to uncharted regions within the country for new opportunities. But unlike the Pilgrims, who fled from religious persecution, these new migrants searched mostly for better economic opportunities. They came from the small towns and cities of the eastern United States to the gold-laden hills of California, and from the centuries-old farms and cities of Europe to the burgeoning young cities of the Northeast and the prairie grasslands of the Midwest. By ship and wagon train, by rail and carriage, they swarmed over the American landscape.

White settlers had been pushing back the western boundaries of the United States since the earliest days of the young republic. In 1803 President Thomas Jefferson purchased the Louisiana Territory, the expanse of land extending west from the Mississippi River to the Rocky Mountains and north from the Gulf of Mexico to the border of Canada. Then he dispatched two explorers to survey what he had bought. With the Louisiana Purchase, the United States doubled its size, and fertile new farm and grasslands became available for settlement.

As settlers pushed farther west, beckoned by the promise of new land for crops and livestock and new opportunities for commerce, they wrote glowing letters to friends and family back home. "We had heard so much of the beautiful prairies of Iowa," a young girl from Pennsylvania wrote in the 1840s. "We could see for miles and all my longings for the vast open spaces were satisfied."

Starting in the 1840s, Americans believed that their nation was destined to expand all the way west to the Pacific Ocean. Their eyes lit up at the prospect of the abundant land and natural resources awaiting development, and they were eager to spread the ideas of democracy and Christianity to native peoples—who already had their own highly developed cultures. This belief in what Americans called "manifest destiny"—the steady, inevitable expansion of the nation all the way to the Pacific shores—propelled the U.S. government in 1845 to annex the Republic of Texas, which had recently won its independence from Mexico, and to foment a bloody war with Mexico in 1846 to capture more territory. When Mexico surrendered in 1848, the United States acquired the sprawling expanse of what is now California, Nevada, Utah, Arizona, and part of Colorado and New Mexico.

Unbeknownst until the discovery of gold in California in 1848, the country also gained a treasure trove of precious minerals. The brilliant sparkle of those golden ores flashed as far away as the hills and valleys of New England, and gold seekers eager for instant riches immediately set out for California. The gold rushers who went to California were mostly men, but soon more families began to migrate west for new economic opportunities. From 1850 to 1852, the number of families who went west surged. In 1852 a correspondent for the *Daily Missouri Republican* observed, "A marked feature of the emigration this year is the number of women who are going out by the land route." Indeed, families stood a better chance of acquiring more land than single people. In Oregon the Donation Land Act of 1850 granted families twice the amount of land that single men received.

Both single and married women made the journey. Throughout the 1840s, educator and writer Catharine Beecher trained and dispatched hundreds of single, young female teachers to open schools in frontier regions. There they lived among pioneer families, boarding for a time with each family in the new community.

Some homesteading wives reluctantly went along with their more enthusiastic husbands, dreading the hardships and uncertainty that lay ahead. In 1853, before heading west from Kansas to Oregon, Elizabeth Goltra mournfully wrote in her diary, "I am leaving my home, my early friends and associates never to see them again, exchanging the disinterested solicitude of fond friends for the cold and unsympathetic friendship of strangers." She continued, "Shall we all reach the 'El Dorado' of our hopes or shall one of our number be left and our graves be in the dreary wilderness?"

Other women, however, were as eager as their husbands, sharing their hopes for a better life. "Ho—for California—at last we are on the way," an excited Helen Carpenter wrote in her diary in 1857, "and with good luck may some day reach the 'promised land.'" The excitement of heading for this promised land did not ease the hardships along the way. Travelers had to be prepared for changing weather and terrain, and they also lived with the ever-present fear of attacks by Indian tribes angered by this invasion of their ancestral lands. When Mary Jane Caples met a group of Pawnees during her journey to California in 1849, she was overcome by fear. "They were the first Indians I had ever seen," she recalled later, "and to my frightened vision . . . they looked ten feet high—my thought was that they would kill us all, and take my baby in captivity."

On the trail, women performed many of the same duties they had done back home—cooking, washing, and caring for their children. But the conditions under which they worked were far more primitive. They had to convert the small space of a tent or wagon bed into a temporary home, stretch out limited amounts of water for cooking and cleaning, cook outdoors over an open fire while fighting dust and insects, and make tasty meals with a minimum of ingredients. As Helen Carpenter ruefully noted in her diary, "One does like a change and about the only change we have from bread and bacon is to bacon and bread." Women gathered wild fruits and berries along the way to bake into pies and tarts to add variety to their families' diets.

Yet there were moments of relief from these burdens. Crossing the Great Plains or the desert could be monotonous after endless days of unchanging landscape— or it could be a magical journey into a mysterious new land. As she crossed the Plains to California in 1860, Lavinia Porter could not get over the sheer "beauty . . .

surrounding us on all sides." She exclaimed, "The air was filled with a balmy sweetness, and yet so limpid and clear that even in the starlight we could catch glimpses of the shimmering trees in the distant river."

On the trail, women spent some of their most pleasurable moments in each other's company—around a campfire at night, knitting and talking over the day's events, cooking, or washing together. Catherine Haun, who crossed the Plains in 1849, recalled, "During the day, we womenfolk visited from wagon to wagon or congenial friends spent an hour walking, ever westward, and talking over our home life back in 'the states' . . . voicing our hopes for the future and even whispering a little friendly gossip of emigrant life."

Finally, after the long days on the trail, after endless hours of wondering what their new homes would look like, travelers arrived at their destinations—only to discover more hardships ahead. Even the hardiest woman was brought down by the sight of her new home—a crude log cabin without doors or windows; a shack with tar paper walls, canvas ceiling, and a dirt floor; or a dirty brown soddie—a dwelling made out of hard-packed soil—which often housed insects and snakes in its four walls. Many settlers had no home at all until the family built one. Mary Rabb spent her first weeks in Texas "spinning under a tree," with only "a quilt and a sheat [sic] for a tent."

But women made do. Just as they did on the trails, they set up homemaking in their new dwellings. They tried to make their homes cheerful and cozy by arranging the few treasured possessions they had brought from home and covering the walls with newspaper, muslin, even geological maps as decoration. Many dwellings became very homey. Hannah Anderson Ropes, a black woman who settled in Kansas in 1855, wrote to her mother in Massachusetts that she hoped to establish a "proper" home in her new surroundings. She reported that she hung "Bay State Shawls" on her cabin walls like tapestries and displayed her "choice China" as decoration. "How we begin to look forward to a condition of civilized housekeeping!" she declared.

While the men cleared the fields for farming or panned for gold and silver, women did the work of homemaking. They cooked and cleaned, baked bread and pies, sewed their families' clothing, preserved foodstuffs for the winter, made soap and candles, and raised chickens and vegetables. Because of the spartan conditions under which they worked, they took special pride in a well-made pair of trousers or a good meal. Women also shared the hard, physical labor with their husbands. They helped construct homes, drove plows, sawed and hauled timber, and stood guard at night for fires or predators. As one Oklahoma woman recalled, "In those days the wife had to help do everything."

Still, women were primarily responsible for the essential work of homemaking. They even turned some domestic tasks into an opportunity to relax and socialize. Quilting parties, for example, were a favorite pastime in which women visited together while working on a quilt. For some, the process of making a quilt symbolized their new lives on the frontier. As one woman homesteader in Kentucky recalled, "You see you start out with just so much [calico]; ... the neighbors will give you a piece here and a piece there, and you will have a piece left every time you cut out a dress, and you take what happens to come and that's predestination ... and that is just the way with livin'. The Lord sends in the pieces, but we can cut 'em and put 'em together pretty much to suit ourselves."

Black women had less opportunity to attend quilting parties and other social events because few other blacks lived nearby. Both black and white women settlers experienced the painful loneliness and physical hardships of living on the frontier. But black women felt even more isolated because of their small numbers and because most whites did not want to live and work with them. Some whites—even those who opposed slavery—did not want to compete against blacks for land and work, and they supported efforts to restrict blacks from migrating or purchasing land. In Iowa free blacks were required to show a certificate of freedom before being allowed to settle, and most western states and territories in the 1850s and 1860s prohibited black inhabitants from testifying against whites in court or riding stagecoaches and streetcars. Black and white settlers alike shared the hardships of homesteading, but rarely did these shared difficulties blossom into mutual support or friendship.

Throughout the frontier, from the lush green valleys of Oregon to the flat, arid lands of the desert Southwest, both black and white women settlers used their talents and resources to help their families and communities. A higher percentage of free black women worked outside of their homes because of economic necessity. Most black women worked as domestics, while others became washerwomen, cooks, dressmakers, and nursemaids. Like black domestics and laundresses back home, they toiled long hours for meager wages and endured their employers' demeaning treatment. But on the frontier, they worked under far more primitive conditions. A small number of black women also ran boardinghouses or taught black schoolchildren.

White women worked by preparing meals for single men in the community or selling home-baked bread and pies. They also sold cloth they had spun, made shirts and trousers for sale, or took in laundry. Women who had extra room took in boarders. Other women worked as cooks, waitresses, and chambermaids in inns and boardinghouses, or opened their own boardinghouses or taverns.

Educated white women became columnists for the "Ladies' Department" of western newspapers or wrote novels about life on the frontier. From 1854 to 1857, Elizabeth Barstow Stoddard wrote as "our Lady Correspondent" for the San Francisco daily *Alta California*. Women taught, both in frontier schools and in mission schools set up by religious orders to educate and convert Native American children. They also pursued less genteel professions, such as prostitution and brothel-keeping.

A woman at a California gold mining camp, 1852. Life in frontier outposts was harsh and lawless because of "the want of respectable female society," according to one miner. This camp, however, seems an exception.

As they put their cabins and shanties in order, women also tried to bring order to their new communities. Like their urban sisters back home, both black and white women settlers organized schools, churches, and clubs in their frontier communities. These various institutions were segregated by race, and far fewer community groups existed among black settlers because of their small numbers. Until homesteaders could afford to build a school or church, they conducted prayer meetings and schools in their own tiny dwellings. Women sponsored box suppers, theatricals, and other events to raise money for a schoolhouse and teacher. They also organized and taught Sunday schools, planned church socials, and participated in missionary societies.

In time, homesteading women organized other social activities, such as reading clubs, literary and debating societies, and amateur musical and dramatic groups. Women's charitable groups also sprang up to assist widows, care for orphaned children, and distribute Bibles among local Native American populations. Women strove to bring civility and morality to their own communities by decrying the gambling, drinking, and general lawlessness that men had introduced to the frontier. Julia Lovejoy, a migrant to Kansas in the 1850s, lamented that in Kansas City the "inhabitants and the morals, are of an indescribably repulsive and undesirable character."

Lovejoy and other homesteaders who hoped to civilize the western regions pointed to the wilderness itself as the cause of the "undesirable character" of many of its inhabitants. Although they admired its natural beauty and abundant resources, the wilderness also represented godlessness and the dark, mysterious aspects of existence. At the center of this frightful setting, to their way of thinking, stood Native Americans, who had lived in the western regions for centuries, wresting their livelihoods and cultural and spiritual traditions from the land.

Most settlers did not understand or respect the Native Americans' way of life, a life dependent upon the bounty of the earth. While Native American men hunted game, women collected seeds and roots and harvested crops. Native Americans looked to the sky and the soil for spiritual sustenance as well. The natural world embodied their deities, and their religious traditions and folkways expressed a respectful love of the earth and all things natural—a reverence that homesteaders who wanted to exploit the land for commercial gain did not share.

By the 1840s and 1850s, homesteaders crossing overland began to encounter large numbers of Native Americans. In Iowa and Kansas, homesteaders came upon Pawnees and Winnebagos. The Sioux predominated in the Great Plains and Minnesota, while the Cheyenne tribes made their homes in Wyoming, Montana, Colorado, and Kansas. Apache tribes inhabited the dry, arid desert lands of Texas, and both Apaches and Pueblo tribes lived in New Mexico. Farther west, the Nez Percés populated the Blue Mountains of Oregon. Other tribes also inhabited the western lands. For centuries, until the first white settlers encroached upon their lands, these tribes had coexisted with each other, sometimes peacefully, sometimes warily, occasionally at war, farming the land and hunting great herds of buffalo, whose bodies they used for meat, clothing, and shelter.

Lurid accounts of Indian attacks filled white children's schoolbooks and the novels their parents read, and fed homesteaders' fears and prejudices against Indians. As the homesteaders came into contact with Native Americans in towns and camps where they stopped to replenish supplies, their fears gradually gave way to a mixture of curiosity and contempt. Harriet Bishop, a missionary who taught in a Minnesota mission school in the 1840s, described the Native Americans she met as "disgustingly filthy," "extremely unchaste" in their manner of dress, and "imbedded in moral pollution." Missionary and nonmissionary women alike regarded the religious beliefs and practices of Native Americans as inferior to their own. "The Indians' ideas of the creation of the world were ludicrous and absurd," Mary Sagatoo, another missionary, wrote. "As a race they are . . . without power of mind or hand to record truthfully events as they occur."

But friendships between Native Americans and homesteaders occasionally flourished. Sometimes they traded foodstuffs and supplies, such as Native American baskets or moccasins for flour, sugar, or coffee. And sometimes neighboring Indians generously supplied fish, game, and wild fruits and berries to homesteaders living on scanty diets. Southwestern tribes taught homesteaders how to build adobe dwellings, and elsewhere Native American neighbors helped settlers find temporary shelter; during the Civil War, a group of Arkansas women fleeing from oncoming Union troops took shelter with a Cherokee family. Native Americans also hired themselves out as domestics, ranch and farm hands, and nursemaids for settlers' children. But these rare, fragile instances of goodwill between Native Americans and homesteaders could not repair the profound sense of loss and displacement that Native Americans endured as settlers moved in on their ancestral and farming lands and wantonly destroyed the land and game that had sustained them. Between 1845 and 1860, in California alone, 115,000 Native Americans died from disease, malnutrition, and murder as homesteaders and gold rushers moved in on their land.

Native Americans and settlers engaged in bloody conflicts, and innocent people on both sides were massacred. As white settlers advanced, claiming Indian tribal lands as their own and breaking the terms of treaties they had signed, Native Americans tried to defend their land. In the 1850s, Pacific Northwestern tribes rose up to defend their homes, and in Minnesota the Sioux fought mightily against oncoming settlers. Cheyenne and Arapaho tribes in Colorado raided settlements to drive homesteaders away. In Apache tribes, some women joined their men on the battleground, while others served as messengers and emissaries between Apache warriors and U.S. military officers. Native American women shared their brethren's contempt for the way that white settlers plundered the land and mocked their centuries-old traditions. And just as white women feared assault by Native American men, Indian women had far greater reason to fear white men, who freely raped them or forced them into marriages.

Armed conflict, disease, famine, and forced resettlement gradually destroyed the communal, agrarian way of life that Native Americans had known for centuries. The Promised Land of opportunity to which homesteaders flocked—the land that Native Americans had cultivated and venerated for so long—became a trail of tears watered by the bloodshed and anguish of native peoples driven from their homeland.

While homesteaders streamed across the American landscape to settle the western regions, another hardy group of migrants journeyed across the Atlantic Ocean to America. Like the homesteaders, they came to seek a better way of life. And they, too, endured a long, hard journey. But they did not see a changing landscape or stop to pick wildflowers along the way. Their only scenery was endless miles of water, or the filthy, airless rooms below deck where they ate and slept. Sometimes the ocean was a placid place to be and sometimes it was terrifying, especially during a storm. Elise Isely, an immigrant from Switzerland who came to the United

States in 1855, described how her ship tossed and turned during a storm like a toy boat. "Salt water was spurted in.... The breaking waves boomed like never-ending thunder."

Once they landed, immigrants had to be wary of swindlers and thieves eager to trick them out of their money and possessions. Sometimes local hotels and boardinghouses hired "runners," who "greeted" immigrants at the docks by grabbing their baggage and demanding that they follow them to nearby lodgings. If the immigrants did not want to lose their bags, they had no choice but to follow obligingly. In 1855 New York City, the major port of entry, built facilities in lower Manhattan to process immigrants and their possessions in an orderly manner and provide them with information on how to meet family members and travel to inland destinations. As a result, swindlers had a harder time taking advantage of newcomers.

In 1840 84,000 immigrants entered the United States. Ten years later, in 1850, 369,000 immigrants came to America. Between 1840 and 1860, approximately 4.2 million newcomers journeyed to the United States. About 40 percent of them were Irish refugees escaping a devastating famine in Ireland. For years, potatoes had been the staple food of the Irish. But in 1845, a terrible blight wiped out Ireland's potato crop. Millions of people went hungry or lost their chief occupation—potato farming. Between 1847 and 1854, the worst years of the famine, more than 1.25 million people fled Ireland to the United States, hoping to find work. Many of the Irish immigrants were single young women forced to support themselves. Immigrants from Germany, Norway, Sweden, Scotland, Wales, and England also came to the United States.

Most immigrants came over simply to make more money. Many, such as the Irish, remained in this country, but other immigrants stayed long enough to earn a substantial amount of money and then returned to their homelands. Most immigrants settled in towns and cities, especially New York and Boston. Others, however, journeyed to the West to start a farm or small business. Colonies of German immigrants headed for Texas in the 1840s and Wisconsin in the 1850s, while Swedes and Norwegians settled in large numbers in Minnesota, Iowa, North and South Dakota, Wisconsin, and Nebraska. Except for the Irish, who for the most part avoided rural life and settled in industrial towns and cities in the North and Midwest, immigrants from other ethnic backgrounds fanned across the American landscape, as far west as California and Oregon. Wherever they settled, in cities or out on the frontier, they sought out family, friends, and other newcomers from back home. They wanted to live among their own.

Newcomers were astonished by the abundance of food and the higher standard of living among Americans in general. Jannicke Saehle, a young Norwegian woman who came to Wisconsin alone, wrote home about the many tasty dishes she ate in her new homeland. "My greatest regret here is to see the superabundance of food, much of which has to be thrown to the chickens and the swine, when I think of my dear ones in Bergen, who like so many others must at this time lack the necessities of life." Immigrants also discovered new food in America. They marveled over wild raspberries, strawberries, and asparagus, and stumbled upon watermelons, a fruit they did not have back home, "as big as a child's head."

Like American-born homesteaders, immigrant homesteaders also flinched at the untamed features of the western region. Elisabeth Koren, from Norway, cried out in her diary, "This is really too much! . . . A snake in the house! . . . It was probably one of those harmless grass snakes, but it was at least two feet long, and it is horrid that such visitors can get into the house."

More worrisome, however, especially for immigrants who lived in towns and cities, was the prejudice of Americans who feared or disliked people different from themselves. Many Americans wanted to reduce the political power of foreign-born voters by extending the waiting period from five to twenty-one years before immigrants became eligible for American citizenship and voting rights. In some states, some people wanted to prevent any foreign-born citizens from holding public office. By restricting immigrants' voting rights and political power, they hoped to discourage immigration to the United States, especially by the Irish, the immigrant group whom they most despised.

As more Irish immigrants poured into the country, anti-Irish sentiment grew even more intense. When Americans referred to Irish neighbors or employees, they used such belittling nicknames as "Bridget" or "Paddy." Irish men and women seeking work in American towns and cities encountered signs declaring "No Irish Need Apply." In 1860 an Irish immigrant who had worked on the railroads poured out his frustration in a letter back home: "It would take more than a mere letter to tell you the despicable, humiliating, slavish life of an Irish laborer on a railroad in the States; . . . everything . . . is against him; no love for him—no protection in life; can be shot down, run through, kicked, cuffed, spat on; and no redress."

Other immigrants besides the Irish endured similar prejudice. Many factories refused to hire any immigrants and those that did assigned them to the lowest paying, least skilled, and most dangerous work. But for immigrants desperate to work, these obstacles were not insurmountable. And America offered most of them more economic opportunities, a higher standard of living, and more independence than they had known in the countries they had left.

Irish women, for example, were expected to be economically independent at an early age and to contribute to their families' upkeep. Thousands of single young Irish women came to America to work, make a new life for themselves, and send money home to their families. And, indeed, they sent most of the millions of dollars that flowed from America to Ireland during the 1840s and 1850s. They prided themselves on their ability to learn new skills and earn money.

Single Irish women fared better in America than married or widowed Irish women. A husband's desertion or death usually rendered a married woman penniless, but a single woman could always find work as a live-in domestic. A married woman with children did not have this choice. She needed to earn enough money to support both herself and her children, and few women had the skills to do so. More than any other destitute women, widowed or abandoned Irish women relied on some form of charitable assistance.

In 1843 an order of nuns, the Sisters of Mercy, settled in Pittsburgh, Pennsylvania, and opened a Mercy House, where women in need could find refuge. Soon they opened Mercy Houses in other major cities, including New York, Chicago, Baltimore, San Francisco, St. Louis, and Philadelphia. They also established training programs in nursing and clerical work, employment agencies, boardinghouses, and day nurseries for the children of working mothers. Although the Sisters of Mercy offered their services to any women in need, Irish and non-Irish, Irish women were their most numerous recipients.

Whether migrants came from the Old World to the New or from the towns and cities of one side of America to the other, all migrants harbored bright hopes for a better way of life for themselves and their families. Some migrants never completed the journey. They died along the way, either on the boats navigating the Atlantic Ocean or on the dusty overland trails. And some regretted having made the journey once they had reached their final destinations. But other migrants fought off the powerful waves of homesickness and regret that occasionally washed over them and eagerly applied themselves to their new lives. The words of one anonymous Norwegian immigrant woman perhaps expressed the thoughts of thousands of other migrants: "When I think, however, that there will be a better livelihood for us here than in poor Norway, I reconcile myself to it and thank God, who protected me and mine over the ocean's waves and led us to a fruitful land."

Searching for a Vocation

In the mid-nineteenth century, a young woman's eighteenth birthday marked a milestone—a rite of passage from childhood and the strong hand of parental authority to the sober concerns of adulthood. At eighteen, women came of legal age. If unmarried, they were entitled to keep any property or earnings they acquired, and they could marry without their parents' permission. Beyond that, they possessed no rights as citizens. Like their mothers and other older women, they could not vote or serve on a jury. In practice, coming of legal age mainly freed young women from parental authority, though many daughters who worked continued to contribute their wages to their families or helped their parents in other ways.

Still, for some women, turning eighteen marked a divide in their lives, a chance to make their own decisions and determine how to spend their adult years, within the limited number of choices available to them. Frances Willard, a future social reformer, used the opportunity of turning eighteen to read a novel that her parents had earlier forbidden her to read. When her father scolded her, she reminded him, as she recalled later, that "I am eighteen—I am of age—I am now to do what I think right, and to read this fine historical story [*Ivanhoe* by Sir Walter Scott] is, in my opinion, a right thing for me to do."

But this exhilarating sense of freedom was overshadowed by a painful awareness of how limited freedom was for women. They watched brothers choose from among a variety of colleges and vocations that were closed to them or, in later years, go off to vote for the first time. When Frances Willard's brother went to vote, Willard turned to her sister, Mary, and tearfully asked, "Wouldn't you like to vote as well as Oliver? Don't you and I love the country just as well as he, and doesn't the country need our ballots?"

For young women who had completed their schooling and who did not marry or were not already working, graduation posed a big question mark as they pondered their next step. Willard, for example, later described the two years following graduation as "often very dull and sometimes very gay" but also "the most difficult" in her life because she had not yet found her "vocation." She felt adrift, without direction or purpose: "I remember that I used to think myself smart. I used to plan great things that I would do and be.... But it is over. The mist has cleared away and I dream no longer, though I am only twenty-one years old." In fact, Willard did find her vocation, though not right away. She eventually became a teacher and, in later years, the president of the Woman's Christian Temperance Union (WCTU). Under her leadership, the WCTU developed an ambitious program of social reform to improve all aspects of women's lives.

Willard was one of many middle-class young women who bemoaned their seeming lack of purpose after graduation. At twenty-five, Emily Blackwell confided in her journal that she had "reached the age for action, for great deeds and what is accomplished? How terrible it must be to look back upon a long life of error and failure." But Blackwell went on to live a remarkably accomplished life. Both she and her sister Elizabeth became physicians. They established one of the first medical schools for other women doctors, the Women's Medical College of the New York Infirmary for Women and Children. Emily Howland, who loved the independence and sense of accomplishment in being away at boarding school, drifted for years after graduation without any sense of purpose. She continued to live with her parents until she was thirty-one, occupying her time with household tasks and family responsibilities. Finally, in 1859, she found her "object in life"—a position as assistant teacher in a school for young black women in Washington, D.C. She devoted the rest of her life to educating and assisting African Americans.

Although they drifted through years of despair and uncertainty, Willard, Howland, Blackwell, and other women eventually found the work that gave meaning and purpose to their lives. Each had received an education that had prepared and propelled her out into the world. Just as the women's rights movement had begun to raise women's expectations for greater social and political equality, expanding educational opportunities also raised women's aspirations for interesting and useful work—although opportunities to do such work were slow in coming.

All of the women graduates of Oberlin College, class of 1855, along with the principal and a member of the Ladies' Board, sat for a commemorative daguerrotype. The three women in the left of the front row graduated from the regular college department but were nontheless supervised by the Ladies' Department, which had a more traditional curriculum.

By the early nineteenth century, parents were willing to send daughters as well as sons to school, and by the 1850s more academies—such as Mary Sharp College in Winchester, Tennessee; Oxford Female College in Cincinnati, Ohio; and Elmira College in Elmira, New York—had sprung up to educate women. In addition, in 1855, the University of Iowa began to admit both women and men. Antioch College, a private college founded in Yellow Springs, Ohio, in 1852, was also coeducational. Slowly, American women were dismantling the barriers that had prevented them from getting an advanced education. Most of the nation's elite private colleges, such as Harvard, Yale, Princeton, and Amherst, would remain closed to women well into the twentieth century, but in the antebellum years a growing number of institutions were opening their doors to women.

African-American women had fewer educational choices because most public schools and colleges did not accept black students. A few northern cities, such as Boston, established a separate public school for black pupils. Elsewhere, students went to private schools established by black residents or white benefactors. In New Jersey, Sarah Grimké and her sister and brother-in-law, Angelina and Theodore Weld, established an integrated boarding school for both black and white students. The school in Washington, D.C., where Emily Howland taught was the first school to educate black students in that city, which was home to more than 10,000 free blacks.

Another institution that welcomed African-American students of both sexes was Oberlin College. For black female students in particular, Oberlin offered opportunities unmatched by any other college of the time. Founded in 1833 as a coed institution, Oberlin was the first college to actively recruit both black men and women students. From 1835 to 1865, at least 140 black women attended Oberlin. Most of these students took one or two classes in basic skills, such as reading and writing. Twelve women completed a special "ladies' course," a curriculum that was not as rigorous as the course of study required for a bachelor's degree, and three received their B.A. degrees.

Although Oberlin's black female students usually came from relatively affluent families, some black students at Oberlin had known their share of hardship, including impoverishment or slavery. Frances Jackson, for example, was born into slavery but was freed when her aunt purchased her freedom for $125. The older woman, a former slave herself, had carefully saved the amount out of her own meager wages of $6 a month. After being freed, young Frances Jackson worked as a servant for a wealthy New England family, where she was allowed to study for one hour every other afternoon. In this way, she prepared herself to attend Oberlin. Her aunt provided her tuition.

Jackson's course work was demanding: She studied Latin, Greek, and higher math; took private French lessons; and studied piano and guitar. In addition, she taught evening classes to newly freed slaves who were attending a special program at Oberlin, and she was the first black student to teach a preparatory class of both black and white students. Jackson felt tremendous pressure to succeed—as if she had, in her words, "the honor of the whole African race upon my shoulders. I felt that should I fail, it would be ascribed to the fact that I was colored." After graduating, she moved to Philadelphia, where she taught in a black school. Eventually, she became the principal. She was a dedicated educator who inspired her students to become doctors, lawyers, engineers, and teachers.

How did other American women use their educations in the years before the Civil War? They had few choices. Like Jackson, they became teachers because teaching was the principal means of employment for educated women. Unlike a legal or business career, it did not challenge traditional ideas about women's maternal qualities. Teachers, like mothers, were responsible for educating and instilling a moral code in children. Teaching was regarded as an extension of the mother's role into the classroom.

In the 1830s and 1840s, more teaching opportunities opened up for women because more states required pupils to attend classes for longer terms. During this period, wages for women teachers rose to between $1.50 and $2.00 a week plus board. But women teachers continued to be paid about one-third less than men teachers—another reason why school boards chose to hire more female teachers.

Like Emma Willard and Mary Lyon, founders of the Troy Female Seminary and the Mount Holyoke Female Seminary, respectively, Catharine Beecher felt that women were uniquely suited to become teachers because of their superior maternal and moral instincts. She wanted teaching to become a "profession for woman, a profession as honorable and as lucrative for her as the legal, medical and theological professions are for men." But instead of establishing one single institution to train women as teachers, she trained and dispatched teachers to open schools throughout the country. She was especially successful in raising money to establish schools in frontier communities. During the 1850s, some 450 teachers trained by her methods opened schools in these towns.

In 1852 Beecher also established the American Woman's Educational Association to finance a women's college that she had established in Milwaukee, Wisconsin. She wanted this college to be the centerpiece of a nationwide system of schools to train women for their "true profession" as educators and homemakers. Although Beecher did not achieve her goal of establishing such a network of schools, she made an immeasurable contribution to opening up more teaching opportunities for women.

As more free black women acquired an education, they became teachers within their own communities. For them, teaching was both a livelihood and a way to help their enslaved brethren. Matilda A. Jones, a star pupil in the only school for blacks in Washington, D.C., explained to a white correspondent, "We need [education] more than your people do, & ought to strive harder, because the greater part of our people, are yet in bondage. We that are free, are expected to be the means of bringing them out of Slavery, & how can we do it, unless we have proper educational advantages? We must get the knowledge, & use it well." During and after the Civil War, scores of dedicated northern black women went South to teach the newly emancipated slaves.

Besides teaching, nursing gradually emerged as another occupation for more educated women. Female relatives generally bore responsibility for nursing sick family members, but in the years before the Civil War families occasionally hired nurses. Not until after the Civil War, however, were professional nursing schools established. Until then, nurses learned from experience. Nursing was demanding work. Like a servant, the nurse was on call twenty-four hours a day. Her status was not as lowly as that of a servant, but she did not enjoy the prestige of a cook. Like a servant or a cook, though, a nurse required great reserves of patience and energy. She spent long hours watching over her patient, preparing special foods and tonics, changing dressings and applying plasters and poultices, and giving massages. A nurse also had to cope with intrusive family members and learn how to bear her patient's suffering and perhaps a lingering death. This was not a job for the timid or weak-hearted, and most paid nurses were older white women who had had years of experience and did not shrink from the sight of a patient's naked body, male or female. Sometimes, the nurse commanded as much authority and respect as a physician, especially when no doctor was available. Nurses earned about three or four dollars a week plus room and board. Employers occasionally added small tips to these wages.

Women who wanted to be doctors instead of nurses faced greater opposition. Until the early part of the nineteenth century, midwives—women with some medical knowledge—performed deliveries and other medical procedures. Medical practices were based on tradition and folklore, or on what seemed to work best. The practice of medicine was a craft or an art as much as a science. By the 1830s, however, male physicians were turning medical practice into a profession by requiring special training in accredited schools and special licensing procedures.

These new standards did not necessarily improve the practice of medicine. Even the most educated doctors in these years knew nothing about antibiotics—drugs that kill bacteria and other microorganisms that cause disease—and had only a basic understanding of how the body worked. Doctors used dangerous and painful procedures, such as "bleeding"—the application of leeches to suck out diseased blood from the patient's system—and relied on heavy dosages of laudanum, an addictive drug, to treat pain. The new standards did, however, succeed in excluding midwives from medical practice. Medicine was rapidly becoming a profession dominated by men because the new medical schools would not accept women students. In 1847 Elizabeth Blackwell managed to get into Geneva Medical College in upstate New York, despite the faculty's disapproval, because her fellow students, all men, fought for her admission. But when she walked into her first class, as an eyewitness later recalled, a "hush fell upon the class as if each member had been stricken with paralysis." A few years later, Geneva refused to admit any more women.

By the 1850s, enough women, and perhaps some men, believed that women doctors must be trained to treat female patients. Victorian values, which emphasized modesty and little physical or emotional intimacy between men and women, gave further strength to this idea. Male doctors shied away from discussing intimate physiological details with female patients. Indeed, male physicians often conducted examinations of female patients with eyes averted or while the woman was fully clothed—hardly the most effective way to uncover health problems. Although Victorian values defined women's primary role as that of wife and mother, Victorian social practices also paved the way for female doctors who could treat female patients with far greater ease than male doctors could.

Women helped other women receive a medical education. Ann Preston, a Quaker activist in Pennsylvania, solicited funds from more affluent women for a women's medical college in Philadelphia. The school that they endowed, the Female Medical College of Pennsylvania, opened in 1850 and was the first American medical school for women in the United States. Ten years later, the Philadelphia County Medical Society still refused to grant accreditation to the school. In 1855 Preston sent Emmeline Cleveland to France to study obstetrics at a maternity hospital in Paris. Two wealthy women paid for Cleveland's education because they wanted to improve the practice of obstetrics at the Female Medical College. When Cleveland returned, she became head of the school's obstetrics department and one of America's first female physicians.

Other women's medical colleges were also established. In 1856 the New England Female Medical College opened, followed by the Homeopathic New York Medical College for Women in 1863. After the Civil War, more all-male medical schools grudgingly opened their doors to women students.

Law, the other male-dominated profession, adamantly refused to accept women lawyers until the late 1860s and 1870s. Before the Civil War, the primary way to become a lawyer was by studying law independently and then passing the state bar exam, whereupon the candidate was admitted to the bar. Male law students also received practical experience by working as clerks in law offices. Women who had educated themselves in the law were not allowed to take the exam and apply for admission to their state bar. Even Virginia Perry, a strong advocate of opening up more professional opportunities for women, cautioned women against pursuing a legal career because it was not fitting. "The noisy scenes witnessed in a courtroom," she wrote in 1861, "are scarcely compatible with the reserve, quietude and gentleness that characterize a woman of refinement." After the war, however, American women began to challenge the exclusionary practices of their state bars.

Refined women could be writers, and many women earned a living with their pens. Perhaps the most successful novelist of the day was Harriet Beecher Stowe. Sister of Catharine Beecher, Stowe was so moved by a true account of the dramatic escape of a young slave woman and her infant that she sat down and wrote a novel about the evils of southern slavery. She drew on her own observations of slavery while visiting Kentucky and on her years of helping runaway slaves. The result, *Uncle Tom's Cabin*, ran in serial form in an antislavery newspaper for nine months before being published as a book in the spring of 1852. Readers shuddered as they read about the young Eliza's escape across treacherous ice floes and the cruelties visited upon the gentle Tom by his loathsome master, Simon Legree.

Stowe wished to arouse the nation's conscience to the sin of slavery, and she succeeded spectacularly. The novel was an instant success. Within a year, it had sold 300,000 copies in the United States. Northerners snatched up the novel as proof of the immorality of slavery, while Southerners lambasted Stowe as a "vile wretch in petticoats" for writing such "falsehoods" and "distortions." The novel drew equal attention in Great Britain and was translated into several foreign languages. When President Abraham Lincoln met Stowe in 1862, he reportedly told her, "So you're the little woman who wrote the book that made this great war." Lincoln was only joking, but he, like others, recognized the novel's powerful impact upon people's awareness of slavery.

Other women, African-American as well as white, devoted themselves to writing or lecturing about the evils of slavery. Some earned a modest income from their antislavery work. Mary Ann Shadd, the daughter of free blacks who were active in the abolitionist movement, lived for a time in Canada, where she established and edited the *Provincial Freeman* from 1854 to 1859. Shadd believed that blacks would find better employment opportunities and less prejudice in Canada, and she used

The Webb family toured the country giving public readings from *Uncle Tom's Cabin*. Mary Webb (center) also gave readings in England, where the book was a best-seller.

her journal to urge America's free blacks to migrate to Canada. She also traveled extensively in Canada and the midwestern United States to lecture and raise money for her newspaper. After the war, she helped convert black women to the cause of women's rights.

Frances Ellen Watkins was one of the most effective African-American female lecturers for abolition. Watkins, a poet and former teacher, went on tour for the

Maine Antislavery Society. Everywhere she spoke, audiences were mesmerized by her strong voice and eloquent words. She used vivid images and uncompromising language. "A hundred thousand new-born babies are annually added to the victims of slavery," she told an audience in 1857. "Twenty thousand lives are annually sacrificed on the plantations of the South. Such a sight should send a thrill of horror through the nerves of civilization and impel the heart of humanity to lofty deeds."

Like their white sisters on the antislavery circuit, Shadd and Watkins braved hazardous winter weather and hostile crowds to bring their message of freedom. But they also suffered from one other hardship—racial prejudice. Watkins described the ordeal of traveling: "On the Carlisle road [in Pennsylvania] I was interrupted and insulted several times. Two men came after me in one day. . . . the shadow of slavery, oh, how drearily it hangs."

Other women wrote novels, but their books had none of the fire or drama of *Uncle Tom's Cabin*. Writers such as Fanny Fern, Mrs. E. D. E. N. Southworth, Caroline Kirkland, Catherine Sedgwick, and Caroline Lee Hentz portrayed the peaceful haven of middle-class family life—a home in which a gentle, pure, and morally superior wife and mother reigned supreme and triumphed over the dangerous ideas of male scholars and artists. With their pat characters and plots, these sentimental stories hardly qualified as great literature. But concealed within the sugary prose were some acerbic and astute observations about the powerlessness and sense of entrapment that women felt at home, especially women who had borne large families. Although their books sold well, the contemporary press and some male writers scorned these women. The novelist Nathaniel Hawthorne dismissed them as "scribbling women."

Women artists also took their themes from the domestic setting of the home. In the 1850s, Lilly Martin Spencer (1822–1902), a self-taught artist, shifted her subject matter from still lifes and themes drawn from mythology and religion to the dailiness of the homemaker's life—cooking, doing laundry, playing with her children. In one painting, a woman wipes her eyes as she peels onions, and in another a housewife extends a flour-covered hand in greeting.

Women painters chose subjects that appealed to their artistic sensibilities and also to popular taste. Although a few women achieved modest success, most female artists lacked the opportunities available to male artists, such as the freedom and means to travel to Europe for study and inspiration. Nor were they allowed to attend classes on figure drawing, where nude male models posed before the class. But Harriet Hosmer (1830–1908), sculptor and daughter of a physician, managed to take private lessons in anatomy and also traveled to Rome for further study. Working each day from dawn to nightfall, Hosmer dedicated her life to her art. She shocked male critics by displaying casts of female nudes in her studio. Complained one critic: "As for Miss Hosmer, her want of modesty is enough to disgust a dog." Male sculptors did not endure such criticism; instead, they were expected to draw inspiration from the human body, clothed or unclothed.

Although young women received instruction in painting and needlework at school, few were encouraged to pursue their talent as a career, especially if they married. Jane Swisshelm, a journalist, later bemoaned how she had sacrificed her artistic powers to her marriage. "I put away my brushes; resolutely crucified my divine gift, and while it hung writhing on the cross, spent my best years and powers cooking cabbage." Like Swisshelm, other educated and talented women put away their brushes or their pens to cook cabbages and change diapers. Woman's place, proclaimed the social and religious mores of the day, was in the home as wife and mother. But some women learned to extend the boundaries of women's role to provide more opportunities for women to earn a living.

In years to come, women would take up the banner of motherhood to expand their social roles and political power. As earlier generations had discovered, the same ideas about women's domestic sphere that had the power to keep women confined to the home as mother and wife also had the power to expand their role in American life.

Weavers, Stitchers, and Domestics

The mid-nineteenth century was not an easy time for workers, male or female. Single wage earners as well as entire families were barely making ends meet on meager wages, and thousands of Americans lived in damp, overcrowded, and unventilated cellar rooms. In Boston the Committee on Internal Health reported that residents in slum districts were "huddled together like brutes without regard to sex, age or a sense of decency, grown men and women sleeping together in the same apartment, and sometimes wife, husband, brothers and sisters in the same bed."

In 1851 Horace Greeley, editor of the *New York Tribune,* estimated that $10.37 was the minimum weekly wage necessary to support a family of five. This would pay for rent, food, fuel, and clothing. But, Greeley observed, this income allowed for no luxuries and no money left to pay medical bills. Yet, in 1851, most urban workers hardly made $10.37 a week. A shoemaker or printer averaged $4 to $6, and a cabinetmaker made about $5 a week. Male textile workers made $6.50; female textile workers averaged about $3.50. To make ends meet, entire families—children as well as adults—went to work in factories or did piecework at home. They often worked twelve to sixteen hours a day, and earned a dollar a day between them.

Single factory women were especially hard-pressed. Although their wages did not rise, their cost of living did. In 1845, according to the *New York Tribune,* the average female factory hand made $2 a week, but room and board cost about $1.50 to $1.75 a week, leaving only 50 cents or less for clothing, medicine, church dues, leisure activities, and savings. Even a brief period of unemployment could be disastrous because it could use up all of a worker's savings. By 1861 average wages had not risen, but the cost of room and board in urban areas had increased to about two dollars, the same as a wage earner's weekly income. Women workers now had no money left for other expenses.

In almost every industry, women usually earned only half to two-thirds of what men earned. Even the most highly skilled women often did not earn as much as the lowest-paid man. Employers justified paying lower wages to women because they, and most of American society, viewed them as temporary workers whose true place was in the home.

This narrow view of women's lives prevented people from improving working conditions for female wage workers or insisting that more occupations open up for women workers. Just as women were not suited to the noisy scenes of the courtroom as lawyers, people argued, neither were their "delicate" natures suited to the hurly-burly of the factory floor. And, indeed, most women stopped doing regular wage work once they married. Only the poorest married women continued to work outside of the home.

The impact of both new technology and the growing influx of immigrant workers can best be seen in the New England textile mills. In the 1820s and 1830s, the mills had been worked by young women from the farm country of New England. Until 1847 the women worked twelve hours a day, six days a week. That year they received an extra half-hour for dinner, reducing the workday to about eleven hours. The working day usually started at 5:00 A.M. and ended at 7:00 P.M. Workers had a thirty-five-minute break for breakfast at 7:00 A.M. and a forty-five-minute dinner break at noon. In 1853 the workday was cut again, to eleven hours, six days a week.

Until the early 1850s, female mill workers were expected to live in the boardinghouses provided by the mill owners. Built of brick, these structures lay across from the mills. Separate tenements housed the families of married workers, who, until the 1850s, were mostly men. Female mill hands shared tiny rooms—usually four to a room—and took all of their meals at the boardinghouse. Mill owners insisted that their female hands be in their boardinghouses by ten o'clock each evening, and they urged boardinghouse keepers, usually older women, to report any violators to the management. In the early years, women were required to attend church services regularly, and some mill owners even deducted pew rent from the women's earnings and paid it directly to local churches.

These close living and working arrangements created a camaraderie among the women workers, a community of like-minded women who eagerly wanted to improve their minds and their lives. Throughout the 1830s and 1840s, they organized and attended lectures, language classes, sewing groups, and literary "improvement circles"—after working a twelve-hour day. From one of these circles was born the *Lowell Offering*, the first journal written by and for mill women. The journal published poetry, short stories, and commentary penned by the female workers.

Workers also organized themselves into labor-reform groups to crusade for better working conditions and shorter workdays. As technological innovations enabled women to work faster and produce more, mill owners assigned more machines to workers—without raising wages. For example, at Hamilton Company,

The *Lowell Offering* published the writing of "factory girls." After working twelve hours a day, these inspired young women wrote poetry, fiction, book reviews, and articles in support of women's rights. Bravely, they also urged reforms in the workplace, such as a shorter workday and higher wages.

one of the mills in Lowell, the average number of looms per weaver more than doubled between 1840 and 1854. The workload for spinners increased as well. Workers were expected to operate more machines at a faster rate. But wages remained the same—although the company reaped higher profits from the workers' increased productivity. Indeed, in the fall of 1848, wages were reduced in all of the Lowell mills, but the workload was as demanding as ever. Mary Paul, from Vermont, wearily wrote her father on November 5, 1848, "I never worked so hard in my life but perhaps I shall get used to it." Throughout the 1840s, every year brought new pressures on mill workers to work harder, faster, and longer. And every year, starting in 1842, workers circulated petitions for a ten-hour day. Some female workers, however, were reluctant to complain because they planned to work only a few more years before marrying and did not want to jeopardize their opportunity to make as much money as they could.

By 1848 native-born farm women no longer flocked to the mills at Lowell or elsewhere. The notorious workload, made worse by assigning more and faster machines to each worker, and the opportunity to secure other work, such as teaching, drew women away from the mills. In their place came immigrant men and women. By 1852 half of all factory operatives in the New England mills were foreign born. Most of these new mill workers were Irish, and they snatched the lowest-paying and least-skilled jobs, such as carding and spinning, while native-born women monopolized the more skilled jobs. Irish workers also lived separately from native-born women, who refused to live or work with them. Gradually, Irish operatives moved into higher-paying positions.

Like other working-class families in the 1850s, immigrant families made mill work a family affair. From the ages of six to nine, immigrant mill workers' children attended school. But by thirteen, girls began to work in the mills. Boys, by contrast, started working around age fifteen. Families wanted their daughters to work as long as possible before they left the work force to marry. Unlike American-born workers, who generally kept all of their earnings, an immigrant daughter turned over a large part of her earnings to her family out of economic necessity as well as a strong sense of family obligation.

New technology also altered women's work in other industries. As more women sought work as seamstresses, sewing women's wages declined. In 1845 the *New York Daily Tribune* estimated that twice as many women were seeking work as seamstresses "as would find employment at fair wages." On the average, dressmakers who worked in factories sixteen hours a day made $1.25 to $2.50 a week in the 1850s. Those who worked at home, sewing bundles of cloth picked up from contractors—middlemen who represented garment manufacturers—made even less. Capmakers, who worked fifteen to eighteen hours a day, usually at home, were the lowest paid of all garment workers. Their average wage was fourteen cents a day, or about eighty-four cents a week.

Out of these meager wages, all sewers paid for thread and needles and any damage to the garment, such as tears. In cities such as Boston and New York, where a single woman needed to earn at least three dollars a week, these wages were hardly adequate. Some women turned to prostitution to supplement their wages. How others survived is a mystery.

A poem by Edward Zane Carroll, published in 1849, aptly described the seamstress's plight:

> We are many in the city
> Who the weary needle ply;
> None to aid and few to pity
> Tho' we sicken down and die;
> But tis work, work away
> By night and by day
> Oh, tis work, work away
> We've no time to pray.

In 1846 Elias Howe introduced the first sewing machine. Five years later, in 1851, the addition of a foot treadle for easier operation made the machine an indispensable tool. But instead of easing the sewer's burden, the sewing machine increased it. Hand sewers could no longer compete with the sewing machine. In one day, one sewing machine operator could do as much work as six hand sewers. Hand sewers were forced to buy or rent sewing machines, or work in garment factories, where they had no control over their wages or hours. To make matters worse, seamstresses, like the mill workers of New England, were expected to work faster and produce more while working for the same wages. New technology, such as the sewing machine or improved looms, enabled consumers to buy manufactured goods at reasonable prices—but at the expense of factory workers, who were not paid a fair wage for operating this new technology.

Some sewers took matters into their own hands. In 1850 women tailors in Philadelphia organized a cooperative to make and sell clothing as well as to hire out their services for mending and tailoring. "We are industrious and willing to work," they declared, "but paid as we are, we can not get enough to support life." Lucretia Mott and others assisted them in organizing. The cooperative lasted at least two years, then lost momentum and disbanded.

In 1851 6,000 stitchers in New York City followed suit and united to form the Shirt Sewers Cooperative Union. They decided to divide both the work and profits among themselves. Through letters in sympathetic newspapers, they appealed for public support and contributions to help them get started, and the funds came pouring in. The union hired a director, rented a store, and began to fill orders for shirts. According to the *New York Daily Tribune,* the Shirt Sewers Cooperative

Union was "among the successful combinative efforts at work in this city." Again, the cooperative seems to have dwindled and disappeared within a few years of its founding.

The mere act of joining a cooperative required great courage. Many parents, religious leaders, newspaper editors, and factory owners disapproved of any challenge to authority, especially from women, who were supposed to cultivate the proper feminine traits of deference and daintiness. Moreover, factory owners and managers did not care about their employees, who worked in ill-ventilated and ill-lit rooms at machines that could ensnare fingers or long hair. Workers were cogs in a machine that was devoted to production and profits. "I regard my work-people just as I regard my machinery," claimed one factory supervisor. "When my machines get old and useless, I reject them and get new [machines], and these people are part of my machinery."

In other industries, the story was much the same. New technology undercut the independent worker, forcing people to work in new factories or to purchase expensive machinery to use at home. Until 1852 women shoebinders in Massachusetts worked mostly part time at home, sewing the upper part of the shoe by hand. That year, a new Singer sewing machine, able to stitch leather, was introduced in the shoe factories of Massachusetts. Some female shoebinders feared the new machine would displace them. At one demonstration of the new equipment in 1853, according to an eyewitness account, female onlookers "shook their fists" at the agent demonstrating the equipment because he was destroying their livelihood.

Soon, however, women began to work in the factories using these new machines. Although they earned higher wages working full-time in the factory, the fears of those fist-shaking women came true. One woman working full-time at her machine accomplished as much as eleven shoebinders working by hand. Consequently, the number of women employed in shoe manufacturing declined dramatically throughout the 1850s. Even worse, the increased productivity of these female machine operators created a greater demand for male workers, who did the skilled work of cutting the leather and making the parts of the shoe. Fewer female operators were hired, but additional male shoemakers were recruited. And though wages almost doubled for female operators throughout the 1850s, women who continued to sew at home by hand received lower wages because they could not maintain the pace or productivity of their factory counterparts.

For a time, however, female shoebinders who sewed by hand at home and those who sewed by machine in the shop joined forces. In 1860 male and female shoe workers in Lynn, Massachusetts, struck for better wages. This was the largest labor protest by American workers before the Civil War. As many as 6,000 workers—5,000 men and 1,000 women—joined the strike, carrying banners proclaiming "American Ladies Will Not Be Slaves." The female factory shoebinders realized that their work was crucial to the total production process. They urged shoebinders who worked at home to join them in demanding higher wages for all female shoe-binders, those who worked at home as well as in the factory. As the strike spread to other shoe-producing towns in eastern Massachusetts, the Lynn shoebinders attempted to recruit shoebinders in these other towns to join them.

Their coalition thrived briefly, but male strikers insisted that wage increases for men were more important because higher wages for them meant they could better support their families. They convinced many women shoebinders that increasing the wages of male factory workers would eliminate the need for women to work at home part-time to supplement their husbands' higher earnings. They hearkened back to an earlier time when men were the main breadwinners and women, as sub-ordinates to men, worked only part-time while tending to their families.

Deserted by their fellow shoebinders who worked at home, the factory shoe-binders beseeched their former allies to support them once again. But the home workers stood firm, and the factory shoebinders dropped out of the strike. Upholding traditional images of women, the home workers supported the male strikers by carrying banners that proclaimed "weak in physical strength but strong in moral courage, we dare to battle for the right shoulder to shoulder with our fathers, husbands and brothers." With them went a powerful source of labor protest that could have strengthened the grievances of all the workers—male and female—against the unfair labor practices of factory owners.

Despite the long hours and low wages, women still preferred working in facto-ries to being domestic servants. At least factory workers had some free time; ser-vants were on call twenty-four hours a day. Domestics worked up to sixteen hours a day, with one afternoon off each week, and earned $1 to $1.25 a week plus board. Servants' duties varied according to their employers' requirements and the number of other servants employed in the house, but in general the work was as demand-ing as an earlier generation had found it.

Servants also had to endure the snobbery of their social "superiors." During the colonial era, servants were treated as part of the family and joined in all household activities. By the mid-nineteenth century, however, they were regarded as mere hired hands and were viewed as an inferior class. The Boston census of 1845 cate-gorized servants as part of the "unclassified residue of the population." No wonder that young women wanted to avoid the social stigma of being a domestic. Mary Paul, who left the Lowell mills to live and work in an experimental community, observed that many women "would live on 25 cts per week at sewing, or school teaching rather than work at housework . . . This all comes from the way servants are treated."

But Irish and free black women often had no choice because they could find no other work. They made up the bulk of women domestics. Some Irish women even preferred domestic work because the free room and board enabled them to save more of their wages and learn about American customs and manners more easily. By 1855 25 percent of all Irish immigrant women and 50 percent of all free black women worked as servants. Domestic service employed the largest number of all working women. Free black women also worked as washerwomen, seamstresses, and dressmakers. All of these jobs were laborious and low-paying.

When they could not make ends meet on meager salaries, some female wage earners turned to prostitution as a last, desperate resort. In 1859 William Sanger, a social investigator, published a report of his research into the lives of two thousand female prostitutes serving time in New York's Blackwell's Island prison. He discovered that nearly a fourth of the women had worked in the sewing trades and that almost half of the prostitutes had been servants, making five dollars or less a month. Many of the women claimed they were destitute when they turned to prostitution and had no other way to earn enough to support themselves.

As the storm clouds of Civil War gathered over the nation, the final curtain on this difficult era for wage-earning men and women came, fittingly enough, in the form of a tragedy. On January 10, 1860, the Pemberton Mill, a textile mill in Lawrence, Massachusetts, collapsed. Like a structure made out of matchsticks, the mill folded in on itself. About nine hundred workers were inside—mostly women. Throughout that day and into the night, the townspeople of Lawrence frantically dug through the rubble of brick and twisted, torn machinery to rescue the trapped mill workers. At eleven o'clock that night, a huge fire erupted, but the rescue work continued. Eighty-eight mill workers had died, 116 were severely wounded, and another 159 workers had sustained less serious injuries. An investigation followed and the accident was attributed to faulty construction. The engineer in charge of construction, who had known that the foundation was not strong enough to withstand the weight of the building, was merely censured.

Although mercy was shown to the engineer, little or none was extended to the victims of the tragedy. Workers who survived the collapse were left unemployed, with no savings to support them until they found other work. One female worker told a relief committee that she owed her boarding lady for her room and board, but, according to a relief committee report, the woman was "unwilling to keep her as she is out of work."

American workers did achieve some small victories during the late 1840s and 1850s, however. In Pennsylvania, Massachusetts, New Hampshire, and some other states, workers succeeded in passing state laws providing for ten-hour workdays and longer periods of schooling for children who worked. But their victory was incomplete. With reduced hours came reduced wages, and some employers made workers sign contracts agreeing to work longer days when necessary.

Growing industrialization did provide women with new ways to earn a living— but the living they earned in those noisy, dangerous factories barely supported them. And the relentless factory bell and production quotas harshly reminded them of their lack of power over working conditions and hours. Women left the factories as soon as they could, by marrying or by finding better-paying or more desirable work, such as teaching.

The vast majority of working women had neither the luxury of an education nor a breadwinner who could support them. By 1860 only about 15 percent of all American women worked for wages, and most of them were among the poorer classes—free black and immigrant women, widows, and rural migrants to the growing cities. But the guns of war would soon change the kind of jobs available to women. From the terrible tragedy of Civil War would come new and different wage-earning opportunities for all women.

Women at War

Like a fire bell in the night—to which Thomas Jefferson, many years before, had likened his terrifying thoughts on the unresolved issue of slavery—shots pierced the dawn silence in Charleston, South Carolina, on April 12, 1861. Confederate troops had fired on a U.S. garrison at Fort Sumter, in Charleston Harbor. Although no one was killed in the ensuing skirmish, those early-morning shots ignited the bloodiest war in the nation's history.

After thirty-three hours of constant bombardment, Major Robert Anderson, commander of the U.S. garrison at the fort, surrendered. On April 14, the Stars and Stripes was lowered and the Confederate stars and bars triumphantly raised over Fort Sumter. The Civil War had begun, and both sides—Union and Confederacy—erupted in celebration, as if a giant party had commenced. In Richmond, Virginia, the Confederate capital, everyone "seemed to be perfectly frantic with delight," an observer wrote. "I never in all my life witnessed such excitement." Troops drilled and marched through the city to the fervent cheers of thousands of bystanders. "The town is crowded with soldiers," Mary Boykin Chesnut reported in her diary. "These new ones are running in. . . . They fear the war will be over before they get a sight of the fun."

The news of Sumter's capture electrified Northerners as well, and a wave of patriotic fervor swept through the North. In New York City, a quarter of a million people flocked to a giant rally for the Union. Across the North, people swarmed into the streets waving Union flags. "The people have gone stark mad!" exclaimed a woman in the Midwest.

Both the North and the South were jubilant about going to war. Northerners believed that they were fighting to preserve the country, while Southerners believed that they were putting their lives on the line to preserve not only slavery but a whole way of life. Each side believed that the war would be over in a matter of weeks and that its soldiers would win, resolving once and for all the long years of debate and painful compromise over slavery. Abraham Lincoln's election to the presidency had brought this agonizing drama to its climax. Southerners portrayed him as a "Black Republican" who would overthrow slavery and give all African Americans as much, if not more, political power than whites. "Do you love your mother, your wife, your sister, your daughter?" a Georgia official demanded of nonslaveholders after Lincoln's election. If Georgia remained in a Union "ruled by Lincoln and his crew . . . in TEN years or less our CHILDREN will be the slaves of negroes."

Events moved rapidly toward disunion after Lincoln's election. On February 9, 1861, Jefferson Davis, a senator and former secretary of war, was elected president of the Confederate States of America (CSA). The CSA consisted of South Carolina, Georgia, Florida, Alabama, Mississippi, Louisiana, and Texas. Virginia joined the Confederacy three days after Fort Sumter was captured, and North Carolina, Tennessee, and Arkansas did the same over the next three months. The rest of the slaveholding states—Delaware, Maryland, Kentucky, and Missouri—remained in the Union, but their loyalties lay partly with the Confederacy. Ironically, although Lincoln opposed slavery, he had no intention of interfering with it in the states where it already existed. He even believed that the Constitution protected slavery in those states, though he hoped that slavery would eventually die out on its own.

Southern women zealously supported the southern cause of independence. A Georgia woman wrote her local newspaper, "I feel a new life within me, and my ambition aims at nothing higher than to become an ingenious, economical, industrious housekeeper, and an independent Southern woman." Throughout the South, women urged their menfolk to enlist in the Confederate military. A Selma, Alabama, woman even broke off her engagement when her fiancé failed to enlist. She sent him a skirt and pantaloons with a note attached: "Wear these or volunteer."

Up North, women also showed passionate support—for the Union. Shortly after the war began, Louisa May Alcott, who later wrote the novel *Little Women*, confided in her diary, "I long to be a man; but as I can't fight, I will content myself with working for those who can." Harriet Beecher Stowe called the Union effort a "cause to die for," and a woman in New York declared, "It seems as if we never were alive till now; never had a country till now."

As their husbands and sons drilled and marched and prepared for battle in opposing armies, women of the North and South swung into action. Throughout the North, women organized soldiers' aid societies to sew uniforms, assemble medical supplies, and knit scarves, socks, mittens, and other items for Union soldiers. In Troy, New York, educator Emma Willard became president of her newly organized society. Her group immediately applied for a government contract to sew soldiers' uniforms and give soldiers' wives paid employment. In New York City, about sixty women met at the New York Infirmary for Women and Children, the hospital founded by physicians Elizabeth and Emily Blackwell, to organize the relief efforts of New York City's women. Within a few days, the Woman's Central Association of Relief (WCAR) was formed with an initial membership of 2,000 to 3,000 women. Befitting a city the size of New York, the WCAR became the largest women's organization to carry out soldiers' relief work.

Unlike earlier volunteer groups, these soldiers' relief societies introduced a new concept to volunteer work: efficiency. During the antebellum years, women who did volunteer work were inspired by religious and moral ideals, and were infused with moral and spiritual zeal. Now, as the huge task of supplying the food, clothing, and medical needs of northern soldiers got under way, volunteers were inspired by the precepts of business rather than religion. They felt an abiding, even motherly concern for the soldiers' welfare, but discipline and efficiency, cooperation and coordination, became the watchwords on their lips.

Free African-American women of the North also did relief work, primarily for former slaves who had escaped North or who were liberated by Union troops as they advanced into Confederate states. In Lawrence, Kansas, for example, the Ladies' Refugee Aid Society helped former slaves find housing in Kansas. Elsewhere, free black women raised money to assist ex-slaves.

Harriet Jacobs, a former slave herself, assisted freedpeople who were flocking to Washington, D.C., in search of shelter and employment. At Freedmen's Village, a temporary community where more than one thousand former slaves were raising food for the Union army, she distributed clothing to the needy, nursed sick refugees, helped other refugees find work, and organized sewing circles and schools. Jacobs derived great satisfaction from her work. "The good God has spared me for this work," she wrote a correspondent. "The last six months have been the happiest of all my life."

Sojourner Truth, the former slave who mesmerized audiences with her eloquence, also worked as a counselor at Freedmen's Village. There, she instructed former slaves "in the habits of industry and economy," as she wrote a friend. "Many of them are entirely ignorant of housekeeping [but] they all want to learn the way we live in the North," she explained. Truth also taught home economics and personal hygiene to freedwomen. Like Jacobs, she felt truly fulfilled by this work. "I think I am doing good," she wrote. "I am needed here."

In the South, white Confederate women were immersed in soldiers' relief efforts as well. Indeed, in Charleston, South Carolina, women had started rolling bandages in January 1861, three months before the war had even begun. Shortly after the war started, women throughout the Confederacy organized hundreds of local soldiers' relief societies. In South Carolina alone, more than 150 such societies sprang up in the first two months of war. Women in Petersburg, Virginia, met every day, including Sundays, to sew uniforms and knit socks and blankets for Confederate soldiers. Many of these soldiers' relief groups had once been benevolent reform and missionary societies. Now they turned from raising money for their churches or charitable activities to outfitting their soldiers. Knitting needles flew like whirligigs and sewing machines whirred nonstop as women dashed off one uniform after another.

But Southern women did more than knit socks—they also filled cartridges and made sandbags for fortification. Because the South had fewer factories than the North for making weapons and other war supplies, those back home—mostly women—were pressed into volunteer service to make vital war materiel. Some women were paid for their efforts, especially when they worked in the few factories that did exist, but most women volunteered their services.

Through their soldiers' relief work, both northern and southern women, African-American as well as white, developed valuable administrative skills. They learned how to coordinate the flow of money and supplies from their groups to other agencies or to the soldiers themselves. They also learned how to keep records, act as leaders of their own groups, and make important decisions regarding the way they used their time, energies, and money. Like their sisters in the women's rights movement and in earlier volunteer groups, they were learning how to be leaders and policymakers.

During the war, women's rights activists continued to draft petitions and collect signatures—but on behalf of African-American slaves instead of for themselves. In 1863 Elizabeth Cady Stanton and Susan B. Anthony organized the Women's Loyal National League to work for the abolition of slavery in all states, including slave-holding states that supported the Union. Both abolitionists and women's rights activists joined the league, and its membership quickly rose to four thousand. In less than a year, the league collected almost 400,000 signatures on petitions urging Congress to pass a 13th constitutional amendment abolishing slavery. Like soldiers' relief societies, the league drew on the efforts of thousands of women in towns and villages throughout the North.

Women also took over the work of men who had gone off to fight. Across the North and South, women took charge of family farms and plantations as their men battled in Antietam or Chancellorsville or Gettysburg—or lay languishing in makeshift army hospitals or military prisons. Some women despaired at the enormous responsibilities of planting, plowing, and running a farm, but other women met the challenge head on—and discovered new strengths and abilities in the process. Sarah Morgan of Baton Rouge, Louisiana, marveled at how much she accomplished in one day—"empty a dirty hearth, dust, move heavy weights, make myself generally useful and dirty, and all this thanks to the Yankees."

Throughout the North, scores of women worked in government offices for the first time to replace male clerks who had enlisted in the Union army. They worked as clerks and copyists, copying speeches and documents for government records. They also became postal employees and worked in the Treasury Department cutting apart long sheets of paper money and counting currency. Salaries ranged from five hundred to nine hundred dollars a year by 1865. Although this was more than what most other female employees made at the time, women still earned half of what men had earned for the same work.

Northern women also worked in factories sewing uniforms. Despite the increased demand for their talents, there were always more seamstresses plying their trade than there was work available for them. Soldiers' wives and widows all sought paid work, and sewing was often the only skill they had. Even when they did work, seamstresses seldom made enough to support themselves. The amount of work available to sewing women—and the wages they were paid—actually declined during the war. Working fourteen to sixteen hours, many seamstresses earned only seventeen to twenty-four cents a day. From that, they had to pay for the thread they used and any damaged goods.

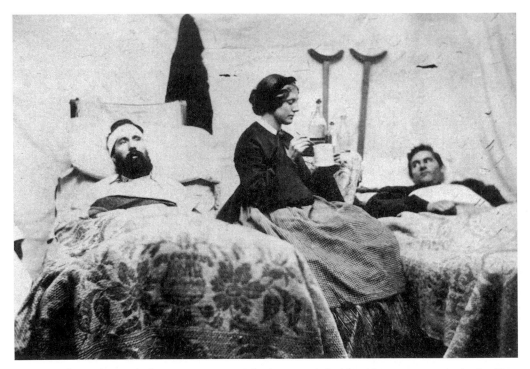

At a Union hospital in Nashville, Tennessee, a nurse feeds a wounded soldier. Nurses were required to be thirty years old and "very plain-looking women. Their dresses must be brown or black, with no bows, no curls, no jewelry and no hoop skirts."

Women found a special kind of power—an inner power of pride and accomplishment—through serving as military nurses. Shortly after the war began, Union military officials established the Department of Female Nurses. Dorothea Dix, who had earlier dedicated herself to improving conditions in the nation's insane asylums, became superintendent of this new department. She took on the formidable task of recruiting and training nurses for the Union army. Dix, who was gravely solemn in appearance and manner, recruited only women who were at least thirty and "plain in appearance," rejecting applicants who were too fashionably dressed or adorned in jewelry. Dix wanted to make sure that her nurses were above reproach in appearance and manner, and that they dedicated themselves to their work. Under Dix's supervision, more than three thousand female nurses joined the Union effort. They earned a monthly salary of twelve dollars.

But one of the most distinguished Union nurses during the war was not affiliated with Dix's Department of Female Nurses. Instead, Clara Barton sallied forth on her own, working in Union battlefield hospitals and sometimes on the battlefield itself. Barton was a slender, petite woman with a round, open face and a gentle, caring countenance. But this mild exterior concealed an iron will and an abundance of energy. When the war broke out, she collected supplies from soldiers' relief organizations throughout New England and distributed them herself to Union army camps.

Soon she was nursing wounded and dying men as they were brought in from the battlefield. On her own, she learned how to dress wounds, tie a tourniquet around bloodied limbs to stem the bleeding, and cut a bullet out of human flesh when no doctor was available. Barton called the soldiers "my boys" and ministered to them with a mother's love. She bathed their perspiring faces with wet rags, stroked their hair and read to them, and gave them small dosages of whiskey to ease the pain. Barton herself was never far from the dangers of battle. One day, as she held a wounded soldier in her arms, a bullet whizzed through the sleeve of her dress and killed him.

Sometimes it took all the inner strength that women could muster to perform their nursing tasks. They coped with the tormented screams of men enduring an amputation without the benefit of anesthesia, the ravings of other soldiers delirious from fever and infection, the quiet stoicism of those soldiers who knew they were dying, and the grim reality of death and disease. But nurses and doctors also became accustomed to such overwhelming suffering. Kate Cumming, a Confederate nurse at the Battle of Shiloh in Tennessee, reported in her diary, "The foul air from this mass of human beings at first made me giddy and sick, but I soon got over it. We have to walk, and when we give the men anything kneel, in blood and water; but we think nothing of it at all." After the ferocious battle of Gettysburg, in which 51,000 Union and Confederate soldiers were killed or wounded over three days of fierce fighting, Cornelia Hancock, a volunteer nurse from New Jersey, wrote to her sister, "I feel assured I shall never feel horrified at anything that may happen to me hereafter. . . . I could stand by and see a man's head taken off I believe—you get so used to it here."

Nurses in the Civil War seldom questioned whether they had stepped beyond women's sphere in performing such "indelicate" work. Whether they hailed from the Union or the Confederacy, their patriotic commitment and also their hearts told them they were in the right place during the war.

If some women found their calling as nurses, other women discovered adventure and fulfillment teaching the former slaves. As the Union armies advanced deeper into the South, capturing Confederate territory and liberating slaves in the process, hundreds of black and white women, mostly in their twenties, followed closely behind to teach the former slaves, many of whom were illiterate. Women risked danger and hardship—and sometimes their families' disapproval—to venture South. They went under the auspices of the American Missionary Society, the Pennsylvania Freedmen's Relief Association, and other agencies that recruited teachers and paid their monthly wages of ten to twelve dollars.

Teachers admired their students' eagerness to learn. "It is a great happiness to teach them," wrote Charlotte Forten to a friend in November 1862. Forten, an African-American woman, taught in the Sea Islands off of South Carolina. "I wish some of those persons at the North who say the race is hopelessly and naturally inferior, could see the readiness with which these children, so long oppressed and deprived of every privilege, learn and understand." Adult ex-slaves, too, were willing students. Of one of her grown-up students, Forten remarked, "I never saw anyone so determined to learn."

Nursing and teaching were traditional forms of women's work, performed in the rush and excitement of war. But women also did untraditional work during the war. Both black and white women worked as spies, scouts, and smugglers. Mary Elizabeth Bowser, a former slave, became a servant in the home of Confederate president Jefferson Davis—so that she could relay military information overheard in the Davis household to the Union side. Two other former slaves, a husband and wife, cleverly devised a system in which the wife, who got herself hired as a laundress for the family of a southern officer, sent messages via the clothesline to her husband, who worked on the Union side. Each article of clothing that she hung on the line represented a movement of Confederate troops. As her husband explained, "That there gray shirt is [Confederate general James] Longstreet; and when she takes it off, it means he's gone down about Richmond." In general, ex-slaves spied for the North because they wanted to help defeat slavery.

About four hundred women disguised themselves as Union or Confederate soldiers and fought in the war. With the proper attire, some could easily pass for men. Women enlisted for a variety of reasons. Some believed in the cause so deeply that they would not let being a woman stop them from fighting as soldiers. Others craved the adventure or could not bear to be apart from husbands or other loved ones who had joined the army. No doubt some women were killed in battle and went to their graves with their true identities concealed. Other women soldiers were forced to reveal their secret when they were wounded. A female Union soldier, wounded in the battle of Chickamauga in Tennessee, was captured by Confederate troops and returned to the Union side with a note: "As the Confederates do not use women in the war, this woman, wounded in battle, is returned to you." When a Union nurse asked her why she had joined the army, she replied, "I thought I'd like camp life, and I did."

For the first two years of the war, Confederate forces won most of the major battles. The Union army, even with its superior resources, floundered from one battle to another under a succession of inept Union generals. Finally, on September 18, 1862, the Army of the Potomac achieved its first significant victory—at Antietam Creek in Sharpsburg, Maryland. The cost of victory was enormous. In one day, nearly six thousand men on both sides were killed and another seventeen thousand were wounded.

But the victory impelled Lincoln to do something that he had been contemplating for a long time: issue an Emancipation Proclamation to free southern slaves. On September 22, 1862, he issued a preliminary Emancipation Proclamation that warned the Confederate states that all slaves held in any state still in rebellion against the Union on January 1, 1863, would be "thenceforward, and forever free." With one stroke of the pen, Lincoln had turned the Civil War into a war to abolish slavery as well as to preserve the Union. By giving the war this added moral purpose, he infused new fighting spirit in Union troops, won the support of other nations that condemned slavery, such as Great Britain, and gave southern slaves renewed hope that the "day of jubilee"—freedom—would soon arrive.

But for most slaves, the outward circumstances of their lives changed little. Most of them stayed on their plantations, some journeyed to refugee camps set up by the Union army, and some went in search of family members who had been sold to other plantations. For all slaves, the war brought new hardships and new challenges. On plantations the work load seemed to double as white men went off to fight and slave men were either forced into service by the Confederate army or recruited by the Union army. Eliza Scantling, who was fifteen in 1865, recalled that in the early months of that year, she "plowed a mule an' a wild un at dat. Sometimes me hands get so cold I jes' cry."

When slave fathers joined the Union army, slave mothers and children suffered the wrath of cruel owners. In 1863 one slave woman wrote to her soldier husband: "I have had nothing but trouble since you left. . . . they abuse me because you went & say they will not take care of our children & do nothing but quarrel with me all the time and beat me scandalously the day before yesterday."

Despite such ill treatment, or the upheaval of living in refugee camps, or the uncertainties that lay ahead, slaves rejoiced at their emancipation because it meant that their families could be together. Hundreds of black couples began to legalize marriage ties. In slavery they had married without benefit of a prescribed civil or religious ritual that was legally binding, and planters were free to break up these marriages. Now, as free people, couples yearned to make their marriages legal and to reunite family members who had been sold among various plantations.

As the war dragged on, African-American and white women on the southern homefront bore the worst hardships, because the war was fought mostly on their soil. Union forces moved farther south, and entire homes, neighborhoods, and towns were destroyed. Almost as difficult to bear were the constant shortages of food and the astronomical price of everyday items. The Union blockade of southern ports deprived Southerners of both the necessities and luxuries they had always taken for granted. Because food was scarce and an unstable Confederate currency continually drove prices higher, basic foodstuffs became unaffordable. People gave up drinking coffee, because the cost of beans had skyrocketed to seventy dollars a pound. Instead, they made do by brewing okra seeds, toasted yams, and roasted corn. In Richmond a barrel of flour cost as much as seventy dollars—beyond the means of most families. By early 1865, bacon and butter in Petersburg, Virginia, cost twenty dollars a pound, and chickens ran as high as fifty dollars apiece.

Worries over how to stretch meager dollars and provisions, and how to protect their homes and possessions from ruin, took a terrible toll on southern women. "I experience such constant dread and anxiety," Lila Chunn wrote her soldier husband, William, in the spring of 1863, "that I feel all the time weary and depressed." One southern woman was so despondent that she felt as if she "could willingly say 'good night' to the world and all in it." Other southern women aimed their wrath at Union soldiers occupying their cities. In her journal, Eliza Andrews fumed, "If all the words of hatred in every language under heaven were summed up together into one huge epithet of detestation, they could not tell how I hate Yankees. They thwart all my plans, murder my friends, and make my life miserable." In New Orleans, women showed their back sides to Union general Benjamin Butler in public and pasted his picture in the bottom of chamber pots.

Northern women suffered too, though they experienced far less hardship than southern women. Up North, everyday items were also scarce because so many goods were being redirected to the war front. As a result, the cost of living also rose beyond the means of many people. Thousands of soldiers' families went hungry, and women who had never had to ask for charity were mortified that they now had to seek assistance.

In 1863 women in New York City went on a rampage. In the South, women had rioted for food; in New York they joined men, mostly Irish, who were protesting against a federal provision that allowed draftees to hire substitutes. The protest quickly erupted into a riot against the city's blacks. The protesters, who feared competition from black workers, resented being drafted to fight a war for the slaves' freedom. Even more so, they resented upper-class Yankee Protestants who could afford to pay substitutes three hundred dollars to fight in their places. Over four days, rioters looted stores and beat innocent blacks. Angry mobs lynched about six blacks, destroyed the dwellings where blacks lived, and burned down the Colored Orphan Asylum. They also set fire to several businesses that employed blacks and destroyed the homes of prominent Republicans and abolitionists. Women took part in the plunder, venting their rage at a government and a war that sacrificed their men and impoverished their lives.

But for all women, North and South, the hardest part of war was losing beloved husbands, sons, and fathers in battle. This cruelty knew no boundaries. Across the battered nation, women feared receiving telegrams with the dreaded news. "A telegram comes to you," wrote Mary Boykin Chesnut, a Southern woman who kept a diary throughout the war, "and you leave it in your lap. You are pale with fright. You handle it, or dread to touch it, as you would a rattlesnake—worse—worse. A snake would only strike you."

Sometimes women found out not from a telegram but from a list published in the newspaper or posted at the train depot. Harriet Beecher Stowe learned that her son Fred had been wounded at Gettysburg from her morning paper. In 1862 an Arkansas woman learned the awful news in a more devastating way—by stumbling upon the bodies of her husband and two brothers on the battlefield at Prairie Grove, Arkansas. By the end of the war, almost every American family had lost a

Along with a clergyman, Southern women tend the grave of Confederate hero Stonewall Jackson. Southern women showed their devotion to the Confederate cause by organizing memorial associations to maintain the graves of their fallen heroes

dear relative or friend; and thousands of families coped with the formidable task of caring for a loved one maimed in battle.

A religious person might have looked for some higher meaning or purpose in this unfathomable suffering. That is precisely what Lincoln did as he stepped forward on a windy, gloomy March day in 1865 to take the Presidential oath of office once more. "Fondly do we hope," he said, "fervently do we pray—that this mighty scourge of war may speedily pass away. Yet, if God wills that it continue, until all the wealth piled by the bondsman's two hundred and fifty years of unrequited toil shall be sunk, and until every drop of blood drawn with the lash, shall be paid by another drawn with the sword ... it must be said 'the judgments of the Lord, are true and righteous altogether.'" Then the President appealed for a speedy end to the war and a "just, and a lasting peace, among ourselves, and with all nations."

As the mighty Union forces encircled the battered Confederate army, a speedy end was indeed in sight. On April 9, 1865, Robert E. Lee, commander of what was left of the Confederate forces, surrendered to General Ulysses S. Grant, commanding officer of the Army of the Potomac. While southern women remained closeted in their homes, the window blinds tightly shut as if they were in mourning, a joyous North erupted into celebration. People thronged the streets, laughing, hugging, greeting one another like old friends, and bells merrily pealed atop church steeples. But this gleeful, noisy spectacle was abruptly silenced by an assassin's bullet. On the evening of April 14, 1865, Lincoln was shot by John Wilkes Booth, a loyal Confederate. The President died quietly the next morning without regaining consciousness, and Northerners mourned their fallen leader.

Women in both the North and South anxiously awaited the return of their menfolk from the battlefields and tried to put their own lives back in order. For Southerners, the immediate task was to repair their shattered homes and cities and eke out a living. Most of the South had been reduced to rubble. Mail service, police protection, bridges, roads, and public buildings—all were in disarray. Local and state governments were in chaos, and the Confederate currency was worthless. The North, while mostly untouched by the physical devastation of war, shared in the shocking number of casualties. No war before or since has cost so many American lives. More than 600,000 soldiers were killed—more than one out of every five soldiers nationwide. Countless others were crippled for life.

As women across the nation reflected upon the last four years of Civil War, upon all the sacrifices and hardships, perhaps they took pride in the vital roles they had played during the war. Now it was time to set their sights on the future. Slavery had been abolished and all African Americans were legally free. But the battle for a "new birth of freedom," as Lincoln had eloquently declared at Gettysburg, was not yet finished—certainly not for America's women. They had yet to achieve the fruits of victory in their struggle for political, economic, and social equality. The coming years would be busy ones indeed, as American women labored to extend the democratic ideals and hopes nobly expressed during the war to their own lives.

CHAPTER 6

Laborers for Liberty

1865–1890

Harriet Sigerman

I n the closing days of the Civil War, a young Southern woman witnessed the occupation of the Confederate capital, Richmond, Virginia, by Union troops. Her heart sank as she watched the Confederate flag taken down from atop the Capitol and the Stars and Stripes raised in its place. "We knew what that meant!" she recalled years later. "Richmond was in the hands of the Federals. We covered our faces and cried aloud. All through the house was the sound of sobbing." But one little girl clapped her hands in delight, because the coming of "the Yankees" meant food for the citizens of this desolate city. "Now we'll get something to eat," she exclaimed. "I'm going to have pickles and molasses and oranges and cheese and nuts and candy until I have a fit and die."

In the North, the citizens of Boston rejoiced at the fall of Richmond. This latest victory meant that the war was almost over. Across the city, people swarmed into the streets, jubilantly blowing soap bubbles and snatching up newspapers to read the latest reports from Richmond. In the distance, bells rang and cannons roared to announce the downfall of the Confederate capital. The entire North was awash in celebration. In Washington, D.C., a reporter wrote, "The air seemed to burn with the bright hues of the flag. . . . Almost by magic, the streets were crowded with hosts of people, talking, laughing, hurrahing and shouting in the fullness of their joy." Throughout the North, in cities and villages alike, flags snapped crisply atop buildings, bells pealed, homes and buildings were aglow, and torchlight parades turned the night into a brilliant burst of color and light.

For former slaves, the end of the war held a more personal meaning. When asked why she wanted to leave her former master's South Carolina plantation, Patience, a freed slave, replied, "I must go; if I stay here I'll never know I'm free." An elderly African-American woman eagerly left her former owner's plantation to join a small community of freed people near Greensboro, Georgia, so that she could, in her words, "Joy my freedom!" She and scores of other former slaves fled from plantations that reminded them of the dark, dreadful days of slavery.

On April 9, 1865, Robert E. Lee, commander of the Confederate army, surrendered to General Ulysses S. Grant, the commander of the Union forces. The long, bloody war was over, and now began the task of rebuilding the shattered nation. Lincoln's untimely death was a tragic event for both the victorious North and the vanquished South. His passing deeply saddened Northerners, and thousands turned out to pay their last respects as the train carrying his body slowly wound its way from Washington, D.C., to Springfield, Illinois, his hometown. For the South, his death was a disastrous turn of events, and fearful Southerners wondered if they would be blamed for Booth's villainy. Indeed, his death aroused their alarm that Reconstruction—the process of restoring the South to membership in the nation—would be unduly harsh. Although he had not completed the plan before his death, Lincoln had envisioned a process in which Southern states would take an oath of loyalty, emancipate their slaves, and allow literate blacks and all black soldiers to vote. After his assassination, Southerners feared that the North would seek vengeance by demanding a high price for Southern reentry into the Union.

The Aftermath of Civil War

In the aftermath of war, Southerners faced the immediate task of repairing an entire region crippled by four years of war. The Civil War exacted a terrible toll on the nation as a whole; no war before or since has cost so many American lives. In 1860 the total population of the United States was about 31 million people, including approximately 3.5 million African-American slaves in the South. From 1861 to 1865, more than 3 million men went to war; this number included 189,000 African-American soldiers who fought on the Union side. Nearly 2 million white men fought for the North, and 900,000 men joined the Confederate cause. Of this total more than 600,000 soldiers were killed, but the burden of casualties fell more heavily on the South. Among Confederate forces more than one out of four soldiers died. Countless other soldiers were crippled for life.

Because the war was fought mainly on Southern soil, the South bore most of its ravages. More than 250,000 Southerners were displaced by the war. Either their homes had been destroyed in battle or they were forced to flee from Union troops who had captured their towns. At least half moved several times within the former Confederacy; others fled to the North or West or even abroad. Varina Davis, wife of former Confederate president Jefferson Davis, aptly described this unsettling period: Everyone, she said, was "uprooted and floating."

Entire Southern cities were destroyed: Columbia, South Carolina, and Richmond, Virginia, had been burned; Atlanta, Georgia, was reduced to rocks and rubble; and after repeated bombardment and two major fires, Charleston, South Carolina, was hardly recognizable. During Union general William Tecumseh Sherman's 1864 march to the sea, from Atlanta to Savannah, Georgia, 285 miles away, his soldiers—along with some Confederate deserters and stragglers—had looted, plundered, and set fire to farms, plantations, and even some slave cabins.

For those left behind—mostly women, children, the elderly, and former slaves who did not flee to other regions—this destruction resulted in lost livestock, homes unfit for habitation, and the loss of cherished possessions as well as the necessary tools for everyday life. Mary Boykin Chesnut toured her ruined plantation after a contingent of Union soldiers had destroyed what Sherman's troops left unfinished. She described the desolation: "On one side of the house every window was broken, every bell torn down, every piece of furniture destroyed, every door smashed in. Our books, our papers, our letters, were strewed along the Charleston road." Union troops also burned the Chesnuts' mills, cotton gins, and a hundred bales of cotton. "Indeed nothing is left now," she lamented, "but the bare land and debts."

Chesnut's experience was only one of many tales of woe. Throughout the battle-scarred nation, the war changed the lives of women from all regions and economic classes—African-American as well as white women. But, in general, Southern women, black and white, suffered far more than Northern women. In many respects, the South had been reduced to a frontier: Local and state governments were in disarray; the Confederate currency was worthless; and bridges, roads, railroads, and public buildings were in disrepair. The few private relief agencies that existed were flooded with requests for help. One Louisiana widow told the New York Ladies Southern Relief Association, established in December 1866, that she needed everything.

Poverty, brutality, the ravagement of their homes and land, the humiliation of defeat and occupation—this was the aftermath of war for Southern white women. As a result, some developed a deep hatred for the North. "Every day, every hour, that I live increases my hatred and detestation, and loathing of that race," declared Mary Steger. "[Northerners] disgrace our common humanity. As a people I consider them vastly inferior to the better classes of our slaves." Sarah Morgan of New Orleans, Louisiana, declared that she remained a "Rebel in heart and soul" and that she would never forget "the cruel wrongs we have suffered."

Meanwhile, the process of Reconstruction fell into place. Despite Southerners' hatred of the occupying troops, the Reconstruction of the South proceeded without revenge in the early postwar years. President Andrew Johnson carried out Lincoln's goals by pardoning all Southerners who took an oath of allegiance to the United States (except for Confederate government officials and military officers above a certain rank) and by establishing temporary governments composed of Southerners in the Southern states. These governments were required to draft new constitutions, but they resisted granting voting and other citizenship rights to African Americans. As a result, Congress carried out a harsher Reconstruction by reestablishing military rule in the South and organizing ex-Confederate states into five military districts under the command of major generals. Former Confederate states were readmitted into the Union only after state legislatures had ratified the 14th Amendment to the Constitution, which granted citizenship to African Americans, and the 15th Amendment, which safeguarded voting rights for black males.

Gradually, these military governments stepped aside, and reconstructed state governments were formed by blacks, who were newly eligible to vote, Southern whites, and Northern "carpetbaggers" who came south to exploit new business and political opportunities for themselves—the name came from the large cloth bags in which many of these travelers carried their belongings. These governments ruled the South for periods ranging from one to seven years. Although some of them were incompetent or corrupt, they introduced important reforms, such as establishing a system of public education, providing farmland to some of the former slaves, setting up charitable institutions, and encouraging blacks to vote.

Daily life continued amid the upheaval of Reconstruction. Still, the defeat and destruction of the South caused much pain and despair for Southern white women. "To have every thing we hold sacred sneered at—& every calamity to our poor country," Mary Boykin Chesnut mourned in her diary. "I said I wished now, as Mother prayed two years ago, that we might all be twenty feet under ground before we were subjugated." Chesnut failed to observe that the Southern way of life, whose passing she now mourned, had depended upon the subjugation of another race of people.

For former slaves, the end of the war meant many things, but above all it meant that they were no longer slaves bound to a master. Instead, they were free human beings able to work for wages, however meager, to support their own families. Although Lincoln's Emancipation Proclamation of 1863 had outlawed slavery in the states that had left the Union to form the Confederacy, he had no constitutional power to enforce his edict until those states were defeated and under Union military control. As Union forces captured Confederate regions during the war, slaves "demonstrated with their feet," as one said, by abandoning Rebel farms and plantations. Union forces also liberated those who still remained on plantations. But not until the Confederacy surrendered was slavery finally abolished. Even then, the abolition of slavery was not made the law of the land until the 13th Amendment to the Constitution was ratified on December 6, 1865.

Throughout the first year of Reconstruction, as during the last two years of the war, ex-slaves flocked to ministers and judges to legalize their marriages. Officials of the Freedmen's Bureau, a network of agencies established by the U.S. government to monitor the former slaves' transition to freedom, urged ex-slaves to do so, but the former slaves did not need much urging. Legalizing marriages and family ties guaranteed that neither the state nor former planters could break up the family. One woman who had been married for thirty-five years and had borne twelve children explained to a teacher that she wanted a marriage license because "all 'spectable folks is to be married, and we's 'spectable." The teacher to whom she addressed this remark, like government officials, reporters, interviewers, and others who recorded what ex-slaves said, wrote down the words spoken by the woman according to the way she heard them.

Although former slaves rejoiced over being free, the outward circumstances of their lives changed little. During the first few months of freedom, many black women and men left the plantations on which they had toiled as slaves. Moving away meant that they were truly free. They also searched for family members who had been sold to other planters. "Every mother's son seemed to be in search of his mother," wrote an observer from the North. "Every mother in search of her children."

Freedom, however, offered few economic rewards. Southern plantation owners refused to sell land to former slaves, and the federal government assisted only half-heartedly in redistributing abandoned land to them. In fact, the government returned to Southern white planters most of the land that had been abandoned during the war or confiscated by Union forces. The Freedmen's Bureau attempted to guarantee fair negotiations for paid work between former slaves and their new employers—in many cases, their former masters. Planters had land but little money and no laborers to work the land, and ex-slaves had neither land nor money. Planters needed laborers to plant and harvest their crops, but most ex-slaves refused to consider themselves employees of white planters because such working arrangements reminded them too much of slavery.

Consequently, a system developed by which black laborers rented the land of white planters to plant and harvest crops, mostly cotton. The laborers paid for use of the land by dividing the proceeds of the crop with the planter. A common arrangement was a "fifty fifty" division in which planter and sharecropper each received 50 percent of the proceeds. From their share, however, laborers also had to pay planters for housing and supplies, such as fertilizer, farm equipment, seeds, and cloth to make clothing for their families. As a result, sharecroppers seldom had any money left and sometimes ended up in debt to the planter.

Sharecropping was a hard life. Indeed, for many former slaves it was not much different from slavery. They had to promise not to be "strowling at night" and needed written permission to go into town or visit relatives nearby. Moreover, planters continued to use corporal punishment to keep their workers in line. Both women and men were subject to this brutal treatment. Caroline, a freedwoman, filed a claim with the Freedmen's Bureau in Greensboro, North Carolina, to force her employer, Thomas Price, to pay her for her work. The next time that she showed up at work, Price was waiting for her. According to testimony in the records of the Freedmen's Bureau, he "knocked her down and beat her with his fist," then ordered his overseer to bring him "the strap." Holding her head between his knees, "he whipped her . . . on the bare flesh by turning her clothes up." Then he told the overseer to "ware [sic] her out" with more lashes, which the overseer obligingly did.

Sharecroppers not only had to endure brutal treatment by former masters; they also received little economic advantage. The best that most such freed slaves

The Freedmen's Bureau built schools that allowed black children in the Reconstruction South to get a formal education. Schools were strictly segregated, however.

could expect was a meager, hardscrabble life. A black family's last, best hope for independence was its own patch of land. The son of one sharecropper recalled his family's modest dream—"the prospect of owning a wagon and a pair of mules and having only our father for boss."

It would seem, then, that little had changed since slavery for black women and men who were aspiring toward a better life. But with freedom black women enjoyed a new role: as nurturers of their own families. In slavery black women worked long hours for the planter and his family and had little time or opportunity to make a home for their own husbands and children, nor could they protect members of their families from the planter's harsh treatment. For the ex-slave woman the true benefit of freedom was the opportunity to be a homemaker for her own family. Throughout the South, freedwomen devoted what little spare time they had to taking classes in homemaking, where they learned new ways to sew and cook. Teachers hired by the Freedmen's Bureau taught these classes.

Planters, however, still wanted black women to devote all of their time to working in the fields. They complained that black women were "putting on airs" by trying to act like white women, who, to the planter's way of thinking, did not engage in such grubby work, although in reality many white farm women did. One ex-slave recalled that on some plantations on the Red River, in Louisiana, he saw white men "drive colored women out in the fields to work ... and would tell colored men that their wives and children could not live on their places unless they work in the fields."

Few freedwomen could indulge in full-time homemaking, because their families needed their economic contribution. Most black women did the same work in freedom that they had done in bondage—they worked in the fields or as midwives or domestic servants. Or they peddled poultry, eggs, fruit, and vegetables along the roads or at markets. But, with freedom, something was different: To their way of thinking, they worked for their families, not for their employers, and these women organized their working life around family needs. Their sense of well-being was closely linked to their families' well-being. One mother, a cook, claimed that she could die happy, though she had spent much of her life in bondage, because her children would grow up in freedom.

Generally men and women performed different tasks. As one black man from Georgia explained, "The able-bodied men cultivate, the women raise chickens and take in washing; and one way and another they manage to get along." And sometimes they did whatever had to be done: "We had to work mighty hard," Fanny Hodges recalled of those early years after the war. "Sometimes I plowed in de fiel all day; sometimes I washed an den I cooked." Frances Ellen Watkins Harper, a free black woman who became a lecturer and poet, shared these impressions about former slave women in the Reconstruction South: "There are many women around me who would serve as models of executiveness anywhere. They do double duty, a man's share in the field, and a woman's part at home. They do any kind of field work, even ploughing, and at home the cooking, washing, milking, and gardening."

Children helped out. Betty Powers, who was eight when the war ended, later recalled the excitement of helping her family make a new life in Texas, where her father bought a plot of land: "De land ain't clear, so we 'uns all pitches in and clears it and builds de cabin. Was we 'uns proud? There twas, our place to do as we pleases, after bein slaves. Dat sho' am de good feelin." But some children resented having to work in the fields when they wanted to go to school. Ann Matthews told an interviewer that she could not get an education because "mah daddy wouldn't let me. Said he needed me in de fiel wors den I needed school."

In many respects, then, the black family in freedom resembled the traditional white family; the husband strove to be the major breadwinner, though women also worked, and he represented the family at political conventions and African-American community affairs, while his wife remained in the background. In church men held leadership positions, and wives were expected to defer to their husbands' authority. But black women also exerted considerable influence over their people's lives. In larger towns and cities throughout the South, free blacks organized groups to help one another secure work or medical attention or any of the many other needs facing a newly liberated people. These mutual aid societies shielded the black community from the hostility and bigotry of white society, and black women from all economic backgrounds held leadership positions in them. Such organizations as the United Daughters of Ham, the Sisters of Zion, the Daughters of Zion, and the Ladies Benevolent Society cared for the sick and impoverished. They also launched educational projects. Women who toiled long hours as laundresses, ironers, and domestic servants became active leaders of these organizations. As the caretaker of her family in freedom, the free African-American woman broadened her understanding of family to include the entire black community.

Women also offered spiritual guidance within their communities. Drawing on ancient African religious practices, elderly women often served as herb doctors and fortune-tellers or used old African spells and charms for medicinal purposes, and their black neighbors eagerly sought their assistance. Although whites dismissed them as ignorant hired hands and "aunties," black women commanded respect and deference within the African-American community.

Relations between husband and wife and parent and child, however, bore many of the scars of bondage. Poverty, uprootedness, and white hostility trailed the former slaves in freedom and shadowed their relations with one another. Some African-American husbands resorted to violence in attempting to assert their authority over their wives, and parents, who had been raised in slavery under the threat of the lash, in turn used corporal punishment on their children. But for every case of family violence, there were scores of loving couples who relished the opportunity to make a life together in freedom. And in the minds and hearts of many black parents, their role as protectors of their families and communities was indisputable. Many a black mother who whipped her children would not allow her white employer to lay a hand on them. Her new status as an emancipated person granted her the right to protect her family from harm as best she could, and she extended her concept of family to her kin and community. Out of the ashes of slavery and Civil War rose a generation of African-American women who would dedicate themselves to the betterment of their race.

In the North, women who rejoiced in the victory of the Union side also faced a new era, one filled with uncertainty. Like Southern women, many Northern women had to wait months before finding out whether a missing soldier was dead or alive. Women searched the battlefields for the bodies of loved ones. An elderly woman from New York searched for three weeks in May 1865 around Petersburg, Virginia, before finding her son's remains.

Some women in the North jumped right into relief work. Harriet Tubman—the legendary conductor of the Underground Railroad—returned to her home in Auburn, New York. Using income from her writing, she converted her house into the Home for Indigent and Aged Negroes. There, she provided board and lodging for former slaves and black war veterans. Other women organized soldiers' and

When her services were no longer required to help slaves escape from bondage, Harriet Tubman used her organizational talents to help needy free blacks by opening a boardinghouse. She also promoted the establishment of schools for former slaves in the South and supported woman suffrage.

orphans' homes and provided jobs and relief for widows of Union soldiers killed in battle. Some Northern women traveled to the South to work as teachers for the Freedmen's Bureau or stayed up North to raise money for freed slaves. The end of the war brought no end to Northern women's volunteer activities.

Rebecca Rouse, president of the Cleveland Ladies' Aid and Sanitary Society, continued to volunteer at the soldier's relief home established by her society. Three months after the war ended, her husband, Benjamin, wrote their daughter, "Mother is just as busy as she can be feeding soldiers on their [way to] return home to different western states and taking care of the sick and wounded at the Soldier's home . . . during the month of June they fed 1,900 soldiers." He continued, "Mother wishes me to say she works so hard at the home days she's too tired to write you at night."

Indeed, some women felt that the most urgent work had just begun. Mary Livermore, who had worked for the Sanitary Commission, a highly organized voluntary agency that provided Northern soldiers with food, clothing, and medical services during the war, realized that the nation needed women's services more than ever. "During the war," she wrote later, "I became aware that a large portion of the nation's work was badly done, or not done at all, because woman was not recognized as a factor in the political world." Livermore devoted the rest of her life to working for women's social and political equality and for the prohibition of liquor.

Although the ravages of war affected the North far less severely than the South, Northern women endured numerous trials in returning to a normal life. For many women, holding on to wartime jobs or finding work was their number-one concern. Some women had to work for the first time to support husbands wounded in the war, and others lost their wartime jobs to returning veterans. Northern women had worked during the war as clerks, bookkeepers, stenographers, and receptionists. They also served as nurses and worked in factories. When the war ended, many women workers were dismissed from their jobs, and female factory and clerical workers who managed to keep their jobs were paid less than during the war.

In the postwar years, women reformers showed little interest in the cause of working women. Harriet Beecher Stowe, who had exposed the cruelty of slavery in *Uncle Tom's Cabin*, was silent about the slavery of wage labor. For a time suffrage crusader Susan B. Anthony expressed concern and even helped to organize working women into their own cooperatives, but she committed most of her energies to fighting for women's right to vote. Some working-class women took matters into their own hands by organizing protests for better wages, shorter hours, and safer, more sanitary working conditions. Garment workers formed their own associations during and after the war. Many of these associations charged membership dues to support their workers who went on strike. Other associations provided sick benefits to workers who were unable to work. A few associations established uniform wage scales and insisted that employers pay the same rates to all association members.

These associations achieved modest gains for their female workers, despite the opposition of skilled male workers who questioned why women needed to work at all. During the war, as women's labor made the uniforms that Northern soldiers wore and printed bonds to pay for the war effort, *Fincher's Trades' Review*, a labor newspaper, proclaimed, "We shall spare no effort to check this most unnatural invasion of our firesides by which the order of nature is reversed, and women, the loveliest of God's creatures, reduced to the menial conditions of savage life."

How shocked the paper's editors would have been had they foreseen what toil "the loveliest of God's creatures" down South would engage in after the war! From the lowliest farm woman to once wealthy planters' wives, Southern women did "anything and everything we could to make a living," according to Myrta Lockett Avary, who lived in Richmond. She recalled seeing a white woman driving a plow to which her young daughters, one of whom was nursing a baby, were hitched. "The great mass of southern women had to drop books for broomsticks, to turn from pianos and guitars and make music with kettles and pans," Avary declared.

Southern women used ingenuity in earning a living. Some women became peddlers and sold clothing, pies, and preserves. Others ran post offices, set type, made shoes, took in laundry, or did sewing. Many tried to revive farms and plantations that had been destroyed or fallen into disrepair. To be sure, women toiled long and hard for mostly meager earnings. Seamstresses who sat hunched over needle and thread from dawn to dusk, straining their eyes and muscles, rarely made more than fifty cents a day. This was hardly an adequate income when a bar of soap cost twenty dollars because of the scarcity of such items and the chaotic state of the Southern economy.

Many poor white Southern families lost their farms after the war. Like the former slaves, they were forced to work or sharecrop for white planters and never regained their own land. A poor white woman's life was as difficult as that of a black woman. She had to stretch meager earnings to feed a typical family of eight or nine, and she did all of the household chores of washing, sewing, cooking, and cleaning. During the busy season, white sharecropping women worked in the fields, but at other times they added to the family income by selling eggs or produce at market.

Although poor white and black women shared similar economic hardships, they seldom interacted. Poor white men regarded blacks as competition for a limited number of jobs and tried to drive them away. Economic desperation made enemies out of two poor groups of people who shared more hardship than the surface difference of skin color would suggest.

Yet poor people were not alone in suffering the economic misfortunes of war. Throughout the postwar South, the standard of living declined for all economic classes, even for affluent planters. In a frightening new world without slaves, planter women had to fend for themselves as they tried to run households and manage plantations. For some, the work was overwhelming. One Louisiana plantation mistress confessed, "I never even so much as washed out a pocket handkerchief with my own hands, and now I have to do all my work." Elsewhere, a young girl did not know how to comb her own hair, and a matron cried at night because no slaves were available to wash her feet.

There were success stories as well. Some women discovered new strengths and talents in coping with the hardships of daily life. Four months after the war ended, a Virginia woman wrote in her diary: "I little thought this time twenty-one years ago when I was putting on my white satin slippers that I should ever cook a dinner for myself, and now I do it every day, & am as happy in these new circumstances as ever before." During the postwar years, Ella Gertrude Thomas of Georgia gradually became the main breadwinner in her family. As her husband sank into despair and gambled away the family's small savings in bad investments, Ella took up teaching and wrote a newspaper column. While her husband's health and hopes ebbed and their savings dwindled, she marshaled new inner resources to keep the family going. "I think and think boldly," she wrote in her journal. "I act— and act boldly."

Confederate men who were once powerful and wealthy, as well as poor and middle-class farmers, scrambled to find whatever work they could. One formerly wealthy planter peddled flowers, another sold tea and molasses to his former slaves, and a former general caught fish and oysters and sold them at market. Like women, men were also forced to lower their sights and do work that, in better times, would have been beneath them.

For Southerners, the war did bring one welcome result—the spread of public education throughout the region. Before the war, public schooling was not available in many Southern communities, and the schools that did exist were usually inadequate. After the war, newly drafted state constitutions provided for a system of public education. As Southerners began to acknowledge the necessity of public education in rebuilding their economy, another form of employment opened up to women: teaching. Upper-class women in particular—"members of the most elegant and cultivated families in the State," according to one school official—flocked to this occupation.

Women seized whatever opportunities they could to teach. Sophie Bell Wright, a young woman from New Orleans, opened a school around her mother's dining room table. Twenty students each paid fifty cents a month. Later she taught mathematics to help pay her way through teacher-training school. In 1894 she opened a night school for working men and boys who were too poor to pay for an education. By 1903 fifteen hundred students were enrolled in the night school. Teaching offered fulfillment and professional advancement, but it was hard work—especially when pupils were unruly and resistant to learning and represented all levels of ability. In addition, many parents were too poor to pay the full tuition. One teacher was forced to reduce her tuition from $12 a month per student to $1.50 a month for poor students.

African-American women also taught. Black communities throughout the South chose representatives, or trustees as they were called, to work with the Freedmen's Bureau in establishing schools for former slaves, both children and adults. Although white men and women journeyed South to educate the former slaves, free blacks from the North felt a special obligation to assist their Southern brethren. For African Americans in the postwar South, teaching or getting an education amounted to an act of courage. White Southerners feared that an educated black population would be "uppity," and they resorted to violence to frighten African Americans away from the schoolroom.

But many would not be frightened away. By 1869 9,000 teachers had been recruited to instruct the former slaves, and 600,000 African Americans of all ages were enrolled in elementary schools. In addition, four universities had been established to train black teachers: Howard University in Washington, D.C.; Hampton Institute in Hampton, Virginia; Morehouse College in Atlanta, Georgia; and Fisk University in Nashville, Tennessee. Besides land, the one other opportunity that most former slaves craved was an education. "The colored people are far more zealous in the cause of education than the whites," wrote an agent of the North Carolina Freedmen's Bureau in 1866. "They will starve themselves, and go without clothes, in order to send their children to school."

Teaching former slaves was a formidable challenge. Like white teachers, black teachers of former slaves had little equipment to work with, and they were forced to devise ways to educate students who lacked even the most basic skills. Most students, including adults, did not know how to read or write because laws in the prewar South had prohibited the education of slaves. Teachers drew reading lessons from the Bible and taught their students to memorize biblical passages that instilled the message of equality. Many of them used up their low salaries—about ten dollars a month—to buy school supplies and assist destitute students.

To make matters worse, their own lives were constantly endangered by violent groups who opposed their efforts. Edmonia Highgate left New Orleans, Louisiana, after white rioters attacked black and white delegates to a constitutional convention to readmit Louisiana into the Union. She moved to a country parish two hundred miles away, hoping to find a safe haven, but violence overshadowed her life there as well. Ruffians shot at her school and students and threatened to burn down both the school and the home in which she boarded. Yet she was determined to stay: "I trust fearlessly in God and am safe," she wrote in a letter. Many teachers were not so confident. They eventually gave up and went back North, overwhelmed by the task and the dangers inherent in their work. But a few teachers felt challenged and profoundly rewarded by their work—even "blessed in the effort," as one dedicated black woman teacher claimed.

Reconstruction brought citizenship to all freed African Americans and the right to vote to African-American men, but it also brought a fierce backlash against these developments—the rise of the Ku Klux Klan. Shortly after the war ended, several leading white Southern men gathered at a hotel in Nashville, Tennessee. There they drew up a constitution for "an institution of Chivalry, Humanity, Mercy, and Patriotism," and stated as their main purpose "the maintenance of the supremacy of the white race." The Ku Klux Klan, as this "institution" was called, was one of several racist groups that sprang up to preserve the political and economic power of white Southerners who were alarmed by the prospect that blacks would vote, prosper economically, demand equal rights, or take any other actions that threatened the political and economic dominance of whites. Other groups included the Knights of the White Camelia, the White Brotherhood, the Society of the Pale Faces, and the White League.

But the Ku Klux Klan, or KKK, struck the greatest terror among black Southerners. Dressed in long white gowns with pointed hoods to disguise their true identities, Klan members rode through the countryside at night spreading terror. In their quest for "humanity" and "mercy," they committed murder, pillaged and burned people's homes, and raped and brutalized innocent black women. The Klan's membership included professional men, such as doctors and lawyers, as well as merchants and poor farmers. From 1868 to 1871, the KKK's membership grew, and its members committed crimes without fear of prosecution. Finally, in 1871, Congress passed a law that imposed fines and imprisonment for "those who go in disguise" to violate other people's "equal protection of the laws."

Although most of the Klan's victims were black men and whites who were willing to share power with blacks, some black women were also targets. Other black women had to stand by helplessly watching as the Klan tortured or killed their husbands. In the early 1870s, many women testified at a congressional inquiry conducted in the South, and their testimony was dramatic and poignant. One black woman, whose husband had been elected constable, an official responsible for maintaining public law and order, testified that the Klan forced her and her children to "wrap our heads up in bed-quilts and come out of the house, and they then set it on fire, burning it up, and my husband in it, and all we had."

Other women told of being beaten when the Klan could not find their husbands, who were the real targets. Still other women were beaten simply for acting "uppity" or for rejecting sexual advances by white men. Hannah Tutson of Clay County, Florida, was whipped from "the crown of my head to the soles of my feet" merely because she and her husband, Samuel, had worked hard and acquired a large parcel of land. In the early years of Reconstruction, the terror of the Ku Klux Klan threatened the already precarious lives of free African-American women and men throughout the South.

The postwar years set the stage for important advances in American women's lives, although many men—and women—continued to define women's role primarily as that of wife and mother. But the times were changing. The fiery trial through which the nation had passed would spark in many women greater recognition of their talents and abilities and fan their desire to lead more active and visible public lives.

Women Fight for Their Rights

After the Civil War ended, American women had battles to wage on other fronts—for the right to vote, to attend college, and to gain greater control over their lives. As Ernestine Rose, a leader in the women's rights movement, once proclaimed, "Freedom, my friends, does not come from the clouds, like a meteor. . . . It does not come without great efforts and great sacrifices; all who love liberty have to labor for it." In the afterglow of victory for the Union and peace for the entire nation, she and other champions of women's rights forged ahead, ready to labor for their freedom. From their battles emerged many new ideas for achieving social and political equality for women.

During the war, leaders of the women's rights movement, such as Elizabeth Cady Stanton and Susan B. Anthony, had shifted their efforts from fighting for women's political and economic rights to campaigning for the abolition of slavery. Now that slavery had been abolished, they confidently expected fellow abolitionists to work for women's right to vote. But they would be sadly disillusioned—a long, hard struggle for woman suffrage lay ahead. Their disillusionment was even more keen because the origins of the postwar women's rights movement lay in the prewar abolition movement, and the two movements had been closely linked for thirty years.

After the Civil War, leaders of the women's rights movement looked to a new source for inspiration: the United States Constitution. They adopted the very same rationale for female suffrage used by proponents of suffrage for African Americans—that the right to vote was the individual's right as a citizen and provided the foundation for democratic government, which the North had just fought to protect in the Civil War. In the immediate post–Civil War years, women's rights leaders maintained that voting was a basic right shared by all citizens, men and women, white and black. Ernestine Rose declared, "Human beings are men and women, possessed of human faculties, and understanding, which we call mind; and mind recognizes no sex, therefore the term 'male,' as applied to human beings—to citizens—ought to be expunged from the Constitution and laws as a last remnant of barbarism."

To achieve this goal, Stanton, Anthony, Antoinette Brown Blackwell, Lucy Stone, and other suffrage fighters established the American Equal Rights Association in 1865 to campaign for both black and female suffrage. Lucretia Mott was elected president, Stanton served as first vice president, and Anthony became corresponding secretary. The creation of this organization was a milestone in the struggle for female equality; it was the first organization formed by American women and men to fight for the right to vote.

Divisions soon emerged within the American Equal Rights Association over the best way to achieve suffrage for all Americans. Some members were willing to support the Republican party's strategy of working first to enfranchise black men—that is, grant them the right to vote—while postponing efforts to enfranchise women until they had achieved their first goal. In contrast, other members continued to support efforts to enfranchise both African-American men and all women. The first major conflict between proponents of black male suffrage and proponents of suffrage for all Americans erupted in 1867 in Kansas. There, two proposals—one that granted female suffrage and one that provided for black male suffrage—came to a vote. Stanton and Anthony campaigned for both, but two of their political partners—Lucy Stone and Henry Blackwell, prominent activists in the prewar abolition movement—supported Republican abolitionists whose first priority was black male suffrage.

Stanton and Anthony were astonished that their fellow reformers would abandon the fight for female suffrage. For their part, Stone and Blackwell were unwilling to divert popular support for black male suffrage. They feared that supporting female enfranchisement would undermine any public support for black male suffrage. As it turned out, both proposals were defeated.

The fight for suffrage for all Americans suffered another blow with the ratification of the 14th Amendment to the Constitution on July 9, 1868. This amendment shattered the common basis of female and black suffrage—natural rights—by affirming black men's status and rights as American citizens while remaining silent about the citizenship rights of women. It did this by introducing into the Constitution the distinction of gender and penalizing states for denying to any of their "male inhabitants" the right to vote. It was the "Negro's hour," insisted former abolitionists—the freedman needed the ballot to protect him from physical harm and political injustice. When women were "dragged from their houses and hung upon lamp-posts" like black men, declared the great orator and former slave Frederick Douglass, then they, too, would need the ballot's protection as much as black men did.

On February 3, 1870, nearly three years after the 14th Amendment was passed, the 15th Amendment was ratified, making women's political invisibility complete. It prohibited states from denying to citizens the right to vote "on account of race, color, or previous condition of servitude" but remained silent about gender prohibitions. In effect, both the 14th and 15th Amendments excluded women from the fundamental right of citizenship—voting.

But the growing division within the women's rights movement and the blow dealt to woman suffrage by the 14th and 15th Amendments did not discourage African-American women from supporting female equality. Sojourner Truth pointedly reminded audiences of black women's need for equal political rights. She claimed that slavery had been only partly abolished because black women did not share the same rights as black men. But she wanted slavery destroyed "root and branch. Then we will all be free indeed."

Other prominent African-American women shared Truth's views. Mary Ann Shadd Cary, a teacher and one of the first women lawyers in the United States, joined the Universal Franchise Association, a suffrage organization composed of both black and white members in Washington, D.C., and represented it at conventions of African-American organizations. Along with other members of the Universal Franchise Association, she addressed the House Judiciary Committee of the U.S. Congress on behalf of woman suffrage. She also helped to organize the Colored Woman's Progressive Franchise Association, a group that set out to challenge the assumption that "men only may conduct industrial and other things." The association hoped to establish newspapers, banks, cooperative stores, and a printing press, all owned and operated by women.

Frances Ellen Watkins Harper was also an outspoken supporter of women's rights. In the following excerpt from her poem "Dialogue on Woman's Rights," she explained why black men should support woman suffrage:

> Some thought that it would never do
> For us in Southern lands,
> To change the fetters on our wrists
> For the ballot in our hands.
> Now if you don't believe 'twas right
> To crowd us from the track
> How can you push your wife aside
> And try to hold her back?

By the late 1860s, Elizabeth Cady Stanton had adopted a new strategy in fighting for female suffrage. Like Sojourner Truth, she no longer emphasized women's common humanity with men and therefore women's common right to suffrage. Instead, she drew on the decades-old arguments that celebrated women's unique intellectual, emotional, and moral qualities to argue that women were *different* from men, and for that reason they were particularly worthy and needful of having the right to vote. In an address to a women's rights convention, she proclaimed, "There is sex in the spiritual as well as the physical and what we need today in government, in the world of morals and thought, is the recognition of the feminine element, as it is this alone that can hold the masculine in check."

Throughout American history, this celebration of women's unique qualities has helped to expand women's influence beyond the home and into the community. Although women were prohibited from voting, serving as legislators, and fighting for the defense of liberty because of their sex, they were obligated to raise liberty-loving sons who dutifully discharged these tasks of citizenship.

In the antebellum years of the 1830s, women had used the same argument to create more visible roles for themselves: As pious, virtuous, and kindly maternal figures, they were obligated not only to raise patriotic sons but to devote themselves to the public good—to extend a helping hand to widows, orphans, "fallen women," and others in need of their excellent influence. Middle-class women had organized or joined charitable societies to spread the moral standards of the home throughout the community. Now, in the post–Civil War era, Stanton and others once again elevated women's "feminine element" into a virtue that would protect the nation's moral life.

Stanton claimed that voting was both a basic right and the most effective way for women to exert their moral influence. In 1868 she and Susan B. Anthony established their own newspaper, the *Revolution,* to promote their campaign for women's rights. In a letter to Anthony, Stanton explained the significance of the newspaper's name and offered her vision of the struggle ahead: "The establishing of woman on her rightful throne is the greatest revolution the world has ever known or will know," she declared. "A journal called the *Rosebud* might answer for those who come with kid gloves and perfumes to lay immortal wreaths on the monuments which in sweat and tears others have hewn and built; but for us . . . there is no name like the *Revolution.*" The motto on the *Revolution*'s masthead read: "Men, their rights and nothing more; women, their rights and nothing less." Anthony managed the office, handled the bookkeeping and bills, and hired the typesetters and printers, while Stanton served as senior editor and primary writer.

Although it lasted for only two and a half years, the weekly newspaper became a mouthpiece for some of the most prominent, creative, and uncompromising members of the women's rights movement. Matilda Joslyn Gage, Paulina Wright Davis, and Ernestine Rose—all highly dedicated and visionary leaders for women's rights—were regular correspondents. More important, the paper, under Stanton's direction, dealt with controversial issues that other papers and forums only touched upon gingerly. Abortion, regulation of prostitution, divorce, and prison reform—all were discussed openly in the *Revolution*'s pages as reasons why women needed political power.

Nor did the paper shrink from condemning the "degrading" legal position of married women and disputing the traditional view of marriage as sacred and indissoluble. Stanton advocated more liberal divorce laws and better legal protection for married women and concluded that giving women the vote would help to rectify married women's legal inequities. The *Revolution* steadily focused the women's rights movement on the need for female suffrage, especially at a time when other reformers supported suffrage only for black men. The newspaper also linked female suffrage to dramatic and controversial reforms for women—reforms that more conservative factions of the movement were unwilling to champion.

The *Revolution* broke other new ground by reaching out to working-class women, whom the women's rights movement had previously ignored. Anthony, in particular, set out to capture working-class women's support. In September 1868, she helped to organize the Working Woman's Association "for the purpose of doing everything possible to elevate women, and raise the value of their labor." The *Revolution* reported on all proceedings of the Working Woman's Association, and Stanton and Anthony established a column entitled "The Working Woman" to highlight issues and events of concern to working-class women. They did not shy away from advocating policies that were highly unpopular, including equal pay for equal work and access to jobs traditionally reserved for men—goals that today's working women are still struggling to achieve.

Meanwhile, the conflict between those who supported women's immediate enfranchisement and those who chose to work for black male suffrage first and woman suffrage later on turned into a bitter schism. By 1869 two organizations had emerged with differing visions and strategies. In May 1869 Stanton and Anthony founded the National Woman Suffrage Association (NWSA). This group refused to support the 15th Amendment—the amendment granting black male suffrage—unless it also enfranchised all women. NWSA members lobbied on a national level for a constitutional amendment to enfranchise women in all states.

In contrast, the American Woman Suffrage Association (AWSA), which was founded by Lucy Stone and Henry Blackwell in November 1869, supported passage of the 15th Amendment. Rather than seek a constitutional amendment to give women the ballot, members of AWSA appealed to individual state legislatures to pass state laws granting female enfranchisement. Members of AWSA published their views in their own newspaper, the *Woman's Journal*. Like its parent organization, the *Woman's Journal* spoke to a more conservative and narrow vision of women's rights. It tried to cultivate the support of conservative middle-class readers by linking suffrage to middle-class benefits, such as higher education for women, professional advancement, and protection of married women's earnings and property from their husbands.

The *Woman's Journal* also avoided discussion of controversial issues, such as abortion and prostitution. It took a chattier, more compromising tone than the *Revolution* and focused strictly on suffrage news—debates, speeches, conventions, and political platforms favoring suffrage. Despite financial reverses and frequent staff changes, the *Woman's Journal* outlasted its rival, the *Revolution*, and eventually became the main organ of the women's rights movement. Lucy Stone was its chief editor, and former abolitionists William Lloyd Garrison, Henry Blackwell, T. H. Higginson, and Julia Ward Howe served as assistant editors.

For twenty years, NWSA and AWSA pursued their separate goals, holding conventions, sponsoring debates, and sending speakers out on the lecture circuit. In 1887 Alice Stone Blackwell, daughter of Lucy Stone and Henry Blackwell, launched a campaign to merge the two organizations. Three years later, in February 1890, the

WOMEN VOTE
FOR
PRESIDENT
And for All Other Officers in All Elections on the Same Terms as Men in
Wyoming, Colorado, Utah and Idaho
WHY NOT IN NEBRASKA?

The women of Nebraska campaigned hard for the right to vote but did not receive it until the 19th Amendment to the Constitution was ratified on August 18, 1920.

two associations joined hands to become the National American Woman Suffrage Association (NAWSA). Elizabeth Cady Stanton served as the first president of NAWSA until 1892, when she withdrew from active involvement in organized suffrage efforts. When Stanton died in 1902, the women's rights movement lost one of its most original and uncompromising voices. Anthony followed her into the presidency of the National American Woman Suffrage Association and remained at its helm until 1904. She died two years later. Although she was more cautious than Stanton in her thinking, Anthony was a courageous and tireless fighter for female equality.

American women had not yet received the constitutional right to vote, but in the two decades between the founding of the National Woman Suffrage Association and the American Woman Suffrage Association in 1869 and their merger into the National American Woman Suffrage Association in 1890, the cause of female suffrage achieved important successes, especially in the West. The first victory for woman suffrage in the United States occurred in the Wyoming Territory, a sparsely settled region with few political traditions in place. The conditions of this region—the absence of long-standing political traditions and greater frontier opportunities for women—proved fertile ground for voting rights for women. In 1870 the tiny legislature in Wyoming passed a female enfranchisement bill, and the governor, John A. Campbell, who some years earlier had watched women conduct a women's rights convention in Salem, Oregon, signed it.

The neighboring territory of Utah followed suit in 1870. Most of Utah's settlers were Mormon. Although women held no important positions in the church hierarchy, they played an active role in community and church life. Church leaders encouraged women to serve as nurses and midwives, and some women even went to medical school. Mormon women also attended church meetings and voted on church matters, taught the younger children in their settlements, raised money for the church, and educated themselves about government, history, and parliamentary law. The Mormon community's acceptance of women's public responsibilities no doubt contributed to winning female suffrage in Utah.

In the Northwest—the region now comprising Oregon and Washington—Abigail Scott Duniway, a brave and feisty woman, led the fight for woman suffrage. In 1852, at the age of seventeen, she journeyed with her family by wagon train to the Oregon Territory. There she married and raised five children and discovered firsthand what it meant to toil long hours for no wages. She also discovered that even though wives had no legal rights, a wife was responsible for any financial obligations undertaken by her husband. When Duniway's husband became disabled in an accident, she was forced to pay his debts.

By the age of thirty-six, Duniway was ready to dedicate her life to woman suffrage. She established her own newspaper, the *New Northwest*, to convey her ideas and provide a forum for suffrage events out West. She also wrote and published vivid accounts of her travels throughout the Northwest. Duniway crisscrossed the region to give speeches and help organize suffrage events.

Duniway also clashed with East Coast suffrage leaders. She staunchly rejected their strategy of portraying women as morally superior to men in order to win public approval for female suffrage. She argued that this strategy perpetuated women's unequal political and economic status by sentimentalizing them. Instead, she urged, suffrage was the way to end the sexual and economic exploitation of women and give women a measure of control over their lives. Like Stanton, Abigail Scott Duniway was a clear-eyed, tough-minded, and dedicated suffrage leader whose unorthodox views did not always sit well with her more conservative suffrage sisters.

Southerners were even more resistant to women's rights. Because many early suffrage advocates had also been abolitionists, some Southerners regarded the movement as "a heresy that has a real devil in it," according to one suffrage worker traveling in Mississippi. Still, there were pockets of support for female suffrage throughout the South. Some Southern women joined the American Equal Rights Association, and in 1869 suffrage resolutions were offered at constitutional conventions in Texas and Arkansas, two former Confederate states applying for readmission into the Union. Although the resolutions did not pass, suffrage leaders were heartened that they had at least been introduced.

Southern women increasingly demanded their rights more forcefully. In 1871 a Virginia woman was turned away from the ballot box. Unimpressed, she ceremoniously dropped a slip of paper into the box to assert her right to vote. But elsewhere in the former Confederacy, old "chivalrous" notions about gallant men and weak women died hard. "We do not need the ballot in Louisiana to protect any of our just rights and privileges," insisted one woman. "Every Southern woman has a protection and champion in every Southern man."

Although suffrage was the cornerstone of American women's campaign for political, social, and economic equality, it was not the only cause for which they fought. Suffrage fighters also envisioned ways to create more fulfilling lives for women. Antoinette Brown Blackwell challenged the traditional notion that women's destiny lay in full-time homemaking. She praised the value of homemaking but urged women to seek employment outside of the home. "Women need a purpose," she declared, "a definite pursuit in which they are interested, if they expect to gather from it tone and vigor, either of mind or body."

Blackwell exhorted women to embark upon all endeavors—"industries, science, art, religion, and into the conduct and government of the State." So that women would not be overwhelmed by both household responsibilities and workplace obligations, she urged husbands to share housework and neighbors to share childcare responsibilities. She suggested that workers share jobs, such as carpentry and blacksmithing, so they could experience greater variety in their daily lives.

The sisters Victoria Woodhull and Tennessee Claflin, who ran a stock brokerage in New York in the early 1870s, were satirized in this 1870 newspaper cartoon, entitled "The Bulls & Bears of Wall Street."

Blackwell not only envisioned social and political equality for women but also desired to bring about a more humane social order in which both men and women could lead joyous, productive lives.

After the Civil War, some crusaders for women's equality resumed the attack on confining clothes. In 1871 Tennessee C. Claflin, an outspoken and controversial advocate of women's rights, proclaimed dress reform to be "one of the most important Humanitarian movements of the age"—indeed, perhaps as important as the crusade for woman suffrage. She condemned current fashions for endangering women's health and that of the children they bore and for contributing to the image of women as sexual objects who dressed only for men's pleasure. Claflin urged women to cast off these life-threatening garments and dress for their own comfort, health, and pleasure.

Her sister, Victoria Woodhull, urged women to cast off not only confining clothing but also confining marriages. Woodhull was a proponent of free love, a movement that challenged the power and authority of organized religion and wanted to abolish the institution of marriage because it stifled true love. Woodhull based her idea of free love on her view that the Constitution protected women's individual rights. Both women and men had the inalienable right to begin or end any intimate relationship, including marriage, because they were free and independent individuals. "I have an *inalienable, constitutional* and *natural* right to love whom I may . . . to *change* that love every *day* if I please," she declared.

Woodhull's opinions caused the women's rights movement acute embarrassment because free lovers were lambasted in the popular press for their radical views. Woodhull herself earned the dubious title of "Mrs. Satan" and "Queen of Prostitutes." But the public's disapproval did not discourage her and Claflin from publishing *Woodhull & Claflin's Weekly*, the journal in which they espoused their controversial beliefs on free love, legalized prostitution, dress reform, and world government.

Woodhull was a fiery orator with a fiery message. In 1871 she addressed a meeting of the National Woman Suffrage Association, declaring, "We mean treason; we mean secession. . . . We are plotting revolution; we will . . . [overthrow] this bogus Republic and plant a government of righteousness in its stead." A year later, she made good on her words by running for President of the United States as a candidate of the newly organized Equal Rights party. Personal problems and scandals, along with the disapproval of her ideas among more conservative suffrage leaders, isolated Woodhull. She and her sister spent their last years in London, where Woodhull continued to lecture and espouse controversial views. She was a brilliant, provocative woman who was far ahead of her time.

The late-nineteenth-century women's rights movement included many such extraordinary and controversial fighters. In the 1870s and 1880s, Spiritualism provided some of the most effective speakers to promote female suffrage and other progressive ideas of the women's rights movement. Suffrage leaders in California relied greatly on Spiritualists and trance speakers in 1870 and dispatched three women mediums to present the first woman suffrage petition to the California state legislature. In Connecticut, New Jersey, Indiana, New York, and Michigan, mediums also played an active role in state suffrage campaigns. They were polished speakers who skillfully appealed to a moral authority higher than the power of the state; but they did so as moral guides themselves, not merely as vehicles for the spirits' ideas.

Despite the efforts of scores of individuals and suffrage groups, many years would pass before women won a constitutional amendment granting them the right to vote. In other respects, some women gained greater control over their lives, usually by becoming economically independent or by enjoying more equality and autonomy within their marriages, an accomplishment that the Spiritualists and others championed. In general, however, women failed to achieve many of the reforms that women's rights supporters called for.

One arena in which women *did* make significant strides, however, was in their ability to get a college education. Women had greater opportunity during the twenty-five years following the Civil War to pursue an education and attain eco-

For a geology field trip at Smith College in Massachusetts in the 1880s, the students sported stylish hats and brought along wicker picnic hampers.

nomic independence and professional fulfillment than ever before. Between 1870 and 1900, the number of women college students throughout the country increased eightfold, from 11,000 in 1870 to 85,000 in 1900. In 1870 women constituted 21 percent of the college population. By 1900 they represented 35 percent. The postwar need for more teachers and for women who were able to step into positions left vacant by men lost in war contributed to this growing influx of female students. Moreover, women who had lost husbands or fiancés in the war now faced the daunting task of supporting themselves. To do that, they often needed more education. Other women, especially from middle-class families, simply thought that an education was their birthright.

Women could take two pathways toward a formal education. They could choose the less expensive teacher-training and business schools, or they could attend four-year colleges. Although coeducation for women and men became more acceptable by the 1870s, many parents preferred to send their daughters to all-female schools. After the war, newly established women's colleges thrived. In 1865 Vassar College in New York State was established. Ten years later, in 1875, Smith College and

Wellesley College, both in Massachusetts, welcomed their first classes. And in 1884 Bryn Mawr in Pennsylvania opened its doors. In the South, the Women's College of Baltimore, now Goucher, opened in 1884. Although professing to train women to be good "Christian" wives and mothers, these schools also offered young women a rigorous academic education in a supportive setting. Their creation was a critical milestone along the path of women's access to higher education.

The elite men's schools—Harvard, Yale, Princeton, and Columbia—still resisted admitting women. In 1874 Harvard faculty began to offer examinations but no instruction to women. A few years later, they instituted a comprehensive academic curriculum without granting degrees. Finally, in 1894, the Harvard Annex, as it was called, was chartered as Radcliffe College, with the power to grant academic degrees. Similarly, at Columbia, women took examinations from the college's professors, though they were not allowed to attend lectures. They protested, and Barnard College, the female affiliate of Columbia, opened in 1889. Other all-male colleges also established separate colleges for women to avoid admitting women into their schools.

In addition to the women's colleges, a few private and state universities began to admit women. These included Boston University, a private college established in 1873 that was coeducational from the start, and several state universities. The University of Iowa had begun to admit women in 1855, and other state universities followed suit. The Universities of Kansas, Indiana, and Minnesota began admitting women in 1869, and state universities in Missouri, Michigan, and California followed a year later. Public universities in the South were more resistant, and many did not admit women until the early twentieth century.

College administrators and educators put forth a variety of reasons to justify excluding women students. Among the most persuasive arguments in its time was the idea that a college education could damage a woman's ability to bear children. Dr. Edward Clarke, a retired Harvard Medical School professor, was a chief proponent of this theory. He argued that women needed to save their "limited energy" for childbearing. If they used it up by studying, they would, in his words, damage their "female apparatus." In 1873 he set forth his ideas in his widely read book, *Sex in Education.* In 1885, however, a survey of coeducational institutions highlighted the positive effects of coeducation on both male and female students. Despite Clarke and his followers, higher education for women was here to stay.

American women would not gain the constitutional right to vote until 1920, when the 19th Amendment to the Constitution granted female enfranchisement. In 1890 this constitutional right was not yet in view. But women had asserted their claim to equal social and political rights and had organized a movement complete with competing organizations and strategies. They had gained crucial political and organizational skills, and many had found their life's work as speakers or writers for female suffrage and equality. By 1890, when the National Woman Suffrage

Association and the American Woman Suffrage Association merged into the National American Woman Suffrage Association, there was no turning back to the days when women devoted their time to doing genteel good works, paid their taxes, or signed away their legal rights in marriage while silently bemoaning their lack of political power. As women waged the struggle to vote and to take greater control of their lives, they had other battles to fight as well—on the job, in their communities, and in defense of new visions of women's lives.

New Employment Opportunities

When the guns of battle were silenced at the end of the Civil War, another kind of roar could be heard—that of the mighty engines of industrial production as the reunited nation entered a period of unprecedented industrial growth. Iron, steel, textiles, lumber, meat packing, flour milling—these were just a few of the industries that mushroomed after the war. They relied on new forms of mass production and, in the process, transformed the artisan, craftlike nature of many occupations into industries that relied on new technology and assembly lines, factories full of workers performing one task over and over.

In Paterson, New Jersey, for example, four silk mills employed 590 workers before the war. Soon after the war, ten more mills sprang up, and 8,000 workers operated the mills. The one machine shop that had employed ten workers before the Civil War employed 1,100 a few years later. And Paterson itself grew from a small town of 11,000 to a city of 33,000. Throughout the country, other towns and villages were undergoing equally rapid growth. Most of this growth took place in the North because the South was still recuperating from the devastation of war. Between 1860 to 1870, the total number of manufacturing companies in the North alone increased by 80 percent.

The expansion of the railroad system helped to knit the country together and enabled goods to travel from one area to another. On May 10, 1869, the finishing touches of a transcontinental railroad system were put in place. At Promontory Point, Utah, the Union Pacific Railroad, originating in Council Bluffs, Iowa, and the Central Pacific Railroad, whose starting point was in California, met as the last spike was nailed down. With this latest engineering feat, businesses were able to find newly accessible markets for their goods.

Although the poet Walt Whitman decried the "depravity of the business classes of our country" and Mark Twain, the renowned satirist, pronounced the country's political and commercial methods bankrupt, other public figures praised the nation's feverish rush to get rich. Throughout the 1870s and 1880s, a Baptist minister, Russell H. Conwell, traveled around the country preaching the gospel of wealth. "I say that you ought to get rich," he exhorted audiences. "It is all wrong to be poor." Such sentiments encouraged a growing social and economic gulf between the rich and poor. With the emergence of big business came the concentration of

In the mid-nineteenth century, urban women began to find work in offices. Women employees of the U.S. Treasury Department printed certificates for bonds that helped finance the Civil War.

great wealth in the hands of a very few. In 1884 a newspaper reporter described the grand setting of a banquet at Delmonico's, a fashionable New York restaurant: "The room was festooned with flowers in every direction. . . . And then the feast! All the dishes which ingenuity could invent or the history of past extravagance suggest were spread before the guests." In wide-eyed delight, the reporter went on to describe the costly wines served. Elsewhere in the nation, another New York paper reported that same year, 150,000 people were out of work, while another 150,000 earned less than sixty cents a day—many of them young women working eleven to sixteen hours a day. During that year, 1884, 23,000 families were evicted from their homes because they were unable to pay the rent.

To be sure, the country's industrial growth had begun even before the war. And the war itself gave a giant boost to the nation's industrial life. Old factories were retooled and new ones were built to produce weapons, ammunition, machinery, clothing, ships, and canned goods. This expansion in industrial production provided new jobs for both men and women. During the war, women from the North, where most of the industrial production took place, found work replacing men who had gone to war. In the following two decades, women continued to seek new forms of employment. They were forced, however, to protect themselves against efforts to give their jobs to returning soldiers or restrict them from entering new occupations. The postwar era was a time of opportunity for women seeking work, but along with the opportunities came new resistance to women as wage earners.

After the war, more young women lived and worked away from their families. Rural women, in particular, migrated to the country's urban industrial centers in search of work. Rural areas offered few ways to earn a livelihood, and opportunities to grow and experience the world seemed far more limited on the farm. Single young women migrated at a greater rate and earlier age than single men to seek work in the cities. On the average, single urban women were eighteen years old while men were twenty.

Although cities offered more employment opportunities, women's choice of occupations was limited primarily to jobs that men would not take or to work that seemed appropriate for women, according to the social standards of the day: work that duplicated women's domestic and caretaking role, such as teaching, nursing, sewing, and domestic service. Women with few skills and little or no education had even fewer choices. Factory work, waitressing, and domestic service were among their few options.

Many women preferred factory work because they regarded it as less demeaning than housework. Yet factory work was arduous. Although most female factory workers were employed in the garment industry, women also worked in factories that made boxes, artificial flowers, canned foods, and other products. For all factory workers the hours were long—anywhere from ten to twelvehours a day—and the loud clack-clack-clack of machines echoed in their ears as they sat hunched over their work for wages of less than a dollar a day. One female garment worker from Brooklyn, New York, told a magazine reporter: "The machines go like mad all day, because the faster you work the more money you get. Sometimes in my haste I get my finger caught and the needle goes right through it. . . . I bind the finger up with a piece of cotton and go on working."

In 1869 sewing women in New York City who worked at home were paid four cents for each pair of undershorts they made. Although the sewing machine, which was invented in 1846, speeded up their work, they were still able to make only five pairs a day. This earned them twenty cents. On top of that, they had to pay for heat, light, and thread, reducing their final paychecks even more. At this time, the cheapest rooms in New York City cost about a dollar a week. Once they paid their rent, they had only a few cents left over for food, clothing, medicine, and transportation. As a result, many single women shared rooms and beds with other working women. Even with this arrangement, they barely had enough money left for food. In 1869 one experienced seamstress declared, "I have worked from dawn to sundown, not stopping to get one mouthful of food, for twenty-five cents. I have lived on one cracker a day when I could not find work, travelling from place to place in pursuit of it."

Twenty years later, the standard of living for urban factory women was no better. In the late 1880s, the urban woman worker was paid an average of $5.58 a week, in contrast to $7.50 to $8.00 a week for a male worker. A woman's salary could drop to $5.24 if she had missed work because of illness or because she was laid off during a slow period at the factory. Yet the average cost of supporting herself in a city was about $5.51 a week. Employers justified paying low wages to women by claiming that women were not supporting families and were working only for "pin money" to buy luxuries. But surveys of working women in the 1870s and 1880s found that most women who worked had no choice. Many supported themselves, and some contributed to family finances. In 1888 the United States Bureau of Labor reported that more than half of the working women surveyed, including women who lived at home, helped to support their families.

Besides a woman's skills, her class and ethnic background determined the work she could find. Starting in 1880, a large influx of immigrants from eastern and southern Europe migrated to the United States. Most came from Russia, Poland, Bohemia, and Italy. They often joined friends and relatives who had immigrated earlier and found jobs in the factories where they worked. Like native-born American women, immigrant women chose factory work over domestic service because it felt less demeaning. Rose Cohen, a Jewish immigrant from Russia, recalled in her autobiography how disappointed her mother was when Rose took a job as a domestic. "Is that what I have come to America for, that my children should become servants?" her mother lamented.

Most Jewish and Italian immigrant women in large cities worked in the garment industry and in artificial flower-making. Polish and Slavic women worked in the textile mills of New England and the South or in meat-packing and food-processing plants in the Midwest. Women from Bohemia who were skilled cigar makers worked as cigar rollers in their new country. Irish and Scandinavian women in the North and African-American women in the South occupied the bulk of domestic service positions.

Most white domestic servants were young and single and lived with the families for whom they worked, usually in a small back or attic room. They earned from two to five dollars for a workweek that was even longer than the sixty- to seventy-hour workweek of most female factory workers. They usually had one afternoon off a week and had to be available to their employers the rest of the time. One young woman servant claimed that her employer would "sit in her sitting-room on the second floor and ring for me twenty times a day to do little things, and she wanted me up till eleven to answer the bell." To make matters worse, "I had no place but the kitchen to see my friends."

African-American women also chose domestic work as a last resort. To them, the relationship between employer and servant was painfully reminiscent of the relationship between mistress and slave. Most black women in Southern cities, however, could find no work except domestic service. But black domestics usually refused to live in their employers' homes and instead worked strictly as day ser-vants. Cooks and maids earned between $4.00 to $8.00 a *month*, and nursemaids earned about $1.50 to $3.00. The workday generally lasted twelve to fourteen hours, at least six days a week. Black women with children had to leave their own children with family or neighbors or all alone.

Although a black woman might be hired as a cook, she could also find herself watering the garden, cleaning house, or running errands. Her title may have spec-ified a certain task, but her duties were as varied as her employer decided. Like white servants, she had to deal with impersonal and sometimes abusive behavior from her employer. She was variously called "cook," "girl," "Mammy," or by her first name, even by her employer's children.

In the South, mostly in Virginia, North and South Carolina, and parts of Ken-tucky and Tennessee, African-American women also worked in tobacco factories. Here, the worst jobs were reserved for them. These included sorting, stripping, stemming, and hanging the leaves—all tasks that required direct contact with the harsh tobacco leaves. Rehandlers, as workers who did this work were called, typi-cally worked five and a half days a week for nine months of steady work. In 1880 tobacco workers in North Carolina earned forty to eighty cents a day for a twelve-hour day. They toiled under terrible conditions: The workrooms were dim and sweltering because sunlight and fresh air were shut out for fear of drying out the tobacco. In some factories, the fetid odor of an overflowing toilet filled the airless rooms. Other black women took in laundry, and those who lived in coastal areas gathered and shucked oysters in factories. This work was as burdensome as tobac-co stripping; shuckers stood at work benches all day and either steamed or pried the shells open to dislodge the precious oysters inside. Their weekly wages averaged between five and six dollars.

Until the 1910s, when thousands of African Americans migrated to Northern cities in search of work, most American blacks continued to live in the rural South, mostly in the former slave Cotton Belt states. There, African-American women shared with husbands, brothers, and fathers the hardscrabble life of sharecropping. For most black sharecropping families, a single misfortune, such as a flood, drought, fire, or illness, could bring financial ruin. Most families lived a stone's throw from starvation.

Throughout the last two decades of the nineteenth century, black sharecroppers continued to live and work at the mercy of the white landlord. He could force them to buy their farm implements and household supplies from him at inflated prices and compel their children to work. William Pickens, the sixth of ten children in an Arkansas sharecropping family, recalled how their landlord in 1888 closed the neighborhood school to force the young people to work. "Very small children can be used to hoe and pick cotton," Pickens remembered, "and I have seen my older sisters drive a plow."

Besides helping out in the fields, the rural African-American woman often lent a helping hand to others—perhaps to a sister recuperating from a difficult pregnancy or to neighbors who needed her homemade herbal medicines. Her day usually began at four in the morning and ended long past midnight. Because she lacked the conveniences that middle-class urban women increasingly enjoyed—such as running water, gas for heat and light, and ready-made clothing—she had to collect firewood and fetch water, prepare meals from scratch, and sew all of her family's clothing, on top of helping out in the fields about twelve hours a day. As one mother of nine later told an interviewer, "I worked many hours after they [her husband and children] was in bed. Plenty of times I've been to bed at three and four o'clock and get up at five, the first one in the morning."

When they were not toiling in the fields, African-American women also took in laundry or sold homegrown produce or eggs from their hens. The saying "chickens for shoes" aptly described black women's desire to earn money from selling chickens and eggs to buy shoes for their children so they could attend school. Frances Ellen Watkins Harper observed that black mothers "are the levers which move in education. The men talk about it . . . but the women work most for it." They equated education with a better life and viewed their own toil as an investment in their children's future. Maude Lee Bryant, a sharecropping mother in Moncure, North Carolina, told an interviewer, "My main object of working was wanting the children to have a better way of living." She hoped that "the world might be just a little better because the Lord had me here for something, and I tried to make good out of it, that was my aim."

Parents seemed especially eager for their daughters to attend school. They knew that with an education their daughters could find work later on as teachers within the African-American community. From 1880 to 1915, more African-American girls than boys attended school, mainly because parents needed the labor of their sons in the fields. Even with an education, however, young black women had little hope of finding professional work outside of the African-American community. Schools and businesses in the white community refused to hire them.

In contrast, white women with more education or the means to pay for business courses found new employment opportunities in office work. In 1870 there were only 19,000 female office workers nationwide; by 1890 this number had multiplied to 75,000. In 1870 only 4.5 percent of office stenographers and typists were women. Ten years later, women held 40 percent of these positions.

Although the workday was long—usually about ten hours—the working conditions were more desirable and less hazardous than factory work, and salaries were relatively high. Moreover, the work was steady; unlike factory workers, office workers were seldom laid off during slow periods. In the 1870s, female office clerks who worked for the federal government could earn as much as nine hundred dollars a year. Although women government workers earned less than men holding equivalent government positions, government jobs paid more than other professional work for women. A female teacher, for example, earned only five hundred dollars a year.

Store clerking was another occupation that opened up to women. In 1870 10,000 women worked as sales clerks. By 1890 that number had grown tenfold, to 100,000. Although the prospect of working in an elegant department store appealed to some women, in reality the work was very arduous and wages were low—about five or six dollars a week. On this meager salary, employees had to pay for room and board and purchase more expensive clothing suitable for work. Saleswomen stood behind the counter for twelve or more hours a day. Until the 1890s, few stores permitted their saleswomen to sit down during business hours, and some clerks fainted from exhaustion. Like most companies that hired women to fill clerical and administrative positions, department stores hired no black women. Immigrant women who spoke fluent English without an accent were hired occasionally.

The post–Civil War era opened up new employment opportunities for women in nursing and teaching. Traditionally a job performed by women at home, nursing evolved into a profession after the Civil War, complete with professional training and accreditation. In 1873 Linda Richards became the first American woman to receive a degree in nursing. She graduated from Dr. Susan Dimock's nursing program at the New England Hospital for Women and Children in Boston, Massachusetts, and went on to teach at newly established nursing schools in New York, Boston, and Japan. She also founded several nursing programs. By the mid-1880s, twenty-two schools for nurses had opened in the United States.

African-American women had always ministered to their people's medical needs. In slavery they nursed sick or injured slaves and served as midwives and wet nurses to other enslaved women and to white mistresses. In freedom they continued to care for ailing members of their communities, using herbs and potions in their treatments. But in the postwar era, they faced obstacles if they wanted to acquire a formal nursing education—most white nursing schools refused to admit black students. One exception was the New England Hospital for Women and Children, which admitted one black student and one Jewish student each year. In 1879 one of its students, Mary Eliza Mahoney, became the first African-American woman to receive a nursing degree.

By 1892 black women could choose from nursing programs at four black colleges: Spelman College in Atlanta, Georgia; Dixie in Hampton, Virginia; Provident in Chicago, Illinois; and Tuskegee Institute in Tuskegee, Alabama. The training was rigorous. At Spelman, for example, graduates took oral examinations before an audience of local citizens and dignitaries. Students were quizzed by faculty and visitors alike and had to demonstrate proficiency in bathing an infant, changing bed linen with a patient in the bed, and preparing and serving meals. These examinations served two purposes: Educators regarded them as an accurate measure of a student's nursing skills and knowledge and as a way to showcase their black students' intelligence and ability before skeptical visitors.

After graduation most black nurses sought employment in private homes. Some went on to teach at other nursing and medical schools or joined the staffs of all-black hospitals. Black nurses also worked to improve public health within African-American communities, especially in the rural South. But nursing remained predominantly a white woman's occupation. In 1910 fewer than 3 percent of the trained nurses in the United States were black.

Besides nursing, teaching was the most acceptable profession for women. American women had taught since before the Civil War. But the enormous need to educate former slaves in the South, as well as to expand public schooling throughout the former Confederacy, created new opportunities for both Northern and Southern women to teach in the South. As immigrants flowed into the country during the 1880s and 1890s, Northern teachers also found plenty of opportunity to teach in the urban schools of the Northeast and Midwest. By the 1880s, two-thirds of the nation's public school teachers were women, and some women even moved up to the powerful position of school superintendent.

For African-American women in particular, imparting knowledge to a generation of black children who may have been born during slavery—when educating blacks was forbidden by many state constitutions—became a form of community service. Both Northern and Southern African-American teachers taught in segregated schools. They bravely coped with inadequate supplies, overcrowded classrooms, inferior buildings, and uncooperative white administrators—many of whom were deeply prejudiced. But the rewards outmatched the drawbacks of such work. The children were eager to learn—in Richmond, Virginia, alone 96.5 percent of all black children attended school in 1890—and teachers were keenly aware of their responsibility to promote the advancement of their race. Fannie Jackson Coppin, a teacher and principal in Philadelphia, was fond of saying that "knowledge is power." To her, education was the bootstrap by which African Americans would pull themselves up the social and economic ladder. She tried to break down all employment barriers against blacks by urging students from even the most impoverished and illiterate families to aim high—to be doctors or lawyers, engineers or authors, or teachers for their own people. Writing to Frederick Douglass in 1877, Coppin passionately described the purpose of an education: "I need not tell you, Mr. Douglass, that this is my desire to see my race lifted out of the mire of ignorance, weakness and degradation: no longer to be the fog end of the American rabble; to sit in obscure corners in public places and devour the scraps of knowledge which his superiors fling him. . . . I want to see him crowned with strength and dignity; adorned with the enduring grace of intellectual attainments."

Because nursing and teaching were considered natural extensions of women's maternal and caretaking nature, women who wanted to go into these professions faced far fewer obstacles than women who wanted to become doctors or lawyers, two professions reserved almost strictly for men. A handful of women doctors had gone into practice before the war and paved the way for women's entry into the medical field. These included the diminutive but formidable Harriot K. Hunt, who taught herself medicine before attending lectures at Harvard University, and

Elizabeth Blackwell, who was forced to go to Europe for her medical training. With her sister, Emily, Blackwell established the Woman's Medical College of the New York Infirmary for Women and Children.

By 1890 the University of Michigan had graduated 88 women doctors, the Woman's Medical College of the New York Infirmary had produced 135 women doctors, and the Women's College of Philadelphia had trained 560. In addition, hundreds of other women were beginning to enroll in medical school. Mary Putnam Jacobi, a doctor who taught at the Woman's Medical College in New York, explained why more women were entering the medical field: "Women have always worked," she observed. "But they demand now . . . a free choice in the kind of work, which, apart from the care of children, they may perform. The invasion of the medical profession is one of the more articulate forms of this demand." Hospitals balked at admitting female physicians to their staffs. As a result, the vast majority of female physicians went into private practice, where they continued to fight an uphill battle to attract patients, or joined the staffs of all-female hospitals.

If white female medical students and physicians faced resistance from a medical establishment rigidly dominated by men, then African-American women who aspired to be physicians encountered even more obstacles because of their skin color. But, undiscouraged, they forged ahead, establishing clinics and hospitals and serving the medical needs of their people. By 1890 115 African-American women doctors were practicing in the United States. One was Rebecca J. Cole, who graduated from the Female Medical College of Pennsylvania in 1867 and then worked with Elizabeth and Emily Blackwell at the New York Infirmary for Women and Children. Dr. Cole was a pioneer in practicing preventive medicine. She made house calls to tenement districts, where she taught basic hygiene and child care to women. She fought against overcrowded housing and became a formidable spokesperson for civil and economic rights for African Americans.

Like female physicians, women scientists and lawyers helped to dismantle the barricades against women's professional advancement. Astronomer Maria Mitchell, born in 1818, never attended college; instead, her father taught her astronomy. When she discovered a comet in 1847, she gained international acclaim. In 1865 she joined the faculty at the newly established Vassar College, an all-women's college. Over the next several decades she trained other female astronomers, including her successor at Vassar, Mary Watson Whitney.

In the eyes of the male-dominated legal profession, women who sought to become lawyers were indeed scorning their "womanly duties." In 1869 Arabella Babb Mansfield petitioned the Iowa bar and became the first American woman to be licensed to practice law. She had taught herself law, a common practice before the turn of the century, and passed the Iowa bar examination. Mansfield encountered little hostility to her admission to her state bar. Other women were not as lucky. Myra Bradwell of Chicago, organizer of her local chapter of the American Woman Suffrage Association and editor of a weekly legal journal, was refused

This advertisement for a lecture by Belva Lockwood trumpeted her as "The Great Washington Lawyer." Other advertisements also listed her more traditionally female accomplishments as "The Teacher and Lover of Children" and "The Untiring Friend of the Sick and the Poor."

admission to the Illinois bar because of her sex. She even appealed her case to the U.S. Supreme Court, but the Court also ruled against her. In 1872, however, while her case was still pending before the Supreme Court, the Illinois legislature passed a bill to admit women to the state bar, and she was admitted. Other similarly self-educated women challenged existing restrictions against admitting women to the bar and became lawyers. But until the late 1890s, most law schools still refused to admit women.

When Belva Lockwood applied to the law school at Columbian College, later George Washington University, she was rejected because, according to the admissions committee, she would "distract the attention of the young men." She attended one of the few law schools that did admit women, National University Law School, and graduated in 1873, only to be denied the right to practice before two higher courts, the Court of Claims and the U.S. Supreme Court. Lockwood fought this discrimination and lobbied for a bill to allow any woman lawyer to appear before the Supreme Court after she had practiced in the highest courts of her own state or territory for at least three years. Congress passed the statute in 1879, and Lockwood became the first woman lawyer to argue before the Supreme Court.

Lockwood made news in other ways as well. In 1872 she supported the presidential campaign of women's rights advocate Victoria Woodhull, and in 1884 Lockwood herself was nominated as a presidential candidate by a group of women in California who had organized themselves as the National Equal Rights party. Her platform advocated equal civil rights for women, African Americans, and Native Americans; temperance; standardized marriage and divorce laws throughout the country; and universal peace. She received 4,149 votes in six states. After running for President again in 1888, she resumed practicing law.

Black law schools were not above practicing sexual discrimination either. In 1869 Mary Ann Shadd Cary, teacher and suffrage fighter, was the first woman to enroll in Howard University's law school. She studied law for two years but withdrew when the school denied her a law degree because of her sex. By 1872, however, the school had changed its policy, and Charlotte E. Ray, who graduated from Howard that year, became the first African-American woman lawyer. Cary returned to Howard many years later and received her Bachelor of Laws degree in 1883. She spent the rest of her life practicing law in Washington, D.C.

In other ways as well, women were making their voices heard. The postwar era was an extraordinarily rich one for women speakers, writers, and artists. Women such as American Red Cross founder Clara Barton and Frances Ellen Watkins Harper went on the lecture circuit to recount their wartime experiences or endorse female enfranchisement. Barton gave hundreds of speeches and usually charged $100 to $150, though she gave veterans' groups a discount. Scores of other women published autobiographies and memoirs about the war. Between 1865 and 1914, more than a hundred books and even more articles about women's wartime exploits were published.

Women wrote about other subjects, too. Louisa May Alcott, born in 1832, is best known for her moralistic novel *Little Women*, which was published in 1868 and became an instant success. It glorified the traditional domestic ideal by portraying a cozy family of four sisters and their mother during the Civil War; faith, love, and hope pull them through difficult times. Alcott was a prolific writer who wrote several other novels for young readers and even tried her hand at some horror stories.

Emily Dickinson, born in 1830 in Amherst, Massachusetts, took inspiration from her beautiful surroundings for her lyrical nature poetry and her more brooding meditations in verse on love and life's transience. She penned more than seventeen hundred poems, but only two were published in her lifetime. As the years passed, she became ever more reclusive and avoided developing close friendships in person, although she conducted a lively correspondence by mail and refined her poetic sensibilities. Her poems were her "letter to the world," as she declared in one verse. After her death in 1886, her sister discovered Emily's poems, neatly bound in packets in her dresser drawer, and pleaded with friends to have them published.

Authors Helen Hunt Jackson (1830–1885) and Sarah Orne Jewett (1849–1909) sought inspiration for their writings in their connection with the land and the people who cultivated it. Like Dickinson, Jackson was born in Amherst, Massachusetts, but she lived for a few years in Colorado, where she learned firsthand about the injustices perpetrated against Native Americans. She confirmed her findings with further research in the New York Public Library. In 1881 she published *A Century of Dishonor*, a scathing indictment of government policy toward Indian tribes. At her own expense, she sent copies to numerous government officials and every member of Congress. Jackson undertook other fact-finding projects on behalf of Native Americans, then changed her creative focus to fiction. In 1884 she published *Ramona*, a historical novel about a Native-American woman in California. Though simplistic and sentimental, the novel focused public attention on the injustices borne by Native Americans. Jewett, chronicler of rural life in Maine, celebrated the quiet virtue and dignity of rural people. She tried to capture the texture of unremarkable, deeply rooted lives in fictional sketches and such novels as *Deephaven* (1877) and *The Country of the Pointed Firs* (1896). Her stories celebrated the land and captured a sense of place, illuminating as well the character of the people who lived there. Looking back, she described what she was trying to achieve in her writing: "I determined to teach the world that country people were not the awkward, ignorant set those persons seemed to think. I wanted the world to know their grand, simple lives."

Women also created other kinds of art. Edmonia Lewis, born in 1845 to an African-American father and Chippewa Indian mother, became a renowned sculptor in the 1860s and 1870s. Many of her works celebrated the emancipation of American slaves. *Hagar in the Wilderness*, completed in 1868, was a dramatic depiction of the biblical female slave. Lewis felt moved to undertake this work out of a "strong sympathy for all women who have struggled and suffered," as she put it. At the Centennial Exposition of 1876 in Philadelphia, which commemorated the hundredth anniversary of the Declaration of Independence, six of Lewis's sculptures were displayed.

Lilla Cabot Perry (1848–1933) and Mary Cassatt (1844–1926) both studied painting in France and were among the few women artists associated with Impressionism. Cassatt was the first American artist to show her work in an Impressionist exhibition. Unlike many other Impressionists, she depicted women and children in her work; her paintings portray gentle, loving moments between women and their young children. Both she and Perry knew the great master of French Impressionism, Claude Monet, and their paintings reveal the Impressionist's broad brush strokes, brilliant use of color and shading, and desire to paint the fleeting moment. Despite their talent, Cassatt, Perry, and other women artists faced many obstacles in gaining acceptance in a male-dominated vocation. More ornamental arts, such as painting china, were among the few socially approved ways for women to express their artistic talents. Women who wanted to be serious artists seldom had the financial resources and encouragement to achieve their goals. Many art schools would not even admit women students.

Women also tried their hand at inventing. American women had invented labor-saving devices since the early nineteenth century, but an outpouring of women's inventions—especially those that made domestic chores such as cooking, cleaning, and sewing easier—occurred in the postwar era. After four long years of war, with its discomforts and deprivations, women were eager to restore order and convenience to the domestic realm. Advances in tools, materials, and machinery enabled inventors to tinker with new possibilities for labor-saving devices.

In 1867 Margaret Knight of Massachusetts introduced a machine that made more durable paper bags. Helena Augusta Blanchard invented the first sewing machine that could sew complicated zigzag seams, and Amanda Theodosia Jones developed a method for canning and preserving fruit without first having to cook it. Other women devised undergarments made without bone or wire to allow women to move around more easily. Women inventors had a variety of motives for introducing their inventions. Some were shrewd businesswomen who realized their ingenuity could make money for them. Others, especially inventors of less confining corsets, hoped their inventions would enhance the quality of women's lives. They expressed a feminist desire to give women more freedom of movement and control over their lives—in this case, through less restrictive and more comfortable clothing. Women inventors demonstrated that women's creative and inventive abilities knew no bounds, and they proved that women were equally at home standing over a cookstove or drafting a blueprint of a new mechanical device.

"Women have always worked," declared Dr. Mary Putnam Jacobi. And indeed they have, but in the aftermath of the Civil War and during the nation's inexorable march toward industrial growth, women found growing opportunities to earn a living. However, America was not ready to grant women all of the opportunities for gainful employment and professional advancement that men enjoyed. Many women and men still viewed the occupation of mother and wife as women's chief role in life. Only when women argued that their work was an extension of their maternal role did they gain professional acceptance by male peers. The quest for professional advancement and for equal pay for equal work swept postwar American women into the twentieth century—and continues to this day.

Toilers on the Land

Although the nation rapidly developed into an industrial power in the years after the Civil War and many young men and women migrated to the cities to work in new factories, others continued to live in rural areas. Some people even left the cities to seek a better life in the still undeveloped western region of the United

States. In 1860 almost half the United States, from the western border of Missouri to the shores of California and from the U.S.–Canadian border to lower Texas, was settled only sparsely.

Several states in this territory had already been admitted into the Union. California was admitted in 1850, Texas in 1845. As their populations soared, other territories also became states. In 1867 Nebraska entered the Union, and Colorado followed in 1876. North Dakota, South Dakota, Montana, and Washington all entered in 1889, Idaho and Wyoming the following year.

The West had been populated long before it was carved up into states. Hispanic peoples had moved up north from Mexico into Texas and then pushed into California and New Mexico, and before them Native Americans had long called the western lands their home. The Sioux, biggest and most powerful of the western tribes, inhabited the woodlands of Minnesota and the Great Plains; the Cheyennes dwelled in the region of the Powder River and Bighorn country of Wyoming and Montana, while farther south, other Cheyenne tribes established villages on the Colorado and Kansas plains. The Apaches occupied the arid southwest region of Texas and New Mexico, the Pueblos lived in New Mexico, and the Nez Percés claimed the Blue Mountains of Oregon and the Bitterroot Range of the Rocky Mountains between Idaho and Montana. Many smaller tribes also inhabited the western lands.

Starting in the 1840s, the trickle of settlers onto the lands of Native Americans and Hispanics turned into a steady stream. The California gold rush of 1849 brought the first flood of migrants from the East Coast and Europe. Other settlers came in search of more fertile farmland and grasslands for their cattle and sheep to graze on. On the Texas Panhandle and the plains of Kansas, Nebraska, and North and South Dakota, they built farms and ranches and set their livestock free to roam and graze on open land. The populations of all of these areas surged. During the 1870s and 1880s, for example, the population of the predominantly farm states of Minnesota, Kansas, Nebraska, the Dakotas, Colorado, and Montana soared from 1 million to about 5 million—eight times the rate of increase of the country as a whole. By the mid-nineteenth century, the West was the most ethnically diverse region of the United States, a mosaic of people from across the globe. From 1860 to 1900, between a quarter and a third of the western population had been born in another country.

By 1890 the flow of migration out west had begun to wane. The buffalo—the main staple of Native Americans—had been wiped out by thoughtless sportsmen, and Native American tribes had endured many bloody clashes with the U.S. military and had been forced to resettle on reservations, patches of land that hardly sustained their physical and spiritual needs. Their former lands were overtaken by settlements ranging from primitive outposts to thriving cattle towns. For women of all ethnic backgrounds—Native American, Hispanic, white, Asian, European,

Wichita women construct a grass lodge in Omaha, Nebraska. In many tribes, women had the responsibility of home building, though the materials and skills they used varied from place to place.

and African-American—who were part of the mosaic of western settlement, the feverish activity of these years had a profound impact upon their lives.

Although customs and practices varied among tribes, Native American women enjoyed greater social equality with Native American men than white women experienced. They worked together to plant, harvest, and grind the corn. As an old woman, Buffalo Bird Woman of the Hidatsa tribe of North Dakota vividly recalled how the women of her family planted corn together in the late nineteenth century. "I liked to go with my mothers to the cornfields in planting time, when the spring sun was shining and the birds singing in the tree tops," she remembered. "We cared for our corn in those days, as we would care for a child; for we Indian people loved our fields as mothers love their children." In winter, especially when game was less plentiful, the corn that Native American women harvested, along with seeds and roots that they gathered, sustained their tribes.

Women played crucial spiritual and economic roles in their tribes. Indeed, the social life of the tribe often revolved around matrilineal clan groups, in which people divided themselves into kinship groups and related women, their husbands, and their children lived together. A family's ancestry was traced through the female line, and children belonged to the mother's clan group. This arrangement did not give Indian women special power over Indian men, but it indicated that women were valued and influential members of their tribes. Though few women chiefs and warriors were to be found, Native American women served their people in equally important ways.

As settlers advanced farther west, Native American women found their important tribal roles gradually changing and disappearing, especially as their tribes lost control of their lands. Up until 1867, the U.S. government maintained treaties with Native American tribes. These treaties specified which regions remained under tribal control and which were open to settlement by other people. But after 1867, Congress abolished the treaty system and devised a reservation plan by which Native Americans were forced to leave their native lands—usually under armed escort by the U.S. military—and relocate in smaller areas reserved for them.

Sarah Winnemucca of Nevada witnessed the forced resettlement of her people in 1878 from their Nevada homeland to the Yakima Indian reservation in eastern Washington. They had only three days to prepare for the treacherous journey over snowbound mountains in midwinter. They traveled by wagon and camped out at night in frigid weather. Upon reaching the reservation, the tribe discovered that their new lodgings were wholly inadequate. They were crowded into a makeshift shed and did not have enough clothing or fuel among themselves to keep warm. "Oh, how we did suffer with cold," Sarah Winnemucca remembered. "There was no wood, and the snow was waist-deep, and many died off just as cattle or horses do after travelling so long in the cold." Sarah Winnemucca recorded her experiences and the sufferings of her people in her book *Life Among the Piutes: Their Wrongs and Claims* (1883). She also traveled to Washington, D.C., in the early 1880s to protest government policies toward Native Americans, and she lectured around the country.

Her startling facts aroused public sympathy, but the government did not change its policies. Indeed, its callous disregard for the rights of Native Americans came to a head at the massacre of Wounded Knee in 1890. After capturing a band of Sioux near Pine Ridge, South Dakota, a contingent of U.S. cavalry marched the group of 350 men, women, and children to a camp near a creek called Wounded Knee, where they attempted to disarm the Indians. A gun owned by one of the Indians went off. Some witnesses said that the Indian fired it; others maintained that it went off when soldiers tussled with the Indian as he tried to put it down. The truth remains unknown. The soldiers immediately opened fire and within minutes 153 Indian men, women, and children were dead. "We tried to run," Louise Weasel Bear remembered, "but they shot us like we were a buffalo."

In the last decades of the nineteenth century, Native Americans continued to be herded off their lands and forced into reservations. They tried to maintain their intimate and cooperative relationship with the land, but reservation officials discouraged them from establishing cooperative farms and instead encouraged them to farm individual plots. As a result, Native American women gradually lost control of the land, and their social power within their tribes diminished. The equal relationship between Indian women and men changed and began to resemble the marital relations of the white settlers, in which a husband held economic and social power over his wife. As their way of life eroded, both Native American women and men were forced to enter into a servile relationship with white settlers. Indian women, and some men, washed clothes and dishes and did other household chores for settlers. Some Indian women worked as nursemaids for white women. As their lands were scooped up by non-Indians eager to wrest a profit from the land, Native Americans' communal, agrarian way of life vanished—and with it, the Native American woman's prominent tribal role.

Hispanic peoples suffered a similar displacement from their land and culture. From the sixteenth century onward, Spanish conquerors and explorers in Mexico married into Native American cultures. The offspring of these marriages became the Hispanics, who migrated up north over the centuries from Mexico to settle in the arid deserts of the American Southwest, the region comprising what is now New Mexico, Arizona, Texas, Colorado, and part of California. Like Native Americans, Hispanics lived and worked cooperatively and relied on the land for their livelihood. In most villages, each family owned a small lot, a house, and the land immediately surrounding the house. The remaining land, along with all water rights, were owned by the villagers together. In this way, a system of private property coexisted with shared property. Villagers pooled labor as well as natural resources. Women worked together to plaster houses, bake bread, spin wool, and stuff mattresses. Men also shared tasks, such as plowing, hoeing, harvesting, and caring for livestock. Sometimes families bartered goods; for example, one family might exchange wool for foodstuff.

Farming tasks were also divided between women and men. Men chose the crops for communal fields, and each wife took exclusive control of the family's garden plot, which produced most of the family's food. When men were away, women also took charge of the village's communal fields. Like Native American women, Hispanic women contributed significantly to their villages' sustenance. One indication of women's important village role can be seen in inheritance practices; unlike Anglo inheritance practices, which favored sons over daughters in dividing up an estate, Hispanic custom was for daughters and sons to inherit equally, although daughters sometimes inherited livestock, furniture, and household goods instead of land. Among the villagers themselves, there were few differences in economic status. Wealthier families lived apart and rarely mingled with their neighbors of more modest means.

In the 1870s, Hispanic villages remained almost untouched by the growing presence of white, or Anglo, settlers. Some Hispanic men performed seasonal work for Anglo settlers for extra cash, then returned to their villages with extra income to purchase additional livestock or open a store. By the 1880s, however, an expanding railroad system brought more white settlers to the Southwest. As more Anglos arrived, they forced their cultural values and business practices on Hispanics: private property, the use of property for commercial gain rather than for subsistence, and an economy based on money instead of barter. Most important, they simply took land that had been commonly owned by Hispanic villagers. Lacking sufficient pastureland, villagers could hardly sustain their agrarian way of life on their small individual plots. Gradually, Anglos gained control over the local village economy throughout New Mexico, Arizona, Colorado, and California. With insufficient land to support themselves, Hispanics had no choice but to work for the new landowners.

Hispanic women were no longer able to help support their culture's communal way of life. They began to work for whites as seamstresses, cooks, launderers, domestics, hotel keepers, and even prostitutes. Like Native American women, they worked as day laborers for someone else instead of as farmers for their own people. They had no control of the hours or terms of their work, and they lost their important role in their own communities as food producers. Like Native American women, Hispanic women relinquished a life rooted in the land for one based on wage labor.

In contrast, white and black women homesteaders heading west faced a life very much dependent upon the bounty of the land. Men and women went west for a variety of reasons—for the adventure, for a fresh start in life, to follow friends or family members who had preceded them, and mostly to seek a better livelihood. Southerners recovering from the wartime devastation of their economy saw in the West an opportunity to regain the wealth that they had lost in the war. Settlers received plenty of encouragement for these hopes. In Colorado and New Mexico, promoters advertised in pamphlets "Where to Go to Become Rich." The governor of New Mexico boasted about enormous reserves of gold, silver, and copper to lure settlers to his region. For people barely scratching out a living, such grandiose promises of instant wealth were irresistible. Promoters also assured settlers that the clear, dry climate of the West would bring instant good health.

White native-born women made up the bulk of women journeying west. African-American women also made the arduous journey but in far fewer numbers, although from 1878 to 1880 hundreds of them headed for Kansas along with their men, seeking greater economic opportunity and freedom from racial prejudice. Some even emigrated in organized groups. By 1880 fifteen thousand black migrants in Kansas were trying to scratch out a living as farmers and laborers. Called Exodusters, they built huts made out of sod bricks and planted wheat. Some organized self-sufficient colonies or worked for white settlers as farm laborers or servants.

For most Exodusters, Kansas proved to be no refuge, and some moved on to Nebraska and Oklahoma or returned to the South. Luckier migrants managed to stay and make homes for themselves. Willianna Hickman, an Exoduster who migrated to Kansas from Kentucky in 1878, recalled that she cried from despair when she saw her new community, a collection of dugouts built against sloping dirt. But the "days, weeks, months, and years passed and I became reconciled to my home. We improved the farm and lived there nearly twenty years." The Exodusters, however, were a tiny minority. Most African Americans could not afford the journey out west and remained in the cities and rural hamlets of the South.

Both single and married women made the journey west. Some married women went reluctantly, knowing they had little choice but to follow their husbands. Others eagerly shared their husbands' dreams of a new life on a new land. Still others stayed behind while their husbands went ahead, waiting and wondering what their new homes would look like. Maggie Brown of Virginia waited a year and a half before joining her husband, Charles, in Colorado. During that time, she feared that he was becoming immoral and unfaithful to her. Nothing Charles wrote in his letters could reassure her until she joined him and saw for herself that Charles had remained faithful.

The trip out west was very hard. Travelers relied on several kinds of transportation: train, stagecoach, wagon, or ship. Traveling by ship was faster, but most travelers chose to go by land because that was less expensive. If they brought livestock with them, they walked most of the way to shepherd their animals along. Although men mostly handled this task, women also took their turn on foot, prodding their cattle or oxen along, while the men drove the wagons that held their belongings.

On the journey, women who traveled as part of a wagon train often carried out the same responsibilities that they did back home—cooking, washing, and caring for children—but under much more primitive conditions. They had to contend with constant dust and cramped quarters. For some, their first big test of withstanding the frontier came when they had to collect dried buffalo dung for fuel. Some women could not bring themselves to touch the dried droppings, but they had no choice if they wanted to make a fire for heating water or cooking. They cooked under crude conditions, with few ingredients, supplementing staple diets of beans, bread, and bacon with wild berries gathered along the way. Occasionally they served a few luxury dishes, such as canned oysters or eggs that had been carefully packed, and they used game and fish caught nearby.

Women shared household responsibilities along the way and welcomed one another's companionship. At night, around the campfire or at crude inns where travelers stayed, women eagerly visited together, knitting, crocheting, or merely resting their tired feet. They confided in each other, sharing thoughts they were perhaps reluctant to admit to their husbands. Annie Green, a homesteader from Pennsylvania, struck up an acquaintance with a "very dear lady" who was also heading out to Colorado. "We spoke to each other of our future prospects, mingled with hopes and fears," Green later recalled. But five weeks after they had all arrived, her friend died of pneumonia.

Such were the uncertainties of women and men who went west. Friendships made along the way abruptly ended when fellow travelers died or went their separate ways. The ever-present threat of illness and the fear of attacks by Indians haunted travelers. The eerie howl of wolves at night, the fear of poisonous snakes and prowling bears, the relentless desert sun beating down, and the bitter cold nights up in the mountains—all of these fears and hardships tormented travelers. Even the desolation of the landscape itself seemed threatening. Riding through South Dakota's Black Hills, Annie Tallent recalled, "I could not help glancing furtively from side to side of the ravines to see whether there were any gnomes or hobgoblins peering out at us from between the crevices of the great rocks."

Women's responses to the landscape and especially to their new homes out west varied widely. Of her new surroundings in Colorado, Annie Green wrote, "Not a tree, plant nor shrub on which to rest my weary eye, to break the monotony of the sand beds and cactus of the Great American Desert." In contrast, Mary Ronan, who lived on an Indian reservation in western Montana in the late 1870s, loved the surrounding countryside, especially the tangy fragrance of June roses and the colorful patches of blue lupine. When she saw her new homeland for the first time, she was enchanted: "So beautiful the valley was that it seemed to me I had entered a place like the Garden of Paradise."

The hardships of the journey itself often paled in comparison to the hardship of setting up a home in a wilderness land. Depending on where they settled, a family's lodgings varied dramatically. In the deserts of New Mexico and Arizona, "home" might be a log cabin with dirt floors or a tiny adobe cottage. In Kansas, many settlers lived in soddies, dwellings dug out of hard-packed soil. These makeshift dirt homes leaked or even dissolved in rainstorms, and snakes, worms, and centipedes made their homes in the walls and dirt ceilings of these dwellings. Many a pioneer woman awoke in the morning to discover she was sharing her bed with a snake that had fallen from the ceiling the night before.

Other families lived in tents or in their wagons until they could build a suitable shelter for themselves. Annie Green of Colorado recalled, "After securing several lots in the new town, we pitched our tent, which was almost daily blown to the ground. To say that I was homesick, discouraged, and lonely, is but a faint description of my feelings." Malinda Harris, a black Exoduster in Kansas, actively discouraged others from coming to Kansas. She wrote in a letter: "dont study a Bout coming away. if I knowed what I know no Body could not Pull me a way [from her former home].... Pray for me for I kneed [sic] Prayers."

Most women who went west believed that their main responsibilities revolved around homemaking—taking care of husbands and children. Back home, such beliefs had perhaps limited their choices by discouraging them from doing work that was not deemed appropriate for women. But in their new homes, these beliefs provided a sense of stability that offset their feelings of uprootedness from familiar surroundings and family and friends. Cooking, cleaning, sewing the family's

The dugout of the Mead family near Bloom, Kansas, housed several generations. Its single room, chock-full of furniture and cooking equipment, was a study in contrasts, containing a primitive washtub alongside an ornate stove and good china. Women did their best to make these damp, dirty hillside dwellings as homelike as possible.

clothing reassuringly linked them to the routine of earlier and easier times. And, as they did along the journey, women shared their chores with other women if possible, visiting as they washed clothes in a nearby creek or baked bread together.

Women, then, understandably took pride in making a home under difficult circumstances; a well-baked pie or well-made shirt were true accomplishments. These homemaking activities were also potential sources of income. Annie Green baked and sold bread. Not only did she earn four dollars in profit but, she claimed, she had "gained the reputation of giving larger loaves than any other person engaged in the business in town." She regarded her labors as both a right and an extension of her domestic responsibilities; to her way of thinking, her earnings helped improve her family's standard of living. Women settlers believed that their obligation to create a healthy and stable home life justified their desire to earn money for their families' benefit.

Their sense of domestic responsibility also justified their desire to build institutions and create organizations that improved their communities. Sunday schools, prayer meetings, church socials, reading clubs, debating societies, amateur musical and dramatic groups, and libraries—women took the lead in organizing these groups and institutions because they desired to bring culture, stability, and morality to an untamed land, especially for their children's benefit. Within a year after settling Kansas, women had organized charitable societies and a local chapter of the Woman's Christian Temperance Union.

With such institutions women quietly challenged the values of a social and political order dominated by men. They celebrated the way in which they were different from men. Men were physically strong and could do the physical work of building homes and schools, but women perceived themselves to be morally and spiritually strong; their vision and guidance created the schools built by men, and it also obligated them to rid their frontier communities of such undesirable practices as excessive drinking, gambling, and prostitution. Just as urban women used the values that defined the ideal domestic realm—purity, piety, moral goodness— to justify their volunteer activities in their communities, so women settlers drew on these very values to establish social order on the frontier. As wives and mothers, or simply as women, they felt obligated to play a vital role in their young communities. Indeed, for some women, the landscape itself strengthened their resolve to fulfill their moral duties. In 1872 Sister Blandina Segale journeyed from Ohio to Colorado and New Mexico to establish missions. "The immense expanse of the plains, the solid Rockies, the purity of the atmosphere, the faultlessness of the canopy above, will stretch the mind toward the Good," she wrote to another nun. "I wish I had many hands and feet, and a world full of hearts to place at the service of the Eternal."

The frontier provided many ways for women to earn a livelihood while they also worked for the common good. Women started schools in their cabins or were dispatched by school boards to teach in designated regions. Women also cooked, sewed, and did laundry for others, especially for single men. Some took in boarders or became innkeepers; others peddled produce from their gardens to earn extra money. Some women found more unusual forms of employment. Maggie Brown, of Rincon, New Mexico, slaughtered her own pigs and cured and sold the meat at market, while other women became trail guides, newspaper editors, or professional writers. Some succeeded as ranchers or mine owners, either after their husbands died or because they simply had better business skills than their spouses. Women doctors and lawyers also went west.

Women actively participated in politics as well. Mary E. Lease of Kansas and Luna Kellie of Nebraska both served as speakers and recruiters for their state chapters of the Farmers' Alliance and the Populist party, which was established in 1890. The Alliance developed programs to benefit farmers, including educational programs; associations for cooperative buying, marketing, and warehousing; and other strategies to improve farmers' economic status. Its successor, the Populist party, converted these individual programs into a wide-ranging political platform designed to protect farmers' interests in an economy that catered increasingly to industrial and financial interests—"a government of Wall Street, by Wall Street, and for Wall Street," as Mary Lease bitingly declared. The Alliance and the Populist party recruited women as lecturers and organizers and supported woman suffrage. The Alliance, in particular, recognized the vital importance of rural women's economic activities and their keen interest in economic reforms that helped farmers.

Woman also earned their livelihood in more dubious ways. In the mining camps of Butte, Montana, as well as in the desert outposts of New Mexico, women worked as prostitutes and owners of brothels and saloons. Women became prostitutes for a variety of reasons—to rebel against strict parents, to experience the adventure of a mining camp, or simply to earn a living when no other choice of work was available. Some prospered and turned their earnings into lucrative real estate investments, but many felt socially outcast and were at risk of contracting venereal diseases, which were often fatal, or of being physically abused by male customers. Prostitution was a lonely, insecure life spent mostly in dark, shabby hotel rooms.

A shameful chapter in the settling of the West concerns Chinese women who were sold into prostitution. These unsuspecting young women were either kidnapped in China and smuggled into American ports, or they were deceived by agents posing as matchmakers who lured them to America. Either way, they became virtual slaves, forced to service the sexual needs of Chinese immigrant male laborers working on the railroads and ranches of the West. Some found sympathetic support from female missionaries who sheltered them in special group homes and trained them to be wives and mothers. But the missionaries pressured them into entering marriages that were not always happy or compatible, and these unfortunate young Chinese women still had little control over their lives.

Whether women worked directly on the land or in country schoolhouses and newspaper offices, nature's cruelty and its bounty had an indelible impact on their lives. Western farmers, ranchers, and miners relied on the kindness of nature to yield profitable crops, livestock, and minerals. A fire, flood, or illness could wipe out a family's livelihood. When Annie Green's husband contracted typhoid fever, she had to spend all of her time nursing him, and their crops went to ruin from neglect. Green was devastated. "Sinking to the earth, I wept and prayed to God for a change in my wretched life," she said later.

Maggie and Charles Brown of Virginia moved back and forth across Colorado and New Mexico twenty-four times over twenty-seven years in search of a better life. Between them, they worked as physician, miner, carpenter, housepainter, farmer, mail clerk, poultry farmer, laundress, baker, and day servant. For a time, they prospered, but unyielding mines, drought, poor business sense, and sheer bad luck played havoc with their finances and their lives. They lost six children to illness, and by her mid-thirties Maggie looked old and haggard. In a letter to her father, she confided, "I don't see any likelihood of times ever being any better. I feel if I do stay here two years longer I will be lost body and soul." Life on the land had not been kind to them.

Closely linked to how comfortable and secure women felt in their new homes was how trusting or distrusting they felt toward Native Americans and Hispanics. Before embarking on the journey out west, travelers heard frightening stories about Indian attacks, especially on women and children. These stories preyed upon their fears and prejudices. Angeline Mitchell Brown of Arizona described an encounter with several Native American men who had broken into the cabin that she shared with two other women. Clearly frightened by this encounter, she gave full vent to all of her prejudices about Indians. Coming face to face with one of her invaders, she "looked at him then straight, & unflinchingly in his cruel gleaming eyes & I know I wondered if Satan in all his kingdom had a more fiendish looking devil." In contrast, Mary Ronan, the wife of a government agent at the Flathead Indian Reservation in western Montana, claimed that she never shut or locked a door in her house and that Indians walked in anytime. But Ronan's trust and good feeling toward her Native American neighbors was tinged with condescension. Whenever she asked them to leave, she always gave them a little gift—"a bit of sugar, a piece of bread or an apple"—like a parent bribing a child with a treat. Most white men and women did not regard their Indian neighbors as equals. Instead, they condemned them as savages or treated them as exotic strangers or ignorant half-people needing instruction in the ways of white Christians.

Yet some white women managed to overcome cultural blinders and develop special friendships with Native American women. Indian women shared homemade remedies with white women or took them on expeditions to gather herbs and roots. Louise S. Gellhorn Boylan, an Iowa settler of the 1870s, "treasured greatly" some beads given to her by neighboring Indian women. And some white women eagerly attended Native American ceremonies and gatherings. White settlers also hired Native American men and women as domestics or nursemaids. From these employment arrangements emerged some friendships between employer and employee.

For their part, Native American women scorned white culture for its materialism, disrespect for the land, and disregard for Native American culture. Although individual Indian women befriended white women and even married white men, Native American women had a long tradition of defending their people's birthright to their ancestral lands. As early as 1818, a delegation of Cherokee women vigorously urged their men to resist U.S. soldiers who were forcibly uprooting them from their homeland. In 1883 the eloquent Sarah Winnemucca pointed out the hypocrisy of a white society that called itself civilized but left a trail of blood as it invaded and plundered her people's homes.

Garden of Eden or land of desolation, good neighbor or savage, trusting white friend or invader—women's responses to the West and to one another were as varied as the terrain itself. Although women from all cultural backgrounds harbored fears and prejudices toward one another, friendships among individual women flourished as surely as the fragrant flowering desert cactus—and as rarely. More often women from different backgrounds and races coexisted uneasily. But the common force in all of their lives was the land and the gifts that it yielded for making a way of life.

Working Together for Social Change

During the postwar years, women who lived in the dusty towns of Kansas as well as the burgeoning neighborhoods of New York City discovered new and different ways to make their voices heard and to enlarge the scope of their lives. Throughout the last three decades of the nineteenth century, a remarkable movement swept the country—women across the nation organized clubs to develop common interests and work together to improve their communities.

These clubs took various forms. Some were study clubs devoted to learning; others were fund-raising organizations designed to raise money for building schools, hospitals, orphanages, and other public institutions. In still other clubs, women became involved in local political causes or investigated working conditions in factories. Whatever the club's goals, its members seized the opportunity to enlarge their interests beyond their homes and families. In the process, they also challenged social practices and ideas about women's lives, although many women did not challenge their role as wives and mothers. Instead, they believed that their maternal concerns obligated them to help improve the quality of life in their communities and neighborhoods.

In the postwar years, the first significant attempt to establish a women's club was Sorosis. Journalist Jane Cunningham Croly organized the club in New York City in 1868 after she was barred from attending a dinner hosted by the New York

Press Club—of which she was a member—because she was a woman. Croly envisioned a group composed only of professional and other self-supporting women that, in her words, "should manage its own affairs, represent as far as possible the active interests of women, and create a bond of fellowship between them." After much debate, club members chose the name Sorosis, a botanical term for plants with a profusion of flowers that bear fruit. (It comes from the Latin *soror,* "sister.") Members of Sorosis organized themselves into four groups—literature, art, drama, and music—and chose topics within those categories to study.

Most topics related in some way to women's lives. Although the club occasionally invited outside speakers, such as astronomer Maria Mitchell, members usually conducted the discussions themselves. According to their first president, Alice Cary, they aspired to teach themselves how to think more deeply and determine what subjects merited attention and debate. Sorosis meetings were not an occasion for "idle gossip," claimed Cary. But Sorosis members did not talk only about paintings and books. Throughout the club's existence, its guiding spirit, Jane Croly, urged members to study and act on reform issues from female labor to public sanitation and education. This philosophy is key to understanding the importance of Sorosis and other women's study clubs, for in offering women a forum for intellectual inquiry and discussion, these clubs urged women to first take their own ideas seriously and then to act upon those ideas.

Study clubs sprang up throughout the nation, especially in the Northeast and Midwest. Unlike Sorosis, these clubs were open to full-time homemakers as well as to professional and other wage-earning women. Like a spreading fever, women who visited friends and attended meetings of their clubs went home and established their own. The clubs' goals were as numerous as the clubs themselves. Some focused on several general subjects, such as art, literature, music, and politics; others focused on a single topic. The Great Expectations Club of Thomaston, Maine, studied English literature and history up to the Victorian era. The Portia Club of San Francisco, which had several women lawyers as members, endeavored to master principles of legal and political theory, and the Heliades Club of Chicago explored world geography. The variety and range of topics within the study club movement were as wide as women's interests and eagerness to learn. In general, however, study clubs focused on literature, the arts, and history—subjects that members, most of whom lacked a formal education, had never had an opportunity to study. Many study clubs survived for a decade or more, and as their members gained greater self-confidence their critical thinking and writing skills greatly improved.

Study clubs, however, had their critics. In 1868, after Julia Ward Howe, author of the "Battle Hymn of the Republic" and an avid club woman herself, established the New England Women's Club, the *Boston Transcript* warned, "Homes will be ruined, children neglected, woman is straying from her sphere." But many club members had no intention of neglecting their domestic responsibilities. Instead, some women justified their club activities as ways to improve home and community life.

While attempting to quiet critics by emphasizing the value of clubs for home and family life, women also recognized the clubs' impact upon their own lives. They met women from different walks of life—older and younger women, professionals as well as full-time homemakers. Though study clubs were composed primarily of middle-class women and were seldom if ever integrated by race, members encountered a variety of life experiences and opinions different from their own. "I went to a Sorosis meeting the other day," declared one club woman. "And nothing ever impressed me so much. The fraternity, the versatility, and the spontaneity of those women was a revelation! A new life tingled through me from head to foot; my horizon broadens."

Study clubs offered many women exposure to new ideas, new friendships, and above all renewed respect for their own talents and abilities. As members gained new self-confidence and organizational skills, they looked beyond their own intellectual improvement to find ways to improve their communities. By the 1880s, many study clubs had begun to transform themselves into community service clubs. By 1889, for example, the Chicago Woman's Club, established in 1876 both to perform "practical work" and engage in intellectual study, had appointed a night matron in the city's prison and women physicians in the county insane asylum, introduced a system of kindergartens into Chicago's public school system, and established a school for male juvenile offenders.

Club women now expanded their domestic sense of responsibility to the entire community. They continued to feel their place was in the home, but home extended beyond the four walls of their private houses to the community. The Woman's Christian Temperance Union (WCTU), established in 1874, reflected this idea of women as caretakers of their communities. The WCTU started in Ohio when women embarked upon a campaign to close all of the saloons in the state because they identified alcohol as the source of family strife and the cause of immoral behavior in the home and community. Although temperance societies had existed before the Civil War, this latest effort to outlaw alcohol had spectacular success. Within several months, the women had closed down more than a thousand saloons and bars through prayer meetings, petitions, and intense pressure on customers and owners of bars.

Like the prewar abolition movement, this temperance crusade was a grassroots effort that drew on religious precepts. Protection of the home and family from the irresponsible and violent behavior of men under the influence of alcohol was a moral and religious cause. Rebecca Felton of Georgia claimed that she joined the WCTU "because it represented organized Mother-love as opposed to this liquor curse." Like the study club movement, the temperance crusade ignited middle-class women's commitment, and the Woman's Christian Temperance Union rapidly grew in membership. Only women were eligible to join.

In 1879, after moving steadily up the leadership ranks, teacher Frances Willard became the WCTU's energetic president. Willard infused new life into the WCTU,

Frances Willard may have been uncertain on a bicycle, but she was resolute in her leadership of the WCTU from 1879 to 1898.

creating new goals and strategies. She espoused a "Do Everything" policy, urging members to work to improve all aspects of women's lives. In 1884 she offered an explanation of her philosophy: "Were I to define in a sentence, the thought and purpose of the Woman's Christian Temperance Union, I would reply: 'It is to make the whole world *homelike*.'"

Inspired by her vision, WCTU members worked not only for temperance but for a variety of causes: boys' and girls' clubs, homes for alcoholic women, and evening schools for working women. They also campaigned for better working conditions in factories, more humane prisons, health education in public schools, and public drinking fountains. But, Willard realized, the WCTU had no real power to bring about these changes until women could vote, and she made female enfranchisement a prime goal of the WCTU. "The Ballot for Home Protection," she declared, gave women their most potent weapon for combating the "tyranny of drink."

Women who had once opposed female enfranchisement became convinced of its necessity. Traditional in their outlook, they had once feared that the ballot would, in their view, "unsex" women—that is, draw women away from their role in life as wives and mothers. To endorse female suffrage, then, was a dramatic step forward. To the new way of thinking, the ballot would not unsex women; instead, voting would help them carry out their moral mission as women more effectively because they now had the political power to implement temperance and other reforms.

The WCTU was only one of many women's organizations dedicated to spreading the values of the home into the community. Another active organization was the Young Women's Christian Association (YWCA). Founded by middle-class women in Boston in 1867, the YWCA endeavored to assist young single women who had migrated from the farm to the city for work. The organization defined its goal as protecting the "temporal, moral, and religious welfare of young women who are dependent on their own exertions for support." To this end, YWCA representatives stationed themselves at bus and train depots, advising young women about employment opportunities and places to live. Eventually the YWCA established its own boardinghouses to ensure that women were living in morally respectable lodgings.

The Working Girls' Society was yet another attempt by middle-class women to be public mothers toward younger working-class women. Founded in 1885 by Grace Hoadley Dodge in New York City, the society attempted to instill proper middle-class values in working-class women. Club activities included lectures and group discussions on topics such as "Purity," "Womanhood," "How to Get a Husband," and "Money—How to Get It and Keep It." A few clubs maintained their own boardinghouses, with libraries and classes in millinery and dressmaking, stenography, literature, physical education, and medical hygiene. By 1890 seventy-five chapters of the society had been established around the country. Dodge called the New York chapter a "home to all its members" and hoped that girls would learn the proper manners, form of dress, and language that their own parents had failed to teach them.

Dodge, who came from an affluent New York family active in charitable causes, hoped to persuade her charges that their true fulfillment lay in becoming genteel women like herself—"not desirous for man's work or place, but remaining where circumstances have placed them . . . developing and enlarging the power God has given them." But working-class members held fast to their own aspirations; they challenged Dodge's emphasis on a life of domesticity by insisting on their right to work and be financially independent.

Jewish and African-American women established clubs as well. Jewish women, in particular, drew on religious values that enshrined women's special role as guardian of the home. In addition, they were also influenced by American middle-class perceptions of women's domestic role. By the 1870s, every sizable American Jewish community had a Ladies Temple Aid Society, Ladies Auxiliary, Passover Relief Fund, or Deborah and Leah lodges. These organizations raised money for local synagogues, assisted needy or ailing Jewish women, helped find employment for Jewish newcomers, and assisted a growing influx of east European Jewish immigrants with housing and educational needs.

American Jewish women went about their club work quietly and deferred to the authority of rabbis and other male leaders. But these grassroots volunteer organizations of the 1870s and 1880s served as a prelude to the emergence of a more comprehensive and ambitious program of political and social reform work initiated by Jewish women in the 1890s.

The National Council of Jewish Women, established in 1893, did more than organize local charity drives within Jewish neighborhoods. Its members educated themselves on public policy, testified before congressional committees, and tried to combat such social ills as poverty and juvenile delinquency within the Jewish community. Although the Council expanded the sphere of women's volunteer concerns and voiced new ideas about female power and equality, its members did not challenge traditional notions about Jewish women's primary domestic role. Like the small, grassroots Jewish organizations that preceded it, the Council tried to expand the values of the home into the community.

African-American women also combined a desire to use their special gifts as women with an explicit aim to help their own people. And like the Jewish women's club movement, African-American women's club activities grew into a more ambitious program of social reform in the 1890s. Many groups were affiliated with black churches. From the earliest days of Reconstruction, female members of the African Methodist Episcopal, Baptist, and Congregational churches organized ladies' benevolent societies that hired physicians and teachers to serve the congregations of their own churches, provided financial aid to sick or impoverished church members, and raised funds for new church buildings and schools. Every black community had one or more women's benevolent societies, and these church-based groups guided their brethren through the difficult transition from bondage to freedom. By the 1880s, however, African-American women were ready to help themselves, although they continued to perform volunteer services for their communities. In 1880 Mary Ann Shadd Cary and other black women organized the Colored Woman's Progressive Franchise Association, the first major organization created and led by black women. Although it strove to help African-American women secure economic, political, and social equality for themselves, it also aimed to give black women the tools to help their own communities more effectively.

To this end, the association endorsed female suffrage. Like the WCTU, black women regarded the right to vote not as an abstract, universal right to which they were entitled as members of the human race, but as a powerful tool to improve their own lives and those of their people. Throughout the 1880s, African-American women pressed their claims for economic, social, and political equality, and they gradually entered professional fields. But central to their own sense of power was their obligation to their communities. In 1886 Anna Julia Cooper, a black writer and educator, eloquently proclaimed this very idea. "Only the *Black Woman* can say 'when and where I enter . . . then and there the whole *Negro race enters with me.*'"

Within a few years, several prominent African-American women, including author and social worker Victoria Earle Matthews, physician Dr. Susan McKinney, and journalist and civic leader Josephine St. Pierre Ruffin, acted upon Cooper's vision. They organized clubs to improve the social, economic, and educational programs within their communities. In Atlanta, Georgia, for example, black women established a local Chautauqua study circle, using readings from the national adult education program based in Chautauqua, New York. Besides implementing educational and social welfare programs, black women's clubs served another purpose: to disprove whites' racist views of black women as immoral and ignorant.

In the South, white women's club activity followed a somewhat different direction. Women also organized study clubs, and by the 1880s several Southern states had chapters of the Woman's Christian Temperance Union. The WCTU, however, had a harder time gaining a foothold in the South because of its support for woman suffrage. According to one Tennessee woman, even ministers opposed the WCTU. "They quote St. Paul," she remarked drily, "and tell us we are wonderfully out of our places."

Southern women organized other clubs as well. In New Orleans, clubs for working-class women helped them find employment and develop more marketable skills. Like the YWCA and other organizations for working-class women, the New Orleans Woman's Club, established in 1885, ran an employment bureau that placed women in jobs from teaching to office work and dressmaking.

In general, however, Southern white women's clubs were religious in aim and organization. Their club work often resembled the activity of black women's church groups. Like African-American women, Southern white women organized clubs to raise funds for rebuilding churches and assisting destitute citizens. They also joined a movement then sweeping the nation, embracing both black and white women's church groups in its wake—foreign missionary work.

Between 1870 and 1910, female missionary societies from across the nation sent missionaries throughout the world to spread the gospel of Christianity. They transformed the foreign-missionary movement into a systematic program of fund-raising and education. Local missionary societies for each religious denomination organized into federations, and each federation published a magazine that offered detailed accounts of the geography and social customs of the countries to which missionaries were sent. These federations, however, were not integrated—black women's missionary societies remained separate from those of white women.

But black and white female missionary societies shared similar concerns, especially in regard to the status of women in non-Christian countries. They decried the inadequate education, social isolation, and harsh treatment that they perceived to be the plight of foreign women. Amanda Smith, an African-American missionary in Liberia, observed, "There is so little attention paid to the education of girls; not a single high school for girls in the whole republic of Liberia. It is a great shame and a disgrace to the government."

Female missionaries also deplored certain cultural practices that physically harmed women, such as foot-binding in China. Although their concerns were based on fact, they glorified the treatment of women and girls in the United States by contrast, without questioning the hard lot of many American women. Yet some of their concerns, such as protecting women and girls from heavy physical labor, found their way into the social programs of reformers in America who opposed child labor and lobbied for better working conditions and higher wages for American women.

Although some women extended the values of the home into the community and the world, others brought the community into the home. In 1889 Jane Addams and Ellen Gates Starr established Hull House in a poor immigrant neighborhood in Chicago. In the same year, Vida Scudder, an English professor at Wellesley College, and six other women rented a tenement building in New York City's Lower East Side, a community composed mostly of Jewish immigrants from eastern Europe. They named their settlement house the College Settlement Association. The settlement house movement had begun. Trained workers lived in both settlement houses and taught local residents cooking, sewing, hygiene, and English. They also provided day care for children of working mothers. Settlement houses provided meeting places for trade unions and helped settle labor disputes between employers and employees.

Settlement houses drew young college-educated women workers who aspired to improve the living and working conditions of poor people. They believed that, with the proper assistance, people could help themselves. By living and working in crowded immigrant neighborhoods, they hoped to bridge a growing economic and cultural gap between rich and poor and share in the community life of local residents. Settlement worker Mary McDowell expressed the idealism behind the movement: "Here was something I had been looking for all my life, a chance to work with the least skilled workers in our greatest industry; not for them as a missionary, but with them as a neighbor and seeker after truth." Although settlement workers confronted appalling poverty in these tenement neighborhoods, they achieved modest gains in helping people improve their lives. By 1906, seventeen years after Hull House and the College Settlement Association opened their doors, nearly two hundred settlement houses existed in the United States, staffed mostly by women who, like club women, desired to improve community life.

Women also brought their maternal values to bear on a subject of great concern for all women—birth control. Before 1873 women could learn about ways to regulate reproduction through advertisements in women's and general-interest magazines, but in that year access to birth control information was dealt a severe blow when Congress passed the Comstock Act. Named after Anthony Comstock, secretary of the New York Society for the Suppression of Vice, the law prohibited selling, distributing, or mailing obscene literature. The Comstock Act expressly defined all contraceptive devices, and any information about them, as obscene. It also forbade any birth control advertisements in magazines, newspapers, books, and other forms of reading material. The law reflected a pervasive belief that both contraception and abortion thwarted a divinely inspired plan of procreation. Comstock was commissioned as a special agent of the Post Office Department to help enforce the provisions of the law named after him. Between 1873 and 1880, he and his associates zealously pursued and helped to indict fifty-five persons whom Comstock identified as abortionists.

An unusual coalition of reformers from many causes got around this law by advocating a form of birth control that gave women the right to say no to their husbands' sexual advances. These advocates argued that a woman had the right to decide when to bear a child. Women would bear healthier, happier children because they were willing and able to care for those children. Far from advocating a woman's freedom to have sex whenever she wished, supporters of "voluntary motherhood," as it was called, argued that women must have the freedom not to have sex and that husbands cannot impose their sexual will on their wives.

Advocates of voluntary motherhood represented a range of causes and points of view: They included feminists, such as Elizabeth Cady Stanton, who strongly affirmed women's right to reject men's sexual advances; free-love advocates, who opposed legal marriage because it stifled true love; and conservative religious crusaders who opposed woman suffrage but endorsed voluntary motherhood as a way to restrict "sexual excess." There is no way of knowing to what extent women successfully relied upon the strategy of voluntary motherhood to regulate their sexual relations; law and custom upheld men's right to demand sexual relations with their wives. But women found ways to control the number of children they bore. From 1800 to 1900, the birthrate among American women declined by about one half. In 1800 the average birthrate was 7.04 children for every married woman; by 1900 it had dropped to 3.56. Between 1860 and 1910, the number of children born to white women dropped by about one-third, from 5.21 to 3.42. Exact figures are not available for African-American women; for the period between 1880 to 1910, however, the birthrate among black women also declined by about one-third. This dramatic decline in birthrates suggests that American women were using new forms of contraception, such as douches, pessaries, suppositories, and abortion. Condoms for men also became more widely available by the 1880s because of the invention of the vulcanization of rubber.

Contraception techniques were not always reliable, especially when people were not adept at using them correctly, and women resorted to abortions. Among physicians there was growing opposition to abortion on moral grounds, and the

Comstock Act prohibited advertising for all forms of birth control, including abortion. Nevertheless, from about 1840 to 1880 physicians and public health officials reported a rising number of abortions among American women, especially middle-class married women. No doubt, more cases went unreported—especially among working-class women who could not afford abortions and resorted to homemade and often tragically dangerous methods of ending a pregnancy. In 1858 the price of an abortion ranged from twenty-five to sixty dollars. By the 1870s, the price had fallen to about ten dollars. Still, ten dollars was a hefty amount for a domestic or female factory hand who was barely surviving on her meager wages.

Clearly both black and white women relied on new forms of birth control and also abortion to limit the number of children they bore. To what extent they adopted the precepts of voluntary motherhood as a form of birth control cannot be determined, but the idea was an important first step toward recognizing women's right to control their reproduction, even if they did not yet have the social or legal power to act on that right. Sexual intercourse in the late nineteenth century carried many risks, including venereal disease, pregnancy, and childbirth. Any step toward giving women greater ability to regulate their sexual and reproductive activities also gave them a measure of control over their lives.

In addition to trying to improve their lives and communities, American women attempted to improve their homes. The postwar years ushered in an array of labor-saving conveniences, such as electricity, running water, refrigerators, washing machines, cream separators, and processed and canned foods. But operating some of these devices, such as hand-cranked washing machine wringers and boilers, was still time-consuming, and many women could not afford these new contraptions. Nor did all households, especially homes in rural areas and less affluent families, have access to electricity or running water. In the 1870s and 1880s, many women still spent long days doing their own sewing, washing, and cooking.

Catharine Beecher, who had earlier proposed ways to help women manage their homes, continued in the late 1860s to devise methods for both simplifying and dignifying housework. In 1869 she and her sister Harriet Beecher Stowe published a book entitled *The American Woman's Home*, a guide to creating the ideal American home. It had detailed floor plans showing careful organization of work space and appliances for cooking and laundry, and urged readers to use the most advanced household technology to save time and create a cleaner, more comfortable home. The Beecher sisters offered both rural and urban variations of this ideal home, and went on to describe a "Model Christian Neighborhood." In this idealized village, ten to twelve families shared the services of a commercial bakery and laundry so that homemakers were not burdened by the chores of doing laundry or baking bread. Neither Catharine nor Harriet Beecher questioned women's domestic role. Instead, they hoped to strengthen women's control over their households and endow the homemaker's role with greater respect, dignity, and proficiency.

Other women developed an even more cooperative vision of homemaking. In 1868 Melusina Fay Peirce, a housewife from Cambridge, Massachusetts, decided that she had had enough of "the dusty drudgery of house ordering." She proposed that women organize cooperative associations to share the task of doing housework in buildings equipped for such purposes. She also proposed that they charge their husbands for their services. Peirce suggested that all members be paid wages out of the fees they collected from their husbands and that they charge competitive retail prices for cooked meals, laundry, and sewing—cash on delivery. Peirce had two goals in mind: to compensate homemakers for their labor and to free them from long days of household drudgery so that they could pursue other interests. Peirce organized her own association, the Cambridge Cooperative Housekeeping Society, in May 1869. It eventually failed because of members' lack of commitment and men's opposition, but Peirce's ideas spurred other thinkers to develop ways to make domestic life less exploitive and time-consuming. She believed that women must earn their own living and organize among themselves in order to lead happy, productive lives.

Marie Stevens Howland, a former mill worker, carried Peirce's vision of cooperative homemaking even further. Howland envisioned cooperative communities in which women found paid employment in fields other than housework. These communities would also provide professional child care and housekeeping services—cooking, cleaning, and laundry—for working mothers. Howland wrote two novels about her ideas and helped organize an experimental community in Mexico. Like Peirce, Howland believed that women must be financially independent. She was among the first American women to challenge the sanctity of the nuclear family—a mother and father and their children living in a separate household—and to urge both men and women to find more than one sexual partner. She envisioned a community in which women were free to work at any job without worrying about cooking and cleaning and taking care of their children, because all of these services would be available to them.

Working-class women were also organizing to fight bread-and-butter battles for fair wages. In 1868 the Working Women's Protective Union was established to fight for higher wages and shorter working hours. All working women, except household servants, were eligible to join the union, which helped working-class women collect unpaid wages from dishonest employers, ran an employment bureau, and tried to develop new kinds of jobs for women. The New York branch collected thousands of dollars in unpaid wages for women and placed fifteen hundred to two thousand women in jobs each year. In 1883 its director noted, "We do not give shelter, and we do not give charity. We furnish employment and we furnish advice and protection and open, as far as we can, avenues of labor to women."

Working-class women wanted more than protection—they sought justice on the job as well. To this end, they joined or formed their own unions to represent their interests as workers. The Daughters of St. Crispin, a union of female shoe-makers, became the first national labor union of women workers in the United States. It demanded equal pay for equal work but softened the demand by claim-ing that equal pay would make women better homemakers. Union members par-ticipated in two strikes for higher wages. They lost one and won the other, and then severe economic depression in 1873 halted their activity. Workers were so desper-ate to keep their jobs that they curtailed union activism that antagonized employ-ers. Other women workers also left their jobs and went on strike for higher wages, with mixed results. Still, despite setbacks on the picket lines, women workers clear-ly demonstrated their ability to organize themselves and demand better wages and working conditions.

Early attempts at organizing unions paved the way for women's entry into two major labor unions: the Knights of Labor, in 1879, and the American Federation of Labor (AFL), in 1886. The Knights of Labor was the first major labor union to actively recruit both white women and African-American men and women. Even housewives were eligible for membership. Although only 2 percent of women workers—approximately fifty thousand female wage-earners—ever joined the Knights during its peak years of activity, the organization fought for equal pay for equal work by men and women and established a permanent women's committee to investigate any wage inequities between men and women workers. The Knights also emphasized cooperatives, much like Melusina Fay Peirce's vision of coopera-tive housekeeping, in which women workers joined together to provide a service or a product rather than work for someone else. This working arrangement appealed to women workers, and a number of cooperatives operated by women arose. The Knights of Labor appealed to the interests and needs of women who desired equal wages but recognized women's homemaking responsibilities as well.

Several factors brought about the demise of the Knights of Labor: unsuccessful strikes, financial problems from investing in cooperatives that failed, an embattled and inept leadership, and growing competition for workers' loyalties from the emerging American Federation of Labor. By the late 1880s, the Knights no longer commanded the loyalty of most working-class women and men.

Women received a less enthusiastic welcome from the American Federation of Labor (AFL), a loosely knit body of independent national and international unions that reached out primarily to skilled workers. Women workers in industry general-ly held jobs that required no special skills or training. For the first few years, women actually felt unwelcome at AFL meetings, which were held at night, when most women did household chores. Sometimes women could not afford the membership dues. When they received a discount on their membership they also received fewer benefits and fewer opportunities to speak out on union matters. By 1890, however, women workers began to demand more recognition in the AFL.

But they fought an uphill battle because the AFL, unlike the Knights of Labor, refused to acknowledge that women were wage-earners as well as wives and moth-

Members of the National Council of Jewish Women meet immigrants as they arrive at Ellis Island. The NCJW's Americanization program helped the new arrivals find housing and jobs, learn English, and otherwise adapt to life in the United States.

ers. Their traditional perceptions of women's roles blinded them to the growing numbers—and militancy—of women workers. By the early twentieth century, women factory workers, especially those who worked in the garment industry, had proved willing to put their jobs and lives at risk to protest their low wages and intolerable working conditions. Eventually, the AFL recognized women workers' commitment to the goals of unionizing and began to recruit more women workers for membership.

In the last three decades of the nineteenth century, American women discovered the power of collective action—to educate themselves, to improve their communities and crusade for suffrage and other rights, to seek fair wages and better working conditions, and to make housework in the private household less time-consuming and odious. Women were coming together, even as greater class barriers, ethnic and cultural diversity, sectional and political loyalties, and philosophical differences regarding women's social roles undermined any kind of unified outlook. Peering into the future, Antoinette Brown Blackwell, the visionary women's rights activist, observed in 1875, "It is a general impulse, and one of those tidal waves in social life, which is impelling so many women into such varied fields of activity. What influence is powerful enough to arrest it?" As American women from across the country strode toward the twentieth century, bringing with them different hopes and visions of women's lives, what indeed could possibly hold them back from joining that vast tidal wave of activity?

CHAPTER 7

New Paths to Power

1890–1920

Karen Manners Smith

I n the summer of 1893, more than 27 million women, men, and children from all over the world visited the World's Columbian Exposition in Chicago, the United States's unabashed proclamation to the rest of humanity that the young democracy had arrived and was ready to join England and France and Spain as a great world power. President Grover Cleveland laid claim to the nation's new status when he opened the Chicago fair on May 1, 1893: "Surrounded by the stupendous results of American enterprise and activity ... [we] stand today in the presence of the oldest nations of the world and point to the great achievement we here exhibit, asking no allowance on the score of youth....We have built these splendid edifices, but we have also built the magnificent fabric of a popular government, whose grand proportions are seen throughout the world...."

Smallest among the "splendid edifices" was the Woman's Building. The lengthy struggle to build it—and, indeed, the whole battle to include women in the planning and administration of the fair—were proof that there were persistent inequalities under President Cleveland's "magnificent popular government." In fact, the women seeking space at the Exposition fared better than 9 million African Americans, virtually excluded from the fair except for displays of handcrafted items in two small exhibits. Few African Americans could be seen attending the fair, though it was open to all who could pay admission, and even black porters and janitors were in short supply.

Women had begun lobbying for a role in the world's fair in 1889, when Congress started to plan the four hundredth anniversary celebration of Columbus's arrival in the Americas. A coalition of woman's rights activists and working women demanded exhibit space for women equal to that being given to men, as well as assignments for women on all the governing boards of the fair. An equally determined group of public-spirited socialites and clubwomen, mostly Chicagoans, pressured Congress for a place at the fair that would include a separate women's building. An act of Congress created the World's Columbian Exposition and awarded the fair site to Chicago. A small amendment inserted at the last moment allowed for the appointment of a separate Board of Lady Managers to handle all business concerning women at the fair. Congress also allotted enough money to construction a "Woman's Building." The men in power thus found a way to include the women while excluding them from the real centers of decisionmaking and establishing them in a separate domain. The all-male fair commission also retained veto power and full financial control over all projects .

The 117 members of the Board of Lady Managers included representatives from all the states and territories, as well as a core group of nine from the host city. Among them were housewives and professional women, business owners, art patrons, and the wives and widows of mayors and governors. From the western states came a woman mine owner and at least one woman rancher. The women ranged in age from twenty-five to seventy; all were educated, though not all were college graduates; and they came from the middle and upper classes of society. The board included both suffragists and anti-suffragists, but there were no black women, despite concerted pressure for representation from African-American women's organizations. The board as a whole was anxious not to antagonize its white Southern members. Nor did the Board of Lady Managers contain any working-class women. The lady managers and the congressmen who appointed them assumed that an "industrial woman" could neither afford the loss of wages nor find the time to attend board meetings. The board was socially quite homogeneous, though regionally and politically diverse.

At its first meeting the Board of Lady Managers set up committees and elected its president, Bertha Honoré Palmer, the wife of one of Chicago's wealthiest men. Palmer was a clubwoman and a patron of the arts. She was not a suffragist, but she was an able politician, in the broadest sense of the term, and an advocate of women's labor reform. Palmer was a very hard worker, as were the other members of the Board of Lady Managers. They were determined that whatever they produced for the fair should be the achievement solely of women. To that end, they found twenty-one-year-old Sophia Hayden, the first woman graduate of the four-year architecture program at the Massachusetts Institute of Technology (MIT), who designed a classical building. Like other fair buildings, it was constructed of staff, a plaster compound not designed for permanence. Its columns, friezes, and ornamental roof sculptures were the work of Enid Yandell and Alice Rideout, both nineteen years old, and the interior decoration and assembling of exhibits became the responsibility of noted art experts Sara Hallowell and Candace Wheeler. One of two enormous murals that decorated the central rotunda was the work of Mary Cassatt.

The Board of Lady Managers also had to raise funds for two other buildings: a much-needed Children's Building, which became a large child-care center for fairgoing mothers, and a women's dormitory near the fairgrounds, for women who were traveling alone or with children. The dormitory also turned out to be popular with young college women visiting the fair in pairs or small groups.

Showcases in the Gallery of Honor at the World's Columbian Exposition displayed the work of women from many countries, primarily fine arts and needlework. Other works of art and portraits of notable women lined the walls.

When their own building was completed, the lady managers filled it with exhibits sent in by auxiliary women's committees in each state. Among the displays were photographs of the Grand Canyon submitted by a woman in Arizona, who had taken them while suspended over the edge in a rope sling with her camera tied to her shoulders. An embroiderer from North Dakota sent a silk opera cloak covered entirely in prairie-chicken feathers. Huge crates of material arrived from foreign countries, including a number of exhibits of women's work that had been denied space in other national and international pavilions.

Decorating the main hall were women's paintings and fine arts, among them some watercolors by England's Queen Victoria. Weaving, fine sewing, intricate lacework, and ceramics were distributed throughout the building. There was an Iowa Corn Kitchen for cooking demonstrations, and a roof garden café that became a popular restaurant for fair goers. The library contained some four thousand books by women, as well as an enormous compilation of American women's labor statistics, gathered by women on the state boards. It contained the first-ever directory of women's organizations in the United States.

In the Organizations Room several dozen women's organizations displayed books, pamphlets, posters, and other paraphernalia of their work. The National

American Woman Suffrage Association (NAWSA) had one small booth, under the auspices of the National Council of Women, an umbrella organization of more than fifty women's groups. NAWSA had reluctantly agreed to keep a low profile in the Woman's Building, mostly in deference to Bertha Palmer's desire not to antagonize fair goers by including politics in the exhibits. Despite its size, the NAWSA booth was much visited, and the suffragists were satisfied. Their more resounding successes lay elsewhere, in the women's branch of the World Congress Auxiliary, which held a series of conventions and meetings in conjunction with the exposition. The largest and best-attended of all the congresses was the World's Congress of Representative Women of May 1893. Nearly five hundred American and European women speakers, meeting in eighty-one sessions, spoke on an enormous variety of women's concerns.

Frances Ellen Watkins Harper of the National Council of Women was one of a handful of well-known black American activists who addressed the congress. Jane Addams of the settlement house movement gave a speech, as did Mary Kenney, a bookbinder and union organizer. A session on suffrage featuring Susan B. Anthony and Lucy Stone, two of America's most famous suffragists, was so crowded that one of the younger speakers fainted while the seventy-two-year-old Anthony was briskly clearing a path to the podium. Susan Anthony was much beloved; her enthusiasm for her cause was notoriously infectious, and she made her audience feel that women had made a great deal of progress in the forty-five years that she had been laboring for woman's rights. Always happy to declare even a small victory, she told her audience that the Woman's Building and the women's congresses had given suffrage a big boost. One member of the press declared, "the day of jubilee has come for that plain, tough, staunch, clear-headed and steel-nerved old lady, Miss Susan B. Anthony." Later in the summer, when she was repeatedly swamped by hand-shaking admirers on the fairgrounds, Anthony was asked if all the attention did not tire her. She replied that, yes, it did tire her, "but not half so much as it did thirty years ago to stand alone with no hands to shake at all."

When the Exposition ended, the exhibits were packed up and shipped back to their donors. Many of the lovely white buildings burned; others were torn down. Mary Cassatt's mural was lost in the chaos and never recovered. Plans for a Woman's Memorial Building did not materialize, and the members of the Board of Lady Managers and all their state auxiliary helpers went back to their own lives as wives and mothers, reformers, clubwomen, missionaries, teachers, doctors, farmers, suffragists, and socialites.

In the main, the women of the fair had accomplished what they had set out to do: they had convened, without male escort or assistance, from every corner of the country; they had run offices, signed contracts, and paid their workers; they had spent their resources wisely, whereas many subcommittees of the national exposition organization had gone into debt; they had built not one but three buildings; they had mounted a vast international display of women's arts and accomplishments both ancient and modern; and they had run conferences that attracted worldwide attention to a number of women's causes. They had also argued about everything; they had been bigoted and exclusionary; they had not changed history or even, as Susan B. Anthony had claimed, made a great deal of progress for woman suffrage. They had, however, made a tremendous statement about the value of women's public activity, a sort of century's-end summation of decades of women's voluntary work and association building, and of their progress in education and the arts.

The 1893 fair was emblematic of much that was relevant in the lives of American women during the Progressive Era, the years between 1890 and 1920. Many who would be principal players during the next thirty years—both individuals and organizations—were on hand for the exposition; their concerns, conflicts, and ambitions, as well as their accumulated accomplishments, were clearly on display. Equally clearly, the achievements of many women were ignored, their concerns glossed over or downplayed. Like their work and their issues, African-American women, working-class women, and, to a certain extent, recent immigrants were conspicuous by their absence. Exclusivity, racism, and class prejudice were stubborn curses that would continue to blight women's advances in the years to come. Nevertheless, many American women—whether together or separately—would find growing personal opportunities. All would face new challenges and continuing struggles to make changes in the American scene.

Women's World in 1890

In 1890 the United States boasted a population of almost 63 million, nearly half of whom lived in urban areas. The Civil War was twenty-five years in the past. The country's continental landmass had been mapped in detail from sea to sea and its western acres parceled out among settlers. The frontier was officially declared closed.

Over the next thirty years, an astounding number of social, political, and technological changes were to reshape the nation. Between 1890 and 1910, millions of new immigrants entered the country, most of them from Europe. In 1898 and again in 1917, the United States became involved in foreign wars in which nearly 120,000 Americans lost their lives. By 1912 the last six western territories had joined the Union. Labor unrest flared up around the country, culminating in dozens of strikes, many of which turned violent when factory owners brought in strikebreakers. White Southern vigilante gangs lynched an average of eighty-five African Americans each year, some of them women and children. A crippling four-year depression hit the country, beginning in the very week that the World's Columbian Exposition opened. Another began in 1907. And, in this same brief, turbulent span of thirty years, a country still becoming accustomed to the potential benefits of the new utilities—gas, electricity, and the telephone—witnessed the invention of the automobile, the airplane, the wireless radio, and the moving picture.

A mother's hard work is evident in the original caption for this photo supplied by a real estate company: "The house is small, but the children are healthy. The stacks are plenty, and the citrons show how gardens flourish in Morton County, North Dakota."

Against this broad background, a generation of American women lived and worked, married, and bore children. Many tried to change the world, either by seeking better work and trying to make a better life for themselves and their families or by tackling social problems that had arisen in the young country as a result of its rapid growth. Many tried to make a better world for women, who made up more than half the population but did not have full rights as U.S. citizens. The Progressive Era did not bring women either liberation or full social and political equality, but it was nevertheless aptly named, for it was a time when an unprecedented number of women began to find new paths to power and fulfillment.

At the end of the nineteenth century, when slightly more than half of all working people were still engaged in agriculture and the nation's population was still concentrated mostly in the Eastern states, the statistically and geographically average American woman would have been a thirty-eight- to forty-year-old white farmer's wife with four or five children, living in southwestern Ohio. Like 98 percent of married white women in 1890, this "average" American woman did not work for pay outside of her home. In addition to housekeeping, cooking, and child care, though, she probably performed a great deal of farm labor and may have sold eggs and butter to make a little cash. She may also have been involved in local church work, or a temperance group, or a ladies' auxiliary of the county Grange, an organization that encouraged farmer cooperatives and agitated for farmers' political rights. Our typical mid-continent woman was probably not an immigrant, but she might well have been the offspring of German or Scandinavian immigrants, the groups that had dominated the settlement of the Midwest after the Civil War. Her daughter, coming of age in the 1890s and educated in a local township school, might have more opportunities than her mother. Unless she married a farmer, or her parents needed her labor at home, she could move to Chicago or some other large city and take up work in a factory, shop, or office.

This picture of the statistically average American woman and her daughter does not tell the whole story. In fact, a white American woman in 1890 was just as likely to be a young working-class woman—a Russian-Jewish or Italian garment worker in New York City, a Polish meat packer in Chicago, or an Irish domestic servant in Boston—as she was to be a farmer's wife in Ohio or Nebraska, because immigration was changing the population so rapidly in 1890. The waves of British, Irish, and German immigration had ended in the 1880s. Now the immigrants, who arrived each year in the hundreds of thousands, came mostly from eastern and southern Europe—Russia, Poland, Serbia, Hungary, Greece, and Italy. Driven out of their native lands, in some cases by ethnic violence and in others by land shortages, population increases, and the loss of village economies to manufacturing, these European men and women came to a country where they had heard they could find both freedom and work. Many newcomers—mostly men—intended to go back rich, and some did. But most immigrants stayed, sending back to Europe for their parents, husbands, wives, and children, or for brothers and sisters and cousins. The 1890s found immigrants squeezed into teeming cities in the Northeast and the Midwest, living largely in ethnic neighborhoods and working in factories or sweatshops—small, privately owned workshops where men and women sewed clothing together piece by piece, usually working long hours at low wages. By 1910, nearly 80 percent of the population of New York City consisted of immigrants and their families.

Even in the most crowded tenement apartments, married women earned money at home by taking in boarders or by sewing or manufacturing small items such as hatboxes or artificial flowers, often employing their young children as assistants. Many of these women remained virtual strangers in their new land, uneducated and unable to speak English, their world limited to the tenement and the few city blocks that made up their ethnic neighborhoods. It was their daughters who went out to work, made friends, learned to speak the language, and contributed their pay packets to the family income.

In large Eastern and Midwestern cities thousands of unmarried women over the age of sixteen had jobs outside the home. In 1890 40 percent of all single white women were in the labor force; 60 percent of single nonwhite women; and 70 percent of single foreign-born women. These young women would join the growing ranks of the labor movement in the next thirty years to fight for a wide range of rights for working women.

Swelling immigrant populations often pushed Northern middle-class white families into better neighborhoods or out into suburbs, connected to the business and shopping districts of the cities by railroads and horse-drawn (later electrified) trams. Women in these suburban families spent their days at home engaged in child care and housework, usually assisted by one or more servants. By the 1890s, middle-class women had learned to relieve the isolation of long days at home with visiting and shopping expeditions and with memberships in women's clubs and civic reform groups. Such groups would experience astounding growth and increasing social and political influence after 1890.

Most white middle-class women still believed in the paramount importance of their function as mothers and homemakers: Women were responsible for the health and spiritual well-being of their families, and the family was, as one historian put it, "the principal adornment of Christian civilization and the bedrock upon which society rested." It was a growing impulse to extend this domestic moral guardianship to society as a whole that led so many of these women into the reform movements of the Progressive Era.

Increasingly, the daughters of white middle-class Northern women were well-educated, and they expected to earn high school or boarding school diplomas. It was no longer uncommon for young middle-class women to attend college, either at one of a growing number of women's colleges or at a coeducational university. In 1890 63 percent of the more than one thousand degree-granting colleges in the country were open to women. By the turn of the century, 40 percent of all college students would be women, though that figure represented less than 4 percent of all American women between the ages of eighteen and twenty-one.

Women's lives in the South at the turn of the century differed in several significant ways from those of their Northern counterparts. Recovery from the Civil War had been slow and incomplete, and the South did not share the industrial prosperity of the North. Society was sharply divided along racial lines, and white racism had become steadily worse after Reconstruction ended in the late 1870s. African-American parents could hope that the *next* generation of black women might escape sharecropping or working in white men's houses, where they were subject to insult and frequently in danger of sexual assault. There were, of course, middle-class black families in the South, and even some that were quite well off. Some daughters of these families attended all-black colleges or teachers' colleges. A very few even went to integrated colleges in the North. These women, along with others who had struggled through poverty to educate themselves, became nurses, doctors, social workers, and teachers; founded schools and missionary societies; and initiated black women's social reform efforts in the 1890s.

Not all white Southern women were middle-class. White tenant farmer families and white sharecroppers lived in dismal circumstances resembling those of their black counterparts. White women living outside agricultural areas sometimes sought jobs in cotton mills, though they often found the working conditions poor and the wages low. Southern white women of the middle and upper classes remained largely homebound, trapped by prewar notions of genteel Southern ladyhood and by white male chivalry, in which men assumed near total control of women's lives in exchange for "protection" of their supposed fragility and their sexual purity. State laws discriminated against women, making it especially difficult for them to obtain divorces and keep custody of their children. In one or two states, married women had only limited control over their own property. Some educated Southern white women had begun to join women's associations well before the 1890s. In these missionary societies, village improvement associations, church groups, and temperance leagues they found identities as reform workers that were acceptable in their restrictive society and that would lead them, after the turn of the century, to more politically charged public activity.

Compared to their Southern counterparts, many Western white women in 1890 found their lives full of opportunity and relative freedom. In the twenty-five years since the Civil War, cities on the Great Plains had grown like mushrooms. Coal, lead, and silver mines pockmarked the landscape from the hills of Appalachia to the slopes of the Rockies and Sierras. Railroads crisscrossed the entire country, tracing the routes where ox-drawn wagon trains, not fifty years before, had struggled to move pioneer families and their goods a few miles a day. Rapid continental travel was now available to anyone who had the price of a train ticket. By 1890, new farming families from Germany, Scandinavia, Poland, and Bohemia had joined earlier settlers, and farms and ranches blanketed the wide prairies with endless acres of wheat and vast herds of cattle. Independent women ranchers and farmers were by no means uncommon. The Homestead Act of 1862 had enabled the head of any family to claim and work 160 acres of western land, and many single women and widows eagerly took advantage of the opportunity to become landowners.

A number of married women followed their husbands to mining towns in the Rockies, while single women and widows gravitated to growing cities—such as Denver, Salt Lake, San Francisco, and Seattle—to work in laundries and other service occupations. Many women ended up working as prostitutes in Western cities. For others, there were opportunities to start small businesses, and some entrepreneurial women owned their own hotels, restaurants, or boardinghouses. Here, as in the East, most women who worked outside the home were domestic servants or teachers, though the Far West had a disproportionately large number of the country's professional women—authors, journalists, doctors, lawyers—who were attracted, perhaps, to a section of the country that still breathed an atmosphere of freedom and adventure.

Western coastal states were especially attractive to Asian immigrants, though the influx of Chinese laborers had slowed to a trickle after the Chinese Exclusion Act became law in 1882. Filipino immigration increased significantly after the Spanish-American War in 1898, and by the end of the nineteenth century, Japanese immigrants had established substantial communities in California. Although the Chinese and Filipino immigration was at first mostly male, Japanese immigration was more evenly balanced between men and women. The Asian groups tended to remain isolated from the larger society, which regarded their different physical characteristics, as well as their languages and customs, with deep suspicion and contempt. Like women in other immigrant cultures, Asian women remained more isolated and less assimilated than men, remaining homebound or working in restaurants, laundries, or small industries run exclusively by members of their community. Many new brides went straight from the boat to the farms of central California, where they picked fruit and vegetables alongside their husbands by day and cooked meals and cared for their children and living quarters the rest of the time.

Western white expansion in the United States had irreparably disrupted the lives of American Indians. By the 1890s, government authorities had confined nearly all tribes to reservation lands. Whites found Native American culture incomprehensible, unclean, and immoral. The impulse to fence it in was accompanied by the desire to eradicate it through conversion to white, Christian ways. Government agents and missionaries, a number of them women, had been at work among Native Americans of the West for several decades, stressing assimilation and the abandonment of native religions, languages, dress, and sexual customs.

Native American women resisted assimilation in a number of ways. Sioux women, for example, maintained their right simply to walk away from unsatisfactory marriages, much to the scandalized horror of white missionaries. Many Indian women also resisted pressure to abandon traditional methods of food preparation. Others learned to exploit the off-reservation marketplace to their advantage. In the 1890s, for example, Navajo women weavers began producing richly patterned rugs for sale in trading posts, providing much-needed cash for a number of Navajo families. In the long run, there was no way Indian women could redeem the losses they had suffered from a century of cultural destruction, but their selective approach to adaptation helped preserve vital remnants of traditional culture and kept their families alive.

By 1890 it had become clear to many that the nineteenth-century "Woman Movement" was entering a new phase of broadened aims and growing public acceptance. Poised to enter the twentieth century, the movement was endowed with a complex legacy of woman's rights issues and an array of both old and new women's associations that were primed for action.

Since the first Woman's Rights Convention in Seneca Falls, New York, in 1848, women had been arguing that male dominance and female submission were neither just nor God-given. While agreeing that women were different from men, woman's rights advocates insisted that as human beings women deserved the same natural rights as those enjoyed by men and guaranteed to men by the U.S. Constitution. Gradually, women's advocates expanded their arguments in favor of equality to include a discussion of woman's unique potential for social contribution, insisting that because of woman's special nature—her qualities as a nurturer and moral leader—she should be given full political and social parity with men, including the right to vote.

Like jugglers keeping several different balls in the air at one time, the leaders of the Woman Movement kept their somewhat contradictory arguments alive simultaneously, though not without a great deal of contention and confusion. They continued to insist on their natural entitlement to social and political equality with men. But it was their skillful promotion of the public use of women's special talents that won wider acceptance for women's reform efforts during the Progressive Era.

Organizations such as the Woman's Christian Temperance Union (WCTU) and women's clubs began to address civic concerns near the end of the nineteenth century. These groups had enjoyed phenomenal growth, and in 1890 more than two hundred local clubs came together in a national federation, which they called the General Federation of Women's Clubs. Like the WCTU, the clubs made it safe for traditional women to engage in political behavior and to see themselves not simply as housewives and mothers but as citizens. Black American women, unwelcome in the white women's club movement, formed their own federations in the 1890s. The most important of these was the National Association of Colored Women, an organization dedicated to political and educational reform and to improving the lives of black men, women, and children.

Woman suffrage, foremost among the demands of the earliest generation of woman's rights activists, had long been the stepsister of the Woman Movement. Many Americans, both men and women, found this direct demand to share political power with men especially threatening. The suffragists' demand for equal voting rights produced a prolonged storm of opposition because it constituted both a real threat to men's exclusive political control and a perceived threat to cherished ideas about woman's nature and social function.

After its formation in 1890, the National American Woman Suffrage Association (NAWSA) was the beneficiary of the decades in which the WCTU, the club movement, and other women's associations had made women's public activity increasingly acceptable. In addition, many women reformers, perceiving that they would be unable to bring about significant change if they lacked the most basic of political rights, soon allied themselves with NAWSA. With its membership on the increase on both state and local levels, NAWSA prepared to focus national discussion of woman's rights on the issue of suffrage and to lead the battle for the vote into the twentieth century.

For the new generation of women, these were heady times. By the mid-1890s, the ideals of the Progressive movement had begun to capture the American imagination, leading concerned men and women to the recognition that their young nation could not, without intervention, overcome the problems created by rapid industrialization and urbanization, the rising tide of new immigration, and the excesses of capitalism. Progressive leaders directed attention to the problems of

American cities—centers of poverty, overcrowding, poor sanitation, and exploitative employment practices—and to the injustices of the nation's economic system. They pointed out that money and property were so badly distributed in the United States that 1 percent of the population owned more than 85 percent of the wealth, while hundreds of thousands lived in poverty.

Books by "muckraking" Progressive journalists, such as Jacob Riis's *How the Other Half Lives* (1890), Ida Tarbell's *History of the Standard Oil Company* (1904), and Upton Sinclair's *The Jungle* (1906), exposed corrupt municipal governments and squalid living conditions among city tenement dwellers, monopolistic business practices, and filth and danger in the industrial workplace. Farmers and political orators in the new Populist party denounced both banks and railroads, which they blamed for agricultural depression and rising farmers' debt. Miners and factory workers went out on strike time and time again to draw attention to their low wages and hazardous working conditions. In every corner of the land, middle- and working-class Progressives trumpeted the need for social change, convinced that society could be transformed if enough people worked to make it happen. For the Progressives, social reform required government intervention on state and local levels, including the passage of regulatory legislation, the funding of government assistance programs, and the creation of government bureaus for social investigation. Reformers also promoted privately run charities and social service organizations, such as settlement houses, which were residential forerunners of the modern community center.

Almost all the new public and private avenues of reform would attract women. For working-class women, the Progressive Era was a chance to focus their energies on the labor movement and the crusade for workers' protection and child labor laws. For middle-class women, the chance to join the attack on the evils of industrial society was an unprecedented opportunity: The possibilities for personal and social progress seemed endlessly exhilarating. It was an eager and purposeful generation of women that swept out of the house during the 1890s and marched on to the next stage of freedom and responsibility.

At Home

The women who filled their lives with public activity from 1890 to 1920 were in a minority. The vast, and mostly silent, majority of American women did not seek changes in gender roles or the existing social order. Many were unable to envision any life other than the one that they currently shared with their families and other members of their class and region. What forces and choices shaped the lives of these women, who kept house for their families, shopped, cooked, raised children, and were largely uninterested in ideas about paid employment, higher education, or voting rights? And what was life like for women who lived in rural isolation, trapped in the unending struggle for daily survival? What about women who could not speak English or those whose most cherished beliefs and customs were alien to the mainstream of American culture? These women, too, are part of the Progressive Era story, for it is their largely unrecorded lives that form the backdrop for the achievements of pioneer educators, suffragists, labor leaders, artists, and rebels. Before we look at the lives and work of activist women, it is important to know how the majority lived and how ideas about women's roles both sustained and limited those lives.

For most of the nineteenth century, the social doctrine of "separate spheres" had promulgated the notion that only men were strong enough to survive daily contact with the dirty world of commerce and industry. The home was a sanctuary from the outside world, where wives, mothers, sisters, and daughters were safely distant from the cash economy and where world-weary men might find peace and a renewed sense of honor in the sympathy and love dispensed by the women of their families, women whose lifelong training taught them that piety, purity, and submissiveness were inborn attributes of the female character. These same wives and mothers were also expected to be able to cook, to clean, and to raise both male and female offspring in an atmosphere of religion and morality. Even the legal system seemed to concur in this conception of woman's nature and work. In an 1873 opinion, the U.S. Supreme Court perfectly described the prevailing idea of womanhood: "The paramount destiny and mission of women are to fulfill the noble and benign offices of wife and mother. This is the law of the Creator." The doctrine of separate spheres required women to dedicate their lives exclusively to unpaid housework and child care, regardless of their individual personalities, tastes, and abilities. A man might measure his life success in any of a multitude of different professions or crafts, but a woman was considered successful only if she were a good wife, mother, and homemaker.

Catharine Beecher and others had tried to reconcile women to the limitations of the household sphere by glorifying their duties. In the 1890s, the home economists—a group of professional women, largely academics—gave much wider meaning to Beecher's ideas about professionalizing housework. Led by Ellen Swallow Richards, the first woman professor at MIT, proponents of home economics developed the field into an academic discipline and built whole departments in colleges and universities dedicated to training domestic science teachers. Home economists thought that homemaking was too complex and too important to be left to chance transmission from mother to daughter. Their solution was to train mothers and daughters in the classroom and the chemistry lab so that they could run their homes according to the most up-to-date scientific knowledge. Characteristic of this new professionalized approach to housework was the application of business and industrial management techniques to the homely tasks of cleaning and cooking. Home economics enlarged the whole topic of housekeeping by bringing it into the public education system and giving it scientific legitimacy. The new discipline helped to transport woman's domestic role into the twentieth century and further cemented the relationship between the American woman and her home.

Assumptions about woman's domestic nature and responsibilities were middle class in origin, but by the end of the nineteenth century they had come to transcend class boundaries and regional differences. Disseminated across the United

States in schoolrooms, sermons, women's magazines, household manuals, and etiquette books, the domestic ideal of American womanhood was almost universally accepted by both men and women. However, like all ideals, it was never perfectly attainable. Although it represented a goal for many women, to others it was an imposition—someone else's idea of what they ought to be and do.

Even among women whose financial circumstances required them to work for wages in factories or shops, or to perform farm chores, the domestic ideal had tremendous influence; the ideal of ladyhood and domesticity became a distant dream. One widowed young black woman, who told her story to the *Independent* magazine in 1912, explained that the opportunity to run her own home and look after her own children was out of the question. She was a children's nurse who worked for a white family from fourteen to sixteen hours a day. She was often up in the night with the baby, who was the youngest of the family's four children. The nurse's own children, left in the care of an older sister, were not allowed to visit their mother at her job, so she only saw them by chance in the street, or every other Sunday afternoon, which she had off. She was never allowed to spend the night in her own home. The nurse was paid ten dollars a month for her work, far from enough to support the children she was not allowed to nurture.

For black domestic servants who did not live in the employer's household, work hours were frequently so long that they, too, were concerned about neglecting their own families. For these women, and for women farm laborers, tobacco factory workers, and many others, the fulfillment of the womanly ideal might have been the opportunity to devote to their own homes and families the same long days of drudgery they were already putting in for white people. However, in rural areas all over the country, black and white families typically mixed work and family life. In the South, in particular, where many African Americans worked in agriculture and only low-paying jobs were available, both men and women worked to provide the family income. Most women found ways to share part of the domestic work with other women relatives, and neighboring aunts and grandmothers often helped with child care. The shape of family life for most black Americans, blended as it was with the life of kin and community, was an arrangement dictated by necessity. Quite different from the middle-class domestic ideal of full-time mother and homemaker, it was a workable alternative.

Middle-class black women had their own difficulties in relating to the standards of domesticity set by white society. Mary Church Terrell was a college-educated clubwoman and spirited social activist, married to a black judge in Washington, D.C. Terrell, who had been raised by well-to-do parents to be a respectable lady, daily encountered the effects of racism in her reform efforts on behalf of African-American women. She was also deeply troubled by her own inability to find a well-built, comfortable house in which to raise her children. The Terrells could afford a substantial house in a nice neighborhood, but for years no one would sell to them because they were black.

This Japanese immigrant family, photographed in 1901, is clothed in American style.

Like black women, many immigrant women found the reality of their lives at odds with the middle-class American domestic ideal. For some, especially for Asian women arriving on the West Coast around the turn of the twentieth century, the important thing was to look like an American lady as quickly as possible. Japanese immigrants, aware that Chinese immigration had been restricted after 1882, were anxious to prove that they could be quickly assimilated into American life. One young bride described her first hour in California: "I was immediately outfitted with Western clothing at Hara's Clothing Store. Because I had to wear a tight corset around my chest, I could not bend forward. I had to have my husband tie my shoe laces. . . . In my case I wore a large hat, a high-necked blouse, a long skirt, a buckled belt around my waist, high-laced shoes, and of course, for the first time in my life, a brassiere and hip pads." New clothing was only the first of many adjustments that the Japanese bride would have to make. Wed to a man she had never seen because her marriage had been arranged by mail, she would be expected to keep house, raise her children, and work among strangers for the rest of her life.

Other newcomers from eastern and southern Europe took up housekeeping in large American cities, where they settled with their families by the hundreds of thousands around the turn of the century. Their ideas about woman's role had been shaped by their centuries-old cultures. These ideas echoed middle-class beliefs that woman's primary functions were domestic and maternal, but immigrant women often had notions of housekeeping and ideas about marriage and childrearing that seemed strange to native-born Americans. For example, New York City social workers, raised in a culture protective of girls and women, often questioned the wisdom of Jewish mothers who sent young teenage girls out into the work force to help support the family while their brothers were encouraged to remain in school and continue their religious studies.

As for housekeeping itself, even experienced immigrant homemakers could find their adjustment to American life full of painful complexity. A Sicilian woman, recalling her home in the old country, told an interviewer: "We had no blinds, no curtains, and the floors were all made of stone. You have no idea how simple life is over there. Here one must wash [laundry] two or three times a week; over there, once a month." Frequently, immigrant housekeeping methods earned the disapproval of middle-class settlement-house workers and schoolteachers who, though essentially sympathetic with the difficulties of the immigrant families that they were trying to help, thought immigrants' decorating tastes were garish and disapproved of their preferences in dress and diet.

Eager to turn their parents into Americans, the children of immigrants sometimes grew impatient with old traditions, feeling that the crafts and skills their mothers had developed in the Old World had little relevance in America or in the lives of the younger generation. Many immigrant women found cherished needlecraft and other rural domestic industries scorned by their daughters, who could buy the kind of finery they valued very cheaply in department stores.

As the quality of tenement housing slowly improved during the early decades of the twentieth century, immigrant women learned to accept not only new housekeeping techniques made possible by gas, electricity, and running water, but also the changing standard of cleanliness and family care that social reformers and their own Americanized children had been urging upon them for years. At the same time, these women, who had come to the United States from cultures where they produced nearly all the items essential to family survival—food, clothing, farm products—gradually became consumers of domestic goods. In this role they joined their middle-class sisters, adopting an aspect of American life that would grow increasingly important during the twentieth century. In *Breadgivers*, an autobiographical novel of immigrant life in New York in 1900, Anzia Yezierska describes the first stages of the process by which immigrants became consumers: "But the more people get the more they want. We no sooner got used to regular towels then we began to want toothbrushes, each for himself. . . . We got the toothbrushes and we began wanting toothpowder to brush our teeth with, instead of ashes. And more and more we wanted more things, and really needed more things the more we got them."

Embraced by the larger American culture and enthusiastically promoted by the experts, the domestic ideal for women was remarkably persistent. Women of various classes and ethnic groups struggled to live up to it. As late as the 1920 census, more than 75 percent of all adult women reported that they functioned exclusively as wives, mothers, and housekeepers in their own homes. The home, however, was changing. By 1900, the domestic role of women was already beginning to reflect the long-term effects of social and technological changes that had been taking place since the Civil War.

Most significantly, women's marital and maternal roles were different from those of their grandmothers. Marriages were not as permanent as they had been in the past. By 1900 the divorce rate had risen to one in twelve couples; by 1915 the rate was one in nine. Two-thirds of divorces were sought by women, a clear indication that a growing number of women were unwilling to accept unsatisfactory marriages and that, increasingly, they had the courage and the means to obtain their independence. The proportion of women choosing never to marry at all had risen from 6 percent throughout the nineteenth century to 10 percent in the 1890s. This new group of women who never married included many educated professionals and others who felt that they could find satisfactory lives, work, and companionship without husbands and children.

Among married white women of childbearing age, the birthrate had dropped from seven children for each woman in 1800 to three to four children in 1900. Among African-American women the birth rate began to decline dramatically after 1900, and by the 1920s about half of all married black women in northern cities were remaining childless, compared to only one-fourth of married white women. The birthrates of immigrant groups also decreased as they became more assimilated into American culture.

These figures suggest to historians that women were exercising increasing control over marriage and reproduction, that they wanted smaller families, and that they were using available methods of birth control. Because medical advances and improvements in nutrition were also making it possible for women in the early twentieth century to live into their sixties and seventies—an increase of ten years over their nineteenth-century life expectancy—they could reasonably expect to have a number of years free from child care responsibilities. Fewer children and longer lives added up to opportunities to engage in work or social life beyond the home and family. For middle-class women, this meant free time to participate in clubs, church groups, and other associations; for working-class women, increased opportunities for picnics in parks, visits to kin, meetings of mutual aid societies, or, after 1905, an occasional trip to the movies.

Along with the social changes that were opening new vistas of independence for the domesticated American woman came a number of late-nineteenth-century industrial and technological advances. However, change that affected household work was slow and uneven, and at the turn of the century many women in the United States labored over the same kinds of cleaning, laundry, and cooking chores that their grandmothers had performed in the middle of the nineteenth century.

Utopian schemes for the radical alteration of domestic work, such as those proposed by social critics Edward Bellamy and Charlotte Perkins Gilman, had appealed to both social visionaries and practical reformers but never seemed to catch on with the general public. Americans simply were not comfortable about exchanging family meals for community kitchens and dining halls, or raising their children in community dormitories. For some Americans "communalism" sounded too much like "communism." For others, the idealized private home—a separate dwelling for each family—was sacred, even though removing some of its most tedious labor would have saved wives and mothers considerable drudgery.

Constant hard work remained a fact of life for most women. It was especially burdensome for those without domestic servants or household help other than their children. In her memoir, *Womenfolks* (1983), Shirley Abbott described a typical Sunday morning in the life of her grandmother, Lavisa Loyd, a farmer's wife who was raising eleven children in rural Arkansas in 1914. Loyd rose at dawn, as she did every day, made a trip to the outhouse, carried a pail of water from the well, and then nursed, washed, and dressed her twin infants. She woke the other nine children and sent them scurrying for more water, wood and kindling for the stove, and milk and butter. Together they shook out the feather-bed tickings and made the beds. Some of the children watched the babies while others helped Lavisa cook the breakfast. There were mounds of bacon, eggs, and potatoes to fry, and gravy to be made; three or four dozen biscuits to be cut and baked, and coffee to set boiling. In the half hour after breakfast Lavisa washed, dried, and put away every single dish, cup, and pan, and swept and mopped the floor. She next saw to it that every child was dressed in a freshly ironed shirt or cotton dress and that faces, hands, and ears were scrubbed clean. At nine o'clock Loyd and her husband drove their eleven children to church in the farm wagon pulled by a team of mules.

From Abbott's description, Lavisa Loyd might as well have been living in 1874 as in 1914. In rural Arkansas, as in rural Arizona, or Montana, or even in parts of Maine, many people lived as if gas, electricity, telephones, and automobiles had not been invented. On the other hand, city people were already acquainted with these wonders, and with movies and airplanes as well. As a rule, innovation happened more quickly in cities than in rural areas, and new technology was available to the well-to-do many years before it reached the homes of working people. Few of the new home utilities and labor-saving machines were ready for mass consumption before 1920. In the case of laundry, all but the wealthiest housewives did some laundry themselves or assisted their domestic servants with the backbreaking labor. Any family who could afford it hired a laundress to come in by the day or take clothing to her own home to wash. By 1910, commercial steam laundries—staffed mostly by women workers—had become big business in cities and large towns, easing the chores of wash day for housewives. In later decades, automatic washing machines would return laundry to the home, making it, once again, the responsibility of the housewife.

The ready-to-wear garment industry had begun to relieve some of women's burdens in home clothing manufacture well before 1890. By 1910 women's clothing was available off the rack in department stores and through catalog sales from Sears Roebuck and other large mail order companies. Clothing came in many styles and all sizes, and it was cheap even by the standards of the day: children's underwear was twelve cents per piece; men's denim overalls sold for forty-eight cents; and ladies' all-wool, two-piece suits for between ten and seventeen dollars. By 1920, most American women were happily buying rather than making their clothing.

Food preparation remained a great consumer of the housewife's time. Most items had to be made from scratch. Even bread, available at pennies a loaf from commercial bakeries, was baked weekly in many middle-class homes. According to such experts as Marion Harland, author of *Marion Harland's Complete Cookbook* (1903), the housewife who made her own bread was demonstrating both her love for her family and her mastery of homemaking skills. In fact, almost all home cooking was a challenge, given the uncertain temperament of most turn-of-the-century cookstoves and the culinary tastes of most husbands and children, who expected to be served three cooked meals a day. In 1900, nearly all American homes had cast-iron stoves, which had replaced fireplace cooking and heating in all but the most primitive houses. Stoves made cooking much easier and used fuel economically, and their temperature could be more or less controlled through the manipulation of a set of dampers. Many kitchen stoves had attached water-heating and storage reservoirs, which made dish washing and laundry easier than they had been in the days when all water had to be hauled and heated in kettles over the fire.

Commercially canned goods—fish, meats, soups, and tomatoes—had been available since the Civil War but became cheap enough for mass consumption only after 1890. The invention of the refrigerated railroad car brought to market an expanding variety of fruits and vegetables in all seasons, although goods that had traveled from California and Florida were not always inexpensive. Most housewives had to plan daily purchases of fresh foods, especially meat and dairy products, either at the market or grocery store, or from vendors who sold foods door-to-door in cities and suburbs. The home icebox, cooled by hundred-pound blocks of ice delivered to the home twice weekly, kept perishables from spoiling immediately in warm weather. Because iceboxes were relatively cheap (five dollars to twenty dollars), all but the poorest families had them. Electric refrigerators did not become widely available until the 1930s, and even in the 1950s some American homes still had iceboxes.

Most Americans used coal for heating and cooking, though families burned wood in parts of the country where trees were still abundant. Coal and wood smoke left a thin film of grime on furniture and windowsills and embedded itself in carpets and curtains, making housecleaning a repetitive and thankless task. Coal-fired furnaces and central heating systems, which burned more cleanly than small stoves and had been available for decades, were still so expensive in the 1890s that they were found only in the urban homes of affluent people. By the 1920s, as a result of changes in steel manufacture and new techniques of mass production, costs came down, and central heating became a standard feature of new houses and apartment buildings. Suburban homeowners also sought ways to install furnaces and hot-air vents or radiators in existing houses. The basement furnace was far from universal in this period, however. Many middle- and working-class folk still had to haul wood from the woodpile or coal from the basement to the stove several times a day.

In the early 1890s, the new gas appliance industry began a massive marketing campaign to get homeowners to use gas for heating, cooking, and lighting. Gas lighting had been a feature of city streets and other public places since before the Civil War. Now there were gas cooking ranges for homes, as well as gas space heaters and furnaces, gas hot-water heaters, gas wall lamps, gas-fired laundry room boilers, and even gas toasters and hair-curling irons. With gas, kitchens would stay cool in summer, and living and sleeping rooms could be warmed rapidly. A 1896 promotional pamphlet from a large gas company included a testimonial promising the housewife a kind of kitchen salvation to be obtained by installing a gas stove: "I looked into my kitchen this morning an hour after breakfast and found it clean, shaded, and cool, although the September heat is intense out-of-doors. As soon as the meals are sent to the table every bit of heat is shut off from range and room. . . . Think of having no coal to bring upstairs; no dampers to regulate (and to break); no ashes to take out; no kindling wood to buy or chop; no fretting because the fire is too low to toast your bread and to broil your steak. . . ."

Gas for cooking certainly made a difference. But gas had to be piped into homes, and for a long time it was available only in major metropolitan areas. Although gas was a cleaner fuel than wood or coal, gas lamps did produce soot, and small gas appliances were not portable. By the 1920s, gas was firmly established in urban areas as an excellent fuel for cooking and heating, but it had lost a significant part of its domestic market to the new technological wonder, electricity.

Electric lighting, invented by Thomas Edison and developed by his financial backers in the 1880s, was available in large cities in the 1890s. In a remarkably short span of years, the Edison electrical system was in place throughout much of the country. The electrical future became the present, as Americans wired their homes for electricity in ever-increasing numbers. By 1920 34.7 percent of urban and suburban residences nationwide had electrical wiring. During the next two decades, as manufacturing boomed and prices fell to meet middle-class incomes, people began to acquire motor-driven washing machines and refrigerators in addition to electric light.

Compared to the complexities of the Edison electrical system, the engineering required for basic household plumbing was not a difficult technology. Piped water and flush toilets had been available to the rich since the Civil War. But indoor plumbing and appliances—sinks, bathtubs, and toilets—were not mass-marketed nationally until after the turn of the century. Many rural families continued to rely on a backyard pump or well, or even, in some cases, a nearby stream or pond for all their water needs. Like the hand pump, the outdoor toilet was a common feature of rural life and remained so in some places until after World War II. Major cities and towns, responding to public health concerns about sewage and disease, had installed basic municipal water and waste systems during the nineteenth century, but these were seldom connected to either the tenements or small single homes of the urban poor until after 1900.

In sophisticated cities like New York and Philadelphia, where hot and cold running water and full bathrooms were becoming standard equipment in most middle-class houses and apartment buildings, the woman whose home was a tenement might find herself hauling all her water for cooking, dishwashing, and laundry from a single cold water faucet in the hallway, and disposing of it by dumping it out the window, just as her ancestors had done for centuries in the old country. The tenement's single toilet per floor might also be in the hallway, shared by as many as four or five families and numerous paying boarders.

Urban housing improved rapidly in the prosperous years just before and after World War I; rural areas modernized much more slowly. People whose fortunes were on the rise, many of whom were immigrants, found new apartments with electric light, gas cooking stoves, hot and cold running water in both kitchens and bathrooms, and giant basement furnaces that heated whole buildings. Ironically, the opportunity to improve housekeeping with new sources of energy and new appliances actually made housework more complex, multiplying some tasks while relieving the burdens of others. Hot running water meant washing and cleaning were easier, but also suggested the need to take more baths or to mop the floor more often. Washing machines made it possible to wash the same clothes more frequently than before. Easily regulated gas or electric ovens meant the housewife could attempt more elaborate cooking and baking than her mother had been able to produce in her day. Despite its heavily advertised promises, the new domestic technology did not actually liberate women from housework. Rather, it intensified the importance of the home and woman's role in it by suggesting that housework could be scientifically perfected.

All the domestic experts and professional home economists promoted scientific housekeeping and the consumption of new appliances and energy sources. In magazines and books, on the lecture circuit, and in secondary schools, where domestic science became part of the required curriculum for girls, these authorities encouraged homemakers and potential homemakers to time their tasks, to break household jobs into segments, and to follow strict sanitary guidelines, especially in cleaning bathrooms and kitchens, potential sources of infectious disease.

"You will send it by special messenger? Thank you."

The Telephone Assists Housewives

THE affairs of the household make the **telephone** a valuable assistant to housewives. It has so many uses in making home management easier and more convenient.

The telephone puts the home within instant reach of all up-to-date stores; with the doctor, lawyer, dentist; with the husband at his place of business; in fact, the telephone keeps the home in touch with everyone who can add to its comfort or offer it protection.

Why not have a telephone in YOUR home?

Just telephone, write or call at our nearest Commercial Office for further information regarding residence telephone service

NEW YORK TELEPHONE CO.

In their early days, telephone companies had to convince consumers that their product was useful. Manufacturers made a particular appeal to women, assuring them that the instrument would give them security and convenience.

Mothers were instructed to keep infants on strict scientific schedules for eating, sleeping, and playing. Girls learned the chemistry of foods and cooking, reinterpreting recipes and even entire menus according to their caloric values, often with little regard for their taste. By 1920 housewives had more rules to follow, more goods to purchase and consume, more technological help and fewer domestic servants, and—because they knew more and could do more—an even stronger sense of responsibility for the health and well-being of their families than they had had thirty years before. Some tasks had moved outside the home, but more elaborate cleaning, cooking, and child care techniques had replaced them. No longer the family's moral guardian, as she had been in the nineteenth century, the twentieth-century housewife had become the guardian of family health and psychological well-being as well as the keeper of the family purse and chief of expenditure. Her title, hours, work load, and "wages" were the same, even if the equipment and the instruction booklet had changed.

In 1920 hardly anybody talked about "woman's sphere" anymore. The new American homemaker had fewer children than her predecessors, more free time, and a more companionable relationship with her husband. Increasingly, married women were entering the paid work force. Indeed, the essential identification of woman with home was in the process of being challenged by women's growing presence in the professions and by their new participation in public life. Broad-ranging role changes, however, lay in the future. For the vast majority of women in 1920, domesticity was still destiny in America.

At Work

Marriage, home, and family were universally acknowledged to be the goals of young women in turn-of-the-century America, whatever their backgrounds. In fact, fully 90 percent of all American women could expect to be married at some time in their lives. For most middle- and upper-class women, domesticity would become a full-time occupation. But for working-class women, most of whom spent their adolescent years engaged in some form of wage work, marriage and motherhood did not necessarily mean that paid labor ceased altogether. Their lives told a different story, one in which earning income was linked to the fulfillment of their roles as wives, mothers, and daughters.

In the majority of immigrant families and for many working-class families of native-born Americans, the standard middle-class pattern, in which an entire family lived on the income of one man, was completely unachievable. The wages paid to a semiskilled working man in 1909, for example—between twelve dollars and fifteen dollars a week—were simply not enough to sustain a family. In large cities, rent often took between a quarter and a third of the family income and frequently did not include heat or fuel for the stove. Food, purchased daily to avoid spoilage, was relatively expensive. A chicken cost twenty-five cents, and potatoes were two cents a pound. Pennies for the newspaper, nickels for carfare, loaves of

A mother holds her baby on her lap while assembling cigarettes on her kitchen table. It was customary for young children to assist their mothers in such home enterprises, as the young son does here.

bread, and cups of coffee added up fast. Many families had bought their furniture on the installment plan, and many belonged to unions or mutual benefit societies. These payments and dues had to be met monthly.

Families adopted a variety of strategies to expand their incomes. In African-American families, where education was prized as a way out of poverty and second-class citizenship, children and teenagers remained in school while their mothers sought work as field hands, domestics, or laundresses. In Northern mill towns, where entire families worked at the textile mill, parents made child care arrangements with neighbors and relatives for the youngest children so that the mothers could work. In the large immigrant communities in major cities, especially among Jews and Italians, Old World traditions demanded that married women and mothers stay at home and that children, especially daughters, be taken out of school and sent out to work, sometimes as young as thirteen or fourteen years old. Daughters were expected to hand over their weekly pay packets, unopened, to their mothers. Usually they received back only carfare and lunch money, and perhaps fifty cents spending money, from an entire week's wages of some six to eight dollars. The rest was applied to family living expenses. Married women worked at home to supplement the family income by taking in laundry or garment-making piecework, by rolling cigars, or constructing artificial flowers. Fully 12 percent of American working women were employed in home work, usually making or finishing items for which an outside contractor paid them by the piece.

Perhaps the most common way for married women to augment the family income was by taking in boarders. In immigrant communities all over the country, where men heavily outnumbered women, it was a typical practice for a working-man to board in the home of a fellow immigrant and his family while saving money to bring his own family to America. Women who took in boarders were expected to provide two or three meals a day and clean laundry, as well as a bed, possibly a room. Many families had several boarders, each paying a weekly fee and often sharing tiny tenement apartments with the family. Some New England textile communities surveyed in 1909 had an average of 2.4 boarders per family.

While mothers stayed at home and brought in money, their daughters were out working in the industrial world. According to the census of 1900, about 5 million women worked for wages outside the home—approximately one in every five women in the country. By 1920, the nonagricultural female labor force, largely urban and white, had swelled to 7.5 million. Most white working women were under twenty-five years of age; three-quarters of them were single. For these women, industrial jobs tended to concentrate in the production of textiles, shoes, shirts, and accessories such as hats, gloves, stockings, and collars. They also worked in canning, bottling, and meat-packing factories and in bookbinding and cigar making. Ten percent of America's working women were professionals, mostly teachers, and another 10 percent were clerks and saleswomen.

Until the middle of World War I, African Americans were excluded from all but the most menial of manufacturing jobs—sweeping, scrubbing, and cleaning factory rest rooms—because of their race. Unlike most working-class white counterparts, African-American women could expect to work for wages outside their homes throughout their single and married lives. In Southern cities and towns, widows and grandmothers often took jobs in old age to support themselves and dependent relatives who had been thrown out of work by the unstable labor economy.

By far the largest employment sector for young American women, both black and white, was domestic service. In 1900 one-third of all wage-earning women— nearly 2 million of them—worked either as servants in private homes or as waitresses in hotels and restaurants. The great majority of household servants in the North, Midwest, and West were white immigrant women or their daughters, though native-born white women continued to work as domestic servants in country towns and villages. In the South, white middle-class families almost exclusively employed black women as maids, nurses, cooks, and laundresses.

Because weekly wages were comparable to those of factory hands but room and board were free, domestic service gave immigrant women a chance to save money. Among Irish servants it was common to send money back to relatives in Ireland or to pay ship's passage for parents and siblings who wanted to immigrate to America.

Women from other immigrant groups—Germans, Scandinavians, and Slavs, for example—went into domestic service because they spoke little or no English and were unqualified for many other jobs. For some new arrivals domestic service provided a chance to learn a little English and become familiar with American culture.

Though some middle-class households employed more than one domestic servant—cooks, nursemaids, laundresses, and handymen were often hired as supplemental help—the most common type of domestic was the general servant, or maid-of-all-work. She labored alone at any and all tasks her employer designated as hers, including all the cleaning and cooking and often the laundry. Fourteen-hour days were not unusual, and few servants had more than two afternoons or one afternoon and one evening off a week. Even with the long hours, domestic service was generally thought to be healthy work, partly because a middle-class diet gave servants improved nutrition and partly because the clean, middle-class home in a good neighborhood was considered a morally and physically safe environment for a young woman who had to earn her living.

For most young women, however, the negative aspects of domestic service—drudgery, loneliness, the lack of personal freedom, and the sense of social inferiority—seriously outweighed the positive ones. Few remained long in any one household, and fewer still saw domestic service as any kind of lifework or career. Even though middle-class housewives kept up a constant demand for maids and cooks, and service jobs were always available, most urban young women preferred to take their chances with industry and commerce, where health hazards and fluctuating wages constituted the price they were willing to pay for after-hours freedom and the right to choose where and with whom they lived, what they ate, and who their friends were.

By 1920, as job opportunities in clerical, sales, and manufacturing work expanded, the proportion of full-time live-in household workers had dropped to less than one-sixth of all wage-earning women. Domestic service did not disappear, but it became increasingly and then overwhelmingly the province of African-American women, who performed domestic service in Northern cities just as they had done it all over the South for more than half a century. Except when caring for very young white children, Southern black domestics had insisted on their right to live away from the job, an arrangement that gave them freedom from the constant supervision of the white employer and allowed them to maintain families of their own. When black women began to move to the North during World War I, they replaced white live-in domestic workers who moved to newly available jobs in industry and business.

In the first decade of the twentieth century, women represented at least half of all workers in textile mills and tobacco factories, and in the garment industries they outnumbered men. About a third of all immigrant women who worked found "unskilled" jobs in factories. They tended to congregate in certain industries by region and by ethnic group. Textile mill work in New England, for example, was performed largely by French-Canadian and Polish immigrant families; both single and married women worked at the looms to supplement the family wage. In New York City, the headquarters of the garment industry, the dominant work force was Italian and Russian Jewish. In large Midwestern cities such as St. Louis, Minneapolis-St. Paul, and Chicago, women from middle-European families—Poles, Czechs, and Bohemians—worked as meat packers and canners.

In Pittsburgh, some 122,000 working women packed crackers and canned molasses, or worked at simple (and low-paid) "women's" jobs in the steel industry. In California, coastal women canned fish, and others packed fruit and vegetables in the fertile Central Valley farmlands. In the South, textile mills hired white women exclusively, but Southern tobacco-processing plants hired both black and white women, allocating the poorest-paid, dirtiest, and most noxious jobs to the African-American workers; the relatively higher paying jobs, and the clean work, such as rolling cigarettes and operating machinery, were reserved for white women workers. All over the Northeast, Midwest, and Far West, in major cities and in large towns, white women of almost every ethnic background worked in commercial steam laundries, outnumbering better-paid male laundry workers by a ratio of eight to one. By 1910 the number of women employed in steam laundries had grown astronomically, and there was one laundry worker for every 152 people in the population.

Not only were women's industrial work choices governed in large measure by ethnic clustering and racial segregation, but the occupations employing the most workers were segregated by sex as well. The positions women could get were frequently limited by traditionally conservative ideas about gender. Work deemed appropriate for women tended to be menial or to resemble housework and other traditional women's concerns, such as needlework or food preparation. Women's jobs also paid much less than those of men doing the same or similar kinds of work in the same trade.

New machinery and scientific management contributed to the "de-skilling" of labor, either by eliminating tasks formerly done by hand or by breaking the tasks down into ever-smaller segments. In many factories, no worker completed a whole garment or shoe by himself, and no one needed more than a day's training to learn the simple, repetitive work. With all these changes in the technology and management of the factory system, some men did lose jobs to less-skilled women, who would accept cruelly low wages in order to help their families survive. When working men blamed women for taking their jobs or depressing their wages, they failed to see that it was not the fault of women who needed to work, but the fault of an industrial system organized solely for profit.

Few industrial jobs for women held any possibility of advancement, and it was not until after World War I that women became job foremen or floor managers to any appreciable extent. Many jobs, like candy making and bookbinding, were subject to seasonal rushes and slack times; women garment makers often found they worked a fourteen-hour stretch for three days and then had no work—and no pay—for the rest of the week. But work hours grew shorter, and by 1920 the fifty-four-hour week had become the legal standard in New York and a number of other states.

Although working conditions improved gradually in the first two decades of the twentieth century, they remained a source of concern for investigators as well as for workers and union organizers in a number of industries. Dorothy Richardson, a journalist from rural Pennsylvania, described the conditions she encountered in several New York industries while looking for work in 1903 and 1904. In a cardboard-box factory, where the speed of the work was set by the rapid pace of the machinery, she found her skirt quickly covered with glue, her hands blistered, and her legs and ankles in agony from standing without a break. She was faint from the heat, the noise, and the foul-smelling air—and all of this happened before lunch!

In the garment industry, the sweatshops of the 1880s and 1890s—small, ill-lit, poorly ventilated, and overcrowded—were gradually replaced by larger factories. Sometimes working conditions were not much improved by the move to larger premises. The most infamous of all garment industry workplaces was the Triangle Shirtwaist Company on Washington Square in lower Manhattan. The Jewish and Italian women who made white cotton blouses trimmed with pleats or ruffles worked long hours for Triangle in the upper floors of an unheated building. Their pay, usually no more than six dollars a week, was docked for lateness, for spending two or three minutes too long in the rest room, for talking on the shop floor, and for mistakes in sewing. The air at Triangle was filled with cotton dust, the floor stained with oil from the sewing machines and cluttered with rags. Foremen routinely locked the fire doors to prevent petty pilfering and unscheduled breaks.

On March 25, 1911, a fire broke out on the eighth floor of the Triangle Company's building. With the doors locked on the outside, the workers were trapped in rooms where the oily floors and lint-filled air soon burst into flames. Those who reached the rusted fire escapes found the structures crumbled under their weight. Some women suffocated or were burned to death at their sewing machines; others jumped from the windows, their hair and clothing in flames. Hoses and ladders were too short to reach the floors where the fire was raging, and the firefighters' nets were not strong enough to hold the weight of the plunging women. Soon the pavement was littered with charred and broken bodies. Frantic family members, rushing to Washington Square to see if their loved ones were still alive, had to fight their way through crowds of onlookers, who stared at the carnage, horrified and helpless.

In all, 3 men and 143 women and girls died in the fire, making it one of the worst disasters in industrial history. At a memorial service held in the city's Metropolitan Opera House, city fathers proposing changes in fire laws and equipment were booed by angry workers. Rose Schneiderman, a young immigrant labor organizer for the International Ladies Garment Workers Union, came forward to

This rare photograph documents the tragedy of the Triangle Shirtwaist fire: the bodies of young women who jumped to their deaths lie lifeless on the sidewalk. The police and bystanders are watching for other victims trapped in the upper stories of the flaming building.

speak. Her solemn words struck a deep chord with the assembled workers: "I would be a traitor to these poor burned bodies if I came here to talk good fellowship. We have tried you good people of the public and found you wanting. . . .This is not the first time girls have been burned alive in the city. . . . Every year thousands of us are maimed. The life of men and women is so cheap and property is so sacred. . . . it little matters if 143 [*sic*] of us are burned to death. . . . I know from my own experience it is up to the working people to save themselves. The only way they can save themselves is by a strong working-class movement."

Rose Schneiderman's words were more than prophetic. The movement was already under way, and women were militantly involved as they had never been before. Scores of new unions in dozens of industries would be born and grow stronger in the period leading up to World War I. Their efforts were inspired by the new generation of immigrant workers, who combined radical traditions they had brought from Europe with a faith in freedom and possibility that was distinctly American. The new labor leaders, many of them women, dedicated their lives to the belief that working-class solidarity would transform the existence of the American poor.

For a few years in the 1880s, before it collapsed under its own size and increasing competition from the new American Federation of Labor (AFL), the Knights of Labor had successfully organized hundreds of thousands of skilled and unskilled workers, both men and women, black and white. The AFL, meanwhile, concentrated its energies on organizing unions for skilled male craftsmen. The AFL was not interested in industrial unionism—the organizing of masses of unskilled workers, such as miners or mill workers, by industry rather than by specialized craft. Many Americans, including the AFL leadership, felt that industrial unionism was under the control of revolutionary socialists. They were deeply suspicious of the socialist Industrial Workers of the World, or Wobblies, who were successfully organizing miners and mill workers in the opening years of the twentieth century. Unlike the Wobblies, the AFL ignored African Americans for many years. And, though it did charter a number of women's local unions between 1890 and 1920, it was heavily biased against women workers. The AFL leadership believed that women should be at home and not in the workplace, and feared that women's willingness to accept low wages constituted a threat to male jobs and wage levels. The AFL would be very slow to realize that encouraging divisions between men and women workers only retarded the progress of labor unionism as a whole, for women were in the workplace to stay.

Difficulties with the AFL and the hostility of working men encouraged working women to organize independent, single-sex unions and to seek leaders from among their own ranks. In the Midwest in the 1890s, these efforts enjoyed some success under the leadership of female socialists and union organizers such as Elizabeth Morgan, Lizzie Swank Holmes, and Mary Kenney O'Sullivan. By 1903, the Ladies Federal Labor Union and the Illinois Woman's Alliance had organized some 35,000 women workers in thirty-six different trades, and they had won substantial gains: Women's wages had risen between 10 percent and 40 percent, and their hours had dropped to fifty-three per week. Child labor had been almost eradicated, thanks to a push for factory inspection and legislative change, which was a big part of the organizers' strategy.

Working-class women began to form alliances with middle-class women reformers such as Jane Addams, who were concerned about the condition of women and children working in industry. In 1903, Mary Kenney O'Sullivan, in concert with William English Walling, a socialist intellectual and settlement house worker, and Leonora O'Reilly, a former garment worker and schoolteacher, established the Women's Trade Union League (WTUL), with offices in Boston, New York, and Chicago. The AFL endorsed the league but did not give it much financial support. Middle-class women reformers, social activists, and a few wealthy philanthropists joined the WTUL. Some, like Margaret Dreier Robins, league president after 1907, and her sister, Mary Dreier, president of the New York branch, dedicated many years of their lives to the WTUL. Working women such as Rose Schneiderman, who became president of the league in 1927, and Leonora O'Reilly, its finest orator, labored throughout their lives for the league and related women's causes, never marrying and retiring only in their final illnesses. "I thought, as a young girl, that I would get married, too," wrote Mary Anderson, a Chicago shoe worker and league member who became, in 1920, the first director of the Women's Bureau of the U.S. Department of Labor, "but somewhere I lost myself in my work and never felt that marriage would give me the security I wanted. I thought that through the trade union movement we working women could get better conditions and security of mind."

Within the WTUL, working-class women and affluent women discovered they shared common disabilities related to gender: political powerlessness, limited options for jobs or careers, and family claims upon their time and attention. However, the league motto, "The eight hour day; a living wage; to guard the home," made it clear to doubters that this alliance did not intend to threaten the sacred precincts of domesticity or woman's traditional role. The goals of the WTUL would include both trade union organization for women and the integration of working women's concerns into programs for women's rights. Through the WTUL, working women were called upon to support the fight for woman suffrage.

Despite points of disagreement and the failure of some of the middle-class "allies" to understand working women's backgrounds and aims, the WTUL was a highly effective alliance between middle- and upper-class women and those of the working class. In its support of a massive strike by New York's garment industry workers in 1909, the WTUL not only won support for the workers but also organized the complex strike shifts and tactics of thousands of women picketers. The league initiated a heavy leafleting campaign, and it publicized the strikers' wage and hour demands, as well as descriptions of their miserable working conditions, in the pages of its magazine, *Life and Labor*. WTUL officers put up bail for some of the jailed strikers, and several of the league's upper-class "allies" joined picket lines and were arrested along with working women picketers. These arrests delighted the press, which brought the plight of striking workers to public attention in an unprecedented array of stories and articles. The strike ended in February 1910, with many of the workers' demands met. The real heroines had been the young women picketers, who, though harassed, beaten, and repeatedly jailed, had stuck it out on the picket line through the worst days of a bitterly cold winter, but the workers owed much of their success to the organizational talents of the WTUL.

The WTUL continued to participate in labor actions around the country, though, in the second decade of the twentieth century, it began to turn much of its attention to suffrage, to lobbying for legislation to protect women and children in the workplace, and to training women labor leaders. During a famous strike of textile mill workers in Lawrence, Massachusetts, in the winter of 1912–13, the WTUL took a back seat, unwilling to associate itself with the radical Wobblies who were organizing the strike. The Wobblies brought in a fiery young orator and organizer, Elizabeth Gurley Flynn, who was an inspiration to the militant working women at

Lawrence. Provoking their own arrests and refusing bail, the women risked their lives as well as their livings in confrontations with police and militia sent in to break up the strike. After eight weeks of violence on both sides, the mill owners capitulated, and the Lawrence strike was settled—a great victory for the striking workers and a boon to mill workers all over New England.

One of the longest-running labor crusades on record involved women steam-laundry workers in California. In actions begun in 1900, women secretly organized the industry in San Francisco, winning the right to live out (they had been required to live in company boardinghouses), as well as a wage increase, nine paid holidays a year, and a number of other concessions. That took six years. In the next six years, they won an eight-hour day, a 30 percent wage increase, including overtime pay, and the installation of modern safety measures in all the plants. They were one of the few unions in such a low-wage, unskilled industry to last so long and accomplish so much.

Turn-of-the-century union organization tended to touch African-American women peripherally, if at all. In the few industrial occupations open to them, black women continued to be paid about half of what white women earned, and no attempts were made to organize black home workers or domestics, though there had been sporadic attempts by black laundresses to organize and strike in Southern cities in the late 19th century. Southern AFL affiliates did not include black men or women, and even unions that did organize black men tended to keep them in separate all-black locals. In Richmond, Virginia, some 367 black men and women tobacco workers successfully maintained a local organization of the Tobacco Workers International Union, but most black women's labor actions in the South consisted of offering support services to black men involved in strikes or walkouts. In both the South and the North, black women were sometimes played off against whites: They were offered jobs as scabs when white women workers went on strike. If they took the jobs, black women usually found that they were fired the minute white women came back to work.

Beyond factory work lay the newly expanding field of white-collar work. The rapid evolution and tremendous growth of the white-collar sector was the most dramatic aspect of change in working women's opportunities between 1890 and 1920. Like their sisters in industrial work, white-collar women found that, wherever they worked, their pay was considerably less than that of men doing the same jobs. Partly as a result of pay discrepancies, some white-collar jobs became "feminized" over time, as companies replaced relatively expensive male employees with a lower-paid all-woman work force.

Women flocked to white-collar work, which carried status and, except for sales-clerking, was better paid than factory labor. By 1910, more than 700,000 women worked as trained nurses and schoolteachers; 77 percent of teachers were women. Another 475,000 women were salesclerks, and nearly 600,000 worked in offices. More than 88,000 women were employed as telephone operators, an increase of

475 percent from 1900. By 1917 this occupation had become so completely feminized that women accounted for 99 percent of all switchboard operators in the United States.

Before 1917, white-collar work was almost exclusively reserved for native-born white women. Immigrants, even second-generation daughters of immigrants who spoke with an accent or had noticeably "foreign" or Jewish names, usually found it impossible to get sales or office jobs. Black women knew that discriminatory hiring practices in both the North and the South made it useless for them even to apply for white-collar office or clerical work in any but black-owned businesses. Increasingly, and mostly in the South, black women were hired to teach black children. By 1910, 22,547 of the nation's 29,772 black teachers were female. Similarly, black women entered nursing in growing numbers around 1900, after the founding of a number of black nursing schools in the 1890s. Black nurses worked in the black community and as private nurses; they were denied jobs in white hospitals and in the Army Nurse Corps and the Red Cross. Excluded from membership in the American Nurses Association, they formed the National Association of Colored Graduate Nurses in 1908.

By 1915, approximately 50 percent of all office workers, and nearly 85 percent of all typists and stenographers, were women. Rather than replacing male office workers altogether, women were moving into new jobs created by the specialization of clerical tasks, jobs that had less overall responsibility than those of male office workers and paid much less, but were still highly desirable. Office work was clean and largely sedentary. Therefore it was "genteel," and in terms of status it ranked just below professional work for women. For young working-class women who finished high school, the move into office work was a chance to bridge the gap into the middle class, with the possibility of making new friends or an advantageous marriage.

Women's wage work, whether "white" or "blue" collar, domestic service, industrial labor, or home sewing, was an integral part of family life for many Americans in the early years of the twentieth century. To working mothers, sisters, and daughters, supporting the family was part of caring for it, just as much as the middle-class woman's single-minded preoccupation with homemaking demonstrated her own adherence to a womanly role and her love for her family.

In Public Life

Both middle-class and elite women came to the Progressive years from a history of involvement with women's associations of the 1870s and 1880s: the women's foreign mission crusade, the women's club movement, the Woman's Christian Temperance Union (WCTU), the Young Women's Christian Association (YWCA), and others. By the mid-1890s, however, women's associations had extended the borders of woman's sphere to include involvement in many outside concerns. They insisted that women were not only uniquely fitted to take a public role in reforming society, but were morally obligated to do so. The new generation of women reformers, whose immediate predecessors had attacked public evils that threatened the home—child labor, prostitution, alcoholism, and poor education—began to embrace a broader range of projects in the 1890s. Claiming that their reform activities constituted a form of "municipal housekeeping," women's organizations seized the opportunity to tackle a variety of urban, industrial problems. The moral and political issues that concerned women shaped the aims of all Progressives, male and female, as well as providing the momentum for Progressive reform programs and much of the volunteer labor.

Women's associations, both old and new, experienced tremendous growth throughout the Progressive period. By the first decade of the twentieth century, the foreign mission crusade had grown to astonishing proportions, with nearly three-quarters of a million members enrolled in local church auxiliaries all over the country. Foreign missionary work—the worldwide endeavor to convert unbelievers to Christianity—was organized independently by each of the major American Protestant denominations. Missionary enterprises connected American women to the rest of the world and also confirmed their sense of American cultural superiority. The women's enthusiasm provided public support not only for missionary work in other countries, but also for the growth of American imperialism during the years in which the United States first joined other Western military powers in the conquest of weaker nations and the attempt to westernize their societies.

Like the foreign mission crusade, the women's club movement expanded rapidly in turn-of-the-century America. The General Federation of Women's Clubs (GFWC), founded in 1890 with about twenty thousand members in some two hundred local clubs, represented nearly 1 million women by 1910. For a majority of women's clubs, the formation of the GFWC coincided with a change in emphasis from self-culture and amusement to service and reform. Clubwomen set up libraries, university extension courses, trade schools, and home economics classes for girls. They raised money for city parks and playgrounds. They lobbied state legislatures and city councils for clean water and better disposal of refuse and for laws to eliminate sweatshop abuses and provide fire inspection for tenement houses. Clubs concerned themselves with the creation of a juvenile court system and joined the fight for federal public health legislation such as the Pure Food and Drug Act of 1906.

Before the turn of the century, the largest organization of American women was unquestionably the WCTU, which drew members from every region of the country and from every social class, although middle-class, white Protestant women predominated, as they did in the women's club movement. The Union's family-centered philosophy and its emphasis on women's right to participate in public affairs that affected the welfare of homes and families made it a "safe" organization for women to join. Its motto was "For God and Home and Native Land"; its badge was a bow of white ribbon, symbolizing the purity of the home; and its rallying cry was "Home Protection." By the early 1890s, the WCTU had 150,000 members, and, through its overseas missions, claimed millions worldwide by the turn of the century. In Chicago, the WCTU had its own office building, called the Woman's Temple, ran its own publishing company, and operated a medical center. All the work was done by women, and women held all the union's executive positions.

Under the twenty-year leadership of Frances Willard, the WCTU took on an ever-increasing array of projects that led it far beyond its original commitment to the prohibition of alcohol. The WCTU was organized into nearly forty departments, each with its own superintendent, and this structure was repeated in the local chapters. Dealing with areas as diverse as labor reform, health and hygiene, social purity, peace and arbitration, prison reform, and education, women learned the techniques of public involvement and political action: lobbying, organization, canvassing, and public relations. The suffrage department became increasingly active and important as the years went by.

The WCTU was particularly important to Southern white women, who saw it as a respectable way to become publicly active and to escape some of the constraints of their protected lives. To women like Belle Kearney and Sallie Southall Cotten, who later became leaders in Southern reform movements, the WCTU was, as Kearney said, the "generous liberator, the joyous iconoclast, the discoverer, the developer of Southern women." Membership in this large national organization also helped to put isolated Southern women in touch with their counterparts in the North, facilitating the exchange of ideas and, eventually, the entry of Southern white women into the suffrage movement.

Although Southern black women were excluded from white chapters of the WCTU, there were some separate chapters for black women in the South, as well as a number of segregated Northern chapters. Frances Ellen Watkins Harper was the only African American on the WCTU's executive committee and frequently criticized the racism of the organization's members, though she was a firm believer in the need for temperance among black Americans.

Temperance was only one of many issues that attracted the attention of black women activists. The antilynching campaign of African-American journalist Ida B. Wells in the 1890s was one of the most dramatic episodes of the black women's reform movement. Lynching, or mob murder of black men (and some black women and teenagers), had become a regular feature of the post-Reconstruction South. It was a tactic of terror and intimidation, and black men who had done well in business or other enterprises and were beginning to have influence in the community were often the targets of lynch mobs. With the tacit consent and all the power of white Southern society behind them, mob members had little need to justify their acts of violence against black men, but they frequently claimed that a white woman had been sexually assaulted by the lynching victim.

The 1892 Memphis, Tennessee, lynching of Thomas Moss, a black grocery store owner, along with his two associates, was directly related to white jealousy of their business success. On a Saturday night in March, an angry white mob attacked the grocery store. Three of the attackers were shot by black men defending the store, and Moss and his partners were arrested and jailed. Kidnapped from jail by the mob, all three were murdered on the railroad heading out of town. Moss left a little girl and a pregnant wife. He also left two very angry friends: Mary Church Terrell and Ida B. Wells.

Memphis-born Terrell, a childhood friend of Moss, was an educator who would soon become a nationally prominent clubwoman and reformer. After the lynching, she and the revered abolitionist leader Frederick Douglass quickly arranged an audience with President Benjamin Harrison, imploring him to publicly condemn lynching. Harrison did nothing, but Terrell, horrified by this latest evidence of the worsening condition of black Americans, embarked on a life of activism to help her race. Wells was a journalist and part owner of the *Memphis Free Speech*, a black newspaper. Outraged by the murder of Thomas Moss, she began a series of antilynching articles that were published in the *Free Speech* and other papers and magazines around the country. She also launched an investigation of white mob violence throughout the South, researching 728 lynchings that had taken place in the preceding decade. A segment of her study was later published as *A Red Record* (1895). What Wells discovered, among many other things, was that not only had the alleged rapes hardly ever taken place but that fewer than a third of all the murdered men had even been accused of assaulting white women. Most had been charged with crimes like "making threats," or "quarrelling with whites," or (amazingly) "race-prejudice."

While Wells was lecturing in Philadelphia, the *Free Speech* offices were looted and burned, and her partners fled for their lives. Warned that she would be hanged from a lamppost if she returned to Memphis, Wells knew that she could never go home again. She waged her antilynching campaign in the North, winning support from blacks and whites alike through her lectures and writings. Although lynching would not be fully eradicated for several decades, Wells's campaign had undermined the stereotype of the sexually violent black male. Her intelligence and personal integrity also encouraged many white Americans to question their racist assumptions about the supposed laziness and immorality of black women. She inspired many black women to take action against racial injustice.

Many women of the established black middle class responded to rising racism in the 1890s by joining the black women's club movement, whose growth paralleled that of the federated club movement of white women. From their very beginnings, most black women's clubs were more radical and more activist than their white counterparts. Although the clubwomen were mostly middle-class and educated, their concerns were for the race as a whole and for the elevation of all black women, regardless of class. Their practical efforts were concentrated in education, health, housing, domestic training, and prison reform. The slogan of the movement, "Lifting As We Climb," reflected the clubwomen's recognition that, although they were themselves privileged, their own survival and advancement, both as women and as African Americans, depended on helping their less fortunate sisters. They knew that all black women were judged by the poorest and most disadvantaged of their sisters. They also knew that all black women were victims of the prevailing stereotype of black female immorality, a relic of the days of slavery when African-American women were at the mercy of white owners' sexual demands. Challenging decades of racist public opinion and discriminatory practices became a key part of the black woman's movement.

In 1895, under the leadership of Fannie Barrier Williams and Josephine St. Pierre Ruffin, some thirty-six women's clubs from twelve states formed the National Federation of Afro-American Women. They elected Margaret Murray Washington, the wife of the influential black educator Booker T. Washington, as the federation president. That same year, in Washington, D.C., Mary Church Terrell was organizing women's clubs into the National League of Colored Women. In 1896, the federation and the league united to form the National Association of Colored Women (NACW), with Terrell as its president. The NACW became the most powerful African-American women's organization in the country—a training ground for leaders, educators, and reformers, for political action on behalf of black women and men, and a springboard for the black woman suffrage movement, which was organized by state and local clubs. On the eve of World War I, the NACW had fifty thousand active members. A number of its programs were used as models by two new civil rights organizations founded in 1909 and 1910: the National Association for the Advancement of Colored People (NAACP) and the National Urban League.

Women's reform activities of the Progressive Era were linked to the advances in women's higher education since the 1870s that had produced a generation of college-educated women possessed of a desire to help and a need to find meaningful work. Although the overall proportion of American women who attended college was very small—7.6 percent of all women aged eighteen to twenty-one in 1920—the increase in attendance was significant: by 1920 women made up nearly 50 percent of all enrolled college students.

Most college women were middle-class daughters of professional men and businessmen. Considering its middle-class clientele, college was expensive: tuition, room, and board at Wellesley in 1906, with pocket money and books, never cost less than $350 annually. At the University of California at Berkeley, students spent between $90 and $495 a year. In an era in which annual middle-class family incomes ranged from $1,000 to $3,000, college for daughters was often out of the question. Scholarships were still rare. As time went by, it became increasingly respectable for a young woman to work her way through college.

After graduation, many women progressed to good jobs as teachers, accountants, private secretaries, librarians, or journalists. Others sought advanced study in science and liberal arts, training that would lead to professional careers in medicine and academia. Women college graduates who went to work tended to marry later than their non-college-educated counterparts. More than half of college-educated women with full-time professional careers never married. For women graduates without the prospect of marriage or any specially chosen career, or for those whose tradition-minded families wanted them to come home, the possibility of a future of aimless leisure and financial dependence loomed unpleasantly. Such women maintained the settlement house movement, the best known of all Progressive Era reforms.

Jane Addams, who opened Hull House on Chicago's West Side in 1889, would later be regarded as the pioneer of the American settlement-house movement, but she had joined an urban reform movement already under way. By 1891 there were six settlements in the United States; by 1900, more than one hundred. Besides Addams, leaders of American settlements included Lillian Wald, who started the Henry Street Settlement in New York City; Mary Kingsbury Simkhovitch, the founder of Greenwich House on New York's Lower East Side; and Mary McDowell, who ran the University of Chicago Settlement House near the Chicago stockyards. Most settlements were run by college graduates, both women and men, and many functioned as short-term residences, where college students could work in a variety of social assistance programs during the summer or for a year or so after graduation.

Over the years, many reformers—men as well as women—joined Addams at Hull House, some as residents, some as regular visitors. Distinguished guests included philosophers William James and John Dewey and President Theodore Roosevelt. For the residents and workers, Hull House provided an exciting intellectual life, a place to discuss social and philosophical issues, and an experimental station where efforts to bridge the gaps between classes were not only talked about, but were put into practice.

Yet it soon became apparent to Jane Addams that clubs and neighborhood services were not enough to counter the poverty and problems of her neighbors. She and a group of Hull House companions pioneered a study of the social conditions in Chicago's 19th Ward, with its tenements, sweatshops, and exploitive child labor. The study was published under the title *Hull-House Maps and Papers* (1895). After this, Hull House residents regularly became involved in political battles for factory inspection and industrial safety, child labor laws, better working conditions for women, the recognition of labor unions, compulsory school attendance, and improved city sanitation.

One of Addams's greatest gifts was the ability to attract capable people and put them to work. It would be difficult to imagine a more impressive group of women than those Addams gathered at Hull House in the 1890s and early 1900s. The brilliant and energetic Florence Kelley, educated in Europe, was the divorced mother of three and a socialist. At Hull House, Kelley led an investigation of Chicago sweatshops, and she later was appointed Illinois state factory inspector for child

A singing class at Hull House in Chicago involves neighborhood residents of all ages. The photographer, Lewis Hine, noted that the music school was "characteristic of the friendly, constructive work that had always been done at Hull House."

labor. When she moved to New York in the late 1890s, Kelley became secretary of the powerful National Consumers' League, a woman-led reform organization that used the boycott—a refusal to buy certain goods or services—to pressure businesses and industries that exploited workers. Julia Lathrop took a job with the Illinois Board of Charities and pioneered investigations of the conditions in poorhouses and mental asylums. She and Addams pressured the state legislature into establishing the first U.S. juvenile court, and she was instrumental in founding the Immigrants' Protective League, which provided information, legal services, and employment referral for newcomers to Chicago. In 1912, Lathrop received a Presidential appointment as head of the new U.S. Children's Bureau, a federal agency within the Commerce and Labor Department that had been designed by Florence Kelley and New York settlement leader Lillian Wald. Alice Hamilton, a doctor from Indiana, became an expert in industrial medicine. Nebraskan Edith Abbott produced a number of classic books on social welfare and became dean of the School of Social Service Administration at the University of Chicago. Her sister, Grace Abbott, headed the U.S. Children's Bureau from 1921 to 1934. Sophonisba Breckinridge, a lawyer from Tennessee, helped Julia Lathrop to found the Chicago Immigrants' Protective League and later became a professor of social economy at the Chicago School of Social Service Administration. Breckinridge was an early and active member of the NAACP and an officer of both the National American Woman Suffrage Association and the American Association of University Women.

The women of Hull House, with the exception of the divorced Florence Kelley, who never remarried, chose lives as single women. Theirs was an era that still found it difficult to accept the possibility that educated middle-class and elite women might combine marriage and family with a career, although such a pattern was becoming increasingly common for married working-class women. Instead, the Hull House women and other unmarried settlement workers found richly rewarding lives in the company of like-minded women. They devoted themselves to the causes they cared about, establishing successful careers and earning the respect of political leaders and socially conscious men and women.

In the process of defining their own lives and helping others, these turn-of-the-century career reformers created the profession of social work. Wherever their later lives took them, they never failed to credit the congenial atmosphere of Hull House, where their talents and abilities had matured and responded to the encouragement of Jane Addams. Addams herself, often called "Saint Jane" by the public and the press, was neither saintly nor self-sacrificing, but was, in fact, a woman who took tremendous pleasure in her life and friendships. A consummate organizer, compromiser, fund raiser, and strategist, a compelling writer and speaker, she was the glue that held everything together. Addams became, for many Americans, the symbol of an age of progress and reform.

Increasingly, as women worked through settlement houses and other reform organizations to improve social conditions, they realized that they could not accomplish all they wanted to do in public life without being able to vote. Powerless either to endorse or unseat the men in power, they were wearied by endless, and often futile, petition drives and lobbying campaigns to persuade legislators and civic leaders to enact reforms. Between 1890 and 1915, most newcomers who joined the fight for woman suffrage would claim that women needed the vote to help clean up America and solve its problems.

The woman suffrage movement had gone through a long period of discouragement. As late as 1905, the membership of the National American Woman Suffrage Association (NAWSA) numbered only seventeen thousand. Wyoming Territory had entered the Union as a state in 1890, retaining the full woman suffrage it had had since 1869. Three more states—Colorado, Utah, and Idaho—enfranchised women between 1893 and 1896, giving them the right to vote in all local, state, and national elections. A few states, mostly in the Midwest, allowed women to vote in school or municipal elections, but between 1896 and 1910 nothing but defeat rewarded the petition drives, speaking tours, and lobbying efforts of NAWSA's workers trying to enfranchise women in state-by-state campaigns.

The Western suffrage campaigns of the 1890s and early 1900s were alternately heartening and discouraging. They also taught young NAWSA leaders a number of significant lessons, including the importance of forming individual clubs of suffragists in every voting precinct in the state and the need to win the support of husbands, fathers, and brothers.

The suffrage campaign in South Dakota, waged during the blistering hot summer of 1890, was marked by squabbling between local and national suffrage workers and by the disappearance of promised support from farm and labor organizations. It was a bitter and expensive defeat. Susan B. Anthony, then seventy, returned home looking old for the first time in her life, and Carrie Chapman Catt, a young Iowan who would be elected president of NAWSA in 1900 and again in 1915, fell ill with typhoid fever, which nearly killed her. Catt returned to the suffrage movement determined to put the hard lessons of the South Dakota campaign into practice. In 1893, as chairman of NAWSA's business committee, she offered her assistance to the Colorado state suffrage referendum campaign. Without much assistance from the national organization, a small cadre of dedicated Colorado suffragists had quietly maneuvered a woman suffrage bill through the sleepy state legislature. The bill had been signed by the Populist governor. The women then organized the state referendum campaign in local precincts in sixty-three Colorado counties, while Catt embarked on a speaking tour in twenty-three crucial areas. She spoke two or three times in each county, helping to organize fifty new suffrage clubs and enlisting the support of influential men in each key community. She maintained an exhausting pace, traveling by train and horse-drawn wagon in the Rocky Mountains, determined to keep every appointment where voters were waiting for her. In November 1893 the referendum passed, and Colorado became the second star in the woman suffrage constellation.

A Kansas referendum was defeated in 1894, but woman suffrage passed in Utah and Idaho in the next two years. A hard-fought, carefully conducted California campaign in 1896 looked promising until the final few weeks, when anti-suffrage forces poured a lot of money and publicity into a successful last-minute attack on the women's interests. California would not enfranchise its women until 1911.

Anti-suffrage forces were everywhere, though they tended to surface mostly in response to specific campaigns in the states. Especially powerful in the Northeast, anti-suffragists called themselves "remonstrants," though the suffragists liked to call them "antis." Most anti-suffragists believed that woman's subordinate position in society was ordained by God and that woman's weak, gentle nature did not fit her for active participation in the world beyond the home—most especially not for the man's world of politics, with its smoke-filled conventions, rough language, and "shady" transactions. Some argued that if women wanted the vote they would have to bear arms in defense of their country, a possibility few Americans could even contemplate in 1900. Others based their arguments on the nineteenth-century belief that the basic unit of society was not the individual but the family—which needed only one voting member: its male head. Particularly painful to suffragists

At a woman suffrage rally at the capitol building in Richmond, Virginia, a banner maps the progress of woman suffrage around the country. Despite the best efforts of suffragists, the state of Virginia would hold out against women's voting rights throughout the national campaign to pass and ratify the constitutional amendment.

was the antis' argument that women did not want suffrage. Indeed, there was plenty of apathy among women, and the number of registered suffragists was undeniably small.

Anti-suffrage sentiment found powerful and influential supporters among conservative clergymen, businessmen, and political and social leaders. Many anti-suffragists were women. Anti-suffragism was also backed by those who made and sold alcoholic beverages, because they tended to associate suffrage with prohibition. The liquor interests feared that if women got the vote they would find a way to ban the sale and consumption of alcohol and their businesses would be ruined. Many suffragists were indeed prohibitionists, but by no means all; and many anti-suffragists were prohibitionists.

For both suffragists and anti-suffragists, race, social class, and ethnic origin were difficult issues. Both sides tended to fear the voting power of recent immigrants (although laws varied from state to state, male immigrants who had applied for citizenship were allowed to vote after a relatively short residence in the United States). Immigrants were often unsophisticated and largely uneducated; their European peasant customs, dress, and speech aroused suspicion and bigotry in middle-class, native-born Americans of both sexes. Anti-suffragists argued that enfranchising

women would double the voting power of the "unwashed masses," while suffragists insisted that it was important to let educated women vote so that they could
defeat the votes of ignorant foreigners, whom they would outnumber even if
immigrant women also received the franchise.

Like the immigrant issue, the subject of votes for African-American women was
a complicated one for white suffragists. NAWSA leaders frequently responded neg-
atively to black women's demands for inclusion in suffrage organizations. This
practice reflected badly on many otherwise admirable suffrage leaders. Further-
more, as white Southern women began to join the ranks of suffragists in growing
numbers around 1900, Northern suffragists found themselves supporting racist
arguments in order to win allies for woman suffrage in Southern states. Southern
white women activists were certain that the only way to sell woman suffrage to
Southern legislators was to convince them that enfranchising white women would
guarantee continued white supremacy in the South. Even if black women were to
be simultaneously enfranchised, they reasoned, the individual Southern states
could find ways to keep them from voting, similar to those they were already using
quite successfully against black men. After the turn of the century, Northern white
women suffragists found it expedient to distance themselves from all African-
American issues and to allow their white Southern sisters to promote woman suffrage as a tool for white supremacy in their region.

Although some black women suffragists, including Ida B. Wells and Mary
Church Terrell, retained more or less cordial relationships with some of the
NAWSA leadership and continued to address suffrage conventions, African-
American women generally formed their own suffrage organizations. By the early
1900s, there were black women's suffrage clubs and state suffrage organizations all
over the country, from Massachusetts to Idaho. Not surprisingly, there was little
opposition to woman suffrage among black men, who understood that black
women's empowerment would be beneficial to the race as a whole. "Votes for
women means votes for Black women," asserted political leader W. E. B. Du Bois.

Between 1896 and 1910, when no new states were enfranchised, NAWSA
remained a battleground for arguments about race, class, and ethnicity. It was also
prey to an ongoing internal dispute between those who wished to push for state-
by-state enfranchisement of women and those who wanted to work exclusively for
a constitutional amendment, which would bring the vote to every woman in the
country. Frustration and discouragement for NAWSA coincided with problems at
the highest levels of leadership. Carrie Chapman Catt's replacement as president,
Anna Howard Shaw, who held both divinity and medical degrees, was a brilliant
and inspiring orator but not a gifted organizer. Susan B. Anthony, who had been
for so long a leader, had died in 1906.

It was time for younger suffragists, charged with the enthusiasm of Progres-
sivism, to inject life into the suffrage movement. Early signs of new life included
the creation of two important new organizations in 1901: the Boston Equal

Suffrage Association for Good Government and the College Equal Suffrage League. Both of these groups grew rapidly and experimented with bold new methods of campaigning: canvassing door to door in city and suburban neighborhoods, staging open-air meetings (suffragists had always previously met, with ladylike decorum, in rented halls or private homes), and touring the state on public transportation to give speeches at every stop. They brought the message to women who might never have gone to a suffrage meeting on their own, and they made many converts.

In 1907, Harriot Stanton Blatch, the daughter of Elizabeth Cady Stanton, started the Equality League of Self-Supporting Women, an alliance of elite women, career women, and working women from factories, laundries, and garment shops in New York. Blatch was convinced that career women and wage-earning women had much in common, and she felt that women should base their demands for political equality on their increasingly important economic role in society. During many years of residence in England, Blatch had been impressed by both the British labor movement and the British woman suffrage campaigns. Under her leadership, the Equality League invited English suffragists to speak at their assemblies, where they were enthusiastically received. The league was also the first to send working-class women to address a state legislature on behalf of woman suffrage. By late 1908, the league had a membership of some nineteen thousand.

Like the other new suffrage organizations, the league favored open-air meetings, and it was the Equality League that initiated the grand suffrage parades of the 1910s. Parades had a significant impact upon the public consciousness: The spectacle of thousands of working- and middle-class women marching with immense dignity before awed and enthusiastic crowds, and the occasional glimpses of wealthy social leaders among the ranks, were a tremendous boost for the suffragists' cause. Gradually, woman suffrage was becoming "fashionable," and, after more than half a century of struggle, it was now becoming respectable. When the General Federation of Women's Clubs finally endorsed woman suffrage in 1914, the cause had found the mainstream acceptability it had sought for so long.

In 1912, two young suffragists, Alice Paul and Lucy Burns, appeared on the scene, eager to reinvigorate NAWSA with campaign tactics they had learned from frontline participation in the militant wing of the British woman suffrage movement, the so-called suffragettes. Paul and Burns persuaded the NAWSA leadership to let them run NAWSA's Congressional Committee in Washington, D.C., to organize a new drive for a federal constitutional amendment. NAWSA committees around the country would continue to work simultaneously for state-by-state enfranchisement.

The British suffragettes who served as models for Paul and Burns favored the tactics of guerrilla warfare in their fight to force the British Parliament to enact woman suffrage. They had become adept at disrupting the meetings of male political organizations and regularly provoked their own arrests to gain publicity. Later, they took to breaking windows, pouring acid in mailboxes, and attacking members of Parliament with whips. One suffragette died after she threw herself under the flying hooves of a racehorse owned by King George V. When jailed, the suffragettes were treated not as political prisoners, as they had demanded, but as common criminals. When they went on a hunger strike to protest they were held down and force-fed. Although Burns and Paul and the other members of the Congressional Committee did not immediately adopt the militant tactics of the British suffragettes, they did make a lot of noise in Washington. They lobbied congressmen unceasingly and, the day before President Woodrow Wilson's inauguration in March 1913, they staged a huge suffrage parade down Pennsylvania Avenue through hostile crowds. The parade culminated in a violent riot when bystanders attacked the suffragists; police were forced to call in the cavalry to quell the disturbance.

Paul and Burns had a political philosophy antagonistic to that of their more mainstream allies at NAWSA. They believed that the suffrage movement should hold the political party in power responsible for the failure to enact woman suffrage. In the United States in 1913 that meant the Democrats. The committee's plan was to embarrass President Wilson, who had not been particularly friendly to woman suffrage, and to work to defeat the Democrats in Congress in the next election. NAWSA, however, had friends and enemies in all parties and insisted on remaining nonpartisan. Because of this irreconcilable issue and other disagreements, the NAWSA leadership disowned the Congressional Committee. In 1914, Burns and Paul set up a separate suffrage organization. Their Congressional Union, which later became the National Woman's Party, remained headquartered in Washington, D.C., where it attracted the most radical elements of the suffrage movement. Once again the suffrage movement was divided. However, the passions and concerns that had brought about the split were signs of increasing vitality in the movement as a whole. In the long run, passage of the federal amendment would be the work of both groups.

In the meantime, NAWSA was emerging from years of discouragement. After two cleverly run campaigns based on local appeals featuring billboards, plays, cookbooks, editorials, and church sermons urging voters to "Give the Women a Square Deal," Washington and California had voted for the franchise in 1910 and 1911. These victories were part of a strong Western grass-roots revival that also saw women enfranchised in Kansas, Oregon, and Arizona in 1912. That same year, the Progressive party endorsed woman suffrage during its unsuccessful third-party campaign to elect Theodore Roosevelt, and in 1913 Illinois enacted a law that allowed its women to vote in Presidential elections. The Illinois suffrage victory, though limited, broke the solid anti-suffrage opposition that had long prevailed east of the Mississippi River.

Woman suffrage headquarters in Cleveland, Ohio, in 1913. Sporting a slogan popularized by President Theodore Roosevelt, its sign demanded that men give women a "square deal" by giving them the right to vote.

In 1915, Carrie Chapman Catt was persuaded to resume the presidency of NAWSA on the retirement of Anna Howard Shaw. At this point, no one seriously doubted that women would win the right to vote; it was just a question of time. In 1916, Carrie Catt told a friend she thought it would take six more years.

In Rebellion

Throughout the Progressive Era, the crusade for social reform and women's rights inspired the hard work and dedication of many women. Most reformers were content to work within the existing social and legal systems, but a handful of rebels made it their mission in life to defy society's most basic conventions and to challenge time-honored assumptions about women and women's roles. This small group of writers, artists, philosophers, and radicals proposed sweeping social changes that most turn-of-the-century Americans regarded as threatening and outrageous, if not downright revolutionary.

The radical activities of such women as Charlotte Perkins Gilman, Emma Goldman, Margaret Sanger, and Isadora Duncan—their scandals, their challenges to the law, and their arrests—coincided with the emergence of America's first self-described "feminist" movement, which began its organizational life in the 1910s among a group of freethinkers in New York City's Greenwich Village. These feminists were professionals, writers, journalists, social workers, and labor leaders. A number of them met weekly, calling their group "Heterodoxy" to indicate that only unorthodox opinions would be encouraged. They argued that women's ingrained ideas of appropriate "femininity," their submission, self-sacrifice, and submergence in the family were all harmful and outmoded; they demanded full, individual freedom and self-development for all women. Many feminists also sought sexual freedom outside of marriage, risking social condemnation by daring to flout convention and respectability with their love affairs.

Early-twentieth-century feminism had roots in socialism and links to the suffrage movement, though not all suffragists were feminists by any means. Although feminist demands for personal freedom, meaningful work, and free sexual expression shocked many, feminism gave heart to others. After 1920, it became the vanguard of the twentieth-century women's movement.

When Charlotte Perkins Gilman joined Heterodoxy in 1912 she was already one of the most important social theorists of her era. Born in 1860, she was the grandniece of Catharine Beecher and Harriet Beecher Stowe, and very proud to be a Beecher—though she turned out to be a far more original thinker than either of her eminent aunts. Her childhood was clouded by her father's desertion and the family's consequent descent into genteel poverty. Charlotte's education was erratic and limited, and after attending the Rhode Island School of Design, she supported herself by teaching art and designing greeting cards until she married Charles Walter Stetson in 1884.

A daughter, Katharine, was born a year later, and Charlotte, not temperamentally equipped to cope with the demands of motherhood, soon suffered a nervous breakdown. An expert on nervous conditions prescribed bed rest and isolation and ordered her never to paint or write again, but to devote herself solely to the care of her husband and baby. To Charlotte, who had been painting and writing since before her marriage and who loved swimming and gymnastics, the prescription was like a death sentence. She grew worse instead of better. Within a matter of months, she found the courage to disobey the doctor's orders. She separated from her husband and, taking little Katharine, went to live in California, where she became attracted to the work and ideas of suffragists and labor leaders and to a popular new form of socialism. This new American version promoted a global, cooperative society to be achieved through gradual, peaceful change, not through class struggle and violence. Charlotte began to write and then to lecture, becoming well known as a speaker on economic and social topics. She was soon totally self-supporting and grew stronger and saner with each passing week.

In 1892, the year in which she published her most famous short story, "The Yellow Wallpaper," a fictional account of her breakdown, Charlotte divorced her husband. Not long afterward, she sent her daughter to live with him and his new wife. The choice to surrender custody of her child created a scandal that swirled around Charlotte's head for several years: Not only had she rejected an apparently amiable husband, but she had abandoned her child and repudiated the cherished American domestic ideal. Nearly ten years later Charlotte took another chance on marriage. This time she chose her first cousin, George Houghton Gilman, seven years her junior and a lifelong friend. This marriage was a success, bringing companionship and full support for her work.

Gilman's books and short stories, and her magazine, *The Forerunner,* reflect her own struggles as a woman and her perceptions of women's role in history and society. In *Women and Economics* (1898), her most important book, she concluded that women's historical dependence on men for sustenance had warped their potential to be fully human, because sexual and reproductive characteristics calculated to attract men had evolved at the expense of women's intellectual and spiritual qualities. Men, in turn, had been cheated of life's fullness by their need to dominate women and deny their humanity.

As a solution to fundamental inequities, Gilman proposed in her later writings a communally organized society that would liberate women from full-time domestic service to men. The private home and monogamous marriages would continue to exist, but women would be freed from cooking, cleaning, laundry, and child care by the reorganization of those jobs within the community. Women would be able to develop their fullest capacities and find meaningful work and economic independence. The home would be a place of rest and congeniality rather than a workplace, and women, now fully equal to men, would be far better mothers and happier wives.

Born in 1869, Emma Goldman, the daughter of a Jewish shopkeeper, spent her childhood in the repressive atmosphere of czarist Russia. As a teenager in St. Petersburg she read radical literature and befriended revolutionary students. In 1885 she emigrated to the United States, where she found work in a factory in Rochester, New York. After a brief, unhappy marriage and divorce, she settled in New York City. Goldman's combative spirit was fired by social injustice and by the huge gulf that she saw between the American dream and the American reality for those on the bottom of society. She loved America, but she wanted to improve it. Before long, she had become involved with Johann Most and Alexander Berkman, leaders of the American wing of the international anarchist movement, which envisioned a world organized into small, cooperative industries, farms, and villages operating without any coercive laws or government intervention. Everyone would be equal, and no person would grow rich from another person's labor. If necessary, anarchists argued, this ideal world would have to be brought about by the destruction of the existing order through revolution and individual acts of violence.

In 1892, Goldman offered her support to Berkman when he attempted to assassinate industrialist Henry Clay Frick. When the attack failed, Berkman went to jail for fourteen years and Goldman, who had not actually participated, fell under the intense scrutiny of police and federal authorities. Surveillance would dog her for the rest of her life in America, and she was arrested and jailed on many occasions. In 1901 authorities even tried—unsuccessfully—to link Goldman to the assassination of President William McKinley, though she had long since abandoned her belief in violence as a tool for social change.

Through much of her career, Goldman focused her considerable talents on social ills and women's emancipation. She published a radical magazine, *Mother Earth,* and crisscrossed the country delivering lectures on labor and anarchism; on birth control, which she felt would free women from their historical bondage to reproduction; and on marriage, which she labeled legalized prostitution, a parasitic relationship based on the treatment of women as property. Goldman favored free love—not promiscuity, as her critics feared, but a free association of equally independent men and women. She herself had many lovers in her lifetime, and a host of loyal friends.

In general, Goldman was impatient with Progressive Era politics and women's reform organizations. Suffrage, she felt, was a distraction from the real need to change society at its roots. She had her doubts about settlement work, too, asking what use it was to teach the poor how to eat with a fork "if they have not the food." Goldman was one of the most charismatic and magnetic speakers America had ever seen and an avid champion of free speech. In one town, threatened with arrest if she appeared on the speakers' platform, she walked in with her hands raised and a handkerchief stuffed in her mouth. The crowd was ecstatic, and Goldman made her point without uttering a single word.

Nearly everyone had an opinion about Emma Goldman. To some, like journalist William Marion Reedy, she was one of the world's greatest living women, an enlightened soul born "eight thousand years ahead of her age." To others she was the most dangerous "Red" in America. Both evaluations were true. Goldman was dangerous, not because she embraced anarchism, but because she presented a real challenge to people's ideas about the fundamental values of American culture: gender relations, materialism, the class structure, and the role of government in free society. In 1917, Goldman and her old friend Alexander Berkman were arrested and imprisoned for their active opposition to the military draft for World War I. When they were released two years later, in the middle of the United States's postwar "Red Scare," the government deprived them of citizenship and deported them to Russia, along with a number of other radicals. Goldman spent the rest of her life in exile in Europe.

Margaret Sanger, born in 1878, owed a significant debt to Emma Goldman, who was promoting birth control in the United States before Sanger adopted the cause and made it her life work. But Sanger, though she had been a socialist in the 1910s,

MOTHERS!

Can you afford to have a large family?
Do you want any more children?
If not, why do you have them?

DO NOT KILL, DO NOT TAKE LIFE, BUT PREVENT

Safe, Harmless Information can be obtained of trained
Nurses at

46 AMBOY STREET
NEAR PITKIN AVE. — BROOKLYN.

Tell Your Friends and Neighbors.   All Mothers Welcome
A registration fee of 10 cents entitles any mother to this information.

מוטערס!

זייט איהר פערמעגליך צו האבען א גרויסע פאמיליע?
ווילט איהר האבען נאך קינדער?
אויב ניט, ווארום האט איהר זיי?

מערדערט ניט, נעהמט ניט קיין לעבען, נור פערהיט זיך.

זיכערע, אונשעדליכע אויסקינפטע קענט איהר בעקומען פון ערפארענע נוירסעס אין

46 אמבאי סטרים ניער פיטקין עוועניו ברוקלין

מאכט דאס בעקאנט צו אייערע פריינד און שכנות.   יעדער מוטער איז וילקאמען

פיר 10 סענט איינשרייב־געלד זיינט איהר בערעכטיגט צו דיזע אינפארמיישאן.

MADRI!

Potete permettervi il lusso d'avere altri bambini?
Ne volete ancora?
Se non ne volete piu', perche' continuate a metterli
al mondo?

NON UCCIDETE MA PREVENITE!

Informazioni sicure ed innocue saranno fornite da infermiere autorizzate a
46 AMBOY STREET   Near Pitkin Ave. Brooklyn
a cominciare dal 12 Ottobre. Avvertite le vostre amiche e vicine.
Tutte le madri sono ben accette. La tassa d'iscrizione di 10 cents da diritto
a qualunque madre di ricevere consigli ed informazioni gratis.

Margaret H. Sanger

This circular, printed in English, Yiddish, and Italian, advertised Margaret Sanger's clinic in the Brownsville section of Brooklyn, New York. This was the first birth control clinic in the country.

was not a revolutionary, and she succeeded where the defiantly radical Goldman could not, eventually making the birth control reform movement acceptable to large numbers of Americans.

As a young woman, Sanger witnessed the premature death of her own mother, who had been worn out by multiple childbirths and the strain of raising eleven children on her husband's artisan wages. A few years later, married and working as a nurse in New York City's immigrant slums, Sanger saw firsthand the unhealthy children and squalid, foreshortened lives of women whose families were too large; she witnessed the pain in which many died from clumsy, back-room abortions. Ignorant herself about effective methods of birth control and powerless to help her patients, Sanger seethed with frustration. In 1913, seeking some answers in Europe, she found government-sponsored birth control clinics, staffed by doctors and nurses, where married women could receive information about limiting the size of their families and be fitted with devices to prevent conception.

Sanger was frustrated in all her early attempts to make birth control systematically available to American women. Written information about contraception was considered obscene and classed with pornography; it was illegal for anyone to tell another person anything about contraception or provide contraceptive materials. Historically conservative, not to say prudish, Americans were reluctant to discuss sexuality or its consequences, and many feared that the limitation of family size among the white middle classes would amount to a form of "race suicide," in which the "best" people would rapidly be outnumbered by the offspring of poor, immigrant, or black Americans. But Margaret Sanger was interested in birth control for all women, especially the poor, who had so few choices in their lives. In 1914, she was arrested and her birth control publications banned from distribution under the obscenity regulations of the U.S. Post Office Department. Given insufficient time to prepare her legal defense, Sanger avoided a jail sentence by fleeing to Europe for a few months, though it meant leaving her three young children behind. In 1916, Sanger and her sister, Ethel Byrne, a nurse, were arrested for opening an experimental birth control clinic in the slums of Brooklyn, New York. The clinic was closed down, to the despair of its women clients, and Sanger and her sister went to jail.

Public support and sympathy for Sanger's crusade grew rapidly after 1916, involving the efforts of both college-educated and working-class women. By the 1920s, there were national and international birth control leagues, and little by little the U.S. legal system gave way before insistent demands for reproductive control from women's organizations and from physicians. Margaret Sanger remained active in the promotion of birth control and the pioneering of new contraceptive methods until her death in 1966.

Isadora Duncan (1878–1927) was born to break the rules. Raised in San Francisco after her parents' divorce, she and her sister and brothers were brought up by their antimaterialistic and atheistic mother, who instilled in them a love of poetry, dance, music, and nature. As a very young girl, Duncan decided it would be her mission to rescue the art of dance from what she saw as the unnatural rigidity of classical nineteenth-century ballet. She hoped to restore the expressive qualities dance had lost since the time of the ancient Greeks. Duncan studied sculpture and nature and the organic movements of the human body, always seeking ways to make dance express the meaning of music, great ideas, or profound and primitive human emotions. She was convinced that all energy and movement originated in the solar plexus, rather than the spine, which was the center of all balletic dance movements; toe dancing she dismissed as ugly and artificial. Her use of prone or supine positions, bent backs and knees, her abandonment of frothy tutus in favor of tunics, flowing draperies, and bare feet, have all become part of modern dance.

Duncan never found support among American audiences. Turn-of-the-century Americans were not comfortable with her unorthodox style of movement or with her diaphanous draperies, deliberately designed to reveal the body as it moved. Briefly, at the beginning of her career, Duncan attracted the attention of a few rich New York socialites, who hired her to dance as salon entertainment; a few years later, Americans would be shocked by her numerous, highly publicized love affairs and by the births of her illegitimate children. Europeans were far more welcoming; they found Duncan colorful and daring and seemed to appreciate her art. After 1900, Duncan lived most of the rest of her life in Europe, where she toured with her performances and ran dance schools for gifted young girls. Duncan was frequently acclaimed, and European artists, from musicians to painters, saw her as the embodiment of the future of art. The French sculptor Auguste Rodin said that he sometimes felt Duncan was the greatest woman the world had ever known.

The triumphs of Duncan's life were counterweighted with tragedy. In 1913, in France, her two little children were drowned when a car they were sitting in slipped its brakes and rolled into the River Seine. Duncan never recovered from their deaths and was haunted until the end of her life by her last vision of their faces in the car window as the chauffeur drove them away. Her own death at age forty-nine came in 1927, just a few weeks after she had completed her autobiography, *My Life*. Climbing into an open sports car in the French Riviera town of Nice, she called out to some friends seated in a sidewalk café: "Adieu mes amis. Je vais à la gloire!" ("Good-bye my friends. I am going to glory!") A moment later, as the car pulled away, her long, fringed scarf caught in the spokes of a rear wheel and broke her neck. She died instantly.

It would be decades before the achievements of Isadora Duncan and other cultural radicals were fully appreciated in America. However, their courageous rejection of conventions in both art and life was already beginning to find echoes in the larger society in the years just before World War I. Symbolized by new fashions in women's clothing and by changes in manners and behavior, women's tentative rebellion against the rigid morality of the nineteenth century had begun—not just among a small cadre of urban feminists, but among well-brought-up young ladies all across the country. Respectable women everywhere abandoned their corsets and began to wear skirts that exposed their ankles; all over the country young ladies joined the dance craze, hopping, stepping, and gliding to the Bunny Hug and the Turkey Trot, often in close proximity to their partners. Gradually, ordinary middle- and working-class women were altering the social definition of sexual morality and stretching the boundaries of female respectability. These cultural changes would shortly find even more dramatic expression in the era known as the Roaring Twenties.

War and Peace

In 1914, across the Atlantic Ocean from the United States, a small conflict in the Balkan countries escalated into a continental war involving most of Europe and pitted the Central Powers—Germany, Austria-Hungary, and the Ottoman Empire—against the Allies—England, France, Belgium, Russia, Serbia, and Montenegro. Before long, the effects of the European conflict began to touch the lives of distant Americans, impinging upon the national sense of safety and forcing conscientious men and women to choose between militarism and pacifism. The war altered the work and family lives of women of all social classes; it also challenged the strategies of both factions of the woman suffrage movement, even as it provided the stage for the final campaign.

President Woodrow Wilson found it impossible to sustain American neutrality after German submarines began to attack American shipping in 1915. In April 1917, he asked Congress to declare war on Germany. Among the few dissenting votes in a chorus of support for this popular war was that of Jeannette Rankin, a representative from Montana and the only woman in Congress.

U.S. involvement in World War I lasted only nineteen months, but some 4 million American men were drafted, and more than half were sent overseas to the battlefields of France. Enlisted to serve in the armed forces as support staff and nurses were the women of the Army Nurse Corps and some eleven thousand Navy "yeomanettes." There were also 305 Marine Corps "marinettes." Professional nurses for the army were recruited through the Red Cross, which enrolled more than twenty thousand of them. The Red Cross also recruited a large number of aides, clerks, and social workers to assist with the war effort at home and abroad. Molly Dewson and Polly Porter, two social workers from Massachusetts, served with the Red Cross in France for fifteen months, engaged in the task of resettling French and Belgian refugees who had fled their homes in the war-ravaged areas of the battlefront. Dewson and Porter were stationed so far behind the front lines that they never even heard gunfire, yet they were glad they had been given a chance to be useful.

American women who did not go abroad were encouraged to serve their country in a variety of voluntary ways. Many started victory gardens to grow their own food, and many canned what they had grown to help save commercial supplies for the troops. Housewives invented ways to serve meatless, wheatless, or butterless meals. Some women started wearing shorter skirts in order to save cloth. Women's clubs and church and civic groups organized war bond drives to help raise funds for the war effort; they rolled bandages and prepared supplies for the Red Cross;

and they worked for government war relief agencies. As in all wars, women took over the management of farms and small businesses that their husbands left behind when they enlisted.

Not all American women supported their country's participation in the war. As early as 1915, in response to escalating violence in Europe and widespread apprehension that the United States would soon be directly involved, a number of prominent women activists had created the Woman's Peace Party (WPP). The three thousand original members of the WPP—among them such notable figures as Jane Addams, Carrie Chapman Catt, and Charlotte Perkins Gilman—adopted a peace platform that called for arms limitation for all nations and for immediate and ongoing mediation of the European conflict. They linked their demand for a voice in the decision making with a protest of the atrocities of war: "As women we are particularly charged with the future of childhood and with the care of the helpless and the unfortunate. We will no longer endure without protest that added burden of maimed and invalid men and poverty-stricken widows and orphans which was placed upon us [in past wars]. . . . We demand that women be given a share in deciding between war and peace." In April 1915, American delegates from the WPP traveled to an International Congress of Women in the Netherlands, attended by women from both the Central Powers and the Allied nations. Chairman Jane Addams, who represented the largest neutral nation, told a reporter, "The great achievement of this congress is . . . the getting together of these women from all parts of Europe when their men folks are shooting each other from opposite trenches."

A number of American women withdrew from the peace movement when their country joined the Allied forces in 1917. Sadly, but wholeheartedly, they offered their assistance in what President Wilson called a war to "make the world safe for democracy." Those who remained pacifists were reviled in the press and greeted with jeers when they spoke in public. Hysterical patriots waged a campaign of suspicion and resentment against Jane Addams and others whom they considered "reds" or even German sympathizers. "Saint Jane," the woman who had represented nobility and unselfishness to a whole generation of Americans, was branded a coward and a traitor. More than a decade would pass before Addams's reputation was restored and her pacifism understood. In 1931, she received the Nobel Peace Prize.

For American working women, World War I brought an unprecedented boon in employment opportunities. As men enlisted in the armed forces or were drafted, they left behind jobs in industry and business that had never previously been open to women. The departure of the regular workers, combined with the enormous Allied demand for munitions and war support materials, helped to produce a labor vacuum that women rushed to fill. Tens of thousands of new jobs opened up. Iron and steel mills, munitions factories, chemical and electrical industries all sought women workers. Women happily shifted from traditional women's jobs in domestic service and unskilled factory labor to the more demanding and better paying wartime jobs. A number of women were joining the paid labor force for the first time, but most of the growth in women's work took place among those who were already working for wages. At one point during the war, women comprised 20 percent or more of all workers manufacturing airplanes, electrical machinery, leather and rubber goods, food, and printed materials. Women in industry ran presses and drills, lathes, welding tools, and milling machines; a few even operated cranes.

Labor unions, which enrolled nearly 3 million new members during the war, increasingly included women members. The U.S. Department of Labor opened a subdivision called the Woman in Industry Service to oversee working conditions and hours of labor for women. The service later became the Women's Bureau of the Department of Labor.

The U.S. government recruited thousands of young typists and stenographers for wartime clerical service in Washington, D.C. Another attractive opportunity for women came from the railroads, which had been placed under government control in late 1917. Women railroad employees worked as station clerks and dispatchers, car cleaners, and as rail yard laborers. By the end of the war, more than 100,000 women were employed in railroad work, where they were given good wages, an eight-hour day, and opportunities for promotion. Even in the relatively enlightened railroad industry, however, women still encountered job segregation and sexual harrassment, and craftsmen still maintained exclusive access to many skilled jobs, just as they had in the prewar workplace.

In their home communities, women took jobs as conductors, ticket takers, and station agents in public transportation. Conducting was particularly attractive because its hours could be structured around family needs and it paid more than twice as much as most women's work—an average of twenty-one dollars a week instead of eight to ten dollars. In general, wages for women war workers were higher than anything that they had previously experienced, often two or three times what they earned in traditional women's jobs—though unless the industry was unionized or under government control, wages were not necessarily as high as those of men in the same jobs.

For many African Americans, the war brought geographical changes as well as changes in employment. During the Great Migration of 1915 to 1920, some 500,000 Southern black men and women left for Northern cities, where industrial labor shortages caused by the call-up of white men had created unheard-of opportunities. As white women replaced white men in industry and business, black women were able to move into the jobs that the white women had vacated. The wages were especially attractive: A cook or a laundress could earn in a day what she earned in a week in the South; in industry she could earn three dollars a day, compared to fifty cents for picking cotton. Domestic service paid twice what it did in the South. Railroads hired black women as cleaners and yard workers and paid

As white women moved into men's jobs in skilled trades, black women also took untraditional work, but in lower-level and more physically strenuous jobs. Here, black women load wheelbarrows in a brickyard.

government-regulated wages. Despite these advantages, the persistence of racism in the North meant that many black women were paid 10 to 60 percent less than white women doing similar work and that they were always assigned to the hottest, dirtiest, and most disagreeable tasks available. Although African-American women increased their participation in Northern industry by 100 percent, they remained less than 7 percent of the women's industrial labor force.

When the armistice was signed on November 11, 1918, and soldiers returned home, women everywhere were unsurprisingly reluctant to give up their wartime jobs. Those who had joined unions specifically to protect their jobs often found that male union leaders were as anxious as the rest of society to see women return to domestic life. For most women, losing a wartime job meant a return, not to domestic chores—which they would be performing in any case—but to low-paid, sex-segregated women's work. In the end, women were unable to hold on to most skilled jobs in heavy industry, in steel, or in railroad work, though they did manage to preserve gains that they had made in the food and garment industries.

Telephone operators and office workers, whose job market had been expanding even before the war, continued to make gains. Black women at every level of the labor force dropped a few notches, and those at the bottom were pushed out altogether. Some went home to the South, but many more stayed in Northern cities, piecing together lives that included both work and family. They reproduced in their city neighborhoods the same sort of supportive networks of kin and friends that had helped to sustain them in the South.

The last campaign in the fight for woman suffrage took place amid the tensions and excitement of war and the immediate postwar years. In 1915, state suffrage referenda in New York, New Jersey, Massachusetts, and Pennsylvania had been defeated. The supporters of woman suffrage still did not have a single urbanized, industrialized Eastern state in their camp. Undeterred, suffragists regrouped, raised more money, and plunged back into the fight. Under the new NAWSA leadership, with Carrie Chapman Catt as president and Maud Wood Park in charge of the congressional lobbying operation in Washington, D.C., NAWSA adopted the "Winning Plan": Suffragists would continue to work for suffrage in the individual states because they needed the expanded electorate that newly enfranchised states would bring, and they would also increase the pressure on the U.S. Congress to pass the constitutional amendment. Park and her fellow lobbyists maintained extensive files on each congressman and senator and carefully selected individual women to talk with them in an attempt to win them over.

In the course of the 1916 election campaign both the Republican and Democratic parties had endorsed woman suffrage but left the decision up to the individual states. Once safely reelected, Wilson let the subject of woman suffrage drop. During his first address to Congress after the election, Wilson pretended to ignore a large banner unfurled from the gallery by Alice Paul and members of the National Woman's Party, the radical faction of the suffrage movement. The banner read, "Mr. President, What Will You Do for Woman Suffrage?" A few weeks later, in early 1917, the National Woman's Party began systematically to picket the White House, and on Wilson's inaugural day a thousand women marched solemnly around and around outside the heavy iron fence.

No one, including the President, would be able to ignore woman suffrage much longer. The campaign was receiving front page coverage in newspapers all over the country; it was featured prominently in popular magazines; the national environment was growing daily more supportive; and 4 million women in eleven states could now vote. If they could add one large Eastern state, women would have enough political power to push toward the amendment and to unseat congressmen and senators who refused to convert to the cause. With 2 million members, NAWSA itself was now the largest women's voluntary organization in the country. As their cause made increasingly visible progress and their work intensified, suffragists grew more and more exhilarated.

In 1917, the war intervened in the rush to the finish line. Catt and the NAWSA leadership decided that the most appropriate response to the national crisis would be to throw NAWSA's support behind the war effort and, at the same time, to continue the fight for suffrage. Those who disagreed could quietly step aside. Catt herself resigned from the Woman's Peace Party that she had helped to found and encouraged NAWSA members to aid in war work. NAWSA funded and sponsored a hospital in France, and both Catt and Anna Howard Shaw served on the Women's Council for the National Defense, which was organized to integrate women into conservation, farming, and other kinds of war relief work. Its cooperative stance on the war effort gained NAWSA many valuable supporters and put President Wilson in its debt. A stunning victory in New York State late in 1917 not only confirmed the positive popular response to NAWSA's war work, it also brought suffragists the electoral power of the largest state in the Northeast.

Leaders of the more militant National Woman's Party decided against official participation in the war effort. They stepped up their picketing and carried increasingly provocative placards, which called the President "Kaiser Wilson" and accused him of betraying democracy by continuing to exclude women. Skirmishes with male onlookers led to the arrests of more than two hundred picketers in the summer and fall of 1917. Nearly half of these women went to jail. There they were treated roughly amid miserable living conditions. Like their British sisters, the women demanded to be classed as political prisoners, and when political status was denied, a number of them went on a hunger strike. Force-feedings made front page news. Within weeks, a huge public outcry about the treatment of these American suffragists embarrassed the authorities into releasing them.

Leaders in NAWSA and their allies in Congress quickly distanced themselves from the militant suffragists of the National Woman's Party. Catt denied any connection with the other group, although they were fighting for the same cause, and she did not protest their brutal treatment. In the end, however, the episode helped rather than hurt the suffrage cause. First, it was a tremendous source of publicity, and second, many Americans were appalled that such outrages had been perpetrated against women peacefully demanding their rights in a democratic country. Many others—including some cautious congressmen who had been sitting on the fence—simply decided to embrace the more conservative suffragists of NAWSA as the lesser of two evils.

Mary Church Terrell and her daughter were among the few African-American women who joined the picketers around the White House, though they were not arrested. Black women, in general, continued to pursue suffrage in segregated organizations and through a growing number of black woman suffrage leagues in the North and the South. Such leagues were repeatedly snubbed by the leaders of both NAWSA and the National Woman's Party, who were still trying to win support for suffrage in the South and among Southern senators and congressmen.

In early 1918, suffragists and members of both political parties realized that the woman suffrage amendment finally had enough support to make it through the House of Representatives. President Wilson advised fellow Democrats to vote for the amendment "as an act of right and justice to the women of the country and of the world." On the morning of January 10, Jeannette Rankin rose in the main chamber of the House to introduce the Anthony Amendment, as it had been called for many years. Women from both NAWSA and the National Woman's Party packed the visitors' galleries, waiting anxiously; they knew that they had not a single vote to spare. One congressional supporter, who was very ill, was brought in on a stretcher to cast his vote; another man had broken his shoulder but waited to go to the hospital to have it set until after the vote was taken. A New York congressman came from the bedside of his dying wife, who was a suffragist and had insisted that he go. He returned to New York after the vote to attend her funeral. When at last the vote was tallied, it won by 274 to 136, exactly the two-thirds majority required to pass a constitutional amendment. Momentarily stunned by their first national victory, the women started to leave the gallery, and then spontaneously broke into a hymn of praise that filled the House chamber and echoed through the hallways.

The suffrage amendment moved on to the Senate, where it would remain bogged down for a year and a half before the women could muster sufficient votes to ensure the needed two-thirds majority. In the 1918 elections, NAWSA worked systematically to defeat four anti-suffrage senators, and the National Woman's Party once again took up its picketing campaign.

Black women's suffrage organizations continued to pursue some measure of just treatment or inclusion from white suffragists. In 1919, hoping to demonstrate the political power their organizations had amassed, the NACW's Northeastern Federation of Colored Women's Clubs applied for membership in NAWSA. The leaders of NAWSA panicked. How would the addition of six thousand black women to their ranks look to the Southern senators whose votes they were courting? Pleading the need for political expediency, NAWSA's embarrassed leaders begged the federation to postpone its application. Ultimately, the federation agreed to withdraw in exchange for a promise from NAWSA that it would not support any last-minute attempts to rewrite the constitutional amendment to include a states' enforcement clause that would give the states, rather than Congress, the power to enforce the new law, thus allowing Southern states to find ways to keep black women from voting. In June 1919, after a string of negative votes, the Senate finally approved the suffrage measure. Scarcely pausing for breath, suffragists fanned out across the country to help secure the needed ratification by three-quarters of the states. In less than a year, thirty-five of the necessary thirty-six states had ratified the amendment.

National attention then focused on Tennessee, the only remaining state in which anti-suffrage was not so firmly entrenched as to make ratification impossible. Still, the opposition was fierce, and representatives of the anti-suffrage interests poured into the state capital of Nashville, alternately threatening the legislators and plying them with liquor. On the last day of the special session, the vote came down to a single undecided representative, twenty-four-year-old Harry Burn, the youngest member of the legislature. Just hours before the vote, Burn had received a letter from his mother, a suffrage supporter, urging him to "be a good boy and help Mrs. Catt put 'Rat' in Ratification." Burn voted "Yes," and the amendment passed. A few days later, on August 26, 1920, the Secretary of State issued a formal proclamation declaring the elective franchise to be the right of every adult woman citizen of the United States. It had been seventy-two years, one month, and one week since the meeting in Seneca Falls, New York, on July 19, 1848, when American women had first convened to demand their "sacred right" to vote.

Exhausted and elated, suffragists shared a moment of accord, though there would be no permanent unity in the women's movement in the decades to come and, for many years, no women's victories as spectacularly satisfying as the achievement of suffrage. An English suffragist might have been speaking for her American sisters when she wrote: "All the time, watching, attacking, defending, moving, and counter-moving! . . . how glorious . . . those days were! To lose the personal in the great impersonal is to live!"

For the rest of their lives, suffragists and other Progressive women would remember the years of struggle and female solidarity with powerful nostalgia. Not only had the work itself been liberating, but women could point to real changes that they had made in American society and politics between 1890 and 1920. American women opening doors, pushing at the boundaries of traditional roles, emerging into public life in unprecedented numbers had set the tone and the agenda for those reforms in labor, politics, and urban life that became the dominant characteristic of the Progressive Era. Looking at the long years that lay ahead in the twentieth century, at the new campaigns for justice and equality that would demand their attention, American women could confidently tell one another they had made a splendid beginning.

CHAPTER 8

From Ballots to Breadlines

1920–1940

Sarah Jane Deutsch

Our images of the 1920s, when we have images, are filled with young women with short hair and short skirts. They are kicking up their legs and kicking off a century of social restrictions. They smoke. They dance. They read racy literature. And they do it all in public. They have "advanced" ideas about sex, too. They have taken the socially outrageous, bohemian behavior of the previous generation's Greenwich Village set, and, to the horror of their parents, have brought it to Main Street.

What was going on with women in the 1920s and 1930s was, of course, more complicated than these images of "flappers," which tend to be of young, white, middle-class women. African Americans, Chicanas, Asian Americans, and other women aspired to be or were flappers, too, but most women of any race or ethnicity lived quite differently. Their lives, like our visions of the past, were affected by these images, but they did not mirror them. Although the 1920s did abound with flappers and would-be flappers, the decade also hosted mothers, professionals, women struggling in poverty, and women asserting new power.

Above all, in the 1920s, there was a pervasive sense of newness. To many it seemed that the world was made new after the massive destruction of World War I ended in 1918—and that women were made new too. What was the "new" woman, this creature who, by 1920, could legally vote in national elections on the same basis as men everywhere in the United States? She was the result of competing desires, visions, and needs from a variety of sources. She looked different to different eyes.

When historians discuss such transformations, they like to talk about the way we, as a society, construct ideas about what a woman is. It is perhaps easiest to understand what historians mean by the social construction of womanhood by looking at the literal construction of woman. Both of the figures on the next page were literal constructions of women. People created fashions that demanded a certain "look" from women, then designed clothing to create that look by shaping

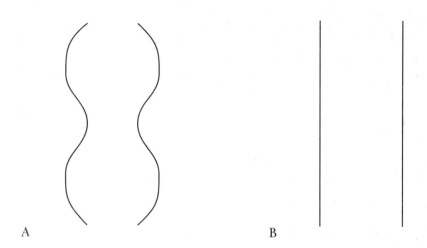

A   B

women's bodies in certain ways. Neither Figure A nor Figure B looks very much like women's own bodies. The first one, the nineteenth-century hourglass figure, took twenty-five pounds of pressure per square inch, in the form of tightly laced whalebone corsets, to create. The second one, the figure of the 1920s new woman, required breast binders and girdles, which were more comfortable, perhaps, but no more natural.

Why would anyone do this to women? The woman in Figure A could not breathe well with all that pressure and could not move freely without fainting. But women were not supposed to. That figure represented the ideal of nineteenth-century womanhood—a homebound, domestic creature unfit (thanks in part to corsets) for the rough world outside the home. She was a creature for a private world and a sign that her husband or father was making enough money to spare her any need to put forth physical effort.

Women without such providers had to do a substantial amount of physical labor themselves. They could not wear tight, confining corsets and were not seen by the upper classes as being "real" women; they were too free with their actions, too free with their bodies, too free altogether.

On the other hand, in the 1920s the new woman, represented by those two straight lines in Figure B, was clearly not a domestic woman. Like men of the day, she was a public figure, so her public figure would be like men's. But the reconstruction of the concept of "woman," of what it meant to be female, even in the ideal, was not as easy as the reconstruction of fashion.

Images and Lives

World War I had wrought dramatic changes in the United States, changes with vital implications for the lives of women. In its year and a half of active participation in

Three women prepare for a trip to California. The independent "new" women of the 1920s felt free not just to shorten their skirts but to abandon them. For the first time more women, like men, wore trousers.

the war, the government vastly increased its armed forces, took over the running of the railroads and telephones, began some basic health services in remote rural areas, controlled prices for food and other commodities, negotiated with representatives of business and workers over working conditions and pay, created new government departments to look after the interests of women workers, and generally entered into the daily economic, social, and political lives of its citizens in newly intimate ways.

For many workers, the government was a far better boss than the private individuals who had been in charge of their lives. It paid better, set better hours, and was more responsive to their complaints. These and other workers faced the postwar world with increased expectations. They had worked hard. They had sacrificed for the war. They had been told they were fighting to save democracy. Now they expected a better world.

The war had also moved people around from place to place and job to job. As men of all races were called up to fight, companies that had previously hired only white men for well-paying jobs found themselves short of labor. For the first time, they began to hire white women and black men. Such jobs as streetcar conducting and railroad work paid more than these women had earned before. For black men, this was often their first chance to move from day labor or agricultural work into steadier, better-paying factory jobs. Some black women managed to break into these newly available jobs, particularly on the railroad, but most of the jobs they found available were the ones white women had left. Even these jobs, even domestic service, in the North tended to pay better and offer better conditions than the ones southern African Americans could find at home. Since before the Civil War a steady stream of black men and women had left the South for the North. Now that stream became a torrent. At the same time, the United States made special arrangements with Mexico to bring Mexican workers across the border to work on railroads, in construction, and in harvesting. What began as wartime migrations continued throughout the 1920s.

All this movement brought new groups of people together and gave them new ways to think about their roles in society. There were racial tensions and sudden strikes by whites protesting the employment of blacks and by blacks protesting discrimination. Black women, whom whites were used to thinking of as quiet and obedient, threw down their tools and quit when foremen cursed at them for protesting conditions or when companies hired white women to supervise them. And white women and men also struggled over what their new working positions would mean after the war. The men of the Amalgamated Association of Street and Electric Railway Employees in New York City were so worried about the changes that they wrote a poem:

> We wonder where we are drifting, where is the freedom of the stripes
>   and stars
> If for the sake of greed and profit we put women conductors on the cars
> When our dear brothers left us, shouldered their guns and went to war,
> Little did we think street railway kings would use women like a squaw.
> Woman is God's most tender flower, made to blossom and to bear
> She was made by God the weaker, like a vine on man to lean
> She was meant to work like her nature, tender sweet and clean. . . .
> We pray God to protect and keep women off the cars.

Many women had a different notion of their "nature," however. As if in answer to the men's poem, women machine tool workers retorted:

> The simple, tender, clinging vine,
> That once around the oak did twine
> Is something of the past;
> We stand now by your side

And surmount obstacles with pride,
We're equal, free at last
And I would rather polish steel,
Than get you up a tasty meal.

Changes had occurred during the war, and life would not be the same again. In the two years after the war ended, the United States witnessed perhaps its greatest upheaval. In 1919 alone, 4 million workers, or one out of every five workers, went out on strike, and there were major race riots in twenty-five towns and cities, including Charleston, South Carolina; Washington, D.C.; and Chicago. In Chicago, five hundred people were wounded, and twenty-three blacks and fifteen whites were killed. The number of lynchings of black citizens, many of the victims still wearing their army uniforms, skyrocketed.

In April 1919, the women of the New England Union of Telephone Operators went on strike. Postmaster General Albert Burleson, who still retained his temporary wartime control over the telephone industry, refused to negotiate. He hired company spies to infiltrate the strikers' ranks and used armed force. What had started as a struggle over wages became a fight to defend the right to bargain collectively. The women presented a solid front, and the male phone workers joined them. When Burleson threatened to replace them with soldiers, one hundred women picketers, accompanied by male relatives in uniform carrying military service flags, blocked their way. The disgusted soldiers said they had not expected to come home from the war to fight women. Nor would the Boston police arrest the strikers. Women doctors gave the strikers free medical care, and restaurant owners kept them fed. Burleson brought in scabs from out of town, but no one would serve them or work with them. The solidarity of the workers and community support brought the strikers victory in only five days.

Few other strikes enjoyed similar success. When a general strike in Seattle peacefully shut down the city, the mayor called in the troops. In the steel industry, where more than half the common laborers were immigrants, employers played up an image of the strikers as foreign agitators. In the wake of the 1917 Russian Revolution and the creation of an international Communist party in 1919, the employers labeled the strikers radical revolutionaries.

To much of the public witnessing the strikes and riots, it did seem as though the United States was verging on revolution. Steel-plant employers succeeded in convincing federal agents to round up and deport thousands of immigrant strikers with no proof of wrongdoing, and the general public did not protest. This anti-Communist fever, known as the Red Scare, raged in 1919 and 1920. Americans watched in near silence as government agents invaded private homes and raided not just union offices but also the offices of dissenting political organizations, arrested and deported members, and destroyed records. They held people on false charges and denied them lawyers in the name of restoring order. No one who had ever raised a voice in protest was safe. By the end of 1920, all was quiet. Yet no one could know what the future would hold. It was into this uneasy peace that the new woman would emerge.

Inventing a Public Woman

When the Tennessee state legislature ratified the national woman suffrage amendment in August 1920, American suffragists had won a seventy-year battle. Suddenly, it was over. What had the victory meant? By the end of the 1920s, the united power of American womanhood that had fought the battle seemed scarcely visible. The promises of unity would not be met in succeeding decades. During the 1920s, the country moved from an era of intense, collective action by women on behalf of women to an era when women's groups had little visibility and limited validity in the eyes of most people. It was not clear whether gaining the vote had liberated women or whether liberation had changed its meaning.

Americans had high expectations of woman suffrage. The world, they were convinced, would be a different place once women had the vote. After 1920, politicians began to respond more carefully to women's grievances. For a time, it seemed safest to do so. Yoncalla, Oregon, woke up after the election of 1920 to a "feminist revolution," according to one journalist. In this town of 323 residents, men outnumbered women by almost two to one, but the *Literary Digest* reported that the women had "risen in their wrath, stirred by the alleged inefficiency of the municipal officials, and swept every masculine office-holder out of his job." The women of the town had worked in absolute secrecy, not even telling their brothers and husbands. Only the town's women were in on the secret, and they prevailed at the polls. Mrs. Mary Burt, a university graduate, was the new mayor. She had lived in Yoncalla for forty years and had long been active in the community. Also elected to the town government was Mrs. Laswell, wife of the ousted mayor. The only thing Mr. Laswell and his assistants could find to tell the press was that they were "much surprised."

At the other end of the country, in Washington, D.C., a spate of legislative and other victories also greeted women. The women's peace movement succeeded in getting the United States to host and participate in an international disarmament conference in 1921. In the same year, the Sheppard-Towner Act allotted the first federal money for health care. Also called the Maternity and Infancy Act, it provided federal matching funds to states to improve prenatal care and infant health. (The program lapsed in 1929.) The Cable Act of 1922 gave married women independent citizenship; no longer would women who married foreigners lose their United States citizenship. And the Women's Bureau of the federal government, created during the war to look after the interests of women workers, became a permanent part of the Department of Labor in 1920.

U.S. Representatives Alice May Robertson, Mae Ella Nolan, and Winifred Huck (left to right) in front of the Capitol in 1923. All Republicans, they represented Oklahoma, California, and Illinois, respectively.

Women streamed into public office in the 1920s, the largest single increase in women's officeholding to that date, leveling off only after 1930. The Democrats and Republicans began to mandate equal representation of men and women on party committees. Altogether, these achievements covering peace, politics, labor, health care, and the home seemed to indicate a wide acceptance of women's significance in the public arena.

Yet by 1924 popular magazines were running articles (written by men) with such titles as "Is Woman Suffrage a Failure?" and "Women's Ineffective Use of the

Vote." There were signs, even early on, that not all was going according to plan. The only woman in Congress in 1921, Alice Robertson, was an anti-suffragist. Women vastly increased their numbers in office, but the meaning of that increase must be set in a wider context. In 1924, there were eighty-four women legislators in thirty states. Five years later there were two hundred, an increase of almost 250 percent. But while there were two hundred women in office, there were ten thousand men. The numbers were similar at other levels of government. In New Jersey, for example, only 19 of 788 county officeholders were women. At the federal level, there were just ten women in Congress in 1926; that year only two women were reelected to Congress in their own right, and only one was elected without the benefit of having completed a dead family member's term. The gains women sought could obviously not rely on strength at the top.

Political parties were reluctant to nominate women for offices that mattered. After arguing for so long that they were above politics, that they were interested in human welfare, not part of self-serving party political machines, women would have to prove to the men controlling political parties that they knew how to play the game. They had to prove that they could be loyal to the party and not just to principles. They had to prove that they represented a separate constituency, a group of voters they could mobilize to support them.

But women did not vote as a bloc; the fragments that had come together for the suffrage fight once more went their separate ways. As the 1920s wore on, an increasing number of delegations of women came to party conventions, only to have the party leaders pay less and less attention to them. The 1924 Democratic convention had 180 women delegates and 239 women alternates. Eleanor Roosevelt, long active in politics and social welfare, headed a subcommittee to gather suggestions from women's organizations for planks on social welfare. But, as she recalled in her autobiography, *This Is My Story*, at the convention itself the women "stood outside the door of all important meetings and waited." Their turn never seemed to come.

Some activist women had long foreseen that the right to vote would not be a miracle cure for social ills, including the inferior status of women. Rose Schneiderman, an activist for the rights of working women, declared of the vote, "Men had it all these years and nothing of great importance had happened." The population in general, men as well as women, seemed to echo her disillusionment. Smaller and smaller percentages of those eligible to vote did so. The number had been declining since 1896, when it had peaked at 79 percent. In 1912, before the passage of the woman suffrage amendment, only 59 percent of all people eligible to vote did so. By 1920, the number had sunk to 49 percent.

At the same time, government officials and most of those who elected them were retreating from a vision of government as an instrument to change society. They looked instead to a government that would restore law and order and protect business. They cared more about assisting employers than protecting the welfare of employees and the unemployed. The Republicans held the Presidency throughout the 1920s. Calvin Coolidge, who became President when Warren Harding died in 1923, believed in business and in businessmen. He stocked his cabinet with businessmen and made them at home in the Republican party. As their money poured into Republican coffers, protective tariffs on industrial goods rose and the courts made it harder for workers to strike. The *Wall Street Journal* happily announced, "Never before, here or anywhere else, has a government been so completely fused with business."

The new attitudes were reflected in the rulings of the courts, as they consistently overturned two decades of reform legislation aimed at regulating business, such as laws setting maximum hours or minimum wages for women. There was no federal minimum-wage or maximum-hour law; workers simply struck the best bargain they could with their employers. Often they worked twelve-hour days, six or seven days a week, and earned only enough to provide them with food and shelter. Workers who belonged to strong unions could get better conditions. Most unions, however, organized only skilled workers, and even among those unions, few organized women workers. Most women lacked the resources, education, or skills to have strong bargaining positions on their own.

Reformers looked to the government for a remedy, recognizing that only the government could set uniform minimum standards that would cover working women. The courts had always struck down such protective legislation for men, on the grounds that it interfered with men's freedom to make their own bargains. But in 1908, the Supreme Court, in *Muller* v. *Oregon,* decided to distinguish between men and women. In part, the Supreme Court argued that women were potential mothers of future citizens, so the government had a special interest in their well-being. The *Muller* ruling opened the way for legislation that would protect women's working conditions.

By 1923, forty states regulated the hours of women's work, and fifteen states as well as the District of Columbia regulated their wages. But two years earlier, an unemployed female worker had petitioned the federal district court for the District of Columbia to keep the minimum wage board of Washington, D.C., from enforcing its decisions on wages for women. She claimed that such enforcement had cost her a job. The Children's Hospital also brought action to prevent the minimum wage board and the board's chairman, Jesse C. Adkins, from forcing the hospital to pay higher wages. The case went to the Supreme Court on appeal. When it decided the case, *Adkins* v. *Children's Hospital,* in 1923, the Supreme Court struck down the Washington, D.C., minimum wage law for women, threatening all the protective legislation that progressive politicians and citizens had fought for and won in the previous twenty years.

The Supreme Court ruled that minimum wage boards were an arbitrary government interference in private affairs, infringing on freedom of contract. Justice George Sutherland, writing for the majority of the justices, struck over and over at what he considered false distinctions between women and men. Women, he declared, "are legally as capable of contracting for themselves as men." Giving women the vote had, according to Sutherland, eradicated differences in the civil status of men and women. With that in mind, he concluded that the law was unfair to the employer, "compelling him to pay not less than a certain sum . . . irrespective of the ability of his business to sustain the burden." Sutherland's claim regarding women's equality with men was ironic given the vast number of inequalities that remained embedded in the laws of the states and in the practices of governments as well as private corporations. Among other restraints, women found certain jobs legally closed to them, companies legally paid them less than men for the same work, some states barred them from serving on juries, and most states denied them equal access to credit.

To some triumphant suffragists the next logical step was an equal rights amendment, which would sweep away all remaining forms of discrimination at once. Activist Alice Paul spearheaded the drive for the Equal Rights Amendment (ERA). She presided over the National Women's Party (NWP) when in November 1923, the seventy-fifth anniversary of the convention at Seneca Falls, it announced the text of the ERA: "Men and women shall have equal rights throughout the United States and every place subject to its jurisdiction." A month later the amendment was introduced into Congress. To Paul, it was logical that the ERA should succeed suffrage as the focus of the NWP. Like suffrage, the ERA was only part of the feminist agenda, but it would give women power, which they could then use as they pleased.

Instead of becoming the new mass women's movement, however, the NWP dwindled. It emerged from the suffrage fight in 1920 with 35,000 members; by the end of the decade, it had 1,000. The problem lay partly in the tactics of the party, which neglected the local precinct-by-precinct organizing that had helped suffrage succeed and instead recruited highly visible celebrities, such as the artist Georgia O'Keeffe, the writer Edna St. Vincent Millay, and the aviator Amelia Earhart. Symbolic of women's advances rather than representative of most women's lives, these women could not help broaden the base for a mass movement.

There were other problems as well. Crystal Eastman supported the Equal Rights Amendment but found it too narrow. A labor lawyer, social investigator, and the first female member of New York's Employer's Liability Commission, Eastman had written in 1918, "Life is a big battle for the complete feminist." For someone like Eastman, the ERA was not the ultimate solution to women's inequality. It touched only on legal issues, not on social relations. It neither affected such concerns as birth control nor required a change in the social roles of men and women in the family. Referring to the NWP convention that had adopted the ERA, Eastman wrote, "If some such [broader] program could have been exhaustively discussed at that convention we might be congratulating ourselves that the feminist movement had begun in America. As it is all we can say is that the suffrage movement is ended."

The ERA's narrowness was particularly evident in regard to race. Alice Paul tried to ensure that the NWP, unlike some other suffrage groups, did not discriminate on the grounds of race. In 1921, the party encouraged black women to attend its national convention as delegates and speak there. But when Addie Hunton, a field secretary for the National Association for the Advancement of Colored People (NAACP), led a delegation of sixty black women from fourteen states asking Paul to throw the party's energy into fighting against southern regulations and terrorism that kept black women as well as men from voting, Paul refused. That, she insisted, was a racial issue, not a women's issue. Paul drew a distinction between racial and gender-based injustice that African-American women could not make in their daily lives.

Increasingly impatient with organizations, from the NWP to the Young Women's Christian Association (YWCA), that insisted they patiently wait until the nation was ready for further progress, black women turned to their own organizing. Lugenia Hope had led Atlanta's Neighborhood Union during World War I when it had teamed up with the newly formed Atlanta Colored Women's War Council to further the war effort. The Neighborhood Union organized each neighborhood to work for community betterment in education, morals, food conservation, employment, health, housing, and entertainment. By 1922, its campaigns had resulted in streets being paved, sewers installed, houses repaired, and classes given on health, wages, and citizenship. Two years earlier, Hope had written Eva Bowles at the national YWCA board, demanding that "full recognition of leadership be given Negro women."

In September 1922, Mrs. Robert M. Patterson, a black socialist candidate for Pennsylvania's General Assembly, declared in the newspaper *Women's Voice:* "Never was there a time in which there was greater need for sane and sober thought on the part of Negro women. . . . We need women who will not sell their rights for a mess of pottage. . . . We must not permit the fight for equal civil rights to cease until it will be possible for every citizen, without regard to race, to have complete civil rights granted to him or her."

Yet white women quarreled among themselves over what civil rights for women meant. At the very moment when social reformer and activist Florence Kelley was marshaling her forces to try to avert the overturn of protective legislation in the *Adkins* case, the NWP submitted a brief on the other side. It was, after all, an unemployed woman who was co-petitioner against the minimum wage for women. In the NWP, Paul and Eastman both had worked closely with working women. They now believed that protective legislation—not just for the minimum wage but also laws against women working at night—prevented women from getting the most lucrative jobs and justified persistent inequalities. On the other hand, Kelley had as allies the Women's Trade Union League, an organization partly made up of and led by wage-earning women. To them, protective legislation acknowledged the realities of unequal social and economic power; the ERA did not. If woman suffrage could produce the kind of damage evident in Justice Sutherland's argument, the ERA seemed to them even more potentially damaging in his hands. Caught by the reality of women's diverse social and economic situations and needs, women divided instead of uniting over the ERA and protective legislation.

Divisions among women were not all caused by the women themselves. For one thing, the raids and prosecutions of the Red Scare had a chilling effect on women's groups. Facing possible jail terms or deportation simply for associating with radical women, some women turned a cold shoulder to former friends. In an era in which organizing at all was suspect, women in the 1920s could either organize together for equality and rights and be labeled "red" and fired, or they could try to go it alone.

Unsurprisingly, women in their twenties and thirties who wanted to succeed in the public world of business or politics believed the most important thing to leave behind was "sex-consciousness," their sense of themselves as women who shared interests with other women. They abandoned any organized quest for general social reform and opted instead for individualism. "Breaking into the human race," as they put it, and individual success in the world as it was became their goals. In 1927, journalist Dorothy Dunbar Bromley wrote in "Feminist—New Style," in *Harper's:* "The pioneer feminists were hard-hitting individuals, and the modern young woman admires them for their courage, even while she judges them for their zealotry and their inartistic methods. . . . They fought her battle, but *she* does not want to wear their mantle." These women wanted to emancipate themselves from each other, from their families, and from the assumption that women were more virtuous than men and more responsible for social welfare. For them, individuality became a way to allow for diversity among women, and it would lead to models of individual accomplishment. It would not, however, lead to the betterment of the group.

The rejection of an older style of feminism and virtuous womanhood came at a time when there was not yet an alternative with which to replace it. In opting to make it in a man's world without changing that world, these women had to try to become like men. Feminists had not yet succeeded in creating a third category, though they desired it, of the "human" sex. Even when coalitions of women formed to support the ERA, they did it, they claimed, so that they could be treated "just like men."

Despite antagonism toward feminist groups, the 1920s found activist women not so much absent as scattered. No longer were they the "woman movement," as they had been in the nineteenth century; now they were women. They still organized, but in a multitude of smaller groups that often opposed each other. Every woman seemed to belong to at least one group, and often to several. There were church groups, parents' associations, self-improvement clubs, and civic leagues. Many women returned to the causes that had most concerned them before the peak of the suffrage movement. Some threw all their efforts into the peace movement. Others returned to such issues as social reform, hours and wages for women, clean city streets and water, adequate schooling and playgrounds, and safe factory conditions, for example. In the South, new interracial efforts against lynching occupied some women. In the Southwest, some Hispanic women worked for bilingual education.

Still other women lobbied for their professional interests. The members of Business and Professional Women, founded in 1918, had originally promoted a broad program to make marriage and divorce laws the same in all states, to gain higher status for home economics in federal aid to state education, and to pass laws regulating the use of child labor. In the 1920s, they increasingly focused on their own interests as professional women and office workers. All this activity, though scattered, was still movement.

Women's Work

In 1921, a Chicago telephone operator reported the inside scoop on her job to the Women's Trade Union League paper, *Life and Labor*. She found the phone company to be not just an employer but a nosy and demanding parent. When she had applied to the company, she had had to undergo a medical examination and take psychological tests and answer such questions as whether she lived with her husband and whether he objected to her working. She spent three weeks in training, during which gum chewing was strictly forbidden. The classes taught more than how to handle telephone equipment; they also instructed operators how to talk. She learned to reply to callers with a particular singsong set of phrases. Unshakably polite, musical tones were required.

When not in classes, and later, on their breaks, the telephone operators could enjoy the company's recreation room, with comfortable couches and chairs, reading lamps, magazines, a piano, and a record player. It also had spotlessly clean, spacious bathrooms with lots of large mirrors and all the modern conveniences. Moreover, the company provided free lunches, free medical service, and reduced prices for theater tickets and groceries. It did not pay wages as high as work that required less education and less expensive clothing and placed fewer restrictions on language and behavior, but the operator wrote that few of the girls would complain. They did not seem to share her opinion that "those of us who retain any sense of independence and self-respect would prefer to have our salaries large enough so that we could pay for our own lunches and medical service."

This description encapsulates much about women's paid work in the 1920s. As a married woman, this particular operator had plenty of company; the percentage of wives working for pay soared in the decade, especially among those aged twenty to thirty-five. But this shift was not matched by a change in attitudes toward women. One national advice columnist claimed that the question she was asked most frequently was, "Should a woman work outside the home after marriage?" despite the fact that increasing numbers of women were already doing so. By 1930, 40 percent of white and black working women were wives, one-third with children

NEW JOBS FOR WOMEN

Everyone is getting used to
overalled women in machine shops

Women have made good as
Street Car Conductors and Elevator Operators

Clerical Work
quite a new job for Negro Girls

Slav, Italian and Negro Women
making bed springs

The war brought us
Women Traffic Cops and Mail Carriers

Laundry and domestic work didn't
pay so they entered the garment trade

A Department of Labor publication illustrates the progress of women's employment after World War I.

under age thirteen, but they still constituted only 11.7 percent of all wives. Several states still banned married women from holding government jobs. Though the percentage of married women teachers doubled, the majority of school boards refused to hire them.

When they worried about wives working outside the home, most people were thinking of *white* married women. Black married women had long been forced by economic necessity to work for wages, and among agricultural worker families, 60 percent of Chicanas with children worked in the fields. Japanese immigrant women had been partners in their husbands' businesses, domestic servants in other people's homes, and agricultural laborers ever since their arrival in large numbers between 1907 and 1921. Married Puerto Rican women in New York City contracted with textile manufacturers to make garments, fine lace, and other goods in their homes. The press and policymakers had never worried about what those women's work would do to their families. Only when white married women began to work outside the home in larger numbers did the issue become a public one.

The work that married or marriageable white women did had to be seen as compatible with older notions of proper womanly behavior. A telephone operator had to have her husband's permission to work. She had to dress with decorum and maintain a sweet temperament. Indeed, the telephone company used the very assumption that women were by nature sweet and submissive to justify hiring women as operators. The company then converted this assumption into fact by training its employees to sound sweet and submissive on the phone and firing those who did not.

The telephone industry formed just one part of an expanding service sector in the 1920s. New forms of communication and new business technologies, such as typing and stenography, vastly increased the number of clerical jobs available. As such jobs became dead-end, fewer men and more women wound up in clerical positions. Clerical work thus became a larger and larger proportion of the posts women held, outdistancing domestic service, teaching, and industrial jobs. By 1930, 2 million women, or one-fifth of the female labor force, were office workers.

As more women came to hold these positions, the jobs became redefined. The secretary was no longer the man on the rise, but the office wife, radiating sunshine and sympathy. Women uneasy about becoming mannish by being on male terrain helped along the redefinition. They wore unbusinesslike clothes—soft and stylish dresses, for example. For the men in management, redefining clerical workers made women less threatening by clearly distinguishing their separate roles. Clerical work, previously a man's job, became "women's work," something requiring a "woman's touch."

There were still tensions in the workplace. As women increasingly dominated clerical positions, businesses were enlarging. Women got stuck in low-paying office jobs, but men could now get stuck in middle management, without much freedom to do the job as they wished. Men felt hemmed in and blamed their new office wives. For their part, secretaries found men they worked for moody, difficult, and irrational. Grace Robinson, a former secretary, complained to the readers of *Liberty* in 1928 that "the man one works for has, more than likely, a healthy, well nourished temper that all its life has been permitted to cavort about naked, untrammeled, and undisciplined." Male bosses began to prefer their female office workers to have only a high school, not a college, degree and to be young enough that the term *girl* could become just another word for *clerical worker.* Youth and education would make the hierarchy in the office clearer. By the decade's end, this equation was so thoroughly cemented that no matter how old the secretary was, she was still a girl to her boss.

It was not only in the "girlishness" of telephone operators that they typified some aspects of the 1920s. Part of the appeal of telephone work undoubtedly lay in the well-appointed lounge. At the turn of the century, young working women had most often lived at home or as boarders with other families. Now, between school and marriage they lived in their own apartments, which they often shared with other young working women. Having their own apartments gave them a sense of autonomy, of young adulthood, of being unsupervised and unrestrained. It gave their parents a lot of worry.

At the same time, young working women hardly lived in the lap of luxury. At fifteen dollars a week, their wages supported only tiny, often ill-lit apartments with sparse furnishings. For women doing dull work and living in dingy, dark apartments on boring, cheap food, the phone company's lounge and benefits gave them as close a glimpse as they might ever have of the middle-class world many wanted. Whenever they sought more from life, to take in the new movies or go to amusement parks, or have a decent dinner, they had to find a better-paid man to treat them. Young working women had started dating men to whom they had not been introduced, without supervision, almost a generation earlier. By the 1920s, this practice was widespread.

Lounges, theater tickets, and lunches formed part of the new strategies by which large corporations had responded to strikes in 1919. Many adopted something called the American Plan of corporate welfare. Instead of paying higher wages, companies provided increased benefits to workers, perhaps subsidized housing or loans. Such benefits made it harder for workers to leave the company, no matter what the conditions of the work itself, and they were less likely to risk losing their benefits by striking. Only large companies could afford such programs, and most women who worked in industry worked for smaller firms. Women of color, in particular, rarely found such enlightened employers.

During World War I, half a million black southerners moved to northern cities. More followed them after the war. They thought they were heading toward the Promised Land, where they could work as well as vote on equal terms with whites.

Mothers labored outside the home so that their daughters could stay in high school long enough to qualify for clerical work. Yet they found, in the North as in the South, that few white people would hire them as anything but domestic servants or manual laborers. As African-American neighborhoods in northern cities expanded, some black women found opportunities as teachers, but the few black-owned businesses large enough to employ clerical workers often hired male office workers, as educated black men found their job options just as tightly restricted. The only place large numbers of black women office workers found employment was Montgomery Ward in Chicago, which employed 1,050 in 1920. Because it was a mail-order business, customers had no direct contact with and never had to know they were served by black clerical workers.

In the 1920s, large numbers of Puerto Ricans also came to the urban North seeking economic opportunity. By 1930, there were fifty thousand Puerto Ricans on the mainland, 81 percent of whom lived in New York City. Almost half were women. The Puerto Rican women, like African-American women, found their opportunities curtailed. Honorina Irizarry left her job as a secretary in Puerto Rico to join her brother in Brooklyn, New York, where she became a bilingual secretary and a Democratic activist. But she was exceptional. In 1925, only 3.4 percent of all Puerto Rican women in New York, and about 15 percent of the women who worked outside the home held clerical positions. Language formed one barrier, but race also played a part.

Despite the tendency to redefine jobs women entered into as "women's work," and despite the prevalent racism, women of all races and ethnic groups did make some headway in the professions in the 1920s. Although the percentage of women workers in the professions grew only from 11.9 percent to 14.2 percent, that rise represented an increase of 50 percent in the number of women professionals. By far most were teachers; the next largest number were nurses, but there were also lawyers, social workers, engineers, and professors. Only the percentage of female medical doctors fell; medical schools imposed a quota on women of no more than 5 percent of a class from 1925 to 1945, and few hospitals accepted female interns.

Professional women came largely from the ranks of college graduates. By the 1920s more than 40 percent of college students were women. They were still the privileged few, however. The proportion of college-age women in the United States who entered college rose from 3.8 percent in 1910 to 7.6 percent in 1920 but would increase to only 10.5 percent by 1930. Not all women had an equal chance of entering college, even if they could afford it. Many colleges carefully controlled the number of Jewish students on campus, and only at Oberlin did black students constitute even 4 percent of the student body. Black women found black colleges more receptive; by 1929, women formed the majority at some coeducational black colleges. Catholic women also found their options enlarged by special schools. The number of Catholic women's colleges rose from 14 in 1915 to 37 in 1925.

Many women faced cultural as well as gender and racial battles. After years of schooling in Kansas and Los Angeles, Polingaysi Qoyawayma, a Hopi Indian, returned to her reservation in Arizona in the late 1920s to become a teacher and missionary. These jobs gave her a chance to have what she had always dreamed of building, her own house, but they also brought tensions. Told she could not speak the Hopi language to her Hopi first graders, Qoyawayma decided at least to use Hopi legends to teach them to read. In her autobiography, *No Turning Back,* she confessed that she was not sure the missionaries would like the burrowing owls song, which began, "We are little burrowing owls, children of Germinating God." It was hostility from Hopi parents, however, that caught her by surprise. They complained, "What are you teaching our children? . . . We send them to school to learn the white man's way, not Hopi. They can learn the Hopi way at home."

Many professional and businesswomen faced tensions regarding marriage and career. Sue Shelton White, a lawyer born in 1887, had led the southern wing of the National Women's Party and was a Democratic party politician. Poverty and discrimination had kept her from getting her law degree until she was thirty-six. Her mother, she wrote for a special series on modern women in the *Nation* in 1926, "drew few distinctions between her boys and girls. I have seen my brothers sweep, wipe dishes, and even cook." When her brothers left home, it was Sue who had to carry the water from the well and cut the kindling. By 1926, however, she considered marriage and a career a difficult combination: "Marriage is too much of a compromise; it lops off a woman's life as an individual. Yet the renunciation too is a lopping off. We choose between the frying-pan and the fire—both very uncomfortable."

Though many professional women continued to find satisfaction in lifelong support from other women, a growing minority of professional women married in the 1920s. In 1910, only 12.2 percent of professional women were married. In 1920, 19.3 percent were; in 1930, 24.7 percent. Psychologist Phyllis Blanchard earned her doctorate from Clark University, where she met a graduate student in chemistry, Walter Lucasse. When the couple married in 1925, Blanchard kept her own name and continued her career as a child guidance counselor. "He respects my work as much as I do his," she told the *Nation's* readers. "If he does not feel quite so keenly as I the need of economic independence after marriage, he is more eager that I have leisure for creative work than I am myself." Blanchard was typical of the new generation of women professionals. In the 1920s, most were not active in social reform, which had gone from being a task of amateur middle-class women to a new profession, social work, with its own college courses and degrees. Many professional women still wanted to increase women's economic status, improve women's sense of their own worth, reorient family life, and redefine sex roles, but they did so only as individuals.

Although clerical workers and businesswomen were newly conspicuous among women workers in the 1920s, most women workers remained in domestic service, agricultural labor, and certain manufacturing jobs. For them, wage labor was a matter of necessity. In the 1920s, 71 percent of U.S. workers earned less than the wage required to support what the government defined as the minimum acceptable standard of living for their families. As a result, in low-income families, 25 percent of all married women worked for wages.

In 1920 five times more married black women than women of any other racial or ethnic group worked outside the home. More than 50 percent of adult black women earned wages. In rural areas most performed back-breaking labor in the fields. In the cities most performed domestic service or laundering. Only 5.5 percent were able to gain employment in manufacturing, a better-paid sector, by 1930. As the total number of servants declined, black women became a larger and larger share of those remaining. Between one-fifth and one-half of the domestics in New York, Chicago, Philadelphia, and other cities were black women. Almost two-thirds of all gainfully employed black women in the North worked as servants or laundresses. In Pittsburgh, for example, 90 percent of black women earned their way as day workers, washerwomen, or live-in servants.

In service, as in other areas of black life, the growth of black enclaves in the North and the greater degree of freedom there than in the South encouraged a new generation of black female northerners to be more assertive in their relations with whites, to join civil rights groups, such as the National Association for the Advancement of Colored People, and to make their relations with their employers more professional. But by the end of the decade, black women still earned only 20 cents, and white women 61 cents, for every dollar that white men earned.

Domestic service meant something different for the fourteen hundred Japanese immigrant women who worked in such positions during the 1920s, making up slightly more than one-fourth of the gainfully employed among them. As with black women and other domestic servants, Japanese women found that sometimes employers became like additional family members, visiting them when they were sick, teaching them English, and giving them gifts. Other employers spied on them constantly, suspecting them of stealing or laziness. For the Japanese, however, domestic work was something new and seen as strictly temporary. Mrs. Uematsu told an interviewer, "My husband didn't bring in enough money, so I went out to work. I didn't even think twice about it." Though the husbands of Japanese immigrant women expected them to contribute to the family income, domestic service, unlike helping in the family business or doing farm work with the family, gave these women an independent wage and time away from their families.

For many black women, on the other hand, domestic service was not a new opportunity to work away from the watchful eye of a husband and to earn an independent income. Rather, it was all that had been available to them for generations. It meant stealing time from their own families and giving it to the families of the very people who foreclosed other opportunities.

In the Southwest, Chicana employment patterns tended to mirror those of black

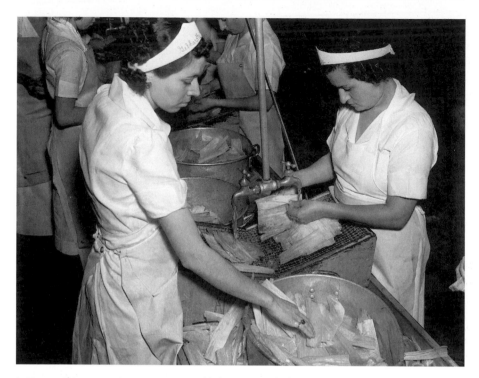

In Texas, Chicana women separate corn shucks in a tamale factory.

women in the East, except that a larger percentage were employed in industrial work, particularly in food processing and garment making. The situation for them varied more than for black women. In San Antonio, Texas, Mexican women worked in pecan shelling and clothing factories while black women could get only domestic service jobs. In Colorado, however, the situation was virtually reversed. Chicana migrant farm workers faced broken-down shacks for housing, long hours in the fields, and wages that would not keep the family warm and fed and the children clothed decently enough to stay in school through the winter. As a result, they tried to earn money in the winter as domestic servants or laundresses if they could not get work in the canneries, which they preferred.

When black and white women, or Anglo and Chicana women, mingled in factories, the outcome was sometimes predictable but sometimes surprising. In the tobacco factories of Durham, North Carolina, the white women workers arrived from a countryside where whites had gone to great lengths to ensure that blacks held only menial jobs. Their own status depended on being different from the black women who worked in the same factory. In an interview, one worker recalled that black women had to "press hard to hold [themselves] up" against the harassment of white bosses and coworkers, even at the risk of losing a job. "You're over here doing all the nasty dirty work," another recalled of the blacks' assignment, the gritty work of stripping the stems off tobacco leaves. "And over there on the cigarette side ... The white women over there wear white uniforms." On the other hand, in the canneries of southern California some Anglo women and Chicana workers developed friendships at work. "I had a Jewish friend," Maria Rodriguez told an interviewer. "She was my work buddy. . . . I never saw her outside the cannery but we were friends at work. . . . We broke the ice by talking about Clark Gable. We were crazy about him."

The 1920s was a hard time to be a factory worker, even without racial tensions. The corporations, courts, and government had made it harder to strike or to protest conditions. Efforts to organize women met with hostility not only from the employers but from male union organizers. Ann Washington Craton, a union organizer herself, reported to the *Nation* in 1927 what happened when one woman organizer got arrested in the course of her job. A small flood of working girls rushed into the union office, demanding that the union pay her bail. But the union men took the news cheerfully. The official in charge told them, "Let her stay in jail. . . . She's all right. Let her stay until we can have a nice, quiet little executive board meeting without her. Then we will get her out. Ladies should stay at home. If ladies won't stay at home, let them stay in jail." When Craton and a coworker wanted to organize women in Newark, New Jersey, a union official complained, "Why don't you forget all this business and leave the labor movement to men? It's too rough for women. Why don't you get married?" Craton and her colleague responded, "Perhaps we are married. . . . We still want to organize women into trade unions in Newark."

Despite all the difficulties, there were strikes of women workers in the 1920s, emerging from the desperation of white as well as black women. In March 1929, the women in the inspection room of an Elizabethton, North Carolina, textile mill walked off the job. All but 17 of the 360 walked out, and the next morning they gathered at the factory gate. When the plant manager did not arrive to negotiate, they rushed through the plant and persuaded their coworkers, women and men, to join them.

The young women of Elizabethton wanted more from life than an endless round of low pay; they wanted more than their mothers had. On the picket lines they were feisty, bold, assertive, saucy, firm, and, above all, funny. Trixie Perry and Texas Bill were ringleaders and friends on the picket line. Both women were brought to court when they were accused of taunting the National Guard and blocking the way to the mills for new, replacement workers; women had marched in front of the National Guard draped in the American flag, forcing the guardsmen to present arms each time they passed. In court, Trixie Perry wore a cap made out of the U.S. flag. When the prosecuting attorney questioned her, she replied, "I was born under it, guess I have a right." When asked if she had blocked the road, she

A Fighting Organization Controlled by the Workers

National Textile Workers Union
OF AMERICA

National President
JAMES P. REID

Vice-Presidents
GUSTAVE DEAK
ELLEN DAWS
WILLIAM T. MURDOCH

Secretary-Treasurer
ALBERT WEISBORD

District Organizer
Fred Erwin Beal

GASTONIA OFFICE—DISTRICT NINE
1242 WEST FRANKLIN STREET

National Office:
104 Fifth Avenue
New York City

Telephone: Watkins 0021

April 13, 1929

To the Editor of the Gastonia Gazette,
Sir:

Since you have been taking such a militant stand in favor of the manufacturers and are understood to be their mouthpiece the Manville-Jenckes local of the National Textile Workers Union of America now on strike for better living conditions request you to publicly answer the following questions

1. WHAT HAVE YOU AND YOUR PAPER EVER DONE TO BETTER THE CONDITIONS OF THE WORKERS, SUCH AS LESSENING THE VERY LONG HOURS, INCREASING THE WAGES, DOING AWAY WITH THE DOUBLING OR STRECH-OUT SYSTEM AND BETTER HOUSING CONDITIONS, IN GASTONIA, WHICH YOU ARE FORCED TO ADMIT EXIST?

2. YOU SAY IN ONE OF YOUR ISSUES THAT THE TEXTILE WORKERS ARE GOING TO HAVE A UNION. WHY IS IT THAT YOU FAVOR THE UNITED TEXTILE WORKERS UNION (U.T.W.) AT THIS PERIOD OF TIME WHEN THE WORKERS ON STRIKE ARE ALREADY ORGANIZED IN THE NATIONAL TEXTILE WORKERS UNION (N.T.W.U.) IS IT YOUR PURPOSE TO SPLIT THE WORKERS SO AS TO BREAK THE STRIKE? WHY DIDN'T YOU THINK THE WORKERS SHOULD HAVE A UNION BEFORE THE STRIKE TOOK PLACE?

3. IN A LIBELOUS FULL PAGE ADV. YOU AND YOUR BOSS FRIENDS CLAIM BEAL TOLD THE STRIKERS TO "CRACK THE HEADS OF OFFICERS AND KILL IF NECESSARY" WE CAN GET 1,000 WITNESSES TO PROVE HE SAID NO SUCH THING, CAN YOU GET ONE STOOLPIGEON TO SAY HE DID?

4. YOU AND YOUR BOSS FRIENDS SAID THE UNION LET THE STRIKERS STARVE AFTER THREE DAYS BEING OUT OF WORK. IF THIS WERE TRUE DON'T YOU THINK THIS IS A TERRIBLE INDICMENT AGAINST YOUR FRIENDS-MANVILLE AND JENCKES, THAT THE WORKERS BEGIN TO STARVE AFTER THREE DAYS UNEMPLOYMENT?

5. WHY DO YOU RAISE THE QUESTIONS OF COMMUNISM, FREE LOVE, RUSSIANISM AND RELIGION WHEN THE ISSUES FOR WHICH THE WORKERS WENT OUT ON STRIKE, AND FOR WHICH THE UNION STANDS, ARE FOR HIGHER WAGES, AND LESS HOURS AND RECOGNITION OF THE UNION.

6. DO YOU KNOW THAT YOUR FRIENDS-MANVILLE AND JENCKES WILL NOT PERMIT WORKERS IN THIER PLANT TO BELONG TO A UNION OF THEIR CHOICE. IS THIS WHAT YOU MEAN BY AMERICANISM?

7. ARE MANVILLE AND JENCKES AMERICANS OR FOREIGNERS?

8. WHY DO YOU NOT TELL YOUR READERS THAT AT EVERY MEETING THE LEADERS HAVE COUNCILED AGAINST VIOLENCE?

This letter from the National Textile Workers Union to the editor of the *Gastonia Gazette* in North Carolina demonstrates these women's determination to demand their rights as workers.

retorted, "A little thing like me block a big road?" Texas Bill was equally unshakable. Asked what she was doing on the road in the early morning, she responded with great dignity, "I take a walk every morning before breakfast for my health." The guards had threatened the picketing women with guns, used tear gas on them, and arrested them, and the women answered them with laughter.

Like the new generation of black domestic workers and the frustrated union organizers, Trixie Perry and Texas Bill represented a new, more aggressive woman worker. They wanted part of what the 1920s had to offer—not just movies and fine clothes, but independence and the wherewithal to buy those goods for themselves.

Fun, Fads, Family

It wasn't just the Trixie Perrys in North Carolina or the cannery workers in California who wanted more from life and dreamed of movie stars. In remote Hispanic New Mexican villages, young women had abandoned their sandals and shawls for high heels and elaborate hats. They learned the new, fast, provocative dance steps of the shimmy and the Charleston, and in villages where there were cars, they even went on dates. Before World War I, flappers had started to appear in certain city neighborhoods; now they were everywhere.

Flappers were women who lived—and lived it up—in public. They wore short skirts that exposed their legs and made them freer than prewar styles had allowed. They bobbed their hair, shearing off the long Victorian tresses that had distinguished them from men and taken so much time to maintain. They wore makeup and flesh-colored stockings. It was still close enough to a time when "painted women" had been actresses and harlots to make wearing makeup seem daring, sexually aware, and definitely modern. These women even smoked in public. In recognition of the new womanhood, in 1925 Bryn Mawr College for women lifted its ban on smoking.

Not everyone agreed on the new rules for America's young women. That same year another women's college, Vassar, instituted a ban on smoking. The editor of the student paper of the University of Illinois called the shimmy "that insult to our whole moral code." But these critics were waging a losing battle. Young women and men were redefining what was proper and seemed to assume that the older systems of order, control, and communication had been destroyed by the war.

Young working women modeled their behavior and their dreams on the movies. In the 1920s, polls showed that movie stars had replaced political, business, and artistic leaders as role models for young people. Ironically, the movies had in turn picked up their themes from the lives of the young working women who made up a large proportion of their audience and had simply glamorized them. The film stories were often created by such women writers as Anita Loos, who wrote *Gentlemen Prefer Blondes* (1925). Fan magazines let their readers know that stars had come from their own ranks: Joan Crawford began as a shop girl in Kansas City, Janet Gaynor as a clerk in a shoe store.

Like the lounge at the telephone company, the new picture palaces gave working women a few hours in opulence. In that luxurious atmosphere they watched films like *Ankles Preferred* (1926), in which a bored Madge Bellamy waited on customers in a department store. In *Soft Living* (1928), secretaries labored over long columns of numbers. It was not the life of the working girl that the movies glamorized; it was the chance for escape; in *Soft Living*, Bellamy, who portrays a secretary for a divorce lawyer, hunts for a millionaire and lands one. Office workers and department store clerks, the films showed, worked amid wealthier male bosses and customers. Through spunk and cleverness, according to the movies, they could use their positions to escape the boring monotony of their work. In *Ankles Preferred*, Bellamy becomes successful in the retail trade in her own right and rejects her wealthy suitors, who are interested only in her body. Instead she turns to a trustworthy young man from a lower-class boardinghouse. But the themes of the two films were the same; they echoed the enormously popular novels that Horatio Alger had written fifty years earlier about poor young men who, through luck, pluck, and virtue, became rich. Usually, their success was assured in part by marrying the boss's daughter. In the 1920s, it was working women who embodied this spirit of entrepreneurial drive. But instead of being the passive maidens rescued by Alger's heroes, now they were in charge of their own futures. Success for them meant marrying the boss, not the boss's daughter.

Reassuringly, the movies tended to end with marriage. Many Americans had begun to fear that the family was being destroyed. If women were free to vote and to live in apartments on their own, and if wives were working outside the home in increasing numbers, then who would keep the home fires burning? The mass media responded by making actual working mothers virtually invisible. Instead, at the same time as the flapper flounced into view, a new glorification of motherhood and marriage emerged. It seemed that after a period of youthful independence and indiscretion, women were to go back home.

It would be a different home, one with fewer children and more machines. Manufacturers found housewives eager for new household technology. With immigration on the decline in the 1920s, fewer white women were available for domestic service. The black, Asian, and Mexican women who took their places did not quite fill the gap. They, too, wanted their independence. They were less willing to be full-time help and live in the homes of their employers. They preferred day work. In response, fewer homes had servants' quarters, and more women became their own maids.

Many of these women worked for wages outside the home as well as doing housewifery within it. Working-class and middle-class women justified going out to work in terms of their families' needs. Their work tended to be intermittent. It most often hinged on their husbands becoming unemployed, a frequent occurrence in the 1920s. Others worked themselves, rather than withdrawing their children from school to work. "It takes the work of two to keep a family these days,"

Anita Loos (standing on the ladder) on the set of *Gentlemen Prefer Blondes,* in which working women try to nab rich husbands. As a professional writer, Loos produced scripts that were considered witty and modern.

claimed one Muncie, Indiana, woman in *Middletown,* Robert and Helen Lynd's pioneering 1929 study of a "typical" American town. Whereas in earlier decades the two workers would have been a father and a child, it would now be a husband and a wife, because more jobs required a high school education.

For many of the families the Lynds interviewed, however, family needs now meant more than just putting food on the table. "An electric washing machine, electric iron, and vacuum sweeper" also had become necessities for working mothers. "I don't even have to ask my husband any more," revealed another Muncie wife, "because I buy these things with my own money. I bought an ice box last year. . . . We own a twelve-hundred-dollar Studebaker [car] with a nice California top, semi-enclosed. . . . The two boys want to go to college, and I want them to. I graduated from high school myself, but I feel if I can't give my boys a little more all my work will have been useless." To many women, being a good mother increasingly meant earning an income to provide purchasing power for the family.

Yet despite all the new technology, the women surveyed by the Lynds claimed that they spent more, not less, time on housework in the 1920s than before. Indeed, the time had almost doubled, from 44.3 to 87.5 hours a week. Standards, it seemed, had risen. At the very moment technology could have freed women from much household drudgery, suddenly their wash had to be whiter than white. Advertisers played on women's guilt. "What do the neighbors think of *her* children?" read one 1928 detergent's ad copy in the *Ladies' Home Journal.*

Advertising reached new levels of psychological sophistication. Because women made most consumer decisions, advertisers took aim at them, giving housework a new, exalted meaning. Suddenly, washing clothes was not simply laundering, as it had always been, but an expression of love. Getting the gray out of a man's collar was not simply an issue of cleanliness; it was saving the American home. Cooking, cleaning, and other housework all fell into the same category. By 1931, *American Home* could declare that "the careful housekeeper ... will know that prime rib roast, like peach ice cream, is a wonderful stimulant to family loyalty."

These advertisements also indicated the increasing degree to which mothering was seen as a full-time job. More household technology could have given women more time to spend outside the house. So could the declining birth rate. In 1900, white women had given birth to an average of 3.56 children each; in 1929, 2.4. Birth control was still controversial, even illegal in many states, but middle-class women were able to get birth control devices from their private physicians, and in large cities some clinics opened to serve working-class women. This left many working-class women without birth control. Even when they could get birth control information, they often found their husbands uncooperative. Yet, even though they continued to have more children than middle-class women, birth rates among the working class also declined. No sooner were there fewer children in the home, however, than experts began to agree that mothers should pay more attention to each one. As advertisements for a laundromat in Muncie asked, "Isn't Bobby more important than his clothes?" And one ad selling electricity declared of the "successful mother" that "she puts first things first. She does not give to sweeping the time that belongs to her children. ... The wise woman delegates to electricity all that electricity can do."

Women involved in charitable work, social and political service, and even wage work—despite the fact that most working mothers took paying jobs only out of dire need—were attacked as selfish, as taking jobs away from men who needed them to support families, and as undermining the stability of the home. It was argued that having a woman in the home would keep a child off the streets. "I accommodate my entire life to my little girl," one middle-class woman boasted to the Lynds. With these new ideas, it was hard for working women to feel that they were also successful mothers, particularly when they lived in homes without electricity—like almost half the homes in the country in 1925.

These new ideas of what women should be sharpened social divisions in the United States. One indication of these divisions was the rapid development of ethnically and economically homogeneous suburbs in the 1920s. The new suburbs were linked to choices about technology and policy that affected women's lives and options. New household technology could have been used, for example, to enhance urban apartment life, which had been on the rise in the previous decades. It could have helped create communal day care facilities and laundries that would have left women freer for other activities. In their zeal to save the family from absent mothers, however, policy makers focused on the private home. Each family was to have its own home, and each home its own mother taking care of her own children, using her own kitchen and laundry.

Increasingly, such individual homes were in suburbs. From 1920 to 1930 the population of New York City rose 21 percent; in the same period the population of one of its suburbs, Scarsdale, soared 176 percent. The allure of suburbs lay in their very sameness. Suburban developers promised buyers spacious houses with children's playrooms and private lawns. They promised to remove and protect women and children from the dirt and tensions of the city. The suburbs also created another social division: masculine cities and feminine suburbs. Men would leave home for work all day, and women would remain home to tend the children. In the newly ubiquitous automobiles, women spent their time driving their children from store to store or to school, all of which had been within walking distance in the city.

Despite the confining aspects of marriage and suburbia, most college women surveyed claimed they aspired above all else to the role of wife. The percentage of women who never married had risen throughout the nineteenth century to a high of 20 percent; now it dropped to 5 percent. The women's average age at marriage also fell.

The 1920s saw the popularization of Sigmund Freud's brand of psychology, particularly its emphasis on the pivotal role of sex in mental health and its depiction of women as incomplete and envious of men. Moreover, at the very moment when women no longer seemed to need marriage on economic or political grounds, people began to define "normal" sexuality in new, narrower terms and to give it increased attention. Despite evidence from a 1926 study that more than one-fourth of adult college-educated women had enjoyed intense emotional relations with other women after puberty, including overt sexual practices, women who never married began to be defined as unfulfilled and neurotic. In an economy built around gratification rather than thrift, women's activism outside the home was taken as a sign of an unfulfilled life.

Women did not cease, of course, to rely on other women for support and intimacy. As with politics, however, the range of tolerated behavior shrank, and what had been acceptable before the war now was questionable. Some young women even feared to share apartments with each other lest they be suspected of homosexuality. And, in the same way that new fears of radicalism split women's political organizations in the 1920s, new fears of homosexuality made it harder for women to form women's groups whose purpose was women's equality and independence.

Women's focus was not supposed to be other women. According to the advertisers and the new psychologists, their emphasis was supposed to be on how to attract men. Women could find fulfillment, the argument went, only through marriage. In the nineteenth century, marriage had been expected to involve women's self-denial and self-sacrifice; now, particularly for the highly educated middle class, it was supposed to provide sexual satisfaction and self realization. Marriage was supposed to be the gateway to a fuller life, not just for women with low-paying, monotonous jobs but also for college-educated women. Sexual fulfillment in marriage, not a career, was depicted as the ultimate fulfillment for women.

Increasingly, businesses used sex and the desire for sexual attraction and passion in their advertisements. Women's appearance, rather than women's virtue, would secure their husbands' fidelity. Cosmetic companies began to sponsor the first beauty contests. "The first duty of woman is to attract," ran one advertisement. Women had been liberated from the corset only to be entrapped by breast binders, dieting, and makeup. They were told that by purchasing the right goods they could create the proper effect. "Your masterpiece—yourself," another advertisement promised its readers. Men as well as women were affected by these trends. Advertisers insisted that the proper collar and the right deodorant would gain a man the desired job, but while men were to use goods to re-create themselves in order to gain jobs, promotions, and public esteem, women were to use goods to re-create themselves in order to get men.

It was in part this focus on sexuality that increased the pressure to legalize birth control. Sex was no longer simply about creating children. With the popularization of psychology, it was about necessary release and pleasure and self-determination. The original birth control activists had aimed to put control of reproduction into the hands of those who had to bear the children—women. By the 1920s, however, the movement had attracted strange bedfellows. Doctors who wanted to legalize birth control tended to want to control it themselves. Other activists, many of them racist, favored it to keep the "unfit" from reproducing. On the other side, William Henry Cardinal O'Connell of the Catholic church in Boston called a bill to legalize birth control a "direct threat . . . towards increasing impurity and unchastity not only in our married life but . . . among our unmarried people."

Yet, as the decade progressed, more and more birth control clinics opened. In Chicago a judge ruled in 1924 that the health commissioner could not deny a license to a clinic, because to do so amounted to enforcing religious doctrines, an illegal joining of church and state. In 1929, when Margaret Sanger's New York City birth control clinic was raided by the police for illegally dispensing birth control devices, the case was thrown out of court, and the plainclothes policewoman who had first entrapped the clinic returned later, in her off-duty hours, to seek treatment. Middle-class women could get birth control devices from their private physicians, but only the clinics gave the poor access to contraceptives. By 1930, fifty-five birth control clinics served the public in twenty-three cities in twelve states.

Despite the increasing availability of birth control, a new focus on sexuality, and a redefined concept of housework, marriage had a hard time living up to its reputation. Not all women found it a way to a fuller life. Tensions arose around consumption. Raising children became more and more expensive, and working-class women continued to have less access to money and birth control. Fears of conceiving another child they could ill afford affected these women's sexual pleasure. And expectations of a way of life that did not materialize led to disappointment. In a 1920s study that asked working-class women what gave them the courage to go on in life when they had become thoroughly discouraged, not one mentioned her husband. In difficult times, husbands became not so much individuals as the focus of their wives' problems and fears about jobs and conception.

The divorce rate rose steeply. From 1870 to 1920, the number of divorces in the United States increased by a factor of fifteen. In 1924, one marriage in seven ended in divorce. More wives than ever before had done paid work during marriage and knew they had options other than staying in an unsatisfactory marriage. Life was not easy for divorced women, but no longer was divorce the disgrace it had been in the previous century.

The rise in divorce prompted attacks on women's education, particularly colleges, for not preparing women for their proper vocation: motherhood and wifehood. A few rebels replied by creating institutes like the one Ethel Howe headed at Smith College, the Institute to Coordinate Women's Interests. It aimed to enable college-educated wives to have professional careers by helping to found cooperative nurseries, laundries, shopping groups, and kitchens. Most women's colleges, however, seemed eager to offer some sop to their critics. In 1924, Vassar's board of trustees created a whole interdisciplinary school of "Euthenics" focused on the development and care of the family, including such courses as "Husband and Wife," "Motherhood," and "The Family as an Economic Unit." At the University of Chicago, Dean of Women Marion Talbot pioneered a graduate program in home economics.

The trajectory from flappers to home economics epitomized an essential dilemma in the 1920s. If women could support themselves and represent themselves politically, why should they bother getting married? In the 1920s, prompted by the mass media and advertising, the family had had to change its meaning. No longer would it be portrayed as a necessary economic unit, though it often still was, or as a microcosm of the social and political structure. Now family was about self-fulfillment, consumption, and nurturing the newly discovered psyche of the child. Writing on women and the state in the mid-1920s, journalist Suzanne LaFollette saw marriage as an economic trap that stifled the independence of both men and women. But marriage did not end in the 1920s. Individual "new women" might get divorced, but marriage as an institution changed its rationale and endured.

Rebels

While her husband went to Europe in 1925, anthropologist Margaret Mead set off for Samoa to study adolescent girls; she published her results in *Coming of Age in Samoa* (1928), a best-seller. In her autobiography, Mead offered this advice: "Women must learn to give up pandering to male sensitivities, something at which they succeeded so well as long as it was a woman's primary role, as a wife, to keep her family intact, or, as a mistress, to comfort her lover." Modern women, Mead implied, had a larger role, and men would have to look after their own sensitivities.

Mead was not alone in her rebellion against the 1920s formula of man-centered woman. When New York lawyer Crystal Eastman and her husband had to move out of their apartment because the building was to be torn down, they moved into two places instead of one. It was Eastman's idea. "You're breaking up our home," her husband had said. But according to an article she wrote for *Cosmopolitan* in 1923, she had replied staunchly, "No I'm not. I'm trying to hold it together." She took a small apartment for herself and her children, and her husband moved to a rooming house near his office. "Every morning," she told her readers, "like lovers, we telephone to exchange the day's greetings and make plans for the evenings. . . . It is wonderful sometimes to be alone in the night and just know that someone loves you. In other moods you must have that lover in your arms. Marriage under two roofs makes room for moods." In a decade when the country had decided that marriage was about sex and romance but that life was about the struggle for individuality, Eastman's solution seemed fitting, if unorthodox.

Other rebellions also took into account 1920s sensibilities and options. Tennis champion Helen Wills personified vigorous, rather than delicate, womanliness. Wills at least had the support of her family in shaping her career. Her father, a physician, had taught her all he knew of tennis, and when she could beat him he set her up with coaches who helped her, at age seventeen, win the 1923 National Women's Championship. Zelda Fitzgerald, on the other hand, was a southern belle, trained to be beautiful, decorative, and amusing. Her husband, the novelist F. Scott Fitzgerald, expected a companionate marriage; he wanted her to amuse herself quietly when he worked and to play when he played. Her sense of emptiness in this life, however, led her into an affair and then to ballet and writing. Even though he wrote novels that chronicled the new morals of the 1920s, her husband objected to her writing in traditional terms: "I am the highest paid short story writer in the world. . . . That is all my material. None of it is your material. . . . I would like you to think of my interests. That is your primary concern, because I am the one to steer the course, the pilot. . . . I want you to stop writing fiction."

Many women did not stop writing fiction in the 1920s, no matter who told them to, and many of the writers were black women who joined Harlem's literary

Black intellectuals and artists often met in the Dark Tower, a salon in Harlem. Poems by Langston Hughes and Countee Cullen were painted on the walls.

circles. Harlem had only recently ceased to be a Jewish immigrant enclave, becoming a large black community within New York City. For both blacks and whites it was a symbol of African-American aspirations and possibilities, the one place an African American could be anything. College-educated black men and women flocked to Harlem from all over the nation. Most other towns had room for perhaps one black doctor or lawyer, who would then serve primarily—and sometimes only—the black community. In Harlem, the largest black community in the country, blacks owned businesses and real estate, were librarians and teachers, and ran literary magazines and cultural gatherings.

In the Harlem of the 1920s, the women and men writers of the Harlem Renaissance also worked to create a new image of blackness. They were a varied lot. Louise Thompson's family had moved to the Far West as domestic help. She grew up in Oregon and California with few other blacks, and often was taken for white or, sometimes, Mexican. When "passing" for white she could not recognize her black friends in public. She began to long for a stronger race identity. While Thompson was studying at the University of California, she heard a speech by W. E. B. Du Bois, a black equal rights activist and scholar who had been instrumental in founding the National Association for the Advancement of Colored People (NAACP); it was the first time she had seen a black man appear in public without self-effacement.

After earning a degree in business administration, Thompson taught at Hampton Institute, a black college in Virginia founded by white philanthropists after the Civil War. She supported a student strike against the school's paternalism, and then headed for Harlem.

Another Harlem writer, Jessie Fauset, came from an old Philadelphia family and graduated Phi Beta Kappa from Cornell. She served as literary editor of *The Crisis*, the NAACP's journal and the most common outlet for Harlem writers. She also wrote four novels, as well as poems and stories. Fauset's novels portrayed middle-class African Americans in middle-class professions striving for middle-class goals, emphasizing similarities between blacks and whites. In her foreword to *Chinaberry Tree* (1931), she declared that the black man "started out as a slave but he rarely thinks of that. To himself he is a citizen of the United States whose ancestors came over not along with the emigrants in the *Mayflower*, it is true, but merely a little earlier in the good year, 1619. . . . And he has a wholesome respect for family and education and labor and the fruits of labor." Although Fauset criticized white society in her novels, she refused to go beyond a mild rebuke.

Others took the rebellion further. Harlem was no paradise. The death rate for blacks in New York City was almost twice that for whites; 60 percent of the black working women in New York City worked as laundresses or servants. Although blacks in New York appeared in 316 of the 321 possible occupations in the 1920 census, they could not be served in many of the Harlem theaters where they performed.

Yet some whites flocked from their homes in Manhattan to Harlem's nightlife. Tired of and alienated from the modern industrial world—especially after witnessing the carnage of World War I—some whites were on the prowl for something fresh, for a less complicated existence, more in harmony with nature and each other. Aided by popularized anthropology and psychology, many looked to the poorer Harlemites for their spiritual salvation. They dipped into Harlem for an evening, making up audiences that, as Walter White, then head of the NAACP, put it, "receive [blacks] as artists but refuse to accept them as men."

The Harlem Renaissance writers rejected the white image of blacks as primitive, one-dimensional, and uncomplicated. "For generations in the mind of America," wrote Rhodes scholar and Harvard graduate Alain Locke in his essay "The New Negro," "the Negro has been more of a formula than a human being." For poet Langston Hughes, the literary movement was a declaration of independence, a chance for black people to create their own images. In 1926 he wrote, "If white people are pleased we are glad. If they are not, it doesn't matter. We know we are beautiful. And ugly too. . . . If colored people are pleased we are glad. If they are not, their displeasure doesn't matter either. We build our temples for tomorrow, strong as we know how, and we stand on the top of the mountain free from within ourselves."

Reality was more complicated than Hughes's declaration. Writers needed money to survive. For a time, Hughes, Thompson, and Zora Neale Hurston shared the same patron, a wealthy, white Park Avenue matron named Mrs. Rufus Osgood Mason, who was both generous and controlling. Mason tried to ensure that her protégées stuck to the image of the simple, emotional primitive, and Hurston had to tread a fine line to write what she wanted. Like Margaret Mead, Hurston had studied anthropology at Columbia University. Unlike Mead, she returned to her own roots, an all-black town in Florida, to collect folklore, funded by Mason. Hurston's novels were not filled with middle-class blacks striving for acceptance in the white world. Instead they depicted, often in dialect, a black world with little direct interaction between blacks and whites. Her characters filled many Harlem Renaissance writers with dismay. As one critic complained, "Her darkies always smiled through their tears, sang spirituals on the slightest provocation, and performed buck dances when they should have been working."

This criticism missed the essential point. Hurston's stories were radical both in their blackness and in their feminism. Indeed, that combination may have been one source of her friction with Harlem's black intellectual elite. As Hurston depicted the world, the competition among blacks and black men's subordination of women stemmed from their relations with white society. Her novels showed African Americans left to themselves, in towns like the one in which she had been born, developing an alternative to white society, a communal culture of social equality. If Hurston's characters spoke in dialect, they were not mindless primitives. Her characters and their thoughts were complex, but it was not a white world that she described. Nor was it a man's world. The men in Hurston's stories had a noticeable tendency to die off, while women survived. Hurston's struggle, like that of Langston Hughes, was for autonomy, but it seemed that she could not conceive of a way for women to achieve full growth and become fully human without writing off the men who, in her stories, kept trying to define them.

Other women sought refuge and self-definition in Harlem, which in the 1920s hosted a lesbian subculture. Lesbian communities also existed in Salt Lake City, Greenwich Village in New York City, San Francisco, and other cities, but Harlem's was the largest. For the first time, in the 1920s, love between women was assumed to be sexual, even when it was not, and "homosexual" was becoming an identity. At this stage, the popular fascination with Freud had two opposing effects. On the one hand, it made people more comfortable with sexual experimentation; in this view, bisexuality became an adventure. On the other hand, popular Freudian psychology defined exclusive homosexuality as a disease. The writer Edna St. Vincent Millay, resisting pressure to add men to the women she loved, referred to Freud's ideas as an "attempt to lock women up in the home and restore them to cooking and baby-tending."

Harlem, already identified with primitivism in the minds of many whites, seemed the ideal place to give in to sexual desires. Although blacks in general shared the mixed feelings of whites toward homosexuality, a series of bars catering particularly to homosexuals opened their doors to all comers.

Both white and black women enjoyed the lesbian subculture, in which many black blues stars participated. Blues had reached its first great popularity in the 1920s, and blues singer Bessie Smith was among the most highly paid women entertainers. She and Ma Rainey, another blues singer, both of whom were married, found a way to keep their lesbian affairs in Harlem from harming their popularity with their audiences. Ma Rainey recorded "Prove It on Me Blues," about a woman who preferred women, but she carefully cultivated an image of herself as being interested in men too. Bisexuality could simply seem twice as sexy.

Concern with individualism and sexuality dominated the decade. Even the rebellions of the 1920s took their shape from those impulses, yet the decade did not resolve the dilemma its opening years had raised. With Zora Neale Hurston able to have women achieve fulfillment only by killing off men, with "New Style" feminists thinking they had to be like men, with no legitimacy granted to organized feminism, with no good fit between ideology and reality, women had only a fragile foothold in the brave new world. Despite having the vote, despite having broken into the human race, they would be ill-equipped to face challenges that the 1930s depression would bring.

Making Do with Disaster

In the mid-1930s, scholar Margaret Jarman Hagood drove deep into rural North Carolina to talk with more than 250 white farm tenant families for her book *Mothers of the South* (1939). In it she described the life of a typical woman named Mollie, from when she was ten years old until Hagood met her at age thirty-seven. Mollie was pregnant again and wishing, she told Hagood, that "doctors would tell you what to do when they say, 'Now you shouldn't have any more children.'"

As a child, Mollie had stayed home from school on wash days to help her mother scrub her father's and brothers' overalls and the baby's diapers in a huge wash pot on top of a wood fire her brothers kindled before school. She worked in a dress worn and outgrown, saving the year's two new dresses for school and church. In 1920, when Mollie was sixteen, she heard about a neighboring girl who had moved to a town to work in a tobacco factory, about the money she made, and the things she could buy. Telling no one, Mollie made a bundle of her clothes and left one morning. For four months she boarded with a relative of her father and made twenty dollars a week. She bought a coat for fifteen dollars, high-top shoes for eleven dollars, and a hat for eight dollars and spent the rest on all the small items denied her on the farm. She reveled in this taste of "urban" culture and the freedom to buy what she chose. She ate store-bought food for the first time and shared meals and good times with the five other women boarding in the same house.

But then her father called her back home and forbade her to return to the factory. She married before the age of twenty, and by the time she was twenty-three she was pregnant for the third time. Her husband, Jim, bought her one Sunday dress each year, when he could afford it. At the time she talked with Hagood, she and Jim lived in a three-room log cabin, and Mollie sold eggs to bring in some extra money. She was determined that her little girl would go to school regularly and get a wage-earning job, far from farming.

Life had changed little for Mollie over twenty years. For many rural women, the drastic economic downturn of the Great Depression started long before the stock market crashed in 1929. Tenant farmers in particular had experienced hard times ever since the Civil War, and farmers in the rural West had never recovered the prosperity they had enjoyed during World War I. Black families fared particularly badly. In Macon County, Georgia, for example, most black farm families lived in houses with dirt floors. Only one-fifth of these homes had indoor water, and three fourths had no sewage disposal. Black income in Macon County averaged less than a dollar per day.

Young women like Mollie were part of a family economy in which their labor helped the family survive but gained them no cash. Young men could work for pay in the fields of more prosperous farmers, but if women wanted to earn money— and be able to spend it—they had to head for town. Hopeful rural migrants who arrived in the cities after 1929, however, confronted an urban America reeling from an economic collapse that touched every sector of the economy. Factories closed. Businesses failed. When one-fifth of the country's banks failed, 9 million families lost their savings. As many as one-third of all workers were either unemployed or on short hours and reduced wages. In some places and for certain groups, the numbers were even higher. By the end of 1930, 70 percent of the African Americans in Charleston, South Carolina, and 75 percent of those in Memphis, Tennessee, were jobless. So were more than half the black women in Chicago and three-fourths of them in Detroit. Only eight states offered workers any form of unemployment insurance. There was no federal unemployment program. Workers' families lost the furniture and cars they had bought on installment plans because they could not meet the payments. Many also lost their homes. By 1934, in Indianapolis, Indiana, and Birmingham, Alabama, more than half the home owners had defaulted on their loans. So had 40 percent of home owners in twenty other cities.

If the 1920s had been a time of optimism and energy for many people in the United States, the 1930s began with fear and desperation. The basic assumptions of the previous decade—that technology was the answer to all problems, that businessmen knew best how to run the country, and that women's and men's greatest duty to society was to seek their own personal satisfaction—tottered.

As for the new women of the 1920s, what had looked like vigorous independence and strong-mindedness in the flapper now seemed careless, selfish, and superficial. A whole generation was tempted by an older, comforting vision of mom as a plump, slightly frazzled woman who could be relied on to sacrifice herself to nurture others and make it all better. That shift, along with the economic realities of the depression, created a different set of possibilities and limits for women.

Families coped with economic disaster in different ways. Helen Hong Wong had come to the United States in 1928 from Hong Kong dreaming of luxury. Instead she found herself, as she told an interviewer, working "like a slave" in her husband's restaurant and laundry. "I was not prepared for such a hard time," she recalled. "I found no streets paved with gold." Despite all the potatoes she peeled and the vegetables she chopped, the couple lost their restaurant in Fort Wayne, Indiana, during the depression. "People couldn't afford to eat," she concluded. Helen and her husband moved to Chicago but could find no work and could not collect welfare. Finally, her husband went to Chinatown and borrowed money from gamblers.

Other families also relied on ethnic connections. Many Americans were only a generation away, if that, from immigration. They still lived in neighborhoods where the shopkeepers and the customers alike spoke Polish, Italian, Spanish, or Yiddish. In Chicago, Mary Rupcinski and her husband had taken in tenants for years. During the depression, they let them stay on for months, even though the tenants could not pay their rent because they had lost their jobs. Neighborhood grocers often carried people on credit as long as they could, and neighborhood banks sometimes held off foreclosing on homes. Relatives doubled up, moving their families together into a single apartment or house. People shared.

Women often had a strong role in keeping such relationships alive. They visited, watched each other's children, and shared recipes. Women needed such networks because they could not make as much money as men could, but the depression proved the fragility of these networks. Without the rent from their tenants, the Rupcinskis ultimately could not make their mortgage payments, and they lost their house. Neighborhood banks closed. Ethnic organizations went bankrupt. When their neighborhood networks failed, women turned to other avenues for help. They cashed in insurance policies, and they visited welfare agencies.

It was hardest for single women to get food, shelter, work, or money from welfare agencies. Policymakers assumed that these women all had families somewhere that would care for them. In New York City, the $8 million government work-relief program focused on helping male heads of families. It took the private effort of well-known women to raise $350,000 to provide work for what they called the unemployed "army of women clerical workers." Men could sleep in flophouses, places charging twenty-five cents a night to sleep on a mattress in a large common room, but there were no flophouses for women. In 1930 the mayor of Minneapolis offered them the city jail.

Women continued to come to the city seeking work, but there was little to be had. In January 1930, one agency in Minneapolis could place only seventy of the three hundred women who applied. Women factory workers, teachers, and clerical workers who had lost their jobs turned to domestic service. Some women, in desperation, turned to prostitution.

At the unemployment bureaus, women waited for hours, day after day. Journalist Meridel Le Sueur wrote of one woman who "went crazy yesterday at the YW[CA]." She had had no work for eight months. As she kept saying, "You've got to give me something," the woman in charge of the agency began scolding the girl for her scuffed shoes. According to Le Sueur, "they were facing each other in a rage both helpless, helpless."

The Great Depression reached into every corner of the country, but it did not affect all people equally. For many middle-class women of all races, the depression required certain changes in spending patterns: buying cheaper cuts of meat, feeding the homeless men who stopped at the back door, and doing without new clothes. Some of these women continued to do community volunteer work, raising money for the unemployed. They saw the food lines, but they did not have to join them.

Among women workers, race played an important role. The fierce competition for jobs fueled racial resentments. Mexican-American and African-American women were the first to lose their jobs and the last to get relief from welfare agencies. Often, they were already living on the margin of survival. Before 1933, when the Prohibition amendment making the manufacture or sale of alcoholic beverages illegal was repealed, many of these women turned to bootlegging, making their own beer or liquor and selling it.

Other women struggled to survive within the bounds of the law. On street corners in the congested neighborhoods of the Bronx in New York City, black women, old and young, dressed as neatly as they could and stood ready to sell their cleaning services for an hour or two, or even for the whole day, for as little as fifteen cents an hour in an arrangement called the Bronx Slave Market. The two black women who investigated the Market for the NAACP's *Crisis* in 1935 found that these low rates had produced a new set of employers. Women of the lower middle-class who could not have dreamed of affording a servant during the 1920s could afford one now.

The number of married women in the labor force increased by 52 percent during the 1930s. By 1940, although the percentage of single women who worked for wages had dropped slightly, 15.6 percent of married women worked for pay. Most of the increase consisted of white native-born women, who provided only 43 percent of the total female labor force in 1930 but 70 percent in 1940. Of these white working women, the fastest-growing group was that between the ages of twenty-five and forty-five, the group most likely to have children at home. Their ability to hire African-American and Mexican-American women for extremely low wages made it easier for them to leave the home.

Not all married women coped with hard times by leaving the home. Many women took in home work. In Durham, North Carolina, women who had worked in tobacco factories now tagged tobacco sacks at home. In Rhode Island, women who had lost their jobs in the textile mill took home worsted wool to mend. Home work networks relied on ethnic neighborhood ties. In West Warwick, Rhode Island, the lace makers for American Textile were Portuguese women; the lace pullers who worked at home for Rhode Island Lace were Italian women; and the lace pullers who worked for Richmond Lace in the rural southwestern part of Rhode Island were descended from English, Scots, or Irish immigrants. There were advantages to home work for women. It allowed them to tend their own children, gather in chatty groups with other home workers, and barter among themselves, using their receipts for work completed as a kind of currency.

Home work had disadvantages, however. In San Antonio, Texas, the presence of thousands of temporarily unemployed families, largely Mexican-American, attracted home work industries from as far away as New York. Garment makers fleeing New York's higher labor costs joined the local pecan-shelling companies that were providing home work in San Antonio. As in Rhode Island and New York, where Puerto Ricans worked in the garment industry, the sewing required was hand work, in this case including embroidery. As the depression took hold, prices dropped continually. Between 1929 and the mid-1930s, employers cut the rates by 50 percent. For Chicanas, as for other home workers, the lack of alternatives kept them on the job. In 1936 the Women's Bureau of the U.S. Department of Labor interviewed home workers in San Antonio and Laredo, Texas. It found that many of the workers lived in one- or two-room shacks without plumbing or electricity. In one home/workshop there was no light source and the renter had to cook all her meals outside and share water and toilet facilities with fifteen other families. Moreover, home work encouraged competition among women. Factory women complained that home workers undercut their wages and their working conditions. Competition between cities also affected women, as garment manufacturers pitted Puerto Rican home workers in the East against Chicanas in the Southwest.

Despite all the rural women fleeing the farms, a Hispanic woman who lived in northern Colorado during the depression told an interviewer, "People on the farm were better off than downtown; we had our gardens." Even relatively prosperous farm women—owners, not tenants—in general produced as much as 70 percent of what their families consumed in clothing, toys, and food. They not only gardened but raised poultry. During the depression, women increased the size of their gardens and the number of their hens. They made more butter from their dairy cows and sold it. They cut up the sacks that held large amounts of flour and sewed them into underwear. In the previous decade, they had proudly begun to participate in a culture of store-bought goods. Now they began to can food again. Government agents dragged huge canning kettles across the mountains of northern New Mexico and eastern Tennessee so that women in remote farming villages could preserve their food.

Rural women canned and preserved fruits and vegetables during the depression, even though many had hoped in the 1920s to start buying some of their food and other goods from stores.

Even with all this work, rural children suffered from malnutrition, and rural women faced childbirth without a doctor or midwife because they could afford neither the medical fees nor the gasoline for transportation. The women resented their declining standards of living, particularly whose who owned their own farms and had, during the 1920s, aspired to participate in the new domestic technology of indoor bathrooms, modern stoves and heating, and superclean-liness. Through national women's magazines and the Sears Roebuck catalogs, these women had internalized the 1920s message that women's duty was to create a beautiful home and a beautiful self. The women writing the advice columns in farm magazines held each other to city standards of tidiness. Women without toilets or sinks, without running water in their homes, who nevertheless preserved fifteen hundred quarts of food a year, were advised to try wearing powder and rouge to please their husbands.

In the 1920s, people had worried about how to keep the family together when faced with women's increasing independence. Now they worried about how to keep men in the family as it became clear that many women still depended on the income of men, after all, and many men were now unemployed. Powder and rouge were not enough. Divorce rates dropped in the 1930s, more because people could not afford the costs of an official divorce than because families were staying together. Desertion ran rampant. Men went out to look for work and never returned, leaving their wives to try to convince increasingly suspicious and underfunded charity agents and city officials that they were virtuous enough to be worthy of aid. Families that stayed together tried not to add new members. The birthrate, which had been declining steadily for a century, hit its lowest point in 1933, when only 75.7 of every 1,000 women of childbearing age gave birth.

In 1936 a federal appeals court overruled an earlier law that had classified birth control information as obscene and thus illegal to dispense, although the decision left state laws intact. The number of birth control clinics nationwide rose from fifty-five in 1930 to three hundred by 1938, but in some states and in many rural areas women still had no access to birth control. In 1937 North Carolina became the first state to provide contraceptives with tax dollars, and six others soon followed. Ironically, North Carolina's reasoning was not that birth control was a human right but that birth control would reduce the black population. Despite statistics showing that black women had fewer babies than white women with similar incomes and living situations, many white southern officials in states with large black populations feared a black population explosion. In 1939 the Birth Control Federation of America responded to eager southern state governments by developing "The Negro Project," a program to disseminate birth control information, which they carefully staffed with local black community leaders.

Whatever the logic, one quarter of all women in the United States in their twenties during the depression never bore children—the highest rate of childlessness for any decade. Many people simply decided not to get married, and marriage rates fell.

With men unable to fulfill their traditional roles as providers and many deserting their homes, women were increasingly left to run the family, with little money and few opportunities. Many people worried that chaos would follow. To them, orderly society depended on a family organized around a strong, dominant father. A few people did suggest that the solution might lie in providing more opportunities for the women left running the family, but most focused on men's unemployment and on how to keep the family together. They tended to decide that the real culprits were married working women, stealing jobs from married men.

The media, which had made married working women invisible in the 1920s, now often vilified them. During the 1920s, married women had experienced discrimination at the local level, particularly as teachers. By the early 1930s, public officials such as New York Assemblyman Arthur Swartz were calling them "undeserving parasites." Several cities ordered the dismissal of wives whose husbands earned what they defined as "living wages." In 1931 legislators in Massachusetts,

New York, and California introduced bills to limit government employment of married women. The federal government's 1932 Economy Act required that when personnel reductions took place in the executive branch, married persons be the first discharged if their spouse also worked for the government. Women earned less than men, even for the same job, so given the choice, a family would logically retain the higher-salaried man's job and let the wife go unemployed.

Many women's groups rallied in opposition to this legislation. The leaders of the Business and Professional Women's Clubs declared in their journal, *Independent Woman*, "Such legislation is not only a blow to married women, but through implication to all women workers and to marriage itself." Women in government work had to choose between a job and a husband.

Despite mounting protests, the controversial clause of the Economy Act was not repealed until 1937. In 1936 George Gallup, witnessing the results of his new public opinion polls, in which 82 percent of the respondents agreed that wives should not work if their husbands were employed, observed that he had "discovered an issue on which voters are about as solidly united as on any subject imaginable—including sin and hay fever."

Local governments followed the lead of the federal government. During the 1920s, the proportion of female teachers who were married had almost doubled, reaching more than 150,000 by 1930. The depression saw communities cut back on school funds, reduce the number of teachers, and slash their salaries. They also reduced the number of married teachers. By 1940 only 13 percent of communities would hire wives as teachers, and only 30 percent would retain women teachers who got married. The percentage of male teachers rose from 19 percent to 24.3 percent of teachers during the 1930s. Married women teachers, however, did not disappear. Indeed, over the same period they increased from 17.9 percent to 22 percent of all female teachers, but the absolute number of women teachers had dropped by 81,000.

On the other hand, women retained their hold on clerical positions, which steadily increased in number in the 1930s. Advocates of women's employment found themselves making a virtue out of the fact that women were by and large limited to certain jobs. The number of women in male-dominated professions, including science and college teaching, decreased in the 1930s. Because all women's jobs were threatened, women who were trying to salvage these jobs reinforced the notion that some occupations were particularly suited to women. Running beauty salons, of which there were forty thousand by 1930, or working as dental hygienists and occupational therapists all offered women increased opportunities and had the added advantage of placing women where they would not compete with men. The proportion of women working outside the home rose only slightly from 1930 to 1940, from 24.4 percent to 25.4 percent, a far smaller rise than in previous decades.

Women seemed to receive mixed messages from the mass media. On the one hand, in 1930, the *Ladies' Home Journal* featured a former career woman confessing, "I know now without any hesitation . . . that [my husband's job] must come first." In 1931 the popular magazine *Outlook and Independent* quoted the dean of Barnard College, a women's college in New York City, telling her students that "perhaps the greatest service that you can render to the community . . . is to have the courage to refuse to work for gain." And on its front page in 1935, the *New York Times* reported that women "suffering from masculine psychological states" and an "aversion to marriage" were being "cured" by the removal of their adrenal gland. In this atmosphere, not only were women workers under fire, but women who centered their lives on women rather than on men came under attack. Lesbianism was no longer chic. Lesbian bars almost disappeared. Homosexuality was now seen by many people as just one more threat to the family.

On the other hand, movie houses showed zany screwball comedies with more complicated lessons. Often, deliciously ditsy, incompetent women were rescued by sensible, capable men—yet men were also frequently portrayed as bumbling or slower-witted than the women. Sometimes the men needed joy and whimsy restored to their lives, not an unexpected theme for a nation in the throes of an economic depression.

In other movies, women were by no means incompetent. The women portrayed by Katharine Hepburn, Bette Davis, and Joan Crawford in the 1930s were often intelligent but needed men to tame and soften them. At the other end of the spectrum, in the dancing movies of Ginger Rogers and Fred Astaire, Rogers often played the responsible, capable, working partner while Astaire's devil-may-care ways needed reforming. Their movies usually ended not with blissful domestic life for her but with successful professional partnership for them both.

How were women to understand their roles through these films? Were they to go from the free but irresponsible flapper to the submissive, nurturing wife who could lighten the burden of dark days but stay safely in her place? Or was there another model still available? It was, after all, in the 1930s that Babe Didrikson emerged as a sports hero, winning two gold medals at the 1932 Olympics, in javelin and hurdles, and a silver in the high jump, and eschewing all feminine wiles. What society demanded of women in the 1930s was complex and contradictory, but it did not completely erode the image of confident, competent, public womanhood created in the 1920s.

Women and the New Deal

In 1931 Emily Newell Blair, a former national vice-chairman of the Democratic party, wrote an article entitled "Why I Am Discouraged about Women in Politics." "Now at the end of ten years of suffrage," she confessed, "I find politics still a male monopoly. It is hardly easier for women to get themselves elected to office than it was before the Equal Suffrage Amendment was passed. Women still have little part in framing political policies and determining party tactics." Indeed, Blair claimed

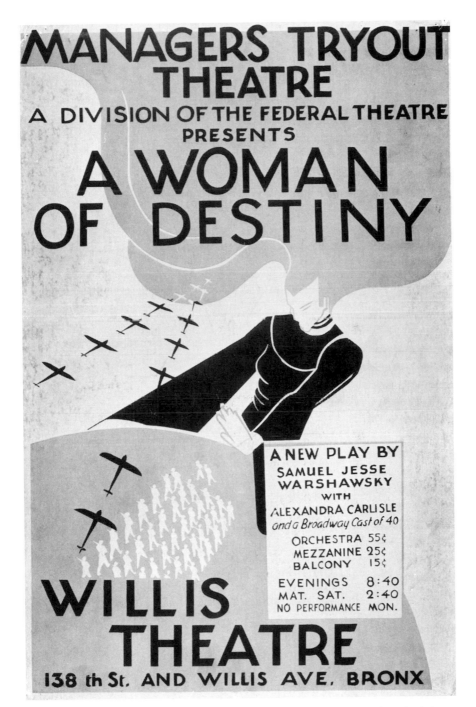

A poster for a 1936 production of *A Woman of Destiny* in New York, sponsored by the Federal Theatre, a New Deal agency. The play tells the story of a woman antiwar activist who becomes president.

that women had less of a voice in party leadership than they had in 1920, when, as an unknown quantity, they had been courted by male politicians.

In the 1930s, few women held elected office. Of the dozen women who served in Congress at some point during the decade, only two were active on women's issues. Blair lamented, "Unfortunately for feminism, it was agreed to drop the sex line in politics. And it was dropped by the women. Even those who ran for office forgot that they were women." Yet the 1930s saw a dramatic increase in women's political influence through appointed, rather than elected, offices. It came as the fruit of Franklin Delano Roosevelt's program, the New Deal that he promised Americans when they elected him President in 1932. The increase in influence was also the result of his wife Eleanor's strong and deeply rooted networks among women reformers and her political abilities as a shaper of New Deal policy.

By early 1933, when Roosevelt took office, the depression was four years old. Herbert Hoover, elected President in 1928, had hesitated to intervene drastically in the economy. Hoover had created public works projects that erected large dams but employed few workers. He had provided some support for banks and had said many encouraging things, but the economy went from bad to worse.

Faced with declining opportunities and increased racial hostility, ten thousand Puerto Ricans headed for home, and many Chinese returned to China. Unable to create jobs or to meet the needs of the unemployed, officials in the Southwest closed ranks against Mexicans and Mexican Americans, accusing them of stealing jobs and using up relief dollars. In 1932, officials in Los Angeles rounded up all the Mexicans they could find, put them and their American-born children in boxcars, and sent them to Mexico. In all, across the United States, these deportations affected approximately 400,000 Mexicans. They solved nothing. Indeed, many "Mexicans" on relief roles were, in fact, U.S. citizens, born and raised on this side of the border. To the officials responsible, however, they all looked alike.

Many Chicanos made their way to the cities in search of opportunities or help. They were joined by 400,000 African Americans migrating from the South to the North for the same reason. And farmers who had lost their homes, along with tenant farmers unable to get leases, rolled west, as one observer noted, "like a parade." Whole counties hit the road.

The cities offered no respite from the hard times. In 1933 half the workers in Cleveland were unemployed, as were 80 percent of those in Toledo. Average family income plummeted from $2,300 in 1929 to $1,500 in 1933. In 1932 28 percent of U.S. households had no employed worker at all. Even those who had work suffered. Stenographers in New York who had made forty dollars a week in 1929 were making only sixteen dollars four years later. Most working women in Chicago earned less than twenty-five cents an hour. Unable to pay their teachers, school districts cut school to three days a week, to two months a year, or simply closed them altogether, depriving a third of a million children of school in 1932.

People looked to Roosevelt's administration to make order of the chaos, to reopen the banks and schools, and to put people back to work. In the process of accomplishing these tasks, the Roosevelts and their allies changed the relationship between individuals and the government. With her long history of work in social welfare, Eleanor Roosevelt stood at the center of that change.

Anna Eleanor Roosevelt had been born into an old, wealthy, and distinguished New York family. By the time Eleanor was ten, both her parents had died—her mother after an operation and her father from alcoholism. She spent the rest of her childhood with relatives. When she reached fifteen, she was sent to a London boarding school. When Roosevelt returned to New York to enter high society, she plunged into social service activities. At the age of eighteen, she worked at the Rivington Street Settlement House, teaching calisthenics and dancing to the impoverished neighbors. She also joined the National Consumers' League, which used the power of consumers to try to better the conditions of workers, particularly women. Employers who met the Consumers' League standards could use the League label, and consumers could buy the goods they produced knowing they had been produced under decent conditions. Roosevelt visited the clothing factories and sweatshops that the League targeted and never forgot what she saw.

Roosevelt married her cousin, Franklin Roosevelt, an ambitious young Harvard graduate, in March 1905. For the next ten years Eleanor was either pregnant or recovering from pregnancy. She helped Franklin's early political career by organizing and hosting social and political gatherings. Then, in 1917, she discovered that her husband was having an affair with her trusted friend, Lucy Mercer. Devastated, she offered him a divorce, but a divorce would have ruined his political career and deprived him of a valued friend and partner. The couple reconciled, and both plunged into politics.

Even the setback of Franklin's lifelong paralysis from a polio attack in 1921 could not stop the Roosevelts. During the 1920s, Franklin played an ever-increasing role in the Democratic party, and Eleanor joined reform organizations, including the Women's Trade Union League. She discovered in the women reformers a warm, supportive network of friends and an astute set of politicians. This warmth sustained her in the rough and tumble political world. In particular, her intimate relationship with journalist Lorena Hickok provided the essential emotional support she could no longer get from her husband. In turn, as early as 1924, women reformers saw Eleanor Roosevelt as a major leader. By 1928 she expressed her frustration that these women politicians met with so few rewards. She would carry this sense of politics and reform—and this network of women—with her into the White House in 1933.

The women who would join Eleanor Roosevelt in Washington were not new to politics. In overlapping networks, they had been building connections and careers throughout the 1910s and 1920s. For example, Mary W. Dewson started her career in Massachusetts reform and suffrage circles. In the 1920s in New York, she served as the civic secretary of the Women's City Club and the research secretary of the National Consumers' League. By 1929 Dewson knew all the leading women reformers in the city. With these connections in mind, Eleanor Roosevelt recruited her into Democratic politics. By 1937 Dewson was vice chairman of the Democratic National Committee and on a number of government advisory boards. Dewson wanted to use political appointments both to get nonpartisan women reformers into the government and to reward loyal Democratic women. For his part, Franklin Roosevelt wanted to be the first President to appoint a woman to the cabinet. In Frances Perkins he found an ideal candidate with connections to both political and reform networks.

Perkins had graduated from Mount Holyoke College in 1902, worked in settlement houses in Chicago, and then studied and conducted research for her master's degree in sociology and economics at Columbia University. She had worked for the Consumers' League as a lobbyist. In 1918 Governor Al Smith appointed her to the New York State Industrial Commission. In 1928 the new governor, Franklin Roosevelt, appointed Perkins Industrial Commissioner, a promotion. After he was elected President, Roosevelt agreed to nominate Perkins as secretary of labor, and Dewson launched a nationwide campaign in her support.

Other women received posts in every agency from the diplomatic corps and the U.S. Mint to the Consumers' Advisory Board of the National Recovery Administration (NRA), an economic agency that was part of the New Deal program. Under Roosevelt, a higher percentage of women received government appointments than ever before, except during World War I.

Women fared best in new agencies. In the seven newest New Deal agencies, including the Social Security Board, the Works Progress Administration, and the Home Owners' Loan Corporation, women made up 44.4 percent of the employees in 1939. The ten executive departments were another story. In the Departments of Labor, State, and Interior, women constituted more than one-third of the employees, but in the Departments of War, Navy, Commerce, and the Post Office, they ranged from 15.2 percent to only 5.5 percent of employees.

Some women had built up political networks over the previous decades whose networks touched, rather than overlapped, those of Eleanor Roosevelt and Mary Dewson. Mary McLeod Bethune was one such woman. Born in South Carolina in the 1870s, the fifteenth of seventeen children, she was the one chosen to attend school and teach the others. A determined mother and scholarships helped Bethune, who was proud of her African heritage, attend a seminary, a bible school, and a number of mission schools in pursuit of her desire to be a missionary in Africa. During her training, Bethune married and had a child. As her efforts to go to Africa failed, she realized that her true mission was in the United States and founded a school for girls in Daytona, Florida; in 1929, it became Bethune-Cookman College.

Eleanor Roosevelt (right) supported Mary McLeod Bethune in her fight to advance the rights of women and African Americans. Roosevelt also encouraged her husband to respond to the concerns of blacks.

But Bethune's activities ranged far beyond her school. A vital force in women's clubs, in 1924 she was elected president of the National Association of Colored Women (NACW). Like all Bethune's organizations, it had a large vision, working to secure a federal antilynching bill, helping rural women and women in industry, training clerks and typists, and raising the status of women in the Philippines, Puerto Rico, Haiti, and Africa. Bethune knew that the number of black women graduating from college was increasing but that the status of black working women had declined in depression conditions. She wanted to mobilize the power of college women on behalf of the others. She felt frustrated with the lack of progress, the conservatism of the NACW, and the difficulties of working in mixed-race organizations such as the Association of Southern Women for the Prevention of Lynching, whose white members had refused to support a federal antilynching law, claiming it violated states' rights. Though Bethune remained more friendly to such groups than did many black women leaders, she decided to found her own organization. On December 5, 1935, she held the founding meeting of the National Council of Negro Women at the Harlem branch of the YWCA.

Bethune's stature had led to her involvement in national-level politics. In 1928, she had participated in the White House Conference on Child Welfare. Yet the New Deal was slow to call on her. As late as 1929, Franklin Roosevelt had boasted that he had never lunched with an African American. He ignored NAACP requests to support a civil rights platform. African Americans supported Roosevelt only because of his job creation and welfare programs. Then, in 1934, Eleanor Roosevelt began taking public stands on racial issues. Unlike her husband, she lent her public support to the antilynching bill. Finally, in 1936, when 76 percent of the black vote returned Roosevelt to office, despite the defection of white Southern Democrats, Roosevelt responded with black political appointments.

The press called the new appointees the "Black Cabinet." Bethune was among them. She directed the Negro Division of the National Youth Administration (NYA), whose mandate was to find jobs for people between the ages of sixteen and twenty-four. Bethune soon made her mark. Seeing the Black Cabinet divided by internal disputes, she organized its members into the Federal Council of Negro Affairs to achieve consensus on policy issues. She also made certain that black universities benefited from the NYA, implementing a small, special scholarship fund for African-American college students because of their greater need. In the 1930s, 48 percent of the fathers of black college students worked in unskilled, low-paying jobs; only 4.7 percent of white students' fathers did.

Many black southern women with fewer connections, less education, and less power than Bethune, surrounded by the terrorist, racist activities of the Ku Klux Klan, felt they had no choice but to repress their anger and resentment in order to keep their jobs and provide for their families. Bethune would have to express their feelings for them. She did not hesitate. In a typical moment, she wrote to Secretary of War Henry L. Stimson on learning that the War Department had failed to invite black women to a 1941 conference on organizing women for the war effort, "We are not humiliated. We are incensed."

Together these women, black and white, tried to ensure that other women benefited from New Deal programs. They were consummate lobbyists. Eleanor Roosevelt had unprecedented access to policymakers, addressing committees of the House of Representatives, conferring with committee chairmen, and sending members of Congress letters demanding the appointment of a coordinator of child care—all the while claiming to act only as a private citizen.

With public charities running dry and states going bankrupt, the federal government swept in like a benign wind. The New Deal created massive temporary job programs and provided relief payments, first through the Federal Relief Administration (FERA), created in March 1933 with $500 million, and the Public Works Administration (PWA), which funded major construction projects with $3.3 billion. Then, in the desperate winter of 1933–34, the Civil Works Administration (CWA) was established; it hired 2.6 million people within a month. At its peak in January 1934, the CWA employed more than 4 million people with wages averaging about fifteen dollars per week, twice the usual FERA rate. When the depression lingered, at Roosevelt's request Congress passed the Emergency Relief Act, under which Roosevelt created the Works Progress Administration (WPA) with the largest single appropriation to that date, $4.88 billion, in order to create jobs.

The New Deal also attempted a more permanent restructuring of the economy. In 1933 the Agricultural Adjustment Act (AAA) and the National Industrial Recovery Act (NIRA), which created the National Recovery Administration (NRA), tried to stabilize production on farms and in factories. These agencies tried to ensure decent working conditions by bringing consumers, employers, and workers together to create codes for the industries and prices and quotas for the farmers. They also made it harder for employers to discriminate against workers for joining a union. These measures were so popular that when the Supreme Court declared the laws unconstitutional in 1935 and 1936, new, more carefully drafted laws swiftly replaced the major provisions of the AAA and the provisions of the NIRA that protected workers' rights. Industrial codes were abandoned, but in 1938 the Fair Labor Standards Act legislated minimum wages and maximum hours, and this time the Supreme Court let the act stand.

The federal government also entered more permanently and more broadly into social welfare. Finally, the United States, like most European countries, had unemployment insurance, old age insurance (Social Security), and aid to dependent children. The last was a provision of the 1935 Social Security Act drafted by the reformers Grace Abbott and Katherine Lenroot, who headed the Children's Bureau. For the first time, the U.S. government became a major guarantor of family welfare.

Some of these programs greatly benefited women; others had mixed and often unexpected consequences. New Deal programs employed countless numbers of women. They also kept many women in college; 45 percent of the college students helped by the NYA in 1936–37 were women. The number of women in college rose almost as fast as the number of men, from 480,000 in 1930 to 601,000 in 1940. For many women, New Deal programs made the difference between starvation and survival, or between despair and self-respect. Stella Boone and Ethel Stringer took time out from their new jobs as WPA Adult Education teachers at a Hispanic secondary school in San Antonio to write to Eleanor Roosevelt in 1936. "Many of us were desperate," they explained, "the unhappy victims of circumstances over which we had no control.... It is unalterably true that shabbiness and hunger are the foes of self-respect. With our homes broken, our children scattered, our souls torn with anguish and desperation ... Some of us had lost our homes which were nearly paid for, had sold our furniture, piece by piece, our jewelry, and even most of our clothes.... Just when all seemed lost and maddened by grief and fear we were ready for anything, this Adult Educational Program came, providing us with a means of livelihood, a ladder up which we could climb again to patriotism and self-respect."

In such programs, Hispanic and Anglo women in San Antonio studied business and clerical subjects in the hope of obtaining white-collar employment. With its vast bureaucracy, the New Deal did provide many clerical and professional jobs throughout the government. At the state level, women ran the WPA's Division of Women's Work. They also participated in the WPA's writing, music, and theater projects. Zora Neale Hurston collected folklore from African Americans in Florida for the WPA Writers Project. Photographers Dorothea Lange and Marion Post Wolcott took pictures for the Farm Security Administration. Other women worked in government-funded positions in hospitals, nursery schools, and cafeterias or cleaned public buildings and organized city records.

Most women's work projects consisted, however, of sewing rooms, where workers made garments for relief recipients; food processing, such as canning factories; health care; and domestic-service training programs. In San Antonio, for example, by early 1936, the WPA employed 1,280 women and just over twice that many men in professional projects. On the other hand, a single sewing room in that city employed 2,300 people. In the country as a whole, 56 percent of the women employed by the WPA worked in sewing rooms.

New Deal policies focused on promoting domestic roles for women; administrators tended to see women as temporary workers who were helping out in an emergency and would return to the home after the depression. Why teach them nondomestic skills they would never use again? Operating procedures in the WPA mandated that job preference be given to male family heads or, if none existed, to adult male children in the household. Only if a husband were absent or disabled and no adult sons lived at home could women receive a high priority at the agency. Even in the National Youth Administration, men received preference over women in job placement. The WPA limited the proportion of jobs it opened to women to between 12 and 16 percent.

There were other limits to the New Deal programs. Social Security excluded domestic servants and agricultural workers, and by doing so excluded most black female and Chicana workers; in the 1930s, 90 percent of black women worked in agricultural labor or domestic service. No code and, later, no minimum wage or maximum hours law covered these workers. Nor was government relief evenly distributed. It went disproportionately to whites. Black women in the South and Chicanas in the Southwest found themselves ousted from work relief programs and had to take poorly paid domestic work or labor in the cotton or vegetable and fruit fields. In addition, the New Deal's crop reduction policies, geared toward increasing agricultural prices by reducing supply, led landowners to evict large numbers of black women who had raised crops on their land as tenants or sharecroppers.

The administrators of government programs were overwhelmingly white. They had little interest in creating jobs programs that would pull women of color away from domestic service, and they were thoroughly imbued with the racial attitudes that dominated their regions. In 1935 *Opportunity,* the journal of the Urban

League, quoted a Georgia black woman who complained, "When I go to them for help they talk to me like I was a dog." Some government officials simply refused relief to black or Chicano clients. Mosel Brinson of Georgia wrote to the U.S. Department of Agriculture in 1935, "I am a widow woman with seven head of children, and I live on my place with a plenty of help. All are good workers and I wants to farm. I has no mule, no wagon, no feed, no grocery, and these women and men that is controlling the Civil Work for the Government won't help me." She added a telling postscript: "P.S. These poor white people that lives around me wants the colored people to work for them for nothing and if you won't do that they goes down to the relief office and tell the women,—'don't help the colored people, we will give them plenty of work to do, but they won't work.'"

Yet white program directors continued to create programs that channeled women of color into domestic service. Mary Katherine Dickson, who administered federal relief programs in San Antonio in 1937, complained that "the majority of housewives in San Antonio have a very real servant problem on their hands and, at present, no means of solving it satisfactorily." She offered her proposal for training black adults in domestic service as the best solution to their unemployment and white housewives' needs, because "between 75% and 85% of persons employed in household service are black." She condemned the public school system for providing the same curriculum and the same expectations for black and white students.

In Denver, officials found they could not fill the classes they had created to train Chicanas in domestic service. Chicanas and black women found almost any other kind of work preferable. Some of these women benefited from New Deal–sponsored classes in clerical skills, but most avoided domestic work by finding jobs in WPA sewing rooms, and even some sewing rooms discriminated. In Fayetteville, North Carolina, officials closed the sewing project and opened a cleaning project for black women. And, unlike white women, black women in the WPA were often assigned to heavy outdoor labor. A physician in Florence, South Carolina, complained to the WPA in 1936 of a "beautification" project where "women are worked in 'gangs' in connection with the City's dump pile, incinerator and ditch piles."

Some programs not particularly aimed at women had unexpected results. The Indian Reorganization Act of 1934 aimed to give Native American tribes increased autonomy by creating tribal governments built around newly written constitutions. Although the underlying sentiment of the act was a new respect for tribal cultures, the new constitutions tended to be built on white models. In tribes where women had been excluded from formal political participation, they gained new voting power, and new women leaders emerged. In other tribes, women lost economic rights and political power. Among the Navajo, for example, New Deal policies of reducing stock in the name of conserving overgrazed land lessened the economic power of women, who were the traditional tribal stock owners. At the same time, jobs programs favoring men made the Navajo men less dependent economically on the clan's women and less willing to contribute their income to the extended family.

Even industrial codes aimed at improving work conditions could backfire. Wages increased rapidly. Between July 1933 and August 1934, southern women textile workers doubled their hourly wages, a more rapid increase than the men's. Even so, however, the twelve dollars a week they now received would scarcely make ends meet. Besides, most received only three-fourths of that amount because, to meet code requirements regarding the number of work hours per week, many mills closed every fourth week. Short hours and production cuts undermined women's wage advances. Increased demands for productivity, on the other hand, made a mockery of the reduction to an eight-hour day. Higher wages could also lead to mechanization and layoffs as machines became cheaper than human workers. In 1935 a black woman worker told an NRA investigator, "They laid off one-fourth of the people in my room after the last raise we got."

Secretary of Labor Frances Perkins may not have been entirely satisfied with the treatment women got from the New Deal. In her papers at the National Archives there is an unsigned, unattributed, undated "Resolution on Unemployment and Working Women." According to that document, "They have been thrown out of jobs as married women, refused relief as single women, discriminated against by the N.R.A. and ignored by the C.W.A." Pondering these issues in 1935, writer and editor Genevieve Parkhurst wondered in *Harper's* magazine whether feminism was dead. After all, almost one-fourth of the NRA codes established wage rates for women that were 14 percent to 30 percent lower than those for men, and southern codes for laundries established earnings for black laundresses below precode levels.

The emphasis throughout the Roosevelt administration, including that of Eleanor Roosevelt and Frances Perkins, remained on providing male workers with jobs and supporting families. Single women earners were invisible; married women workers existed only as mothers or wives. WPA rules prohibited the agency from providing work for women eligible for aid from the Aid to Dependent Children program as well as for most married women. Such policies aimed at curbing the seeming trend of women becoming the family breadwinner; if there was no man to do so, the role would be assumed by the state.

With the tremendous anxiety over social stability and fears for the family as the core of social order, few spoke for the woman workers, and feminist individualism was rarely seen. In 1935 the *New York Herald Tribune* reported that the president of the national League of Women Voters, the organizational heir to the suffrage movement, was defining "a 1935 new-style feminism." This new feminism, she insisted, did not demand that women disappear into their kitchens. Instead, it required "women making good in positions of responsibility, other women backing them up, and all preparing themselves for similar service," as they did in Roosevelt's administration. Yet the new focus was less on personal achievement than it had been in the

1920s. Women social reformers had achieved high visibility and power with the New Deal, and those focusing instead on equal rights for women were in disarray.

The social reformers saw themselves as bettering the world for women, helping women and children fend off economic disaster, fostering the success of women in government positions, and safeguarding the welfare of working women. But in Frances Perkins's Department of Labor, the Children's Bureau expanded rapidly, while the Women's Bureau remained small. That policy decision left childless women stranded and left little room for a notion of women's rights that did not depend on their family roles. Despite its powerful women, the New Deal did not revolutionize the position of women in relation to men or the family.

For all its contradictions, however, the New Deal had drastically changed the relationship of women to the state. By providing Social Security, however limited, unemployment insurance, jobs, NRA hearings where workers could air their grievances directly to federal officials, wage and hour legislation, and other programs, the New Deal altered what people believed they could expect and took new responsibility for the welfare of families and workers. These heightened expectations, particularly among working-class women, led them to take matters into their own hands.

Taking Matters into Their Own Hands

Throughout the 1930s, impoverished and unemployed people found that those from whom they sought help—charity agents, local, state, and federal officials, and employers—all sought to define their needs, aims, and the limits of their aspirations. Some women resisted such definitions and insisted on defining their own needs, desires, and identities. Many went beyond writing letters. They joined together, sometimes with men, sometimes without them, to protest as a community.

Eviction protests offer an example. In journalist Caroline Bird's memoir of the Great Depression, *The Invisible Scar,* she recalled, "Eviction was so common that children in a Philadelphia day-care center made a game of it. They would pile all the doll furniture up first in one corner and then in another." Rents dropped precipitously during the 1930s, but however low they fell, unemployed workers could not afford to pay them. Tired of moving, desperate for housing and self-respect, they began to fight the evictions. Women played a central role in eviction protests. They had built up neighborhood networks over the years, visiting, sharing work with and caring for neighbors, gossiping, distributing home work, and taking in boarders. Now these women's neighborhood networks were matched by newer networks of unemployed men. With the help of the Communist party, they united into Unemployed Councils. These councils organized the bulk of the eviction protests, but it was the neighborhood networks that made them successful. In cities as different as New York, Baltimore, and Sioux City, Iowa, women and men would gather up the neighborhood and march to a site where a city official, on behalf of a landlord, had just thrown a family into the street. Vastly outnumbered, the city official could only leave or watch helplessly as the crowd took the tenant's belongings back into the apartment. Eviction proceedings took two or three months, which gave unemployed tenants valuable breathing space before the city marshal would again appear to evict them.

In such community protests men made most of the street-corner speeches, but women maintained the picket lines. They did so even when, as the Communist paper the *Daily Worker* reported in 1933 about a Brownsville, New York, rent protest, "day after day thugs and police beat women and children who picketed in front of the house." Black women organized neighborhood Housewives Leagues over jobs as well as housing. Discrimination ran rampant in the job market, and many employers refused to hire African Americans. In Chicago, Baltimore, Detroit, Harlem, and Cleveland, Housewives Leagues used their power as consumers to launch "Don't Buy Where You Can't Work" campaigns. Stores in black neighborhoods would either have to employ black workers or lose black business. These boycotts resulted in as many as 75,000 new jobs for blacks during the 1930s.

Women also took the power of their neighborhood networks beyond their own streets. As members of women's auxiliaries to largely male unions, they played a vital role in supporting the major men's labor strikes of the decade, including the Minneapolis general strike and the Flint, Michigan, sit-down strike at General Motors. But the women also organized on their own behalf, as workers.

In 1933 in St. Louis, Missouri, nine hundred black women pecan workers walked out of seven factories owned by the same man. They demanded higher pay and better working conditions—pay and conditions equal to those of white women workers. Connie Smith, a middle-aged black woman, led the protest, and she secured widespread cooperation, including that of the Unemployed Councils. When the factory owner tried to pit whites against blacks by offering white women a wage increase if they would return to work, a group of fifteen hundred black and white women marched together to City Hall to refuse the offer. Faced with solidarity between black and white women, the owner surrendered on all counts—equal treatment, higher wages, and better conditions.

Determined to take advantage of the ferment, in 1934 William Green, head of the American Federation of Labor (AFL), announced a campaign to bring women into the unions. Yet just bringing them in as members did not guarantee them a voice in policy-making. At Philco, the nation's leading radio maker and Philadelphia's largest single employer, even with the union, women and men had different assignments and were subject to different wage rates. Although women made up about half of Philco's six to seven thousand employees and half the union members of the United Electrical, Radio and Machine Workers of America, men held the offices, including those in departments with large female majorities.

Few women protested the distribution of labor. As former worker Catherine McGill told an interviewer, "At that time, you were glad to have a job." And most of

Philco's women workers believed that some jobs were more appropriate to women and others to men. They accepted that those jobs labeled "women's jobs" had lower wages. Ironically, at Philco this acceptance of jobs and wages defined by sex, which had started as a way to keep women from competing for "men's jobs," resulted in men losing jobs to women after all. An unsuccessful strike by the union at the end of 1937 led to a reclassification of fifteen hundred positions from "men's jobs" to "women's jobs" at correspondingly lower pay, and women became the majority of workers at the plant.

In the same year that Green announced his policy shift, the International Ladies' Garment Workers Union (ILGWU) began organizing women workers in San Antonio. They struggled to unite Anglo and Mexican-American women factory workers with the largely Chicana hand sewers and embroiderers who worked at home, but high unemployment made it easy for employers to fire or otherwise harass union members and replace them. No lasting success was achieved until 1935, when New Deal legislation made company harassment of union members illegal. From 1936 to 1938, the union helped garment factory workers make steady gains in San Antonio.

The changes in labor legislation fostered dramatic growth in union membership and the formation of a new Committee on Industrial Organization of the American Federation of Labor. It soon split off, amid bitter disputes, to become the Congress of Industrial Organizations (CIO). The CIO proved more hospitable to women workers because it organized by industry rather than by skills, many of which had excluded women. Of course, this shift did not change the prevalent ideas about men's and women's work overnight, and even CIO unions approved settlements with employers that allowed lower wages for women than for men in the same jobs. Stella Nowicki, an organizer in Chicago meat-packing plants at the time, recalled, "Women had an awfully tough time in the union because the men brought their prejudices there." Moreover, after a day's work many women still had to care for children, make meals, and clean the house. "The union didn't encourage women to come to meetings," Nowicki said. "They didn't actually want to take up the problems that women had." And most women workers remained in fields that were hardly touched by union organization.

Yet over the decade women's union membership tripled, reaching 800,000 by 1940. Two hundred thousand of them were in the ILGWU, but women also organized in a wide variety of occupations and industries, from domestic work to clerical work, canning to radio manufacturing. Often women were hungry for unions. United, they had a chance to take some control over the conditions of their work and livelihoods. Instead of depending solely on their employers, they could depend on each other and bargain with their employers.

Despite continued wage inequities, the unions, new legislation, and federal attempts at regulating the workplace gave women workers an expanded vision of their rights and a sense that their government would hear them and act. In NRA

Hispanic men and women gather for a 1935 meeting of the National Miners Union in Gallup, New Mexico.

hearings, for example, women complained again and again about sexual harassment. In textile mills, men used profane and vulgar language, which the women found humiliating and degrading. Worse yet, bosses pressured young women workers into sexual relations and fired them if they did not comply. Mothers who tried to protect their daughters were turned away and told it was none of their business. These issues still lay outside the formal codes and contracts affecting workers. Women used these new forums to make this hidden abuse, this particularly female problem, visible and to demand remedies.

Sexual harassment was one of the shared experiences that bound cannery workers at the California Sanitary Canning Company (Cal San) together. In 1939, during a record-breaking heat wave, nearly all 430 women workers, most of them Mexican Americans, walked off their fruit-canning jobs. The tremendous solidarity of this union local was built on ethnic, kinship, and neighborhood as well as gender lines. Sometimes three generations of women worked in the plant. They shared the experience of slippery floors, itchy peach fuzz, and the ever-swifter pace of production, in addition to sexual harassment. Those workers who were not

Chicanas, the Russian Jews, lived in Boyle Heights in East Los Angeles. The two ethnic groups lived on separate blocks but met at the same streetcar stops in the early morning.

Twenty-four-year-old Dorothy Ray Healey, an international vice president of the United Cannery, Agricultural, Packing and Allied Workers of America (UCA-PAWA) and a cannery worker organizer since the age of sixteen, led the campaign. The strikers established a twenty-four-hour picket line to demand that the company recognize their union and that all workers be union members. Although the workers had walked out at the height of the peach-canning season, the factory owners, the Shapiros, refused to negotiate. Neighborhood grocers donated food to sustain the strikers. Many grocers refused to stock Cal San products. The National Labor Relations Board reprimanded the Shapiros for refusing to bargain, but the stalemate continued. After two and a half months, one morning the Shapiros awoke in their comfortable house to an unusual sight. A small group of children in orderly picket lines on the Shapiros' well-manicured lawn carried signs saying "Shapiro is starving my Mama" and "I'm underfed because my Mama is underpaid." Surprised and moved, many of the Shapiros' neighbors brought the young picketers food, and several members of the Shapiros' synagogue reproached them. Finally the Shapiros agreed to meet with the union representatives. The cannery workers' success had hinged on a strategy of incorporating women workers as parts of entire kinship and friendship networks, rather than as isolated individuals. In that way, the union represented these women's own sense of themselves as whole people. Unlike many relief and welfare policies, it did not force them to choose between being workers or wives, daughters or mothers.

For women textile workers too, the boundary between "mother" and "worker" was fuzzy. By 1940 72 percent of the women workers in North Carolina's textile mills were married, up from less than half ten years earlier. To these women, having a working husband was no guarantee of security. Even if a man neither drank nor gambled away his earnings he could fall ill, and in this delicately balanced economy every cent was essential. One unemployed widow told the editor of the Greenville, North Carolina, *News* that she valued the security that came from knowing she herself was a good mill hand. What she and other women wanted was not a handout, but "a chance to earn our bread." Laid off for their inability to match the speedup of machinery or by reduced mill hours, these women wanted work, not welfare or charity.

In the South and West, some new unions attempted to organize across racial lines. Sometimes they tried more than they succeeded. When the Tobacco Workers International Union (TWIU) won a major strike in Durham, North Carolina, against Liggett & Myers in 1939, the union readily sacrificed black women workers to secure their contract. They allowed the company to mechanize the stemming department swiftly and to fire the large number of black women who worked there.

But some unions went in the other direction. The ILGWU had excluded black women from its Boston union as recently as 1933, and a victorious strike there had put black presser Mary Sweet out of work. However, a coalition of unions in New York City had created the Negro Labor Committee to advance the condition of black workers, and in 1934 the ILGWU asked Sweet to help them organize black women into the union. By the end of the year, ILGWU locals—not only in Boston but in New York, Chicago, and Philadelphia—included black women, and some had black officers. The union wage scale made some black garment workers among the best-paid women in Harlem, earning forty-five to fifty dollars for a thirty-five-hour week.

Still, the cavalier treatment of black women by many organizations dominated by white men and women contributed to the special allure of the Communist party for black women and men in the 1930s. The Communist party (CP), more than any other organization in the decade, outspokenly supported black civil rights. Even the NAACP recognized by mid-decade that it was losing its role as primary civil rights advocate to the CP. The CP also paid at least lip service to equality between men and women. In the South, it created organizations where whites and blacks worked together.

Members of the CP came from a variety of backgrounds. Mary Leonard, the widow of an Alabama druggist, had a solidly working-class background, but through her speaking abilities and her base of support among poor white house-wives she became a party leader. Jane Speed was more demure in appearance than Leonard. Born into a wealthy southern family and educated in Austria, where she and her mother picked up left-wing sympathies, she appeared refined and unthreatening. Among the African-American women in the party, Estelle Milner, daughter of an Alabama sharecropper, played a vital part as a young schoolteacher in linking black farmers to Communist leaders in Birmingham, Alabama. And Eula Gray, who at age nineteen in 1931 held together the Communist-aided interracial Sharecroppers' Union and spurred the organization of twenty-eight locals and twelve women's auxiliaries, came from a long line of black Alabama militants. Her great-grandfather had been a state legislator shortly after the Civil War. Her uncle Ralph, an independent farmer, was assassinated by white officials in 1931 for his role in organizing sharecroppers, and her father continued to risk his life for the same cause.

The women's auxiliaries met separately from the men in the Sharecroppers Union, both so that one parent could always stay home with the children and to divert the suspicions of local white authorities, who were hostile to this attempt on the part of sharecroppers to drive a better bargain. But the women involved them-selves as intimately as the men in the main business of the union. They read the Communist newspapers and kept up a correspondence that linked them to the national and international Communist movement. Like many neighborhood women who organized in the 1930s, they emphasized their need to feed and care for their families and their inability to do so under current conditions.

Perhaps the most telling protests of the decade, the ones that brought together the threads of women's roles, the New Deal, and worker relations, were the protests by WPA sewing project workers in 1939. In that year, Congress passed a relief appropriations act that cut WPA programs in half by revising eligibility requirements for WPA employment. Among other groups, the act barred workers who could receive Aid to Dependent Children (ADC). In Minneapolis, WPA officials dismissed nine hundred women workers in early 1939, assuming they were eligible for ADC. Even if these women had been eligible, they would first have had to have ADC interviews and then await processing before they would receive any money, and the process was delayed because other people had recently been transferred into the system. Moreover, even if these women had ultimately gotten ADC, after weeks or months of no income, ADC still paid less than the WPA's work relief.

Many of the remaining women working in the sewing project, who were the chief support of their families, viewed themselves as the prime targets of the policy. WPA cuts continued into the spring. In May, fifteen hundred WPA workers voted to take a one-day holiday to protest the cuts. They formulated demands for the reinstatement of laid-off workers and an increase in relief work budgets, and they planned a march for June 2. On that day, more than five thousand workers gathered in front of the Minneapolis WPA office. Yet on July 5 there were more layoffs and wage cuts. Workers on the Minneapolis state fairgrounds put down their tools and drove from one WPA project to the next, urging a general WPA strike. The next day, eight thousand Minneapolis workers stayed away from work, nearly closing all of the city's projects, and joining almost 125,000 relief workers on strike across the country.

After three days, the mayor of Minneapolis ordered police to go to the north Minneapolis sewing project, where fights began between women strikers and those women who continued to work. Despite a police escort through the strikers' lines, striking women harassed the non-strikers. Minnie Kohn organized a squad of women strikers who rushed the entering women workers and tore their clothes off. As one witness told the press, "It was quite a sight. The strike-breakers naked amidst the jeers of the strikers."

Even this tactic failed. On July 21 the WPA workers agreed to end the strike, having made no gains. Strikers who had missed more than five days of work were fired. At least 160 people, about one-third of them women, were brought to trial on felony charges of conspiracy to intimidate relief clients. Most of them had worked on the WPA project and were more than fifty years old. Some were self-supporting single women, and many others had families dependent on their WPA wage. Normally, they would have fit perfectly the image of crusading motherhood, as defenders of hearth and home. Instead, by taking matters into their own hands they threatened the New Deal image of women as helpless victims needing assistance.

At the trial, the attorneys and the press portrayed Kohn and her allies either as self-seeking individuals who had misled their followers (the prosecution's view) or as the victims not of job cuts but of jealous coworkers (the defense view). In neither case were they presented as working women defending their right to jobs because of their need to feed themselves and others. Minnie Kohn was sentenced to forty-five days in the workhouse. The self-expressions of militant women workers had not succeeded in altering the dominant stereotypes of women or the policies based on them.

The women who took part in these protests had refused to accept invisibility as their fate. They had taken matters into their own hands, including the matter of what it meant to be a woman struggling to survive in the 1930s. They rejected New Deal distinctions between women as workers and women as mothers, and they drew support from networks that related instead of separated neighborhood and workplace. These women met with many defeats, but they did enjoy some successes. Evictions were postponed. Wages were raised. And perhaps most important of all, women workers had made themselves seen and heard.

CHAPTER 9

Pushing the Limits

1940–1961

Elaine Tyler May

When the Japanese attacked the United States at Pearl Harbor in 1941, the country went to war, fighting Nazi aggression and genocide in Europe and Japanese expansion in Asia. Peace came in 1945, but it was a tense and fragile peace marked by what was called the Cold War between the two new superpowers, the United States and the Soviet Union, which lasted until the late 1980s.

As soon as the nation entered the war, the worst economic depression in the nation's history ended suddenly, to be followed by decades of prosperity with a booming economy. These were the years of the major demographic upheaval of the century: the Baby Boom. Marriage rates increased, men and women married younger, the divorce rate declined, the birth rate soared, and Americans streamed into rapidly expanding suburbs. Technological advances came rapidly. The United States dropped the first nuclear weapons on Hiroshima and Nagasaki at the end of World War II, unleashing the atomic age; television came to American homes in 1950; houses filled with appliances.

Mainstream politics dwindled to a call for unity and patriotism in defense of war and Cold War aims, but beneath the surface, artists, activists, and those excluded from the bland political mood of the Cold War consensus planted the seeds of massive social change. The civil rights movement took shape in the South and began the agitation that would transform race relations more profoundly than anything since the Civil War. It also laid the groundwork for other movements that would emerge later on behalf of women, farm workers, American Indians, gays and lesbians, and other groups seeking their rightful place as full American citizens.

American women were part of all these dramatic events and developments. They shaped them and were also affected by them. Some women had more choices than others, but they all took advantage of new opportunities and pushed against the constraints that remained. They were not watching from the sidelines; they were on the march. Often their choices were limited. These were not years of steady progress. Opportunities opened in some areas for some women, and shrank or closed for others. As a result, women developed creative strategies for their lives and sought to transform the institutions in which they lived and worked.

During these mid-century decades, individual opportunities were determined largely according to gender and race. Although there had already been decades of effort on behalf of the rights of women and people of color, equal opportunity was a long way off. In some ways, the postwar years actually represented backward steps on the path toward full equality. These were decades when racial and gender divisions became rigid, even though class divisions—especially between the prosperous working class and the comfortable middle class—softened.

Most of the changes involving American women in the early 1940s resulted from the wartime emergency. Emergency was nothing new to the young women and men coming of age, who had been reared on the trials and hardships of the Great Depression. Dreams for a better life—a good job for the man, a life as homemaker for the woman—were the goals of many depression-weary Americans. In these dreams lay the seeds of the postwar era, when men would try to provide for their families in ways that were so difficult for their fathers during the depression, and women would finally have the luxury to stay home with their children. But there were other legacies of the depression. The 1930s was a time not only of economic hardship and misery, but of tremendous energy and radicalism. Many believed that fundamental flaws in the American economic and political system were responsible for the crisis, and that the only cure would be a complete overhaul of the system. Those reform-minded citizens believed that recovery would be achieved not simply by returning to the ways of the past, but by changing the system.

Another legacy of the depression was the increased role of the government in private life. The New Deal did a great deal to ease the suffering of many during the depression, but it did nothing to eradicate poverty or solve the economic crisis. As late as 1941, 40 percent of all American families lived below the poverty level, and almost 8 million workers earned less than the legal minimum wage. The depression did not affect everyone in the same way, but it created a general state of crisis that altered daily life for millions of women and men.

One role that changed was the place of marriage in people's lives. The marriage rate had plummeted to an all-time low during the early 1930s, the birthrate had declined, and divorces had increased as families collapsed under financial strain. Many young single women took jobs to help support their parents and siblings. Employment offered an alternative to young marriage and economic dependence. One young woman was in no hurry to marry: "It's not that I didn't want to get married, but when you are working and have your own money . . ." she did not feel compelled. Many others of her generation made similar decisions. One explained, "During all the years I worked, I had a boyfriend, but we both had responsibilities at home. . . . Now they say 'career woman' but at the time you wouldn't call yourself that. It's just because you felt you had a responsibility at home, too." These women felt a sense of obligation to their parents, but they also took pride in their economic contributions. In spite of the discrimination women faced in the paid labor force, many achieved some measure of independence they were not so eager to give up to become dependent in someone else's home—especially with men's employment as precarious as it was. As a result, more than 6 million single women in the 1930s were making it on their own and contributing to the support of their parents' households.

The popular culture at the time, particularly movies and fan magazines, glamorized single working women and affirmed their active role in public life. Radio soap operas featured independent career women such as "Dr. Kate," "Hilda Hope, M.D.," and "Her Honor, Nancy James." Some of these programs continued into the war years, such as "Joyce Jordan, Girl Intern," which became "Joyce Jordan, M.D." four years later in 1942. "Ma Perkins," about operator of a lumber yard, began in 1933 and lasted twenty-seven years. Movies featured similar heroines. In *His Girl Friday*, a popular film of 1940, a feisty reporter who has just divorced her work-obsessed boss proves her grit by rescuing a hapless criminal and outwitting her male colleagues. Even though she agrees to marry again at the end of the movie, she has established herself as a smart and tough professional who can do a "man's job." It is not at all clear, however, that she will settle down into marital bliss. Similarly, Scarlett O'Hara, the shrewd heroine of the popular novel and film *Gone With the Wind*, survives hard times through her intelligence and determination, although in the end her marriage is in shambles. Hollywood encouraged the independence of women and the equality of the sexes but failed to portray families that included independent women. Rather, these tough and rugged heroines were admired as *women*, not as wives.

These ideas prevailed in the world beyond Hollywood as well. Even the most radical measures of the New Deal, created to ease hardship, failed to promote the possibility of a new family structure based on gender equality. The government provided relief for families in need, but not jobs for married women, and the New Deal also failed to remedy wage inequities. Men still earned much more than women, even if they held similar jobs. By ignoring the plight of working women, the government actually contributed to the deterioration of their economic status.

The depression opened the way for a new type of family with shared bread-winning and an economy based on equality of the sexes, but it also created the wish for a time when fathers alone could provide a decent living and mothers were freed from outside employment. In the end, that wish for separate roles for women and men won out over the potential for equality. If the paid labor force had been a more hospitable place, and if public policies had fostered equal opportunities for women, young people in the 1930s might have been less inclined to set their sights on becoming breadwinner-husbands and homemaker-wives. Realistic long-term job prospects for women might have prompted new ways of structuring the family and the economy. In the face of persistent obstacles, that potential withered. But when World War II brought a sudden end to the depression, bringing full employment and a booming economy, many of these obstacles would be removed.

World War II and the Chance for Change

World War II ushered in sudden, dramatic changes for American women. One young woman recalled the breathless excitement of life in wartime Chicago: "Chicago was just humming, no matter where I went. The bars were jammed, and unless you were an absolute dog, you could pick up anyone you wanted to.... There were servicemen of all varieties roaming the streets all the time. There was never, never a shortage of young, healthy bucks.... We never thought of getting tired. Two, three hours of sleep was normal.... I'd go down to the office every morning half dead, but with a smile on my face, and report in for work. There was another girl there who was having a ball too, and we took turns going into the back room and taking a nap on the floor behind a desk."

Work changed, too. When the men left to fight the war, women took jobs that had never been available to them in the past. Almira Bondelid recalls what happened when her husband left for overseas: "I decided to stay in San Diego and went to work in a dime store. That was a terrible place to work, and as soon as I could I got a job at Convair [an aircraft manufacturer].... I worked in the tool department as a draftsman, and by the time I left there two years later I was designing long drill jigs for parts of the wing and hull of B-24s."

With these new opportunities for work and play, women during the war glimpsed the possibility for long-term changes that might have led to full equality for women. But wartime needs caused a temporary crisis, and women's new activities were expected to last only "for the duration." Some changes turned out to be much more lasting, but the upheavals that brought sexual adventure to the single woman in Chicago and exciting new work to the wife in San Diego ended after the war.

When war broke out, women rapidly entered jobs in war-related industries. Many had been employed before the war, mostly in low-paying, nonunion jobs in laundries, department stores, restaurants, and hotels, where they earned an average of $24.50 a week, compared to $40.35 a week for wartime manufacturing jobs. During the war, 300,000 women worked in the aircraft industry alone. Many assembled B-29 bombers, the mainstay of the U.S. Air Force. Others—welders, draftswomen, and machinists—built tanks and warships and made ammunition. Women also worked in nondefense industries such as machine shops, steel mills, oil refineries, railroad roundhouses, and lumber mills. In all, women comprised half of this work force. The Office of War Information noted that war production work had "disproved the old bugaboo that women have no mechanical ability and that they are a distracting influence in industry."

Nevertheless, the nation remained uneasy about these new work roles for women. As large numbers of married women took jobs for the first time, many observers expressed alarm. *Fortune* magazine reported, "There are practically no unmarried women left to draw upon. . . . This leaves, as the next potential source of industrial workers, the housewives. . . . We are a kindly, somewhat sentimental people with strong, ingrained ideas about what women should or should not do. Many thoughtful citizens are seriously disturbed over the wisdom of bringing married women into the factories." Eventually, the stigma attached to employment for married women evaporated, and women were urged to work as a patriotic duty, in order to keep the war economy booming while the men went off to fight.

As women rushed eagerly to take challenging and well-paying defense jobs, recruiters did their best to claim that the work would not diminish their femininity. "Rosie the Riveter," a young woman in overalls working to build ships and planes, became a national symbol; pictures of attractive "Rosies" graced magazine covers and posters. Marilyn Monroe first gained attention when her photograph appeared in *Yank*, a magazine for servicemen. She was pictured not as the Hollywood sex goddess she would later become, but as a typical Rosie the Riveter, in overalls at her job in a defense plant. Employers and recruiters insisted that women's new jobs merely extended their domestic skills. Boeing Aircraft boasted of "pretty girls in smart slack outfits showing how easy it is to work on a wiring board." These women would remain glamorous, as one advertisement for cleaning noted in verse:

> Oh, aren't we cute and snappy
> in our cover-alls and slacks?
> And since the tags say 'Sanforized'
> we'll stay as cute as tacks!

Women faced constant reminders that they were different from the male workers they replaced. Even when viewed in the most positive light, their work appeared as a temporary interruption of their feminine routine. As *Life* magazine noted, "Girls are very serious about their chance to fly for the Army at Avenger Field, even when it means giving up nail polish, beauty parlors, and dates for a regimented $22^1/_2$ weeks. . . . They each have on the G.I. coveralls, called zoot suits in Avenger Field lingo, that are regulation uniform for all working hours. Though suits are not very glamorous, the girls like their comfort and freedom."

Dressed like men and doing traditional "men's work," these women were not treated like men. They earned less than men earned for the same work, and they often faced unwanted male attention. One female war worker complained, "At times it gets to be a pain in the neck when the man who is supposed to show you work stops showing it to you because you have nicely but firmly asked him to keep his hands on his own knees; or when you have refused a date with someone and

"Rosie the Riveter" had many roles: doing metalwork at the Marinship Corp. (top left), cleaning furnaces at a U.S. Steel factory (top right), and preparing machine screws to be dipped in a protective coating (bottom).

ever since then he has done everything in his power to make your work more difficult. . . . Somehow we'll have to make them understand that we are not very much
interested in their strapping virility. That the display of their physique and the lure
of their prowess leaves us cold. That although they have certainly convinced us that
they are men and we are women, we'd really rather get on with our work."

In spite of the harassment, teasing, and unwanted sexual advances women war
workers faced, they enjoyed their new jobs, and most wanted to keep them after the
war. Unlike the depression, the war emergency opened the way for a new labor
force that could no longer be divided into "men's jobs" and "women's jobs," but
would instead bring men and women into the same jobs, working side by side. In
addition, because so many men went into the armed forces, and so many women
went to work, young Americans might have postponed marriage and childbearing,
just as they had in the depression. But that did not happen. Instead, ironically,
wartime encouraged family formation. The return of prosperity made it easier for
young men and women to marry and have children.

Young married women, those most likely to have children at home, made the
smallest gains in the labor force; young mothers were encouraged to stay home.
Although the Federal Works Agency invested nearly $50 million in day care centers
to accommodate employed mothers during the war, such centers were generally
considered harmful to a child's development. In all, only three thousand day care
centers were established by the federal government, and even these were not filled
to capacity.

Older married women who did not have young children at home were the
fastest-growing group in the paid labor force. By the end of the war fully 25 percent of all married women were employed—a huge gain from 15 percent at the end
of the 1930s. But they worked for low wages. In 1939, the median annual income
for women was $568, compared to $962 for men—and for black women it was a
mere $246. By 1940 women comprised less than 10 percent of union members,
although they were 25 percent of the workers.

Because women were still clustered in lower-skilled, lower-paying jobs, they had
few bargaining levers to use to improve their working conditions. Relatively few
held jobs like Rosie the Riveter. Most held the kinds of jobs women had always
been able to get. If they worked in factories, their jobs were the lowest skilled and
lowest paid. If they worked in white-collar jobs, they were most likely to be secretaries, clerks, and saleswomen. Or they worked in "pink-collar" service occupations
such as waitressing or hairdressing. In spite of these limitations, women took
advantage of wartime opportunities to earn better wages and enter new occupations. Even for women of color, who were usually given the least desirable and most
menial jobs, often as cleaning women or chambermaids, the war offered the possibility of improved conditions.

American Indian women, for example, found new opportunities for work as
well as political activism. World War II had a profound and lasting effect on the

Menominee women working for the tribal lumber industry clear diseased plants from timberlands.

lives of American Indians. As men left the reservations to join the armed services or to take jobs in the cities, women moved into areas of activity previously closed to them. Along with male enlistees, eight hundred Native American women joined the armed forces. Hundreds of others went to work in West Coast aircraft industries, where they worked along with white women as riveters, inspectors, and machinists. Approximately twelve thousand Indian women left the reservations for war-related work.

Native American women assumed new leadership positions on as well and off the reservations. Many became teachers in Indian schools, while others took over farming chores that in some tribal communities had become men's work in the prewar years. In many communities, the war loosened traditional work roles for men and women. Several Navajo women, for example, mastered traditionally male crafts such as silversmithing. In Wisconsin, Indian women began working in the lumber mills on the Menominee reservation for the first time. Indian women as well as men went back and forth from cities to reservations during the war, establishing ties to urban communities that would grow after the war.

Wartime also broke down traditional tribal boundaries for many Indians. The National Congress of American Indians (NCAI) was founded in 1944 to work on behalf of Indian people of all tribes, and women were central participants. Ruth Muskrat Bronson, an Oklahoma Cherokee and Mount Holyoke College graduate, became volunteer executive secretary and opened an office in Washington D.C., where she embarked on an energetic public relations campaign. A year later, at the second national convention of the NCAI, the delegates adopted a policy to elect at least one woman to the executive council each year. The war sparked a new militancy among American Indian activists. As Robert Yellowtail, a member of the NCAI council, wrote after the war, "What did 30,000 Indian soldiers fight for in the recent war? Surely it was for liberty and freedom of the American kind."

Those words resonated among African Americans as well, many of whom fought courageously in the war. The fight against fascism abroad brought home painfully the need to overcome racism at home. Membership in the National Association for the Advancement of Colored People (NAACP) rose dramatically during the war, and the Congress of Racial Equality (CORE) was founded in 1943. Although it would be another decade before the civil rights movement captured the attention of the entire nation, the struggle for racial equality continued throughout the war. Foreshadowing the courageous acts of civil disobedience that would later become the hallmark of the movement, during the war a black army nurse in Alabama brazenly boarded a bus in front of white passengers, and was beaten and jailed as a result.

African Americans joined the armed services as well as the ranks of industrial workers during the war, contributing to the war effort in important ways. But wherever they went, they faced racist policies, segregation, harassment, poor pay, and the worst jobs. Although wartime offered some improvement for impoverished blacks, the system of segregation prevented them from reaping the same benefits as their white counterparts. The reality of wartime left many blacks feeling bitter.

African Americans learned that they would have to fight for their own rights. As early as 1940, at a civil rights convention in Chicago, a black woman delegate suggested, "We ought to throw fifty thousand Negroes around the White House, bring them from all over the country, in jalopies, in trains and any way they can get there . . . until we get some action from the White House." She was calling for integration of the defense industries, where blacks were segregated into the worst jobs with the lowest pay. The very threat of such a demonstration proved to be effective: President Roosevelt issued Executive Order 8802, which outlawed discriminatory hiring practices by defense contractors and established the Committee on Fair Employment Practices.

More than half a million African Americans migrated out of the rural South during the war to work in defense industries. Racial tensions worsened as competition for jobs and housing between blacks and whites exploded in urban riots in New York City, Detroit, and other cities. Even in the armed services, where black men served just as willingly and courageously as white men, blacks were subjected to verbal and physical attacks by their white counterparts. Nevertheless, the armed forces, like the war industries, provided steady income throughout the war.

Women were among the thousands of African Americans who migrated to northern cities during the war. Lillian Hatcher was one of the first black women to be hired above the service level in the Detroit auto industry, and her new job in the factory paid her twice what she was earning previously as a cafeteria worker. She later recalled, "I was working not for patriotic reasons, I was working for the money. The ninety-seven cents an hour was the greatest salary that I had earned." African Americans had to fight for the jobs they wanted. Poet Maya Angelou became the first black streetcar conductor in San Francisco during the war, but not without a struggle. She made herself a promise that "made my veins stand out, and my mouth tighten into a prune: I WOULD HAVE THE JOB. I WOULD BE A CONDUCTORETTE AND SLING A FULL MONEY CHANGER FROM MY BELT. I WOULD." And she did.

Many were not as fortunate as Angelou. Black women in wartime industries were given the most dangerous jobs in the factories. In airplane assembly plants, black women worked in the "dope rooms" filled with poisonous fumes of glue, while white women were in the well-ventilated sewing rooms. In every industry, the lowest paying, most difficult, most dangerous, hottest, and most uncomfortable jobs went to black women—and they often worked the night shifts. Sarah Killingsworth, an African-American woman working in a Los Angeles defense plant, came from Tennessee, where she made $2.50 a week. In her new job, she earned $40 a week, even though she had the most menial of jobs: tending the ladies' rest room during the night shift. But she did not find the work itself oppressive. Rather, she saw it as a way to help other women workers. "I would give them a No-Doz so they could stay awake all night," Killingsworth recalled. "This was the graveyard shift. Some of 'em had been out drinkin', and we would let them take a nap for about fifteen minutes. We would watch out for them, so their supervisor wouldn't miss 'em. We put the sign out: Closed. We'd wake 'em up, and sometimes they'd give us tips. They would give me fifty cents for a tablet or a cup of coffee, so they could stay awake." Overall, she believed the war benefited black people. "They didn't mix the white and black in the war. But now it gives you a kind of independence because they felt that we gone off and fought, we should be equal. Everything started openin' up for us. We got a chance to go places we had never been able to go before."

New opportunities emerged for African-American women in the growing black communities as well. In Richmond, California, for example, black migration contributed to the transformation of a small town into a bustling metropolis. Before the war, there were only 270 blacks in Richmond. But when the city became a war production center, African Americans from the South came there to work in the shipyards. By 1943 the black population had increased by 5,000 percent. Slightly more than half of the southern black migrants to Richmond during the war were women. The presence of blacks was apparent not only in the factories, but in the social and cultural life of the city, most notably in the blues clubs that began to proliferate. Many of these clubs were owned and operated by African-American women from Arkansas. One such female entrepreneur was Margaret Starks, manager of Tappers Inn, the most popular club in North Richmond. Starks also served as a talent booking agent for a number of local clubs and published the city's first black newspaper on the premises of the Tappers Inn. Starks's business acumen fed into her political activities, and she served as the secretary of the Richmond branch of the NAACP during the war years. Along with the newspaper, she also located the NAACP offices in a room at Tappers. "Everybody would know where to find me if they needed any [business] done," she said, explaining the various activities she ran out of the inn. Women like Margaret Starks, and the blues club scene they helped to create, provided an arena where African-American people exerted some power over their lives and developed community institutions. In spite of the city's official discrimination and segregation policies, within the African-American community blacks could organize politically and form networks for their own social and economic needs.

Like African Americans and Native Americans, Mexicans and Mexican Americans had long been isolated from mainstream American society and segregated into menial jobs. Mexican women in the Southwest were overwhelmingly segregated in garment and food-processing firms. During World War II, however, women took advantage of the wartime demand for their labor to advance their interests. The activism of women working at the California Sanitary Canning Company provides one dramatic example. Energetic labor organizers like Luisa Moreno and Dorothy Ray Healy built a powerful union of women workers who were able to achieve a wage increase and recognition of their union. Family and community networks helped support and strengthen the union. Although their union could not be sustained after the war in the face of mounting opposition by anti-Communist crusaders, the successes of this union during the war demonstrate how much control these women were able to achieve over their work lives.

Seventy-five percent of all workers in the California canneries were women. Because women formed the majority, their segregation from male employees allowed women to work in the plants in an atmosphere of little interference from men. In other industries where men were in the majority, however, the segregation of women was a disadvantage. Automobile manufacturing, for example, remained male dominated. Before the war, women accounted for only 10 percent of all auto workers, where they were concentrated in a relatively small number of jobs. After an initial shutdown, the industry retooled for war production. When the plant doors reopened in 1942, male workers were in short supply and women were hired in unprecedented numbers. By the end of 1943, a fourth of the industry's workers were female. Throughout the war, the automobile industry maintained women in certain jobs and men in others. Despite the dramatic upswing in women's participation in the work force, unions had not developed strategies that included a place for women's concerns in their negotiations with the companies, nor had a strong feminist movement come together to assert women's needs, such as child care and equal access to good jobs. As a result, gender division of labor survived the war.

Despite women's dramatic contributions to the war effort, they were not able to achieve equal pay or working conditions. Unequal treatment led to a campaign for equal rights. The Republicans in 1940 and the Democrats in 1944 supported the Equal Rights Amendment (ERA), but the two major union federations, the American Federation of Labor (AFL) and the Congress of Industrial Organizations (CIO), opposed it. Even Secretary of Labor Frances Perkins and First Lady Eleanor Roosevelt, two activists on behalf of women's rights, refused to support the legislation because they feared that women workers would lose legal protections against long hours and health hazards. In 1945, Congress considered a bill that would have required equal pay for women. But even with a fair amount of bipartisan support and some union backing, that measure failed. When the ERA finally reached the Senate in 1946, it received less than the two-thirds majority necessary to pass, although a majority of senators voted for it.

These measures met defeat in large part because women's war work was expected to end. The War Manpower Commission assumed that "the separation of women from industry should flow in an orderly plan." Frederick Crawford, head of the National Association of Manufacturers, found a point of agreement with his usual adversaries, the union leaders, when he said, "From a humanitarian point of view, too many women should not stay in the labor force. The home is the basic American institution." Many women rejected this notion. As one argued, "War jobs have uncovered unsuspected abilities in American women. Why lose all these abilities because of a belief that 'a woman's place is in the home'? For some it is, for others not." But her words would be drowned in a sea of voices calling upon women to prepare to assume their places in the kitchens and bedrooms of returning servicemen.

Winding Down

During the war, as women streamed into the paid labor force, some observers feared that women might not be willing to settle down into family life once the emergency ended. Single women now became targets of campaigns that would continue after the war, urging women back into their domestic roles.

Single women also caused alarm because of their perceived or potential sexual activity. A typical wartime pamphlet warned, "The war in general has given women new status, new recognition. . . . Women are 'coming into their own' in this war. . . .

Yet it is essential that women avoid arrogance and retain their femininity in the face of their own new status. ... In her new independence she must not lose her humanness as a woman. She may be the woman of the moment, but she must watch her moments."

This theme echoed throughout the war. One college textbook for family life courses, *Marriage and the Family* (1940), explained why women had to watch their moments so carefully: "[T]he greater social freedom of women has more or less inevitably led to a greater degree of sexual laxity, a freedom which strikes at the heart of family stability. ... When women work, earn, and spend as much as men do, they are going to ask for equal rights with men. But the right to behave like a man meant [sic] also the right to misbehave as he does. The decay of established moralities came about as a by-product." The authors of the textbook state as if it were a scientific formula their opinion that social freedom and employment for women would cause "sexual laxity," moral decay, and the destruction of the family.

Writers like these urged women to stay "pure" for the soon-to-be-returning veterans. At the same time, they warned soldiers to avoid sexual contact with women who hung around army bases to prevent catching venereal diseases from them. Wartime purity crusades marked a revision of the germ theory: Germs were not responsible for spreading disease; "promiscuous" women were. Widely distributed posters warned that even the angelic "girl next door" might carry disease. "She may look clean, but ... ," read one caption next to a picture of everybody's sweetheart. Wartime ushered in an anxious preoccupation with all forms of nonmarital sexuality, from concern about prostitution to fierce campaigns against homosexuals and other so-called "deviants" in military as well as civilian life.

Although the alarmists' fears were exaggerated, it was true that wartime opened up new possibilities for sexual experimentation. More young people moved into cities and away from neighborhood and parental supervision. Many now earned their own money and took charge of their own leisure time and behavior. For many young women experiencing this new independence, men in uniform held special appeal. "When I was sixteen," recalled a college student a few years later, "I let a sailor pick me up and go all the way with me. I had intercourse with him partly because he had a strong personal appeal for me, but mainly because I had a feeling of high adventure and because I wanted to please a member of the armed forces." With so many girls in this adventurous spirit, one teenage boy described wartime as "a real sex paradise. The plant and the town were just full of working girls who were on the make. Where I was, a male war worker became the center of loose morality."

Wartime changes in women's behavior aroused concern. Nowhere was this ambivalence more obvious than in the military itself. In a major change from the past, women entered every part of military service except combat. One thousand civilian female pilots joined the Women's Airforce Service Pilots (WASP), 140,000 women joined the Women's Army Corps (WAC), 100,000 entered the navy as WAVES (Women Accepted for Voluntary Emergency Service), and others enlisted with the marines and coast guard. A few were physicians, and many were nurses. Although a small number of women held dramatic and highly publicized positions in formerly all-male areas such as aviation, most served in administrative, clerical, and communications jobs. Occupations in the military reflected the gender-based divisions in the civilian labor force.

Nevertheless, the military made great efforts to recruit women during the war. Oveta Culp Hobby, director of the Women's Army Corps, proclaimed women "are carrying on the glorious tradition of American womanhood. They are making history! ... This is a war which recognizes no distinctions between men and women." To the female Americans she hoped to recruit, she said, "This is YOUR war." Women of "excellent character" who could pass an intelligence test could join the WACs, provided they had no children under the age of 14. Healthy, unmarried women with no dependents under the age of eighteen could enlist in the WAVES. A WAVE who married might remain in the service, if she had finished basic training and as long as her husband was not in the service. The birth of a child brought an "honorable discharge."

Although the armed forces offered women alternatives to full-time home-making, it was virtually impossible to combine a job in the military with family life. Nevertheless, the armed services presented the image of the female recruit as very "feminine" and domestically inclined. Every effort was made to dispel prevailing notions that military work would make women "masculine" or ruin their moral character. A guidebook for women in the armed services and war industries, for example, included a photograph of a young WAVE with a caption that described her as "pretty as her picture ... in the trim uniform that enlisted U.S. Navy Waves will wear in winter ... smartly-styled, comfortable uniforms ... with a soft rolled-brim hat." Women in the military were needed for their "delicate hands" and "precision work at which women are so adept," and in hospitals where "there is a need in a man for comfort and attention that only a woman can fill." Women's corps leaders did little to challenge these images; they assured the public that after the war enlisted women would be "as likely as other women to make marriage their profession."

These publicity measures met with only partial success amid public sentiment suspicious of women in nontraditional roles. In fact, rumors about the supposedly promiscuous sexual behavior and scandalous drunkenness of female recruits were so widespread that the armed forces had to refute the charges publicly. One result was to make into policy the sexual double standard in the military: Men were routinely supplied with contraceptives (mainly to prevent the spread of venereal disease), but women were denied access to birth control devices. In the rare cases in which sexual transgressions were discovered, women were punished more severely than men.

Lesbianism was another reality of wartime that the military took pains to suppress. But the military was an ideal place for lesbian relationships to flourish. Phillis Abry quit her job as a lab technician to join the WACs because she "wanted to be with all those women." Homosexuality was not allowed in the military, of course, but lesbians were not easily identified. "I remember being very nervous about them asking me if I had any homosexual feelings or attitudes," she recalled. "I just smiled and was sweet and feminine."

At the same time that women's war work was given a domestic aura, domestic tasks gained new patriotic purpose. Millions of women were involved in volunteer work during the war, and much of it involved traditional skills such as canning, saving cooking fats, and making household goods last longer. Much as homemakers in the depression recognized the importance of their domestic skills for the survival of their families during the economic emergency, so the homemakers of the war years saw their work as contributing to the success of the war emergency

Still, traditional marriage was not only expected for women, it was one of the primary reasons given for fighting the war. The walls of barracks were decorated with "pinups," photographs of women in alluring poses reminding the men why they were fighting. Movie star Betty Grable was the most popular pinup, not because she was the most sexy and glamorous, but because she had a rather wholesome look. Grable came to represent the girl back home and the "American Way of Life" that inspired the men to fight. As one soldier wrote in a letter to Grable, "There we were out in those damn dirty trenches. Machine guns firing. Bombs dropping all around us. We would be exhausted, frightened, confused, and sometimes hopeless about our situation. When suddenly someone would pull your picture out of his wallet. Or we'd see a decal of you on a plane and then we'd know what we were fighting for."

Grable became even more popular when she married band leader Harry James in 1943 and had a child later that year; it reinforced her image as everyone's sweetheart, future wife, and mother. In order to be worthy of similar adoration, women sent their husbands and sweethearts photos of themselves in "pinup" poses. Betty Grable herself encouraged women to send their men photos of themselves in swimsuits, to inspire them to fight on and come home to an erotically charged marriage. Men at war were encouraged to fantasize about sex that awaited them when they returned—not with the "victory girls" who hung around bases, but with their wives. In the words of one soldier, "We are not only fighting for the Four Freedoms, we are fighting also for the priceless privilege of making love to American women."

Popular culture was filled with many such messages. One example, produced under government sponsorship, was a series of programs aired on all major radio networks in 1942 in an effort to mobilize support for the war. One highly acclaimed segment, "To The Young," included this exhortation:

The crucial wedding scene in the popular 1940 feature *This Is the Army,* starring Ronald Reagan. The movie's theme reinforced the ideal of home and family during wartime.

Young Male Voice: "That's one of the things this war's about."
Young Female Voice: "About us?"
Young Male Voice: "About *all* young people like us. About love and gettin' hitched, and havin' a home and some kids, and breathin' fresh air out in the suburbs . . . about livin' an' workin' *decent,* like free people."

Americans conformed to this expectation. Women entered war production, but they did not give up on reproduction. The war brought a dramatic reversal in patterns of family formation of the 1930s. The depression was marked by delayed marriages and declining marriage and birthrates, yet more than 1 million more families formed between 1940 and 1943 than would have been expected during normal times. The marriage rate was spurred by the draft deferment for married men in the early war years, and also by the imminence of departure for foreign shores. During the war the birthrate also jumped, from 19.4 to 24.5 births per 1,000 population. The 1944 government-sponsored war propaganda film *This Is the Army,* starring Ronald Reagan, was the most successful film of the war years. In this film, the men are center stage as they finish the job their fathers began in World

War I. The plot revolves around the efforts of the central character's sweetheart to persuade her reluctant soldier to marry her. Finally she succeeds, and the duo wed just before the hero leaves to fight overseas.

In spite of all the limitations, women took advantage of every new opportunity available to them. Perhaps the most dramatic example of this resourcefulness can be seen in the experiences of Japanese-American women during World War II. More than any other group of American citizens, Japanese Americans suffered during the war. Following the bombing of Pearl Harbor on December 7, 1941, the United States and Japan were at war. Immediately, a wave of suspicion and hostility toward Japanese and Japanese-Americans surfaced, especially on the West Coast, where their presence was considered a threat to national security. On February 19, 1942, President Franklin Roosevelt signed Executive Order 9066, which suspended the civil rights of American citizens of Japanese descent by authorizing the removal of 110,000 Japanese and their American-born children from western states.

Families were given one week's notice to evacuate their homes and move to assembly centers, fourteen hastily constructed, prisonlike compounds in California, Oregon, and Washington. Many citizens lived in these camps for the duration of the war. Some left in order to serve in the armed forces, attend college, work nearby, or relocate to the East. All were profoundly affected by the disruptions in their lives and the hardships they faced in the camps. As one woman wrote from a camp in 1942, "The life here cannot be expressed. Sometimes, we are resigned to it, but when we see the barbed wire fences and the sentry tower with floodlights, it gives us a feeling of being prisoners in a 'concentration camp.' We try to be happy and yet oftentimes a gloominess does creep in.... I just wonder if all the sacrifices and hard labor on [the] part of our parents has gone up to leave nothing to show for it?"

In spite of hardships and humiliations, the loss of liberty, privacy, and comforts, Japanese-American women made the best of the situation, and even managed to gain some benefits from it. The intimacy of the camps posed a challenge to formal patterns of arranged marriage, and young women asserted more freedom of choice to date and marry whomever they wished. Because most people had access to a wide range of jobs in the camps, young women were able to experiment with a variety of occupations, ranging from mess-hall work to accounting to optometry. Many took advantage of opportunities to go to college.

World War II opened up new opportunities for women, but it also imposed many constraints. The war extended the state of crisis that characterized the depression and disrupted expectations for women and men. Yet many women liked the new freedom they gained during the war, the challenging, well-paying jobs, and the chance to demonstrate their abilities. As the *New York Times Magazine* noted near the end of the war: "Alma goes to work because she wants to go to work. She

A young mother wheels her baby along a makeshift sidewalk in a veterans' trailer park in Charlottesville, Virginia (top). Many returning soldiers and their wives began their postwar lives in veterans' housing assembled from surplus Quonset huts reminiscent of their service barracks (bottom).

wants to go now and she wants to keep going when the war is over. Alma's had a taste of LIFE. She's poked her head out into the one-man's world. . . . Of course, all the Almas haven't thought through why they want to work after the war or how it's going to be possible. But they have gone far enough to know that they can do whatever is required in a machine shop. They've had the pleasure of feeling money in their pockets—money they've earned themselves."

But Alma was in for a rude awakening after the war. She was unlikely to be able to keep that job. Although the vast majority of women who worked for wages during the war wanted to keep their jobs, many lost their wartime positions to the returning veterans. Men and women alike were expected to relinquish their emergency roles and settle into domestic life—men as breadwinners, women as homemakers. In this vision, there was no room for the independent single woman, nor the married career woman. After the war, all the major institutions in which Americans lived and worked came to foster the vision of a nation finding its ultimate security in the traditional American home.

The Nuclear Family in the Nuclear Age

In the summer of 1959, a young couple married and spent their honeymoon in a bomb shelter. *Life* magazine featured the peculiar adventure and quipped that "fallout can be fun." Although the "sheltered honeymoon" was little more than a publicity stunt, it serves as an eerie symbol of the nuclear family in the nuclear age. The young couple, surrounded by consumer goods, spent two weeks in total isolation, protected from the world by the thick concrete walls of a twenty-two-ton steel and concrete box, twelve feet underground. In many ways, the shelter represents the family itself: sealed off from the dangers of the world.

As soon as World War II ended in 1945, the Cold War began. The United States had dropped two nuclear bombs on Japanese cities, ushering in the Atomic Age. The cloud created by those massive explosions lingered in the world's consciousness for decades. Within a few years, the Soviet Union exploded its first atomic bomb, and the arms race between the two superpowers began in earnest. Elsewhere in the world the Chinese revolution overturned a government friendly to the United States and replaced it with a Communist regime. This was quickly followed by Communist North Korea's invasion of South Korea. At home, a fierce crusade against communism led to mass hysteria in which almost anyone who dared to criticize the U.S. government might be labeled a subversive. The peace Americans welcomed after 1945 was a fragile one at best.

The woman in the "sheltered honeymoon" was a far cry from "Rosie the Riveter." Gone was the popular wartime icon in her goggles and overalls using heavy equipment to put together a battleship. For American women, the end of the war brought nearly as many changes as wartime itself. Many had to leave their well-paying wartime jobs to make room for the returning veterans. Nearly all the "Rosies" who had riveted had to find something else to do. A number of women continued to work in the postwar years, often in occupations that did not pay as well. But whether employed or not, nearly all women, and nearly all men, caught the family fever.

During the years after World War II, Americans were more eager than ever to establish families. The family became the ultimate symbol of security for Americans tired of depression and war. As world tensions loomed while the United States and the Soviet Union viewed each other with suspicion and hostility, families could feel safe inside the walls of their houses. They could also feel economically secure with the stable salaries male breadwinners were able to earn in the booming postwar economy. The bomb-shelter honeymooners were part of a generation who lowered the age at marriage for both men and women and quickly brought the birthrate to a twentieth-century high after more than a hundred years of steady decline, producing the famous "Baby Boom" that lasted for two decades.

The divorce rate also declined, after a postwar peak in 1946 (caused, no doubt, by the dissolution of hasty wartime marriages). This peculiar pattern of young marriage, high birthrate, and low divorce was one of the most striking features of the postwar years. It ended as abruptly as it began, lasting only until the Baby Boom children came of age. By the late 1960s, the nation had returned to long-term trends: lower birthrates and higher divorce rates. The 1940s and 1950s stand out as a unique twenty-year era of domesticity. The Baby Boom affected nearly everyone. Although there were deep divisions in society, particularly along racial lines, when it came to having babies, everyone was doing it. If we divide the population according to economic class, religion, racial identification, or any other category, we find that among all groups the birthrate rose in the 1940s and '50s and then declined in the 1960s. The Baby Boom was a statistical indicator of the intense focus on family life that permeated the nation in the years after World War II.

The rush into family life was accompanied by a powerful belief in the idea of "togetherness." *McCall's* magazine celebrated this family ethic in 1954 when it proclaimed to its white middle-class readers that women were marrying younger, raising larger families, and living in affluent homes: "But the most impressive and the most heartening feature of this change is that men, women, and children are achieving it together. They are creating this new and warmer way of life not as women alone or men alone, isolated from one another, but as a family sharing a common experience."

This powerful commitment to family was accompanied by a widely held belief that men should be the wage earners for their families, and women should tend to the home and children. Women of all racial, ethnic, and class backgrounds faced intense pressure to become wives and mothers after the war, and to make homemaking their primary career. Agnes Meyer expressed these sentiments in 1950 when she wrote in the *Atlantic Monthly*, "What modern woman has to recapture is

An Ohio steelworker and his family in a typical postwar housing project. In return for scarce housing, the original residents pledged three thousand hours of labor apiece to help build additional units.

the wisdom that just being a woman is her central task and greatest honor. . . . Women must boldly announce that no job is more exacting, more necessary, or more rewarding than that of housewife and mother."

But working women were not eager to leave the labor force. Four out of five women who worked during the war hoped to keep working after the war, including 69 percent of working wives.

Although more than 3 million women left their wartime jobs, most were rehired into other occupations. By 1947, there were more women in the paid labor force than there had been during the war, and more working wives than ever before. Somehow, home life would have to respond to the increasing number of employed married women. The policies of the government, private sector employers, and even labor unions, however, made it difficult for women to avoid economic dependence on their husbands or their fathers even if they continued to hold jobs. Although it was still possible for most women who wanted a job to find one, these jobs rarely paid well. Women's average weekly pay declined from fifty dollars to thirty-seven dollars, a drop of 26 percent, more than five times the postwar decrease for men. Three quarters of the women who had jobs in war industries were still employed after the war, but 90 percent of them were earning less than they had during the war.

Women also left the military. Public opinion was no longer so willing to tolerate "unfeminine" military occupations for women now that the war was over. Female veterans faced particular hardships. Fewer than half were able to find jobs that made use of the skills they learned during the war, and they were not eligible for many of the important veterans' benefits available to their male counterparts, such as homeowner's loans.

In spite of the huge numbers of women in the paid labor force, female employees found it difficult to combine the responsibilities of a family with a job outside the home. The few child care facilities that the federal government had established during the war closed, and mothers of small children faced even more intense pressures to stay home. As younger women left the paid labor force in order to have babies, they made room for older women whose children were in school. It was not unusual for women to take jobs after their children were grown. Since most women married young and had their children during their early twenties, they were in their mid-thirties when their youngest child entered school. With the life span increasing, many women could look forward to decades of active life when their primary childrearing duties were over. Since very few highly skilled, well-paying, or professional positions were available, most of these women took jobs as secretaries, clerks, saleswomen, and waitresses in the "pink-collar ghetto," poorly paying service jobs held almost exclusively by women. As a result of these expanding job opportunities, the number of employed women continued to rise after the war, even though the range of employment available to them narrowed.

Black women were hit especially hard by the changes in the female labor force. Although they experienced a slight overall gain, their income was still less than half that of white women at the end of the 1940s. The racism they faced felt especially bitter after all they had sacrificed for the country. In 1945, Maya Angelou noted with sadness that former black war heroes were now "hanging on the ghetto corners like forgotten laundry left on a back yard fence ... Thus we lived through a major war. The question in the ghettos was, Can we make it through a minor peace?"

Although wartime brought both black and white women into the paid labor force in record numbers, jobs remained divided according to race. By 1950, 60 percent of all employed black women still worked as maids in private homes or as service workers in institutions, compared with only 16 percent of white working women. In contrast, 40 percent of employed white women held clerical jobs as secretaries, clerks, and saleswomen, compared with only 5 percent of black women.

Black women and white women faced very different choices after the war. White women might decide to forgo paid employment and marry a man with a well-paying job, taking on the role of full-time homemaker and mother in a comfortable suburban home. Black women did not have that choice. Excluded from the suburbs, married to men who faced poorly paid jobs and few chances for advancement, they had to develop different strategies. As one black woman explained, after the war their families were "crammed on top of each other—jammed and packed and forced into the smallest possible space." As they had before as well as during the war, black women continued to seek whatever employment they could get.

For many white women, the need for extra household income made it acceptable to take jobs they enjoyed and gain a respite from household tasks. Married women's wages helped purchase the appliances, automobiles, and other consumer goods that became available in the expanding postwar economy. By 1960, 10 million wives were employed—triple the number in 1940—but fewer than half of them worked full time. Most of their positions were jobs, not careers. In spite of the return to prosperity, there were proportionately fewer women in professions than there had been in 1930.

According to polls taken at the time, half of employed women claimed to be working "to buy something," and only one fifth admitted to "a need for accomplishment." These women were supposed to be working to benefit their families, not themselves. If they said they enjoyed their jobs, they might have appeared selfish. At the same time, many women faced the stress of "double duty," coming home from work to face household responsibilities. Nevertheless, 60 percent said that they found self-esteem in their jobs. For young married women with children at home, the strain of holding a job may not have been worth the meager rewards. But for older married women, a job was an acceptable alternative to full-time homemaking and contributed to the family income as well.

Shrinking job opportunities for women after the war reflected more than efforts to keep women "in their place." Just as important was the need to preserve a place for men. The economic depression of the 1930s had barely lifted before men who were in the prime of their working lives were again wrenched from their jobs. Many of the more than 16 million men who served in the armed forces during the war wondered if they would be unemployed when they returned. Wartime surveys revealed deep fears about postwar life: seven out of ten Americans expected to be worse off after the war, six out of ten anticipated lower wages, and three fourths believed there would be fewer jobs. Many business leaders expected a major depression with high unemployment within a decade. *Fortune* magazine summed it up: "The American soldier is depression conscious . . . worried sick about postwar joblessness."

Although the economy turned out to be much healthier than these pessimistic wartime predictions, returning veterans nevertheless faced many difficulties. Thousands were unemployed in the immediate postwar years, costing the government $2.5 billion in unemployment benefits. There was also a severe housing shortage, forcing many families to double up in cramped quarters. Along with these difficulties were the physical and psychic scars of war. More than half of the veterans who saw social workers for counseling were treated for psychological distress caused by their combat experiences.

Under these circumstances, few begrudged the advantages given to former servicemen, who were considered the nation's heroes. They received housing loans, educational benefits, and medical care. Most of the veterans' benefits were geared toward men, not to women who had served in the armed services. Female veterans, like their civilian sisters, were expected to become wives and mothers after the war, not to compete with men for jobs and training programs. As one marriage counselor put it in a statement addressed to wives and future brides of returning servicemen: "Let him know you now want him to take charge."

The generous benefits available to returning veterans became known as the GI Bill of Rights, or simply the GI Bill. (GI was an abbreviation for "government issue," and was often used to refer to soldiers.) Among its noteworthy features were educational benefits. Nearly half of all veterans, more than 6 million men, flooded into colleges, universities, and other training programs. By 1947, nearly half of all college students were veterans. College enrollments also increased for women during the postwar years, but not at the same rate as for men.

Although more women were enrolled than before, they represented a smaller percentage of the student population. Women had made up 47 percent of college students in 1920; by 1958 they were only 35 percent of the total, and they earned fewer degrees. During the war years, some barriers to women were removed. Harvard Medical School, for example, finally admitted women for the first time in 1945. But as professional opportunities for women shrank, so did the number of advanced degrees they earned. College and professional degrees did not guarantee the same entry into well-paying jobs and careers for women as they did for men. As a result, more than half of all women college students dropped out to marry and become housewives or to support husbands through school. Jokes reflected this trend: Women were said to be pursuing an "MRS. degree," since so many met their future husbands in college, or to be earning their "Ph.T.," for Putting Hubby Through by holding jobs while their husbands completed college. It was expected that a college-educated man could get a better job than a college-educated woman, and would be able to support his family after graduation.

One study showed that young women in an all-white sample were twice as likely to enter college as their mothers had been, but were much less likely to complete their degrees. Instead, they were much more likely to marry highly educated men. Only 37 percent of women college students completed their degrees. It is not likely that the women who dropped out of school did so because they were unable to handle the rigors of academic life. Nor did they simply give up. Rather, they were following the advice of many of their teachers, and considering their opportunities for the future. In 1949, the noted sociologist Talcott Parsons told his students at Radcliffe College that "the woman's fundamental status is that of her husband's wife, the mother of his children." Many undoubtedly took such advice to heart. According to one white woman who graduated from Radcliffe in 1951 and went on to become the wife of a college dean, "We married what we wanted to *be*. If we wanted to be a lawyer or a doctor we married one." In other words, college enabled these white women to find and marry men who had good occupational prospects.

In 1956, presidential candidate Adlai Stevenson spoke to Smith College graduates at their commencement ceremonies, urging them to take up the banner of domesticity with pride: "Once they wrote poetry. Now it's the laundry list. Once they discussed art and philosophy until late in the night. Now they are so tired they fall asleep as soon as the dishes are finished." But "women in the home [can] have an important political influence on man and boy . . . I think there is much you can do about our crisis in the humble role of housewife. I could wish you no better vocation than that." For many white college-educated women, that indeed would be their fate.

For black women, the pattern was very different. Since most black women expected to be employed, like their mothers and grandmothers before them, college degrees would greatly improve their occupational prospects. Although there were far fewer black women than white women in college, more than 90 percent of black women who entered college completed their degrees. Pauli Murray, born into an African-American family in the South, struggled against the double burdens of race and gender. Coming from a long line of activists, she wanted to help sharecroppers and other disadvantaged blacks. In 1941 she entered Howard Law School, the elite school for African Americans at the time. Although she was spared racism at the historically black institution, she ran into her first brush with sexism there. "Ironically," she later wrote, "if Howard Law School equipped me for effective struggle against Jim Crow [the system of racial segregation], it was also the place where I first became conscious of the twin evil of discriminatory sex bias, which I quickly labeled Jane Crow."

Although the men were friendly, sexism took an insidious form. "I soon learned that women were often the objects of ridicule disguised as a joke. I was shocked on the first day of class when one of our professors said in his opening remarks that he really didn't know why women came to law school, but that since we were there the men would have to put up with us. His banter brought forth loud laughter from the male students. I was too humiliated to respond." Murray got the best revenge: She worked her way to the head of the class. Her success at Howard did not provide her with a golden key to the future, however. She faced discrimination once again, this time at an elite white institution, Harvard. Denied the opportunity to continue her legal studies there, not because of her race but again because of her sex, she completed her law degree at the University of California at Berkeley. Later, she wrote an important paper that influenced a landmark 1954 Supreme Court decision, *Brown v. Board of Education of Topeka, Kansas,* which ruled that the "separate but equal" provision that justified segregated schooling was unconstitutional.

Pauli Murray was an exceptional woman, of course, and few women black or white achieved the kind of distinction and influence she achieved. Nevertheless, her story is typical of the drive and determination showed by African-American women in their struggle to achieve education, influence, and a better life for themselves and their children. Although they faced the double burdens of racism and sexism, often compounded by poverty, they were at the same time largely spared what Betty Friedan would later call the "feminine mystique," the trap of domesticity that constrained the lives of educated white women in the suburbs.

For white, middle-class women, college was an entry into affluent domesticity. Many must have believed that if they found a suitable mate at college, it made good sense to quit school and marry. By 1956, one fourth of all urban, white college women married while still in college. To do otherwise was a gamble. A woman who decided to postpone marriage, complete her education, and try to pursue a career during these years was likely to find it difficult, if not impossible, to gain access to a professional school or to find a job in the occupation of her choice. She might also find her chances for marriage reduced if she waited too long.

College-educated women often faced frustration when they tried to develop careers in their chosen fields. A survey of five thousand women who graduated from college between 1946 and 1949 found that two thirds had married within three to six years after graduation. Only half had been able to find the kind of work they had wanted and for which they had been prepared. Those who had chosen occupations traditional for women, such as teaching, nursing, or secretarial work, were largely successful in finding positions, but fewer than half who sought work in science, psychology, music, business, or journalism could find jobs. Many ended up as secretaries, clerks, or receptionists. It is not surprising that these professionally educated women were often dissatisfied with their jobs.

The difficulty of developing a career no doubt encouraged many women to marry during college. Most universities were forced to discontinue their policies against married students and provide places for young couples to live, arrangements that made it easier for women to drop out of school and work or have children while their husbands remained enrolled. Young men and women were both advised that marriage during college was a good idea. Women were warned that their "chances for marriage are greatly reduced if they do not make a permanent attachment during the college years." Men were also encouraged to marry while in school. As one writer in the *Ladies Home Journal* advised, "Many young men find that they can do much better work if they get the girl out of their dreams and into their kitchens."

Vocational guidebooks and counselors urged women to use their college education to prepare themselves to be well-educated housewives, with some skills to fall back on in case of an emergency. This may have been realistic advice, given the limited employment opportunities for women, but it made many college-educated women resent their education for raising their expectations. They felt frustrated and bored because their desire for intellectual and creative work, which had been sparked in college, was unfulfilled. Many female graduates called for changes in the

Training for the steno pool: young women in Minnesota master the fine points of the manual typewriter.

college curriculum that would be more suited to their jobs as homemakers. One female graduate later recalled, "An appalling number of graduates apparently felt that they should be more adequately prepared for their 'roles as wives and mothers' and suggested courses and reading lists to that end. I was horrified."

Dissenting voices were futile against the trend to tailor women's education toward domestic tasks. In 1949, Lynn White, president of Mills College, complained that "women are educated to be successful men. Then they must start all over again to be successful women." The domestic-oriented education that White and others fashioned at the time prompted a critical response from professional women, but it would be decades before feminists in great numbers would protest. And the effort to educate women for domesticity did have a number of advantages for women who would become career homemakers. It helped to professionalize the responsibilities of full-time wives and mothers, and to provide their work with dignity and stature. Improving the lot of the housewife was one way to push against the limits of domesticity. But in the long run, college curricula geared to the profession of homemaking did not solve the problems of frustration and boredom many educated women experienced. One explained her feelings this way: "This problem of the 'educated woman' learning to accept the monotony of housework and child training with cheerfulness and happiness has plagued me. I find much greater happiness now that the children are older," and she felt free to take a job outside the home.

Other housewives were more content. Some found that devoting themselves fully to the tasks of homemaking gave them a deep sense of satisfaction. They looked upon marriage and motherhood not as bliss, but as a challenging career with numerous rewards. One woman, who had seen her share of troubles as the wife of an alcoholic, made the best of it and focused on the positive. She took pride in her "husband and child and the chance to make a home for them … I always wanted marriage more than a career, and I have found the community activities one gets involved in (PTA, Girl Scouts, League of Women Voters, Women's Club, Church), keep you just as busy as a job and are equally stimulating." Although women were excluded from virtually all the positions of power in politics and business, many such career homemakers made an impact on local communities through their involvement in neighborhood voluntary associations.

Women faced choices and trade-offs, and for many, life as a homemaker was preferable to the struggles associated with careers for women at a time when opportunities were so limited. One career homemaker claimed that she sacrificed nothing: "I gained and gained. [My husband] gave me things I longed for. Social position, nice family, background, the kind of home I wanted, money … " As a career woman, these trappings of the good life would have been nearly impossible to achieve. So this woman, like so many others, opted to marry and settle in the suburbs.

Suburbia

In 1959, the same year that the sheltered honeymooners were featured in *Life* magazine, Vice President Richard Nixon traveled to Moscow for the opening of a U.S. trade exhibition. Nixon spent two full days debating with the Soviet premier, Nikita Khrushchev, not over bombs, missiles, rockets, or even forms of government. Rather, they quibbled over who had better washing machines, televisions, and other gadgets. In what became known as the "kitchen debate," the two world leaders ultimately argued over who had better *women.*

Nixon boasted that "our goal is to make life better for our housewives," whose burdens were eased by appliances that would allow them to be attractive wives and attentive mothers. Khrushchev claimed that he did not share Nixon's "capitalist view of women," and instead took pride in the productive women workers who filled Soviet factories. Although neither side triumphed in the skirmish, the debate reveals an important fact about the Cold War era: Families, homes, and consumer goods— along with the proper roles of women—had become high-stakes political issues.

The locale of the appliance-laden American home, complete with perky housewife, was the suburb. Suburban developments sprang up all over the country in the

wake of World War II. As developers rushed to meet the postwar demand for housing, banks, government subsidies, and private investors poured funds into new,
single-family homes. In 1946, for the first time, a majority of the nation's families
lived in homes they owned. Over the next fifteen years, 12 million more families
became homeowners. New houses in expanding suburbs were built with young
nuclear families in mind.

Families did not have to be wealthy to buy houses in the suburbs, but they did
have to be white. Racial minorities were not allowed to purchase homes in the suburbs, even if they could afford them. William Levitt pioneered in the development
of standardized, inexpensive, mass-produced suburban homes available to white
families of modest means. In the first Levittown, on Long Island, outside New York
City, 17,400 houses accommodated eighty-two thousand residents. The structures
were all basically alike, but they had flexible interior spaces that were easy to
expand if the family increased in size. As young parents moved into these homes
with their rapidly growing families, it is no wonder that the first Levittown quickly earned the nicknames "Fertility Valley" and "The Rabbit Hutch."

The homes were not particularly fancy or elegant, but they were filled with
household appliances, the so-called "labor-saving" devices that would, presumably,
lighten the housewife's burden. Appliances were not intended to give women more
free time to develop hobbies, careers, or other interests. Rather, they enabled
housewives to achieve a higher standard of cleanliness and efficiency, while allowing more time for child care. Housework could be more professional.

It is not at all clear that "labor-saving appliances" actually saved housewives any
time, but they did allow women to maintain immaculate houses. Consumer spending also increased the housewife's tasks. Shopping, driving, and selecting goods
from the array of choices available became a major part of the household manager's routine. All together, full-time homemakers, like their mothers before them,
still worked about fifty-five hours a week. Labor-saving appliances actually saved
time only for women who worked outside the home. Employed women spent only
about twenty-six hours a week doing housework. But, of course, that was in addition to the hours they spent at their paid jobs. Employed or not, care of the home
and family remained women's responsibility. Ironically, the husband's place of rest
was the wife's place of labor.

The home was also the center of family leisure. Postwar Americans spent a good
deal of their incomes on items that would make the home comfortable and enjoy-
able: appliances, automobiles, backyard barbecue sets, and of course, televisions.
By the 1950s, televisions were selling at a rate of more than 5 million a year. In their
living rooms, ordinary families watched idealized families in enormously popular
shows such as "Ozzie and Harriet," "Leave It to Beaver," and "Father Knows Best."
These television families all had certain features in common: They were white, they
lived in comfortable suburban homes, full-time homemakers had down-home

wisdom and patience, and fathers always knew best. Curiously, although the fathers in these programs were the breadwinners of the family, we rarely if ever saw them at work. They were home, presiding with kindly, fatherly authority, clearly the head of the household. Nevertheless, mothers were the ones in charge of the daily routines, the running of the home, and the supervision of the children.

Television shows that featured working-class families were often continuations of radio comedy shows from the pre-TV era. Shows like "The Honeymooners" depicted working-class men with real jobs (usually undesirable ones like bus drivers or sewer workers), wives who tolerated their husbands' explosive tempers and rolled their eyes at men's foolishness, and neighbors who shared their struggles. There were no children in these families, typically, but the couples were often preoccupied with purchasing consumer goods. They usually lived in apartments, rather than single-family houses, marking their distance from the child-centered suburban families featured in the middle-class situation comedies.

A few shows focused on ethnic Americans. "I Love Lucy," starring a Cuban band leader and his American real-life wife, made television history when the couple's child was born on the show before a TV audience of millions. "Amos 'n' Andy" featured black Americans who, despite moments of wit, wisdom, and shrewd cleverness, were depicted in stereotyped ways as clumsy bumblers. Television shows of the 1950s reinforced prevailing attitudes about white suburban families, working-class couples, and ethnic minorities. Nevertheless, these shows also brought Americans together around familiar characters and their daily struggles, making them somewhat more human than their stereotypes would suggest.

The struggle to achieve the ideal suburban life took its toll on both men and women. Since the primary goal of the male "breadwinner" was to provide for his family, it was expected that he would work for the best steady pay, regardless of whether he enjoyed the job. The reward was in the quality of life that the man's income could buy—not the intrinsic satisfactions of the job itself. The woman's part of the bargain was to keep the home cheerful and clean, and to be content with the homemaker role. If either partner believed that the other was not keeping the bargain, trouble brewed. The only hope for material security came from the husband's income. If a wife held a job, her income would help but it would not pay the bills. And she would still be responsible for taking care of the home.

If husbands had to work hard and sacrifice in order to earn enough to support the suburban way of life, women at home worked equally hard. In fact, there was no guarantee that affluence lessened their work load. The family's wealth did not provide this wife with much leisure, nor many opportunities to develop her own interests. Even community volunteer work was difficult. As one suburban housewife noted: "Because of the size of our family, we have very little personal fun—I mean no clubs or activities. I used to be very active in PTA, church (taught Sunday school), and garden club, but my last two children, now four and two years old, changed all this. I just stay home with them and taxi my oldest boys around. Our oldest boy, almost fifteen, is away at prep school, but in our rural community I have to drive someone somewhere every day. I expect to get back into community life when my younger children are in school all day. I feel quite stale as though I don't use my mind enough." Still, she felt satisfied with her life, in spite of a "stale" mind and an "overbearing inconsiderate" husband. She had worked hard to achieve the family life they had built on his income and her labor, and she was proud of her efforts.

For white, heterosexual, affluent, married women with children, suburban life had its rewards. It also had its drawbacks. But what about the women who did not have the resources to live the life of the suburban housewife? What about those whose ethnic or racial background, income level, marital status, or sexual orientation excluded them from these communities of nuclear families? For these women, like their white suburban sisters, there were hardships as well as rewards. Oddly enough, being excluded from the world of suburbia also gave these women a certain amount of freedom from its rigid expectations.

African-American women were not likely to avoid full-time domestic work. The difference was, they were more likely to do it in someone else's home. By 1950, 41 percent of all employed black women worked in private homes. Another 19 percent worked in office buildings, restaurants, and hotels as scrubwomen, maids, and housekeepers. Of the remaining 40 percent, many worked in farm labor. In spite of the migration to the North, as late as 1950, 68 percent of African Americans still lived in the South. The lives of southern black women largely resembled that of their female ancestors during slavery: living in shacks, working sun up to sun down, forced to obey local white people or risk severe consequences. In the North, as whites continued to move to the suburbs, blacks became more concentrated in the cities. By 1960 blacks were more urbanized than whites. North as well as South, black men earned less than half of what white men earned, and black women received less than half the amount that white women earned. Black women continued to face the most dismal prospects for paid employment, but they continued to take whatever jobs they could get.

In the postwar years, white women faced pressure to become full-time homemakers, and were often stigmatized if they held jobs. Black women faced no such stigma. Because of economic necessity, African-American women had a long history of combining paid work with domestic responsibilities. One advantage employed black women had over their white counterparts was that wage-earning African-American women commanded a great deal of respect within their communities.

White mainstream journals idealized the stay-at-home wife and mother and sanctioned employment only as an economic necessity. *Life* heaped disdain upon feminists of an earlier era: "Unlike the strident suffragettes who were once eager to

Black schoolteachers enjoyed great respect in their communities. They symbolized the goal of African-American parents for their children to get a good education and rise above jobs in the service economy.

prove their equality with men, the typical working wife of 1953 works for the double pay check that makes it possible to buy a TV set, a car—or in many cases simply to make ends meet. The problems created by her efforts to solve this are what happens to the children and what happens to her marriage. But most working wives, who have no intention of working indefinitely, feel it necessary to risk these dangers and cope with the problems in order to maintain a good standard of living for their families."

In contrast, the black press presented working wives and mothers in a heroic light. Rather than condemning the political agitators of earlier days, the African-American community connected black women's work with the struggle for racial as well as gender equality dating back to the nineteenth century. *Ebony* offered a tribute to "Women Leaders" in 1949: "Their contribution to a fuller, richer life in the American tradition has been two-fold: they have aided in no small way the general fight of Negroes for integration in a living democracy and they have battled against the traditional enforced inferiority to the U.S. male. . . . Today's stout-hearted women who stand at the head of the onward march appropriately look back with pride to the glowing traditions handed down by such sterling heroines as Harriet Tubman and Sojourner Truth, who never accepted the myth that women belong to a weaker sex." But while *Ebony* praised black women with jobs, it also recognized that few black women had the luxury to be full-time homemakers. Poverty and discrimination filled the lives of black women with constant struggle. Some black families were fortunate enough to take advantage of postwar prosperity and allow mothers to stay home. For these women, homemaking represented a double triumph. As *Ebony* noted, "The cooking over which the 'white folks' used to go into ecstasies is now reserved for her own family and they really appreciate it."

At a time when white women were admonished not to compete against their husbands and to direct their career aspirations into the home, black women were encouraged to pursue all opportunities. *Ebony* featured a "Medical Family," Jane and Barbara Wright, sisters who were each physicians married to lawyers. Another article featured "husband and wife teams" of prominent dual-career couples. While whites were warned that such arrangements would lead to neglected children and marital conflict, *Ebony* told its readers that "each couple is daily proving joint interests and twin careers to be both profitable and stimulating."

The families featured in *Ebony* were no more typical of black Americans than the notables featured in the white press were typical of white Americans, but the magazine did reflect a different set of values that extended not only to the wealthy black families featured in the news, but to the majority of black Americans who faced financial hardships. Although these African-American families were deprived of the material benefits available to white Americans, they were also spared some of the drawbacks of life in the suburbs.

Suburbs fostered tightly knit nuclear families in loosely knit communities and extended family networks. People moved often, and ties to neighbors were often weak, since the nuclear family was expected to be self-sufficient and self-enclosed. People did come together in a number of associations, most notably in the churches and synagogues that sprang up across the country. The suburban landscape was dotted with religious institutions, as Americans joined congregations in record numbers. People also came together in local civic institutions. Women joined local PTAs, women's clubs, and charities, and they organized scout troops and other enrichment programs for their children. These efforts provided women with community ties, and gave them the opportunity to shape social, religious, and educational institutions in their neighborhoods. These were important tasks. But deep sources of mutual support and tight networks based on kinship and friendship were difficult to achieve in the suburbs. People moved in and out too quickly, and many left their relatives and ethnic communities when they moved to the suburbs. The isolation of the nuclear family also inhibited the casual visiting that took place on the stoops of urban apartments or the streets of the cities.

Those outside the suburbs were more likely to develop strong ties of support with relatives and friends. It was both more possible and more necessary to do so. Take, for example, the Jacksons, an African-American family from rural Arkansas. Most blacks still lived in the rural South, in spite of the massive migration northward that began early in the century, increased substantially during the war, and continued steadily in the postwar years. Between the mid-teens and the 1960s, ninety-six members of the Jackson family joined that migration and moved North. First they moved to rural areas in the North where they worked on farms. Eventually they settled in cities. Wherever they settled, they clustered with their relatives. While white suburban family arrangements centered around the married couple and their children, this was not necessarily the typical family formation for African-American migrants to northern cities. Often the strongest ties over time were among siblings.

Poverty and discrimination made it extremely difficult for poor African-American women to live according to the suburban ideal. The inability to find adequate jobs broke up many families. Even the welfare system often separated families; for a woman to get welfare, she could not be living with a man. In the postwar years, 25 percent of African-American wives were either separated, widowed, or divorced, compared to 10 percent of white women.

Ruby Lee Daniels struggled against heavy odds to build a secure life for herself and her children. An illegitimate daughter of Mississippi sharecroppers, she came north after the war and moved into an apartment with her aunt. The janitorial job she got at Montgomery Ward paid her four times as much as she had earned as a waitress in Mississippi, but the North was not paradise. She still struggled against poverty. She married young and separated quickly, had two children, and never settled down with a man. Her real family were her female friends and relatives, who helped her find shelter and work, and helped her raise her children. She hoped she would find a good man, a good job, and a home of her own in Chicago. But her dream never came true. For Ruby Lee Daniels, poverty and the difficulties of being a single mother prevented her from achieving her goal.

Family strategies based on strong ties of kinship, functioned well for African Americans who were excluded by poverty as well as racism from white suburban America. But as long as American society was deeply racist, segregation had some advantages for African Americans. It protected them and their children from constant degradation and harassment in their daily lives. As Carolyn Reed recalled of her childhood in a segregated neighborhood, "Teachers then . . . were marvelous—black teachers that were really interested in helping children." She remembers one of her teachers telling her, "You are as good as anyone—you're just as good as anyone, but you're not better than anyone." It is not likely that a white teacher in the early 1950s would have been so encouraging to a young black girl. As we shall see, these strong community supports served them well when African Americans came together in the most powerful grass-roots political movement of the century: the civil rights movement.

Dating, Mating, and the Double Standard

World War II was over and the wartime anxieties about single women out in the world of men seemed to have subsided. American men and women rushed into marriage and retreated into the safety of their own bedrooms—but peacetime did not bring sexual tranquility. Rather, the sexual terrain remained a minefield. Until very recently, sexual restraint was a time-honored moral code in America. Men were usually forgiven their sexual indulgences; it was almost expected that young men would "sow their wild oats" before marriage. But women were not allowed such indulgence. They were expected to be virgins when they married. By the middle of the twentieth century, however, women began to explore their sexuality in new ways, often outside marriage. Although sexual activity among young women was by no means uncommon, it still carried severe consequences. The "double standard" that allowed men more sexual freedom than women was still in full force. As they had tested other restraints, women pushed against the sexual boundaries, too.

Sex and reproduction affected women's lives much more powerfully than men's. The mid-century decades were particularly treacherous ones because the codes of sexual conduct were changing so rapidly. On the one hand, traditional sexual mores and the "double standard" remained so strong that a woman's reputation could be "ruined"—in the lingo of the day—if she behaved in ways that were outside the boundaries of acceptable sexual conduct for women. If she became pregnant as a result, the consequences were extremely dire.

On the other hand, these were the years when sex became big business; sex was used to sell products from cars to toothpaste. It was also a time when sex came to define the cornerstone of marital happiness. Magazines, movies, and every form of advice literature encouraged women to be attractive and sexy to catch a man— but to put on the brakes when it came to sex itself. Birth control devices were becoming more effective and available, but abortion remained illegal except under exceptional circumstances, and illegal abortions were extremely dangerous. If women were confused by all these mixed messages, it is no wonder. As one woman recalled, "Postwar America was a society with Stop-Go lights flashing everywhere we looked. Sex, its magic spell everywhere, was accompanied by the stern warning: Don't do it."

The American sex ethic, like the work ethic, seemed to define central beliefs about the national culture. But when Alfred Kinsey published his now-famous studies of American sex life, *Sexual Behavior in the Human Male* (1948) and *Sexual Behavior in the Human Female* (1953), the nation and the world learned that Americans did not practice what they preached when it came to sex. Kinsey, an unassuming zoologist, wrote these two massive tomes that documented, in hundreds of pages of facts, figures, and tables, American sexual habits. Although these scientific texts were incredibly dry and boring to read, they instantly became bestsellers, so eager were Americans to read about their own private behavior.

Kinsey found that nearly all men engaged in masturbation and heterosexual petting, and that almost 90 percent had premarital intercourse. Half admitted to having extramarital sex, and more than a third had homosexual experience. For women, the numbers were not quite so high, but equally surprising to a society that still believed in female chastity. More than three fifths of the women had engaged in masturbation, 90 percent had experienced petting, half had engaged in sexual intercourse prior to marriage, and a quarter in extramarital sex. These statistics indicate the extent to which Americans violated their own codes of conduct. Kinsey's studies revealed what American men and women *did*—but not how they felt about it. It is in the feelings that went along with the actions—love, anger, guilt, resentment, disappointment, and satisfaction—that the full story of postwar sexuality needs to be understood.

One of the most surprising findings in Kinsey's study was the extent of homosexual activity among Americans. The war and postwar years opened up new possibilities for gay men and lesbians to socialize and form relationships. During the war, the armed services provided places for same-sex relationships to develop, far removed from the scrutiny of family and neighbors. Pat Bond, a wartime teenager who enlisted in the Women's Army Corps, feared that her attraction for women would condemn her to be "forever alone." But when she joined the service, she found a pleasant surprise. "Everybody was going with someone or had a crush on someone," she recalled. "Always the straight women I ran into tended to ignore us, tended to say, 'Who cares? It leaves all the men for us.'" Another woman who joined the navy fell into a relationship with another recruit whom she "admired greatly." She explained, "We didn't talk about what we were doing, we just did it and felt good about it. I just thought, 'Well, this is the way it's going to be forever.'"

Civilians also found new ways to meet partners in the wartime social scene in the cities. One young lesbian was amazed at the boldness she encountered when she moved to Los Angeles to find work and lived in a boardinghouse for single women. She had no idea how to find other lesbians until she overheard a conversation among her neighbors. "I thought, 'Gee, I wonder if these are some of the girls I would very dearly love to meet.' . . . I started talking and finally they asked me, 'Do you like boys, or do you go out strictly with girls?'" Her new friends introduced her to other lesbians and showed her around the lesbian bars that were springing up in Los Angeles. These ties, forged in wartime, continued in the postwar years as the network of lesbian communities grew and flourished. Gay bars were centers of social life for homosexual men and lesbians, but the bar scene did not appeal to all lesbians. Other networks also served their social needs. Among these were business and professional women's organizations and friendship networks. A woman doctor recalled the "wonderful parties where we could be ourselves . . . It gave me an identity, a self-identity and for the first time a community identity."

It was now obvious that homosexuality, once considered a deviant fringe element of society, was pervasive. But in the hostile climate of the Cold War years, this knowledge did little to make life easier for gay men and lesbians. In fact, the postwar era was a time of heightened persecution of homosexuals. Anyone who did not display the appropriate sexual behavior of the era—heterosexual dating, young marriage, and childbearing—was suspected of being a "pervert." This pejorative term was widely used during these years and implied not only sexual deviance, but danger. The Republican party national chairman, Guy Gabrielson, claimed that "sexual perverts . . . have infiltrated our Government in recent years," and they were "perhaps as dangerous as the actual Communists." It was widely believed that only "manly" men could stand up against the threat of communism, and that "perverts" were security risks. The persecution of homosexual men and women became more intense than ever before. Homophobia became ferocious. Male homosexuals were considered the greatest menace. Lesbians were also condemned, but since displays of affection between women were not uncommon, lesbianism more easily went unnoticed.

Lesbianism was the most flagrant violation of the sexual code for women, but there were many other types of violations. Nonmarital sexual behavior of any kind was problematic. There was, of course, one easy way for young women to avoid the difficulty altogether: get married. Even some lesbians used marriage as a cover for their sexuality. But the solution was much easier for young heterosexual women. In the postwar years, teenage sex was considered bad only if the teenagers were unmarried. It is quite possible that one reason the age at marriage dropped so precipitously during these years was that youngsters married in order to engage in sex legitimately. Although the rate of *premarital* intercourse did not rise significantly during these years, the rate of *teenage* sexual intercourse rose dramatically. These teenagers were married.

At the same time, marriage itself was sexualized in new ways. Followers of Freud popularized his ideas that sexual repression was unhealthy. People should enjoy sex—but only in marriage. In fact, good marriage depended upon good sex, according to many experts at the time. A professor of education at Whittier College warned that if married partners were not sexually satisfied, their children would suffer, and he concluded with a statement that summarized much of the thinking of the era: "Wholesome sex relations are the cornerstone of marriage."

But experts continued to contradict themselves and give confusing advice. If sex was so important to marriage, then sexual attraction should play a major role in choosing a spouse. At the same time, young people were warned against putting too much emphasis on sexual attraction. One expert proposed a scientific formula for mate selection: "60 percent profound affection and respect [and] 40 percent intense sex attraction." With this balance, "you can be fairly sure that you'll get the happy, fantastic, fairy-tale result." Unfortunately, he claimed that most marriages were based on 70 percent sexual attraction and 30 percent genuine affection, a formula likely to lead to divorce. All experts agreed on the importance of sexual compatibility in marriage, but they gave no hints as to how that compatibility would be determined prior to marriage.

The path to marriage was expected to start during high school, and young women were to take charge of the matter. The key was allure. Magazines aimed at young girls were filled with tips on "how to catch a husband" or "how to snare a male." But this catching and snaring was supposed to happen passively: Never "give the man the idea you are running after him; pretend to let him catch you." Much of the skill of man-catching involved subordinating the girl's thoughts and feelings to those of her date—good practice for a marriage in which the man was expected to be the head of the household. "Concentrate on your companion's feelings instead of your own. . . . learn to talk about things that interest men," young women were told. The important thing was to "arouse and hold a man's interest."

Dating began the path to marriage. Most young people dated during high school, and many, especially young working-class women who did not go on to college, married right after graduation. The dating system established a certain amount of physical intimacy between unmarried men and women. Although the proportion of young men and women having sexual intercourse did not increase substantially between the 1920s and the 1960s, there was a significant increase in physical intimacy that stopped short of intercourse. As Kinsey noted, on "doorsteps and on street corners, and on high school and college campuses, [petting] may be observed in the daytime as well as in the evening hours." He claimed that petting was "one of the most significant factors in the sexual lives of high school and college males and females."

Dating and petting in high school often encouraged young coupling, and those who were steady dates were more likely to become sexually involved. One teenager explained that it had more to do with love than with sexual experimentation: "Something you go all the way in should only be with someone you really love, not just any date." Although adults at the time were sometimes alarmed at what they saw as promiscuous behavior, dating and petting, and even intercourse between steadies, was part of a system of dating that was expected to lead, ultimately, to the rational choice of a marriage partner.

The dating and petting system, however, contained many dangers for women. It was very difficult for a young woman to know how to avoid being a "prude," and at the same to know how far was "too far" to go and still maintain her reputation and desirability. The "double standard" was fiercely enforced, which meant that boys could experiment sexually with little risk, but girls were condemned if they did so. It was a confusing and stressful situation for young women. Boys were expected to try to go as far as possible with the girls they dated, and girls were expected to set the limits.

Young women who gave in to the pressure often paid a very high price, by losing the boy's affection or her reputation, or, in the worst case, becoming pregnant. Said one pregnant sixteen-year-old, "How are you supposed to know what they want? You hold out for a long time and then when you do give in to them and give your body they laugh at you afterwards and say they'd never marry a slut, and that they didn't love you but were just testing because they only plan to marry a virgin and wanted to see if you'd go all the way." One episode like this was enough to mark a "good girl" as a "bad girl" and destroy her reputation.

"Good girls" did not have sex. Or, if they did, it was only with someone they truly loved. The situation was exactly the reverse for young men. If men dated young women they "respected" and truly cared for, they would not have sex with them. As one male college student explained, "I felt that if I were sexual with someone, that indicated that I didn't respect them. I could be sexual with someone I didn't care for, but not with someone I did care for. The fact that I was never sexual with anyone is because I never dated anyone I didn't care for." This strange logic permeated social relations between young men and women, causing constant tensions and confusions in both the white and black communities. One young southern black man said, "There are some that I run around with and can do anything to, and there are some who won't let you mess with them. I don't mess with girls I go with because they are nice girls, and I don't believe it's nice to bother nice girls."

Young women struggled to assert their own desires for intimacy, affection, and sexual exploration within the double standard. Many bent or broke the rules, or claimed their rights to their own desires in the rapidly changing sexual climate of the era. Gradually they chipped away at the more brutal aspects of the double standard. As one study at the time concluded, "Values have probably changed . . . at least to the extent that more girls accept premarital coitus *if* there is an emotional involvement with the partner and some commitment by him to marriage in the future."

Even sex with a steady boyfriend, or a fiancé, was fraught with potential consequences. Sometimes the commitment to marriage came after the fact. As one woman recalled of her decision to marry her husband, "The fact that we had been intimate, I am certain, made my mind set for marriage to him." Apparently, it was not a good enough reason, for she later regretted her "poor choice of mate" and divorced him. Another woman confessed that even after marriage, she feared that her reputation would be ruined if people knew they had engaged in premarital sex: "I was afraid that someone might have learned that we had intercourse before marriage and I'd be disgraced." These comments indicate the terrible strain a woman was under to be sexy enough to catch her man, but not too sexy to lose him. Women suffered the stigma of "promiscuity," and risked the danger of pregnancy. They had to walk the difficult tightrope between sexual allure and the emphasis on virginity that permeated the youth culture. Kinsey found that half of the men he interviewed wanted to marry a virgin—although it does not appear that he asked the same question of women. Kinsey understood that this pressure to remain sexually chaste might lead to guilt and psychological disorders: "Behavior which is accepted by the culture does not generate psychologic conflicts in the individual or unmanageable social problems. The same behavior, censored, condemned, tabooed, or criminally punished in the next culture, may generate guilt and neurotic disturbances in the nonconforming individual and serious conflict within the social organism." Kinsey's anthropological language described postwar America quite accurately. For women, whose bodies would bear the reproductive consequences of sexual activity, the matter was complicated indeed.

Birth Control, Abortion, and the Baby Boom

For all the confusion and tension surrounding sex outside of marriage, sex was supposed to blossom in marriage. Safely expressed within the home, sex could lead to its ultimate purpose: reproduction. Experts at the time claimed that the fullest expression of a woman's sexuality was motherhood. In 1947, Ferdinand Lundberg and Marynia F. Farnham, two Freudian psychologists, wrote a best-selling book about women's sexuality, *The Modern Woman: The Lost Sex.* They argued that the goal of female sexuality is "receptivity and passiveness, a willingness to accept dependence without fear or resentment, with a deep inwardness and readiness for the final goal of sexual life—impregnation."

Women who did not accept this idea, according to Lundberg and Farnham, "constitute the array of the sick, unhappy, neurotic, wholly or partly incapable of dealing with life . . . They have always been known and simply recognized for what they are—the miserable, half-satisfied, the frustrated, the angered." Much of their scorn was heaped on feminists of an earlier day. With absolutely no evidence, "experts" such as these claimed that feminists, "when they came to perform the sexual act, found that they were frigid." But mothers were sexy. This was a new idea; previously, motherhood had been associated with chastity and purity.

The very meaning of marriage began to be identified with having children, and women were expected to achieve their greatest fulfillment in motherhood. Given the strong connections among female sexuality, marriage, and motherhood, one might expect that the birth control movement would have withered during these years. On the contrary, the movement gained momentum. After birth control became legal under federal law in the 1930s, the number of birth control clinics in the nation grew rapidly, from fifty-five in 1930 to more than eight hundred in 1942. In that year, the Birth Control Federation of America changed its name to the Planned Parenthood Federation of America, signaling a major shift in the movement's philosophy. New goals focused not so much on the rights of women to control their own reproduction, but on strengthening the family through liberating female sexuality in marriage. If women did not fear pregnancy, they would be more likely to enjoy sex with their husbands, leading to happier families.

In addition, birth control made it possible to postpone and space children, so that families could be scientifically and rationally planned. During the 1950s, there was rapid progress in birth control technology. Condoms, diaphragms, jellies, and foams were widely available. Research moved ahead on the intrauterine device (IUD) and on oral contraceptives. "The Pill," as the birth control pill came to be known, was approved by the Food and Drug Administration in 1960. Birth control was not to be used by unmarried women to prevent pregnancy, nor by married women to avoid motherhood. Rather, it was another scientific advance to enhance family life. Like washing machines or vacuum cleaners, birth control devices might be considered "labor-saving appliances" that would make a homemaker's job as wife and mother happier, easier, and more scientific.

Of course, the widespread use of birth control did not result in a declining birthrate. Rather, it may have actually contributed to the Baby Boom by enabling couples to marry young and have the number of children they wanted. When women were asked what they thought was the "ideal" number of children, the most common response went from two in 1940 to four in 1960. Women were marrying and having children younger than their grandmothers had. Most had their children while they were in their twenties, and they used birth control to postpone and space their children as well as to prevent further pregnancies after they had completed their families.

By 1961 the National Council of Churches of Christ had approved the use of birth control devices. Nonorthodox Protestant and Jewish organizations moved from outright hostility to enthusiastic approval, even making it a moral obligation to control family size. The medical profession agreed. At the same time, state legislatures were loosening their restrictions on birth control. Before the war, most states banned the distribution of contraceptive information and materials, even to doctors. But most of these restrictions were eliminated by the 1950s. Now birth control was considered a means of strengthening families. Increased availability and the removal of legal restrictions led to widespread use of contraceptives among married couples. During the 1950s, 81 percent of white wives of childbearing age used birth control. White middle-class Protestant couples were the most likely to use birth control, and contraceptive use among other groups was increasing.

American society was ready to accept birth control as a means to improving marital sex and family planning, but it was not ready to accept its potential for liberating female sexuality outside of marriage. Public opinion, lawmakers, and physicians all did their part to make sure that birth control would encourage marriage and family life. Consequently, one of the most explosive scientific developments of the postwar years, which held the promise of freeing sex from marriage and marriage from procreation, did neither. That potential was not realized for two decades.

Advocates of family planning endorsed contraception but drew the line at abortion. While birth control was promoted as a means to strengthen families, abortion

Margaret Sanger (left) attends the opening of a birth control clinic in Tucson, Arizona, in 1953. She had been an active crusader for contraception and women's rights since the 1920s.

was considered a threat to sexual morality and family life. If birth control was the reward for the virtuous, abortion was the punishment for the immoral. The American Social Hygiene Association warned that illicit sex could lead to the abortionist's door, and illustrated the point in its pamphlet with a picture of a frightened-looking woman walking up a dingy stairway in an obvious slum. Illegal abortions were indeed dangerous, but the association urged sexual restraint rather than legalized abortion.

Legal abortions had been available for several decades, but they became more difficult to obtain in the 1940s and 1950s. Legal abortions could be performed only if physicians decided that continuing the pregnancy would present a danger to the woman's life or health. In most states, physicians were able to interpret the danger as they saw fit, and some women were able to obtain safe, legal abortions in hospitals. But in the postwar years, physicians and hospital boards became increasingly reluctant to approve legal abortions, sending thousands of pregnant women into the back alleys to have dangerous operations performed illegally.

In spite of the risks, abortions were still quite common. There were an estimated 250,000 to 1 million illegal abortions each year during these decades, which were responsible for about 40 percent of all deaths of pregnant women. Among the women surveyed in the Kinsey report in 1953, one in four of all wives said they had abortions by the time they were forty, and nearly 90 percent of premarital pregnancies were aborted. Educated black women were as likely to obtain abortions as educated white women; those with less education were more likely to carry their pregnancies to term. Most abortions were illegal. There were probably fewer abortions performed after the war than before, due in part, no doubt, to the increasing availability of birth control. Nevertheless, sensational articles in the popular press about illegal "abortion rings" increased. This media attention to the subject of abortion warned young women of the dangers of illicit sex. Horrific as stories of botched abortions were, desperate women continued to terminate unwanted pregnancies.

For unmarried women unable or unwilling to have an abortion, having a baby out of wedlock presented enormous difficulties. As with so many aspects of postwar life, the experience of unmarried pregnancy differed greatly for white and black women. Sally B. was white; Brenda J. was black. Both were sixteen years old when they got pregnant in 1957. Both girls' parents were upset by the news. But from that point on, their stories diverged. Sally's parents owned a dry cleaning store in a city in Pennsylvania. When she told them she was pregnant, they were horrified. They were furious at Sally and her boyfriend, Tim, whom they had forbidden her to date. To make matters worse, as soon as she told Tim she was pregnant, he lost interest in her. Sally hardly knew where to turn. Her father, who had done business in the community for twenty years, was very concerned about what their neighbors would think about the disgrace Sally had brought upon her family. He suggested that they send Sally away, and tell their neighbors and friends that she was dead. But Sally's mother offered a different solution. They would tell the school that Sally had been invited to spend spring semester with relatives in San Diego. Then they would send Sally to the Florence Crittenton home for unwed mothers in Philadelphia, where she would stay until the baby was born. Until the time that Sally left, she stayed at home with her angry parents, who refused to let her leave the house. In a few weeks, before Sally began to look pregnant, she was whisked off to the home for unwed mothers.

At the Crittenton home Sally was hidden from public view. She and other girls, most of them white, who had "gotten into trouble" took classes in grooming, sewing, charm, and cooking. Sally told the social worker that she wanted to keep her baby. But the social worker claimed that it was not normal for an unmarried girl to want to keep her baby. She said that Sally was suffering from a number of psychological disorders that caused her to think that she wanted to keep the baby. The social worker met with Sally every week, and by the time her baby was born she had been persuaded to give the baby up for adoption. She had been convinced that she had done something so wrong that she did not deserve to keep her child. "I don't think any unmarried girl has the right to keep her baby. I don't think it's fair to the child. I know I don't have the right," said Sally sadly, after her baby girl was born. The child was adopted by a Philadelphia lawyer and his wife who were infertile. Sally was back home before her seventeenth birthday. Her social worker and her parents warned her severely to keep the entire episode secret for the rest of her life, and to pretend that it never happened.

Brenda J. had a very different experience. Brenda lived in New York with her mother, a sister, and two brothers. Brenda did not have to tell anyone about her pregnancy—her mother figured it out when Brenda was about two months along. Brenda's mother was upset. She was unhappy about Brenda leaving school, and disgusted that Brenda was thinking of marrying the baby's father, her nineteen-year-old boyfriend. She convinced Brenda to give up that foolish idea: "It's better to be an unwed mother than an unhappy bride. You'll never be able to point your finger at me and say, 'If it hadn't been for her.'" Brenda stayed in school until she was expelled by the dean of girls. Brenda's boyfriend continued to spend time with Brenda, but as she got bigger she was sure he was going out with other girls too. After she was expelled from school, Brenda ran errands and helped her mother, who worked as a maid for a middle-class family. As the time for her delivery drew near, she began to worry about how she would take care of the baby. Her family had no extra money and no extra space for a baby. Brenda considered giving up the baby, perhaps to relatives in South Carolina. But her mother told her, "You put your child away, you might as well kill him. He'll think no one wants him." When Brenda's baby was born in the local public hospital, Brenda told the nurse, "I love the baby as much as if I was married." Brenda had no money, and her boyfriend left to find work in Florida. So Brenda went to the welfare office, where she was sternly lectured about girls having sex and taxpayers paying the price. She was told that she had to find the baby's father if she wanted welfare, and that the welfare people would be watching her apartment.

The stories of these two girls describe the dire consequences for young women who got pregnant out of wedlock. Typically, white girls were shrouded in secrecy, banished from their homes and families, and virtually forced to give up their babies for adoption. These girls provided babies for the adoption industry, since infertile white couples during the Baby Boom years were desperate to find healthy white infants. Black girls, on the other hand, were more likely to stay in their families and be encouraged to keep their babies. Most homes for unwed mothers did not accept non-white clients, and the demand for black babies to adopt was not as great as for white babies.

For black and white teenagers, marriage was one solution. If a white girl became pregnant, the father of her child might be forced into a "shotgun" wedding by the girl's parents, but often these marriages did not last long. Other times, the couples decided to marry sooner than they had planned, or perhaps the pregnancy made them decide to get married. In any case, with the marriage age dropping rapidly, marriage was one way to solve the problem of unwed pregnancy. For young white couples who had the resources to marry, marriage avoided the stigma of illegitimacy.

Young couples who could not afford to marry right away might postpone the wedding. One young African-American woman from the South had her baby and continued to live with her tenant-farmer parents. But her relationship with her fiancé was solid: "We was in love and just couldn't wait to get married [before having sex].... He's living out here in the country now, working with his papa.... I still loves Connie. He comes over to see me and treats me and the baby nice. We wants to get married soon's he can make a little more money." In this case, both families supported the young couple as they tried to get established; there was no "shotgun" wedding, and the boy did not reject his girlfriend as soon as she became pregnant. Not all young pregnant women were so fortunate.

The different treatment of black and white unwed mothers reflects how white and black women were regarded almost as sexual opposites. Since African Americans first arrived in this country, they have been treated as though they were sexually more "wild" and "primitive" than whites. This unproven assumption provided the basis for widespread rape of black slave women by their white owners, and the constant suspicion surrounding black men that led to countless lynchings. Myths of black female sexuality also promoted contrasting myths of white female purity. These myths victimized both black and white women: black women were routinely exploited sexually by whites, and white women were routinely denied the expression of their own sexual feelings.

The effects of these long-held beliefs about sex and race continued well into the twentieth century, when they continued to affect young women coming of age. Sally and Brenda both found that once they got pregnant, they had few options.

Their paths were determined largely by their race. And yet both girls grew up during a time when sexual attitudes, mores, and behavior were in flux. Neither girl was "promiscuous," a disparaging term frequently used during these years to condemn young women (but never young men). Both obviously had sex with their boyfriends out of feelings of love, even though both boys ultimately left the women to bear full responsibility for the consequences of their sexual relationships. Throughout these decades, women had to navigate the sexual minefield with great care—for they were at much greater risk of getting hurt than their male peers were.

Although black unwed mothers were more likely to keep their babies, and white women to give them up for adoption, both endured the stigma of unwed motherhood. A study of fifty unwed black mothers in Indiana in 1957 found that two out of three of the girls' families punished them severely, and that most of the girls described their babies as unwanted. Many had tried to get abortions, and when they were unsuccessful, they tried to have their babies adopted. Another study concluded, "Most mothers of children born out of wedlock expressed great feelings of guilt and were fully aware of the stigma in the Negro and general community."

Unwanted babies, of course, were not necessarily unloved; many babies born to married parents were not planned or "wanted" until they arrived. Illegitimate babies may well have been loved, but they and their mothers faced a difficult life. Many pregnant girls felt that the best they could do for their children was to put them up for adoption. During the 1950s, some of the homes for unwed mothers began to provide services to black women as well as white, and some of the facilities became integrated. But few black women were able to take advantage of the opportunities available at the homes. White women suffered the trauma of unwed pregnancy, isolation, and the sadness of giving up a baby. But then they could put the whole episode behind them. Black women who had babies out of wedlock usually faced a long and difficult struggle to provide for themselves and their children.

Unwed pregnancy, like unwed sex, was condemned because it happened outside marriage. Inside marriage, however, both were celebrated. Married couples in the postwar years wanted large families. In one study of middle-class white couples in the mid-1950s, 39 percent wanted at least four children. As one wife recalled, "After the first baby, I wanted company for her and had a second daughter. A miscarriage left me with such a feeling of failure that I wanted the third child. The fourth was a happy accident. So now we're really 'happy' to be blessed with our two boys and two girls." For this woman, a miscarriage represented a "failure," even though she had no control over it. And an unplanned pregnancy was a "happy accident." Her story reflects the ways in which children were seen as blessings; large families were considered to be happy ones.

Of course, not all large families were happy. Children required care, attention, and money. The desire to provide college educations for all of their children was one reason why some parents limited the size of their families. As one mother explained, "I think if money had not been such a worrisome thing and if we had not had so many periods of unsteady jobs, we might have had more children." Another said, "After the first two were born and we appreciated the joys of parenthood it was mutually desired to have more children. We have stopped at four only because we feel the financial burden of educating more than four is more than we can see our way clear to assuming. We would both like six children. And it is not too late to change our minds about stopping at four!"

At a time when motherhood was supposed to provide fulfillment for women, few dared to complain about the stresses of childrearing. Women who chafed against the burdens of full-time motherhood were often accused of being selfish or "neurotic"—another common word at the time used much more frequently to describe the mental state of women than of men. One woman admitted that she believed there was more to life than constant child care: "The expenses of raising a child made us feel two would be enough. For we wanted to give a college education, music lessons, etc. to each child, if he showed interest. Also the interests I have had in church and community activities made me discontent with constant baby or child care." But comments like these were rare.

Why did postwar women and men want, and have, so many babies? There is no simple answer. The Baby Boom of the 1940s and '50s was accompanied by a widespread set of beliefs favoring large families. These ideas were everywhere, from magazines and TV shows to medical advice. Public policies, such as tax breaks for parents with dependent children and financial support for suburban home ownership, encouraged couples to have children. Still, one needs to ask why postwar couples—especially women—wanted large families.

One explanation is that prosperity encouraged people to have babies. There is certainly some truth to this, but there were other prosperous eras that did not spark a Baby Boom. And one study concluded that the evidence provided no support at all for the idea that higher income caused a higher birthrate between 1940 and 1960. Nevertheless, numerous children, like numerous appliances in the home, symbolized abundance.

There are some cultural explanations. Many educated women made homemaking their career, investing it with skill, prestige, creativity, and importance. Considering how difficult it was for women to build professional careers outside the home, it is not surprising that many women poured their energies into their families. As the *Ladies Home Journal* put it, "Increasing numbers of women, disillusioned with their present roles or with what the workaday world can offer, will turn toward motherhood as the happiest road to fulfillment." But motherhood could be full time only as long as there were young children at home. Once the children entered school, motherhood could not be full time, unless the woman had more children. Having additional children could extend the years of one's chosen career as a full-time mother.

With so much emphasis on having babies, those who did not have children faced both pity and scorn. Women in particular suffered if they were unable to have children. Since motherhood was expected to be a woman's main source of satisfaction, many childless women said that they felt "abnormal" and "unnatural." The adoption industry flourished during these years, with most of the demand coming from infertile middle-class couples and most of the supply coming from unmarried white girls and women. At the same time, the treatment of infertility practice became a booming medical field, even though only half of all cases could be diagnosed and treated. Although it was well known at the time that infertility was as likely to result from a problem with the man as with the woman, treatment was usually focused on the woman. Some doctors went so far as to operate on healthy, fertile women before checking to see if the problem might reside with the husband. Many women suffered through the pain and humiliation of infertility treatment in their desperate efforts to become mothers and live out the expected role of postwar women.

As with other aspects of life for American women, women pushed the limits of sexuality and reproduction as far as they could, given the constraints they faced. They struggled to maintain the fine line between sexual allure and sexual misbehavior, while redefining acceptable female sexuality before and during marriage. Those who fell outside the norm of acceptable conduct—single mothers, lesbians, and the childless—struggled to achieve dignity. And those who produced and reared the Baby Boom children put their greatest energies into the task.

Going Against the Grain

While much of white America retreated to the suburbs; conformed to the consumer, corporate way of life; and avoided political activism at a time when anti-Communist crusaders could easily destroy the lives of political dissenters, black America was busy marshaling the most important grass-roots political movement of the century. The civil rights movement captured the attention of the nation in 1955 with the Montgomery, Alabama, bus boycott. It began when Rosa Parks, an African-American woman, refused to give up her seat to a white person on a bus. But the seeds of the civil rights movement had been sown over many decades.

Although she had long been active in the struggle for racial equality, Rosa Parks became famous for her heroic act of defiance. In December 1955, she and two other women, Jo Ann Robinson and Virginia Durr, took action to end the segregation of buses. All three women were born in the South. Parks and Robinson were granddaughters of slaves; Durr was the granddaughter of slaveholders. Durr had been educated at Wellesley College, a women's college in the North, where she first learned to live with blacks as equals. She later married and moved to Washington, D.C., where she worked for the Democratic Women's Committee while rearing four children. Durr worked energetically to abolish the poll tax, a device used mostly in the South to charge money for the privilege of voting, effectively denying the vote to many blacks, poor whites, and women.

The Durrs returned to the South after the anti-Communist hysteria led by Senator Joseph McCarthy became unbearable for them, and they became active in the National Association for the Advancement of Colored People (NAACP). There Virginia Durr met Rosa Parks, who was a seamstress at a local department store and secretary of the NAACP. The third woman, Jo Ann Robinson, was the twelfth and youngest child of a farm family who owned their own farm in Georgia. She was the first in her family to attend college, and like most African-American women who began college, she graduated. She went on to earn a master's degree at the historically black Atlanta University, and in 1949 she joined the faculty of Alabama State College, another all-black institution, in Montgomery.

Robinson was not familiar with the system of segregation on the city buses; she owned her own car. One day, however, she decided to take a bus. Without knowing she was doing anything illegal, she sat down in one of the first ten rows of the bus—those reserved for whites. She did not realize the bus driver was yelling at her until he stood over her shouting, "Get up from there! Get up from there!" with his hand up ready to hit her. In horror and humiliation, she ran from the bus. The pain of that moment stayed with her, and she waited for the right opportunity to challenge the system.

Over the next several years, a number of black bus passengers refused to give up their seats. Each time, the black community wanted to take action, but they were not well enough organized. Finally, the time was right. On December 1, 1955, Rosa Parks left her job and caught the bus home. She sat in the black section of the bus, but the bus filled quickly and the driver demanded that she give up her seat to a white passenger. Technically, according to the law, blacks were not required to give up their seats if there were no other seats available further back in the bus. So Rosa Parks was in fact within her legal rights when she refused to move. Nevertheless, she was arrested and jailed.

Clifford Durr, Virginia Durr's husband and an attorney, bailed her out. Durr could easily have had the charges dismissed, because Parks had not violated the law. She was not required to give up her seat because there were no other seats on the bus. Parks's husband was terrified and wanted the charges dismissed. "Rosa, the white folks will kill you," he begged. But Rosa Parks and her friends were determined: They would not have the charges dismissed but would use the case to test the constitutionality of the segregation system, known as the Jim Crow laws.

While Parks awaited trial, Jo Ann Robinson worked energetically with a few of her students to draft, duplicate, and distribute thousands of fliers urging blacks to stay off Montgomery's buses. Here the active network of organized women moved into high gear. They took batches of fliers all over the city, where members of the Women's Political Council distributed them. Four days after Rosa Parks's arrest, she was tried and convicted. On that day, no blacks rode the Montgomery buses. Parks decided to appeal the decision, and the boycott continued. The night of the trial, more than ten thousand people gathered at Holt Church for a mass meeting. A young minister who had just moved to Montgomery, Reverend Martin Luther King, Jr., spoke passionately to the gathering, urging that the protest continue and calling for nonviolent resistance. From that moment on King was considered the leader of the nonviolent movement for civil rights. But women were powerful rank-and-file activists carrying the movement forward.

The participation of black women was most apparent in the bus boycott. Since they comprised the largest group of bus riders, their refusal to ride the buses made a huge dent in the revenue the buses needed to operate, making the boycott enormously successful. These women sacrificed mightily to participate in the boycott. For an entire year they walked from their homes on one side of town to the homes of their white employers on the other. "My feet is tired, but my soul is rested," said one elderly African-American woman of her daily trek. They had to deal not only with tired feet, but with hostile white city leaders who tried desperately to break the boycott.

The efforts of these women, along with the strength of the networks and political alliances that kept the boycott going, yielded tremendous success. In 1956 the case finally went to the Supreme Court, which ruled in *Gayle* v. *Browder* that Montgomery's Jim Crow laws, which enforced strict racial segregation in public places such as buses, stores, and restaurants, were unconstitutional because they deprived blacks of the equal protection of the laws guaranteed by the 14th Amendment.

By now the civil rights movement was in full swing. Martin Luther King, Jr., and other African-American leaders formed the Southern Christian Leadership Conference, and they hired Ella Baker, head of the New York chapter of the NAACP, as administrative assistant. Although Baker was an experienced veteran of the struggle for civil rights, and was probably the best person for the job as director of the organization, she was given a subordinate position. Baker was resigned to the situation, and explained it this way: "As a woman, an older woman, in a group of ministers who are accustomed to having women largely as supporters, there was no place for me to come into a leadership role." But from her position behind King's limelight, Baker mobilized the movement.

Baker had grown up in the South and had graduated from the all-black Shaw College, but her college degree earned her jobs only as a waitress and factory worker. During the 1930s and the war years, she was an active organizer for civil rights. In 1954, when the Supreme Court decided the *Brown* v. *Board of Education* case, ruling that segregated schools were unconstitutional, she became president of the New York City branch of the NAACP and worked to integrate the city schools. Later, when she helped to found the Student Nonviolent Coordinating Committee (SNCC) in 1960, she encouraged young students to violate segregation statutes all over the South by sitting in at lunch counters and registering voters in areas of the Deep South where blacks had been prohibited from voting for more than half a century.

By the early '60s, the danger and violence faced by civil rights activists had escalated to terrifying levels. But the movement continued, and it began to attract young whites from the North as well as the South. During the early years, few whites were directly involved. Some watched from the sidelines, some provided moral and material support, and some fought aggressively against the protestors. Leaders of a number of white churches supported the cause of equal rights; there were others who were opposed. Women were on all sides of the issue. Some southern white women participated in the bus boycott by driving their maids to and from work, either in sympathy with the effort or simply because they needed their hired help. Others were hostile. A few, like Virginia Durr, were active participants. But by and large, white women, like white men, shunned political activism in the 1950s.

For white Americans, trying to hang on to the fragile prosperity and security postwar life offered, political activism during the Cold War years was dangerous business. The mere suggestion of participation in any left-of center politics could cost their jobs and reputations. African Americans had a great deal to gain and were willing to risk taunts, threats, beatings, intimidation, and even death; whites had little to gain and perhaps much to lose by challenging the system. All across the nation, in Hollywood, on college and university campuses, in government offices, individuals suspected of left-wing sentiments were tarred with the brush of suspicion by the anti-Communist crusaders. Under the circumstances, it was difficult for whites to muster the courage to fight for the rights of African Americans. It was not until the 1960s that whites became active in the movement in significant numbers.

White women found other ways to influence public life, however. One way was through the voluntary organizations that emerged in cities, towns, and suburbs across the country. In churches, schools, charities, scout troops, and numerous civic clubs, women volunteered their time. Many middle-class women built virtual careers, and gained prominence and influence, through their volunteer efforts. As membership in churches and synagogues expanded, women were active in religious groups of all kinds, from choirs to Sunday schools to charities. In these groups, women learned new skills and forged networks that helped them overcome the isolation of their domestic routines.

For some, voluntarism was a direct route to power. Alice Leopold had been president of the League of Women Voters and director of a visiting nurses' program before becoming secretary of state in Connecticut in 1953. Because of her earlier experience as a volunteer, she knew how to get an equal-pay-for-women bill through the state assembly. In 1954 she organized a conference on the Equal Rights Amendment; later in her career she became director of the Women's Bureau in the U.S. Department of Labor.

A few notable women held positions of power in the 1950s, and used their positions to challenge the outrageous conduct of Senator Joseph McCarthy, who from 1947 to 1954 led the anti-Communist crusade against people with liberal views. McCarthy and his followers accused many innocent people of being security risks, disloyal citizens, Communist sympathizers, or "perverts," destroying careers and lives as he went along. Senator Margaret Chase Smith from Maine was one of the few who called upon the country to resist "fear, ignorance, bigotry and smear."

Other women used different channels to raise their voices in protest. Women newspaper publishers such as Katherine Graham, Dorothy Schiff, Agnes Meyer, and Alicia Patterson took liberal stands on issues like civil rights and McCarthyism, as the anti-Communist hysteria came to be called. Author Lillian Smith wrote on behalf of women's rights and racial equality, in spite of hostile critics. Dorothy Day published the *Catholic Worker* newspaper and wrote often about poverty and peace issues.

Mary McCarthy (no relation to Joseph) wrote many essays defending liberals and assailed the loyalty oaths and conformity required by McCarthyism. She was horrified by the attacks on intellectuals and teachers. She claimed that American students were not in danger of indoctrination by Communists, but rather were in danger of "being stupefied by the complacent propaganda for democracy," which was "pious, priggish, and groupy." Women scholars also registered their protest against life as it was. Rachel Carson, for instance, wrote a number of influential books calling for sensitivity to the environment, notably *The Sea Around Us* (1951), capping her career in the 1960s with her powerful warning about dangerous chemicals, *The Silent Spring*.

All across the country and in many different ways, individual women called for change and resisted the most oppressive conditions of the era. These efforts represented a prelude to the major upheavals that would begin in the 1960s. Efforts on behalf of women's rights were not well organized during the fifties. A small group of older women had forged a strong alliance earlier in the century as part of the National Woman's Party and continued to work together in the postwar years, but the momentum for women's rights collapsed. Most of the active women's organizations in the postwar years were apolitical. Groups like the League of Women Voters, Business and Professional Women, and the American Association of University Women were white middle-class mainstream groups that worked in the public interest, but did little to challenge the system. Only a few associations, such as the YWCA, began to build new alliances across race and class that would bring women from different backgrounds together to forge a new agenda.

Signs of stirring, however, were evident beneath the surface of postwar complacency. While most women experienced discontent in isolation, as exhausted housewives or underpaid and exploited workers, a few groups did begin to organize on their own behalf. In 1950, for example, when Chicano miners in New Mexico went on strike to protest wage cuts and unsafe conditions at the Empire Zinc Company, women began to mobilize to change the conditions of their lives. They had long suffered under miserable living conditions in company-owned towns, where they lived in shacks with no running water. They were unable to work in the mines and had no other job opportunities, so they were totally dependent upon their husbands' earnings. During the strike, they began to ask why the striking men were not demanding better housing conditions. The men dismissed the women's concerns as trivial, but soon the situation changed. Miners were forbidden to picket, and the company brought in truckloads of strikebreakers to take their jobs in the mines. Women suddenly took up the picket lines. Drawing upon the skills and friendships developed in their churches and neighborhoods, they bravely faced the police. Now the men, who had laughed at their domestic concerns, found themselves at home changing diapers and washing clothes—with no hot water. Women meanwhile found strength with each other on the picket lines, and in the crowded jails where they were thrown with their babies. Jailers hardly knew what to do with all the women who sang together even as their babies cried. When the women returned home, the men understood their needs, and they had gained new respect.

Another example of women's organizing emerged in the tiny lesbian community in San Francisco, where in 1955 a lesbian couple, Del Martin and Phyllis Lyon, founded the Daughters of Bilitis. They advocated equal rights for homosexuals and provided "a home for the Lesbian. She can come here to find help, friendship, acceptance and support. She can help others understand themselves, and can go out into the world to help the public understand her better."

Like the African-American women in the South who gave birth to the civil rights movement, the wives of the Chicano miners and the lesbians in San Francisco were already so excluded from mainstream American society that their struggles seemed worth the risks involved. They did not reap the benefits of the affluent society. They did not live on tidy, tree-lined suburban streets. They did not suffer from what Betty Friedan would later call the Feminine Mystique. Although the anti-Communist crusaders who followed Senator Joseph McCarthy would consider these women un-American, they were simply asserting their claim as Americans, wanting to be included in the American dream, wanting their full rights as citizens.

Even for those who presumably lived the American dream, discontent was beginning to surface. In March 1960, *Newsweek* discussed the plight of the housewife: "All admit to being deeply frustrated at times by the lack of privacy, the physical burden, the routine of family life, the confinement of it. However, none would give up her home and family if she had the choice to make again." *Redbook* chimed in the same year, offering a five-hundred-dollar prize for the best account of "Why Young Mothers Feel Trapped." More than twenty-four thousand women responded.

By the early 1960s, white middle-class women were beginning to fight back. On November 1, 1961, fifty thousand American housewives walked out of their homes and jobs in a massive protest, "Women Strike for Peace." They were among the first postwar middle-class whites to organize against the militarism of the Cold War. Several strike leaders had been active in the peace movement and other liberal causes during the '40s and '50s, but most were ordinary young housewives. According to *Newsweek*, the strikers "were perfectly ordinary looking women . . . They looked like the women you would see driving ranch wagons, or shopping at

Though properly clad as tidy housewives, women took to the streets to protest the dangers of nuclear testing. Some used their young children as props to demonstrate their stake in the future.

the village market, or attending PTA meetings . . . many [were] wheeling baby buggies or strollers." Within a year their numbers grew to several hundred thousand.

Anti-Communist crusaders worried that Women Strike for Peace signaled that "the pro-Reds have moved in on our mothers and are using them for their own purposes." The Federal Bureau of Investigation (FBI) kept the group under surveillance. In 1962 the leaders of the group were called before the House Un-American Activities Committee (HUAC), a committee much feared and hated by political activists because of the way it had destroyed the lives and careers of hundreds of Americans during the worst years of anti-Communist hysteria. But with the Women Strike for Peace activists, the Committee met its match. The tables were turned and now the women taunted and humiliated the congressmen. For three days, the committee hearing room was in turmoil. Hundreds of women packed the room, hissing, booing, shouting, applauding, and making no effort to quiet their noisy babies. The congressmen who tried to prove that these women were Communists looked ridiculous. The women were not intimidated and frightened the way most of the HUAC witnesses were. Retired schoolteacher Blanche Posner lectured the congressmen as if they were misbehaving school boys. "You don't quite understand the nature of this movement," she told them. "This movement was inspired and motivated by mothers' love for children. . . . When they were putting their breakfasts on the table, they saw not only the Wheaties and milk, but they also saw Strontium 90 and Iodine 131"—radioactive elements sometimes present in milk during this time as a result of atomic bomb testing.

What were the congressmen to do when confronted, literally, with motherhood and apple pie at a time when the virtues of the American home were considered the best antidote to communism? By the end of the third day of the hearings, Chairman Clyde Doyle had completely lost control of the situation. He forbade the spectators to stand. Then he forbade them to applaud. Finally they ran up and kissed the witnesses. The president of Women Strike for Peace, Dagmar Wilson, was called to the stand and presented with flowers by a young mother in the crowd. The dignified woman demolished the strategy of Doyle and his cronies. When asked if she "would knowingly permit or encourage a Communist party member to occupy a leadership position in Women Strike for Peace," she coolly replied, "Well, my dear sir, I have absolutely no way of controlling, do not desire to control, who wishes to join the demonstrations and the efforts that women strikers have made for peace. In fact, I would also like to go even further. I would like to say that unless everybody in the whole world joins us in the fight, then God help us."

These women carried the banner of motherhood into politics, a strategy that their grandmothers had used effectively in the suffrage movement of the turn of the century. Their ability to turn the rhetoric of the Cold War upside down and make a mockery of the dreaded committee hearings signaled that something powerful was beginning to happen among American women. The youth of the 1960s are usually given the credit—or the blame—for the upheavals unleashed during that decade on behalf of civil rights, women's rights, and peace, and for the cultural revolution that shattered the sexual mores and suburban conformity of the 1950s. But it was the parents of that youthful generation—largely their mothers—who paved the way. Women Strike for Peace was one example; the southern civil rights movement another.

Some women who lived the typical housewife life during the postwar years became fiery activists later. Betty Goldstein was one such woman. In 1943 she graduated summa cum laude from Smith College and won a graduate fellowship at Berkeley to complete her Ph.D. in psychology. When she told her boyfriend her good news, he let her know that she could choose between him and the fellowship. Crushed and afraid of becoming an "old maid college teacher," she turned down the opportunity, even though the romance did not last. Goldstein next went to Greenwich Village in New York, rented an apartment with some friends, and went to work as a journalist. But after the war ended and her friends married and moved to the suburbs, she began to fear being left alone. She married Carl Friedan and began having children in the late 1940s. When she was pregnant with her second child, she was fired from her job. For the next several years, Betty Friedan lived the life of a suburban housewife. Yet the education she acquired, her early career as a journalist, and her years of involvement with liberal political causes during the war all set the stage for later activism.

During the dormant '50s, those inclinations were submerged in a sea of domesticity. But in the early '60s, Friedan wrote a book that would capture the attention of educated white women across the country. *The Feminine Mystique* identified the "problem that has no name," the trap of the educated American housewife whose aspirations were stifled within the four walls of the home. Friedan urged her peers to leave their homes, pursue careers, and reject the stifling constraints of postwar domesticity. Her book became an instant best-seller. It was one of the first statements to pave the way for the new feminist movement that would soon erupt.

Soon younger women would organize that movement, which would move well beyond Betty Friedan's call for self-realization into a full-fledged assault on sexism in all its forms. The new feminists would demand access to professional occupations and skilled jobs, protest low wages, and work for pay equity. They would reject the sexual double standard that had plagued their mothers and would claim their rights to reproductive choice and legal abortion. These young women were acting on their own behalf, but they had also taken cues from their mothers. As one feisty member of Women Strike for Peace said in 1963, as she called for an end to the bomb-shelter mentality that had prevailed throughout the early Cold War era: "The thought of spending two weeks with two children in a close dark hole [family bomb shelter] was too horrible to think of and we knew we had to do something. Now that we women have started we will no longer be content to be dull uninformed housewives." Women of the 1940s and '50s kept pushing the limits, and eventually they broke through.

CHAPTER 10

The Road to Equality

1962–TODAY

William H. Chafe

The signs were auspicious for change. "The torch has been passed to a new generation of Americans," the young President John F. Kennedy said. After years of being governed by those born in the nineteenth century, the generation that came of age during World War II had surged to power, bringing a new tone of urgency and activism. "Ask not what your country can do for you," the President said, "but what you can do for your country." As if to symbolize the changing of the guard, people began paying new attention to problems and issues that for too long had been hidden in the shadows.

Although Kennedy was not known as a feminist, one of his first acts was to create a Presidential Commission on the Status of Women, naming Eleanor Roosevelt, the most venerated and admired woman in the country, as its honorary chair. In some ways this initiative was unconnected to Kennedy's far more conventional concerns with foreign policy and economic growth. Nevertheless, the commission reflected the air of unrest that was making its way through society as people awakened to new challenges. Students on the nation's campuses started to discuss political reform and social injustice. Young blacks in the American South boldly announced that black people would no longer accept being seated only in the balconies at movie theaters, using rest rooms marked "Colored Only," or standing up at lunch counters rather than sitting down with other customers. The nation had even started to read again about poverty in America and how more than 20 percent of American citizens—primarily old people and children, women, and blacks—were living below the "poverty level." All this was happening within a framework of excited optimism. Something *should* be done. Something *would* be done.

Let Us Begin

If a group of journalists had gathered around a table in 1962, they would not have been likely to select changes in women's lives as one of the major emerging stories. After all, politics as defined by John Kennedy was still a "macho" game dominated by the Cold War. Events such as the Cuban Missile Crisis were its real testing points. Even civil rights was more a showdown between male rivals than a searching inquiry into how issues such as race could shape and control a society.

Yet by the start of the 1970s few issues would have more prominence or significance than the feminist revolution and the changes taking place in the everyday lives of countless women. It all happened because of the flowering of criticism and reform that came with a new generation. Women's issues could not be ignored once young people started rebelling against social norms, students began challenging discrimination based on race (why not sex as well?), and antipoverty crusaders started examining the roots of economic oppression. Questions of gender and sexual politics may not have been the headlines that seized popular attention in 1962, but they were just below the surface, ready to become the news story that helped define an era.

No dramatic social change occurs for a single reason or springs from one group of people alone. But any effort to understand the transforming power of feminism in the late 1960s and 1970s must begin with the young people who were attending college when John Kennedy was inaugurated. Those college students already reflected a dramatic shift in life patterns. Twenty years earlier, when their parents were their age, only 15 percent of American youth had gone to college. But then had come World War II, the emergence of a fast-paced economy fueled by consumer purchases, a housing boom and technological innovation, and a corresponding explosion of economic and educational opportunities.

The "affluent society" meant more than a mass migration of young families to suburbia, the spread of sprawling shopping malls, and huge growth in automobile ownership and highway construction. It also necessitated a system of higher education that mass-produced the scientists, managers, and technological experts to sustain and expand the gains that had been made. America had become a "knowledge" society, and the university and its residents were a central part of the nation's nervous system. By 1965 45 percent of young people attended college—three times the proportion of a quarter century earlier. Reflecting the vital connection between education and the affluent society, 75 percent of these college students came from families with incomes above the national median. They represented—and were expected to reproduce—the social and economic comfort from which they came.

Yet the experience of having grown up in such comfort also gave young people a different perspective from which to consider their lifetime goals and priorities. Their parents had been raised during the hardships of the Great Depression in the 1930s and the uncertainties of war in the 1940s. They had struggled to win economic security and then prosperity in the postwar era. For the younger generation, material comfort was taken for granted, not a distant prize to be won or an elusive goal that gave life meaning. Perhaps that was why James Dean was such a cult hero for 1950s teenagers, and the film *Rebel Without a Cause* such a powerful generational symbol. Perhaps it was precisely "a cause" that young affluent Americans were searching for.

When they got to college, moreover, many of these students found an environment that encouraged them to be skeptical and critical of the social standards and practices that prevailed in the middle class. This was an era when the most popular book in sociology was *The Lonely Crowd* by David Riesman, a searing account of how Americans seemed to care more about pleasing others in order to get ahead than about standing up for their convictions. History and other disciplines started to focus more attention on such issues as slavery and racism. Universities had been dismissed by critics in the 1950s as mindless mazes through which conformist students moved quietly, like trained rats, toward a predetermined goal. That stereotype had always been overdrawn, but now it became positively wrong as students in different places and in different ways sought new answers and better questions.

In Cambridge, Massachusetts, for example, a group of Baptist students came together to form what was called the Fetter Family. Composed of young people attending Boston-area colleges, the "Family" met on a regular basis to talk about witnessing to their faith and to arrive at a clear commitment about how their religious views should be translated into practice in their communities. Each month members of the group journeyed to a town or village in Massachusetts to "testify" to their faith, agreeing—by prearrangement—to take over the programs of a local church for a weekend and to be in charge of everything from the Sunday sermon to the youth group.

In 1961 the theme of the Fetter Family was "Jesus Christ, the Revolutionary." When they went out to suburban towns and wondered out loud what Jesus Christ, the Revolutionary, might have to say about real estate contracts that barred blacks from moving to decent housing, or moralistic codes that said boys could be sexually active but girls must remain virgins, they were expressing some of the new energy and social criticism that were bubbling to the surface on campuses throughout the country.

That energy received formal expression in 1962 when a group of students from throughout the country came together in Ann Arbor, Michigan, to offer their manifesto for the future. "We are the people of this generation," the Students for a Democratic Society (SDS) declared, "bred in at least moderate comfort, housed now in universities, looking uncomfortably to the world we inherit." Disturbed by the expectation that they should conform to the values and practices of their parents, they insisted on a larger perspective that was critical of technocracy, committed to ending racial and social injustice, and devoted to building communities where people could live "with dignity and creativeness." Some of the young, at least, were ready to declare their agenda for change, and they believed they could achieve it.

A second place to look for the reasons why feminism and women's issues became so visible by the end of the decade is in the civil rights movement. No struggle shaped the 1960s generation as much as that of black Americans to secure full equality and justice. Nor did any other movement capture so completely the

After the lunch counter sit-in at the Woolworth's in Greensboro, North Carolina, the dime-store chain became a nationwide target of protests against Jim Crow policies. This picket line was set up in Jamaica, New York.

desire to create a better world. If white students were ready to criticize the world they inherited, racial discrimination offered them a powerful weapon; if they wished to act on their ideals and religious faith to show they could "make a difference," civil rights offered an ethical case to demonstrate their commitment; and if they hoped to find through their activism a real-life alternative to the world they were now questioning, there was no more inspiring model than that of the "beloved community" where blacks and whites, living and working together, could make peace and love and justice a reality.

The civil rights movement had its own long history, going back well before the 1940s and 1950s. Yet in its more recent existence, the movement provided themes and examples likely to inspire and galvanize the young: the 1955 bus boycott in Montgomery, Alabama, sparked by Rosa Parks's refusal to give up her seat because she was African American; the four black freshmen (all men) in Greensboro, North Carolina, who sat at a "whites-only" lunch counter in 1960 and launched a wave of sit-ins that spread to fifty-four cities in nine states; and the men and women students from all over the South who met in Raleigh, North Carolina, that same year to form the Student Non-Violent Coordinating Committee (SNCC). Its credo, similar to that of Dr. Martin Luther King Jr. was a powerful evocation of the faith, confidence, and spirit that would inspire a generation. "We affirm the philosophical . . . ideal of non-violence as a foundation of our purpose," SNCC leader James Lawson declared, "the presupposition of our faith, and the manner of our action. . . . Love is the central motif of non-violence. . . . Such love goes to the extreme; it remains loving and forgiving even in the midst of hostility. It matches the capacity of evil to inflict suffering with an even more enduring capacity to absorb evil, all the while persisting in love." To people looking for an ideal to live and possibly die for, the SNCC credo embodied the best that America had to offer.

Many of the most important leaders in the civil rights movement were women. Rosa Parks had long been a mainstay of the National Association for the Advancement of Colored People (NAACP) in Montgomery. Jo Ann Robinson and the Women's Political Council had played a key role in organizing the bus boycott there. Ella Baker was in many ways the mother of the civil rights movement. In addition to being one of the NAACP's chief organizers in the South, she also served as the acting executive director of Dr. King's Southern Christian Leadership Conference at the end of the 1950s (male ministers, she found, were more comfortable making her "acting" director rather than director). In Greensboro, a black schoolteacher, Nell Coley, had been a constant source of inspiration to the sit-in students, telling them "the way you find things need not happen. . . . I don't care if they push and shove you, you must not accept [discrimination]. . . . You are who you are."

As some white students came to join blacks in SNCC during the early 1960s, they found black women playing pivotal roles in the movement, roles that demonstrated a new possibility for women's activism, one not usually associated with the roles social convention prescribed for women. Along with the civil rights movement itself, and the growing criticism of societal norms that was emerging in the new generation, this experience of women's leadership would contribute to the gradual emergence of a feminist agenda.

In the meantime, other less visible changes had made the legal and economic status of women a significant concern for policymakers. During the twentieth century the proportion of women in the labor force had been increasing. Before World War II most of these women were young, single, and poor. They worked almost exclusively in sex-segregated jobs, such as domestic service and clerical positions. Where they did occupy jobs similar to those held by men, they were paid only a fraction of the male wage. A disproportionate number of women workers came from immigrant backgrounds or were African Americans or Latinas. Although over time more married women joined the labor force, especially during the Depression when survival required that everyone earn money if possible, society still expected that all but the poorest women should concentrate on homemaking once they married and started to have children.

World War II did not alter this expectation overnight, but it accelerated some long-term trends in women's employment and changed the cultural dynamics affecting women's work. More than six million women took jobs during the labor crisis created by the war—an increase in the female labor force of more than 50 percent. Most important, 75 percent of these women were married and 60 percent were over the age of thirty-five. The end of the war brought a massive propaganda campaign to force women to return to the home, but some effects of the wartime experience remained. The proportion of married women in the labor force had increased from 15 percent in 1940 to almost 25 percent in 1950. The average age of women workers had increased. And more and more women who were middle class and educated were taking jobs.

The aftermath of World War II produced a kind of cultural division in attitudes toward women. On the one hand, psychologists, family "experts," the media, advertisers, and public opinion leaders celebrated domesticity, portraying mothers and housewives as "daily content in a world of bedroom, kitchen, sex, babies and home." Yet at the same time, many women were acting in ways that seemed to contradict the experts' advice. All during the suburban bliss of the 1950s, women were taking jobs at a rate four times faster than men. Frequently, these were not full-time jobs. Rarely were they in fields that offered promotion or high pay. Nor did there appear to be any "feminist" motivation driving women to the work force. In fact, women were taking jobs in order to help the family move one rung higher on the middle-class ladder, afford an addition to the suburban tract house they had just bought, set money aside for a college fund for the kids, or buy a new car. It was part of becoming a member of the affluent society.

Moreover, women—especially middle-class women—were developing a pattern of seeking jobs that had its own clear cultural logic. The greatest increase in employment among women took place among those over thirty-five whose children were in school. The proportion of women at work in that category leaped from 25 percent in 1950 to 39 percent in 1960. Thus young mothers were still staying at home, to do what the magazines said they should do, but once their children started school they were taking jobs on the reasoning that, with another income, the family as a whole could enjoy a better life. By 1960 the percentage of married women at work had doubled compared to 1940 (from 15 percent to 30 percent), and both husbands and wives worked outside the home in more than 10 million families (an increase of 330 percent over 1940).

Some economists and policymakers noted these trends. The National Manpower Council, for example, conducted a lengthy study aimed at improving "development and utilization of the country's human resources." Published when the Soviet Union seemed to be racing ahead of the United States in technology (*Sputnik,* the Soviet space satellite, had been launched in 1957, the world's first such venture), the council's book, *Womanpower,* emphasized that women's talents were essential to winning the competition for control of the world. According to one expert, data from college entrance examinations, administered by the Educational Testing Service, showed that women constituted 98 percent of the bright young people who did not go to college. Was it not time to look anew at the job opportunities available to women, the extent to which they were receiving the training necessary to maximize their abilities, and the degree to which the government bore a responsibility to advance the status of women as a precious national resource?

Against this backdrop President Kennedy appointed his national Commission on the Status of Women in 1961. In part he was paying off a political debt to Esther Peterson, a longtime supporter who for years had worked in the halls of Congress as a lobbyist for garment workers and other labor union women, and whom Kennedy now appointed head of the Women's Bureau of the U.S. Department of Labor. Kennedy also hoped to solidify his position with liberals by making Eleanor Roosevelt the honorary chair of the commission. Hardly a bold or risky maneuver from Kennedy's point of view, examining the status of women seemed an ideal way to signal recognition of an important constituency and support mobilizing the full resources of the country to win the Cold War.

The commission fulfilled Kennedy's hopes, completing in 1963 a comprehensive, balanced, and careful analysis of women's situation. It covered some important new ground on women's issues. For example, it emphasized the critical importance of child care facilities to full utilization of women's resources, recommended paid maternity leave, and supported giving unemployment and minimum wage benefits to large numbers of women previously not covered. Perhaps most important, it focused attention on the pervasive inequities women experienced on the job, preparing the way for the Equal Pay Act of 1963. This act mandated that where women and men did exactly the same job, they should receive exactly the same wage.

On some more contentious issues, the commission embraced compromise. Ever since 1923 the National Woman's Party, headed by Alice Paul, had singlemindedly pursued passage of the Equal Rights Amendment (ERA) to the Constitution. The amendment would have prohibited any law that used sex as a basis for treating men and women differently, but up until the 1960s most women's organizations believed that some laws protecting women were necessary. Widow's pension laws, regulations governing night work, provisions limiting the amount of weight a woman could be asked to carry—all these laws would be abolished under the ERA. Although after 1941 the Supreme Court ruled that minimum-wage and maximum-hour laws could be extended to men as well as women (previously, the Court had said only women could be protected), many women reformers were still convinced that some laws recognizing women's differences were useful.

Confronted with this long-simmering controversy, the commissioners agreed to disagree. Their final report declared that the ERA "need not now be sought,"

President Kennedy signs the Equal Pay Act in 1963. Among the witnesses are Esther Peterson (front row, left, in light dress), head of the Women's Bureau, and Vice President Lyndon B. Johnson (far right).

advocating instead another strategy for promoting women's legal rights. The 14th Amendment to the Constitution guaranteed all citizens "equal protection under the law." The commission believed that this clause could serve as a basis for freeing women citizens from discriminatory treatment—much in the same way that black civil rights advocates had used it.

Yet the commission's most important contribution was not what it said or failed to say, but the fact that it existed. It formally acknowledged the fact that women's rights and opportunities were of critical national importance. The commission had not only gathered information and made recommendations, it had created an organizational structure of people sharing common concerns. These people were committed to working together to develop a common base of data from which to proceed.

A network had been established. Pivotal to that network were a series of state commissions on the status of women. These commissions were created through-out the country to pursue on a local level the same work being done by the nation-al commission. Starting in 1964, the state commissions gathered annually in

Washington, D.C., to assess the progress that had been made on women's agenda of change and to generate strategies for the next step. Such a gathering in 1966 would lead to a result that Kennedy could never have anticipated in 1961—the creation of the National Organization for Women (NOW), which would become the civil rights vanguard of a reborn and revitalized feminism.

The politicians who prepared to take power in the winter of 1961 as representatives of the "new generation of Americans" had many concerns, but it is unlikely that any of them saw women's rights, child care, or gender roles as priority issues. These men, after all, were "technocrats" who prided themselves on "crisis management," "fine-tuning" the economy, and calibrating the most efficient strategy for containing the spread of communism. Yet historical change comes from unanticipated consequences as often as from well-planned designs. Whatever the actual priorities of the Kennedy administration, its leaders and participants conveyed a message of change, of vitality, of confidence, and of commitment. "We can do better," the President said.

To a degree that he would never have foreseen, that sense of commitment—the feeling that people could make a difference—resonated with undercurrents that had already begun to be felt throughout the society. Although the postwar America had been dominated by change, the cultural mood at the end of the 1950s was of complacency, conformity, and comfort—yet many segments of society were prepared to burst that bubble and address some of the contradictions and inequities beneath its surface.

Those who received and interpreted the political messages of change in the early 1960s, rather than those who pronounced them, would make the greatest difference in the nation's social history. By the end of the Kennedy administration, young people, civil rights activists, and women reformers had all given their own meaning to the phrase "we can do better." A common thread running through each was the need to take seriously the issue of equality between women and men in America.

Different Audiences

Late in the 1970s a bumper sticker began to appear regularly on cars owned by feminists. It read: "A Woman Without a Man Is Like a Fish Without a Bicycle." Interpretations of the phrase were as varied as its readers. But one clear message was that women could survive and prosper without men, just as fish could survive and prosper without bicycles. Men and women were of different worlds, with different rhythms, attributes, priorities, and values. In short, they had little if anything to do with each other.

That was a radical message, light-years away from where young students and civil rights workers were in the early 1960s. It would take multiple stages of alienation, anger, and bitterness before such a bumper sticker could emerge. In the meantime, events had to unfold, and a thousand different voices had to be heard.

The overpowering irony of the idea of a woman's movement was that women were everywhere, constituting 51 percent of the population, members of all classes and of all ethnic, religious, political, and economic groups. If, as some argued, women were oppressed like minorities, they surely did not all share the same material circumstances, suffer the same degree of discrimination, or live together in the same run-down neighborhoods as some African Americans did on Chicago's South Side or as Mexican Americans did in the Los Angeles barrios. What, then, did it mean to share an identity? Did a rich, white, college-educated woman who ran the local Junior League have more in common with her Latina maid who had never gone to high school than with her rich, white, college-educated husband? What defined the bonds of gender? And could they be as strong as the bonds of class or ethnicity or religion?

Any movement that developed to address issues of gender inequality had to deal with the question of audience. If a woman without a man was like a fish without a bicycle, it was even more true that a cause without a public to support it was no cause at all. Who, then, were some of the potential audiences among women in the early 1960s that might follow this movement if it came into being? What were their concerns? How ready were they to join a larger political and social revolution? What mattered to them? And were they prepared to share their individual discontents and find in that sharing the basis for collective action based on a common identity?

At least in retrospect, the most striking thing women appeared to have in common in the early 1960s was a sense of relative happiness. In 1962 the George Gallup polling organization asked a cross section of American women whether they were content with their lot. Two out of three women said yes. When the question was posed whether women as a group were victims of inequality or discrimination, only one in three women said yes. From one perspective, of course, that level of discontent was very high, suggesting profound problems. On the other hand, the overall level of satisfaction seemed high, especially in light of other polls in which most women said the greatest fulfillment of their lives was when they gave birth to their children, and a strong majority expressed satisfaction with their roles as homemakers.

One way to read such evidence is to conclude that some, and perhaps many, women did have problems in their lives but that they saw these problems as peculiar to themselves or their own circumstances, not as part of a shared phenomenon based on their being women. They might reflect on their individual situation, even talk about it with their women friends, and still not see their dilemma as a "woman" problem. In the early 1960s there was not yet even a label for such concerns. As feminist author Betty Friedan would describe it, it was a "problem that had no name." Moreover, there was more than one problem—or at least the problem seemed different depending on who you were, how old you were, where you lived, and what you wanted. It was hard to discern unity in the face of such

WHAT KIND OF WOMAN ARE YOU?

FRANTIC COOK?

Chauffeur?

Smothered Mother?

TOO INVOLVED?

Restless?

Interesting?

𝔍nformed?

Responsible Parent?

Motivated?

Satisfied?

BETTY FRIEDAN
author, "THE FEMININE MYSTIQUE"

Betty Friedan will help you decide when she speaks on

"A NEW IMAGE OF WOMAN"

 Attend Temple Emanu-El Sisterhood

DONOR LUNCHEON

Tuesday, October 29, 1963

As she traveled throughout the country to promote the ideas in her ground-breaking book *The Feminine Mystique,* Betty Friedan urged American women to reexamine their lives.

diversity. It was also important to understand how real women, in different circumstances, might perceive the world around them as reflecting or not reflecting issues of gender. The experiences described here and later are those of real people, although their names and some details have been altered.

Laura Whiting was the daughter of English immigrants who came to America in 1903. She was born in 1913. Her father was a night watchman, her mother a cafeteria worker. Bright and energetic, Laura did well in high school. She then went on to take secretarial courses that enabled her to move beyond the occupational level of her parents and get a good clerical position by the time she was in her early twenties. She married on the eve of World War II, had a child within a year, and settled comfortably in the role of wife and homemaker.

Laura's husband came from a slightly better background economically than she did, but he too had taken just a few business courses after high school. Older than she, he did not have to go to fight in World War II but worked in a munitions plant instead. When the war was over he took a job as a bookkeeper, earning less than three thousand dollars a year. The couple rented an apartment and lived on a tight budget, but they worried about money. Eventually he inherited a house, but their budget remained tight, and it was sometimes a strain to find the extra money for new curtains or a vacation trip. With her child now in school most of the day, Laura wanted to go back to work, remembering fondly her job as a secretary and the social pleasures that came from chatting with other employees and making jokes.

But Laura's husband resisted that idea, refusing to give her permission to find a job, even part-time. He was somewhat old-fashioned, and believed that earning an income and providing for the family was a man's role. If she went to work, people might think he was not able to fill that role, that he was not really a man.

Laura went along with her husband's wishes. In the 1950s most people still believed in the sexual division of labor and man's authority in the family. But the disagreement between them was painful and sometimes bitter. She shared her unhappiness with some of her woman friends. They were all part of a woman's club at the church and would get together regularly to cook church suppers, run rummage sales, or have monthly socials. Occasionally, the whole group would talk about family problems and men, sharing a common sensibility about the "war between the sexes." But no one ever uttered the word "feminism," and all the women seemed to feel the situation was perfectly normal. After all, every married couple had problems, and over time, they usually worked out.

In Laura's case, she eventually was able to persuade her husband that it was all right for her to take a part-time job, especially once their son was in college. She enjoyed the work and the people enormously. She had been right. There was a zest and vitality that came from being out in the world. But she had still not made any connection in her own mind between the problem that she had experienced and larger issues that related to gender. She had solved her own problem, as others of her friends had solved theirs, and there did not seem to be a larger, overriding issue.

Hilda Newberry was born in 1930, seventeen years after Laura, just as the Great Depression was beginning. Although Laura's father was out of work for a number of years, Hilda's family survived the economic crisis fairly well. A product of an old-stock upper New York State family, she grew up in middle-class comfort. Because of her background and the expectations middle-class families had for their daughters in those days, Hilda went to an excellent private junior college for women at the end of the 1940s. The intellectual content of the courses was solid. But ordinarily students went there to acquire the kind of education that would prepare them for a brief work career and then marriage to a professional or business person of comparable background.

That was what happened to Hilda. In the early 1950s she fell in love with the son of an advertising executive. After she accompanied him on a brief stint in the army, they settled down in New York, where he began a career in business. He soon became a banker on Wall Street, and with growing success, earned enough so that they could move to a suburb on Long Island. The mothers gathered to keep an eye on the young children, to share gossip, and to have fun. In these backyard get-togethers there was always news to share—whose husband was getting what promotion, the latest addition to the neighborhood, emotional or physical problems among the children. Here they could also talk about their private hopes and dreams or the difficulties they were having in their marriages. Sometimes the conversation would even touch on such topics as sex and divorce. The women formed a close-knit community, solidified each day by shared rituals of coffee, conversation, and child supervision. They were dedicated on one level simply to helping each other get through the day but, in an even larger sense, to building and maintaining the family as a unit and the community as a group enterprise.

Some of Hilda's friends took part-time jobs at the local library and public school. Others devoted long hours to volunteer work with the PTA, Cub Scouts, and Brownies. Most spent endless hours in activities caricatured in novels and high-brow magazines—chauffeuring children to ballet lessons and Little League practice and driving their husbands to and from the commuter train station. But for the most part, suburban women's days were neither mindless nor empty. With the same spirit that animated their backyard conversations, women used their activities to give substance and purpose to a way of life.

But Hilda and her friends shared feelings of anger and alienation about this way of life. Like the college graduates whom Betty Friedan wrote about in *The Feminine Mystique* (1963), they felt that their education and talents had been put on the shelf before even being tried out in the real world. Their days took on a uniformity that discouraged the flowering of individual interests and skills. A person trained in design, literature, or political science could feel that she had entered a time warp upon getting married and moving to suburbia—shut off totally from the life and excitement she had once known.

Problems also came with compartmentalized sex roles—husbands in work situations full of managerial crises, occasional flirtations, and at least the appearance of worldly sophistication; wives frustrated by the inability to have shared experiences to discuss at dinnertime. Where was the partnership everyone talked about in this age of "companionate" marriage? How did people share a life when their existences were so separate and different? Why did she always change the diapers and do the laundry? What was her goal, her objective, to reach? He had his career and the next big law case to spur him on. What did she have, especially when, at the occasional business dinner, she was expected to discuss babies and recipes with the other wives and not to challenge her husband's pompous colleague on subjects about which she knew far more than he?

Thus the conversations in the backyard and over coffee represented a confluence of concerns. On good days, the sense of fellowship, affection—yes, even sisterhood, though that word had not yet become part of a political vocabulary—made the life of community building in the suburbs seem rewarding and self-justifying. On bad days the frustration over the lack of companionship in marriage and the lack of opportunity for achievement and self-expression made living on Long Island more a "suburban captivity," as one sociologist called it, than an exercise in creativity. For Hilda the good days outnumbered the bad. But then, in the early 1960s, there was still no language to label moments of discontent or to define them as part of a collective experience.

Barbara Harris had a life very different from that of either Hilda Newberry or Laura Whiting. Born toward the end of World War II, she was the fourth daughter in an African-American family that eventually included eight children. Her father had migrated to Winston-Salem from Warren County, North Carolina, where his family raised tobacco on a thirty-acre farm. In 1930 Winston-Salem was a fast-growing, "new South" city where life was supposedly better for black people. Barbara's father became a tobacco stemmer in the R. J. Reynolds cigarette factory, and his wife worked as a part-time domestic servant, cleaning the homes of white people five or six hours each day.

Barbara was bright, funny, and very pretty. Like her mother, she became active in the local AME Zion Church, singing in the youth choir, going to prayer meetings, helping with the food preparation and service at the wonderful meals that always seemed to highlight religious gatherings. She felt very well off, at least relative to some of her friends, until her father suddenly left home after his eighth child had been born. From that time on he would pop up periodically in their lives, but he was no longer a stable presence, financially or otherwise.

When it came time for Barbara to go to high school in 1958, there was already talk about demanding that blacks be able to enroll at previously all-white schools. Some of Barbara's friends petitioned to do so in accordance with the Supreme

Court's *Brown* decision, which had mandated an end to segregation, but the process was long and painful and often meant harassment and intimidation from whites. Barbara's mother could not afford the time or trouble of such a struggle, so Barbara went to the all-black high school that her older sisters had attended. But Barbara was very aware of segregation and the growing talk about challenging it. Every time she climbed up to the balcony of the downtown theater to sit in the "colored" section, she thought about the issue.

When Barbara was sixteen, the sit-ins began in nearby Greensboro. One week later they broke out at Woolworth's in Winston-Salem. The sit-in was led by Carl Matthews, a friend of her oldest sister. She and her classmates were thrilled and frightened. Here was a group of students, hardly older than they were, taking on the entire system of racism—defying white policemen, refusing to leave the five-and-dime when ordered to by the manager, sitting there and being spat upon and sworn at by white kids with leather jackets and slicked-back hair. Then one day a classmate of Barbara's suggested that a group of high school students go down to Woolworth's and join the demonstrations. After all, he said, they were part of the new generation too. Why shouldn't they do their part?

Barbara was terrified, but she also was excited. This was the chance of a lifetime, an opportunity to change her life and that of everyone else she knew with black skin. She did not tell her mother about her plans, because she knew she would be worried. With her high school classmates, Barbara went downtown the next day after school and took her place at the lunch counter alongside the college and high school students who were insisting that life be different and better. It was the greatest moment she had ever experienced.

Barbara was smart enough and had good enough grades to go on to college or a technical institute after high school. But in her senior year she met a boy and fell in love. A few months later she discovered that she was pregnant. It was 1961, abortion was not something that people talked about very much, and, besides, having a child was a source of pride and achievement. Barbara had thought about what it would be like to become a civil rights worker in Mississippi or Georgia—like the students she saw on television, demonstrating, being beaten, sometimes being murdered. But now she had a daughter and had to find some way to support her.

As the years went by, Barbara's life did not become any easier. She took a job as a receptionist at an insurance company. She eventually married and had another child. But the relationship was not smooth. Her husband went out with other women, and when she complained, he hit her. After five years he moved out, leaving her to support the children alone. Some of her other women friends had the same kind of problem, and they talked about it together.

On one hand, many things seemed to be changing for the better. A civil rights law, passed in 1964, had abolished separate eating, bathroom, and theater facilities, and a voting rights act, passed in 1965, gave every black person the right to vote. Yet Barbara and most of her friends could still barely survive on a paycheck not much more than the minimum wage. Barbara thought about how good it would be if she had a husband who loved her and could help support the children, and she sometimes wondered whether this problem between women and men was universal and whether anything could be done about it. But usually she worried more about putting enough food on the table and buying winter coats for the kids. The rest seemed almost like a given, the way things were, something you could not really change.

The stories of Laura Whiting, Hilda Newberry, and Barbara Harris exemplify the diversity of experience and background that women brought to the early 1960s. Anyone who talked to these three women about their daily lives would probably be impressed mainly by how distinctive their life histories were. Each was a product of her own time, place, and background.

Yet these women were united as well by common experiences shaped by their gender. They may not have used such a word in 1962—at least in the way it came to be used two decades later—but the reality of their lives reflected some shared concerns. All grew up in a culture that assigned people different roles based on their sex. Women were always expected to do the housework, care for the children, and cook the meals. Women who had men in their lives were also expected to follow their lead and be deferential. No matter what a woman's race, class, or religion, she was limited to certain kinds of jobs, ordinarily segregated by sex, that paid lower wages and had fewer opportunities for promotion than men's jobs.

Perhaps the most important bond uniting women was their relationship to men. The details of individual women's lives might vary enormously, but all experienced the difficulty of negotiating and living with men accustomed to privilege, control, and power based on their sex. For Barbara Harris it might mean being hit; for Laura Whiting, being told she could not take a job; for Hilda Newberry, being expected to keep her mouth shut when one of her husband's colleagues said something stupid. In each case there was a gender boundary that represented a difference potentially far greater than any that might divide the three women from each other.

There was also the opportunity, shared by each of these women, to confide in their sisters—women from the same class, background, or neighborhood whom they knew in many ways far more intimately than they did the men in their lives. Whether it was Hilda in the backyard, Laura at the church supper, or Barbara with her high school classmates, a community existed that offered a sounding board, reinforcement, and emotional sustenance.

Was gender as powerful a source of identity as race or class? Given a choice of which was more important in her life, would Barbara Harris select the gender she had in common with Hilda Newberry, or the color she shared with her husband? If one woman was poor and worked on a factory floor with other poor people, male and female, did she have more in common with them, or with the wife of the factory owner, who was rich?

Whatever their different backgrounds, Laura Whiting, Hilda Newberry, and Barbara Harris each had identified a problem in their lives having to do with men. For every one of them in the early 1960s, it was a "problem that has no name." They talked about it with each other, they described similar situations, but they all saw their predicaments as individual in nature, part of "the way things are," dilemmas to be coped with, each woman by herself.

What would happen when someone gave the problem a name, described its origins and development, and sought to forge a collective voice of protest and action to solve it? When that happened, which would prevail—the voice of commonality, or the voices of difference?

The Rebirth of Feminism

During the 1960s, events sometimes happened so quickly that they almost seemed to outpace the speed of sound. In the fall of 1961 coeducational colleges still had rules regulating the few short periods of the week when men could be in woman's dorms and vice versa. Boys wore ties and button-down shirts and sported "whiffle" haircuts (so short that if you rubbed your hand over the bristles you could generate static electricity); girls wore skirts, starched blouses, knee socks, and pony tails. No one would think of calling a university president a derogatory name or breaking into official files.

By 1969, in contrast, rules had become synonymous with fascism. Male and female students lived with each other in the same dormitory room; a new sexual revolution had swept the country, accompanied by widespread experimentation with drugs. At the legendary rock festival at Woodstock in 1969, thousands of people gathered in open fields to hear their favorite musicians, celebrating not only a triumphant counterculture but brazenly flouting conventional, middle-class behavior. Boys and girls wore jeans patched with fragments of the American flag, smoking marijuana was commonplace, and hair reached the lower backs of men and women alike. Policemen were routinely called "pigs" by some of the best and brightest college students, and one university president, whose office was occupied by demonstrators, received a manifesto telling him: "up against the wall, motherfucker." It was quite a decade.

Nothing changed more quickly, or posed so great a challenge to traditional authority and customs, as the ways some women thought of themselves and their role in society. In 1962 *Harper's Magazine* thought it was being bold in commenting that American women seemed "ardently determined to extend their vocation beyond the bedroom, kitchen and nursery." The editors could not have conceived of the possibility that a few short years later the daughters of some of these same women would demand the abolition of their confinement to the bedroom, kitchen, and nursery, an end to the traditional family, abortion "on demand," and—in some cases—the creation of all-female communities.

Even "moderate" feminists held sit-ins at the editorial offices of *Newsweek* and

In 1968 members of the National Women's Liberation Movement demonstrated outside the Miss America pageant in Atlantic City, New Jersey, on the grounds that it set false goals for women.

the *Ladies' Home Journal*, demanding that women be assured an equitable share of high-level positions. It was a time of extraordinary transformations, from dramatizing the "sexploitation" of the Miss America contest in 1968 to creating the legal and cultural framework to admit women to the military academies at West Point and Annapolis as equals with men.

When the leaders of President Kennedy's Commission on the Status of Women wrote their final report in 1963 demanding equal pay for equal work and an end to discriminatory treatment of women in the legal system and on the job, they were making a natural rights argument as old as the Declaration of Independence. Individuals possessed God-given rights, they emphasized, and it was a violation of universal laws of nature for these to be denied on the basis of such group characteristics as race or sex. As early as the 1940s, when the Carnegie Foundation issued its clarion call, authored by the Swedish sociologist Gunnar Myrdal, to end racial discrimination, sociologists and lawyers had commented that women were examples of an "American Dilemma." Like black people, they were members of a society committed to liberty and personal freedom, yet treated as separate and different because of a shared physical characteristic. The contradiction was profound, striking at the heart of the integrity of the American Creed. Only when all citizens were freed from such categorical discrimination could the American dream be considered workable.

Pauli Murray, a black lawyer who had pioneered the effort to get blacks admitted to Southern law schools in the 1930s, zeroed in on the connection between racial and sexual equality in her work for the Kennedy Commission on the Status of Women. Like black civil rights activists, she declared, women should prosecute their case for freedom by going to court and demanding equal protection under the laws, a right conferred by the 14th Amendment. This amendment, added to the Constitution in 1868, sought to ensure the legal standing of the newly freed slaves by defining their citizenship rights. At the time Congress had inserted the word "male" in front of "citizen," caving in to those who still wanted to exclude women from fundamental rights, such as voting. But the 19th Amendment had altered that by recognizing women's right to vote, and now, Murray argued, women should insist on carrying their case forward on the basis of the civil rights they enjoyed with all citizens under the clause of the 14th Amendment that declared, "No State shall . . . deny to any person within its jurisdiction the equal protection of the laws."

Betty Friedan referred to parallels between racial and sexual equality in her 1963 book, *The Feminine Mystique,* but, more centrally, reached out to galvanize the consciousness of millions of American women by giving a label to "the problem that has no name." The dominant institutions of American culture, Friedan charged, had tried to treat women like children by enclosing them in "comfortable concentration camps" where they were told they must be happy because they were women, not individuals. Assigned a set of responsibilities solely on the basis of their sex, women had been denied the chance to cultivate their individual talents or assert their personal rights.

"I've tried everything women are supposed to do," one young mother wrote Friedan, "hobbies, gardening, pickling, canning, and being very social with my neighbors. . . . But I'm desperate. I begin to feel that I have no personality. I'm a server of food and putter-on of pants and a bedmaker, somebody who can be called on when you want something. But who am I?" The question struck at the heart of all the concerns that produced distress in the lives of Laura Whiting, Hilda Newberry, and Barbara Harris. They were always supposed to accept a man's commands, to fulfill some role society said was theirs, and they were discouraged from claiming their own voices and challenging the status quo.

In the strange way that history happens, the link between civil rights and feminism was enshrined in law by a perverse attempt to derail the 1964 Civil Rights Act. Representative Howard Smith, a conservative Southern Democrat, thought he could ensure the bill's defeat if he added women to its coverage, making sex—as well as race—susceptible to civil rights legislation. That idea would appear so ridiculous, Smith imagined, that Congress would not support it, and the civil rights bill would fail to pass. Instead, an unusual coalition of conservatives and liberals formed to pass the amendment. It was just as logical to outlaw discrimination based on sex as it was to prohibit discrimination based on skin color, and women's rights activists had long understood the analogy. Now that logic was installed in the law, and it became a major instrument for achieving the goals of the President's Commission on the Status of Women.

Unfortunately, many of those responsible for enforcing the new legislation shared Smith's opinion that adding women to the measure was more a joke than a serious public policy. Explicitly and implicitly, those directing the Equal Employment Opportunities Commission (EEOC)—the government agency charged with implementing the civil rights law—gave notice that they would not treat complaints about sex discrimination the same way they would treat grievances based on racial discrimination. Once that approach became known, the network of women reformers nurtured by the President's commission went into action. Meeting in Washington, D.C., in 1966 to monitor enforcement provisions by the EEOC, members of the various state commissions on the status of women—led by Pauli Murray and Betty Friedan—decided the time had come, in Friedan's words, "to take the actions needed to bring women into the mainstream of American society, now, full equality for women, in fully equal partnership with men. NOW. The National Organization for Women."

With the formation of NOW in the fall of 1966, America's women's rights activists had an organization comparable to the NAACP, ready to fight through the media, the courts, and the Congress for the same rights for women that the NAACP sought for blacks. NOW focused on an "equal partnership of the sexes" in job opportunities, education, household responsibilities, and government. Friedan and her allies pressured Kennedy's successor, President Lyndon B. Johnson, to include women in his affirmative action policies, which were designed to speed the movement of minorities to decent jobs, and to appoint feminists to administrative and judicial offices. NOW endorsed the Equal Rights Amendment and made reform of abortion laws a national priority.

Even before NOW formed, a younger generation of women were gaining a new sense of themselves in the civil rights movement. Most of the younger activists joined the Student Non-Violent Coordinating Committee (SNCC), which created an atmosphere in which independent thinking and social criticism could flourish. The majority were black, but a significant minority were white, many of them women, including Sondra Cason (later Casey Hayden) from the Faith and Life community in Austin, Texas, and Mary King, daughter of a Protestant minister. A new sense of empowerment infused the women and men alike. "If you are spending your time [doing] community organization, . . . opening people's awareness to their own power in themselves," Mary King noted, "it inevitably strengthens your own conceptions, your own ability." As women took their turn risking life and limb to make the movement happen, they were transformed in their own sense of who they were and what they could do. "I learned a lot of respect for myself for having gone through all of that," one said.

White women were impressed by the black women they met. Some of the black women were older; black minister Charles Sherrod, the organizer of SNCC's project in southwest Georgia, called them the "mommas" of the movement. "She is usually a militant woman in the community," Sherrod defined such a woman, "outspoken, understanding, and willing to catch hell, having already caught her share." Fannie Lou Hamer of Mississippi was one. Evicted from her land for daring to register to vote, then horribly beaten by a white sheriff, she refused to give in to hate or fear. "Black and white together," she would sing out at civil rights rallies. "We are not afraid." Observing the effect Hamer had on people, the white volunteer Sally Belfrage observed that "a sort of joy began to grow in every face.... For just that second, no one is afraid, because they are free."

Younger black women exhibited some of the same strength and determination. Diane Nash was a Fisk University beauty queen, but what struck her colleagues in the movement was her quiet courage as she insisted on continuing the 1961 Freedom Rides through the South. These courageous bus trips tested the right of blacks to ride interstate buses with whites, in the face of wanton beatings from white thugs armed with steel pipes. In most SNCC activities, women demonstrated that in daring, boldness, and courage, they were the equals of any man.

But some of the women also detected a typical male paternalism in the movement. Ella Baker had seen it when black male ministers refused to acknowledge her authority and talent by giving her the formal title of executive secretary of the Southern Christian Leadership Conference. Women in SNCC saw it when they were treated as though it was natural that they should do the typing and clerical work, or make the coffee, or take notes at meetings. One volunteer said, "The ... general attitude toward the inferiority and 'proper place' of women is disgusting."

These sentiments were held mainly by white women. The movement—including the prominent role played by black women—had heightened their awareness and consciousness about being treated as less than equal. Because the ideals of the "beloved community" were so high, any failure to measure up to those ideals became a crushing blow. Most black women in the movement seemed not to have the same response. They were already a part of the black community, they assumed their leadership roles in a natural and unforced manner, and they had other priorities. White women, less sure of their identity within the movement, were potentially more critical.

The sense of alienation grew during Freedom Summer 1964, when nearly a thousand white volunteers came to Mississippi to join the black struggle and work for voter registration and better schools and health facilities for blacks. It was a summer of extraordinary tension and turmoil. Three civil rights workers were lynched—two of them white, one black. Scores of churches were torched by white terrorists after being used for voter registration rallies. Fear was rife, as bombs were thrown at "freedom houses" where SNCC women and men lived, and shotgun fire rang out regularly in the night. Interracial fissures grew within the movement as well. Black leaders resented white Northern liberals telling *them* what to do, while some Northern whites were distressed that their talents were not fully utilized.

Relations between the sexes caused the greatest trouble. At a time when a new sexual revolution was just getting under way, the old rules and regulations about whom you slept with and after how long no longer seemed so clear. This was compounded by the realization that the biggest social taboo of all—interracial sex—was one of the most suspect and oppressive rules. If the goal of the movement was a truly beloved community, why not extend that to sexual interaction? And how better to show that you meant what you said about integration than to sleep with someone of the other race? Especially in the heat of what seemed like combat conditions, reaching out for love, or even just release, appeared to be a logical and perhaps politically inspired thing to do.

In reality, however, too many women (and some men) became sexual objects. Sexual intercourse could become a rite of passage imposed against one's will as well as a natural expression of bonding and affection. White and black women in particular became suspicious of each other. Black women were sometimes torn between anger at "their" men for choosing white women as sexual partners and anger at white women for seducing black men. The formula could be reversed, depending on which sex and which race you talked about. But the overall result was a new level of awareness that gender, as well as race, was an issue in this movement, and that until the question of treating women as equals became an explicit commitment of the movement, at least some of its ideals would always fall short of realization.

That became the context for the first tentative explorations of the "woman question" within SNCC. Casey Hayden and Mary King described the movement's attitude toward women, arguing that within SNCC women were frequently treated with condescension, as though they were tokens to be tolerated, not respected. "[The] assumption of male superiority [among SNCC men]," they wrote in 1964, "[is] as widespread and deep-rooted and as crippling to the woman as the assumptions of white supremacy are to the Negro." No matter how much they were doing to make the movement happen, women were never allowed to exercise power. "This is no more a man's world than it is a white world," the paper concluded. If SNCC men did not realize that, women would have to force them to change.

As an early statement of feminist principles, the Hayden-King position paper brilliantly seized upon the underlying similarity between the gender and race issues. Its logic and emotion were overwhelming. Yet it came at a time in SNCC's history when the movement was not prepared to give equal treatment of women the same priority as equal rights for blacks. Many SNCC men felt that their record on the issue was already better than that of most in the society; many black SNCC women saw the argument as relevant in a larger sense, but more the product of white women's experience than of their own. After an all-day discussion at a staff retreat, the majority sentiment was to put the question of gender equality aside.

Within a year the Black Power faction of the civil rights movement, led by Stokely Carmichael, had risen to prominence in SNCC. This faction saw integration as a plot by whites to retain control of the movement. Many blacks became determined to seize control of their own agenda and exclude whites. But the white women who had first raised the issue of sex discrimination within SNCC did not lose the voices they had found. Rather, they intensified their efforts to evolve a set of principles on which women could unite for *their* movement in the same way that blacks had united for theirs.

In "Sex and Caste: A Kind of Memo," Hayden and King elaborated on the lessons they had learned. Women, like blacks, they claimed, were "caught up in a common law caste system." Both privately and publicly, they were treated as different and inferior. The only answer to such treatment, they concluded, was for women to organize collectively on their own behalf. "Perhaps we can start to talk to each other more openly than in the past," they wrote, "and create a community of support for each other so we can deal with ourselves and others with integrity and therefore keep working." Hayden and King were talking about the same kind of support and communication that had always been a critical part of women's lives—in Hilda Newberry's life with her backyard community, in Laura Whiting's with her church group, in Barbara Harris's with her work and schoolmates. But now it was a call with an avowedly political purpose—to take the shared issues they and other women had talked about for years and make them the foundation for a collective act of rebellion.

The final ingredient for the rebirth of feminism came from the rapidly expanding student movement in America. That movement was not a unified crusade. It took as many forms as there were issues. Some believed that a new culture, a "counterculture," offered the only way to change America. Others embraced political revolution, even if it had to include violence. Some wore overalls, T-shirts, and love beads and sought to transform the materialism of the middle class by creating an alternative life-style; others chose factory jobs, short hair, and rimless glasses, committed to overturning the system from within.

Some generalizations, however, are valid. Most of the participants in the student movement were white and from middle- or upper-class backgrounds. Children of privilege, they shared something in common with the Fetter Family, the group of Protestant students in Boston seeking reform of the church. But they had gone far beyond the moderate optimism of that group, and even the more pointed skepticism of Students for a Democratic Society's (SDS) 1962 Port Huron statement, with its desire to humanize capitalism and technocracy. By the mid-1960s, when the student movement started to grow with explosive force, more and more young people began to question the very basis for their society. The Vietnam War radicalized youthful protestors, male and female alike. With its use of napalm to burn down forests and search-and-destroy missions to annihilate the enemy, the war seemed to symbolize the dehumanizing aspects of capitalism and Western-style democracy.

As student radicals set out to turn America around from its foreign policy in Vietnam, few constants emerged from the tactics and philosophies of various protest groups. But with virtually no exceptions, the men in the movements treated women as inferiors. "Macho" radicalism seemed the wave of the future—except that the women of the various movements would have none of it.

Some of the paternalism of the student movement reflected classic unconscious assumptions. "We regard *men* as infinitely precious and possessed of unfulfilled capacities for reason, freedom and love," the Port Huron statement had said—as if from the Declaration of Independence in 1776 to the present day nothing had happened to alter the presumption that citizens were men. At other times, though, men in the movement seemed to intentionally regard women as inferior. At one SDS convention, an observer noted, "Women made peanut butter, waited on table, cleaned up, [and] got laid. That was their role." Todd Gitlin, president of SDS in the mid-1960s, noted that the whole movement was characterized by "arrogance, elitism, competitiveness, ... ruthlessness, guilt—replication of patterns of domination ... [that] we have been taught since the cradle." Women might staff inner-city welfare projects and immerse themselves, far more than men, in the life of the community being organized, but when it came to respect and recognition, they were invisible. Women occupied only 6 percent of SDS's executive committee seats in 1964.

Throughout the entire antiwar movement, a similar condescension and disregard prevailed, symbolized by the antiwar slogan, "Girls say yes to guys [not boys] who say no." Always happy to accept the part of the sexual revolution that allegedly made women more ready to share their affection, male radicals displayed no comparable willingness to share their own authority as part of a larger revolution. Women's equality was not part of the new politics any more than it had been part of the old.

No event better symbolized the underlying antifeminist sentiment of the New Left than an antiwar demonstration in Washington, D.C., in 1969. Women felt that some of their concerns as women should be addressed as well. The men resisted but finally agreed that, toward the end of the program, a woman representing these concerns would be allowed to speak. As soon as she took the microphone, men in the audience started to hoot her down.

In the face of such treatment, women members of the student movement began to arrive at the same conclusions reached by Hayden and King in "A Kind of Memo." But the women of the New Left never had the positive experience of the "beloved community" that veterans of the civil rights movement had shared. Consequently, their anger was greater, their radicalism more pointed. The process of finding a collective voice, though, was the same. After a workshop in which women activists expressed their grievances, one participant wrote, "for many ... it was the first [experience] of caring for other women—the feeling that women should organize women and [that] situations had to be developed so women could support other women." The women of the student movement learned from bitter experience that they had to seize their own agenda, organize as separatist groups excluding men, and develop a program for change that dealt exclusively with their interests.

As the women's liberation movement spread from campus to campus and city to city, so too did consciousness-raising groups, the new instrument for mobilizing, then institutionalizing, a sense of collective self. If male values and organizations were the source of the problem with the larger society, women would have to create their own institutions, their own values, and their own way of making decisions and relating to each other. Through this intimate process of self-disclosure and self-discovery women's liberation quickly developed its most famous insight: that the personal is political. Church-activist-turned-radical-feminist Charlotte Bunch declared, "[T]here is no private domain of a person's life that is not political and there is no political issue that is not ultimately personal."

The women in these groups came to understand that they were not responsible for the pain and dissatisfaction of their relationships with men; rather, these problems reflected the whole system of hierarchy and power of a male-dominated system designed to oppress women. To turn the world upside down, women had to begin by creating true democracy in their relationships with each other, then carry those values and ways of making decisions into the public arena and transform it as well.

None of this could happen through traditional institutions with their hierarchies and male values. Women had to occupy their own social space, develop their own definition of who they were, and form their own agenda. This was perhaps the most revolutionary idea of all—taking control of their own lives and refusing to be subservient to what someone else said was their "proper place."

By the end of the 1960s, the foundation had been created for a widespread assault on traditional attitudes and values regarding sex roles in America. The issues could not be summarized easily or quickly. They involved more than questions of equal pay and the chance to compete one-on-one with men for a law partnership or medical residency. The issues were inclusive and varied in nature, ranging from abolishing sexist language like "chick" or "girl" to preserving and protecting woman's reproductive freedom of choice, eliminating sexist stereotypes from children's books, and defending a person's sexual orientation. Some women chose to organize feminist political caucuses, others created committees on the status of women in the professions, and still others organized a woman's legal defense fund to fight in court for women's rights. Countless women joined the battle to heighten public consciousness about rape and domestic violence against women.

Because the issues were so varied, they affected thousands of different groups and virtually every aspect of American life. For the same reason, however, this was no monolithic movement with a single director, program, or credo. The advantage was that women could enter into the movement in many places and feel comfortable. The disadvantage was that at times energies seemed divided, and disagreement rather than consensus prevailed over what needed to be done.

The key issue was how the broad expanse of American women (and men) would receive these varied messages. Because women were part of every class, religion, and ethnic subgroup in the United States, the array of messages and issues would increase the chance of positive responses. On the other hand, if the various women's movements seemed to ignore or condescend to those not yet "enlightened," they could set in motion a powerful backlash. In geological terms, the women of NOW, the civil rights struggle, and the student movement had created the basis for a seismic shift in the political and cultural landscape of America. Whether it would become an earthquake or just a tremor depended on how people responded.

Which Road to Travel

Ultimately, accounts of change in gender relationships after the 1960s would depend on the standard of measurement being used. If a woman defined equality as having her husband share responsibility for feeding and diapering a baby, then drawing up a weekly schedule for such tasks could qualify as an earthquake. But if she defined equality as an end to male-dominated institutions shaped by "masculine" values of competition and winning, then a change in one's household's division of labor would seem fairly trivial. Part of the problem the new women's movement faced was that people started from different places and had different goals. And goals could change over time: The woman who in December 1968 believed that more help from her husband was revolutionary might conclude a year later that marriage was the source of all oppression and that reform of existing institutions was just a trick to perpetuate the status quo.

From the time the women's rights movement started in the United States in the 1840s, there had always been a division between those who believed fundamentally that women were *individuals* and should be treated exactly the same as men and those who believed women were different, biologically and psychologically, and should be allowed to act *collectively* to implement their distinctive mission. The division of opinion shaped the arguments made for the 19th Amendment, which granted woman suffrage. Some said women should have the vote because it was their natural right as individual citizens to participate in the electoral process; others insisted that women needed the vote so that they could fulfill their special task of overseeing the national family's moral and spiritual health.

This distinction continued to shape divergent approaches to feminism. It helps explain the difference in goals and tactics between liberal feminism, with its focus on individual rights, and radical feminism, with its concern for group advancement and activities. The liberal National Organization for Women became the premiere civil rights group fighting for individual advancement for women.

NOW used court cases, lobbied with Congress, and pressured the President to lower barriers against women. One of NOW's central demands was ratification of the Equal Rights Amendment (ERA)—a measure that would abolish sex as a category for treating women and men differently under the law. The ERA represented an individualist approach to equality: Its goal was a society in which women and men had identical status as individual human beings.

This approach accepted as basically sound the existing structure of the society, including the values underlying social and economic institutions. The plan was to secure women's acceptance as individuals within those institutions on the principle of equal opportunity. Women should be granted the same opportunity as men to become chief executives and board members of corporations. NOW concentrated on destroying obstacles that defined women as different in rights or abilities from men. It forced the *New York Times,* for example, to do away with classified ads that specified "Male Only" or "Female Only" jobs. It also integrated bars and restaurants that in the past had excluded women. But at no time did NOW question corporate domination of American culture or the existing two-party political system. Integration, not separation, and reform, not revolution, were its goals.

In the 1960s it was customary for classified ads to be separated into "Help, Women" and "Help, Men." The eye-catching "Girls Girls Girls" in the left column was a typical come-on for the clerical positions reserved for women.

Radical feminists, by contrast, wanted to change society by acting collectively to attack the roots of women's oppression. For most women who called themselves radical feminists, the problem was the system of patriarchy—social, economic, and cultural institutions that supported male supremacy. As long as women were trained by patriarchal institutions such as schools and churches to defer to men and suppress their own desires, they could not be free.

This approach treated women as an oppressed political "class." Their oppressor, in turn, was "the class of men, or the male role," as one radical feminist put it. One class remained in control of the other by dividing and conquering its victims, or even worse, persuading its victims that they deserved to be subordinate. "The key to maintaining the oppressor role," New York feminist Ti-Grace Atkinson wrote, "is to prevent the oppressed from uniting." In a patriarchy men did this to women by socializing them to believe in "love," using romantic relationships to convince women to accept their own oppression, and creating such institutions as marriage and the family to reinforce their bondage. Other institutions such as corporations, schools, churches, and government echoed this class relationship, creating the equivalent of a closed system in which women, the majority of the world's population, were fooled into accepting an inferior and powerless role.

Radical feminists called for women to unite to throw off their oppression—and to exclude men from the movement. "We need not only separate groups, but a separate movement," one radical feminist wrote. Coalition with men would lead only to a new version of women's subservience and defeat. Women had to fight for themselves. They had different values and concerns than men had. What they needed was not acceptance as individuals into patriarchal institutions, but the kind of class solidarity as women that would permit their distinctive values to flower and triumph. If male-dominated institutions and values were the problem, women must develop their own institutions—reflecting their own values—and make these the cornerstone independence.

Radical feminists thus devoted much of their energy to building woman-defined and woman-run structures. Some were cultural, such as publishing houses, journals, and newsletters. Others were health-related—women-run clinics, for example, or centers for women seeking abortions or needing counseling or assistance in the face of domestic abuse from men.

Lesbians participated in all forms of the women's liberation movement, but during the 1970s, following the emergence of a distinctive "gay liberation" movement, there developed among some lesbians a much clearer sense of the need for a separate movement devoted to lesbian issues and concerns. By their commitment to women as well as their rejection of sexual ties with men, lesbian feminists demonstrated their determination to be independent of patriarchal controls. Moreover, by affirming their own identity, lesbian feminists were claiming a voice and a collective sense of self that significantly broadened and deepened the range of feminist constituencies.

Whatever the importance of these internal differences, most radical feminists were more similar to each other than to liberal feminists. They might eventually want to be equal with men as individuals, but first they sought to be independent from men and to celebrate their collective identity as a class, nourishing those values and attitudes that emphasized their differences rather than their similarity to men.

Adopting a similar antiliberal approach, socialist-feminists also focused on the need for revolution rather than reform. Only for them, the class to be overthrown was capitalism, not men, and the means to secure that end was by uniting with all other oppressed groups of the world. Socialist-feminists believed in solidarity but did not support separatism among women. They would continue to protest against the sexism displayed by men who were oppressed, but they would do so in the context of recognizing that the ultimate source of women's inequality was not men but rather the power of a capitalist class that included women as well as men. The fact that top executives at General Motors might include women did not make GM any less exploitative. "Women's liberation does not mean equality with men," one writer observed, "[because] equality in an unjust society is meaningless."

The socialist-feminists felt that NOW's program could easily be implemented without changing a single power reality. "The establishment will have no problem whatsoever in assimilating [liberal feminists] by meeting their basic demands," Marlene Dixon, a socialist-feminist wrote. "In the future we can expect limited and elitist day-care programs, ... abortion repeal; an effective end to job discrimination at least on the elite level.... All of these programs give the illusion of success while in fact assuring the destruction of any hope for women's liberation." Only when the fundamental institutions of society were overhauled would true equality become attainable.

Socialist-feminists were very different from radical feminists in their assessment of where the roots of oppression lay and how best to secure freedom. Yet both approaches shared a commitment to a collectivist rather than an individualist program of change. And both saw felt that reform could abolish the source of women's inequality. Whatever their conflicts over who constituted a class and what revolution would mean, radicals and socialists seemed to embrace a vision worlds apart from that of the women who started NOW and emerged from the networks of women reformers put in place by the state commissions on the status of women. How could all of them be part of the same movement? What would individual women do when confronted by such diverse definitions of feminism? Above all, how would average women perceive and respond to such a bewildering array of pronouncements?

It was very difficult for women beyond a certain age to identify with radical or socialist feminism. Laura Whiting or Hilda Newberry might decide that the ERA made sense as a long-overdue recognition of women's right to legal equality. They would probably support the Equal Pay Act. They might even imagine themselves as participants in and victims of Betty Friedan's "feminine mystique," sharing with Friedan's characters a "problem that has no name." Perhaps both women were conscious of having encountered the patriarchy—though they never would have called it that. Still, the furthest either would have been likely to go was to have some positive feeling about the ideas that NOW put forward in the late 1960s.

But their daughters might easily have listened more readily to all three versions of feminism: liberal, radical, and socialist. Daughters of women who had taken jobs in the aftermath of World War II were more likely to see themselves as playing a variety of roles in the world and as having a definition of marriage and family in which the husband and wife were equal partners. These same young women—and their brothers—had lived through the civil rights struggle. With possibilities for social change were exploding at an unprecedented rate, a younger generation would feel more comfortable in exploring all the ideas that emerged from the feminist movement.

Despite the differences between various feminist approaches, there was overlap. Radical feminists, for example, took the lead in protesting the Miss America contest in Atlantic City as a "meat market," but other feminists recognized the exploitation involved in such a ritual or the ruthlessness of the female fashion and cosmetics tycoons who promoted products that ensnared women in sexual captivity. And all women activists could easily support abortion reform, the ERA, or the campaign for better day care. One did not have to think that a particular program was a cure-all to see it as a step in the right direction. People found it possible to move in and out of a variety of feminist groups in their quest for the road they most wished to travel.

Jane McCall graduated from college in 1963, the year that Betty Friedan's *The Feminine Mystique* was published. The daughter of a woman who had once aspired to become a doctor, Jane took her own ideas seriously. Although she had conformed to the gender expectations of the 1950s and participated in traditional middle-class female cliques while in high school, she was inspired by the social change movements of the early 1960s to question the structures of the society in which she had grown up.

In college, Jane read Simone de Beauvoir's *The Second Sex,* which describes how women are always treated by men as objects and how men project onto women characteristics and emotions they choose not to recognize in themselves but stereotype as "feminine." Jane became confirmed in her interest in feminist issues. She was especially struck by the way women's roles were confined to the home. Although she planned to set aside a minimum of two years to care for each of her children (she wanted to have four), she was also determined to reenter the work world. She was not ready to buy into the world Friedan had portrayed, where advertisers and social scientists persuaded women to be happy with a lifetime of subservience. Friedan and de Beauvoir had helped to create for Jane a new set of lenses through which she observed her own life and that of the society around her.

Those lenses became more sharply focused when the women's liberation movement entered Jane's life. The movement took root everywhere, but especially in large cities and around college campuses. With a young child, Jane moved with her husband to a small college where she heard about a consciousness-raising ("c-r") group that had just started. She joined immediately. Some of the other women were also married and had children. Others were single.

A radical feminist had started the group and introduced ideas and readings that galvanized discussion. The c-r group became a life-changing experience. The women developed a community of support and revelation as each week they explored their individual and collective experiences of growing up female in America. The topics were endless: "playing dumb" on dates, discovering their own sexuality, inequality in the roles of husbands and wives, snide jokes from comedians, and derisive comments by men on the street.

Sometimes the discussion turned to lesbianism and whether that might not be a better, more rewarding kind of relationship. One or two of the women confessed to their own experiences with homosexuality and their desire to explore that possibility further. At other times the women focused on the complete inequality that characterized their home lives, with men simply assuming they would be waited on, and women expected to do all the cleaning, child care, and shopping.

Because the women in her group had taken vows of confidentiality, Jane shared with her husband only some of the insights she derived from its meetings, but the discussions gave her the support and reinforcement she needed to demand changes at home. One day she compiled a list that showed how many hours she spent on the work of the home and how many hours her husband spent. The ratio was eighty to fifteen. She demanded that changes be made, and reluctantly he agreed, sensing that a sea change was taking place in her life and that he might be washed ashore if he did not respond.

When Jane and her husband moved to a different university, she continued her involvement in the women's movement—and also her effort to build an egalitarian marriage and raise "her" children. For more than a year she helped lead a consciousness-raising collective, with the goal of starting c-r groups that could expand and spread the feminist message of self-organizing. Then she joined a publishing collective that wrote and distributed children's books that avoided sexist stereotypes.

Eventually, Jane made abortion rights her primary political activity; she had pursued graduate training in social work and was now an abortion counselor. A classically "political" task, organizing for abortion rights meant building coalitions, lobbying the state legislature, and closely allying with groups like the National Abortion Rights Action League (NARAL) and NOW.

Over six years Jane had moved from c-r groups to participating in a "separatist" publishing venture to joining an organization that most would have seen as mainstream politics. One could say that Jane had proceeded from a "radical-feminist" starting point to liberal feminism. Yet she did not see those categories as either relevant or meaningful. At each stage she had worked with some women who were lesbian feminists and believed strongly in separatism, and also with "straight" women who saw their feminist work as consistent with marriage. There were so many things to do that there was no point in devoting time to thinking about labels. Jane had simply followed her own interests in women's issues wherever they led her. In the process she explored many of the roads available within the feminist movement.

VOLUME 1, NUMBER 11
SEPTEMBER 30, 1970
WASHINGTON, D.C.

TWENTY-FIVE CENTS

off our backs
a women's liberation bi-weekly

back to school?

The radical feminist publication *off our backs* portrayed in graphic terms the new roles that women were taking on even as they continued to raise their children. Expressing the disaffection of many women fed up with American culture, *off our backs* served as a vehicle for women to communicate with each other about their concerns and potential solutions to their oppression.

Certainly in the larger culture labels became a primary source of contention and division. Some socialist feminists dismissed groups like NOW as substitutes for the establishment that cared only about getting a few more women executives into the exploitative ruling class. Socialists also dismissed radical feminists as being too inward looking and unpolitical. Radical feminists,one socialist said, used celebrations of sisterhood as a basis for "isolating ourselves from issues not directly related to our status as women." Radical feminists, in turn, found it easy to dismiss both liberals and socialists as too male-centered, willing to accept coalition with the oppressor as a vehicle for progress when in fact they were simply perpetuating their own bondage. Liberal feminists, finally, perceived both radical and socialist feminists as indulging in romantic illusion. In 1970 Betty Friedan denounced the "sexual shock-tactics and man-hating" of radical feminists, singling out for rejection the "lavender menace" of lesbian feminists, whom she believed would alienate support for broader women's rights objectives. (Within six months she saw her mistake and NOW changed its tune.) Similarly, liberal feminists rejected the rhetoric of socialist feminists as so much hot air.

Yet real women in real places did not fall easily into such categories of ideological contention. They were as likely as not to have participated in a variety of different kinds of feminism, moving naturally and without great anxiety or stress from one to the other. More often than not, the transitions evolved as part of a progression along a single journey, not a leap from one ideological fortress to another.

On the national level, the divisions remained, and on occasion were highlighted by the pronouncements of prominent individuals such as Betty Friedan or Ti-Grace Atkinson. Yet there was continuity between the different groups of feminists as well. Despite Friedan's concern over the "lavender menace," NOW created a task force on sexuality and lesbianism in the early 1970s and appeared to display a greater commitment to gay rights. Radical feminists and socialist feminists joined liberal feminists on issues from abortion rights to the ERA, child care, and spouse abuse. NOW even emulated its critics on the Left, announcing as its slogan for 1975 "Out of the Mainstream, Into the Revolution." The average citizen saw more to unite feminists than to divide them.

The one glaring flaw that should have concerned all women activists, whatever their ideological persuasion, was feminism's failure to escape its narrow class and race boundaries. Despite the ambitious aspirations of socialist feminists for a cross-class, cross-race coalition, most feminist activists were white, middle class, and college-educated. There were occasional black feminist groups, such as the National Black Feminist Organization, and each feminist organization boasted some participation by African-American or Latina women. Yet on balance, the numbers were infinitesimally small. Both the language and the programs of feminist groups seemed to reflect a white middle-class approach. Until women of all classes and backgrounds felt attracted to and welcomed by feminist groups, there was little likelihood that the promise of a universal sisterhood could become a reality.

Responses

One measure of a social movement's success is the extent to which its ideas affect people's behavior: how they talk, what they wear, what career choices they make, how they conduct themselves in the privacy of their bedrooms as well as on the job. Most social movements also seek to change public policy, hoping that transformations that occur in private life may be reflected in state regulations and programs as well.

By those criteria it seemed that feminism had registered a powerful impact on American society during the 1970s. It was not just that late-night comedians started to make jokes about women's liberation or that talk shows now considered sex equality a "hot" item. Women changed their social and economic behavior, postponing marriage and childbearing and seeking new careers. Some men, at least, became more aware of how language and etiquette reflected sexist assumptions. Politicians began to address issues of gender discrimination directly. By no means had nirvana been reached. When the manufacturer of Virginia Slims cigarettes decided to pitch its product specifically toward a female audience, it chose for its slogan "You've come a long way, Baby," suggesting a dual message—women's lives had changed, but women remained sex objects. Yet even though sexism was still rife, the evidence suggested that change remained the dominant theme of the day.

One sign of change appeared in public opinion polls taken during the 1960s and 1970s. In 1962 George Gallup had found that two-thirds of all women were satisfied with their lives and did not desire major change. Eight years later—three to four years after the women's movement had started—the Roper polling organization posed the same question, finding that 50 percent of women wanted significant changes while 50 percent were satisfied. Four years after that, in 1974, the result was exactly the reverse of what it had been in 1962—two-thirds of women were dissatisfied and wanted to see significant change toward greater equality, while only one-third were content. The turnaround correlated directly with the emergence of an active feminist movement.

Most impressive were the results among younger women, most likely to have grown up with ideas shaped by the women's liberation movement. The pollster Daniel Yankelovich was stunned by the "wide and deep" acceptance of feminist ideas among the young. In two years the number of students who declared that women were an oppressed group had doubled; moreover, approximately 70 percent of women in college expressed agreement with the statement that "the idea that a woman's place is in the home is nonsense." The generation that came of age after Betty Friedan's *The Feminine Mystique* was published had internalized a very different sense of who they were and what they should be doing than their mothers or grandmothers had.

These new attitudes translated quickly into behavior. Throughout the decades following the Great Depression, college-educated women had constituted a smaller proportion of doctors, lawyers, and other high-paying professions than they had in 1920, largely due to discrimination. Hospitals would not accept women interns, and law firms offered few partnerships to women. Cultural attitudes transmitted by teachers and parents also played a part. Guidance counselors told female students that they should be nurses, not doctors, or that they should become secretaries rather than executives. As a result, from 1940 to 1970 the entering classes of medical, law, and business schools were only 5 to 8 percent female. As late as 1970, college men interested in careers in engineering, medicine, and law outnumbered women eight to one.

By the mid-1970s, however, the number of women planning to enter traditionally "feminine" careers, such as elementary school teaching or nursing, fell from 31 percent to 10 percent. In the meantime, women's applications to law and medical schools soared 500 percent. By the mid-1980s, entering classes of medical, law, and business schools were 40 percent female. The percentage of new women doctors increased from 9 percent in 1971 to 22 percent in 1981, while the proportion of women Ph.D.s leaped from 10 percent to 30 percent. Thirty years earlier, virtually all these women would have been entering "women's" jobs, with low prestige, limited chance for advancement, and poor pay. Now they were becoming increasingly competitive with men for high-paying, high-status jobs in the most prestigious professions. The feminist movement seemed to have made a significant impact, supporting a very different idea of who a woman was, and what she could aspire to be, than had existed just a few years before.

Less related to feminism, perhaps more a consequence of the general "liberation" attitudes of the 1960s, was a significant change in women's sexual behavior as well. There have really been two sexual revolutions in the twentieth century. The first came in the early 1900s, when there was a significant increase in the number of women engaging in premarital intercourse and expressing satisfaction with their sexual experiences. Use of birth control also increased at that time. By the 1970s, however, that first revolution seemed mild. The number of women who believed that premarital sex was wrong fell from 75 percent in 1969 to 53 percent in 1974. Among younger women, especially, sexual behavior patterns became much more similar to those of men, with approximately 75 percent of women and men becoming sexually active by the age of seventeen.

The greatest indicator that feminism was now a significant presence in America appeared in the new, respectful attention that public policymakers paid to issues of gender. Largely in response to pressure from NOW, the Equal Employment Opportunity Commission (EEOC) began to devote as much time to complaints about gender discrimination as it had to grievances about racial discrimination. When it was discovered that 7 percent of all gender-related cases involved workers at American Telephone and Telegraph (AT&T), the commission filed a lawsuit on behalf of all women workers at that company. The result was a settlement involving back pay to women workers who had been denied equal treatment and a powerful affirmative action program to attract women employees. (Affirmative action programs provide limited kinds of preferential treatment, such as increased job opportunities and promotions, for members of groups that have historically been victims of long-term racial or gender-based discrimination.) AT&T started to desegregate its work force, with women taking positions repairing telephone lines, traditionally an all-male job, and men being hired as operators, traditionally a female job. The U.S. secretary of labor announced in 1970 that federal contracts would require the employment of a certain percentage of women.

Congress did its part by enacting bills designed to end discrimination against women. It also provided support to programs of special interest to women. Title IX of the 1972 Educational Amendments Act prohibited any college or university that received federal aid from discriminating against women. Among other things, Title IX required that college athletic programs allocate scholarships to women athletes on the same basis as to men athletes. Congress also used the tax codes to provide benefits for young families using child care.

Most impressive was the move in Congress to pass the Equal Rights Amendment (ERA) and send it to the states for ratification. For fifty years the National Woman's Party had been seeking such action. For most of that period the ERA failed because other women's groups opposed it, believing that the amendment would nullify all special legislation designed to protect women's interests. By the late 1960s, however, most women's groups had endorsed the ERA, and Congress responded. In 1972 the ERA passed the House by a margin of 354 to 23, the Senate by 84 to 8. The action seemed to suggest that a feminist wave was sweeping the entire country (but the amendment was never ratified).

In politics as well, women seemed to be making a major surge forward. A new National Women's Political Caucus was formed, representing elected officials as well as policymakers, to lobby for female representation in all government agencies as well as to support legislation of special interest to women. Individual members of Congress—such as Shirley Chisholm (the first black woman in Congress and a presidential candidate in 1972), Bella Abzug (a prominent peace activist), and Sissy Farenthold (a Texas politician whose name was placed in nomination for vice president on the 1972 Democratic ticket)—headlined the growing prominence of women as a political force. The number of women candidates for state legislative positions increased by 300 percent from 1972 to 1974; women's participation in party political conventions skyrocketed (from 13 percent in 1968 to 40 percent in 1972 among Democrats and from 17 percent to 30 percent among Republicans); and parties appeared to be competing to see which could do more to attract women followers.

The federal court system also seemed responsive to the new feminist wave. Pauli Murray had pioneered the strategy of winning legal battles for women by using the equal protection clause of the 14th Amendment. Women lawyers, especially through the Women's Rights Project of the American Civil Liberties Union, brought many successful sex-discrimination cases in the 1970s, establishing that women could not be excluded from juries, that they had the same legal standing as men to administer estates and handle property, that they should be accorded the same status in relation to their dependents as men had always had, and so on.

Perhaps the most far-reaching court decision affecting women's lives was the Supreme Court case *Roe* v. *Wade* (1973). Jane Roe, a fictitious name for a young, single woman who was pregnant, sued on behalf of all other women for the right to have an abortion. Her lawyers argued that anti-abortion statutes violated women's right to privacy. They also contended that the right to privacy was guaranteed, implicitly, by the Bill of Rights of the Constitution. By a seven-to-two vote the Supreme Court upheld their argument, viewing reproductive freedom as a fundamental right. In the specific case the Court ruled that women could have a medically safe abortion until the third trimester of a pregnancy. Women who had been forced to flee the country or resort to back-alley abortionists in order to terminate an unwanted pregnancy now had won the battle to exercise control over their bodies legally and openly.

Even institutions of popular culture reflected the changes. There had always been women's magazines—the *Ladies' Home Journal, McCall's,* and *Redbook,* to name just a few. For the most part they reinforced traditional views of women's place in the social order. Advice columns told how to keep a husband happy or deal with a problem child; recipe pages offered new ideas on how to satisfy the family palate; and advertisements focused on selling products to enhance "femininity" or help women in their ordained social roles as homemakers and mothers. These magazines certainly were not on the cutting edge of feminism.

In 1972 all that changed. Women journalists had already started to challenge the sexist assumptions of traditional journals, holding a sit-in at *Ladies' Home Journal* and suing *Time* and *Newsweek* for not adequately recognizing women's issues and their professional status as reporters. Now a group of women led by Gloria Steinem started to publish a different kind of woman's magazine. Entitled *Ms.,* the new journal identified itself as a voice of the woman's movement, committed in its feature stories and its advertising to reinforce feminism. Steinem had been a brilliant reporter who frequently found herself the victim of discrimination aimed at women. Because of the absence of abortion rights laws in America, she had been forced to have an illegal abortion. Often she had to write about "women's" topics from a traditional perspective in order to sell her stories. Once she had even posed as a *Playboy* bunny in order to write a piece for *Show* magazine.

But increasingly Steinem had been able to focus on political stories about civil rights and other burning social issues, which brought her into the feminist movement. When *Ms.* was first published, as a supplement to *New York Magazine* in 1971, it sold a quarter of a million copies. By 1972 it was on its own, galvanizing women readers with its array of successful writers—such as Alice Walker,

Ms. magazine was founded in 1971 to address issues not covered by the traditional women's magazines, a role it continues to fill today.

Catharine Stimpson, and Letty Cottin Pogrebin—and its systematic evocation of the dynamic changes occurring daily in women's lives.

Ms. was particularly effective in recognizing and endorsing women's gradual yet startling realization of their inequality. The letters columns were full of stories describing the "click" that suddenly made a woman realize she was playing a part assigned to her by someone else, denied her own voice and autonomy. It might come in the middle of the night when a woman's husband woke her saying, "The baby's crying, honey, you'd better see what's wrong" or when a young man persisted in making romantic advances after the woman said to stop. The "click" was there in a thousand manifestations. Through *Ms.* they became the common property of women throughout the land. Not only was it okay to be a feminist, but it was a fact of life and a truth that readers could not imagine having missed for so long. *Ms.* became a staple of many women's lives, just as *McCall's* once had been.

Even Hollywood stars began promoting a different vision of how boys and girls should grow up. Led by actress Marlo Thomas, a group of entertainers concerned about how most fairy tales and children's books socialized children into traditional roles of female passivity and male aggression decided to celebrate diversity and autonomy. A record album, "Free To Be You and Me," was a series of songs, by stars everyone recognized, that told boys and girls it was all right for them to be whoever they wanted to be. Crying was good for both boys and girls. So were sports, playing with dolls, and dressing up. Dr. Benjamin Spock, the pediatrician who had written the nation's leading book on how to raise children, even changed some of his advice to young parents when he became aware that some old ways of treating boys differently from girls were not only wrong but harmful.

No matter where you looked—from the Supreme Court to the White House to the newsstand—women were being treated in a different fashion, demanding a different code of behavior, and translating into their daily lives a commitment to greater freedom than had ever been seen before in America. "I am woman, hear me roar," entertainer Helen Reddy sang. "In numbers too large to ignore, . . . I am strong, I am invincible." There was a determination to reach an audience, to declare a message of independence, to seize a voice, and few could avoid being aware that a cultural revolution was potentially on the way.

Yet for most Americans, male and female, this was still just a news story. It might be interesting to talk about, but what did it mean? After all, women and men had to play different roles in society in order for things to work, didn't they? How could the family survive if women were not ultimately responsible for cooking the meals and raising the kids? And how could men retain their manhood if they were expected to do "women's work," such as cleaning the toilets and doing the laundry? Wasn't there something eternal about Adam and Eve and their differences that made all these feminist slogans more a passing fad than a deepseated change?

It seemed that all the energy and momentum were on the side of women's liberation—but countless Americans had not yet been heard. Millions of women from ethnic and cultural minorities with a different set of traditions than "Anglo" women might not feel the same need to assert themselves as the women in NOW did. And millions more, perhaps, thought there was no reason to consider changing roles they believed to be divinely ordained.

Feminists might laugh scornfully at the advice columns in the *Ladies' Home Journal*, but others saw them as on target and much closer to what really counted than fantasies of independence. The contest was not over. And if in 1973, with the ERA, *Roe* v. *Wade,* and *Ms.*, some feminists felt in command, it was too soon to tell whether they were right.

The Countermovement

The 1960s had brought not only protest movements but also a revulsion at what many saw as the excesses of protest movements. Some were disturbed by the transition within the civil rights movement from passive, nonviolent protest in pursuit of integration to the Black Power rhetoric ("Move on over Whitey, or we're gonna move on over you") of Stokely Carmichael. Others were distressed by the young college students with long hair, love beads, and jeans who hurled the epithet "pig" at police officers, denounced their country as corrupt and brutal, and then seized university offices and trashed their professors' files as a way of expressing disgust with the war in Vietnam. And there now appeared on the scene something called women's liberation. Feminists—at least some of them—celebrated homosexuality, denounced religion and the nuclear family as bastions of patriarchy, and saw salvation in a manless world where women could enshrine their own separate and superior values.

The same people who felt their values and life-styles under attack from Black Power militants were likely to feel threatened by students or by "women's libbers." Social observers gave different names to this phenomenon. Some called those who were angry Middle Americans; others used the phrase the Silent Majority; by the mid-1970s, TV evangelist Jerry Falwell called his followers the Moral Majority. Whatever the name, it usually described people who were working class or lower middle class in background and who had struggled all their lives to become part of the American Dream. They had toiled to buy a small house and perhaps send a child to college; they believed firmly in God and country; and now they saw all that they cherished in life being spit upon.

For many Middle Americans, feminism represented the epitome of what was wrong. After all, were traditional sex roles not the foundation of society? And if people stopped treating women like women, and men like men, everything would fall apart. From such a perspective, everything valuable in society—the family, the church, vows of fidelity, loyalty to country, love of parents—was based on men and women knowing their place and working together to make America great. Feminism was about more than women's right to vote or have a career or manage their own institutions; it was an attack on the very foundations of society. And it must be opposed.

To women concerned with preserving the esteem and recognition conferred by traditional sex roles, the ERA symbolized all that was dangerous in the feminist movement. If the ERA became law, they believed, all differences between the sexes would be abolished, and all institutions based on those differences would self-destruct. The family was based on women and men performing complementary roles, with husbands and wives sharing a loyalty to the family that was more important than their individual lives. By contrast, the ERA seemed to embody individualism run amok. As one antifeminist wrote, "[T]he humanist-feminist view of the family is that it is a biological, sociological unit in which the individual happens to reside; it has no meaning and purpose beyond that which each individual chooses to give it. . . . [In such a situation, the family] becomes an instrument of oppression and denial of individual rights."

Worst of all, from this point of view, was the degree to which feminism destroyed the softer, more nurturing and sacrificing side of women's nature and replaced it with the ideal of women acting like men. This "macho-feminism," as one person called it, "despises anything which seeks to interfere with the desires of Number One." Through such a selfish process, women's true nature was destroyed. "The less time women spend thinking about themselves," Connie Marshner, a leading antifeminist, wrote, "the happier they are. . . . Women are ordained by nature to spend themselves in meeting the needs of others." But if feminists had their way, selfishness would prevail over serving the family, and women would compete with men for dominance and self-assertion rather than uniting with men for the greater good of the family unit.

One of the first movements to counter feminism focused on defeating the ERA. Led by Phyllis Schlafly, a conservative Republican with a master's degree in government from Radcliffe, the anti-ERA forces concentrated on mobilizing grass roots constituencies in each state to petition their state legislators not to ratify the ERA. The organizations had many names: STOP-ERA (STOP meant Stop Taking Our Privileges), WWWW (Women Who Want to be Women), and FLAG (Family, Liberty and God). But all had a common theme: defend the family and preserve the differences between the sexes. "God Almighty created men and women biologically different and with differing needs and roles," Jerry Falwell proclaimed. "Good husbands who are godly men are good leaders. Their wives and children want to follow them." According to Schlafly and her allies, if the ERA were successful, husbands would no longer be required to provide for wives; alimony (a divorced husband's responsibility to provide financially for his ex-wife) would cease; and protective labor laws that aided blue-collar women would be eliminated.

STOP-ERA leader Phyllis Schlafly addresses a rally in the Illinois state capitol in June 1978. The Illinois House of Representatives was scheduled to vote on the Equal Rights Amendment that week.

Most frightening of all, the God-ordained differences between men and women would be dissolved. In phrases reminiscent of the battle over separate facilities for blacks and whites, antifeminists warned of "desexegration," where men and women would be forced to share everything, including combat duty in war. The specter of homosexual marriages hovered over anti-ERA pronouncements, as did concern about men and women using the same toilets—maybe even the same showers. Where would it all end?

Anti-abortion forces played a variation on the same themes. According to Connie Marshner, the essence of the "pro-choice" argument was that women should be able to put Me first, ignoring the fact that the creation of a fetus was divinely sanctioned and that the elimination of the fetus was both a sin and an act of murder. Although Catholics were most likely to become active in "pro-life" groups, as they were called, many Protestants joined also, usually from conservative churches that valued traditional family life as the cornerstone of a virtuous society. According to the National Right to Life group, people who supported women's right to abort a fetus were attacking motherhood, devaluing the sanctity of life, and possibly preventing some future Einstein or Edison from growing to maturity to help the world. By showing motion pictures (based on ultrasound) of a fetus moving around a woman's womb during the third month of pregnancy, these Right to Life groups powerfully portrayed their antagonists as baby-killers.

Clearly, these were neither simple issues, nor were they without transforming emotional force. One could easily become fanatical about women's rights—on either side of the issue. The "click" that a reader of *Ms.* experienced when she heard a male employer refer to his forty-five-year-old secretary as a "girl" could readily occur on the other side if a Roman Catholic mother of four children heard a physician who performed abortions talk about routinely disposing of twenty-five fetuses in one day. At what point did women's rights clash with the rights of religious freedom? And who was to decide what policies most effectively served the greater good of the community?

This turmoil occurred in the midst of a conservative revival. Richard Nixon had won the presidency in 1968 by claiming to speak on behalf of the Silent Majority. Insisting that he would restore law and order, resist permissiveness, and strike out against the excesses of antiwar demonstrators and other protestors, Nixon assumed leadership of a cultural war against the most radical of the 1960s social movements. He promised that as president he would appoint conservative, Southern judges to the Supreme Court; fight busing for purposes of racial integration; and defend traditional family values against feminists and others who demanded more child care centers, abortion reform, and sexual freedom.

The 1972 presidential campaign became a referendum on cultural change. George McGovern, the Democratic presidential nominee, supported amnesty for Vietnam War protestors who had fled to Canada rather than be drafted. He also favored legalization of marijuana. In addition, the party implemented a quota system of representation at the Democratic convention, with racial minorities and women given a larger share of seats than ever before. Nixon, in turn, portrayed McGovern as the embodiment of the counterculture who spoke on behalf of feminism, student radicals, and environmental extremists. As Nixon defined it, the election was to determine whose values would control America—those associated with the traditional family, patriotism, and respect for authority, or those connected to attacks on the family, encouragement of dissent, and rebellion against middle-class morality. Although gender equality was just one of the issues involved, it affected almost every American: It literally entered the most private spaces where people lived, as well as public policy debates.

Dianne Chavis was initially perplexed by the issue. Born in South Carolina in 1953, she had grown up with fairly conventional beliefs. She was not well off, but neither was she poor. After graduating from high school in 1968, she went to a local community college for two years to study to become a dental assistant. Through her training there, she met her husband, who was completing his specialty training in orthodontics. The two moved to the suburb of a larger metropolitan area and within five years had two children. Dianne stayed at home to take care of them. Fully engaged by her activities as a mother and member of the community, Dianne seemed to be the kind of woman *McCall's* would portray as the ideal young wife.

Then two momentous events took place. The first came when Dianne's older daughter was almost killed in an accident. She hovered between life and death, recovering only after months of therapy and care. The second event was in many ways a direct response to the first. Dianne experienced a religious conversion. She had been a routine churchgoer in her youth, and she and her husband occasionally attended the local Methodist church. But when her daughter was injured, Dianne met another woman at the hospital who was a devoted member of a Baptist evangelical church in the area. That woman seemed so enveloped by her faith that it informed and inspired every part of her life. Through long hours of intense and intimate conversation, Dianne became convinced that she too should turn her life over to Jesus. The next month she was baptized at the evangelical church and started to go to weekly Bible study classes as well as Sunday school and church services. She was a "born-again" Christian.

Dianne's new-found faith not only strengthened her in her daily struggle to help her daughter recover, it also gave her a new perspective on some of the issues that she and the other women in her neighborhood talked about in their backyards. Dianne became convinced by her minister that the family was imperiled by the changes taking place in society and that the deepest threat came from those who were trying to unsettle and subvert the roles that husbands and wives played. According to the Bible, Dianne said, God had placed men in charge of the household. They were to act on behalf of the well-being of the family, according to God's wishes. Women, in turn, were to be subject to men, offering support and love in their roles as wives and mothers. Both husband and wife—and their children—were to mirror the dictates of God as reflected in the teachings of the Bible.

Consistent with her new beliefs, Dianne became a subscriber to the Moral Majority newsletter. In keeping with the political agenda put forward by conservative politicians, the Moral Majority set out to fight the evils of secular humanism, including those associated with feminism, the ERA, and the campaign for reproductive freedom. Dianne became convinced through studying her newsletter and talking with her friends at church that the ERA would totally destroy all that gave coherence and meaning to her life. It would fragment and corrupt the discipline and authority that God had ordained for the family. And by sanctioning homosexual relationships, it would undo the only means by which God had provided for the perpetuation of his kingdom—the monogamous, heterosexual family.

Dianne joined the organization committed to defeating the ratification of the ERA in her state, agreed to help send out mailings for the Right to Life group in her community, and took as her personal charge the responsibility to bear witness to her faith in her neighborhood conversations with the other women on her block. Many of them had little sympathy with the Moral Majority, and some believed strongly in the ERA and in a woman's right to control her own body. But they understood at least some of the things that Dianne had been through. And they knew that they would have to consider the depth and conviction of her beliefs on these issues before they could take sides.

Judy Morgan was seven years older than Dianne. She had grown up in a poor household, then had worked her way through college and gotten married immediately after graduation to her college sweetheart, Ted. He was an ambitious account executive who quickly rose through the corporate ranks to become one of the leading officials of his company. He traveled a great deal, frequently taking Judy with him. They had two boys born at the end of the 1960s. The family lived in a New York suburb, not too distant from Ted's office. Judy worked part-time at the local school but spent most of her time in the home, raising the children, helping Ted with his career through entertaining and socializing with other wives, and enjoying their comfortable life-style.

Judy thought of herself as an educated, independent woman. She was active in the local PTA, read magazines like *Harper's* and *The Atlantic*, and ordinarily voted for the Democratic party. She followed closely the emergence of the women's liberation movement, and like most Americans of her class and age group, spent more than a few evenings talking about the new feminism. But Judy was bothered by many of the ideas she associated with the women's movement. It was not that she did not believe women should have equal rights with men or that they should not enjoy equal access to careers and job opportunities. But she resented deeply the implication she heard in much feminist literature that anyone who did not have a career competing with men was a failure and that women who stayed in the home and fulfilled more conventional roles were without value in the society.

Too often, she thought, feminists were not only judging men for being sexist but were also judging women for being behind the times if they did not get on the feminist bandwagon. It was as if a woman who liked to cook, enjoyed raising children, and took pleasure in making a fine home should feel as though she had betrayed her sex. The aura of condescension and snobbishness that seemed to characterize some feminist pronouncements on women's traditional roles was offensive and irritating. If women's rights activists wanted to have a career and challenge men, by all means let them do it. But let them also respect women who made other choices, even if those choices were traditional.

For Judy, the issue was not whether to be a feminist or an antifeminist, but rather how to be herself. She did not want to be told she either had to be for complete freedom of life-style or totally in the other camp. She believed in the rights of consenting adults to practice whatever kind of sex they wished, but she resented those who declared that a gay or lesbian life-style was more conducive to freedom and fulfillment than a heterosexual marriage. She thought that under certain circumstances women should have the right to abort an unwanted pregnancy. But she also believed that certain limits on that freedom were permissible, including waiting periods, counseling, and a restricted time frame within which an abortion could take place. Judy thought the ERA was a good idea, but she did not approve of women going into combat or living in trenches alongside men. In short, she occupied a middle-of-the-road position on most issues involving feminism, and she was angry that people on both her left and her right were denying her the freedom to occupy that space.

Barbara Harris, the African-American woman who had dropped out of high school to have her first child in the early 1960s, occupied yet another position on the spectrum of opinion. She believed strongly in women's rights—in theory. After all, she had demonstrated and crusaded for black rights. But most of what she heard from the new women's liberation movement sounded irrelevant to her life. It was all well and good to talk about having a career and shedding sexual stereotypes. But few black women she knew could take advantage of those opportunities. The main problem in the black community, as she saw it, was the need for more men to remain committed to building and sustaining traditional nuclear families. She wanted black men to assume and carry out the role of breadwinner, not be free of it.

All the criticism of the nuclear family and traditional sex roles that Harris heard from feminists in the media seemed to reflect a distinctly white, middle-class perspective. Black women wanted to preserve and strengthen their relationships with black men, not attack those men. Racial solidarity—not division—seemed the most important priority for African Americans, and to the extent that feminism set women against men, it was a threat to be avoided, not a challenge to be welcomed.

Black women supported better pay and greater job opportunities for all women, and they believed in better and more accessible child care facilities. But in too many instances it seemed that white women wanted careers and high-paying jobs so that they could hire black women to take care of their children, without paying them a decent wage. Even the emphasis on reproductive freedom could mean something different in the black community than in the white. Children were valued highly in the African-American culture. What if the focus on abortion was, as some black men said, simply an effort by white people to prevent the black community from growing in size and strength?

Thus, even as the feminist movement appeared to be the dominant force in American society at the beginning of the 1970s, counterforces were undercutting the likelihood of a feminist triumph. As it turned out, according to the polls conducted in the early 1980s, 20 percent of the American people were *for* abortion under all circumstances and 20 percent were *against* abortion under all circumstances. But that left 60 percent in the middle, willing to consider a variety of restrictions or controls that might modify *Roe* v. *Wade*. Similarly, although a majority of women and men said they supported the ERA, enough opposition existed to pose a serious challenge to ratification. The ERA required approval by three-fourths of the state legislatures to become part of the Constitution. Many of the legislatures that had not approved the ERA by the mid-1970s were in those parts of the South where conservative constituencies were strongest.

Conservatives were not about to roll over and play dead. As Nixon's campaign had shown, a social and cultural war was being waged, and many Americans who believed that Black Power, the student movement, and women's liberation were gnawing away at the vitals of the nation were ready to fight back. They had powerful resources: faith in the traditional family, the authority of religion, and the value of patriotism. Countless Americans shared Dianne Chavis's "born again" beliefs that God had ordained men and women to play profoundly different roles in life. Still others shared the consternation of Judy Morgan at the elitism and judgmental quality of much feminist rhetoric. And many poor women—many of them from oppressed racial groups—had different priorities from white middle-class feminists. Latina and Asian women, for example, took pride in cultural traditions that gave women a special value as mothers and homemakers. And loyalty to family and to racial or ethnic solidarity could easily take precedence over a commitment to a feminist agenda.

The future of women's rights seemed to hinge on how different groups of citizens and policymakers responded to different feminist messages. Despite the commitment of many feminists to the ideal of sisterhood across class and race lines, it seemed that women had as many different responses to issues of sex equality as men. It was also clear that a substantial body of Americans, male and female, was prepared to support political figures like Richard Nixon, Jerry Falwell, and Phyllis Schlafly in their effort to return America to conservative social values regarding sex and family life. For them, feminism was a hostile force. Perhaps the contest of political wills would be resolved by the decisions of those in the middle, not by those who occupied either extreme.

The Persistence of Differences

By the middle of the 1980s two generalizations could be made about women's lives in the United States. First, no group in society had experienced as much change as women had over the preceding three decades. Second, the changes that had occurred affected women in dramatically different ways, depending on whether they were white or nonwhite, rich or poor, married or divorced. Ethnicity, class, and marital status continued to determine what happened to women.

Change was the common thread in analyses of women's sexual and family lives. In the 1950s not even half of women were sexually active before marriage, while by the 1990s considerably more than three-quarters were. At the height of the "baby boom" that lasted from the end of World War II to the early 1960s, the average woman married by age twenty, and bore three or four children fairly close together. Only 5 percent of births took place outside marriage. But as the twentieth century ended, the average woman who married waited until age twenty-five or twenty-six, and had only one or two children, perhaps in her thirties. Only 60 to 70 percent of women in the prime childbearing years of twenty-five to thirty-four were married, as compared to almost 90 percent in the baby boom period. Childbirth was six times as likely to take place outside marriage as it had been in 1960.

Marriage itself was far less predictable, and less lasting, as the divorce rate rapidly rose to equal more than half of the marriage rate. Almost a quarter of Americans did not marry at all, as compared to 15 percent as recently as 1972. Because of this and also because of divorce, more than 40 percent of white women and more than 60 percent of black women in the mid-1990s were not married.

Some of these women might have married had they been able to choose a spouse of their own sex. Since the 1960s, lesbians and gay men had become increasingly accepted members of American society, working, loving, building lives for themselves—and desiring to marry. In the mid-1990s, the courts of Alaska and Hawaii came close to legalizing same-sex marriage on the basis of equal rights laws. Hastily-gathered popular referenda in these states and legislation in more than thirty others forestalled the measure, but the extent of change and acceptance was visible in the state of Vermont's legislative decision in the year 2000 to offer a comprehensive domestic-partnership status, with the rights and benefits of marriage, to same-sex couples.

Employment patterns made the transformations in women's roles material. In 1960 approximately 30 percent of women worked; four decades later the figure was 75 percent, including 60 percent of mothers whose children were not yet of school age, the category of women least likely to take employment in the past. Women not only constituted half the entering classes of law schools and medical schools, but they made up nearly half of the entire labor force. Yet these statistics hid the degree to which gender remained a source of inequality. In the mid-1980s, for example, a woman lawyer earned, on average, $33,000, a male lawyer, $53,000. In 1984 only 4 percent of working women had incomes higher than $28,000 a year. The figure for men was 26 percent. Women's wages progressed from 59 percent of what men received in 1960 to 73 percent of what men earned in 1998.

Work continued to be allocated, designed, and valued differently according to whether women or men performed it. In the history of wage labor there had developed shorthand descriptions to differentiate one kind of work compensation from another. People talked about a "living wage," a "family wage," and then—quite distinct from the other two—a "woman's wage." The first defined what it was society thought to be necessary for a person to live in dignity, modest comfort, and self-respect. The second described what a *man* should be able to earn in order to provide adequate support for his family, four or more people. A "woman's wage" was seen as secondary, something extra that women might earn as "pin money," a popular phrase meaning a little "extra" for purchasing frivolous goods. Even though in reality women toiled, just as men did, to support themselves and their families, they were not treated as if that was what they were doing. Instead it seemed that their work was worth less than men's.

The traditional definition of "women's work" and a "woman's wage" meant that women doing the same work as men received significantly less pay, and women were segregated in certain kinds of jobs that employers, men, and the entire society viewed as "women's work." Many believed that women's delicate fingers and attention to detail made them particularly qualified to do sewing and other chores requiring dexterity. These skills quickly became generalized to such industries as textiles and garment making. The capacity for monotonous and repetitive labor—the jobs of operatives in canneries or of cigarette rollers in tobacco factories—also became identified as "women's work." In each case, the work women did was viewed as something uniquely theirs to perform and was rewarded not with a "living wage" or a "family wage" but with a "woman's wage."

The result was that even after 1960, the jobs women took commonly became defined as "women's work," with low wages, few opportunities for promotion and advancement, and a far smaller range of occupations than for male workers. More than three-quarters of women workers were clustered in just 5 percent of all job types. For example, in 1998 nearly 99 percent of secretaries were female; 93 percent of registered nurses, 89 percent of nursing aides and orderlies, 92 percent of bookkeepers, and 84 percent of elementary school teachers were also. Women dominated the garment industry, they provided virtually all day-care workers, and they monopolized data-entry positions and bank teller jobs. But few of these offered prospects for social or economic upward mobility. Most of the new jobs created in

The monotony of the file room and the miniskirt of the clerk typify a stereotype that persisted in the 1970s.

America after 1970 and filled by women were in the service sector. All too often, these jobs paid wages close to the minimum allowed by federal law—barely enough to feed oneself, let alone anyone else. At the other end of the pay scale women were scarce indeed: only 1% of chief executives and less than 4% of high-ranking corporate officers of the "Fortune 500," the richest corporations in the land, were female, for example. In far too many cases, taking a job defined as "women's work" became a pathway to poverty rather than an open door to self-fulfillment and dignity.

Certainly a feminist could argue that women's increased employment represented a positive development—yet there were caveats. The implications of the rise in divorce were also double-edged. "No-fault" proceedings, instituted in the 1960s and 1970s, allowed divorce if both partners said their marriage had irretrievably broken down. As a result, women were able to leave unhappy marriages and become independent, which seemed a victory for women's freedom—yet women were often divorce's victims. As part of liberal feminism's assault on sexual distinctions under the law, groups such as NOW had pushed for subsequent divorce reforms that put a premium on both spouses' equality without regard to gender. Such traditional practices as having a husband pay alimony to his former wife were abandoned; a husband's obligation to support his wife post-divorce was no greater than her requirement to support him. This meant that unpaid wives and mothers who had sacrificed their own careers to serve their husbands and families often ended up empty-handed if their husbands in middle age—at the peak of their own earning powers—decided to leave. With no financial settlement to fall back on, and no marketable job skills, and frequently with custody of the children, such former wives were likely to experience poverty and despair. Not even half of ex-husbands actually paid the child support costs they were assigned as part of divorce settlements. Far from being a badge of liberation, then, divorces stemming from husbands' dissatisfactions or mid-life crises often greatly disadvantaged women who had entered marriage thinking it was forever. Betty Friedan ruefully noted that "women who had been housewives, who hadn't worked in years, or who made very little money, found themselves divorced with no provision whatsoever for their maintenance or for training for a job to earn real money, and often with the whole responsibility for the children to boot." Ex-wives' standards of living typically dropped sharply after divorce, while their ex-husbands' financial assets rose.

Increasingly, poverty became an experience primarily of women and children. By the 1990s one out of every four children in America lived below the poverty line (up from one out of five in 1980). Seventy percent of adults who lived below the poverty line were women. The picture was most grim for women (and men) who were members of minority groups. From the beginning of American history, race had served as a primary determinant of status, wealth, power, and prestige. It was the basis for eradicating native peoples from the land, for enslaving generations of Africans and African Americans, and for assigning immigrant groups to the most menial and exploitative jobs. Women often fared even worse than men in such ethnic minorities. White masters and overseers systematically took sexual advantage of their female slaves or female house servants. Owners of canneries or sweatshop garment factories paid immigrant women lower wages than men, forcing all to work in disease-producing conditions.

The mid-twentieth century did bring progress. As a result of the labor movement and the civil rights struggle, more minority women gained the chance to work in factories or in offices from which they had been excluded before World War II. After the 1964 Civil Rights Act was passed the number of African-American women employed in clerical and other white-collar jobs zoomed up. Yet by the end of the century black women still earned ten cents less than white women for every dollar earned by the average man, and the earnings gap was even greater for the average Latina.

The impact of race and ethnicity was clear in the feminization of poverty. Through the decades after 1960, the number of female-headed households skyrocketed, driven both by divorce and by lower marriage rates. One-fifth of family-based households among whites were female-headed by the 1990s; among Latino families it was almost one-third, and among African-Americans, almost three-fifths. During these years poverty climbed upward among ethnic minorities, even as it fell overall among whites. In 1998 28.8 percent of white, single mother households with children lived below poverty level, as compared to 47.5 percent for blacks and 52.2 percent for hispanics. The correlation between being a female head of a household with children and being poor was dramatic.

Behind all the stories about a revolution in women's status was a complicated, tortured, and often contradictory reality. Because race and class interacted with gender, some women benefited enormously from the gains that had been won by feminists, while countless others saw no change at all in their lives, and the situation for many worsened rather than improving. To a poor woman struggling to make ends meet while holding down a minimum-wage job at the local fast-food outlet, the promises of women's liberation seemed like a slap in the face. Economic resources and education seemed to be the most important variables. A young college-educated woman from an economically secure background had a world open to her that was strikingly different from her mother's or grandmother's opportunities. If these earlier generations worked outside the home, they were likely to be secretaries, salesclerks, nurses, or teachers. Even then, they were likely to stop work when they married and had a child. The woman with a college degree in the year 2000, on the other hand, could go to law school or get a master's degree in business administration. She might then enter a large corporate firm and make a six-figure salary, doing the same kind of work for the same pay as the brightest young man. If she married, it was probable that her husband would be someone with a comparable background. And if they had a baby, they were likely to pay a child-care worker or a day-care center to take care of the child while continuing to pursue their careers.

A young Latina woman born in the South Bronx, on the other hand, faced a very different situation. If she was like half the young people in New York City's public schools, she would drop out before graduating from high school. There was a good chance she would have a child while still in her teenage years, but would not get married. With no job skills, she could find work only at low-paying service establishments. By the time she was twenty she would be locked into a cycle of work and family responsibilities that seemed to offer little opportunity for improvement. Not only was the life of the South Bronx woman no better than her mother's or grandmother's, but it might even be worse.

There were other possibilities, of course. A white (or black) high school graduate who worked as a secretary for an insurance agency or as a factory operative at General Motors might well find her life better than that of her mother—for which the feminist movement deserved some credit. Greater attention to sexual harassment in the workplace might discourage unwanted advances from male bosses or coworkers. Legal advances for women's rights contributed to higher wages and the opening of some jobs that previously had been restricted to men. If the woman had an unwanted pregnancy, she now could consider terminating it legally.

One of the major problems with feminist advances was that they operated differentially. Their benefits were largely limited to women already in a position to be able to take advantage of the new rights that had been won. Nor did the differential decrease over time. When *Roe* v. *Wade* became the law of the land, for example, poor women as well as rich women had access to an abortion. But by 1978, Congress had prohibited federal funds from being used to pay for abortions for poor women. Then additional restrictions were enacted to circumscribe women's abortion rights, including a twenty-four-hour waiting period and the requirement that teenagers notify their parents and get their permission. Because of threats to their funding and security, abortion providers dwindled in number. Well-off women had little difficulty coping with these restrictions. But women

Dianne Rivera-Jean (top), an electrician's mate/fireman, leaves a California naval base en route to Somalia, where she will assist in relief efforts of Operation Restore Hope. Lieutenant Commander Darlene M. Iskra (bottom), commanding officer of the salvage ship USS *Opportune,* was the first woman assigned to command a U.S. Navy ship.

from culturally conservative and economically disadvantaged backgrounds found the restrictions almost impassable. What had once seemed like a feminist victory for all women had come to have a distinctly middle- and upper-class tinge.

Similarly, government programs designed to force companies and universities to open doors to women had little impact on those clustered in sex-segregated, low-paying jobs. Affirmative action occasionally worked well as a means of giving women lawyers access to jobs at law firms that previously hired only white men, or of giving women professors opportunities to be hired in departments that had never considered women scholars. But affirmative action meant little to women who were data processors working side by side with other women in a giant computer pool (unless it meant that some men were hired), or to operatives at a textile mill who had neither the education nor the training to qualify for a management-level opening. In short, affirmative action—and other equal opportunity programs—tended to benefit those with preexisting credentials that enabled them to move forward. They did less to open new possibilities for people stuck in sex-segregated and low-paying positions.

Programs that might have been of greater value to the mass of women in the workplace either were not implemented or were rejected. Working-class and minority women had no need greater than adequate child care for their young children—child care that would not only permit them to hold decent jobs, but would also give their children the medical care, nutrition, and educational stimulation that might break the cycle of poverty and improve the children's chances for a better life. Congress enacted such a program in 1972. Called the Comprehensive Child Development Act, it would have created day-care centers throughout the country, with places available to all children regardless of ability to pay. But President Nixon vetoed the measure on the grounds that it would undermine the strength of the nuclear family. Well-off people, of course, could afford to pay for their own child care. But poor women did not have that option, and most were forced to rely on makeshift arrangements.

"Comparable worth" was another idea that, if enacted and upheld by the courts, might have significantly improved the economic status of millions of women workers. Equal pay legislation in the past had focused on securing equal compensation for women who performed the same work as men. Yet such laws failed to address the underlying problem of job segmentation—the fact that most women worked with other women and did not hold the same jobs as men. On the other hand, if the skills required for a job could be measured and compared with skills needed for other jobs, it might be possible to arrive at a reliable standard that would lead to people with comparable skills being paid comparable wages. In San Jose, California, for example, job investigators found that the skills and training needed by a nurse were approximately comparable to those required for a fire-truck mechanic. Yet the nurse, a woman, earned nine thousand dollars less than the mechanic, a man. Clearly, given the number of women in skilled positions, whether nurses, secretaries, or data processors, a wage scale adjusted to compensate for comparable worth might bring substantial improvement in wages.

In some cities, such as Minneapolis and Seattle, where comparable worth policies were implemented, it made a significant difference. Yet many government officials criticized the idea as unworkable and a violation of the free market system, and courts were inconsistent in upholding comparable worth laws. What the opponents ignored, of course, was that the so-called free market system was in fact based on old ideas that women should be confined to "women's work" that paid only a "woman's wage."

Poor, working class, and minority women had ample reason to feel that feminism reflected middle-class priorities and values. To be sure, feminist groups from NOW to Redstockings (a radical feminist group) included attention to working-class issues in their literature and did what they could to press for measures that would help the poor as much as the rich. Yet in the end the feminist aims that were achieved seemed to be concentrated in areas designed to promote *individual* rights for those in a position to take advantage of them, rather than on issues that might bring *collective* advancement for women of all classes and races. Justifiably or unjustifiably, "feminism" became associated in the public eye with well-groomed, highly articulate women in business suits who sat around boardroom tables or frequented centers of power. It was not publicly linked to programs that an Irish-Catholic mother of four who worked in a shoe factory, or a black single mother who was a high school dropout, could identify with. Some groups tried to bridge that chasm, and black and Hispanic women occupied prominent positions in feminist organizations. Nevertheless, it was hard to escape the conclusion that impoverished minority women's experiences after 1960 had little in common with those of well-educated middle- and upper-class women; ethnicity and class remained powerful obstacles to women's solidarity.

Where Do We Go from Here?

As the nation greeted the year 2000, few issues seemed as critical to the future direction of American society as what happened to women. Although the previous decades had brought milestone after milestone of progress, women remained the primary victims of economic, social, and political inequality. Even as 40 percent of the black women in the country joined white women as full participants in the middle class and as lawyers, doctors, and business executives, another 40 percent became caught up in an ever-deepening spiral of poverty, unemployment, and social dislocation.

During the administration of President Bill Clinton in the 1990s, opposition to "welfare as we have known it" rose on a flood tide of ill-deserved accusations against teenage single mothers, usually depicted as African-American, although more "welfare mothers" were white. The Personal Responsibility and Work Opportunity Act of 1996—asserting the superiority of the two-parent family—rolled back the federal commitment to assisting single mothers raising children that had been in place since the New Deal of the 1930s. It required that all "welfare mothers" (and fathers) seek employment or job training. Despite some feminists' objections that poor women needed support for their mothering, and that child-care facilities were inadequate for mothers who could earn only the minimum wage, this revision of welfare policy was put into place, removing resources and adding further stress to impoverished female-headed families. If the country was becoming a two-tier society, with little in the way of resources or life-style shared by the two tiers, women's lives displayed the division starkly.

Any social change, good or bad, reveals as much about the larger society as it does about the individuals or groups most involved in the change. The various feminist movements that have been so much a part of change in the status of American women since the 1960s tell us a great deal about what options did and did not exist for those seeking to direct that change. And the way the society responded to different demands and possibilities may help clarify the direction of future developments.

By the mid-1990s policymakers and Americans in general seemed to have struck a compromise on what would be allowed in the way of judicial and constitutional change on women's status. Despite early success in securing support in state legislatures, for example, backers of the Equal Rights Amendment discovered that there was no chance of persuading three-fourths of the states to ratify it. By 1982, time ran out. Part of the reason for the defeat was that on virtually any issue involving traditional values, whether patriotism, prayer in the schools, or sex roles, the Southern states took a more conservative stance than others. These states played a significant role in blocking the ERA—but opposition was more widespread. Behind state legislatures' unwillingness to endorse the ERA lay conservatives' fears that basic distinctions between women and men were going to be thrown out. Ultimately, the ERA failed because individuals like Judy Morgan and Dianne Chavis did not wish their legislators to leave traditional values completely behind.

On the other hand, there seemed to be a consensus that most public advances made during the height of feminist influence should remain in place. Women continued to make slow progress in achieving political offices in the 1990s, both appointive offices in President Clinton's administration and election to state and national legislatures. The gains were far more substantial at local than at national levels, but represented improvement nonetheless. Continued awareness of a "gender gap" in voting—that is, that women were more concerned about social issues such as education, gun control, health care, Medicare, and social security, and would vote their preferences—kept politicians from neglecting women's civic presence.

Reproductive choice continued to be a highly contested issue, a touchstone for political organizing by fundamentalist Christians, who opposed abortion as the taking of human life. The tremendous development of reproductive technologies during the 1990s enabled human ova to be fertilized outside the mother's body and reimplanted in the uterus, thus offering hope of biological offspring to previously infertile couples but also creating ethical dilemmas regarding surrogate mother-hood and parental rights and greatly complicating the question of when life begins. The U.S. Supreme Court, having allowed many states to set restrictive conditions upon women's right to choose an abortion, decided in 1992 in the case of *Planned Parenthood* v. *Casey* to leave intact the heart of the founding decision, *Roe* v. *Wade*. This was in keeping with the apparent sentiments of a plurality of the American people. Yet the intensity of the anti-abortion movement, some of whose adherents used violent and illegal tactics, succeeding in reducing drastically the numbers of abortion providers. Together with the continuing refusal of government Medicaid programs to pay for abortions, this especially compromised the ability of poor women, those in remote geographical areas, and young women without parental support to terminate their pregnancies.

In both the ERA and the abortion instances, there appeared a tendency to round off the rough edges of more extreme positions taken by both pro- and anti-feminists. The larger question was whether programs could be engineered to re-flect feminist concerns for advancing the rights of women along with the concerns of other groups for a more just and fair society. In many European societies, reformers had often sought to incorporate into larger social democratic policies their objectives for women as mothers and members of families. Thus, for exam-ple, Sweden's parental leave provision enabled either parent to stay at home with a new baby for a full year without sacrificing job or seniority and still receiv-ing 80 percent of his or her normal pay (up to a certain limit). Though far more mothers than fathers took time off (reflecting traditional gender roles and men's usually higher earnings), such parental-leave laws made staying home and taking care of a child a basic human and social right. Other European coun-tries, including France, Britain, Germany, Italy, the Netherlands, and Spain, enti-tled new mothers to generous maternity leave with full or nearly full pay, and preserved a parent's job and seniority rights for longer periods, up to three years. By the 1990s U.S. policy mandated twelve weeks of maternity leave, but left pay up to employers. Many European states also provided government-run child-care facilities as a basic educational right. Again, mothers might be the chief beneficia-ries, but the rationale was what was best for the entire society. Such an approach emphasized what joined people together as part of a common society, not what divided them.

There was at least a chance that American society might seek to move in a similar direction. While the idea of government-funded national health care foun-dered in comparison to the rise of private health-care management organizations, commitments to child care, parental leave, and enforcement of child support arrangements seemed politically palatable. These could be presented as pro-family,

Escorted by five of the six women members of the U.S. Senate—from left to right: Carol Moseley-Braun, Barbara Boxer (behind Moseley-Braun), Barbara Mikulski, Dianne Feinstein, and Patty Murray—Hillary Rodham Clinton prepares to talk with the Senate about President Clinton's proposed health care reforms in the early 1990s.

pro-community measures designed to serve the well-being of everyone, even as mothers—and especially poor mothers—would be prime beneficiaries.

No issues have been a greater source of injustice and inequality in the United States than those shaped by gender, race, and class. Through the extraordinary sacrifices of countless activists, American society was persuaded to address persistent race and gender barriers in law and society in the second half of the twentieth century, to reduce the inequalities individual Americans suffered because they were not born male or white. The new, freer America was still a two-tier America, however, with millions of people unable to take advantage of the changes won by civil rights advocates and feminists. If Americans could move with as much energy and purpose in the new century to extend basic human rights and decent living conditions to those on the lower tier, then perhaps the long struggle to secure true equality between women and men, white and nonwhite, could finally be won.

Bibliography

General Histories of American Women

Armitage, Susan, and Elizabeth Jameson, eds. *The Women's West.* Norman: University of Oklahoma Press, 1987.

————. *Writing the Range: Race, Class, and Culture in the Women's West.* Norman: University of Oklahoma Press, 1997.

Axtell, James, ed. *The Indian Peoples of Eastern America: A Documentary History of the Sexes.* New York: Oxford University Press, 1981.

Bataille, Gretchen M., and Kathleen M. Sands. *American Indian Women: A Guide to Research.* New York: Garland, 1991.

Baxandall, Rosalyn, Linda Gordon, and Susan Reverby, eds. *America's Working Women: A Documentary History—1600 to the Present.* New York: Vintage, 1976.

Berkin, Carol Ruth, and Mary Beth Norton, eds. *Women of America: A History.* Boston: Houghton Mifflin, 1979.

Cott, Nancy F. *Public Vows: A History of Marriage and the Nation.* Cambridge: Harvard University Press, 2000.

————, et. al., eds. *Root of Bitterness: Documents of the Social History of American Women.* rev. ed. Boston: Northeastern University Press, 1996.

Cowan, Ruth Schwartz. *More Work for Mother: The Ironies of Household Technology from the Open Hearth to the Microwave.* New York: Basic Books, 1983.

Degler, Carl. *At Odds: Women and the Family in America from the Revolution to the Present.* New York: Oxford University Press, 1980.

D'Emilio, John, and Estelle B. Freedman. *Intimate Matters: A History of Sexuality in America.* New York: Harper & Row, 1988.

DuBois, Ellen Carol, and Vicki L. Ruiz. *Unequal Sisters: A Multi-Cultural Reader in U.S. Women's History.* New York: Routledge, 1994.

Evans, Sara M. *Born for Liberty: A History of Women in America.* rev. ed. New York: Free Press, 1997.

Franklin, Penelope. *Private Pages: Diaries of American Women, 1830s–1970s.* New York: Ballantine, 1986.

Giddings, Paula. *When and Where I Enter: The Impact of Black Women on Race and Sex in America.* New York: Bantam, 1984.

Gordon, Linda. *Woman's Body, Woman's Right: A Social History of Birth Control in America.* New York: Grossman, 1976.

James, Edward, Janet Wilson James, and Paul Boyer, eds. *Notable American Women, 1607–1950: A Biographical Dictionary.* 3 vols. Cambridge: Belknap Press of Harvard University Press, 1971.

Jones, Jacqueline. *Labor of Love, Labor of Sorrow: Black Women, Work, and the Family from Slavery to the Present.* New York: Basic Books, 1985.

Kerber, Linda. *No Constitutional Right to be Ladies: Women and the Obligations of Citizenship.* New York: Hill & Wang, 1998.

———, Alice Kessler-Harris, and Kathryn Kish Sklar, eds. *U.S. History as Women's History: New Feminist Essays.* Chapel Hill: University of North Carolina Press, 1995.

———, and Jane Sherron De Hart, eds. *Women's America: Refocusing the Past,* 5th ed. New York: Oxford University Press, 2000.

Kessler-Harris, Alice. *Out to Work: A History of Wage-Earning Women in the United States.* New York: Oxford University Press, 1982.

Lerner, Gerda, ed. *Black Women in White America: A Documentary History.* New York: Vintage, 1992.

———. *The Female Experience: An American Documentary.* New York: Oxford University Press, 1992.

Matthews, Glenna. *Just a Housewife: The Rise and Fall of Domesticity in America.* New York: Oxford University Press, 1987.

———. *The Rise of Public Woman: Woman's Power and Woman's Place in the United States, 1630–1970.* New York: Oxford University Press, 1994.

Mintz, Steven, and Susan Kellogg. *Domestic Revolutions: A Social History of American Family Life.* New York: Free Press, 1988.

Norton, Mary Beth, ed. *Major Problems in American Women's History: Documents and Essays.* Lexington, Mass.: D.C. Heath, 1989.

———, and Carol Ruth Berkin, eds. *Women of America: A History.* Boston: Houghton Mifflin, 1979.

Ogden, Annegret S. *The Great American Housewife: From Helpmate to Wage Earner, 1776–1986.* Westport, Conn.: Greenwood, 1986.

Ruiz, Vicki. *From Out of the Shadows: Mexican Women in Twentieth-Century America.* New York: Oxford University Press, 1998.

Ryan, Mary P. *Womanhood in America: From Colonial Times to the Present.* 3rd ed. New York: Franklin Watts, 1983.

Sklar, Kathryn Kish and Thomas Dublin, eds. *Women and Power in American History.* 2 vols. Englewood Cliffs, N.J.: Prentice-Hall, 1991.

Solomon, Barbara. *In the Company of Educated Women: A History of Women and Higher Education in America.* New Haven, Conn.: Yale University Press, 1985.

Ware, Susan. *Modern American Women: A Documentary History.* New York: McGraw-Hill, 1997.

Weiner, Lynn. *From Working Girl to Working Mother: The Female Labor Force in the United States, 1820–1980.* Chapel Hill: University of North Carolina Press, 1985.

Wertheimer, Barbara Mayer. *We Were There: The Story of Working Women in America.* New York: Pantheon, 1977.

Woloch, Nancy. *Women and the American Experience.* 3rd edition. New York: McGraw Hill, 2000.

Chapter 1

Anderson, Karen. *Chain Her by One Foot: The Subjugation of Native Women in Seventeenth-Century New France.* New York: Routledge, 1990.

Devens, Carol. *Countering Colonization: Native American Women and the Great Lakes Missions, 1630–1900.* Berkeley: University of California Press, 1992.

Etienne, Mona, and Eleanor Leacock, eds. *Women and Colonization.* New York: Praeger, 1980.

Gutierrez, Ramon. *When Jesus Came, the Corn Mothers Went Away: Marriage, Sexuality, and Power in New Mexico, 1500–1846.* Stanford, Calif.: Stanford University Press, 1991.

Jensen, Joan M., and Darlis A. Miller, eds. *New Mexico Women: Intercultural Perspectives.* Albuquerque: University of New Mexico Press, 1986.

Landes, Ruth. *Ojibwa Woman.* New York: Columbia University Press, 1938.

McLoughlin, William G. *After the Trail of Tears: The Cherokees' Struggle for Sovereignty, 1839–1880.* Chapel Hill: University of North Carolina Press, 1993.

———. *Cherokee Renascence in the New Republic.* Princeton, N.J.: Princeton University Press, 1986.

Namias, June. *White Captives: Gender and Ethnicity on the American Frontier.* Chapel Hill: University of North Carolina Press, 1993.

Nash, Gary B. *Red, White, and Black: The People of Early America.* Englewood Cliffs, N.J.: Prentice-Hall, 1974.

Niethammer, Carolyn. *Daughters of the Earth: The Lives and Legends of American Indian Women.* New York: Collier, 1977.

———. "Cherokee Women and the Trail of Tears," *Journal of Women's History* 1 (1989): 14–28.

———. *Slavery and the Evolution of Cherokee Society, 1540–1866.* Knoxville: University of Tennessee Press, 1979.

Quimby, George I. *Indian Life in the Upper Great Lakes.* Chicago: University of Chicago Press, 1960.

Richter, Daniel K. *The Ordeal of the Longhouse: The Peoples of the Iroquois League in the Era of European Colonization.* Chapel Hill: University of North Carolina Press, 1992.

Riley, Glenda. *Women and Indians on the Frontier, 1825–1915.* Albuquerque: University of New Mexico Press, 1988.

Schlissel, Lillian, Vicki L. Ruiz, and Janice Monk, eds. *Western Women: Their Land, Their Lives.* Albuquerque: University of New Mexico Press, 1988.

Shoemaker, Nancy, ed. *Negotiators of Change: Historical Perspectives on Native American Women.* New York: Routledge, 1995.

———. "The Rise or Fall of Iroquois Women," *Journal of Women's History* 1 (1989): 39–57.

Van Kirk, Sylvia. *Many Tender Ties: Women in Fur-Trade Society in Western Canada.* Winnipeg, Canada: Watson & Dwyer, 1981.

Weber, David J. *The Spanish Frontier in North America.* New Haven: Yale University Press, 1992.

White, Richard. *The Middle Ground: Indians, Empires, and Republics in the Great Lakes Region, 1650–1815.* New York: Cambridge University Press, 1991.

Chapter 2

Histories of the Colonial Period

Axtell, James. *The European and the Indian: Essays in the Ethnohistory of Colonial North America.* New York: Oxford University Press, 1981.

Bailyn, Bernard. *The Peopling of British North America: An Introduction.* New York: Vintage, 1986.

Berlin, Ira. *Many Thousands Gone: The First Two Centuries of Slavery in North America.* Cambridge: Harvard University Press, 1998.

Bonomi, Patricia. *Under the Cope of Heaven: Religion, Society, and Politics in Colonial America.* New York: Oxford University Press, 1986.

Boyer, Paul, and Stephen Nissenbaum. *Salem Possessed: The Social Origins of Witchcraft.* Cambridge: Harvard University Press, 1974.

Cooke, Jacob Ernest, et al., eds. *Encyclopedia of the North American Colonies.* 3 vols. New York: Scribners, 1993.

Fischer, David Hackett. *Albion's Seed: Four British Folkways in America.* New York: Oxford University Press, 1989.

Innes, Stephen, ed. *Work and Labor in Early America.* Chapel Hill: University of North Carolina Press, 1988.

Kulikoff, Allan. *Tobacco and Slaves: The Development of Southern Cultures in the Chesapeake, 1680–1800.* Chapel Hill: University of North Carolina Press, 1986.

Lockridge, Kenneth A. *A New England Town: The First Hundred Years.* New York: Norton, 1970.

Morgan, Edmund S. *American Slavery, American Freedom: The Ordeal of Colonial Virginia.* New York: Norton, 1975.

———. *The Puritan Dilemma: The Story of John Winthrop.* 2nd ed. Reading, Mass.: Addison Wesley Longman, 1999.

Rutman, Darrett B., and Anita H. Rutman. *A Place in Time: Middlesex County, Virginia, 1650–1750.* New York: Norton, 1984.

Sobel, Mechal. *The World They Made Together: Black and White Values in Eighteenth-Century Virginia.* Princeton, N.J.: Princeton University Press, 1987.

Tate, Thad W., and David L. Ammerman. *The Chesapeake in the Seventeenth Century: Essays on Anglo-American Society.* Chapel Hill: University of North Carolina Press, 1979.

Wood, Peter S. *Black Majority: Negroes in Colonial South Carolina from 1670 through the Stono Rebellion.* New York: Norton, 1974.

Women, Family, and Household

Brown, Kathleen M. *Good Wives, Nasty Wenches, and Anxious Patriarchs: Gender, Race, and Power in Colonial Virginia.* Chapel Hill: University of North Carolina Press, 1996.

Dayton, Cornelia Hughes. *Women Before the Bar: Gender, Law, and Society in Connecticut, 1639–1789.* Chapel Hill: University of North Carolina Press, 1995.

Demos, John. *A Little Commonwealth: Family Life in Plymouth Colony.* New York: Oxford University Press, 1970.

———. *The Unredeemed Captive: A Family Story from Early America.* New York: Knopf, 1994.

Earle, Alice Morse. *Colonial Dames and Good Wives.* 1895. Reprint, Bowie, Md.: Heritage Books, 1988.

———. *Margaret Winthrop.* 1895. Reprint, Williamstown, Mass.: Corner House, 1975.

Greven, Philip. *The Protestant Temperament: Patterns of Child-Rearing, Religious Experience, and the Self in Early America.* Chicago: University of Chicago Press, 1977.

Juster, Susan. *Disorderly Women: Sexual Politics and Evangelicalism in Revolutionary New England.* Ithaca, N.Y.: Cornell University Press, 1994.

Kamensky, Jane. *Governing the Tongue: Sinners and Witches in Puritan New England.* New York: Oxford University Press, 1997.

Karlsen, Carol F. *The Devil in the Shape of a Woman: Witchcraft in Colonial New England.* New York: Norton, 1987.

Koehler, Lyle. *A Search for Power: The "Weaker Sex" in Seventeenth-Century New England.* Urbana: University of Illinois Press, 1980.

Morgan, Edmund S. *The Puritan Family: Religion and Domestic Relations in Seventeenth-Century New England.* New York: Harper & Row, 1966.

Narrett, David E. *Inheritance and Family Life in Colonial New York City.* Ithaca, N.Y.: Cornell University Press, 1992.

Norton, Mary Beth. *Founding Mothers and Fathers: Gendered Power and the Forming of American Society.* New York: Knopf, 1996.

Reis, Elizabeth. *Damned Women: Sinners, Witches, and the Discourse of Depravity in Early New England.* Ithaca, N.Y.: Cornell University Press, 1997.

Smith, Daniel Blake. *Inside the Great House: Planter Family Life in Eighteenth-Century Chesapeake Society.* Ithaca, N.Y.: Cornell University Press, 1980.

Spruill, Julia C. *Women's Life and Work in the Southern Colonies.* 1938. Reprint, New York: Norton, 1972.

Thompson, Roger. *Sex in Middlesex: Popular Mores in a Massachusetts County, 1649–1699.* Amherst: University of Massachusetts Press, 1986.

Ulrich, Laurel T. *Good Wives: Image and Reality in the Lives of Women in Northern New England, 1650–1750.* New York: Knopf, 1982.

Wall, Helena M. *Fierce Communion: Family and Community in Early America.* Cambridge: Harvard University Press, 1990.

Woodward, Grace Steele. *Pocahontas.* Norman: University of Oklahoma Press, 1969.

Primary Sources by or about Early American Women

Andrews, William L., ed. *Journeys in New Worlds: Early American Women's Narratives.* Madison: University of Wisconsin Press, 1990.

Boyer, Paul, and Stephen Nissenbaum. *Salem Village Witchcraft: A Documentary Record of Local Conflict in Colonial New England.* Boston: Northeastern University Press, 1993.

Crane, Elaine Forman, ed. *The Diary of Elizabeth Drinker.* 3 vols. Boston: Northeastern University Press, 1991.

Hall, David D., ed. *The Antinomian Controversy, 1636–1638: A Documentary History.* 2nd ed. Durham, N.C.: Duke University Press, 1990.

———. *Witch-Hunting in Seventeenth-Century New England: A Documentary History, 1638–1692.* Boston: Northeastern University Press, 1991.

Hensley, Jeannine, ed. *The Works of Anne Bradstreet.* Cambridge: Harvard University Press, 1967.

Karlsen, Carol F., and Laurie Crumpacker, eds. *The Journal of Esther Edwards Burr, 1754–1757.* New Haven: Yale University Press, 1984.

Pinckney, Elise, ed. *The Letter Book of Eliza Lucas Pinckney, 1739–1762.* Chapel Hill: University of North Carolina Press, 1972.

Ruether, Rosemary R., and Rosemary S. Keller, eds. *Women and Religion in America: A Documentary History.* Vol. 2, *The Colonial and Revolutionary Periods.* New York: Harper & Row, 1983.

Seaver, James E. *A Narrative of the Life of Mrs. Mary Jemison.* Edited by June Namias. Norman: University of Oklahoma Press, 1992.

Shields, John, ed. *The Collected Works of Phillis Wheatley.* New York: Oxford University Press, 1988.

Chapter 3

Histories of the Revolutionary Era

Ahlstrom, Sydney. *A Religious History of the American People.* Garden City, N.Y.: Image Books, 1975.

Bailyn, Bernard. *Ideological Origins of the American Revolution.* Cambridge: Harvard University Press, 1967.

Berlin, Ira, and Hoffman, Ronald, eds. *Slavery and Freedom in the Age of the American Revolution.* Charlottesville: University Press of Virginia for the United States Capitol Historical Society, 1983.

Countryman, Edward. *The American Revolution.* New York: Hill & Wang, 1985.

Cremin, Lawrence A. *American Education: The Colonial Experience, 1607–1783.* New York: Harper & Row, 1970.

———. *American Education: The National Experience, 1783–1876.* New York: Harper & Row, 1980.

Gilmore, William J. *Reading Becomes a Necessity of Life: Material and Cultural Life in Rural New England, 1780–1835.* Knoxville: University of Tennessee Press, 1989.

Graymont, Barbara. *The Iroquois in the American Revolution.* Syracuse, N.Y.: Syracuse University Press, 1972.

Gross, Robert A. *The Minutemen and Their World.* New York: Hill & Wang, 1976.

Gutman, Herbert G. *The Black Family in Slavery and Freedom, 1750–1925.* New York: Pantheon, 1976.

Innes, Stephen, ed. *Work and Labor in Early America.* Chapel Hill: University of North Carolina Press, 1988.

Isaac, Rhys. *The Transformation of Virginia, 1740–1790*. Chapel Hill: University of North Carolina Press, 1982.

Jennings, Francis. *Empire of Fortune: Crowns, Colonies and Tribes in the Seven Years War in America*. New York: Norton, 1988.

Jordan, Winthrop D. *White Over Black: American Attitudes Toward the Negro, 1550–1812*. Chapel Hill: University of North Carolina Press, 1968.

Kulikoff, Allan. *Tobacco and Slaves: The Development of Southern Cultures in the Chesapeake, 1680–1800*. Chapel Hill: University of North Carolina Press, 1986.

Lockridge, Kenneth A. *Literacy in Colonial New England: An Enquiry into the Social Context of Literacy in the Early Modern West*. New York: Norton, 1974.

Morgan, Edmund S. *The Birth of the Republic, 1763–1789*. Rev. ed. Chicago: University of Chicago Press, 1977.

Mullin, Gerald W. *Flight and Rebellion: Slave Resistance in Eighteenth-Century Virginia*. New York: Oxford University Press, 1972.

Nash, Gary B. *Forging Freedom: The Formation of Philadelphia's Black Community, 1720–1840*. Cambridge: Harvard University Press, 1988.

———. *The Urban Crucible: Social Change, Political Consciousness, and the Origins of the American Revolution*. Cambridge: Harvard University Press, 1979.

Pierson, William. *Black Yankees: The Development of an Afro-American Subculture in Eighteenth-Century New England*. Amherst: University of Massachusetts Press, 1988.

Royster, Charles. *A Revolutionary People at War: The Continental Army and American Character, 1775–1783*. Chapel Hill: University of North Carolina Press, 1979.

Silverman, Kenneth. *A Cultural History of the American Revolution*. New York: Thomas Y. Crowell, 1976.

Sobel, Mechal. *The World They Made Together: Black and White Values in Eighteenth-Century Virginia*. Princeton: Princeton University Press, 1987.

Wallace, Anthony F.C. *The Death and Rebirth of the Seneca*. New York: Vintage, 1972.

Wood, Gordon S. *The Creation of the American Republic, 1776–1787*. New York: Norton, 1969.

Zilversmit, Arthur. *The First Emancipation: The Abolition of Slavery in the North*. Chicago: University of Chicago Press, 1967.

Histories of Women

Brekus, Catherine. *Strangers & Pilgrims: Female Preaching in America 1740–1845*. Chapel Hill: University of North Carolina Press, 1998.

Buel, Joy Day, and Richard Buel, Jr. *The Way of Duty: A Woman and Her Family in Revolutionary America*. New York: Norton, 1984.

De Pauw, Linda Grant, and Hunt, Conover. *Remember the Ladies: Women in America, 1750–1815*. New York: Viking Press in association with The Pilgrim Society, 1976.

Hoffman, Ronald, and Albert, Peter J., eds. *Women in the Age of the American Revolution*. Charlottesville: University Press of Virginia for the United States Capitol Historical Society, 1989.

James, Janet Wilson. *Changing Ideas about Women in the United States, 1776–1825*. New York: Garland, 1981.

Kerber, Linda K. *Women of the Republic: Intellect and Ideology in Revolutionary America.* Chapel Hill: University of North Carolina Press, 1980.

Klinghoffer, Judith Apter, and Elkis, Lois. "'The Petticoat Elector': Women's Suffrage in New Jersey, 1776–1807." *Journal of the Early Republic* 12 (Summer 1992): 159–193.

Norton, Mary Beth. *Liberty's Daughters: The Revolutionary Experience of American Women, 1750–1800.* Boston: Little, Brown, 1980.

Salmon, Marylynn. *Women and the Law of Property in Early America.* Chapel Hill: University of North Carolina Press, 1986.

Scholten, Catherine M. *Childbearing in American Society: 1650–1850.* New York: New York University Press, 1985.

Swan, Susan Burrows. *Plain and Fancy: American Women and Their Needlework, 1750–1850.* New York: Holt, Rinehart and Winston, 1977.

Ulrich, Laurel Thatcher. *A Midwife's Tale: The Life of Martha Ballard, Based on Her Diary, 1785–1812.* New York: Knopf, 1990.

Primary Sources Cited in the Text

Condict, Jemima. *Jemima Condict, Her Book: Being a Transcript of an Essex County Maid During the Revolutionary War.* Newark, N.J.: Carteret Book Club, 1930.

Earle, Alice Morse, ed. *Diary of Anna Green Winslow: A Boston School Girl of 1771.* Bedford, Mass.: Applewood Books, 1996.

A Girl's Life Eighty Years Ago: Selections from the Letters of Eliza Southgate Bowne; With an Introduction by Clarence Cook[. . .]. New York: Scribners, 1887.

Greene, Jack P., ed. *The Diary of Landon Carter of Sabine Hall, 1752–1778.* 2 vols. Charlottesville: University Press of Virginia, 1965.

Jackson, John W., ed. *Margaret Morris: Her Journal with Biographical Sketch and Notes.* Philadelphia: George S. MacManus, 1949.

Karlson, Carol F., and Laurie Crumpacker, eds. *The Journal of Esther Edwards Burr, 1754–1757.* New Haven: Yale University Press, 1984.

Parkman, Ebenezer. Diary. Parkman Family Papers. American Antiquarian Society, Worcester, Mass.

Tayler, Mary Hunt. *The Maternal Physician: A Treatise on the Nurture and Management of Infants.* New York: Isaac Riley, 1811.

Wallett, Francis G., ed. *The Diary of Ebenezer Parkman, 1703–1782. First Part: Three Volumes in One, 1719–1755. With a Foreword by Clifford K. Shipton.* Worcester, Mass.: American Antiquarian Society, 1974.

Chapter 4

Histories of the Era 1800–1840

Blasingame, John W. *The Slave Community: Plantation Life in the Antebellum South.* Rev. ed. New York: Oxford University Press, 1979.

Boyer, Paul. *Urban Masses and Moral Order in America, 1820–1920.* Cambridge: Harvard University Press, 1978.

Dublin, Thomas. *Farm to Factory: Women's Letters, 1830–1860.* New York: Columbia University Press, 1981.

Faragher, John Mack. *Sugar Creek: Life on the Illinois Prairie.* New Haven: Yale University Press, 1986.

Genovese, Eugene. *Roll, Jordan, Roll: The World the Slaves Made.* New York: Vintage, 1976.

McCurry, Stephanie. *Masters of Small Worlds.* New York: Oxford University Press, 1995.

Monroy, Douglas. *Thrown among Strangers: The Making of Mexican Culture in Frontier California.* Berkeley: University of California Press, 1990.

Ryan, Mary P. *The Cradle of the Middle Class: The Family in Oneida County, 1780–1835.* New York: Cambridge University Press, 1983.

Walters, Ronald G. *American Reformers, 1815–1860.* New York: Hill & Wang, 1978.

Histories of Women

Boydston, Jeanne. *Home and Work: Housework, Wages, and the Ideology of Labor in the Early Republic.* New York: Oxford University Press, 1990.

Clinton, Catherine. *The Plantation Mistress: Woman's World in the Old South.* New York: Pantheon, 1982.

Cott, Nancy F. *The Bonds of Womanhood: "Woman's Sphere" in New England, 1780–1835.* New Haven: Yale University Press, 1977.

Dublin, Thomas. *Women at Work: The Transformation of Work and Community in Lowell, Massachusetts, 1826–1860.* New York: Columbia University Press, 1979.

Flexner, Eleanor. *Century of Struggle: The Woman's Rights Movement in the United States.* Cambridge: Harvard University Press, 1975.

Fox-Genovese, Elizabeth. *Within the Plantation Household: Black and White Women in the Old South.* Chapel Hill: University of North Carolina Press, 1988.

Jensen, Joan. *Loosening the Bonds: Mid-Atlantic Farm Women, 1750–1850.* New Haven: Yale University Press, 1986.

Lebsock, Suzanne. *Free Women of Petersburg: Status and Culture in a Southern Town, 1784–1865.* New York: Norton, 1985.

Melder, Keith E. *Beginnings of Sisterhood: The American Woman's Rights Movement, 1800–1860.* New York: Schocken, 1977.

Rothman, Ellen K. *Hands and Hearts: A History of Courtship in America.* New York: Basic Books, 1984.

Scott, Anne Firor. *Natural Allies: Women's Associations in American History.* Urbana: University of Illinois Press, 1991.

Stansell, Christine. *City of Women: Sex and Class in New York, 1789–1860.* Urbana: University of Illinois Press, 1987.

White, Deborah Gray. *Ar'n't I a Woman: Female Slaves in the Plantation South.* New York: Norton, 1985.

Biographies, Autobiographies, and First-Person Accounts

Buhle, Mari Jo, and Paul Buhle, eds. *The Concise History of Woman Suffrage: Selections from the Classic Work of Stanton, Anthony, Gage, and Harper.* Urbana: University of Illinois Press, 1978.

Eckhardt, Celia. *Fanny Wright: Rebel in America.* Cambridge: Harvard University Press, 1984.

Greene, Dana, ed. *Lucretia Mott: Her Complete Speeches and Sermons*. New York: E. Mellon Press, 1980.

Hays, Eleanor Rice. *Morning Star: A Biography of Lucy Stone, 1818–1893*. New York: Octagon, 1978.

Lerner, Gerda. *The Grimke Sisters from South Carolina: Pioneers for Women's Rights and Abolition*. New York: Houghton Mifflin, 1967.

Stanton, Elizabeth Cady. *Eighty Years and More: Reminiscences, 1815–1897*. New York: Schocken, 1971.

Sterling, Dorothy. *We Are Your Sisters: Black Women in the Nineteenth Century*. New York: Norton, 1984.

Chapter 5

Histories of the Mid-Nineteenth Century

Attie, Jeanie. *Patriotic Toil: Northern Women and the American Civil War*. Ithaca, N.Y.: Cornell University Press, 1998.

Berlin, Ira, et al., eds. *Free at Last: A Documentary History of Slavery, Freedom, and the Civil War*. New York: New Press, 1992.

Bleser, Carol, ed. *In Joy and in Sorrow: Women, Family, and Marriage in the Victorian South, 1830–1900*. New York: Oxford University Press, 1991.

Braude, Ann. *Radical Spirits: Spiritualism and Women's Rights in Nineteenth-Century America*. Boston: Beacon, 1992.

Clinton, Catherine. *The Other Civil War: American Women in the Nineteenth Century*. New York: Hill & Wang, 1984.

———, and Nina Silber, eds. *Divided Houses: Gender and the Civil War*. New York: Oxford University Press, 1992.

Diner, Hasia R. *Erin's Daughters in America: Irish Immigrant Women in the Nineteenth Century*. Baltimore: Johns Hopkins University Press, 1983.

Faragher, John Mack. *Women and Men on the Overland Trail*. New Haven, Conn.: Yale University Press, 1979.

Foote, Cheryl. *Women of the New Mexico Frontier, 1846–1912*. Boulder: University Press of Colorado, 1995.

Franklin, John Hope. *From Slavery to Freedom*. 5th ed. New York: Knopf, 1988.

Hersh, Blanche Glassman. *The Slavery of Sex: Feminist Abolitionists in America*. Urbana: University of Illinois Press, 1978.

Massey, Mary Elizabeth. *Bonnet Brigades*. New York: Knopf, 1966.

McPherson, James M. *Battle Cry of Freedom: The Civil War Era*. New York: Oxford University Press, 1988.

Myres, Sandra L. *Westering Women and the Frontier Experience: 1800–1915*. Albuquerque: University of New Mexico Press, 1982.

Riley, Glenda. *Women and Indians on the Frontier, 1825–1915*. Albuquerque: University of New Mexico Press, 1984.

Scott, Anne Firor. *The Southern Lady*. Chicago: University of Chicago Press, 1970.

Varon, Elizabeth. *We Mean to Be Counted: White Women and Politics in Antebellum Virginia*. Chapel Hill: University of North Carolina Press, 1998.

Histories of Women

Albers, Annie, and Beatrice Medicine. *The Hidden Half: Studies of the Plains Indian Women.* Washington, D.C.: University Press of America, 1983.

Bartlett, Elizabeth Ann. *Liberty, Equality, Sorority: The Origins and Interpretations of American Feminist Thought: Frances Wright, Sarah Grimke, and Margaret Fuller.* Brooklyn, N.Y.: Carlson, 1994.

Blumenthal, Shirley, and Jerome S. Ozer, eds. *Coming to America: Immigrants from the British Isles.* New York: Delacorte, 1980.

Bynum, Victoria E. *Unruly Women: The Politics of Social and Sexual Control in the Old South.* Chapel Hill: University of North Carolina Press, 1992.

Chambers-Schiller, Lee Virginia. *Liberty: A Better Husband.* New Haven, Conn.: Yale University Press, 1984.

Dubois, Ellen Carol. *Woman Suffrage and Women's Rights.* New York: New York University Press, 1998.

Faust, Drew Gilpin. *Mothers of Invention: Women of the Slaveholding South in the American Civil War.* Chapel Hill: University of North Carolina Press, 1996.

Harris, Katherine. *Long Vistas: Women and Families on Colorado Homesteads.* Boulder: University Press of Colorado, 1993.

Hoffert, Sylvia D. *When Hens Crow: The Women's Rights Movement in Antebellum America.* Bloomington: Indiana University Press, 1995.

Luchetti, Cathy. *Home on the Range: A Culinary History of the American West.* New York: Villard, 1995.

Schlissel, Lillian. *Far from Home: Families of the Westward Journey.* New York: Schocken, 1989.

Sterling, Dorothy, ed. *We Are Your Sisters.* New York: Norton, 1984.

Weatherford, Doris. *Foreign & Female: Immigrant Women in America, 1840–1930.* New York: Schocken, 1986.

Biographies and First-Person Accounts

Alcott, Louisa May. *Hospital Sketches.* Cambridge: Belknap, 1960.

Ames, Mary. *From a New England Woman's Diary in Dixie in 1865.* New York: Negro Universities Press, 1969.

Anderson, John Q., ed. *Brokenburn: The Journal of Kate Stone, 1861–1868.* Baton Rouge: Louisiana State University Press, 1972.

Banner, Lois W. *Elizabeth Cady Stanton: A Radical for Woman's Rights.* Boston: Little, Brown, 1980.

Boydston, Jeanne, et.al. *The Limits of Sisterhood: The Beecher Sisters on Women's Rights and Woman's Sphere.* Chapel Hill: University of North Carolina Press, 1988

Clifford, Deborah Pickman. *Crusader for Freedom: A Life of Lydia Maria Child.* Boston: Beacon Press, 1992.

Fairbanks, Carol, ed. *Writing of Farm Women: An Anthology.* New York: Garland, 1990.

Gordon, Ann D., ed. *The Selected Papers of Elizabeth Cady Stanton and Susan B. Anthony: In the School of Anti-Slavery, Vol. I.* New Brunswick, N.J.: Rutgers University Press, 1997.

Hedrick, Joan D. *Harriet Beecher Stowe: A Life.* New York: Oxford University Press, 1994.

Hudspeth, Robert, ed. *The Letters of Margaret Fuller.* 6 vols. Ithaca, N.Y.: Cornell University Press, 1983–1994.

Kolmerton, Carol A. *The American Life of Ernestine L. Rose.* Syracuse, N.Y.: Syracuse University Press, 1999.

Mohr, James C., ed. *The Cormany Diaries: A Northern Family in the Civil War.* Pittsburgh: University of Pittsburgh Press, 1982.

Oates, Stephen B. *A Woman of Valor: Clara Barton and the Civil War.* New York: HarperCollins, 1994.

Painter, Nell Irvin. *Sojourner Truth: A Life, A Symbol.* New York: Norton, 1996.

Pryor, Elizabeth Brown. *Clara Barton: Professional Angel.* Philadelphia: University of Pennsylvania Press, 1987.

Sklar, Kathyrn Kish. *Catharine Beecher: A Study in American Domesticity.* New Haven, Conn.: Yale University Press, 1973.

Woodward, C. Vann, ed. *Mary Chesnut's Civil War.* New Haven, Conn.: Yale University Press, 1981.

Woodward, C. Vann, and Elisabeth Muhlenfeld, eds. *The Private Mary Chesnut: The Unpublished Civil War Diaries.* New York: Oxford University Press, 1984.

Chapter 6

Nineteenth-Century Histories

Avary, Myrta Lockett. *Dixie After the War.* New York: Da Capo, 1970.

Basch, Norma. *Framing American Divorce.* Berkley: University of California Press, 1999.

Bennion, Sherilyn Cox. *Equal to the Occasion: Women Editors of the Nineteenth-Century Frontier.* Reno: University of Nevada Press, 1990.

Boardman, Fon W., Jr. *America and the Gilded Age, 1876–1900.* New York: Henry Z. Walck, 1972.

Brown, Dee. *Bury My Heart at Wounded Knee.* New York: Holt, Rinehart & Winston, 1991.

Clark, Judith Freeman. *America's Gilded Age: An Eyewitness History.* New York: Facts on File, 1992.

Hartog, Hendrik. *Man and Wife in America.* Cambridge: Harvard University Press, 2000.

Hayden, Dolores. *The Grand Domestic Revolution.* Cambridge, Mass.: MIT Press, 1981.

Hilton, Suzanne. *The Way It Was—1876.* Philadelphia: Westminster Press, 1975.

MacDonald, Anne L. *Feminine Ingenuity: Women and Invention in America.* New York: Ballantine, 1992.

Martin, Theodora Penny. *The Sound of Our Own Voices: Women's Study Clubs, 1860–1910.* Boston: Beacon Press, 1987.

Meigs, Cornelia. *Jane Addams: Pioneer for Social Justice.* Boston: Little, Brown, 1970.

Petrik, Paula. *No Step Backward: Women and Family on the Rocky Mountain Mining Frontier, 1865–1900.* Helena: Montana Historical Society Press, 1987.

Reiter, Joan Swallow, and the editors of Time-Life Books. *The Women.* The Old West series. Alexandria, Va.: Time-Life Books, 1978.

Werstein, Irving. *This Wounded Land: The Era of Reconstruction, 1865–1877.* New York: Delacorte, 1968.

Western Writers of America. *The Women Who Made the West.* Garden City, N.Y.: Double-day, 1980.

Histories of Women

Goldsmith, Barbara. *Other Powers: The Age of Suffrage, Spiritualism, and the Scandalous Victoria Woodhull.* New York: Knopf, 1998.

Hodes, Martha. *White Women, Black Men.* New Haven: Yale University Press, 1997.

Hopkins, Sarah Winnemucca. *Life Among the Piutes.* 1883. Reprint, Reno: University of Nevada Press, 1994.

Jackson, Helen Hunt. *A Century of Dishonor.* 1881. Reprint, Williamstown, Mass.: Corner House Publishers, 1973.

Jones, Jacqueline. *The Dispossessed: America's Underclass from the Civil War to the Present.* New York: Basic Books, 1992.

Mathes, Valerie Sherer. *Helen Hunt Jackson and Her Indian Reform Legacy.* Austin: University of Texas Press, 1990.

Moynihan, Ruth B., Susan Armitage, and Christiane Fischer Dichamp, eds. *So Much To Be Done: Women Settlers on the Mining and Ranching Frontier.* Lincoln: University of Nebraska Press, 1990.

Moynihan, Ruth B. *Rebel for Rights: Abigail Scott Duniway.* New Haven: Yale University Press, 1983.

Murolo, Priscilla. *The Common Ground of Womanhood: Class, Gender, and Working Girls' Clubs, 1884–1928.* Urbana: University of Illinois Press, 1997.

Nelsen, Jane Taylor, ed. *Prairie Populist: The Memoirs of Luna Kellie.* Iowa City: University of Iowa Press, 1992.

Pascoe, Peggy. *Relations of Rescue: The Search for Female Moral Authority in the American West, 1874–1939.* New York: Oxford University Press, 1990.

Peters, Virginia B. *Women of the Earth Lodges: Tribal Life on the Plains.* North Haven, Conn.: Archon, 1995.

Scott, Anne Firor. *The Southern Lady: From Pedestal to Politics.* Chicago: University of Chicago Press, 1970.

Biographies and First-Person Accounts

Bordin, Ruth. *Frances Willard: A Biography.* Chapel Hill: University of North Carolina Press, 1986.

Duniway, Abigail Scott. *Path Breaking: An Autobiographical History of the Equal Suffrage Movement in the Pacific Coast States.* 1914. Reprint, New York: Source Book Press, 1970.

Fox, Mary Virginia. *Lady for the Defense: A Biography of Belva Lockwood.* New York: Harcourt Brace Jovanovich, 1978.

Friedman, Jane. *America's First Woman Lawyer: The Biography of Myra Bradwell.* Buffalo, N.Y.: Prometheus Books, 1993.

Jensen, Joan, ed. *With These Hands: Women Working on the Land.* Old Westbury, N.Y.: Feminist Press, 1981.

Kellie, Luna. *A Prairie Populist: The Memoirs of Luna Kellie.* Edited by Jane Taylor Nelson. Iowa City: University of Iowa Press, 1992.

Kraditor, Aileen S., ed. *Up from the Pedestal: Selected Writings in the History of American Feminism.* New York: Quadrangle, 1968.

Moynihan, Ruth Barnes. *Rebel for Rights: Abigail Scott Duniway.* New Haven: Yale University Press, 1983.

Niederman, Sharon, ed. *A Quilt of Words: Women's Diaries, Letters & Original Accounts of Life in the Southwest, 1860–1960.* Boulder, Colo.: Johnson Books, 1988.

Rhodes, Jean. *Mary Ann Shadd Cary: The Black Press and Protest in the Nineteenth Century.* Bloomington: Indiana University Press, 1998.

Silverthorne, Elizabeth. *Sarah Orne Jewett: A Writer's Life.* Woodstock, N.Y.: Overlook Press, 1993.

Sterling, Dorothy, ed. *We Are Your Sisters: Black Women in the Nineteenth Century.* New York: Norton, 1984.

Whicher, George Frisbie. *This Was a Poet: A Critical Biography of Emily Dickinson.* 1938. Reprint. Hamden, Conn.: Archon, 1980.

Willard, Frances. *How I Learned to Ride the Bicycle: Reflections of an Influential 19th-Century Woman.* 1895. Rev. ed., Sunnyvale, Calif.: Fair Oaks Publishing, 1991.

Chapter 7

Histories of Women

Baker, Paula. "The Domestication of Politics: Women and American Political Society, 1780–1920." *American Historical Review* 89 (June 1984): 620–47.

Bederman, Gail. *Manliness and Civilization.* Chicago: University of Chicago Press, 1995.

Blair, Karen J. *The Clubwoman as Feminist: True Womanhood Redefined, 1868–1914.* New York: Holmes and Meier, 1980.

Bodnar, John. *The Transplanted: A History of Immigrants in Urban America.* Bloomington: Indiana University Press, 1985.

Bordin, Ruth. *Women and Temperance: The Quest for Power and Liberty, 1873–1900.* Philadelphia: Temple University Press, 1981.

Buhle, Mari Jo. *Women and American Socialism, 1870–1920.* Urbana: University of Illinois Press, 1981.

Carson, Mina. *Settlement Folk: Social Thought and the American Settlement Movement, 1885–1930.* Chicago: University of Chicago Press, 1990.

Cirksena, J. Diane, and Valija Rasmussen. *Women in Progressive America 1890–1920: Social Reconstruction.* St. Louis Park, Minn.: Upper Midwest Women's History Center, 1991.

Crocker, Ruth H. *Social Work and Social Order: The Origins of the Settlement Movement in Two Industrial Cities, 1886–1930.* Urbana: University of Illinois Press, 1991.

Deutsch, Sarah. *No Separate Refuge: Culture, Class, and Gender on an Anglo-Hispanic Frontier in the American Southwest, 1880–1940.* New York: Oxford University Press, 1987.

Epstein, Barbara Leslie. *The Politics of Domesticity: Women, Evangelism, and Temperance in Nineteenth-Century America.* Middletown, Conn.: Wesleyan University Press, 1981.

Fitzpatrick, Ellen. *Endless Crusade: Women Social Scientists and Progressive Reform.* New York: Oxford University Press, 1990.

Frankel, Noralee, and Nancy S. Dye, eds. *Gender, Class, Race and Reform in the Progressive Era.* Lexington: University of Kentucky Press, 1992.

Gabaccia, Donna. *From Sicily to Elizabeth Street: Housing and Social Change Among Italian Immigrants, 1880–1930.* Albany, N.Y.: SUNY Press, 1984.

———. *From the Other Side: Women, Gender, and Immigrant Life in the U.S. 1820–1990.* Bloomington: Indiana University Press, 1994.

Ginzberg, Lori. *Women and the Work of Benevolence: Morality, Politics, and Class in the Nineteenth-Century United States.* New Haven, Conn.: Yale University Press, 1990.

Gordon, Lynn D. *Gender and Higher Education in the Progressive Era.* New Haven, Conn.: Yale University Press, 1990.

Greenwald, Maurine Weiner. *Women, War, and Work: The Impact of World War I on Women Workers in the United States.* Westport, Conn.: Greenwood, 1980.

Grossman, James. *Land of Hope: Chicago, Black Southerners, and the Great Migration.* Chicago: University of Chicago Press, 1989.

Guy-Sheftall, Beverly. *Daughters of Sorrow: Attitudes Toward Black Women, 1880–1920.* Brooklyn: Carlson, 1990.

Harley, Sharon, and Rosalyn Terborg-Penn, eds. *The Afro-American Woman: Struggles and Images.* Port Washington, N.Y.: National University Publications, 1978.

Hewitt, Nancy, ed. *Women, Families, and Communities: Readings in American History, Part II.* Glenview, IL: Scott, Foresman, 1990.

Higginbotham, Evelyn Brooks. *Righteous Discontent: The Women's Movement in the Black Baptist Church, 1880–1920.* Cambridge: Harvard University Press, 1993.

Hine, Darlene Clark, Kathleen Thompson, and Hine Thompson. *A Shining Thread of Hope: The History of Black Women in America.* New York: Broadway Books, 1999.

Horowitz, Helen Lefkowitz. *Alma Mater: Design and Experience in Women's Colleges from their 19th Century Beginnings to the 1930s.* New York: Knopf, 1984.

Ladd-Taylor, Molly. *Mother-Work: Women, Child Welfare, and the State 1890–1930.* Urbana: University of Illinois Press, 1994.

Lasch-Quinn, Elizabeth. *Black Neighbors: Race and the Limits of Reform in the American Settlement House Movement 1890–1945.* 1993.

McCarthy, Kathleen D., ed. *Lady Bountiful Revisited: Women, Philanthropy, and Power.* New Brunswick, N.J.: Rutgers University Press, 1990.

Muncy, Robin. *Creating a Female Dominion in American Reform, 1890–1935.* New York: Oxford University Press, 1991.

Niethammer, Carolyn. *Daughters of the Earth: The Lives and Legends of American Indian Women.* New York: Collier Macmillan, 1977.

Riley, Glenda. *Inventing the American Woman, A Perspective on Women's History 1865 to the Present.* Arlington Heights, Ill.: Harlan Davidson, 1986.

———. *A Place to Grow: Women in the American West.* Arlington Heights, Ill.: Harlan Davison, 1992.

Rosen, Ruth. *The Lost Sisterhood: Prostitution in America 1900–1918.* Baltimore, Md.: Johns Hopkins University Press, 1982.

Rosenberg, Rosalind. *Beyond Separate Spheres: Intellectual Roots of Modern Feminism.* New Haven: Yale University Press, 1982.

Rosenzweig, Linda W. *The Anchor of My Life: Middle-Class American Mothers and Daughters, 1880–1920.* New York: New York University Press, 1993.

Smith-Rosenberg, Carroll. *Disorderly Conduct: Visions of Gender in Victorian America.* New York: Knopf, 1985.

Stansell, Christine. *American Moderns: Bohemian New York and the Creation of the New Century.* New York: Metropolitan Books, 2000.

World's Columbian Exposition

Holley, Marietta. *Samantha at the World's Fair.* New York: Funk & Wagnalls, 1893.

Muccigrosso, Robert. *Celebrating the New World: Chicago's Columbian Exposition of 1893.* Chicago: Ivan R. Dee, 1993.

Rydell, Robert. *All the World's a Fair.* Chicago: University of Chicago Press, 1985.

Schlereth, Thomas J. *Victorian America: Transformations in Everyday Life 1876–1915.* New York: HarperCollins, 1991.

Truman, Benjamin Cummings. *History of the World's Fair: Being a Complete and Authentic Description of the Columbian Exposition from its Inception.* New York: Arno, 1976.

Weimann, Jeanne Madeline. *The Fair Women.* Chicago: Academy Chicago, 1981.

Domestic Life

Abbott, Shirley. *Womenfolks: Growing Up Down South.* New York: Ticknor & Fields, 1983.

Dudden, Faye E. *Serving Women: Household Service in Nineteenth-Century America.* Middletown, Conn.: Wesleyan University Press, 1983.

Ewen, Elizabeth. *Immigrant Women in the Land of Dollars: Life and Culture on the Lower East Side 1890–1925.* New York: Monthly Review Press, 1985.

Frankfort, Roberta. *Collegiate Women: Domesticity and Career in Turn-of-the-Century America.* New York: New York University Press, 1977.

Katzman, David M. *Seven Days a Week: Women and Domestic Service in Industrializing America.* New York: Oxford University Press, 1978.

Shapiro, Laura. *Perfection Salad: Women and Cooking at the Turn of the Century.* New York: Farrar, Straus & Giroux, 1986.

Strasser, Susan. *Never Done: A History of American Housework.* New York: Pantheon, 1982.

———. *Waste and Want: A Social History of Trash.* New York: Metropolitan Books, 1999.

Sutherland, Daniel. *Americans and Their Servants: Domestic Service in the United States from 1800–1920.* Baton Rouge: Louisiana State University Press, 1981.

Weatherford, Doris. *Foreign and Female: Immigrant Women in America 1840–1930.* New York: Schocken, 1986.

Women and Work

Baron, Ava. *Work Engendered: Toward a New History of American Labor.* Ithaca, N.Y.: Cornell University Press, 1991.

Benson, Susan Porter. *Countercultures: Saleswomen, Managers, and Customers in American Department Stores, 1890–1940.* Urbana: University of Illinois Press, 1986.

Blewett, Mary. *We Will Rise in Our Might: Workingwomen's Voices from Nineteenth-Century New England.* Ithaca, N.Y.: Cornell University Press, 1991.

Boris, Eileen. *Home to Work: Motherhood and the Politics of Industrial Homework in the United States.* New York: Cambridge University Press, 1994.

Brody, David. *Workers in Industrial America: Essays on the 20th Century Struggle.* New York: Oxford University Press, 1980.

Davies, Marjorie W. *Woman's Place is at the Typewriter: Office Work and Office Workers 1870–1930.* Philadelphia: Temple University Press, 1982.

Dye, Nancy Shrom. *As Equals and Sisters: The Labor Movement and the Women's Trade Union League of New York.* University of Missouri Press, 1980.

Eisenstein, Sarah. *Give Us Bread, But Give Us Roses: Working Women's Consciousness in the United States, 1890 to the First World War.* Boston: Routledge, 1983.

Glazer, Penina M. and Miriam Slater. *Unequal Colleagues: The Entrance of Women into the Professions 1890–1940.* New Brunswick, N.J.: Rutgers University Press, 1987.

Glenn, Susan. *Daughters of the Shtetl: Life and Labor in the Immigrant Generation.* Ithaca, N.Y.: Cornell University Press, 1990.

Goldin, Claudia. *Understanding the Gender Gap: An Economic History of American Women.* New York: Oxford University Press, 1990.

Kennedy, Susan Estabrook. *If All We Did Was to Weep at Home: A History of White Working Class Women in America.* Bloomington: Indiana University Press, 1979.

Meyerowitz, Joanne J. *Women Adrift: Independent Female Wage Earners in Chicago 1880–1930.* Chicago: University of Chicago Press, 1988.

Milkman, Ruth. *Women, Work and Protest: A Century of U.S. Women's Labor History.* Boston: Routledge and Kegan Paul, 1985.

Peiss, Kathy. *Cheap Amusements: Working Women and Leisure in Turn-of-the-Century New York.* Philadelphia: Temple University Press, 1986.

Strom, Sharon Hartman. *Beyond the Typewriter: Gender, Class and the Origins of Modern Office Work.* Urbana: University of Illinois Press, 1995.

Tax, Meredith. *The Rising of the Women: Feminist Solidarity and Class Conflict, 1880–1917.* New York: Monthly Review Press, 1980.

Tentler, Leslie. *Wage Earning Women: Industrial Work and Family Life in the United States 1900–1930.* New York: Oxford University Press, 1979.

Women and Politics

Buhle, Mari Jo, and Paul Buhle, eds. *The Concise History of Woman Suffrage: Selections from the Classic Work of Stanton, Anthony, Gage, and Harper.* Urbana: University of Illinois Press, 1979.

Davis, Allen F. *Spearheads for Reform: The Social Settlements and the Progressive Movement, 1890–1914.* New York: Oxford University Press, 1967.

Flexner, Eleanor. *Century of Struggle: The Woman's Rights Movement in the United States.* New York: Atheneum, 1972.

Ford, Linda. *Iron-Jawed Angels: The Suffrage Militancy of the National Woman's Party, 1912–1920.* Lanham, Md.: University Press of America, 1991.

Gilmore, Glenda. *Gender and Jim Crow: Women and the Politics of White Supremacy in North Carolina 1896–1920.* Washington, D.C.: Smithsonian Institution Press, 1993.

Graham, Sara Hunter. *Woman Suffrage and the New Democracy.* New Haven: Yale University Press, 1996.

Kraditor, Aileen S. *The Ideas of the Woman Suffrage Movement, 1890–1920.* New York: Columbia University Press, 1965.

Lunardini, Christine A. *From Equal Suffrage to Equal Rights: Alice Paul and the National Woman's Party 1910–1928.* New York: New York University Press, 1986.

Newman, Louise. *White Women's Rights: The Racial Origins of Feminism in the U.S.* New York: Oxford University Press, 1999.

Ryan, Mary P. *Women in Public.* Baltimore, Md.: Johns Hopkins University Press, 1992.

Stebner, Eleanor. *The Women of Hull House.* Albany, N.Y.: SUNY Press, 1997.

Terborg-Penn, Rosalyn. *African American Women in the Struggle for the Vote 1850–1917.* Bloomington: Indiana University Press, 1998.

Wheeler, Marjorie Spruill. *New Women of the New South: The Leaders of the Woman Suffrage Movement in the Southern States.* New York: Oxford University Press, 1993.

———. *One Woman, One Vote: Rediscovering the Woman Suffrage Movement.* Troutdale, Oreg.: New Sage Press, 1995.

Biographies and First-Person Accounts

Addams, Jane. *Twenty Years at Hull House.* 1910. Viking Penguin, 1998.

Blair, Fredrika. *Isadora: Portrait of the Artist as a Woman.* New York: McGraw Hill, 1986.

Davis, Allen F. *American Heroine: The Life and Legend of Jane Addams.* New York: Oxford University Press, 1973.

Diliberto, Gioia. *A Useful Woman: The Early Life of Jane Addams.* New York: Scribner, 1999.

Dobkin, Marjorie Housepian. *The Making of a Feminist: Early Journals and Letters of M. Carey Thomas.* Kent, Ohio: Kent State University Press, 1979.

Drinnon, Richard. *Rebel in Paradise: A Biography of Emma Goldman.* Boston: Beacon Press, 1961.

Dubois, Ellen Carol. *Harriet Stanton Blatch and the Winning of Woman Suffrage.* New Haven: Yale University Press, 1999.

Duncan, Isadora. *My Life.* 1927. New York: Norton, 1996.

Falk, Candace. *Love, Anarchy, and Emma Goldman.* New York: Henry Holt, 1984.

Fowler, Robert. *Carrie Catt.* Boston: Northeastern University Press, 1988.

Gilman, Charlotte Perkins. *Herland.* Edited by Ann J. Lane. New York: Pantheon, 1979. First published in "The Forerunner," 1915.

———. *The Living of Charlotte Perkins Gilman.* Madison: University of Wisconsin Press, 1991.

———. *Women and Economics: The Economic Factor Between Men and Women as a Factor in Social Evolution.* Edited by Carl Degler. 1898. New York: Harper & Row, 1966.

Goldman, Emma. *Living My Life.* New York: Dover, 1970.

Horowitz, Helen Lefkowitz. *The Power and the Passion of M. Carey Thomas.* New York: Knopf, 1994.

Jones, Beverly Washington. *Quest for Equality: The Life and Writings of Mary Eliza Church Terrell 1863–1954.* Brooklyn, N.Y.: Carlson, 1990.

Lane, Ann J. *To Herland and Beyond: The Life and Work of Charlotte Perkins Gilman.* New York: Pantheon, 1990.

Richardson, Dorothy. *The Long Day, The Story of a New York City Working Girl.* 1905. Reprint. Edited by Cindy Sondik Aron. Charlottesville: University of Virginia Press, 1990.

Sanger, Margaret. *My Fight for Birth Control.* 1931. Elmsford, N.Y.: Maxwell Reprint edition, 1969.

Sklar, Kathryn Kish. *Florence Kelley and the Nation's Work.* New Haven: Yale University Press, 1995.

Terrell, Mary Church. *A Colored Woman in a White World.* Washington, D.C.: Ransdell, 1940.

Van Voris, Jacqueline. *Carrie Chapman Catt: A Public Life.* New York: Feminist Press, 1987.

Ware, Susan. *Partner and I: Molly Dewson, Feminism, and New Deal Politics.* New Haven: Yale University Press, 1987.

Wexler, Alice. *Emma Goldman, An Intimate Life.* New York: Pantheon, 1984.

——. *Emma Goldman in America.* Boston: Beacon Press, 1986.

——. *Emma Goldman in Exile.* Boston: Beacon Press, 1989.

Yezierska, Anzia. *Breadgivers.* 1925. Reprint, New York: Persea, 1975.

Chapter 8

Histories of the Era 1920–1940

Agee, James, and Walker Evans. *Let Us Now Praise Famous Men.* Boston: Houghton Mifflin, 1941.

Cohen, Lizabeth. *Making a New Deal: Industrial Workers in Chicago, 1919–1939.* New York: Cambridge University Press, 1990.

Kelley, Robin D. G. *Hammer and Hoe: Alabama Communists During the Great Depression.* Chapel Hill: University of North Carolina Press, 1990.

Leuchtenburg, William. *The Perils of Prosperity: 1914–1932.* Chicago: University of Chicago Press, 1958.

Lynd, Robert, and Helen Lynd. *Middletown.* 1929. New York: Harcourt, Brace, 1959.

McElvaine, Robert. *The Great Depression, America, 1929–1941.* New York: Times Books, 1984.

Terkel, Studs. *Hard Times: An Oral History of the Great Depression in America.* New York: Pantheon, 1986.

Histories of Women

Acosta-Belen, Edna, ed. *The Puerto Rican Woman: Perspectives on Culture, History and Society.* New York: Praeger, 1986.

Blackwelder, Julia Kirk. *Women of the Depression: Caste and Culture in San Antonio, 1929–1939.* College Station: Texas A&M Press, 1984.

Chafe, William H. *The Paradox of Change: American Women in the Twentieth Century.* New York: Oxford University Press, 1992.

Cook, Blanche Wiesen. *Eleanor Roosevelt.* Vol. 1, 2. New York: Viking, 1992, 1999.

Cott, Nancy F. *The Grounding of Modern Feminism.* New Haven: Yale University Press, 1987.

Faderman, Lillian. *Odd Girls and Twilight Lovers: A History of Lesbian Life in Twentieth-Century America.* New York: Viking Penguin, 1992.

Hagood, Margaret. *Mothers of the South: Portraiture of the White Tenant Farm Woman.* New York: Norton, 1977.

Hall, Jacquelyn Dowd. *Revolt Against Chivalry: Jessie Daniel Ames and the Women's Campaign Against Lynching.* New York: Columbia University Press, 1979.

——, et. al. *Like a Family: The Making of a Southern Cotton Mill World.* Chapel Hill: University of North Carolina Press, 1987.

Hine, Darlene Clark. *Black Women in White: Racial Conflict and Cooperation in the Nursing Profession, 1890–1950.* Bloomington: Indiana University Press, 1989.

Low, Marie Ann. *Dust Bowl Diary.* Lincoln: University of Nebraska Press, 1984.

Mead, Margaret. *Blackberry Winter.* Magnolia, Mass.: Peter Smith, 1989.

O'Connor, Carol. *A Sort of Utopia: Scarsdale, 1891–1981.* Albany, N.Y.: SUNY Press, 1983.

Qoyawayma, Polingaysi. *No Turning Back: A True Account of a Hopi Indian's Struggle to Bridge the Gap Between the World of Her People and the World of the White Man.* Albuquerque: University of New Mexico Press, 1964.

Roosevelt, Eleanor. *The Autobiography of Eleanor Roosevelt.* 1961. New York: Da Capo Press, 1992.

Ruiz, Vicki. *Cannery Women/Cannery Lives: Mexican Women, Unionization, and the California Food Processing Industry, 1930–1950.* Albuquerque: University of New Mexico Press, 1987.

Sanchez, George J. *Becoming Mexican American: Ethnicity, Culture, and Identity in Chicano Los Angeles, 1900–1945.* New York: Oxford University Press, 1993.

Scharf, Lois. *To Work and to Wed: Female Employment, Feminism, and the Great Depression.* Westport, Conn.: Greenwood, 1980.

Shaw, Stephanie J. *What a Woman ought to Be and to Do: Black Professional Women Workers During the Jim Crow Era.* Chicago: University of Chicago Press, 1996.

Showalter, Elaine, ed. *These Modern Women: Autobiographical Essays from the Twenties.* Old Westbury, N.Y.: Feminist Press, 1978.

Wall, Cheryl A. *Women of the Harlem Renaissance.* Bloomington: Indiana University Press, 1995.

Ware, Susan. *Beyond Suffrage: Women in the New Deal.* Cambridge: Harvard University Press, 1981.

——. *Partner and I: Molly Dewson, Feminism, and New Deal Politics.* New Haven: Yale University Press, 1987.

Chapter 9

Histories of the Era 1945–1960

Bernstein, Alison R. *American Indians and World War II: Toward A New Era in Indian Affairs.* Norman: University of Oklahoma Press, 1991.

Blum, John Morton. *V Was for Victory: Politics and American Culture During World War II.* New York: Harcourt Brace Jovanovich, 1976.

Boyer, Paul. *By the Bomb's Early Light: American Thought and Culture at the Dawn of the Atomic Age*. New York: Pantheon, 1985.

Chafe, William H. *The Unfinished Journey: America Since World War II*. 4th ed. New York: Oxford University Press, 1998.

Daniels, Roger, Sandra C. Taylor, and Harry H. L. Kitano. *Japanese Americans: From Relocation to Redress*. Salt Lake City: University of Utah Press, 1986.

Freeman, Samuel. *The Inheritance: How Three Families and the American Political Majority Moved from Left to Right*. New York: Simon & Schuster, 1996.

Gilbert, James. *A Cycle of Outrage: America's Reaction to the Juvenile Delinquent in the 1950s*. New York: Oxford University Press, 1986.

———. *Another Chance: Postwar America, 1945–1985*. 2nd ed. Chicago: Dorsey Press, 1986.

Hall, Jacquelyn Dowd. *Like a Family: The Making of a Southern Cotton Mill World*. Chapel Hill: University of North Carolina Press, 1987.

Hodgson, Godfrey. *America In Our Time: From World War II to Nixon, What Happened and Why*. New York: Random House, 1976.

Jezer, Marty. *The Dark Ages: Life in the United States, 1945–1960*. Boston: South End Press, 1982.

Kevles, Daniel. *In the Name of Eugenics: Genetics and the Uses of Human Heredity*. New York: Knopf, 1985.

May, Elaine Tyler. *Homeward Bound: American Families in the Cold War Era*. New York: Basic Books, 1988.

May, Lary, ed. *Recasting America: Culture and Politics in the Age of Cold War*. Chicago: University of Chicago Press, 1989.

O'Neill, William L. *American High: The Years of Confidence, 1945–1960*. New York: Free Press, 1986.

Satterfield, Archie. *The Home Front: An Oral History of the War Years in America, 1941–1945*. New York: Playboy Press, 1981.

Terkel, Studs. *"The Good War": An Oral History of World War II*. New York: Pantheon, 1984.

Histories of Women

Anderson, Karen. *Wartime Women: Sex Roles, Family Relations, and the Status of Women During World War II*. Westport, Conn.: Greenwood, 1981.

Chafe, William H. *The Paradox of Change: American Women in the Twentieth Century*. New York: Oxford University Press, 1991.

———. *Women and Equality*. New York: Oxford University Press, 1978.

Foner, Philip. *Women and the American Labor Movement: From World War I to the Present*. New York: Free Press, 1980.

Gatlin, Rochelle. *American Women Since 1945*. Jackson: University Press of Mississippi, 1987.

Gordon, Linda. *Pitied But Not Entitled: Single Mothers and the History of Welfare*. New York: Free Press, 1994.

Hartmann, Susan M. *The Home Front and Beyond: American Women in the 1940s*. Boston: Twayne, 1982.

Kaledin, Eugenia. *Mothers and More: American Women in the 1950s.* Boston: Twayne, 1984.

Kunzel, Regina. *Fallen Women, Problem Girls: Unmarried Mothers and the Professionalization of Social Work, 1890–1945.* New Haven: Yale University Press, 1993.

Lamphere, Louise. *From Working Daughters to Working Mothers: Immigrant Women in a New England Industrial Community.* Ithaca, N.Y.: Cornell University Press, 1987.

Milkman, Ruth. *Gender at Work: The Dynamics of Job Segregation by Sex during World War II.* Urbana: University of Illinois Press, 1987.

Oppenheimer, Valerie Kincade. *The Female Labor Force in the United States.* Westport, Conn.: Greenwood Press, 1970, 1976.

Rosenberg, Rosalind. *Divided Lives: American Women in the Twentieth Century.* New York: Hill & Wang, 1992.

Rothman, Sheila. *Woman's Proper Place: A History of Changing Ideals and Practices, 1870 to the Present.* New York: Basic Books, 1978.

Rupp, Leila. *Mobilizing Women for War: German and American Propaganda, 1939–1945.* Princeton, N.J.: Princeton University Press, 1978.

———, and Verta Taylor. *Survival in the Doldrums: The American Women's Rights Movement, 1945 to the 1960s.* New York: Oxford University Press, 1987.

Tsuchida, Nobuya, ed. *Asian and Pacific American Experiences: Women's Perspectives.* Minneapolis: University of Minnesota Press, 1982.

Van Horn, Susan Householder. *Women, Work and Fertility, 1900–1986.* New York: New York University Press, 1988.

Wandersee, Winifred D. *Women's Work and Family Values, 1920–1940.* Cambridge: Harvard University Press, 1981.

Family, Reproduction, and Sexuality

Bailey, Beth. *Sex in the Heartland.* Cambridge: Harvard University Press, 1999.

———, and David Farber. *The First Strange Place: The Alchemy of Race and Sex in World War II Hawaii.* New York: Free Press, 1992.

Berube, Alan. *Coming Out Under Fire: The History of Gay Men and Women in World War II.* New York: Free Press, 1990.

Brandt, Allan M. *No Magic Bullet: A Social History of Venereal Disease in the United States Since 1880.* New York: Oxford University Press, 1985.

Chauncey, George. *Gay New York: Gender, Urban Culture, and the Makings of the Gay Male World. 1890–1940.* New York: Basic Books, 1994.

Cherlin, Andrew J. *Marriage, Divorce, Remarriage.* Cambridge: Harvard University Press, 1981.

Coontz, Stephanie. *The Way We Never Were: American Families and the Nostalgia Trap.* New York: Basic Books, 1992.

D'Emilio, John. *Sexual Politics, Sexual Communities: The Making of a Homosexual Minority in the United States, 1940–1970.* Chicago: University of Chicago Press, 1983.

Farrell, Betty G. *Family: The Making of an Idea, an Institution, and a Controversy in American Culture.* Boulder, Colo.: Westview Press, 1999.

Fineman, Martha. *The Illusion of Equality: The Rhetoric and Reality of Divorce Reform.* Chicago: University of Chicago Press, 1991.

Gordon, Linda. *Heroes of Their Own Lives: The Politics and History of Family Violence.* New York: Viking, 1988.

Kenney, Sally J. *For Whose Protection? Reproductive Hazards and Exclusionary Policies in the U.S. and Britain.* Ann Arbor: University of Michigan Press, 1992.

May, Elaine Tyler. *Barren in the Promised Land: Childless Americans and the Pursuit of Happiness.* New York: Basic Books, 1995.

Modell, John. *Into One's Own: From Youth to Adulthood in theUnited States, 1920–1975.* Berkeley: University of California Press, 1989.

Reed, James. *From Private Vice to Public Virtue: The Birth Control Movement and American Society Since 1830.* New York: Basic Books, 1978.

Roberts, Dorothy. *Killing the Black Body: Race, Reproduction, and the Meaning of Liberty.* New York: Pantheon, 1997.

Skolnick, Arlene. *Embattled Paradise: The American Family in an Age of Uncertainty.* New York: Basic Books, 1991.

Solinger, Rickie. *Wake Up Little Susie: Single Pregnancy and Race before Roe v. Wade.* New York: Routledge, 1992.

Stack, Carol. *All Our Kin: Strategies for Survival in a Black Community.* New York: Harper & Row, 1974.

Chapter 10

Histories of Women

Berry, Mary Frances. *Why the ERA Failed: Politics, Women's Rights and the Amending Process.* Bloomington: Indiana University Press, 1986.

Davis, Angela. *Woman, Race and Class.* New York: Random House, 1981.

Echols, Alice. *Daring to Be Bad: Radical Feminism in America, 1967–1975.* Minneapolis: University of Minnesota Press, 1989.

Ehrenreich, Barbara. *The Hearts of Men: American Dreams and the Flight from Commitment.* Garden City, N.Y.: Anchor, 1983.

Eisenstein, Zillah. *The Radical Future of Liberal Feminism.* White Plains, N.Y.: Longman, 1981.

Evans, Sara. *Personal Politics: The Roots of Women's Liberation in the Civil Rights Movement and the New Left.* New York: Knopf, 1979.

———, and Barbara Nelson, *Wage Justice: Comparable Worth and the Paradox of Technocratic Reform.* Chicago: University of Chicago Press, 1989.

Faludi, Susan. *Backlash.* New York: Crown, 1991.

Filene, Peter. *Him/Her/Self: Sex Roles in Modern America.* 3d ed. Baltimore: Johns Hopkins University Press, 1998.

Freeman, Jo. *The Politics of Women's Liberation.* New York: David McKay, 1975.

Ginsburg, Faye. *Contested Lives: The Abortion Debate in an American Community.* 2nd ed. Berkeley: University of California Press, 1998.

Harrison, Cynthia. *On Account of Sex: The Politics of Women's Issues, 1945–1968.* Berkeley: University of California Press, 1988.

Hartmann, Susan M. *From Margin to Mainstream: American Women and Politics Since 1960.* New York: Knopf, 1989.

————. *The Other Feminists: Activists in the Liberal Establishment.* New Haven: Yale University Press, 1998.

Hewlett, Sylvia. *When the Bough Breaks: The Cost of Neglecting Our Children.* New York: Basic Books, 1991.

Hochschild, Arlie. *Second Shift: Working Parents and the Revolution at Home.* New York: Viking, 1989.

Hoff-Wilson, Joan, ed. *Rights of Passage: The Past and Future of the ERA.* Bloomington: Indiana University Press, 1986.

Hole, Judith, and Ellen Levine, *Rebirth of Feminism.* New York: Quadrangle, 1971.

Hull, Gloria, et al. *All the Women Are White, All the Blacks Are Men, But Some of Us Are Brave.* New York: Feminist Press, 1982.

Klatch, Rebecca. *Women of the New Right.* Philadelphia: Temple University Press, 1987.

Linden-Ward, Blanche, and Carol Hurd Green. *Changing the Future: American Women in the 1960s.* New York: Twayne, 1992.

Luker, Kristin. *Abortion and the Politics of Motherhood.* Berkeley: University of California Press, 1984.

Mansbridge, Jane. *Why We Lost the ERA.* Chicago: University of Chicago Press, 1986.

Mathews, Donald, and Jane Sherron DeHart. *Gender and Politics: Cultural Fundamentalism and the ERA.* New York: Oxford University Press, 1990.

Petchesky, Rosalind. *Abortion and Woman's Choice: The State, Sexuality and Reproducive Freedom.* New York: Longman, 1984.

Rosen, Ruth. *The World Split Open: How the Modern Women's Movement Changed America.* New York: Viking, 2000.

Rothschild, Mary Aikin. *A Case of Black and White: Northern Volunteers and the Southern Freedom Summers.* Westport, Conn.: Greenwood, 1982.

Rubin, Lillian. *Worlds of Pain: Life in the Working-Class Family.* New York: Basic Books, 1976.

Wandersee, Winifred. *On the Move: American Women in the 1970s.* New York: Twayne, 1988.

White, Deborah Gray. *Too Heavy a Load: Black Women in Defense of Themselves 1894–1994.* New York: Norton, 1999.

Yung, Judy. *Unbound Feet: A Social History of Chinese Women in San Francisco.* Berkeley: University of California Press, 1995.

Biographies, First-Person Accounts, and Feminist Documents

Boston Women's Health Book Collective Staff. *Our Bodies, Ourselves.* Rev. 2nd ed. New York: Simon & Schuster, 1976.

Brownmiller, Susan. *In Our Time: Memoir of a Revolution.* New York: Dial, 1999.

Bunch, Charlotte. *Passionate Politics: Feminist Theory in Action.* New York: St. Martin's, 1987.

Crawford, Vicki, Jacqueline Anne Rouse, and Barbara Woods, eds. *Women in the Civil Rights Movement: Trailblazers and Torchbearers, 1941–1965.* New York: Carlson, 1990.

Daly, Mary. *Beyond God the Father.* Boston: Beacon Press, 1973.

DuPlessis, Rachel Blau, ed. *The Feminist Memoir Project.* New York: Three Rivers Press, 1998.

Firestone, Shulamith. *The Dialectic of Sex: The Case for Feminist Revolution.* New York: Morrow, 1970.

Friedan, Betty. *The Feminine Mystique.* New York: Norton, 1963.

———. *It Changed My Life.* New York: Random House, 1976.

———. *The Second Stage.* New York: Summit, 1981.

Greer, Germaine. *The Female Eunuch.* New York: McGraw-Hill, 1971.

Hoff, Mark. *Gloria Steinem: The Women's Movement.* Boston: Houghton Mifflin, 1992.

hooks, bell. *Ain't I a Woman: Black Women and Feminism.* Boston: South End Press, 1991.

———. *Talking Back: Thinking Feminism, Thinking Black.* Boston: South End Press, 1989.

King, Mary. *Freedom Song: A Personal Story of the 1960s.* New York: Morrow, 1987.

Millett, Kate. *Sexual Politics.* Garden City, N.Y.: Doubleday, 1970.

Moody, Anne. *Coming of Age in Mississippi.* New York: Dial Press, 1968.

Morgan, Robin, ed. *Sisterhood is Powerful.* New York: Random House, 1970.

Murray, Pauli. *The Autobiography of a Black Artist, Feminist, Lawyer, Priest, and Poet.* Originally published as *Song in a Weary Throat.* Knoxville: University of Tennessee Press, 1989.

Reuther, Rosemary Radford. *Sexism and God Talk: Toward a Feminist Theology.* Boston: Beacon Press, 1983.

Robinson, Jo Ann. *The Montgomery Bus Boycott and the Women Who Started It.* Edited by David J. Garrow. Knoxville: University of Tennessee Press, 1987.

Schlafly, Phyllis. *The Power of the Positive Woman.* New Rochelle, N.Y.: Arlington House, 1977.

Steinem, Gloria. *Outrageous Acts and Everyday Rebellions.* New York: NAL/Dutton, 1986.

Picture Credits

Courtesy Department Library Services, American Museum of Natural History: 4, 29; Boston Athenaeum: 202; Boston Public Library / Rare Books Department. Courtesy of The Trustees: 72; British Library: 52; Brown Brothers: 381; Courtesy of the California History Room, California State Library, Sacramento, California: 256; Chicago Historical Society: 355; The Connecticut Historical Society: 175; Cook Collection, Valentine Museum: 294; Department of Defense: 581; Friends Historical Library, Swarthmore College: 157; By permission of the Houghton Library, Harvard University: 72, 78; The Huntington Library, San Marino, California, Rare Book Department: 96; Kansas State Historical Society: 335; The Library Company of Philadelphia: 149; Library of Congress: 9, 20, 57, 80, 106, 126, 134, 170, 192, 218, 234, 238, 249, 398, 419, 451, 478, 555; Library of Congress, Federal Theatre Project Collection at George Mason University, Fairfax, Va: 455; Lowell Historical Society: 222; Lowell National Historic Park: 272; *Man and Two Women*, Peter Rindisbacher, Glenbow Collection, Calgary, Canada: 33; Minnesota Historical Society:49, 415, 499; Museum of American Textile History: ii; Museum of Modern Art Film Stills Archive: 437, 488; Photo by Edward S. Curtis, Courtesy Museum of New Mexico, Neg. No. 143735: 16; Courtesy Museum of New Mexico, Neg. No. 4852: 329; National Archives: 316, 408, 426, 478, 480, 493; National Museum of American History, Smithsonian Institution: 14, 26, 297, 311, 324, 351, 374, 376, 468; Used by permission of the National Woman's Christian Temperance Union, Evanston, Illinois: 342; Nebraska State Historical Society: 308; Collection of the New York Historical Society: 144, 168; New York Public Library, Astor, Lenox, and Tilden Foundations: 391;Oberlin College Archives, Oberlin, Ohio: 263; Courtesy off our backs: 560; Archives & Manuscripts Division of the Oklahoma Historical Society: 42; Courtesy, Peabody Essex Museum, Salem, MA: 64, 118; Pennsylvania Academia of the Fine Arts, Philadelphia. Gift of Paul Beck, Jr.: 183; Reuters/Corbis: 586; The Schlesinger Library, Radcliffe Institute, Harvard University: 536, 539; Schomburg Center for Research in Black Culture: 504, 532; Smith College: 313, 402, 514, 566; Sophia Smith Collection, Smith College: 230; St. Louis Art Museum: 197; State Historical Society of North Dakota Collection 90, Brown Land Collection, #111: 358; Stowe-Day Foundation: 268; Southern Historical Collection, Wilson Library, University of North Carolina at Chapel Hill: 434; Studio Museum in Harlem Archives/James Van Der Zee Collection: 443; Gary Tong: 6, 114, 140; U.S. Army Military History Institute, Carlisle, Pa: 282; University of New Hampshire: 89; VMI archives: 287; Western History Collections, University of Oklahoma Library: 47; UPI/Corbis-Bettmann: 459, 546, 570; University of Rochester: 240; U.T. The Institute of Texan Cultures, *The San Antonio Light* Collection: 432; Valentine Museum: 394; c. Washington Post reprinted by permission of the Washington, D.C., Public Library: 490, 526; Wellcome Library, London: 121; Courtesy, the Winterthur Library: Printed Book and Periodical Collection: 190; Yasui family of Portland, Oregon: 367; Zintgraff Collection, The Institute of Texan Cultures: 578.

Contributors

Nancy F. Cott is Jonathan Trumball Professor of American History at Harvard University and the director of the Schlesinger Library on the History of Women in America at the Radcliffe Institute for Advanced Study. She is the author of *The Bonds of Womanhood: "Woman's Sphere" in New England, 1780–1835; The Grounding of Modern Feminism;* and *Public Vows: A History of Marriage and the Nation,* among other books.

William H. Chafe is Alice Mary Baldwin Distinguished Professor of History and Dean of the Faculty of Arts and Sciences at Duke University. He has also served as director of the Duke-University of North Carolina Women's Studies Research Center. Professor Chafe is the author of *The American Woman: Her Changing Social, Political and Economic Roles 1920–1970; Women and Equality: Changing Patterns in American Culture; Civilities and Civil Rights: Greensboro, North Carolina and the Black Struggle for Freedom; The Unfinished Journey: America Since World War II; The Paradox of Change: American Women in the Twentieth Century;* and *Never Stop Running: Allard Lowenstein and the Struggle to Save American Liberalism.* He is co-editor, with Harvard Sitkoff, of *A History of Our Time: Readings in Postwar America,* and general series editor, with Anne Firor Scott, of University Publications of America's women's studies series.

John Demos is the Samuel Knight Professor of American History at Yale University. He is the author of several volumes of colonial history, including *The Unredeemed Captive: A Family Story from Early America,* which was a finalist for the National Book Award in Non-Fiction (1994); *A Little Commonwealth: Family Life in Plymouth Colony;* and *Entertaining Satan: Witchcraft and the Culture of Early New England,* for which he was awarded the 1982 Bancroft Prize in American History.

Sarah Jane Deutsch is Associate Professor of history at the University of Arizona. She is the author of *No Separate Refuge: Culture, Class, and Gender on an Anglo-Hispanic Frontier in the American Southwest, 1880–1940,* which won the Gustave O. Arlt Award in the Humanities from the Council of Graduate Schools, and the forthcoming *Women and the City: Gender, Power, and Space in Boston, 1870–1940.* Professor Deutsch has worked with the Worcester, Massachusetts, public schools to introduce cultural and racial diversity into the U.S. history curriculum. She previously taught at Yale University, M.I.T., and Clark University. She holds a B.A. and Ph.D. from Yale and an M.Litt from Oxford University, where she was a Rhodes scholar.

Michael Goldberg is Associate Professor of American studies at the University of Washington at Bothell. He is the author of *An Army of Women: Gender, Politics and Power in Gilded-Age Kansas,* which is part of the *Reconfiguring American History* series published by Johns Hopkins University Press, and a contributor to the *American National Biography.* Dr. Goldberg previously taught at New Mexico Tech and Yale University. He holds a Ph.D. in American studies from Yale and a B.A. in American studies from the University of California, Santa Cruz.

Jane Kamensky is Associate Professor of history at Brandeis University, where she has taught since 1993. She earned her B.A. and Ph.D. in History from Yale and is the author of *Governing the Tongue: Sinners and Witches in Puritan New England* and *The Colonial Mosaic: American Women, 1600–1760.* She is currently at work on a book called *The Exchange Artist,* a history of the Boston Exchange Coffee House, which was, ca. 1810, one of the largest and strangest buildings in the United States. Her schorlarship has been supported by grants from the Andrew W. Mellon Foundation, the National Endowment for the Humanities, the American Council of Learned Societies, the Pew Charitable Trusts, and the Bunting Institute of Radcliffe College. She is also co-founder and co-editor of *Common-place,* www.common-place.org, the online journal of early American life.

Elaine Tyler May is Professor of American studies and history at the University of Minnesota. Her publications include *Great Expectations: Marriage and Divorce in Post-Victorian America, Homeward Bound: American Families in the Cold War Era, Pushing the Limits: American Women, 1940–1961,* and *Barren in the Promised Land: Childless Americans and the Pursuit of Happiness.* She is co-editor of *Here, There and Everywhere: The Foreign Politics of American Popular Culture,* and co-author of a college-level United States history textbook, *Created Equal: A Social and Political History of the United States.*

Marylynn Salmon is the author of *Women and the Law of Property in Early America* and co-author of *Inheritance in America: From Colonial Times to the Present,* as well as numerous scholarly articles on early American women's history. Dr. Salmon is research associate in the history department at Smith College and director of the Smith Summer Humanities Program. She was a contributor to *Women of America: A History*, and her study of the legal status of women after the American Revolution was published in the volume *Women, War, and Revolution*. Dr. Salmon was formerly assistant professor of history at the University of Maryland, Baltimore County. She holds a B.A. from Cornell University and a Ph.D. from Bryn Mawr College.

Harriet Sigerman is an independent scholar who has written *Land of Many Hands: Women in the American West* and an award-winning young-adult biography of Elizabeth Cady Stanton, *"The Right Is Ours."* Her most recent publication is *The Columbia Documentary History of American Women Since 1941*. In addition, she is a contributer to the American National Biography and *The Young Reader's Companion to American History*. She has been an assistant editor to *The Papers of Elizabeth Cady Stanton and Susan B. Anthony* at Rutgers University. A graduate of the University of California at Irvine, she holds an M.A. and Ph.D. in American history from the University of Massachusetts at Amherst.

Karen Manners Smith is Assistant Professor of U.S. history and women's history at Emporia State University in Kansas. She holds degrees from Brandeis University and the University of Massachusetts, and is currently completing a life of Mary Virginia Terhune: *"Marion Harland": The Making of a Household Word*. She has delivered papers on Terhune at Winterthur Museum, Radcliffe College, and the 1994 Conference on Southern Women's History at Rice University. Dr. Smith formerly taught U.S. women's history at Smith College.

Index